Haskamot

Dear esteemed reader,

It is my greatest honor to add my voice to this incredible achievement written by my mentor and friend David Woolf. My relationship with David and his eishet chayil Fran spans over three decades when they allowed me to direct NCSY Canada, an organization they built with love. Those early days were so formative for me at the beginning of my career. It was David who drove the organization forward, David who led by example and David who never lost the spark of teaching, educating and inspiring all those he would come in contact with.

It is therefore no surprise that David has taken yet another creative, thoughtful and meaningful way to inspire us all with Torah thoughts for all type of Jews who come from all type of backgrounds. The key to our success as a people and a pillar of our mission is to continue the process of learning, questioning, and growing. The Jewish people are uniquely charged to engage ourselves in inquiry and to challenge ourselves to become better human beings and servants of Hashem. David follows this tradition with his wonderful book.

David taught me that no two Jews are alike and therefore each person's path is unique as they build their relationship with the Almighty. Torah IQ is yet another masterpiece project created by a master educator to help our community master Hashem's holy works.

Rabbi Glenn Black
CEO, NCSY Canada

Haskamot

THE AFIKIM FOUNDATION

December 2020

After reading through the creative and probing riddles that run through so many of the parshiot in "Torah IQ: The Great Torah Riddle Book", I'm left with but one unanswered riddle that continues to stump me.

The riddle? How did David Woolf create such an outstanding work?

Readers will be both challenged and enthralled by this well-researched and meaningful book. An ideal sefer for discussion around the Shabbat family table.

Rabbi Raphael B. Butler
President, The Afikim Foundation

Haskamot

YOUNG ISRAEL OF QUEENS VALLEY
141-55 77th Ave. Flushing, NY 11367
Phone: 718-263-3921 email: yiqvoffice@gmail.com

8 Teves 5781

December 23, 2020

So many of my fondest childhood memories bring me back to Congregation B'nai Torah of Toronto where my father served as Rav for 27 years. The shul was large and diverse - hundreds of members ranging from the older European born immigrants to the younger North American generation, Israeli *shelichim*, Jews of Ashkenazi and Sefardi descent, and children of all ages attending a wide variety of schools.

One figure who stands out prominently in my mind due to his active involvement with and impact upon the youth in particular and the shul as a whole, is David Woolf. His leining was always flawless, his davening was a blend of perfect nusach and uplifting, melodious tunes, and his efficiently run Shabbos youth minyan was always a popular destination for kids and teens.

His enthusiasm and love for Torah knowledge was shared with his young audience through his weekly trivia challenges which he has painstakingly compiled over many years to share with a far larger audience in book form.

I have no doubt his thought provoking riddles will enhance many a Shabbos table by stimulating the inquisitive mind and sparking a fascinating Torah discussion.
I wish him much continued *hatzlacha* in his learning and teaching of Torah.

Shmuel Marcus

With Love and Appreciation

To my son
Yitzi
who, with great professionalism,
artistic expression and inspired creativity,
dealt with the layout, typesetting,
proofreading, and design of this book,
as well as choosing the title Torah IQ.
Yitzi is an incredible graphic artist,
photographer and branding professional
living in Jerusalem Israel.

He is the co-creator of
Let's Bench – custom benchers
(letsbench.com),
and Seek It Tours – experiential photo scavenger hunts in Israel
(seekitisrael.com).

Most important, he is our son
and we are very proud of him!

Thanks, Yitzi!

You are
welcome Dad

TORAH

The Great Torah Riddle Book

PARSHIYOT | GENERAL TORAH
BIGGEST/SMALLEST, LONGEST/SHORTEST, ETC.
HALACHOT, CUSTOMS & BLESSINGS | BRAINTEASERS

DAVID WOOLF

www.myjewishprinting.com

For information, comments, or suggestions, contact:
david@TorahIQbook.com

www.TorahIQbook.com

Cover Design and Typesetting by Yitzchak Woolf

Tellwell Talent
www.tellwell.ca

ISBN
978-0-2288-5302-2 (Hardcover)
978-0-2288-5300-8 (Paperback)
978-0-2288-5301-5 (eBook)

Dedicated

In honour of the matriarch of our family
פרל נחמה בת יצחק צבי וטויבא פייגא שתחי שתחי' – Pearl Woolf

In memory of our dear parents, *aleihem hashalom,*
שמעון בן יצחק גרשון וחיה ע"ה – Sidney Woolf
אלימלך בן דוד וחוה רחל ע"ה – Max Good
רבקה רייצא בת יהודה צבי הלוי ופריידל ע"ה – Regina Good

In memory of our grandparents, *aleihem hashalom,*
Yitzchak Gershon and Chaya Woolf
יצחק גרשון בן שמעון ע"ה וחיה בת יהודה אריה לייב ע"ה

Yitzchak Zvi and Toba Feiga Cannon
יצחק צבי בן הרב נחום ליפא ע"ה וטויבא פייגא בת דוב דוד ע"ה

Dovid and Chava Rochel (Gut) Good
דוד בן אלימלך הי"ד וחוה רחל בת שלום הי"ד

Yehuda Zvi Halevi and Fraidel Woznica
יהודה צבי בן בנימין הלוי הי"ד ופריידעל בת וולף הי"ד

In Loving Tribute

To our children, their partners and all our grandchildren,
who have made our lives interesting, exciting, entertaining
and above all, gratifying. We are proud of them all!

In Appreciation

To my partner, my love, my wife
Fran
– it has been an amazing half century plus!
May we be *zocheh* to share many more years together
in good health, with much happiness,
and *nachat* from our great family.
Thanks for everything!

Haskamot

Haskamot

CONGREGATION B'NAI TORAH

בית כנסת **RABBI**
בני תורה **HARAV YIRMIYA MILEVSKY**

אלול תש"פ

Throughout the ages, Klal Yisrael had great educators who took it upon themselves to transmit Torah to the next generation. A good teacher understands that if one wants to inspire the student, he must recognize the jargon that talks to the pupil.

The questions or riddles that you will find in this book are far more than trivia. It is the language of a very talented and devoted teacher, who for many years taught by understanding how to talk to the future.

When one converses with the hundreds of young men and women who grew up as Torah Jews at Congregation B'nai Torah, David Woolf and the Youth Minyan is always the first memory that is shared. For many, the lifelong appreciation for the richness of Parashat Hashavua, originated at the B'nai Torah Youth Minyan.

Mazel Tov to David on compiling this incredible volume. I have no doubt that with this Sefer in hand, a whole new generation of young men and women will be excited to make our precious Torah part of their life.

Yirmiya Milevsky

Yirmiya Milevsky

CONGREGATION B'NAI TORAH

465 Patricia Avenue Toronto, Ontario, M2R 2N1 | Tel/Fax 416.226.3700 | office@bnaitorah.ca

Haskamot

Beth Avraham Yoseph
of Toronto Congregation
Joseph and Faye Tanenbaum Synagogue Centre

Mara D'Asra - Senior Rabbi
RAV N. DANIEL KOROBKIN

Rabbi Emeritus
RAV BARUCH TAUB

Founding President
JOSEPH TANENBAUM ל"ז

President
JEFFREY BROWN

Immediate Past President
ZAC KAYE

12 Teves 5781
December 27, 2020

David and Fran Woolf, נ"י, have been pillars of the Toronto Jewish community for decades. They are pioneers in Jewish outreach through their various efforts with NCSY, Jewish music, Jewish travel, and much more. The key to their success has been their contagious love for Judaism and Torah. It is truly an honour to count them as part of the Thornhill Jewish community.

Reb David has transferred this contagious love for Torah learning into his new brilliant sefer, *Torah IQ: The Great Torah Riddle Book*. Structured as a "trivial pursuit" game, it engages the reader instantly in the myriad minutiae of Torah knowledge. You will find your curiosity piqued by so many of these questions, which David has culled over the decades. His own fascination with the nooks and crannies of the Beit Midrash appears on every page of the work before you. We owe Reb David a debt of gratitude for collating this information and sharing it with all of us.

This work is an excellent choice for your Shabbos table, and will not only provide hours of fun-filled conversation, but will also fill your soul with enriching Torah knowledge. We wish David, Fran, and all the Woolfs continued bracha and success in their efforts for Klal Yisrael.

Best wishes,

Rabbi Daniel Korobkin

613 Clark Ave W, Thornhill, Ontario L4J 5V3 • Tel: 905-886-3810 Fax: 905-886-5103 • www.bayt.ca
JOSEPH AND FAYE TANENBAUM SYNAGOGUE CENTRE

iv   TORAH IQ: The Great Torah Riddle Book

CONTENTS

Preface, Thank Yous and Introduction

Throughout life, there are many influences that shape us as human beings and as Jews. Where we live; our family; formal and informal education; books, magazines, and newspapers that we read; our friends, *rabbis* and teachers; places to which we have traveled and the people we met along the way; public figures we revere as heroes; the neighbourhood where we live; our country Canada; our homeland Israel; our *shul* and community; our personal history and the collective history of the Jewish people.

It would be impossible for me to thank all those who have influenced me personally, and me and Fran as a couple. But I would like to take a stab at trying to highlight some of those who have had an effect on me as a person and as a *Jew*, and who therefore have all played a significant role in encouraging, inspiring, and motivating me to compile and organize this book.

In most introductions to books and *sefarim* that I have read, (and I generally read the introductions, as I believe that the reader's connection to the content is refined and influenced by getting a feel for the creator of the work), the thanks to the author/editor's spouse is generally the last, preceded by the phrase, "*acharon acharon chaviv*" – "saving the best for last." I am going to defy convention, as I truly believe, in a paraphrasing of *Rabbi Akiva*'s words to his wife "*sheli shelah hu*"–all that I have and all that I have accomplished is a result of the wonderful partnership that Fran and I have had for the more than half a century that we have been together.

People do laugh at us (yes, even our children and grandchildren) because we share a car, a phone, a Facebook account, and spend almost every waking hour together. But we would not want it any other way. We *b"h* have had a true partnership, where we do not look at each other only as our spouse, but also as our best friend, the one with whom you would want to share your every experience. And yes, that encompasses the joyful and the celebratory moments, as well as the challenging and distressing ones. Just as you would want your best friend beside you to share celebrations and festivities; so too, you would want to have the support and comfort of your best friend, in times of stress and need. Thank you, Fran, for being my mate, my partner, and my best friend. I could not have completed this without your love and encouragement.

Our parents and by extension their family history and religious roots, were major influences in our development as individuals, as a couple, and as Jews.

My father, Sidney (Shimon) Woolf *a"h* ("*alav hashalom*" – "of blessed memory"), was born in Manchester, England in 1922. He was one of ten siblings, born to Reb Yitzchak Gershon and Chaya Woolf.

My mother, Pearl Anita (Perel Nechama) *tblct"a* ("*tibadel l'chaim tovim aruchim*" – "she should continue to be blessed with long life"), was born in 1924 in the small Northern England *Torah* community of Gateshead, just across the river from Newcastle-Upon-Tyne, to Reb Yitzchak Zvi and Toba Faige Cannon. She and her sister were raised in Gateshead, which, at the time, was to England, what Lakewood is to the United States today.

My mother and father's formative years coincided with some of the most difficult years in the 20th century; spending their preteen years during the great depression, and their teen years and first years of married life, during the Second World War.

But they were in relative safety in England, compared to Fran's parents, who were both from the same area near Sosnowiec, Poland, whose lives were interrupted by being sent to labour and concentration camps, where they spent the balance of the *Shoah*.

Fran's father, Max (Meilech) *a"h,* was one of nine children born to Dovid and Chava Rochel (Gut) Good. He and his oldest brother were the family's only survivors of the *Shoah*. Fran's mother, Regina (Rivka Raitza) *a"h,* was one of four siblings born to Yehuda Zvi Halevi and Freidel Woznica. Miraculously all four siblings survived the *Shoah*.

Fran's parents had met in the late 1930's but their courtship was interrupted by the outbreak of the *Shoah*, and when the war ended, neither knew if the other was alive. By the grace of *Hashem*, they amazingly and thankfully met again and were married in the DP camp of Bergen Belsen. Their *ketubah* proclaims in bold letters the location of their wedding, Bergen Belsen, where Fran was born in 1948.

We are constantly impressed and amazed by the fact that despite being brought up in the most challenging economic era of the Great Depression, and despite being first hand witnesses to the horrors of the *Shoah* and the near destruction of our people, these two families could march on with *emunah* and *bitachon* and succeed in creating a huge Jewish family, now numbering in the thousands, that respects and reveres our religious traditions. And so, we give *hakarat hatov* to our parents. It is their shining example, their care and concern, their training and their love, that has moulded our lives, our sense of right, our ethics, and our values.

The *neshamot* of Fran's parents and my father, *aleihem hashalom*, should have an *aliyah*, from the *Torah* learning that went into the development of this manuscript. And at the same time, my mother (*tblct"a*) should be blessed with good health, *arichat yamim*, and continued *nachat* from her children, grandchildren, great-grandchildren, and *b"h* great-great-grandchildren.

I must say at this point, that when I had the manuscript partially complete at the beginning of this century, my father Sidney Woolf *a"h* was so proud of my "book" project, that he had the hand typed manuscript permanently on his coffee table and read the riddles from time to time at the *Shabbat* table. He wanted me to finish it and I unfortunately did not do so during his lifetime. My mother, *tblct"a*, used to ask me from time to time how the project was going and hopefully this now completed book, will bring her much happiness, pride, and *nachat*.

Fran and I are both blessed with wonderful siblings; they and their families should be blessed with good health and *nachat* from their children and extended families.

Our children have all grown to create families of their own and have blessed us with much *nachat* and happiness. Utilizing their many talents, we have watched them forge their future, each in their own unique way.

I often joke "if I had known grandchildren were this much fun, I would have had them first." But the truth is that "we are the past, our children the present, and our grandchildren the future." Grandchildren are the dots that connect lines from generation to generation. They are the future link in the glorious chain of our family.

Oftentimes, a grandchild will ask me "Gramps, who is your favourite" and the truth is that each of our grandchildren is special in their own way, and cherished as if they were the only one!

As it says (*Mishlei* 17:6) "*ateret zekeinim bnai vanim*" – "grandchildren are the crown of their elders" and to us, we look at our grandchildren as the icing on the cake. They represent the very significant dividends paid to us for the years that we invested in creating a family and raising children.

We could write a *megillah* on what each of our children, their partners and our grandchildren mean to us; their considerable talents and skills; but in doing so, we would need another complete volume. We give each of them the *beracha* of good health, happiness, and success in all that they do.

Our teachers and *rabbis* helped shape who we are and what we stand for. Their enthusiasm for *Torah* and their special gifts in being able to impart a love of Judaism to each of their students and congregants, played a major role in the creation of this book. Special recognition has to be given to educators Rabbi Chaim Nussbaum; *zt"l*, Rav Akiva Greenberg *a"h*; Rav Shneur Weinberg, Rav Sholom Gold, Rav Chaim Mintz; and to rabbis, Rav Raphael Marcus *zt"l* and Rav Yirmiya Milevsky; each of whom inspired me in their own unique way to grow in *Torah* learning and in *Avodat Hashem*.

Fran and I have had the good fortune of a more than 40 year involvement with *NCSY* and the amazing work they do in connecting Jewish teens to their Jewish heritage. Our relationship with this wonderful organization has allowed us to see young people grow and flourish, and create their own families in communities all over the globe. A bonus for us is that we had the opportunity to work hand in hand with such talented and dedicated leaders as Rabbi Raphy Butler, Rabbi Dr. Nosson Westreich, and Rabbi Glenn Black.

One of the most talented *Torah* leaders around today is Reb Zale Newman and it has been our good fortune to share responsibility for *NCSY Canada* for many decades, as well as developing a strong friendship and ultimately a musical partnership in producing many cassettes and CDs featuring, among others, Reb Shlomo Carlebach *z"l* and Yehuda!

Thanks to Mendel Rubinoff and Rabbi Mordechai Bamberger who share my love of *Torah Trivia* and who graciously shared their riddles with me; some of which are included in this volume.

A special thank you to my daughter Zahava who assisted in the proofreading and editing of the manuscript and to my son Yitzi, whose considerable talents in graphic arts and layout, helped me get this manuscript ready for presentation to the publisher. Thank you Yitzi for your assistance, advice and suggestions, for selecting the name *Torah IQ*, and for an amazing cover.

Finally, I would like to remember seven *B'nai Torah* individuals who, in their relatively short time on this earth, accomplished much and with whom I had the good fortune to interact and to be considered a friend.

Rav Yehoshua Abramoff *zt"l* was a *Torah* scholar par excellence and together with his wife Ayala *tblct"a*, were among our closest friends. Reb Yehoshua was our *posek* for many years; he rose above the crowd through his love of humanity, his family, his enormous *Torah* knowledge, his humility, and his impeccable *middot*.

Rav Raphael Marcus *zt"l* was our *shul* Rabbi at *B'nai Torah* for 27 years. He was a gentle man and a caring soul, and when he entered a room, you inevitably perceived that he had a personal connection to every individual in the room. His ultimate *tzidkut*, though, was his connection, genuine concern, and respect for each and every member of *Klal Yisrael*.

Lawrie Cherniak *a"h* was someone, who, despite his many health issues and years of medical battles, had a heart that was filled with love for *Torah* and dedication to community. When there was a need for organizational involvement, Lawrie was not only ready to step up to the plate, but totally prepared to assume a leadership role. His involvement at *B'nai Torah*, BAYT, and NCSY, among many others, was legendary; his respect for *Torah* and *Rabbonim* was an example for all to follow. Together with Debbie *tblct"a*, they were a formidable team for worthy Jewish causes. He is sorely missed.

Izzy Kaplan *a"h* was a dedicated supporter of Israel and *Zionism*. Many a tourist was asked by Izzy to please find room in their suitcase to take much needed items for individuals and communities, and because you knew the sincerity of the person asking, you immediately grabbed the *mitzvah*. The city of *Sderot* was one of his pet projects and because of his singular efforts, the schools and playgrounds of *Sderot* now have bomb shelters to protect the youth of the city. Izzy's wife Suzie and children *yblct"a* are now living the dream that Izzy unfortunately was never able to realize. *Medinat Yisrael* misses his love, sincerity, and dedication.

Jack Kahn *a"h* was a community leader involved in so many organizations, that you wondered how he had time to eat or sleep. Whether it was *shul, Mizrachi, World Zionism* or the quiet *tzedakah* campaigns that Jack spearheaded, here was a man who did everything with class and dignity. It was our honour to be counted among his and Susan's friends.

Aharon Weisblatt *a"h* was a man of many hobbies and talents; he was a man of action and few words. It was an honour to share "center stage" on the *bima* of *B'nai Torah* with Aharon as *shluchei tzibbur* for the *Yamim Noraim* for about 40 years. His knowledge of *nusach*, his sweet beautiful voice and melodious harmonies are so missed and cannot be replaced. We are so thankful that we had the chance to be part of Anna *tblct"a* and Aharon's world.

Paul Forman *a"h* was a once in a lifetime person. Talented, driven, energetic, sensitive, caring, and dedicated. There are so many more adjectives to describe this amazing human being. If a job needed to be initiated or completed, you just knew that Paul would be the person to undertake the task with excitement and attention to detail. Our more than 60 year relationship with Paul and Annie *tblct"a* is something that we will treasure forever.

I am completing this book around the time of the year, that Paul *a"h* and Aharon *a"h* and I would annually convene, to prepare for the *yamim noraim*, where we would share the *bima*. We would try out new *niggunim*, practice harmonies, and try to create ways, through the power of *niggun* and song, to stimulate participation and *kavanah* in the *kahal hakadosh* of B'nai Torah. This is the first year that we will not be together in many years and I will miss the sweetness of Aharon's voice and the energy of Paul's *hitlahavut* during this *High Holiday* season and for all *Yamim Noraim* in the future.

Yehi Zichram Baruch.

Finally I thank the *Ribono Shel Olam* for the blessings bestowed on me and my family, and for enabling me to complete this volume.

David Woolf

The Book's History

When I first attended *Ner Israel Yeshiva College* of Toronto in the early 1960s, it was a relatively new *yeshiva*. The *yeshiva* began as a branch of *Ner Israel* in Baltimore, and in the first year, had less than 15 students. I began there in the *yeshiva*'s second year of existence. Our second year class was just a bit larger, and as a result, being in the *yeshiva* atmosphere in those early years, meant that you interacted on a daily basis with the *rebbeim* and the *hanhala*.

The *Rosh Yeshiva* at the time was a young, dynamic rav, Rabbi Sholom Gold, and he was joined by a number of other young rabbis and "*elter bachurim*" who succeeded in establishing an atmosphere of a love of *Torah* study and *mitzvah* observance. Not only was Rabbi Gold the *Rosh Yeshiva*, he was also my class *rebbe* for a few years. His classes on *Torah* were literally amazing, filled with deep analysis of the *pesukim* and the stimulating presentation of illuminating and fascinating commentary from the *Torah* giants of yesteryear.

I would have to say that Rav Gold was one of my teachers who inspired me to love the beauty of an intriguing *Torah* "*vort*," and the captivating magic of a *dvar Torah* that clarified a seemingly challenging and problematic portion of the text. And while *Ner Israel* was what one would classify as a "*litvish*" *yeshiva* with its roots in the famous *Torah* centres of *Slabodka* and *Ponevesz*, Rav Gold served us a diverse assortment of *Torah* views that encompassed the world of basic *pshat*, *Chassidism*, mysticism, and "*lomdish*" analyses of the *Torah* text. I was truly living in the "*pardes*" – "orchard" of the *Torah* world, soaking in the *Pshat, Remez, Drush,* and *Sod* (the first letters of each word forming the word "*pardes*") of authentic *Torah* thought.

After leaving the *yeshiva* and getting married, my wife Fran and I moved to Windsor, Ontario where I attended the University of Windsor to complete my MBA degree. To make ends meet, we both taught; she, full time in the Windsor public school system; and both of us, part time, at the *Shaar Hashamayim* Hebrew *School*, under the direction of an amazing educator, Rabbi Chaim Schloss a"h. He was an expert *mechanech*, a wellspring of *Torah* knowledge, and author of a series on Jewish history.

It was in Windsor that we both developed our love of transmitting *Torah* to young people and we were instrumental in assisting in the establishment of a Jewish Day School in Windsor and in the connection of some of our young students to the youth activities of a relatively new youth movement called *NCSY*.

As an aside, when we were downsizing a few years ago, we discovered pictures of some of our former students, and using the tools of social media, made contact with a number of them to catch up after more than half a century. We were proud to discover that many of them were Jewishly connected and even prouder, when some of them attributed a small part of that connection to the "two young teachers" that they had at the *Shaar* from 1968–1971.

When we moved back to Toronto in 1971, we moved into the Willowdale district of Toronto and joined *Congregation B'nai Torah. B'nai Torah* in the early years, in the '70s and '80s, was the place to be, if you had a young family. It was started by a small group of families that took advantage of the new building development going on in the Willowdale district of north Toronto. There was a mix of high rise apartments, large single family and semi detached homes in an area along Bathurst Street, Toronto's major "Jewish" thoroughfare, just south of Steeles Avenue. These were truly pioneers, as never before had Orthodox Jews ventured so far north. The first Rabbi was Rav Shlomo Jakobovits and the *shul* was housed in a number of temporary facilities before it began to build its permanent building at the corner of Patricia and Bathurst.

We decided that this was the place where we would lay down our roots and begin to build our family. Part of the motivation was that Rav Sholom Gold, my *rebbe* from *Yeshiva,* had become the spiritual leader and the *shul* began to grow and flourish. By the time we moved there, there was a growing number of young families already living in the area and what was very visible on a *Shabbat* morning, was a veritable traffic jam of baby carriages.

The membership was *orthodox* yet diverse, as there was a mixture of *kippot serugot,* black hats, *Chassidim* and *Mitnagdim, Ashkenazim* and *Sepharadim,* Israelis, locals, and "immigrants" from Montreal, Jews from Polish and Hungarian backgrounds, along with a smattering of *gartels;* and most surprisingly, everyone got along. The *shul* even went so far as to adopt an *"Ashkefard" nusach,* that was mostly *Ashkenaz* with a number of exceptions, to make the *nusach Sefard* people feel at home; namely, *Hallel* on the first night of *Pesach, Hoshanot* during *Shacharit* on *Sukkot, Yotzrot* on *Parshat Shekalim* and *Parshat Hachodesh,* and *Hakafot* on *Shemini Atzeret* evening. Fifty years later, there are now shuls that are adopting a "unified" *siddur*, due to the intermingling of cultures from among the Jewish world; it seems like *B'nai Torah* was way ahead of its time.

Today, if you speak to people who grew up in *B'nai Torah*, there is almost unanimous agreement that this was the greatest place to build a family. Despite its diversity or perhaps because of it, there was an incredible atmosphere of feeding off of the strengths of everyone and focusing primarily on what unites us as a people, and minimizing the things that divide us. There was no room for classifying everyone as "us" or "them" in neat little boxes. Rather we took what we had in common and built an amazing *shul* with our shared communal values and created an environment and spirit that truly portrayed an atmosphere of "*k'ish echad, b'lev echad.*"

It was in this wonderful *shul*, where, in addition to the spiritual life of *tefillah* and *Torah* learning in the *shul*, two areas of activism were nurtured and cultivated, and in my humble opinion, have become the everlasting legacy of *B'nai Torah*.

First, there was a deep rooted connection and attachment to Israel, with the result today that *B'nai Torah* just might be the synagogue in North America, from which the largest number of families have made *Aliyah*. Second, while many Orthodox *shul* members have great participation in synagogue and yeshiva/day school activities, *B'nai Torah* had many members who made significant contributions to general Jewish communal organizations. Over the years, *B'nai Torah* members were leaders in *Jewish Family and Child Service, UJA, Federation, Mizrachi, World Zionism, Bnei Akiva, OU/NCSY, Jews for Judaism, COR Kashrut*, and many other communal endeavours.

Getting back to the early years, *B'nai Torah* in a short time, became the hub of youth activities for families throughout the city. It was likely the only *shul* at the time that simultaneously hosted *Bnei Akiva* programs, *Pirchei* and *Bnos* programs, and *NCSY Shabbatons*. Children of the *shul* attended the gamut of schools in the city from *Associated* to *Eitz Chaim* to *Bais Yaakov*. Everyone was accepted for who they were and amazingly, we all gelled.

Early on in our time there, I was approached by Reb Baruch Kempinski *a"h*, who was the *gabbai* of the *shul*, who asked me to occasionally assist in the running of the youth *minyan* and to get involved in the Youth Committee of the *shul*. Within a year or two of helping with the *minyan*, I was elected to the board and appointed as Youth Committee Chairman. At this point, I assumed the leadership of the *minyan* and watched it grow to eventually host upwards of 100 participants, male and female, every *Shabbat* and *Yom Tov* morning. It was a *minyan* targeted to grade six and up to university age, so that those beginning to attend were pre *bar/bat mitzvah* and by the time they reached *bar mitzvah* would have seen and heard enough to take a shot at leading the services. In the meantime, they could serve as *gabbaim, daven pesukei d'zimra,* and "get their feet wet."

Part of my goal was to see young people of the *shul* become adept at *davening* and *laining*. I felt very strongly that the youth *minyan* should become a place where the youth of the *shul* could become fully involved and walk away with a positive experience. Participants were encouraged to lead the services and the *laining*. While there were a few adults who attended, they did not get *aliyot* or lead the services, unless one of the youth failed to prepare his part of the *laining* and then the adults pinch hit. At the same time, I did not want it to be the excuse for not being in *shul* or for roaming in late. I therefore established a number of criteria. The *minyan* began at 9:30 in the morning and if you did not show up in time for "*barchu,*" you were not allowed in. There was to be a minimum of talking during *davening*. Before too long, people understood that this was a fun but serious place to attend.

I am proud to say that today there are a number of "graduates" of the Youth *Minyan* who are full time *baalei kriah* in their communities, and there are many shuls where the *baalei tefillah* for *Shabbat, Yom Tov,* and for the *Yamim Noraim,* got their start and their training in the *B'nai Torah Youth Minyan.*

When Rabbi Raphael Marcus became the *Rav* of the *shul* in 1980, he visited the *youth minyan* and noted that while it was nice to experience the decorum, the quality of the *tefillah,* and the *Kriat HaTorah,* he was quite surprised that there was no *dvar Torah* or "sermonette" at some point in the service, and he suggested that I give one every week. I explained to the *Rav* that because we started 30 minutes later than the main *minyan,* I had to "move" the services along, so that we would be finished at the same time as the main *shul,* thereby allowing the kids to go home with their parents. Additionally, because the attendees were almost all Jewish day school or *yeshiva* students, who heard *divrei Torah* all week in school, the last thing they would want to do would be to hear me delivering a *dvar Torah* on *Shabbat* morning.

The *Rav* insisted, so the compromise was that rather than deliver a talk, I would ask three riddles every *Shabbat,* focusing on either the *parshah,* the *chagim,* or *halacha,* and give the youth *minyan* members time to "shout out" the answers on the spot, or to return the following week with answers. I had to prepare interesting and intriguing questions weekly that would stimulate the kids and challenge them.

Over the years, we were blessed with many bright kids, a number of whom were contestants or winners in the *Chidon Hatanach* – the International Bible Contest, held every year in Israel. These were the years when I had to prepare the most challenging riddles, as on a number of occasions, answers were being shouted out from both sides of the *mechitza,* before I had barely finished posing the question.

I prepared questions for close to two decades and at some point along the way, decided to write them down and organize them in a booklet. I even had one of the *minyan* participants, Batya Breslow, work for a summer in organizing and researching, with an eye to one day publishing this work. For some reason, I stopped recording and organizing the work in 2002. This book that you are now reading was partially complete and for about 17 years, sat in a file drawer in our home. This past year, I got inspired and began once again to work on its completion. A few months after I revived the project, the world found itself in the midst of the Covid-19 pandemic and all of a sudden I found myself with lots of time to work on completing the project.

Returning to my partially completed work, I reviewed what I had done until 2002, added areas of the book that appeared sparse, and researched all the sources so that they are properly cited and quoted. I truly hope that you enjoy this book and welcome comments, suggestions and alternate answers as you find them. I hope that it becomes a useful tool to use at your *Shabbat* table, as it was at our family table, as our kids were growing up.

Parts of the book are "original," if you can label reading a *peirush* by a revered and noted *Torah* commentator like the *Chatam Sofer, Ramban, Gra,* or others, taking their remarks and turning their commentary into a riddle, as "original." Some of the questions have been generated by reading a statistic or a *gematriya* of the *Baal Haturim* or the *Chida* or some *chassidic* master and creating a riddle from their comments. Many of the questions in the section called "Biggest, Smallest, Longest, Shortest" came from my many years as a *baal kriah* and a lover of *Torah* trivia.

Some of the questions in the *parshah, halacha,* and *berachot* sections and in the section on the *chagim,* saw their inspiration from reading the now legendary weekly *Torah Tidbits* by Phil Chernovsky of the *OU Israel Center* in *Jerusalem;* the wonderful weekly series *Torah Lodaat* by *Rav Matis Blum, zt"l* of New York; *Torah Q&A* from the *Jerusalem Ohr Somayach Yeshiva,* the weekly *Torah Online* Digest of *BAYT Beth Avraham Yosef* of *Toronto* Congregation, *Chassidic Insights* on the Weekly *parshah* by *Rav Zvi Akiva Fleisher* of the *Shema Yisrael Torah Network,* and from the many *sefarim* on *minhagim* that I have had the pleasure of learning over the years.

But what is clear to me is that without the platform of the *Youth Minyan* at *Congregation B'nai Torah* in Toronto, this book would never have seen the light of day. I have much "*hakarat hatov*" – "gratitude" to the *shul,* to its *rabbis* over the years, and especially to the young *mitpallelim* of the *minyan,* who became the testing ground for almost all the riddles in the book.

As a result of all said above, I do not see myself as the author of this work; rather, I see myself as the compiler and editor of hundreds of questions and answers that will hopefully light up the atmosphere in many a Jewish home in the coming years. Enjoy!

PARSHIYOT

PARSHAT BEREISHIT QUESTIONS

1. Give three instances in the *Torah* where there are five words in a row, each word having two letters?

2. It says in *Tehillim* (119:130) "Your opening words illuminate." What connection is there between the light of *Torah* and its first words?

3. When the *Torah* enumerates the years of *Adam*, there appear to be two superfluous words *"asher chai."* Where else in the *Torah* do we have a similar occurrence and why?

4. Who was the first person to learn *Chumash* with *Rashi*?

5. How old was *David Hamelech* when he died?

6. In *Bereishit* 4:21, *Yuval* is identified as the inventor of the harp. How many strings did the harp have in the *Beit Hamikdash*?

7. How is music and specifically the harp related to the heart and soul of man?

8. Who had the first guard dog in history?

9. Who committed a sin punishable by death when he was only one day old?

10. Who was the first twin in the *Torah*?

11. What was the first case of triplets in the *Torah*?

12. On which day were the sun and moon created?

13. What is the circumference of earth?

14. What two *mitzvot* were granted to women because of *Chava's* sin in the *Garden of Eden* and what *mitzvot* are they excluded from because of the same sin?

15. Three people in the *Torah* were asked rhetorical questions by *Hashem*. Their answers indicate a lack of *"bitachon"* – "trust" in *Hashem*. Who were the three people and what were the questions and answers?

16. All animals were created on the sixth day of creation. Which animal mentioned in *Tanach* had eight legs?

17. Which chapter of *Tehillim* did *Adam* compose?

18. Who was stronger – *Kayin* or *Hevel*?

19. On what date did *Kayin* kill *Hevel*?

20. Did any of *Kayin's* descendants survive the flood?

PARSHAT BEREISHIT ANSWERS

1. The three instances are:
   1. *"Noach et Shem et Cham"* (*Bereishit* 6:1).
   2. *"ki gam zeh lach ben"* (*Bereishit* 35:17).
   3. *"ki yad al kes kah"* (*Shemot* 17:16).

2. The *Vilna Gaon* explains that there is a connection between the first *pasuk* of each of the five books of the *Torah* and the design of the *Menorah*. *Bereishit* has seven words in the first *pasuk* signifying the seven branches of the *Menorah*. *Shemot* has 11 words signifying the 11 knobs. *Vayikra* has nine words signifying the nine flowers. *Bamidbar* has 17 words, which, with its *"kolel"* is 18 (the rules of *gematriya* permit one to add one to the total; e.g., 17 words plus one for the entire sentence = 18), like the 18 cubit height of the *Menorah* and the first *pasuk* in *Devarim* has 22 words signifying the 22 decorative cups of the *Menorah*.

3. We have a similar occurrence in the case of *Avraham* (*Bereishit* 25:7). In both *Adam* and *Avraham*'s cases, they were supposed to live additional years. *Adam* was supposed to live 1000 years but he donated 70 years of his life to *David Hamelech* (*Yalkut Tehillim* 843). *Avraham* was supposed to live 180 years, but his life was shortened by five years, so that he would not witness the wickedness of *Eisav*. Therefore the *Torah* specifies that these were the years that they actually lived. They were assigned additional years, but never lived them out. (*Haktav V'Hakabbalah Bereishit* 5:5 and 25:7).

4. Trick question: *Rashi*'s father studied *Chumash* with him all the time, hence *Rashi*'s father was the first person to study *Chumash* with *Rashi*.

5. He was 70 (*Bereishit Rashi* 47:29).

6. The *Gemara* in *Erechin* 13b relates that the harp used in the *Beit Hamikdash* was a seven stringed instrument. The *gemara* deduces this from the *pasuk* in *Tehillim* (16:11) which speaks about *"sova"* – "joy," which is composed of the same letters as the word *"sheva"* – "seven." However, in the time of the *Mashiach*, the harp will be eight stringed and in *"Olam Habah"* – "the world to come" the harp will be two stringed. *David Hamelech* in *Tehillim* refers to the *"sheminit"* (see examples in *Tehillim* 6 and *Tehillim* 12), which is the eight stringed harp. In *Tehillim* 33, he refers to the *"nevel assor,"* which *Rashi* describes as the 10 stringed instrument.

7. Rav Matityahu Glazerson explains that *Yuval* invented the *"kinor"* – "harp." The harp is the instrument most closely shaped like a human heart. The word *kinor* can be divided into the letters *"kaf vav"* which has the numerical value of 26, equalling *Hashem*'s name; and the word *"ner"* – "candle," which according to *Torah* commentators represents the soul of man, which has

a flame constantly soaring upwards. The harp, the earliest musical instrument, therefore connects man's heart and soul to *Hashem*.

8. The *Ramban* quotes the *Bereishit Rabbah* who says that *Kayin* was given a dog for protection when he was punished and sent into exile for the sin of killing his brother *Hevel* (*Ramban, Bereishit* 4:13).

9. *Adam.* The gemara (*Sanhedrin* 38b) tells us that he was born in the first hour of the sixth day of creation. When he was nine hours old, he was commanded not to eat from the *"etz hadaat"* – "the tree of knowledge" or he would die. By the 10th hour, he had eaten from it. The punishment for eating from the *"etz hadaat"* was death (*Bereishit* 2:17).

10. *Rashi* (*Bereishit* 4:1) tells us that *Kayin* was born together with a twin girl.

11. *Rashi* (*Bereishit* 4:1) tells us that *Hevel* was born as a triplet with two girls.

12. *Rashi* (*Bereishit* 1:14) says that they were created on the first day and were only set in motion on the fourth day.

13. The *Gemara* in *Pesachim* 94a quotes *Rava* who said that the size or circumference of the world is six thousand parasangs. If you check on Wikipedia, there are varying opinions of the length of a parasang, which was a Persian unit of distance. One of the opinions is four statute miles, which would then place the circumference of the earth as 24,000 miles. The actual circumference is 24,900 miles.

14. Women were granted the *mitzvot* of *Shabbat* candles and *Challah*, because *Chava*'s actions spoiled *Adam*, who is described as the *"ner"* – "light" of the world (*Mishnah Berurah* 263:12), and also as the *"challah"* or initial inhabitant of the world (*Mishnah Berurah* 242:6). Women do not participate in the *mitzvah* of *Kiddush Levana* because *Chava*'s actions caused the moon, which was originally the size of the sun, to diminish (*Mishnah Berurah* 426:1).

15. *Adam, Kayin* and *Bilaam*:

    1. After eating from the Tree of Wisdom, *Adam* hides and *Hashem* asks him "Where are you?" *Adam* answered: "I heard the sound of *You* in the garden, and I was afraid because I was naked, so I hid."

    2. After killing his brother *Hevel, Kayin* was asked by *Hashem* "where is your brother *Hevel?*" *Kayin* answered "am I my brother's keeper?" (*Bereishit* 4:9).

    3. *Bilaam* was asked by *Hashem* "who are the people who came to visit you tonight?" *Bilaam* answered that *Balak* had sent them to him (*Bamidbar* 22:9).

    In all three cases, they should have realized that *Hashem* obviously knew the answer.

16. In *Megillat Esther*, we are told that *Achashverosh*'s decree that Jews may defend themselves against their enemies, was delivered throughout the

empire by *"achashtranim"* (*Esther* 8:10). In the *gemara* (*Megillah* 18a), there is a discussion as to whether one fulfills one's obligation to hear the *megillah* if one does not understand Hebrew. The *gemara*, at that point, questions whether anyone really understands the meaning of the word *"achashtranim"*? *Rashi* says they were a type of swift camel. *Saadiah Gaon* says that they were mules. *Elazar* of *Worms*, known by his commentary, *Rokeach*, said that the *achashtranim* were eight legged, two humped camels. He noted that the *gematriya* of *"achashtranim"* is the same as the *gematriya* of *"shel shemoneh raglayim"* – "of eight legs." The *Rokeach* says that this animal was chosen to speedily deliver the message because it would walk on four legs, with the other four legs gathered under its body. When the first four legs became tired, they would switch to the other four legs, and as such, the animal had twice the stamina of other animals (*Rokeach Bereishit* 1:25). *Rav Yaakov Emden* wrote that he found books attesting to this animal's existence, still in his time, in Persia.

17. *Adam* composed Chapter 92 of *Tehillim, Mizmor Shir L'Yom HaShabbat*. There are two versions quoted by *chazal* as to when *Adam* composed this chapter of *Tehillim*:

    1. The *midrash* says that it was the *Shabbat* that saved *Adam* from death. The *midrash* (*Tehillim, Chapter* 92) recounts the events of the first day of *Adam*'s life, hour by hour. "In the tenth hour he sinned, in the eleventh hour he was judged, in the twelfth hour he was thrown out. *Hashem* came to sentence him but *Shabbat* arrived and instead, *Hashem* expelled *Adam* from *Gan Eden*. *Yom Shabbat* came and became his defense attorney, saying before *Hashem*, "Master of the universe, in the six days of creation, no one suffered punishment at all, and You begin with me? Is this my holiness? Is this my rest? And for the sake of *Shabbat, Adam* was saved from *"Gehinnom"* – "hell." When *Adam* saw the power of *Shabbat*, he was about to sing a hymn to *Shabbat* but *Shabbat* said to him, "To me you sing a hymn? Let's you and I sing a hymn to *Hashem*, let it be *"tov lehodot lashem."*

    2. According to *Bereishit Rabbah* (22:13), *Adam* composed this *perek* after *Kayin* told him about the power of repentance or *teshuva*. The word *Shabbat* can be rearranged to form the word *"tashuv"* (return).

18. *Hevel* was stronger. The *midrash* (*Bereishit Rabbah* 22:17–18) comments on the strange usage of the word *"el"* in the *pasuk* *"vayakom Kayin el Hevel achiv"* – "and *Kayin* rose up against *Hevel* his brother" (*Bereishit* 4:8). The *midrash* recounts that when *Kayin* rose up to kill *Hevel, Hevel* overpowered him. When *Kayin* begged to be released, *Hevel* let him go, and with no sense of appreciation for *Hevel*'s mercy, *Kayin* then killed *Hevel*. The *Chafetz Chaim* explains that it was for this reason that *Kayin* was later given a guard dog;

for no animal is more faithful and grateful to its owner than a dog. And no act could be more contrary than *Kayin's* taking advantage of *Hevel's* kindness, and using it to kill him. By giving him a dog, *Hashem* was giving *Kayin* a constant reminder of his lack of "*hakarat hatov*" – "recognition of kindness." In this way, perhaps *Kayin,* too, would learn to show appreciation for the kindness done to him.

19. The *Targum Yonatan* says that the offerings were brought on the 14th of *Nisan* as the *Pesach* offerings. The *Bereishit Rabbah* 22:4 quotes the dispute between *Rabbi Eliezer* and *Rabbi Yehoshua* as to the date of the creation of the world. One said it was created in the month of *Tishrei* and the other says it was created in the month of *Nisan.* The *midrash* then suggests that *Hevel* was only alive for about 50 days and therefore according to the *Tishrei* creation date, he died around *Chanukah,* and according to the *Nisan* creation date, he died around *Shavuot.*

20. One would assume that since only *Noach* and his immediate family survived the flood and since *Noach* was a descendant of *Sheit,* the brother of *Kayin,* that *Kayin's* lineage stopped with the flood. However, one would then be overlooking *Noach's* wife, *Naamah,* (*Rashi Bereishit* 4:22) who was a direct descendant of *Kayin.* Here is the lineage: *Naamah* was the daughter of *Tzilah,* who was the wife of *Lemech,* who was the son of *Metushael,* who was the son of *Mechiyael,* who was the son of *Irad,* who was the son of *Chanoch,* who was the son of *Kayin.*

PARSHAT NOACH QUESTIONS

1. *"Shnayim shnayim ba-oo el Noach"* (Bereishit 7:9) – *Eilu hayamim shegomrim et haHallel.* Explain?
2. What was the date of *Metushelach's yahrtzeit*?
3. Who was *Noach's* father-in-law?
4. Who had a father and father-in-law with the same name?
5. Who in *Parshat Noach* could really call two of his sons *"Bubbie"* and *"Zeidy"*?
6. Can you solve the following?
    Sof sof techilat sh'mi,
    Techilat sof sof sh'mi,
    U'k'sheba Noach el hateiva timtza sh'mi,
    Ma sh'mi?
7. Which year in history is missing in *Parshat Noach*?
8. What role does the number 15 play in *Parshat Noach*?
9. Where is there a hint to *Purim* in *Parshat Noach*?
10. Who was the youngest of *Noach's* three children?
11. From where do we learn the concept of only saying *"miktzat shevach"* – "partial praise" of a person in their presence?
12. How many fish died during the flood?
13. When in the water, how much of the ark was visible above the water?
14. How long did it take *Noach's* vineyard to grow?
15. Who was the first person in the *Torah* to name his son after his father?
16. Darwin proposed that man evolved from monkeys. When in history did men actually turn into monkeys?
17. Who made the nails used in the building of the ark?
18. Which three occupants of the *teiva* were the only ones to mate during the flood?
19. Where is there a reference to *Eliyahu Hatishbi* in the story of *Noach* and the raven?
20. Put the following brothers in order from oldest to youngest: *Avraham, Haran, Nachor.*

PARSHAT NOACH ANSWERS

1. This is one of my all-time favourite riddles. "*Shnayim shnayim ba-oo el Noach*" (*Bereishit* 7:9). The first "*shnayim*" refers to the two days of *Shavuot*; the second "*shnayim*" refers to the first two days of *Pesach*; "*ba-oo*" has the *gematriya* of nine which refers to the days of *Sukkot* in *Chutz La'aretz*; "*el Noach*" is the same *gematriya* as the word *Chanukah*. These then are the days when we recite the complete *Hallel*. Obviously, this riddle only works in *Chutz La'aretz*.

2. The *Torah* tells us that the flood began on the 17th day of *Cheshvan*. The flood should have begun on the eleventh of *Cheshvan* but that was the day that *Metushelach* died and out of respect for *tzaddikim*, the punishment by the flood was delayed (*Rashi Bereishit* 7:4). *Rashi* points out that if you calculate the years of *Metushelach*, you will find that he died in the six hundredth year of *Noach*'s life, which coincided with the date of the Flood (*Gemara Sanhedrin* 108b).

3. *Rashi* in *Bereishit* (4:22) tells us that *Lemech*'s daughter *Naamah* was married to *Noach*.

4. *Noach*'s father was *Lemech*, son of *Metushelach*, and his father-in-law was *Lemech* son of *Metushael* (*Bereishit* 5:28–29)

5. *Bereishit* 10:7 lists the sons of *Kush*. Two of his five sons were named *Svah* and *Savta*!

6. Another of my all-time favourite riddles. *Pinchas* is composed of the name *Noach* surrounded by a *Peh* and *Samech*. Literally translated as: The end of the word *sof* is the first letter of my name (*peh*), the beginning of the word *sof* is the last letter of my name (*samech*), and if you add a *nun* and a *chet* (from the word *noach*) to the middle of the word (alternate translation for the word *teivah*), you will find my name, *Pinchas*.

7. The *Torah* tells us that *Noach* was 600 years old when the flood began (*Bereishit* 7:11) and lived 350 years after the flood (*Bereishit* 9:28). The flood lasted for one year and ten days. That should give us a total of 951 years. But the *Torah* lists *Noach*'s total years as 950 (*Bereishit* 9:29). So there is a year missing.

8. The floor of the *teiva* was 15,000 square *amot* (50 × 300). Cubic area of each of the three compartments was 150,000 cubic *amot* (300 × 50 × 30 = 450,000 / 3 = 150,000). The waters were 15 *amot* above the highest peak (*Bereishit* 7:20) and the waters raged for 150 days. One of the reasons for the flood was a lack of fidelity between husband and wife. The *gemara* (*Sotah* 17a) explains that man (*ish*) and woman (*ishah*) have two common letters, *alef* and *shin*. The two uncommon letters are *yud* and *heh*, which have a *gematriya* of 15 equal to one of *Hashem*'s names. Therefore by bringing *Hashem* (i.e.,

the *yud* and the *heh*) into marriage, we have a successful union of man and woman; without it, we have only fire (*alef* and *shin* or *aish*). The use of 15 in the story of the flood is there to show that the sin of infidelity caused the *yud* and *heh* to be removed from amongst them and therefore *Hashem* brought about their punishment and the salvation of *Noach* in multiples of 15 – *yud* and *heh*. (*Kli Yakar Bereishit* 6:15). The *Kli Yakar* quotes the *pasuk* in *Tehillim* 118:16, "*lo amut ki echyeh, va'asaper maasei kah*" – "I will not die, but rather I shall live, and I will proclaim the wondrous deeds of *Hashem*." Real living, says the *Kli Yakar*, is when families are producing offspring through the union of husband and wife and this is highlighted by the use of *Hashem*'s name "*kah*" comprised of the *yud* and the *heh* in that *pasuk*.

9. There are two:
   1. The tree that was used to hang *Haman* was 50 cubits high supplied by *Parshandata*, governor of the *Mount Ararat* area, from a beam of *Noach*'s ark which was 50 cubits wide (*Medrash Abba Gorion*).
   2. The *Megillah* uses the word "*v'Noach*" (*Esther* 9:17) instead of the more grammatically correct "*v'nachu*," as a description of the peace and tranquillity experienced by the Jews after the defeat of *Haman*. The use of the word "*v'Noach*," to symbolize peace after war, is synonymous with the concept of the dove holding an olive branch in *Parshat Noach*, the universal peace symbol.

10. You might have said *Yefet*, since he is always listed last when the three sons of *Noach* are mentioned. The *Siftei Chachamim* (*Bereishit* 9:24) quoting the *Maharshal* says, however, that *Shem* was the youngest of *Noach*'s three children and cites a genealogical proof from the text.

11. *Rashi* (*Bereishit* 7:1) quotes the *gemara* (*Eruvin* 18b) and says that when *Hashem* called *Noach* "*tzadik*" – "righteous," he held back from using the added praise of "*tamim*" – "perfect," as this conversation took place in *Noach*'s presence.

12. The *gemara* (*Zevachim* 113b) says that no fish died in the flood.

13. Since we know that the total height of the ark was 30 "*amot*" – "cubits" (*Bereishit* 6:15); and that 11 *amot* were below water level (*Rashi Bereishit* 7:17); therefore, when in the water, there were 19 *amot* of ark above the water level.

14. The *Targum Yonatan* (*Bereishit* 9:20) says that *Noach* found a vine in one of the rivers flowing from *Gan Eden* and he planted this vine. The vineyard miraculously grew in one day!

15. *Terach* was the son of *Nachor* and he had three sons; *Avraham*, *Nachor* and *Haran* (*Bereishit* 11:24–26). Unlike common custom, rarely in the *Torah* do we find people naming children for a deceased close relative.

16. The *Gemara* (*Sanhedrin* 109a) states that a percentage of the people involved in the building of "*Migdal Bavel*" – "The Tower of Babel" were punished by being transformed into monkeys.

17. *Rashi* (*Yehayahu* 41:7) identifies *Shem*, the son of *Noach*, as a blacksmith, who made all the nails used in the construction of the ark.

18. The raven, the dog and *Cham*, the son of *Noach*, sinned and mated whilst in the ark (*Gemara Sanhedrin* 108b).

19. The raven circled around the ark "*ad yevoshet hamayim*" – "until the waters had dried up" (*Bereishit* 8:7). *Rashi* quotes the *midrash* that says that the raven was ready for another mission should the waters dry up, and during the days of King *Achav*, it was the raven that brought food to *Eliyahu* (*Melachim* 1:17:6). The *Siftei Chachamim* says that a hint to this is that the word "*yevoshet*" is written without the "*vav*," yielding the letters "*tishbi*," a reference to *Eliyahu Hatishbi*. Furthermore, it is written "the water dried up" rather than "the earth dried up," alluding to the drought in *Eliyahu*'s days. (*Maharshal*)

20. *Avraham* was older than *Nachor* by one year, and *Nachor* was older than *Haran* by one year (*Sanhedrin* 69b).

PARSHAT LECH LECHA QUESTIONS

1. How many individuals in *Parshat Lech Lecha* are referred to by a name different from their normal name?
2. How many individuals of royalty (i.e., king, queen, prince or princess) are mentioned in *Parshat Lech Lecha*?
3. How do we know that *Terach* did "*tshuva*" – "repented"?
4. How long was *Avraham* supposed to live and why were his years shortened?
5. Where do we find a hint to the first *beracha* of *Shemoneh Esrei* in *Parshat Lech Lecha*?
6. How many people in *Tanach* were named before they were born?
7. Who was the first person to call *Hashem* by the name "*Adon*" – "Master"?
8. Who aged 13 years over two *pesukim*?
9. Superman loses his strength when he is near Kryptonite. Who in the *Torah* lost his strength because of his closeness to a particular geographic location?
10. Name a *kohen* whose sons were not *kohanim*?
11. Name *kohanim* whose father was not a *kohen*?
12. Which two *kohanim* are mentioned by name in *Sefer Bereishit*?
13. In Hebrew, the noun normally precedes the adjective; e.g. a good boy is "*yeled tov.*" This is the opposite of English, where the adjective precedes the noun; e.g. good boy. Where in *Parshat Lech Lecha* is there a Hebrew phrase with the adjective preceding the noun?
14. There were 48 male prophets and seven female prophetesses in history. How many of these were husband and wife prophet/prophetess teams?
15. Name three people who resembled *Avraham*?
16. Who became a father at the age of eight?
17. It is a tremendous honour, but I cannot be the recipient of this honour twice from the same donor. What is this honour?
18. What was *Avraham* doing when the "*palit*" – "the giant *Og*," came to tell him *Lot* was captured?
19. Name a father-in-law who was two years younger than his son-in-law?
20. Who was the mother of *Avraham*?

PARSHAT LECH LECHA ANSWERS

1. Four individuals in *Parshat Lech Lecha* are referred to by a name different from their normal name, namely:
   1. *Amrafel* was *Nimrod* (*Rashi Bereishit* 14:1).
   2. *Malki Tzedek* was *Shem* (*Rashi* 14:18).
   3. "*hapalit*" – "the fugitive," was *Og* (*Rashi* 14:13).
   4. The "three hundred and eighteen people" were *Eliezer*, which equals 318 in *gematriya* (*Rashi* 14:14).

2. There are 12 who are named in *Parshat Lech Lecha* and one who was not yet a king, but who would eventually become royalty. They are the nine kings mentioned in the war between the four kings and the five kings; plus *Paroh, Malki Tzedek* and *Hagar*:

1. *Amraphel*	7. *Shinav*
2. *Aryoch*	8. *Shemever*
3. *Kedarlaomer*	9. *Bela*
4. *Tidal*	10. *Paroh*
5. *Bera*	11. *Malki Tzedek*
6. *Birsha*	12. *Hagar* (daughter of *Paroh*).

   Another possible answer is *Og*, the future king of *Bashan*.

3. *Rashi* (*Bereishit* 15:15) explains that *Hashem* promises *Avraham* "And you shall come to your ancestors in peace," hinting to the fact that he would join his father *Terach* who had done *teshuva* (*Bereishit Rabbah* 30:4).

4. *Rashi* (*Bereishit* 15:15) explains that *Avraham* was supposed to live 180 years but his life was shortened by five years so that he would not witness *Eisav's* evil conduct. The very day when *Avraham* died, *Esau* rebelled against *Hashem* (*Bereishit Rabbah* 63:12). *Rashi* also explains that his son *Yishmael* repented during *Avraham's* life-time (*Bereishit Rabbah* 38:12). This was to fulfill *Hashem's* promise "you shall be buried in a good old age."

5. *Hashem* promises *Avraham* (*Bereishit* 12:2) "and I will make you into a great nation" hinting to the fact that in the first *beracha* of *Shemoneh Esrei* we say "*Elokai Avraham*" – "the God of *Avraham*"; "and I will bless you" hinting to the fact that we say "*Elokai Yitzchak*" – "the God of *Yitzchak*"; and "I will make your name great" hinting to the fact that we say "*Elokai Yaakov*" – "the God of *Yaakov*." The *pasuk* then concludes "and you will be a blessing" hinting to the fact that the conclusion of the *beracha* is "*Magen Avraham*" – "shield of *Avraham*" (*Rashi Bereishit* 12:2; *Gemara Pesachim* 117b).

6. There were five; two in the *Torah* and three in the rest of *Tanach*. They are *Yishmael* (*Bereishit* 16:11); *Yitzchak* (*Bereishit* 17:19); *Yoshiyahu* (*Melachim* 1:13:2); *Emanuel* (*Yeshayahu* 7:14) and *Shlomo* (*Divrei Hayamim* 1:22:9).

7. *Avraham* (*Bereishit* 15:8) at the *"brit bein habetarim,"* "the covenant between the pieces."

8. In *Bereishit* 16:16, we are told that *Avraham* was 86 years old and in the very next *pasuk* (*Bereishit* 17:1), he is now 99 years old. Therefore in one *pasuk*, we have seen the passage of 13 years!

9. The *Torah* says that *Avraham* chased the four kings "till *Dan.*" *Rashi* (*Bereishit* 14:14) cites a *gemara* (*Sanhedrin* 96a) that says that he could not proceed further as his strength was sapped by being close to where his descendants would ultimately create an idol.

10. *Malki Tzedek* was a *kohen* (*Bereishit* 14:18) but his children were not (*Gemara Nedarim* 32b).

11. *Moshe* (*see Gemara Zevachim* 102a) and *Aharon* were *kohanim*; yet their father *Amram* was a *levi*.

12. *Malki Tzedek* (*Bereishit* 14:18) and *Potifera, Yosef*'s father-in-law (*Bereishit* 41:45) were both priests.

13. *Yishmael* is described as a *"pereh adam"* – "a wild man" (*Bereishit* 16:12). The *Haktav Vehakabbalah* comments the reason for the adjective preceding the noun in this case, is because *Yishmael* was one who had little value for humanity and therefore the primary description of him was his wildness rather than his basic essence as a human being.

14. There were four prophet/prophetess husband and wife teams in Jewish history. They were *Avraham* and *Sarah, Elkana* and *Chana, David* and *Avigail,* and *Mordechai* and *Esther* (*Rashi Gemara Megillah* 14a).

15. Three people who physically resembled *Avraham* were *Lot* (*Rashi Bereishit* 13:8); *Yitzchak* (*Rashi Bereishit* 25:19); and *Eliezer* (*Bereishit Rabbah* 60).

16. *Haran* was the father of *Yiscah* (*Bereishit* 11:29) and *Rashi* comments that *Yiscah* was *Sarah,* the wife of *Avraham* (*Rashi Bereishit* 11:29). The *Gemara* states (*Sanhedrin* 69b) that *Avraham* was two years older than *Haran* and we know that *Avraham* was 10 years older than *Sarah.* Therefore *Haran* was eight years older than *Sarah* and thus became a father at the age of eight.

17. The honour of being a *"sandek"* – "the one who holds the baby during a *brit* or circumcision ceremony" cannot be given to the same person for two brothers (*Shulchan Aruch Yoreh Deah* 265:11).

18. *Targum Yonatan* (*Bereishit* 14:13) tells us that this occurred on *Erev Pesach* while *Avraham* was busy baking *matzot* in preparation for the *Pesach Seder.*

19. The *Torah* tells us that *Haran* was the father of *Yiscah* (*Bereishit* 11:29) and *Rashi* comments that *Yiscah* was *Sarah,* the wife of *Avraham* (*Rashi Bereishit* 11:29). Therefore *Haran* was *Avraham*'s father-in-law. The *Gemara* (*Sanhedrin* 69b) states that *Avraham* was two years older than *Haran.*

20. *Amatlai bat Karnevo* (*Gemara Bava Batra* 91a). The *gemara* notes that she had the same name, *Amatlai,* as *Haman*'s mother.

PARSHAT VAYERA QUESTIONS

1. From where do we derive the *halacha* that one should always try to *"daven"* – "pray" in a *"makom kavua"* – "the same place"?
2. From where do we learn the importance of escorting guests when they are ready to leave?
3. What three elements of *"hachnasat orchim"* – "welcoming guests" do we learn from the word *Eshel* (*Bereishit* 21:33)?
4. From where do we learn that one should not deviate from the local custom?
5. One of the ten items that was prepared *"Erev Shabbat bein hashmashot"* – "Friday evening at twilight" appears in *Parshat Vayera*. What is it?
6. From where do we learn that we must make a *"seudat mitzvah"* – "ceremonial dinner" for a *Brit Milah*?
7. Bring proof that *Avraham* was a member of *"eidot hamizrach"* – "oriental Jews"?
8. How were *Lot* and *Sarah* related?
9. How old were *Avraham* and *Sarah* when they married?
10. Which two people were brothers, first cousins and uncles to each other?
11. What were the names of *Yishmael's* wives?
12. Why did *Lot's* wife specifically turn into a pillar of salt?
13. Who were the only people to ride on donkeys in the *Torah*?
14. Which of the *avot* learned at the *Yeshiva* of *Shem*?
15. In *Bereishit* 22:14, *Avraham* calls the place of the *Akeida* "*Hashem Yir'eh*" which is better known as *Har HaMoriah, Har Habayit* or *Yerushalayim*. What is the mathematical connection between the name *Hashem Yir'eh*, given by *Avraham*, and the name *Yerushalayim*?
16. Who was the first person in history to be on *Har Hamoriah*?
17. Name three miracles that occurred in the desert that were a result of actions in *Parshat Vayera*.
18. Who in the *Torah* grew?
19. What did *Yitzchak* and *Arpachshad* have in common?
20. Which item in *Parshat Veyera* requires two *berachot* upon seeing it?

PARSHAT VAYERA ANSWERS

1. After praying on behalf of *Sodom, Avraham* returns to the same spot the next day to speak to *Hashem* (*Bereishit* 19:27). The *Radak* comments that it is appropriate for a person to select a specific place where he offers up his prayers on a regular basis (*Gemara Berachot* 6b).

2. *Avraham* escorts the *Malachim* when they left (*Bereishit* 18:16). The *Chida* comments that the *gematriya* of "*holech imam l'shalcham*" – "*Avraham* escorted them as they left" is 613, to teach us that when one escorts guests as they leave your home, it is as important as keeping all of *Torah* (*Chomat Anach al HaTorah, Bereishit* 18:16).

3. *The* word "*eshel*" (*Bereishit* 21:33) *is* spelled *alef, shin, lamed; alef* stands for "*achila*" – "providing food"; *shin* stands for "*shtiya*" – "providing drink" or "*shechiva*" – "a place to sleep"; and *lamed* stands for either "*lina*" – "providing a place to sleep" or "*leviya*" – "escorting guests as they leave" (*Rashi Ketubot* 8b).

4. *Rashi* indicates that the *malachim* who visited *Avraham* were not really eating; they just appeared to be; to teach us that one should not deviate from the local custom (*Bereishit* 18:8).

5. One of the items enumerated in *Pirkei Avot* 5:6 that were created on the eve of *Shabbat* of creation at twilight was the ram that was a substitute for *Yitzchak* at the *Akeidah. Bartenura* comments that it was decreed at the first Friday afternoon twilight that it would be stuck in the thicket by its horns at the time of the binding of *Yitzchak*.

6. The *Torah* records that *Avraham* made a great feast on the day of "*higamel et Yitzchak*." The *Daat Zekeinim* comments that the word "*higamel*" (*Bereishit* 21:8) is made up of the letters *heh* and *gimel*, which numerically equal 8, and the letters *mem* and *lamed* which spell the Hebrew word for circumcision, hinting to the fact that it was the day of *Yitzchak's brit*.

7. When the three angels came to *Avraham's* tent, *Rashi* (*Bereishit* 18:10) comments that this story occurred during *Pesach. Rashi* also comments a few *pesukim* earlier (*Bereishit* 18:7) that *Avraham* ran to the herd and chose three calves, so that he might prepare three tongues for the angels and serve these to them together with mustard condiment (*Bava Metzia* 86b). We know that mustard is generally accepted to be in the category of "*kitniyot*" which is only permitted during the holiday of *Pesach* to Jews of the *eidot hamizrach* community; and not permitted to *Ashkenazi* Jews. Therefore, *Avraham* must have been a member of *eidot hamizrach*. All kidding aside, we do know that *Avraham* came from the region near Aleppo Syria which adheres to the *eidot hamizrach* tradition.

8. They were brother and sister. *Bereishit* 11:27 records that *Haran* was *Lot's* father. Two verses later (*Bereishit* 11:29) we learn that *Haran* also had two daughters, *Milcah* and *Yiscah*; *Rashi* tells us that *Yiscah* was *Sarah* (*Bereishit* 11:29).

9. According to the *Yalkut* (*Lech Lecha* 16:78), *Avraham* and *Sarah* were child-less for 75 years. Therefore *Avraham* was 25 when he married the 15 year old *Sarah*. There are other opinions on this topic as well.

10. Another of my top 10 riddles. The answer is *Amon* and *Moav*. They were brothers because they had the same father, *Lot*. They were first cousins, because their mothers were sisters. They were uncles to each other, if one is considered the son of *Lot*, while the other is the grandson of *Lot* and vice versa.

11. *Yishmael* first married *Adisha*, divorced her, and then married *Patima* (*Targum Yonatan Bereishit* 21:21).

12. The *midrash* (*Midrash Agadah Bereishit* 19:32) relates the following: The city of *Sodom* prided themselves on not being hospitable to visitors, and in fact made it an offense. *Lot* asked his wife for salt for the guests and she replied, "Also this evil custom you wish to introduce into this place?" She had no salt in the house and went from door to door asking neighbours for salt for her husband's guests, letting everyone know that *Lot* had ignored the laws of the city by inviting strangers. A short time later, a mob gathered at *Lot's* door, demanding that he give up his guests to be mistreated. The next morning, as *Sodom* was about to be destroyed, the angels rescued *Lot* and his family. As they fled, the angels warned them not to look back at the city. It was not appropriate for them to stare at the suffering of others. But *Lot's* wife disregarded the warning and, "She looked from behind, and she became a pillar of salt (*Bereishit* 19:26)." The *Midrash* explains, "She sinned with salt, and she was punished with salt." In *rabbinic* language, we call this "*midah keneged midah*" – "measure for measure."

13. The only people who are specifically mentioned in the *Torah* as riding a donkey are *Avraham* (*Bereishit* 22:3), *Zipporah* and her sons (*Shemot* 4:20) and *Bilaam* (*Bamidbar* 22:22).

14. If you answered *Yaakov*, then look again at the reference in *Rashi* (*Bereishit* 28:9) which says that *Yaakov* learned at the *Yeshiva* of *Ever* (no mention of *Shem*). The *Targum Yonatan* (*Bereishit* 22:19) notes that only *Avraham* is mentioned after the *Akeida* and he explains *Yitzchak's* absence due to the fact that angels miraculously transported him through the air to the *beit midrash* of *Shem* where he learned for three years.

15. The name of the city is nearly always spelled in *Tanach* as *Yerushalem*, with the letters *yud, resh, vov, shin, lamed* and *final mem* (without a second *yud*, other than four times when there is a second *yud* between the *lamed* and

the final *mem*). The *gematriya* of "*Hashem yireh*" is 242. The *gematriya* of "*Yerushalem*" is 586 and its square root is 24.2 (to the nearest 10th). Coincidence? I think not! (*L'Orah Shel Torah, Rabbi Yaakov Auerbach*).

16. According to the *Targum Yonatan* (*Bereishit* 3:23), when *Adam Harishon* was exiled from *Gan Eden*, he moved to *Har Hamoriah*.

17. The *Gemara* (*Bava Metzia* 86b) says that *Avraham*'s bringing of butter and milk to the angels was rewarded by the appearance of *mann* in the desert; *Avraham*'s standing before the angels to serve them was rewarded by the Pillar of Cloud that traveled with and protected *Bnai Yisrael*; and *Avraham*'s giving water to the angels was rewarded by the appearance of the well of *Miriam*.

18. The word "*vayigdal/vayigdalu*" – "and he/they grew" is found in connection with *Yitzchak* (*Bereishit* 21:8); *Yishmael* (21:20); *Yaakov* and *Eisav* (25:27); and *Moshe* (*Shemot* 2:10).

19. Both were born to 100 year old fathers. *Shem* was 100 when *Arpachshad* was born (*Bereishit* 11:10); and *Avraham* was 100 when *Yitzchak* was born (21:5).

20. When one sees *Lot*'s wife's pillar of salt, he is required to recite the *beracha* "*Dayan Ha-Emet*" for her and "*Zocher Hatzadikim*" for him (*Berachot* 54b; *Shulchan Aruch Orach Chaim* 218:8).

PARSHAT CHAYEI SARAH QUESTIONS

1. Give six proofs that *Yishmael* did "*teshuva*" – "repented" before he died?
2. The letters of the name *Yishmael* appear three times in the *Torah* in the correct order, but not as a one-word name, but rather grouped into other words. What are the three occurrences and what are their contexts?
3. *Eliezer* is a central character in *Parshat Chayei Sarah*. How many times is his name mentioned?
4. How do we know that *Sarah* recognized *Hashem* earlier in life than *Avraham*?
5. How old was *Rivka* when her father died?
6. Why didn't *Avraham* bless *Yitzchak* before he died, just as *Yitzchak* and *Yaakov* did to their children?
7. Who in the *Torah* had 13 children?
8. No one wants to be known as a number. Who in the *Torah* had a number as his name?
9. The *Vilna Gaon* cites the *pasuk* "*va'Hashem beirach et Avraham bakol*" as proof that *Avraham Avinu* kept the *mitzvah* of *Sukkah*. What is the connection?
10. Who in *Parshat Chayei Sarah* went to *Gan Eden* without dying?
11. What was *Avraham*'s daughter's name?
12. The *Torah* names two women who covered themselves with veils. Both of these women had twin boys. Who are they?
13. It was the first day on the job for someone in last week's *Parshat Vayera* and the first day on the job for someone in this week's *Parshat Chayei Sarah*. Who were the two individuals and what were their jobs?
14. Place in chronological order: birth of *Noach*, birth of *Avraham*, the flood, the tower of *Bavel*, death of *Noach* and death of *Avraham*?
15. Who could not have children as a result of a blessing that she received?
16. *Nezem* can mean nose ring or earring. How many references are there to *nezem* in the *Torah*?
17. How many names of places in the *Torah* have to do with numbers?
18. How many promises in the *Torah* were made by placing a hand on the other person's thigh as in "*sim na yadcha tachat yereichi*"?
19. How many cases of "*kefitzat haderech*" – "miraculous travel between two distant places in a brief time" are found in the *Torah*?
20. Where is there a proof in *Parshat Chayei Sarah* and a proof in the previous *parshah, Parshat Vayera,* that one should not talk when eating?

PARSHAT CHAYEI SARAH ANSWERS

1. The six proofs are:
   1. The *Torah* tells us that *Avraham* died "in a good old age" (*Bereishit* 25:8; *Rashi* 25:9), indicating that *Yishmael* had repented.
   2. *Avraham* was buried by *Yitzchak* and *Yishmael* together and the *Torah* lists the younger *Yitzchak* first, indicating that *Yishmael* had repented and was giving *kavod* to his younger brother *Yitzchak* (*Mizrachi Bereishit* 25:9).
   3. *Yishmael* was listed as "*ben Avraham*" – "the son of *Avraham*" (*Bereishit* 25:12) just as *Yitzchak* was listed as "*ben Avraham*" (*Bereishit* 25:19).
   4. When we look at the way the *Torah* describes the years of *Yishmael* after his death (*Bereishit* 25:17), it is described in the same terms as the years of *Sarah* and of *Avraham* (*Daat Zekeinim Bereishit* 23:1).
   5. The expression "*vayigva*" – "and he expired" denoting dying, is used to describe the death of *Yishmael* and the *gemara* says that "*vayigva*" is only mentioned in the case of righteous people, indicating that *Yishmael* repented before his death (*Rashi Bereishit* 25:17; *Bava Batra* 16b).
   6. When the *Torah* says that *Hashem* blessed *Avraham* "*bakol*" – "with everything," the *gemara* (*Bava Batra* 16b) comments that everything means that *Eisav* never rebelled as long as *Avraham* was living and that *Yishmael* repented while *Avraham* was still alive.

2. The phrase "*levilti shemoa el hakohen*" contains the name *Yishmael* spread over three words (*Devarim* 17:12); the phrase "*lo yishma el*" contains the name *Yishmael* spread over two words (*Devarim* 18:19); the phrase "*v'lo yishma aleihem*" contains the name *Yishmael* spread over two words (*Devarim* 21:18). In each case, the *Torah* refers to a disobedient person and his relationship to parents, to the court and to a prophet. (*Niflat miToratecha*).

3. This is a trick question because anyone who studied the story of *Eliezer* going to find a wife for *Yitzchak* is sure that *Eliezer*'s name is mentioned numerous times in the story. In actual fact, *Eliezer* is never mentioned in *Chayei Sarah*. He is always referred to as "*ha'ish*" – "the man" or "*ha'eved*" – "the servant." What is more surprising is that the only time that *Eliezer* is mentioned in the entire *Torah* is as "*Damesek Eliezer*" (*Eliezer* of Damascus) (*Bereishit* 15:2).

4. There is a *midrash* that says that *Avraham* was 48 years old when he recognized *Hashem*. *Rav Akiva Eiger* says that based on this *midrash*, *Sarah* and *Avraham* lived an equal number of years, and explains: since a "*ger*" – "convert" is like a newborn child, we can say that *Avraham* was "born" at age 48; *Avraham* lived for 127 years after his discovery of *Hashem* (175–48=127).

Therefore, if they "lived" an equal number of years, *Sarah* must have recognized *Hashem* at birth.

5. Three years old. Since we know that *Betuel* died when *Rivka* was leaving to marry *Yitzchak* (*Rashi Bereishit* 24:55), and at that time, according to the *midrash*, she was three years old (*Rashi Bereishit* 25:20, quoting the *Seder Olam*).

6. There are two reasons given for *Avraham* not blessing *Yitzchak*:
    1. Blessing *Yitzchak* would have put *Avraham* in the funny position of having to bless *Yishmael* also. And not wanting to create jealousy between his children, he decided to bless neither (*Targum Yonatan* 25:11).
    2. *Rashi* (*Bereishit* 25:11) comments that *Avraham* did not want to bless *Yitzchak* because he foresaw that *Yitzchak* would have *Eisav* as his offspring, and therefore *Avraham* said that he would leave any blessings to the Master of all Blessings, *Hashem*. Thus, the *pasuk* says that following the death of *Avraham*, *Hashem* blessed *Yitzchak*.

7. While there are *midrashim* that inflate the number of children of *Yaakov*, this question deals with the actual listing of offspring in the *Torah*. There are three people with thirteen children that are all enumerated by name in the *Torah*. *Yaakov* had 12 sons and one daughter for a total of 13 children (all other than *Binyamin* are listed in *Parshat Vayeitzei*; *Binyamin's* birth is in *Parshat Vayishlach*). *Yishmael* has 12 sons and a daughter listed in the *Torah* (*Bereishit* 25:13–15; *Bereishit* 36:3). *Yaktan* (*Bereishit* 10:26–29) had 13 sons.

8. The *Ibn Ezra* points out (*Bereishit* 23:2) that the place *Chevron* was alternately called *Kiryat Arba* because *Arba* was the name of the father of the other three giants (*Achiman*, *Sheishai* and *Talmai*) who, according to *Rashi*, lived there.

9. *Peninim Mishulchan Hagra* relates that at a festive gathering on *Chol Hamoed Sukkot*, the *Vilna Gaon* asked those assembled to bring proof from the *Torah* that *Avraham* observed the holiday of *Sukkot*, and no one was able to present an answer. The *Gaon* noted that there are three phrases in the *Torah* that refer to the *mitzvah* of residing in a *sukkah*. The three phrases are "*basukkot teishvu shivat yamim*," "*kol haezrach b'Yisrael yeishvu basukkot*" and "*lemaan yeidu doroteichem ki basukkot hoshavti*" (*Vayikra* 23:42,43). The three phrases begin with the letters *bet, kaf* and *lamed* spelling "*bakol*," and therefore when the *Torah* says "*v'Hashem beirach et Avraham bakol*" (*Bereishit* 24:1), it is hinting to the fact that *Avraham* observed the *chag* of *Sukkot*.

10. *Eliezer* the servant of *Avraham* is listed among those who entered *Gan Eden* while still alive. The complete list, according to *Derech Eretz Zuta* 1, includes *Chanoch ben Yered, Eliyahu, Mashiach, Eliezer* the servant of *Avraham, Chiram* king of *Tzor, Eved* king of *Kushi, Yaavetz* son of *Rabbi Yehuda Hanasi, Bitya* daughter of *Paroh* and *Serach* daughter of *Asher*. And

continues the *Derech Eretz Zuta,* according to some, *Chiram* king of *Tzor* should be removed and *Rav Yehoshua ben Levi* included instead (*Derech Eretz Zuta* is one of the 15 minor tractates of the *gemara* that were compiled later than the rest of the *Talmud,* but are usually included in printed editions).

11. The *gemara* (*Bava Batra* 16b) says that *Avraham* and *Sarah* had one daughter whose name was "*Bakol*" (see *Bereishit* 24:1).

12. The two women who covered themselves with veils and had twin boys are *Rivka* (*Bereishit* 24:65 and 25:24) and *Tamar* (38:14 and 38:26). They are both in *Sefer Bereishit.*

13. In *Parshat Chayei Sarah,* it is the first day on the job for *Ephron* (*Rashi Bereishit* 23:10) as a "*shotair*" – "police officer" and in the previous *parshah, Parshat Vayera,* it is the first day on the job for *Lot* as a "*shofait*" – "judge" (*Rashi Bereishit* 19:1). In both cases, *Rashi* comments that the word "*yoshaiv*" is written "*chosair*" without a "*vav,*" so that it could be read as "*yashav*" indicating that they were not just sitting, but rather, serving in some official capacity.

14. The proper chronological order for these six events is: birth of *Noach*; the flood; birth of *Avraham*; Tower of *Bavel*; death of *Noach*; death of *Avraham*.

15. *Rivka* received a blessing from her father *Betuel* and her brother *Lavan* when she was about to leave her home to marry *Yitzchak* (*Bereishit* 24:60). The blessing that they gave *Rivka* is repeated at every Jewish wedding "*achoteinu, at hayi l'alfei revava*" – "our sister, you are blessed to merit tens of thousands of offspring." The *Chida* (*Chomat Anach, Bereishit* 24:60) notes that the letters of the word "*revava*" spell "*Rivka bat Betuel Ha'Arami,*" and because the blessing came from her wicked father and brother, she was destined to be barren, unable to conceive. Therefore, this blessing became a curse. It is for this reason that *Hashem* forbade *Lavan* from speaking to *Yaakov* (*Bereishit* 31:24) "*mitov ad ra*" – "on matters good or bad," to indicate that even the good wishes of an evil person can be destructive.

16. There are four. *Rivka* received a nose ring from *Eliezer* (*Bereishit* 24:22); *Yaakov* gathered nose rings and idols from his household and buried them under the *elah* tree near *Shechem* (35:4); *Aharon* collected the earrings of *Bnai Yisrael* for the golden calf (*Shemot* 22:2); and the women of Israel donated their nose rings for the building of the *mishkan* (*Shemot* 35:22).

17. Three places in the *Torah* incorporate numbers. *Kiryat Arba* (*Bereishit* 23:2); *Be'er Sheva* (26:33) and *Meah Shearim* (26:12).

18. There are two places in the *Torah* where people make a promise by placing a hand on the other person's thigh. *Avraham* made *Eliezer* promise that he would not choose a Canaanite woman as a wife for *Yitzchak* (*Bereishit* 24:2); *Yaakov* made *Yosef* promise that he would not bury him in *Mitzrayim*

(47:29). Both were done by placing a hand on the other person's thigh. *Rashi* explains that whoever takes an oath must take in his hand some sacred object (*Gemara Shevuot* 38b). As circumcision was the first commandment given to *Avraham*, and was acquired only through much pain, it was consequently dear to him, and therefore he selected this as the object upon which to take the oath (*Bereishit Rabbah* 59:8).

19. There are three cases of "*kefitzat haderech*" found in the *Torah*:
    1. *Eliezer* reached *Charan* the same day he left *Avraham's* home (*Rashi Bereishit* 24:42).
    2. On the way back to *Avraham's* home, *Eliezer* and *Rivka* traveled from *Charan* to *Chevron* in three hours instead of the normal 17 days according to *Pirkei d'Rabbi Eliezer* 16 and to just one hour according to the *Yalkut Shimoni*.
    3. *Yaakov* arrived in *Charan* the same day he left *Be'er Sheva* (*Targum Yonatan Bereishit* 28:10).

20. In *Parshat Chayei Sarah*, *Eliezer* tells *Rivka's* family "*lo ochal ad im dibarti*" – "I will not eat until I have spoken" (*Bereishit* 24:33). In the previous *parshah* – *Parshat Vayera*, the angels first ate, then spoke with *Avraham*, as it says "*vayocheilu vayomru*" (*Baal Haturim* 18:8–9).

PARSHAT TOLDOT QUESTIONS

1. Name four places mentioned in *Parshat Toldot* that are still names of places today.
2. Which person in *Parshat Toldot* smelled like the "*Ketoret*" – "the incense in the *Beit Hamikdash*"?
3. How many instances of the act of smelling occur in *Sefer Bereishit* and how are they connected?
4. What unintentional curse was said in *Parshat Toldot* that was partially fulfilled?
5. If one used an *etrog* for the *besamim* of *havdalah*, what blessing would one make?
6. At which meal may one not eat from his own food?
7. How do we know from *Parshat Toldot* that a bride and groom are absolved from all their sins on the day of their wedding?
8. What other instances bring forgiveness from sins?
9. In ancient times, before fertility clinics were around, what was one way for a childless couple to assure themselves children?
10. How do we know how old *Yaakov* was when he fled from *Eisav*?
11. How many different ways is the word "*toldot*" spelled in the *Torah*?
12. How many times does the word "*vayivez*" – "and he spurned" appear in *Tanach*?
13. Who told *Rivka* that she was going to give birth to twins?
14. How many times do we find the concept of "those who curse you will be cursed" in the *Torah*?
15. Name the first time in the *Torah* that a reference is made to the similarity of the genetic makeup of a parent and a child?
16. Who were the previous owners of *Eisav's* "*bigdei hachamudot*" – "the desired clothing" (*Bereishit* 27:15) that *Rivka* used to dress *Yaakov*?
17. *Yishmael* was circumcised at 13, *Avraham* was circumcised at 99, *Yitzchak* was circumcised at eight days. At what age was *Eisav* circumcised?
18. How old was the wine that *Yaakov* served *Yitzchak* before receiving the *berachot*?
19. *Yitzchak* looked like *Avraham*. Who did *Yaakov* look like?
20. Where is there a hint to Italy in the *Torah*?

PARSHAT TOLDOT ANSWERS

1. There are four places named in *Parshat Toldot* that still exist today: *Rechovot, Mitzrayim* (Egypt), *Beer Sheva, Meah Shearim.*

2. When *Yaakov* received the blessings from *Yitzchak*, it is written (*Bereishit* 27:27) that "the smell of my son is like the smell of the field." The *Targum Yonatan* comments that this smell was like the smell of the *ketoret* (incense used in the *Beit Hamikdash*).

3. *Hashem* smelled the sweet smell of *Noach*'s sacrifice after the flood (*Bereishit* 8:21) and *Yitzchak* detected the smell of *Eisav*'s clothing, worn by *Yaakov* (*Bereishit* 27:27). In each case, the word *"vayarach"* – "and he smelled" is used and the *Baal Haturim* notes that the aroma was that of *Gan Eden.*

4. In *Rivka*'s goodbye speech to *Yaakov*, as he was leaving for *Lavan*'s home, *Rivka* said, "let me not lose you both in one day!" (*Bereishit* 27:45), referring to *Yaakov* and *Eisav*. As it turned out, *Yaakov* and *Eisav* did not die on the same day; however, they were buried on the same day (*Gemara Sotah* 13a).

5. It depends. If you are *Ashkenazi*, you would recite the *beracha* of *Boreh Minay Besamim*, as the *Rabbis* standardized the liturgy of *havdalah*, because not very many people are experts in the particular blessings on sweet smells. *Sefaradim*, however, would make a *beracha* based on the actual category of sweet smell, *"hanotein rayach tov bapeirot."*

6. The *"Seudat Havra'ah"* – "the meal of recovery," the first meal that a mourner eats after returning from the funeral must be prepared using food that does not belong to the mourner (*Gemara Moed Katan* 27b). In *Parshat Toldot*, *Eisav* comes from the field and sees his brother *Yaakov* preparing a lentil stew (*Bereishit* 25:29). *Rashi* explains that this was the day of *Avraham*'s funeral and it coincided with *Eisav* beginning his degenerate ways. *Avraham* died five years before his time, so that he would not witness *Eisav* veering from the straight and narrow path. *Yaakov* was preparing the special *seudat havra'ah* for his father *Yitzchak*, who, in mourning for his father *Avraham*, was returning from the funeral, and was not permitted to prepare his own meal. The meal was lentil stew, because lentils are round like a wheel, and mourning is a wheel that revolves in the world, touching everyone sooner or later as a revolving wheel touches every spot in its rotation (*Bava Batra* 16b). As well, just as lentils have no mouth, so, too, mourners have no mouth, for they are not permitted to initiate speech during the week of *shiva*.

7. *Eisav* married *Machalat*, the daughter of *Yishmael*. *Torah Temima* quotes the *gemara* (*Yerushalmi Bikkurim* 3:3) which states that her name was in fact *Basmat*, but she was referred to as *Machalat*, from the root "to forgive," teaching us that *Eisav* was forgiven for his sins on the day he married. The

gemara deduces from here, that every *chatan* and *kallah* are forgiven for their sins on the day of their wedding.

8. *Rashi* refers to a *midrash* (*Midrash Shmuel* 17) which lists three classes of people whose sins are pardoned; the bride and groom on the day of their wedding, the convert to Judaism and one who is appointed to a position of leadership in the Jewish Community (*Rashi Bereishit* 36:3).

9. The *gemara* (*Berachot* 31b) tells us that *Chana*, the mother of *Shmuel Hanavi*, desperately wanted to have children and prayed to *Hashem* to grant her wishes. She indicated that should her wishes not be granted, she would arrange to be alone with a stranger against the wishes of *Elkana*, her husband, and upon discovery, would be wrongfully accused. Based on the laws of *Sotah* she would then be forced to drink of the "*sotah* waters" – "bitter waters." The *Torah* says that a woman who is childless and who is wrongfully suspected of being a *Sotah*, will be blessed with children upon drinking the bitter waters. This was what *Chana* had hoped to achieve.

10. He was 63 years old. In *Bereishit* 28:9, we are told that at the time that *Yaakov* fled, *Eisav* married *Machalat* "the daughter of *Yishmael*, the sister of *Nevayot*." *Rashi* comments that the addition of "sister of *Nevayot*" appears to be superfluous. *Rashi* deduces that the *Torah* is teaching us that *Yishmael* died between the engagement and marriage of *Eisav* to *Machalat*. Therefore, working backwards, we know that *Yishmael* was 14 years older than *Yitzchak*. And *Yitzchak* was 60 years old at *Yaakov* and *Eisav*'s birth, making *Yishmael* 74 years old at the time. Since we are told that *Yishmael* lived a total of 137 years, *Yaakov* and *Eisav* must have been 63 years old at the time of *Eisav*'s marriage to *Machalat*, and *Yaakov*'s fleeing *Eisav*.

11. In *Bereishit* 2:4, "*toldot*" is spelled with two "*vavs*." In *Bereishit* 25:12, it is spelled without any *vav* at all. In *Bereishit* 25:19, it is spelled with one *vav*. There are also places in *Tanach* where the one *vav* is the second letter, and places where the one *vav* is the second last letter. The *Torah Temimah* cites a *midrash* (*Midrash Rabbah Shemot* 30) which states that there are only two places in *Tanach* where "*toldot*" is spelled "*malei*" with two *vavs*. The *midrash* proceeds to explain that the first occurrence (*Bereishit* 2:4) describes the creation of heaven and earth which symbolized total heavenly joy, and hence the word is spelled "*malei*" or full, to indicate complete happiness. The only other time that it is written "*malei*" (i.e., with two "*vavs*") is at the end of *Megillat Rut* (*Rut* 4:18) when the genealogy of *David Hamelech* is recorded. Perhaps this explains why, for the birth of *Yishmael*, "*toldot*" is spelled "*chaser*" or lacking any *vav*, as for his birth there was no heavenly joy. In the description of the birth of both *Yaakov* and *Eisav*, it would appear that there was only partial heavenly joy and as such there is only one *vav* in the word "*toldot*" in *Parshat Toldot*. May we experience total joy, when the

future offspring of *David Hamelech* arrives and is proclaimed *Mashiach ben David* (*"yehi ratzon sheyavoh bimhairo b'yameinu"* – "may He come speedily in our days, *Amein!"*).

12. Twice. Once when *Eisav* sells the *"bechora"* – "firstborn rights" (*Bereishit* 25:34), and once regarding *Haman's* resolve to destroy the Jewish people (*Megillat Esther* 3:6). The *Baal Haturim* connects the two with a *midrash* on *Megillat Esther,* which states that *Haman* descended from a concubine relationship of *Elifaz,* the son of *Eisav. Eisav* despised the birthright and *Haman* despised *Mordechai* and the Jewish people. Like grandfather, like grandson!

13. According to *Rashi* (*Bereishit* 25:23), *Hashem* initially revealed *Rivka's* twin pregnancy to *Shem,* who then told *Rivka.* The *Siftei Chachamim* explains that we know that *Hashem* did not tell this directly to *Rivka,* because of the strange construction of the *pasuk.* The *pasuk* says *"vayomer Hashem lah"* – "And *Hashem* said to her." Normally, if *Hashem* was speaking directly to a person, it would say *"vayomer lah Hashem."* Because of the position of the word *"lah," Rashi* realized that this was not direct communication.

14. Three times. The first is *Hashem* speaking to *Avram* in *Lech Lecha* (*Bereishit* 12:3); the second is *Yitzchak* speaking to *Yaakov* in *Toldot* (27:29); and the third is *Bilam* speaking about *Bnai Yisrael* in *Balak* (*Bamidbar* 24:9).

15. *Rashi* quotes a *Midrash Tanchuma* and comments on the repetitive nature of the first *pasuk* in *Parshat Toldot* (*Bereishit* 25:19), "these are the generations of *Yitzchak* the son of *Avraham; Avraham* gave birth to *Yitzchak."* Because *Avimelech* took *Sarah* while she was still barren (*Bereishit* 20:2), and soon thereafter, she gave birth to *Yitzchak,* the rumour began to spread that *Yitzchak* might be from the illegitimate relationship between *Sarah* and *Avimelech.* Therefore *Hashem* made the facial features of *Avraham* and *Yitzchak* perfectly matched so that all would know that there was no truth to the rumour.

16. The *Bartenura Al HaTorah* explains the history and mystery of *Eisav's* special garments that *Rivka* used to disguise *Yaakov* (*Bartenura Bereishit* 27:15). He quotes the *midrash* that says that these were the *"kotnot or"* – "the leather garments" that *Hashem* made for *Adam* and *Chava* (*Bereishit* 3:21). On the garments of *Adam* were images of all the animals in the world, and when *Adam* wished to summon a particular animal, he would simply touch the image of that animal and it would present itself in front of *Adam.* This special miraculous garment made its way into the possession of *Nimrod. Eisav* asked *Nimrod* if he could borrow the garment and when *Nimrod* gave it to *Eisav, Eisav* touched the image of the lion and instructed the lion to kill *Nimrod,* so that he would not have to return the garment. *Eisav,* fearing that one of his wives would use the garment to kill him, stored the garment

at *Rivka's* home and that is why the *pasuk* says *"asher ita babayit"* – "the clothes that were with her in her home."

17. According to the *Daat Zekeinim* (*Bereishit* 25:25), *Eisav* was never circumcised. Since *Eisav* was very red when he was born, *Yitzchak* thought it would be dangerous to circumcise him on the eighth day. After a year or two, when his colour remained the same, *Yitzchak* realized that this was *Eisav's* natural complexion so he could be circumcised, but decided that since he didn't circumcise him when he was eight days old, he would wait until he was 13, the same age *Yishmael* was at his circumcision. However, when *Eisav* turned 13, and *Yitzchak* wanted to circumcise him, *Eisav* refused.

18. Wine which is aged is supposedly very good. This wine was truly very old! In fact, more than 2000 years old. According to the *Targum Yonatan* (*Bereishit* 27:25), it had been preserved since the six days of creation.

19. *Yaakov* looked like *Adam Harishon.* The *gemara* (*Bava Metzia* 84a) says "the beauty of *Yaakov Avinu* is a semblance of the beauty of *Adam*, the first man, who was created in the image of *Hashem*."

20. *Yitzchak* blesses *Eisav* *"mishmanei ha'aretz yihyeh moshavecha"* – "from the fat places of the earth will be your dwelling place" (*Bereishit* 27:39). *Rashi* explains that this refers to Italy.

PARSHAT VAYEITZEI QUESTIONS

1. *Yaakov* surrounded his head with stones. For what were these stones used previously?
2. Who was *Leah* originally supposed to marry?
3. What are the only two *Aramaic* words in the *Torah*?
4. What is the *Arabic* name for the "*dudaim*"?
5. What is the connection between a ladder, money and poverty?
6. Where is there a reference in *Parshat Vayeitzei* to the UN partition vote of Israel in 1947 (which took place during the reading of this *parshah*)?
7. How was *Rachel* rewarded for "stealing" her father's idols?
8. Give three distinct proofs from *Vayeitzei* that *Leah* was a prophetess.
9. Why would one not want to be called up to the *Torah* as "*ploni ben* his grandfather's name"?
10. In *Vayeitzei*, the first *pasuk* tells us that "*vayeitzei Yaakov*" – "and *Yaakov* left *Beer Sheva*." It should have been sufficient to say "*vayelech Charana*," because we knew that he was in *Beer Sheva*. *Rashi* comments (*Bereishit* 28:10), that the *Torah* wants to teach us that the departure of a righteous person from a particular place leaves an indelible impression on that place. Which other person in *Tanach* causes *Rashi* to make a similar comment?
11. In naming her son *Gad* (*Bereishit* 30:11), *Leah* says "*bagad*" – "good luck has come." The two word phrase is written in the *Torah* as one word and *Rashi* says that he does not know why it is written as one word. How many other two word phrases in *Tanach* are written as one word?
12. How many times in *Tanach* do various forms of the phrase "*vayidar neder*" – "and he/she/they made a vow to *Hashem*" appear?
13. The *pasuk* says that *Lavan* was told that *Yaakov* was fleeing. Who was the informer?
14. From where in *Parshat Vayeitzei* is there an indication of the importance of "*tefillah b'tzibur*" – "praying with a *minyan*"?
15. What is the connection between *Reuven, Rut, Shimshon, Shmuel, Beit Shemesh* and *Shavuot*?
16. What did *Yaakov* not do because he married two sisters and what will he not do in the future?
17. What five miracles occurred to *Yaakov* the day he left *Be'er Sheva* for *Charan*?
18. How old was *Yaakov* when he married?
19. Which *pasuk* makes reference to a parent blaming a child for broken dishes?
20. What exactly were the *terafim* that *Rachel* took from *Lavan*?

PARSHAT VAYEITZEI ANSWERS

1. *Ramban*, in his commentary to a later *pasuk* (*Bereishit* 28:17), cites the *Pirkei D'Rabbi Eliezer* which says that these stones which *Yaakov* assembled around his head, were part of the altar upon which *Avraham* bound *Yitzchak* at the *akeida* (*Pirkei D'Rabbi Eliezer* 35). The *Ramban* further cites the commentary as saying that *Yaakov* took 12 stones to indicate that he would later be blessed with twelve tribes, and miraculously, the 12 stones merged into one stone to indicate that the twelve tribes would become one great nation, as stated in the *pasuk* "*mi k'amcha Yisrael goy echad baaretz*" (*Divrei Hayamim* 1:17:21).

2. *Leah* was originally supposed to marry *Eisav*. The *midrash* (*Bereishit Rabbah* 70:16) says that at the same time that *Yaakov* and *Eisav* were born to *Yitzchak* and *Rivka*, *Rachel* and *Leah* were born to *Lavan*. Letters were sent arranging the *shidduchim* of the older boy, *Eisav*, to the older girl, *Leah*, and the younger boy, *Yaakov*, to the younger girl, *Rachel*. When *Leah* began to hear reports of *Eisav*'s ill deeds, she began crying; while *Rachel*, upon hearing reports of *Yaakov*'s righteousness, began to take on a shining aura. Hence the reference "the eyes of *Leah* were tender, while *Rachel* was of beautiful appearance" (*Rashi Bereishit* 29:17).

3. *Yegar Sahaduta* (*Bereishit* 31:47), the name given to the pillar erected at the covenant site between *Lavan* and *Yaakov*, are the two *Aramaic* words in the *Torah*.

4. The *Torah* records that *Reuven* brought *dudaim* to his mother *Leah*. *Rashi* translates the word into Arabic as "*yasmine*" – "jasmine" (*Rashi Bereishit* 30:14 – *Sanhedrin* 99b).

5. The *Baal Haturim* (*Bereishit* 28:12) points out that the *gematriya* of "*sulam*" – "ladder" (*samech, vav, lamed, mem*) and "*oni*" – "poverty" (*ayin, vov, nun, yud*) and "*mamon*" – "wealth" (*mem, mem, vov, nun*), are all equal to 136. This teaches us that wealth is not permanent; one should use it wisely and connect his wealth to those who are poor; the ladder symbolizing the constant ups and downs in one's fortune.

6. *Rav Isaac Halevi Herzog zt"l* (then *Chief Rabbi* of Palestine) noted that the UN vote for the partition plan was 33 in favour and 13 against. He noted the first two letters of *Yaakov*'s reference to the treaty site with *Lavan*, *Gal Eid*, were *gimel* and *lamed* which equals 33, while the first two letters used by *Lavan* to describe the treaty site, *Yegar Sahaduta*, were *yud* and *gimel* which equals 13.

7. *Rachel* hid the idols "*bechar hagamal*" – "in the saddle of the camel" (*Bereishit* 31:34). "*Bechar*" is spelled *bet, chaf, reish*. She was riding the camel and at the same time preventing her father from bowing down to

the idols. *Rachel* had two sons, *Yosef* and *Binyamin*, both of whom would be rewarded through riding and bowing down. In *Yosef*'s case, he rode in the royal chariot and the people were commanded *"avreich"* – "to bow down" before him (*Bereishit* 41:43). The word *"avreich"* contains the same letters as *"bechar."* In *Binyamin*'s case, his direct descendant, *Mordechai*, rode on the king's horse, *"asher rachav alav hamelech"* – "that the king rode upon" (*Esther* 6:8). The word *"rachav"* again contains the same letters as *"bechar."* It is interesting to note that there are only three people in *Tanach* who were given the king's *"taba'at"* – "ring': *Yosef, Haman* and *Mordechai* (and there were actually only two rings, as the same ring that was given to *Haman* was subsequently given to *Mordechai*); and the only two people in *Tanach* who are called by the term *"mishneh l'melech"* – "second in command to the king," and therefore entitled to the same respect given to a king, including bowing down, are *Yosef* and *Mordechai*. The word for saddle *"bechar"* connects all three incidents and is therefore indicative of the ultimate reward that *Rachel* received for her act (*Parshat Hashavua* on the Internet by Rabbi Kalman Kaminer/Dr. Avraham M. Speiser).

8. *Rashi* quotes a *Midrash Tanchuma* (*Rashi Bereishit* 29:34) that all the *Matriarchs* were prophetesses, and therefore *Leah* knew that *Yaakov* would have a total of 12 sons. The three passages that point to *Leah*'s prophesy are:
   1. When she names *Levi*, acknowledging that she now had her rightful share of three sons or one quarter of the total (*Bereishit* 29:34).
   2. When *Yehuda* was born, she thanked *Hashem* for granting her more than her share or one third of the total (*Bereishit* 29:35).
   3. When she was pregnant with *Dinah*, she knew that the fetus was male (*Bereishit* 30:21). *Rashi* quotes the *gemara* (*Berachot* 60a) that *Leah* prayed that it be changed to female so that her sister *Rachel* would not have less of a share than the maidservants, *Bilhah* and *Zilpah*.

9. Because it would mean that his father is a *"rasha"* – "evil person." The *She'elot U'Teshuvot Trumat Hadeshen* 1:21 (attributed to *Rav Israel Isserlin*) rules that in the case where one's father is a *rasha*, the son should be called to the *Torah* as the "son of the grandfather." He cites *Parshat Vayeitzei* (*Bereishit* 29:5) as the source for this *halacha* where *Lavan* is called *"ben Nachor"* (his grandfather) rather than *"ben Betuel"* (his father).

10. The only other person about whom *Rashi* makes a comment that the departure of a righteous person from a particular place leaves an indelible impression on that place is regarding *Rut* when she leaves the Fields of *Moav* with *Naomi* (*Rashi Rut* 1:7).

11. *Rashi* says there are 15 such occurrences in *Tanach* of a word spelled as one word, but read as two. *Rashi* comments on the word *"chaylkaim"* (*Tehillim* 10:10) that this word translated as "helpless," is actually a two-word phrase

"*chayl*" – "*ka'im*" meaning "a broken army." Another well known example in the *Torah* is the word "*aishdat*" (*Devarim* 33:2), read as two words "*aish*" "*dat*" translated as "a fiery *Torah*."

12. Various forms of the phrase "*vayidar neder*" (and he/she/they made a vow to *Hashem*) are found in reference to *Yaakov* (*Bereishit* 28:20); *Bnai Yisrael* (*Bamidbar* 21:2); *Yiftach* (*Shoftim* 11:30); *Chana,* mother of *Shmuel* (*Shmuel* 1:1:11); and the passengers on the boat in *Yonah* (*Yonah* 1:16).

13. The informer was *Amalek*. The *Baal Haturim* notes that there are only two places in the *Torah* that use the phrase "*vayugad...ki barach*" – "and someone was told that someone was fleeing." The first instance is in *Parshat Vayeitzei* (*Bereishit* 31:22), where someone tells *Lavan* that *Yaakov* was fleeing. The second instance is where *Paroh* is told that *Bnai Yisrael* was fleeing (*Shemot* 14:5). The *Baal Haturim* deduces from the common phraseology that there was a common informer, and he quotes a *Midrash Tanchuma* that identifies *Amalek* as the informer in both cases. He further notes that the *gematriya* of "*ki barach*" is equal to the *gematriya* of *Amalek*.

14. The first words of *Bereishit* 28:16 are "*Vayikatz Yaakov mishnahto vayomer*" – "and *Yaakov* awoke from his sleep and he said." The *Baal Haturim* points out that the last letters of the four words spell "*tzibur*" – "congregation" (*tzadi-bet-vav-reish*), to teach us that one's *tefillot* are to be said when rising in the morning and are best heard in a *tzibur* or *minyan*.

15. All six are mentioned in connection with "*ktzir chittim*" – "the wheat harvest." *Reuven* brings the *dudaim* flowers to his mother during "*yemei ktzir chittim*" (*Bereishit* 30:14); *Rut* remains in *Boaz*'s field until the end of the wheat harvest (*Rut* 2:23); *Shimshon* attempts to take back his first wife at this time (*Shoftim* 15:1); *Shmuel* miraculously causes it to rain during this time (*Shmuel* 1:12:17); the *aron* is returned by the *Plishtim* to *Beit Shemesh* while the people are harvesting the wheat (*Shmuel* 1:6:13); and *Shavuot* is celebrated at the time of "*ktzir chitim*" (*Shemot* 34:22).

16. *Yaakov* did not bury both sisters in the *Maarat Hamachpela* in *Chevron* because it would be embarrassing, since the *Torah* forbids marrying two sisters (*Ramban Bereishit* 48:7). In the future, *Yaakov* will not lead the *birkat hamazon* at the "*seudat tzadikim*" – "meal of the righteous," because he married two sisters in their lifetimes. Although at the time it was not prohibited to marry two sisters, this practice would eventually become a serious transgression (*Pesachim* 119b).

17. The five miracles that occurred to *Yaakov* on the day that he left *Beer Sheva* for *Charan* were:
    1. The daylight hours were shortened.
    2. The stones *Yaakov* put beneath his head became one.

3. *Yaakov* was able to remove the extremely heavy stone atop the well with no assistance from others.
4. The waters in the well rose.
5. His journey was shortened and he arrived in *Charan* the same day that he left *Beer Sheva* (*Targum Yonatan Bereishit* 28:10).

18. *Yaakov* was 84 when he married (*Rashi Bereishit* 29:21). *Rashi* tells us that *Yaakov*, realizing that he was first getting married at the age of 84, was worried, because he could not comprehend how such an elderly person could beget the 12 tribes, even though he knew, as a prophet, that this would, in fact, occur.

19. *Bereishit* 30:23. When *Rachel* names *Yosef*, she says *"asaf Elokim et cherpati"* – "Hashem has taken away my disgrace." *Rashi* explains that so long as a woman has no child she has no one to blame for her faults; when, however, she has a child, she puts it on him/her, blaming him/her for broken dishes or treats taken from the pantry.

20. The *"terafim"* were made by beheading a firstborn and then pickling it in salt and spices. They would write some magic phrases on a gold plate and place it under its tongue. They would then hang it on a wall and it would answer questions about the future. *Rachel* took it because she did not want it to reveal to *Lavan* that *Yaakov* and his family were escaping (*Targum Yonatan Bereishit* 31:19).

PARSHAT VAYISHLACH QUESTIONS

1. The first "love" of *Parshat Vayeitzei* was the love of *Yaakov* and *Rachel*. What is the first "love" found in *Parshat Vayishlach*?
2. Who else was born with *Binyamin*?
3. Where is there a hint to *Haman* in *Parshat Vayishlach*?
4. Which place in *Parshat Vayishlach* was named for an incident involving animals?
5. How many kings were there from *Edom* before the first king of Israel?
6. From where in *Parshat Vayishlach* do we learn that it is forbidden to count the Jewish people in the normal manner?
7. On what day of the week did *Shimon* and *Levi* kill the males of *Shechem*?
8. How old were *Shimon* and *Levi* when they avenged the rape of *Dina*?
9. How many times is a tree used as a burial spot in the *Torah*?
10. In the time of the *Mishnah*, the *Torah* reading was simultaneously translated into the language of the time, *Aramaic*, so that the multitudes would readily understand the words of *Torah*. Which part of *Parshat Vayishlach* was not translated?
11. How do we know that Israel is south of *Aram Naharayim*?
12. Who in *Parshat Vayishlach* had the same name as his mother?
13. *Devorah*, the nursemaid of *Rivka*, was buried under a tree. Where else in *Tanach* does that specific tree appear?
14. We are all waiting for *Mashiach* and want to be the first to greet him. Where should we wait?
15. It is important to be humble. However, the *gemara* (*Sotah* 5a) says that a "*talmid chacham*" – "a learned individual" may possess conceit in the measure of a "*shemonah b'sheminit*" – "an eighth of an eighth." How does this Talmudic dictum connect to *Parshat Vayishlach*?
16. *Rashi* (*Bereishit* 32:5) comments on the words "*im Lavan garti*" – "I lived with *Lavan*," that *Yaakov* kept all 613 *mitzvot* while in *Lavan*'s house. If *Yaakov* had gone to *Bavel*, perhaps he would have kept 614 *mitzvot*. Explain.
17. *Rabbi Yehoshua ben Prachia* gave us certain advice in *Pirkei Avot* (*Mishnah Avot* 1:6). Where is there a *pasuk* in *Parshat Vayishlach* that seems to indicate that *Esav* followed this advice?
18. Besides reviewing the *parshah* for "*shnayim mikra v'echad targum*" – "the custom of reading the *parshah* twice with translation during the course of the week," when else would a person read the *parshah* of *Vayishlach*?
19. What name did *Esav* give *Aholivama* and why?
20. Which person mentioned in *Vayishlach* was "of no fixed address?"

PARSHAT VAYISHLACH ANSWERS

1. Trick question: Read "*love*" in this case, as the Hebrew word for negative commandment. Therefore, the first "lav or *issur*" – "negative command-ment" in the *Torah* is *Gid Hanasheh*.

2. He was part of triplets. Two sisters were born with him; while each of the other tribes had one twin sister born with them. (*Rashi Bereishit* 35:17).

3. The *Baal Haturim* (*Bereishit* 32:12) says that the first letter of the three words "*hatzileini na miyad*" – "please save me from the hands of my brother *Eisav*," spell *Haman*. In this *pasuk*, *Yaakov* fears that *Eisav* will kill his family, and enumerates "*eim al banim*" – "women and children." In the story of *Purim*, *Haman*, *Eisav*'s descendant, wanted to kill everyone, enumerating "*hanashim vehataf*" – "the women and children."

4. The place *Sukkot* (*Bereishit* 33:17) was given its name to commemorate the huts that *Yaakov* made for his animals.

5. Eight (*Bereishit* 36:31–39; *Rashi* 36:31). It is the fulfillment of the prophesy given to *Rivka* (*Bereishit* 25:23) that "power shall pass from one to the other"; i.e., there will never be simultaneous kingdoms of *Yaakov* (*Israel*) and *Eisav* (*Edom*). When one is powerful, the other weakens.

6. The *pasuk* says "*asher lo yisapher meirov*" – "which are too numerous to count" (*Bereshit* 32:13). *Rashi* comments in *Shmuel* 1:15:4 that it is from this *pasuk* that one learns that one must not count *Bnai Yisrael* in the normal manner; but rather, should count objects associated with the people, such as hats, articles of clothing or possessions.

7. It was a Sunday, and based on the *gemara*, this was an opportune time to attack the males of *Shechem*. *Rashi* (*Gemara Taanit* 27b) says that since Man was created on a Friday, and Sunday is "*yom hashlishi*" (*Bereishit* 34:25) from the day of creation, Man is always weaker on a Sunday.

8. They were 13 years old. We deduce this from the use of the word "*ish*" (*Bereishit* 34:25) when referring to *Shimon* and *Levi*. *Rashi* (*Gemara Nazir* 29b) says that the *Torah*'s use of the word "*ish*" always refers to age thirteen.

9. Twice and both in *Parshat Vayishlach*. In *Bereishit* 35:4, *Yaakov* buries the idols that were in his household under the terebinth tree near *Shechem* and a few *pesukim* later (*Bereishit* 35:8), *Devorah*, *Rivka*'s nursemaid is buried under the oak tree near *Betel*.

10. The incident of *Reuven* and *Bilhah* (*Bereishit* 35:22) was not translated (*Gemara Megillah* 25a) as it is not to be understood literally based on another *gemara* (*Shabbat* 55b), and if it were merely translated without any explan-ation, we might think of *Reuven* in a derogatory manner.

11. *Rashi* explains (*Bereishit* 35:18) that *"Ben-Yamin"* means "son of the south." Since *Binyamin* was the only one of *Yaakov's* children born in Israel, he was named son of the south as Israel is south of *Aram Naharayim*.

12. *Timna* was the concubine of *Elifaz*, the son of *Eisav*. The *Ramban* (*Bereishit* 36:12) says that she died during childbirth and the son that was born was named *Timna* in her memory.

13. We are told that *Devorah* the Prophetess sat under the *Tomer Devorah* (*Shoftim* 4:5). The *Daat Zekeinim* (*Bereishit* 35:8) says this was the same tree under which *Devorah* the nursemaid of *Rivka* was buried.

14. We should wait at *Migdal Eider,* which is identified by *Targum Yonatan* as the place where *Mashiach* will first reveal himself at the end of days (*Targum Yonatan Bereishit* 35:21).

15. The *Vilna Gaon* explains that if you look at the eighth *pasuk* of the eighth *parshah,* you will find the statement by *Yaakov "katonti mikol hachassadim"* – "I have been humbled by all the kindness that *Hashem* has done for me" (*Bereishit* 32:11).

16. Trick question: The *gematriya* of the Hebrew word *"garti"* is *"taryag"* or 613. *Targum Onkelos* translates the word *"garti"* as *"darti"* which has a *gematriya* of 614. Therefore, if *Yaakov* had lived in *Bavel,* a place where *Aramaic* is spoken, he "might" have kept 614 *mitzvot.*

17. This is a play on words. *Yehoshua ben Prachia* advises *"asei l'cha rav"* – "make for yourself a *rav* or *Rabbi"* (*Mishnah Avot* 1:6). *Eisav* in *Parshat Vayishlach* (*Bereishit* 33:9) says *"yesh li rav"* – "I have a lot," when declining *Yaakov's* gifts, claiming that he already has much wealth. *"Yesh li rav"* can also be translated "I have a *Rabbi."*

18. There is a *minhag* to read from the beginning of *Vayishlach* until the end of *perek* 33 on the *Motzaei Shabbat* before a trip. For this reason, this section of *Torah* appears in many *siddurim* in the service of *Motzaei Shabbat* (*Ba'er Heitev* on *Orach Chaim* 299).

19. *Eisav* called her *Yehudit,* hoping to fool *Yitzchak* into believing that she had given up idol worship (*Rashi Bereishit* 36:2).

20. *Baal Chanan ben Achpor* is the only king mentioned in *Parshat Vayishlach* who does not have a place associated with his name. The *Baal Haturim* explains that he had many enemies and was therefore constantly on the run (*Baal Haturim Bereishit* 36:38).

PARSHAT VAYEISHEV QUESTIONS

1. Somewhere in the first five *pesukim*, there is a word which hints at the number of times that *Yosef* was sold and the people to whom he was sold. What is that word?

2. There is a *pasuk* in one of the five *megillot* that names three of the central figures in *Parshat Vayeishev*. What is the *pasuk* and who are the three people?

3. Name as many incidents cited over the past month's *Torah* readings that feature clothing and deceit?

4. One of *Yosef's* dreams in *Parshat Vayeishev* was instrumental in a miracle which occurred much later in history. What was the miracle?

5. How many dreams are recorded in the *Torah*?

6. Who else in *Tanach* had a "*ketonet passim*" – "coat of many colours"?

7. The baker, the King of *Ai, Bigtan, Teresh, Haman* and his sons. What is the common thread?

8. In one *pasuk*, there are three consecutive words among seven words, one in past tense, one in present tense and one in future tense. Where is this *pasuk*?

9. One person, same *parshah*, two articles of clothing, identical recognition instruction. Explain.

10. Of which two people in the *Torah* can it be said, that their names spelled backwards, are words used by the *Torah* to describe them?

11. How old was *Yaakov* when *Yosef* was sold?

12. What did the brothers of *Yosef* do with the money from the sale of *Yosef*?

13. *Rashi* (*Bereishit* 37:2) explains that part of the "*dibatam ra'ah*" – "evil report" that *Yosef* gave about his brothers was that they were guilty of eating "*eiver min hachai*" – "limbs from live animals." Which limbs did *Yosef* say he saw them eating?

14. Who was *Tamar's* father?

15. What name did *Yaakov* have besides *Yisrael*?

16. What are the first two dippings mentioned in the *Torah* and how are they connected to the *Pesach* story?

17. What is the connection between fire, honey, *Shabbat*, sleep and dreams?

18. *Rivka* and *Tamar* both gave birth to twins. What similarities and differences can you think of, between the two stories?

19. Who was *Bilhah* and *Zilpah's* father?

20. Which of *Yaakov's* sons probably never ate on his birthday?

PARSHAT VAYEISHEV ANSWERS

1. *Rashi* tells us that the word *"pasim"* (*Bereishit* 37:3) stands for *Potiphar, Socharim, Yishmaelim, Midyanim,* who are the four people to whom *Yosef* was sold.

2. *Rut* 4:12 names *Tamar, Yehuda* and *Peretz,* who are all mentioned in *Parshat Vayeishev.*

3. There are four incidents in *Bereishit* that involve clothing and deceit. They are:
   1. The *"k'tonet pasim"* – "coat of many colours" that *Yaakov* gave to *Yosef.*
   2. The *"beged"* – "coat" that *Yosef* left with *Potiphar's* wife.
   3. The *"petil"* – "cloak" that *Yehuda* left as a pledge to *Tamar.*
   4. *Eisav's* clothing that *Yaakov* wore to receive *Yitzchak's* blessings.

   The common thread that runs through these incidents is that they were all used in a deceitful manner. Curiously, the word *"beged"* – "coat" and *"bagad"* – "to deceive" are spelled the same way in Hebrew. There is a concept in Judaism called *midah k'neged midah* – *Hashem* has a master plan which involves a series of events that mirror each other. In this thread, *Yaakov* deceives his father by wearing *Eisav's* clothing and then creates a sense of jealousy against *Yosef,* with the coloured coat he gives him. He is then deceived by his sons with the same coat, which is bloodied to convince *Yaakov* to believe that *Yosef* has been killed by a wild animal. *Yehuda,* who *Rashi* tells us was subsequently blamed by his siblings for not dissuading them in the *Yosef* affair, leaves his coat as security with *Tamar* and that ultimately proves that he made her pregnant. And finally, *Yosef's* coat is left in *Potiphar's* wife's hands, and is used as evidence to convict him.

4. The *Daat Zekeinim* (*Bereishit* 37:9) tells us that when *Yehoshua* ordered the sun to stand still in *Givon,* the sun refused. *Yehoshua* told the sun that based on *Yosef's* dream, the sun is forever subservient to *Yosef* and his offspring. We know that *Yehoshua* was from the tribe of *Efraim,* and is therefore a direct descendant of *Yosef.* As a result, the sun listened to its master, *Yehoshua,* and stood still.

5. The only dreams listed in the *Torah* are in *Sefer Bereishit.* There are ten dreams:
   1. *Hashem's* warning to *Avimelech* (*Bereishit* 20:3)
   2. The dream of *Yaakov* and the ladder (*Bereishit* 28:12)
   3. *Yaakov's* dream of the flock (*Bereishit* 31:10)
   4. *Hashem's* warning to *Lavan* (*Bereishit* 31:24)
   5. *Yosef's* first dream (*Bereishit* 37:7)
   6. *Yosef's* second dream (*Bereishit* 37:9)
   7. The dream of the butler (*Bereishit* 40:9)
   8. The dream of the baker (*Bereishit* 40:16)

9. *Paroh's* first dream (*Bereishit* 41:1)

10. *Paroh's* second dream (*Bereishit* 41:5)

6. *Rashi* (*Bereishit* 37:3) says that *Tamar*, the half sister of *Avshalom*, had a coat of many colours (*Shmuel* 2:13:18).

7. They are all individuals mentioned in the *Torah* as having died by hanging. The only other allusion to death by hanging is a general reference to those executed by *Bais Din* for a capital offense (*Devarim* 21:22).

8. In *Bereishit* 37:17, the man who finds *Yosef* looking for his brothers tells him "...*shomati omrim neilcha*..." – "I have heard them (past tense) saying (present tense), let us go (future tense) to *Dotan*."

9. The person is *Yehuda*; the two articles of clothing are:

   1. The coat that he leaves as a surety with *Tamar*.

   2. *Yosef's* coat of many colours.

   The expression used in both instances is *"haker na"* – "please recognize if you can" (*Bereishit* 37:32 and 38:25).

10. *Noach* and *Er*, son of *Yehuda*. Concerning *Noach*, the verse says (*Bereishit* 6:8): *Noach* found *"chein"* – "favour" in *Hashem's* eyes. In Hebrew, *chein* is *Noach* spelled backwards. Concerning *Er*, the verse says (*Bereishit* 38:7): and *Er*, *Yehuda's* firstborn, was *"rah"* – "evil" in *Hashem's* eyes. In Hebrew, *rah* is *Er* spelled backwards.

11. *Yaakov* was 108 years old when *Yosef* was sold (*Rashi Bereishit* 35:29).

12. The opening *pasuk* of the *haftarah* says that the brothers bought shoes with the money that they received for selling *Yosef* (*Amos* 2:6). This is recounted in the *Asarah Harugei Malchut* portion of the *Yom Kippur Musaf* service and in the *Midrash Pirke D'Rabbi Eliezer* 38, it is explained that each brother took two silver coins from the proceeds of the sale of *Yosef*, to buy himself a pair of sandals.

13. *Targum Yonatan* (*Bereishit* 37:2) says that *Yosef* saw them removing tails and ears from living animals and he assumed that the brothers then ate these limbs. *Perush Yonatan* comments that in his time, Arab shepherds removed the tails and ears from animals in order to cure them. *Yosef* was unaware of the fact that these limbs could be removed for health reasons and instead assumed they were eating the tails and ears.

14. *Rashi* says that *Shem* the son of *Noach* was *Tamar's* father (*Rashi Bereishit* 38:24).

15. The *midrash* says that he was also known as *"Shemesh"* – "sun" by the *"malachim"* – "angels." It brings proof from the *pasuk* "*ki va hashemesh*" – "as the sun, *hashemesh*, had come" – (*Bereishit* 28:11) which refers to *Yaakov's* arrival at *Beit El*. When *Yosef* later retold his dream of the *"shemesh"* – "sun," the *"yareach"* – "moon," and the 11 *"kochavim"* – "stars" bowing down to

him, *Yaakov* knew it was true, because no one else knew that he was referred to as *"shemesh"* (*Bereishit Rabbah* 68).

16. The first dipping mentioned in the *Torah* is when the brothers dip *Yosef's* special coat into the blood of the *"se'ir izim"* – "a kid goat" (*Bereishit* 37:31) and the second dipping is the commandment to dip the *"agudat ezov"* – "bunch of hyssop" (*Shemot* 12:22) into the blood of the *"korban Pesach"* to spread it on the doorposts. The *Ben Ish Chai* explains that the first dipping represents the first instance of *"sinat chinam"* – "baseless hatred" in the *Torah*, which caused the exile to *Mitzrayim*. The second dipping represents the solution to *sinat chinam*. The way to correct baseless hatred and exit the exile is hinted by the *"agudat ezov"* – "the bunch of hyssop," representing the unity of the Jewish people.

17. They are all ⅟₆₀th of something. Fire is ⅟₆₀th of *gehenom*; honey is ⅟₆₀th of *mann*; *Shabbat* is ⅟₆₀th of *Olam Haba*; sleep is ⅟₆₀th of death; and dreams are ⅟₆₀th of prophecy (*Gemara Berachot* 57b).

18. Both wore veils (*Bereishit* 24:65; 38:14). *Rivka* gave birth to a *tzadik* and a *rasha* while *Tamar* gave birth to two *tzaddikim* (*Rashi Bereishit* 25:24); *Rivka* gave birth full term and *Tamar* gave birth prematurely (*Rashi Bereishit* 38:27).

19. *Bilhah* and *Zilpah* were both born to *Lavan* through a concubine (*Rashi Bereishit* 31:50).

20. *Binyamin*, because his mother *Rachel* died while giving birth to him. Therefore, his birthday was also the *yahrtzeit* for his mother and many people have the custom to fast when they are observing a *yahrtzeit* for a parent.

PARSHAT MIKEITZ QUESTIONS

1. What underlying meaning was in *Yosef*'s message when he used the word "*b'zot*" – "with this will you be tested" (*Bereishit* 42:15)?
2. What word in *Parshat Mikeitz* hints at the sources of *Yaakov*'s troubles in his life?
3. Where in the *Torah* are there six words in a row that all begin with an "*alef*"?
4. Give two hints to *Chanukah* from *Parshat Mikeitz*.
5. For the first time, the Children of *Yaakov* are called "*Bnai Yisrael*," a name that will be passed on to describe the Jewish people forever. Why are we not called by the names of the other *Avot*?
6. Where does the word *Chanukah* appear in *Parshat Mikeitz*? (That is, all the letters of the word "*Chanukah*" are written together, although they are out of order.)
7. On what date of the Jewish calendar was *Yosef* released from jail?
8. Why did *Paroh* change *Yosef*'s name?
9. What was the significance of the brothers bowing down to *Yosef* (*Bereishit* 42:6) when they first approached him in *Mitzrayim*?
10. In *Parshat Mikeitz*, who married his niece?
11. Name a male, mentioned in the *Torah*, with a great-great-great-grandmother and great-great-great-granddaughter with the same name? All three names are mentioned explicitly in the *Torah*?
12. How many people hurried in the *Torah*?
13. *Yosef* accuses his brothers of being "*meraglim*" – "spies." What parallels can you find between the brothers of *Yosef* and the *meraglim* that *Moshe* sent?
14. *Yosef* assures his brothers that he fears *Hashem* (*Bereishit* 42:18). How many more individuals (as opposed to the people of Israel, or the nation of *Amalek*) in the *Torah* are associated with the concept of fear of *Hashem*?
15. How many times are the descriptions *yefat* or *yefay to'ar* and *yefat* or *yefay mar'eh* used in *Tanach*?
16. What is the symbolism behind the name that was given to *Yosef*: *Tzafnat Paneach*?
17. How old was *Yosef* when he was put in jail?
18. I am the 11th of 12 and I am also the first born. Who am I?
19. Which *haftarah* for a *Shabbat Torah* reading is read the least amount of times a year?
20. Which command of *Yaakov* in *Parshat Mikeitz* proved to be prophetic?

PARSHAT MIKEITZ ANSWERS

1. *Zot* is equal numerically to 408. The *Bnai Yisrael* will be tested through "*teshuva*" – "repentance," "*tefillah*" – "prayer" and "*tzedakah*" – "charity." In many *machzorim* for *Rosh Hashanah* and *Yom Kippur*, written above "*teshuva*" is "*tzom*" – "fasting"; above "*tefillah*" is "*kol*" – "voice"; and above "*tzedakah*" is "*mamon*" – "money." Each of these three words is equal to 136 numerically. If you combine these, you end up with 3 × 136 = 408, which is the numerical value of "*zot.*"

2. The *Vilna Gaon* explains that when *Yaakov* says to his sons "*alai hayu kulana*" – "upon me has it all fallen" (*Bereishit* 42:36), *Yaakov* was hinting at his mother *Rivka*'s statement to him earlier "*alai kilelatcha b'ni*" – "your curse will be on me, my son" (*Bereishit* 27:13). The *Gra* explains that *Rivka* was telling *Yaakov*, "the trouble you will experience in the course of your life will come from three sources that make up the word '*alai.*'" The *ayin* stands for *Eisav* who tried to kill *Yaakov* physically. The *lamed* stands for *Lavan* who tried to kill *Yaakov* spiritually. The *yud* stands for *Yosef* who symbolized strife between siblings and family. When the brothers told *Yaakov* that *Shimon* was now incarcerated and *Binyomin* was summoned by the ruler of *Mitzrayim*, he exclaimed "my mother assured me that my troubles would come only from *Eisav, Lavan* and *Yosef.*" This was not in the script, so to speak.

3. *Bereishit* 42:21 – "*ish el achiv aval asheimim anachnu.*"

4. *Parshat Mikeitz* is almost always read on *Chanukah*. On rare occasions, *Shabbat Chanukah* has its *Torah* reading from *Parshat Vayeishev*. But since it is mostly *Mikeitz*, many commentators try to find connections between *Mikeitz* and *Chanukah*. The first hint to *Chanukah* in *Mikeitz* is in the beginning of the *parshah*, which speaks about the two dreams of *Paroh*, describing the strong cows being devoured by the weak cows, and the thin sheaves of grain devouring the full and hearty sheaves of grain. This is an allusion to the *Chanukah* story which is the story of the strong being defeated by the weak as stated in the special *tefillah* of "*al hanissim*" – "*masarta gibborim b'yad chalashim*" – "you delivered the strong in the hands of the weak." The second hint at *Chanukah* in *Parshat Mikeitz* is based on an observation of the *Vilna Gaon*. The *Gaon* says that at the end of every *parshah*, many *Chumashim* list the number of *pesukim* in the *parshah*. The only *parshah* that lists not only the number of *pesukim* but also the number of words is *Parshat Mikeitz*. The number of words is listed as 2025. The Gaon says that the word "*ner*" – "candle" is equal in *gematriya* to 250. We light for eight days; therefore 8 × 250 = 2000. *Chanukah* is on the 25th of *Kislev* and therefore 2000 + 25 = 2025, which is the number of words in *Mikeitz*. Other connec-

tions between *Miketz* and *Chanukah* are mentioned in the answer to the first question in the *Chanukah* section.

5. The name *Yisrael* includes hints to the names of all the patriarchs and matriarchs. The *yud* stands for *Yitzchak* and *Yaakov*. The *sin* stands for *Sarah*. The *reish* stands for *Rivka* and *Rachel*. The *alef* stands for *Avraham*, and the *lamed* stands for *Leah*. All are included. Additionally, there is a wonderful explanation of *Rav Shimshon of Ostropoli*, as quoted in the *sefer Talelei Orot*. He says that the total number of letters in the names of the patriarchs is 13. The total number of letters in the names of the matriarchs is also 13. The *gematriya* of "*echad*" – "one" is 13, indicating that the matriarchs and the patriarchs were the ones to introduce the concept of monotheism or one God to the world. Additionally, the number of letters of the matriarchs and patriarchs is 26, which is the *gematriya* of the name of *Hashem* – *yud, heh, vav* and *heh*.

6. *Yosef* said to his attendant, "*u'tevoach tevach v'hachain*" – "slaughter an animal and prepare it" (*Bereishit* 43:16). The word "and prepare" – "*vav-hay-chaf-nun sofit*" plus the last letter "*chet*" of the prior word "*tevach*" – "slaughter" spell "*Chanukah*" when they are rearranged. The *Otzar Chaim* says that this is an allusion to the *Seudat Chanukah* that the *Ramah* describes as a "*ktzat mitzvah*" (*Shulchan Aruch Orach Chaim* 670:2).

7. *Rashi* (*Tehillim* 81:6) says that *Yosef* was released from prison on *Rosh Hashanah*.

8. *Rashi* (*Divrei Hayamim* 2:36:4) says kings would rename their servants in order to show ultimate control over their subjects that they could even change their name if they wished, and as a result, *Paroh* changed *Yosef*'s name.

9. When the brothers bowed down to *Yosef*, it was confirmation of the dreams that *Yosef* had, in the beginning of *Parshat Vayeishev*. The *Baal Haturim* (*Bereishit* 42:6) points out that the *gematriya* of "*vayishtachavu lo*" – "and they bowed down to him" is 772, which is the same *gematriya* as "*b'chan titkayeim hachalom*" – "here the dream was fulfilled."

10. According to *Pirkei d'Rabbi Eliezer* 38, *Osnat* was the daughter of *Dinah* through *Shechem*. Therefore *Yosef* was her uncle.

11. *Menashe*'s great-great-great-grandmother and great-great-great-granddaughter were both named *Milka*. *Menashe*'s father was *Yosef*, his grandfather was *Yaakov*, his great-grandmother was *Rivka*, his great-great-grandfather was *Betuel*, which would make his great-great-great-grandmother *Milka*, "wife of *Nachor*, brother of *Avraham*" (*Bereishit* 22:20). His son was *Machir*, his grandson was *Gilad*, his great-grandson was *Chefer*, his great-great-grandson was *Tzelafchad*, making *Milka*, *Tzelafchad*'s daughter, his great-great-great-granddaughter (*Bamidbar* 27:1–2).

12. Two of the instances of people "hurrying" are in *Parshat Mikeitz*. First, the eleven sons of *Yaakov* who go down to *Mitzrayim*, "*vayemaharu*" – "and they hurry" to unload their sacks when they are accused of stealing *Yosef*'s goblet (*Bereishit* 44:11). Second, *Yosef* hurries to leave the room when he is moved to tears when seeing his brother *Binyamin* for the first time (*Bereishit* 43:30). The other instances are *Avraham*, who hurriedly gives instructions to *Sarah* to prepare cakes for the three angels (*Bereishit* 18:6); *Yishmael*, who hurries to prepare the meal for the three angels (*Bereishit* 18:7); *Rivka* who hurries to serve *Eliezer* and his camels (*Bereishit* 24:18); *Paroh* who hurries to call *Moshe* during the plague of "*arbeh*" – "locusts" (*Shemot* 10:16); and finally, *Moshe*, who hurries to bow down to *Hashem* when He reveals His "*yud gimel midot*" – "thirteen attributes of mercy" (*Shemot* 34:8).

13. There are three similarities and one difference:
    1. There were 12 sons of *Yaakov*, but only 10 are accused of being spies; there were 12 spies but only 10 participated in the negative report.
    2. The only two times the word "*diba*" is mentioned in the *Torah* is *Yosef*'s report about his brothers (*Bereishit* 37:2) and the *meraglim*'s report about the land (*Bamidbar* 13:32).
    3. *Chevron* is mentioned in both incidents. *Yosef* went to find his brothers in *Shechem* by way of *Emek Chevron* (*Bereishit* 37:14) and *Kalev* went to *Chevron* during his mission (*Bamidbar* 13:22).
    4. In the *Yosef* story, *Yehuda* stands up against *Yosef* (*Bereishit* 44:18) and in the story of the *meraglim*, *Kalev*, a descendant of *Yehuda*, and *Yehoshua*, a descendant of *Yosef*, are on the same side (*Rav Ari Kahn, Meorei Ha'Aish, Aish HaTorah*).

14. The following people or groups exhibited fear of *Hashem* in the *Torah*: *Adam* (*Bereishit* 3:10); *Sarah* (*Bereishit* 18:15); *Avraham* (*Bereishit* 22:10); *Yaakov* (*Bereishit* 28.17); *Shifra* and *Puah* (*Shemot* 1:21); *Moshe* (*Shemot* 3:6); and certain servants of *Paroh* (*Shemot* 9:20).

15. The following people or animals are referred to as "*yefat to'ar* or *yefat mar'eh*" – "handsome or beautiful" in *Tanach*: *Sarah* (*Bereishit* 12:11); *Rachel* (*Bereishit* 29:17); *Yosef* (*Bereishit* 39:6); the cows in *Paroh*'s dream (*Bereishit* 41:18); the woman captive in war (*Devarim* 21:11); *David Hamelech* (*Shmuel* 1:17:42); *Avigail*, wife of *Naval* (*Shmuel* 1:25:3); *Tamar*, daughter of *Avshalom* (*Shmuel* 2:14:27); and *Esther* (*Megillat Esther* 2:7).

16. The *Midrash* (*Bereishit Rabbah* 90:4) states that each of the letters of the name *Tzafnat Paneach* stand for another character trait possessed by *Yosef*: *tzadi* – *tzofeh* (visionary); *peh* – *podeh* (redeemer); *nun* – *navi* (prophet); *tav* – *tomech* (supporter); *peh* – *poter* (interpreter); *ayin* – *arum* (astute); *nun* – *navon* (understanding); and *chet* – *chozeh* (seer).

17. *Yosef* was 28. Since we know that he was 30 years old when he was summoned to interpret *Paroh's* dream (*Bereishit* 41:46) and we know that it was after spending two years in prison, he must have been 28 years old when he was originally incarcerated.

18. *Yosef* was *Rachel's* first born and at the same time, was the 11th of 12 sons born to *Yaakov*.

19. There are two possible answers to this riddle:
    1. If you said *V'zot Haberacha,* you might be right, as there is no *haftarah* for that *parshah*. *V'zot Haberacha* is read on *Shemini Atzeret* in Israel and on *Simchat Torah* in "*chutz laaretz*" – "diaspora" and the *haftarah* is the special reading for that holiday. So, in that case, the answer would be zero. However, the question was "a *haftarah* for a *Shabbat Torah* reading" and "*V'zot Haberacha*" is read on *Shabbat* only if *Shemini Atzeret/Simchat Torah* happens to coincide with *Shabbat*.
    2. But in reality, the *haftarah* for *Parshat Mikeitz* is read on the average once every ten years, making it the least read *haftarah* for a regularly scheduled *Shabbat Torah* reading. Since *Parshat Mikeitz* usually coincides with *Chanukah,* the special *Chanukah haftarah* is read. Here's the general scenario: The months of *Cheshvan* and *Kislev* can have either 29 or 30 days each, and there are three different configurations to the year. So, if the first day of *Rosh Hashanah* is on a *Shabbat,* and if the configuration of the year is deficient (i.e., *Cheshvan* and *Kislev* both have 29 days, making the year deficient, resulting in 353 days in a regular year or 383 in a leap year), then the first day of *Chanukah* occurs on a Friday and the last day also on a Friday. In such situations, the *Torah* reading for *Shabbat Chanukah* is *Parshat Vayeishev,* and *Parshat Mikeitz* occurs after *Chanukah* is over. In this rare occurrence, the official *haftarah* for *Parshat Mikeitz* would be read.

20. When *Yaakov* commanded his children to go to *Mitzrayim* and purchase food, he could have used the word "*l'chu*" – "go," but instead used the word "*r'du*" – "go down" (*Bereishit* 42:2). *Rashi* points out that the *gematriya* of "*r'du*" is 210, corresponding to the 210 years that *Bnai Yisrael* were ultimately enslaved in *Mitzrayim*.

PARSHAT VAYIGASH QUESTIONS

1. How do the musical notes on the first *pasuk* in *Vayigash* hint at the meaning of the *pasuk*?
2. How many individuals in *Sefer Bereishit* had their lives shortened and why?
3. *Shaul ben HaCanaanit* is one of *Shimon*'s sons. Name his mother?
4. Who married *Dina*?
5. How did *Yosef* prove to his brothers that he was indeed *Yosef*? How did he prove to his father that he was indeed *Yosef*?
6. In *Vayigash*, we find the phrase "*Yaakov, Yaakov*" (*Bereishit* 46:2). Who else in *Tanach* have names appearing twice consecutively?
7. Where is there a *remez* in *Vayigash* that *Yaakov*'s life was shortened by 33 years?
8. Cite an allusion to the binding of the four species of *Sukkot* in *Vayigash*?
9. At the beginning of *Parshat Vayigash*, *Yehuda* approached *Yosef* with confidence as one king to another. Where is this hinted at in the first three words of the *parshah*?
10. *Paroh* promises that *Yaakov* and his sons would live "*b'meitav ha'aretz*" – "in the best of the land," in the land of *Goshen* (*Bereishit* 47:6). How are these two descriptions redundant?
11. Where is there a hint in *Parshat Vayigash* to the special clothing that one should wear on *Shabbat, Yom Tov* and *Rosh Chodesh*?
12. How many people in *Tanach* "fell on each other's neck," i.e. cried on each other's shoulders?
13. This word is found 4 times in the *Torah*; a) relating to *Binyamin*; b) relating to the smearing of the blood on the doorpost during the Plague of the Firstborn; c) relating to the Four Species of *Sukkot*; and d) relating to the *Meraglim*. What is the word?
14. Which ten brothers were all named in honour of one person?
15. When was all the gold and silver in the world found in one place?
16. Who was the head of his family but was the 7th oldest?
17. How many references are there to the number 130 in the *Torah*?
18. How many of the sons of *Yaakov* were born in Israel?
19. We read in *Parshat Vayigash* (*Bereishit* 44:30) "*nafsho keshura b'nafsho*" – "their souls are bound together." To what is the *Torah* referring?
20. Through *Yosef*'s ingenuity and direction, the House of *Paroh* benefited financially, and yet there was no long term appreciation of all that *Yosef* did for the Egyptian economy. Where in *Parshat Vayigash* is there a hint to the punishment that would be imposed on *Mitzrayim* for this lack of appreciation?

PARSHAT VAYIGASH ANSWERS

1. The *Vilna Gaon* says that the musical notes on the first six words of the first *pasuk* (*Bereishit* 44:18), are *"kadma v'azla revii, zarka munach segol."* He explains that earlier (*Bereishit* 43:9), *Yehuda* promised *Yaakov* to return with *Binyamin,* and if not, *"vechatati lecha kol hayamim"* – "I will have sinned to you for all time," which according to *Rashi* means that *Yehuda* was prepared to give up *"olam habah"* – "his portion in the world to come." Therefore, in *Parshat Vayigash, Yehuda,* the fourth son (logically the first born, *Reuven,* should have approached *Yosef*), pleads with *Yosef,* to release *Binyamin. Olam Habah* is at stake. The translation of the names of the musical notes, *"kadma v'azla revii"* – "the fourth one took the lead and went (to *Yosef*)" is speaking about the fourth son, *Yehuda,* going to plead with *Yosef.* The names of the next three musical notes, *"zarka munach segol"* are translated as "I am throwing away my opportunity for eternal rest with the *"am segula,"* the chosen nation" which, according to the *Vilna Gaon* is a reference to *Yehuda* explaining to *Yosef* that his *Olam Habah* is at stake.

2. Five individuals in *Sefer Bereishit* had their lives shortened:
   1. *Adam* gave 70 years of his life to *David Hamelech* (*Zohar Vayishlach* 1:167b).
   2. *Chanoch* was 'taken' by *Hashem* early because he was liable to go astray (*Rashi Bereishit* 5:24).
   3. *Avraham's* life was shortened by five years so that he would not see *Eisav* sin (*Bereishit* 15:15).
   4. *Yaakov* was supposed to live 180 years but he died at 147 years. His life was shortened by 33 years because he complained to *Paroh* that his years were "few and troublesome" (*Bereishit* 47:9) when in reality, he should have had *hakarat hatov* for being saved from *Eisav* and *Lavan* and for the return of *Dinah* and *Yosef* (*Daat Zekeinim Bereishit* 47:8,9). The *Baal Haturim* (*Bereishit* 47:28) however, offers an alternative reason for the loss of 33 years. He says that since the word of a *tzadik* is always fulfilled, *Yaakov's* promise that the one with whom *Lavan's* idols would be found would die, meant that *Rachel* died as a result of *Yaakov's* curse. The wording used was *"lo yichye"* (*Bereishit* 31:32) and the *Baal Haturim* points out that the *gematriya* of *"yichye"* is 33. (Note: all the patriarchs were supposed to live for 180 years, but only *Yitzchak* did).
   5. *Yosef* was supposed to live 120 years. He heard *Yehuda* and the Egyptian interpreter refer to his father *Yaakov* (5 times each) as 'your servant' and did not object to this verbal humiliation of his father. For this, he lost 10 years and only lived to 110.

3. She is identified by *Rashi* as *Dina bat Yaakov* (*Rashi Bereishit* 46:10).

4. *Iyov* married *Dina* (*Bava Batra* 15b).

5. He proved to his brothers that he was indeed *Yosef* by showing his brothers that he was circumcised (*Rashi Bereishit* 45:4) and that he spoke Hebrew (*Bereishit* 45:12). He proved to his father that he was indeed *Yosef,* when he sent his father "*agalot*" – "wagons," reminding *Yaakov,* that the last topic they had been learning before *Yosef* was sold, was "*eglah arufah*" – "the case of an unsolved murder." *Eglah* is similar to the Hebrew word for wagon (*Midrash Tanchuma*).

6. In addition to "*Yaakov, Yaakov*" mentioned in the question, there are six other instances in *Tanach.* They are:
   1. *Noach* (*Bereishit* 6:9)
   2. *Shem* (*Bereishit* 11:10)
   3. *Terach* (*Bereishit* 11:27)
   4. *Avraham* (*Bereishit* 25:19)
   5. *Yaakov* (46:2)
   6. *Moshe* (*Shemot* 3:4)
   7. *Shmuel* (*Shmuel I* 3:10)

   The only cases where the double usage of the name is similar to ours, in the sense that it is *Hashem* calling out to the person, twice for emphasis, are *Avraham, Yaakov, Moshe* and *Shmuel.* In the other three cases, the two names are separated by a comma, as in "these are the generations of *Noach, Noach* was a *tzadik.*"

7. The *Daat Zekeinim* notes that the two *pesukim* that record the exchange between *Yaakov* and *Paroh,* where *Yaakov* complains about his short and troublesome life (*Bereishit* 47:8–9) total 33 words.

8. The *pasuk* says "*e'e'leh v'agidah*" – "I will go up and I will tell" (*Bereishit* 46:31). "*e'e'leh*" is spelled *alef, ayin, lamed, heh.* These four letters correspond to *etrog, arava, lulav* and *hadas* (*Tikunei Zohar* 29:8). The word "*agidah*" can be translated as "I *will bind*" and "*e'e'leh*" could be a reference to going up to *Jerusalem* on the *chag* of *Sukkot.*

9. The *Baal Haturim* (*Bereishit* 44:18) points out that the final letters of the first three words "*vayigash eilav Yehuda*" spell "*shaveh*" – "equal," indicating that *Yehuda* approached *Yosef* as an equal, as one king to another.

10. The *Baal Haturim* (*Bereishit* 47:6) points out that the *gematriya* of "*b'meitav ha'aretz*" equals the *gematriya* of "*Goshen,*" indicating that the prime real estate in *Paroh*'s land was "*eretz Goshen.*"

11. The *Torah* tells us that *Yosef* gave clothing to each of his brothers. However, he gave 300 silver coins and five changes of clothing to *Binyamin.* The Hebrew word "*chamesh*" – "five" consists of the letters *chet, mem* and *shin,* which stand for *chodesh, mo'ed,* and *Shabbat,* specifically days in the life of

a *Jew* where he is mandated to wear special clothing, out of respect for the holiness of the day.

12. There are three instances in the *Torah* where people fell on each other's necks and they are all in *Bereishit*. *Yosef* and *Binyamin* fell on each other's neck (*Bereishit* 45:14); *Yosef* fell on *Yaakov*'s neck (*Bereishit* 46:29); and *Eisav* fell on *Yaakov*'s neck (*Bereishit* 33:4).

13. The word is *"ulekachtem"* – "and you shall take." The four places in the *Torah* where this word is found are:
    1. *"ulekachtem gam et zeh"* (*Bereishit* 44:29)
    2. *"ulekachtem agudat eizov"* (*Shemot* 12:22)
    3. *"ulekachtem lachem bayom harishon"* (*Vayikra* 23:40)
    4. *"ulekachtem mipri haaretz"* (*Bamidbar* 13:20)

14. *Binyamin* named his ten sons in honour of his older brother *Yosef*:
    1. *Bela*, because he was *"nivla"* – "swallowed" among the nations.
    2. *Becher*, because *Yosef* was his mother's *"b'chor"* – "firstborn."
    3. *Ashbel*, because *Hashem* made him a captive, combination of the words *"shevi"* and *"Keil."*
    4. *Geira*, because he lived as a *"geir"* – "stranger" in a strange land.
    5. *Naaman*, because he was *"na'im"* – "very pleasant."
    6. *Aichi*, because *Yosef* was his *"achi"* – "brother."
    7. *Rosh*, because *Yosef* was a *"rosh"* – "leader."
    8. and 9. *Mupim* and *Chupim*, because he was not at *Yosef*'s *chuppah* and *Yosef* was not at his.
    10. *Ard*, because he *"yarad"* – "went down" to the nations, to *Mitzrayim* (*Gemara Sota* 36b).

15. All the gold and silver in the world was brought to *Yosef* in *Mitzraim* as payment for food during the famine. When *Bnai Yisrael* left *Mitzrayim* at the time of the Exodus, they took it all with them (*Gemara Pesachim* 119a).

16. Trick question: *Binyamin*'s son *Rosh* was the 7th son in the family, but his name literally means "head."

17. There are four references to the number 130 in the *Torah*:
    1. *Yaakov* was 130 years old when he went down to *Mitzrayim* to be reunited with *Yosef* (*Bereishit* 47:9).
    2. *Adam* bore *Sheit* when he was 130 years old (*Bereishit* 5:3).
    3. *Yocheved* was 130 years old when she gave birth to *Moshe* (we know this because she was born as *Yaakov*'s family entered *Mitzrayim* and *Moshe* was 80 years old at the time of the *Exodus* 210 years later).
    4. The weight of the silver platters that the *Nesi'im* donated to the *mishkan* was 130 measures of weight (*Bamidbar* 7:13).

18. Only *Binyamin* was born in Israel. (*Rashi Bereishit* 35:18).

19. The *Baal Haturim* (*Bereishit* 44:30) points out that the word *"keshura"* – "bound together" is equal in *gematriya* to 611, the same *gematriya* as *Torah*, indicating that *Yaakov* and *Binyamin* were bound together through the study of *Torah*.

20. The phrase *"beita Paroh"* – "to the House of *Paroh*," is found in only two places in the *Torah*. Once here in *Bereishit* (47:14), speaking about the vast amounts of money that found their way to the Egyptian treasury through the efforts of *Yosef*; and once by the plague of *"arov"* – "wild animals," that was inflicted upon the Egyptians prior to the *Exodus* (*Shemot* 8:20). The *Baal Haturim* points out that because the Egyptians showed no *"hakarat hatov"* – "appreciation" for the goodness that *Yosef* brought to their country, they were punished through the plagues. The use of the same phrase *"beita Paroh"* connects the two ideas.

PARSHAT VAYECHI QUESTIONS

1. What numerical relationship is there between *Efraim* and *Menashe*, and *Reuven* and *Shimon*?
2. Who was the first person to take *Bnai Yisrael* out of *Mitzrayim*?
3. There are two *parshiyot* whose names contain forms of the word "*chai*" – "life." They are *Chayei Sara* and *Vayechi*. How do the first words in each of these *parshiyot* teach us about true happiness in life?
4. Who was the first person in history to get sick?
5. Where is there a hint in the blessings of *Yaakov* to the length of the lunar and solar calendars?
6. In the entire book of *Bereishit*, how many different instances of sibling strife are found?
7. In many *chumashim*, beside the word "*Yehudah*" (*Bereishit* 49:8) one will find the notation "*b'rosh amud bet, yud, heh, shin, mem, vav, siman*." What does this cryptic phrase mean?
8. What did *Yaakov* plant while in *Mitzrayim*?
9. Which "*minhag*" – "custom" quoted in the Laws of "*milah*" – "circumcision" did *Yosef* not follow?
10. What three letters combine to form a word used by *Yaakov* to describe *Yosef* in his blessings in *Parshat Vayechi*; can also be used to form the subject of one of *Paroh*'s dreams; and also spell one of *Yosef*'s talents which helped release him from prison?
11. Which book is known as "*Sefer Hayashar*" – "the book of the upright"?
12. It's a person, a place, part of the body and a portion. Name a word in *Sefer Bereishit*, appearing four times with these four different meanings?
13. Who is recorded in the *Torah* as having been kissed?
14. During his lifetime, King *David* did not kill *Shimi Ben Geirah*, because of *Shimi*'s future famous descendant, and in *Haftarat Vayechi* asks his son *Shlomo* to care for *Shimi*. Name the famous descendant?
15. Which twins were buried on the same day even though they didn't die on the same day?
16. Where is there a hint to *Mordechai* and *Esther* in *Parshat Vayechi*?
17. Like father like son. Name a father and son in *Bereishit* who experienced a similar physical ailment. Name the ailment?
18. Name two sets of brothers who are mentioned in the same *pasuk*?
19. Name two places in the *Torah* where this person is mentioned twice in each *pasuk*, each time by a different name?
20. How many years were there from creation until *Yaakov*'s family of "*shivim nefesh*" – "70 souls" went down to *Mitzrayim* and *Goshen*?

PARSHAT VAYECHI ANSWERS

1. The *gematriya* of *Efraim* and *Menashe* is 726 while the *gematriya* of *Reuven* and *Shimon* plus its *kollel* (one of the rules of *gematriya* is that one can arbitrarily add one to make the values jive) is 726 giving an additional meaning to the *pasuk* (*Baal Haturim Bereishit* 48:5): "*Efraim* and *Menashe* will be the same as *Reuven* and *Shimon*."

2. *Yosef* was the first person to take *Bnai Yisrael* out of *Mitzrayim* when he led his brothers, (the *Bnai Yisrael*), from *Mitzrayim* to *Chevron* to bury their father *Yaakov* (*Yisrael*) in the *Maarat Hamachpela* (*Bereishit* 50:7–8).

3. The years that *Yaakov* truly lived in tranquillity and happiness were limited to the 34 years when he was together with *Yosef*, 17 years before the brothers sold *Yosef* and the final 17 years when *Yaakov* was reunited with *Yosef* in *Mitzrayim*. Likewise, the years that *Sarah Imeinu* experienced true happiness were limited to the 37 years after she had given birth to *Yitzchak*, from age 90 when she gave birth, to age 127 when she died. The *Baal Haturim* points out that the *gematriya* of the first word in *Vayechi* ("*vayechi*") is 34 (*Baal Haturim Bereishit* 47:28), and the *gematriya* of the first word in *Chayei Sarah* ("*vayihiyu*") is 37 (*Baal Haturim Bereishit* 23:1). Interestingly, the *Baal Haturim* points out these as independent calculations, and does not connect the two.

4. The first person in history to get sick was *Yaakov*. The *Mishnah Berurah* (*Orach Chaim* 230:7) tells us that when one sneezes, we are to say "*l'refuah*" – "be well," and the sneezer is to answer "*baruch tihiye*" – "you should be blessed" and then "*lishuatcha kiviti Hashem*" – "I hope for Your salvation, O Hashem" (*Bereishit* 49:18). He explains that originally people never got sick. When their time came, they would not get sick but would simply sneeze and die. The sneeze was the method by which the breath of life would leave the human being. *Yaakov*, however, wanted to have some indication of his end, so that he would have time to put his affairs in order and give his children instructions for life without him. He therefore prayed that *Hashem* give him warning of the time of his death, to have adequate time to attend to his affairs and his wish was granted.

5. The *Baal Haturim* (*Bersishit* 49:27) notes that the collective numerical value of the first letter of the first word of each of the blessings (not including the names of the children of *Yaakov*; e.g., referring to the blessing given to *Reuven*, the letter would be "*bet*" from the word "*b'chori*") equals 365, which is the number of days in a solar calendar. The collective numerical value of the last letter of the last word of each of the blessings is 354, which is the number of days in the lunar calendar. He cites two *pesukim* in *Yirmiyahu*

(*Yirmiyahu* 31:34–35) which connects the offspring of *Yaakov* to the sun and the moon.

6. There are six instances of sibling rivalry in *Bereishit: Kayin* vs. *Hevel; Shem* and *Yefet* vs. *Cham; Avraham* vs. *Lot* (brother-in-law); *Yitzchak* vs. *Yishmael; Yaakov* vs. *Eisav; Yosef* vs. his brothers.

7. When writing a *Sefer Torah*, the "*sofer*" – "scribe" has to follow certain rules (*Baal Haturim Bereishit* 49:8). One of these rules is that each column in the *Torah* should begin with a "*vav*" except for six specific columns listed below, which must respectively begin with a *bet, yud, heh, shin, mem,* and *vav.* This type of *Sefer Torah* is called a "*vav Sefer Torah.*" The *halacha* is that if a *Torah* is written without a *vav* at the beginning of each of the columns, it is nevertheless *kosher.* However, the six specific columns must begin with the specified letter; otherwise the *Torah* would not be *kosher.* The words that begin these six columns are:

   1. *Bet* in the word *Bereishit* (*Bereishit* 1:1)
   2. *Yud* in the word *Yehuda* (*Bereishit* 49:8)
   3. *Heh* in the word *habaim* (*Shemot* 14:28)
   4. *Shin* in the word *shmor* (*Shemot* 34:11)
   5. *Mem* in the word *ma* (*Bamidbar* 24:5)
   6. *Vav* in the word *v'a'idah* (*Devarim* 31:28)

   In most *Chumashim,* the notation listed in the question will appear in the column beside each of these occurrences, except for the first, *Bereishit,* as this column must obviously begin with a *bet* and not with a *vav.*

8. *Rashi* (*Shemot* 25:5) quotes a *Midrash Tanchumah* which says that *Yaakov* saw "*b'ruach hakodesh*" – "with divine inspiration," that *Bnai Yisrael* would one day build the *Mishkan,* and would need cedar wood. He therefore brought cedar trees with him to *Mitzrayim* and planted them. He left instructions that upon exiting *Mitzrayim,* they were to take the cedar with them, so that they would be able to build the *Mishkan* in the desert.

9. *Shulchan Aruch* (*Yoreh De'ah* 265:11) cites the accepted custom that one should only be honoured as "*sandek*" – "one who holds the baby during the circumcision ceremony," for one son in a family. *Yosef* was either *sandek* or *mohel* at the circumcision ceremonies of his great-grandchildren, the sons of *Machir,* the son of *Menashe* (*Peirush Yonatan Bereishit* 50:23).

10. The three letters are *peh, reish* and *tav.* In the blessings that *Yaakov* gave to *Yosef,* he describes *Yosef* using these three letters (*Bereishit* 49:22) as "*ben porat*" – "one who is filled with grace." *Paroh* dreamt about "*parot*" – "cows" (*Bereishit* 41:2); and *Yosef* was released from prison because he was a "*poter*" – "interpreter" (*Bereishit* 41:8). All of these words use the same three letters *peh, reish* and *tav.*

11. A verse in *Yehoshua* (10:13) mentions *"sefer hayashar."* The *gemara* (*Avoda Zara* 25a) explains that this is the *Book of Bereishit* or the *Book of Avraham, Yitzchak* and *Yaakov,* who were all *"yashar"* – "upright" individuals. There are other commentators who explain that the *Sefer Hayashar* is another name for the entire *Torah* or for the *Book of Devarim.*

12. The word is *Shechem.* In *Bereishit* 9:23 it means shoulder; in *Bereishit* 33:18 it is the name of a city; in *Bereishit* 34:2 it is the name of *Chamor's* son; and in *Bereishit* 48:22, it refers to the portion of land that *Yaakov* gave *Yosef.*

13. In *Parshat Vayechi, Yaakov* is kissed by *Yosef,* after *Yaakov* passes away (*Bereishit* 50:1). *Yaakov* was also kissed by *Lavan* when he arrived in *Charan* (*Bereishit* 29:13); and by *Eisav* when they met on *Yaakov's* return from *Charan* (*Bereishit* 33:4). In *Parshat Vayechi, Yaakov* kisses *Menashe* and *Efraim* before blessing them (*Bereishit* 48:10). The other people who are mentioned in the *Torah* as having been kissed are: *Yitzchak* by *Yaakov* before giving the blessings (*Bereishit* 27:27); *Rachel* by *Yaakov* when he first meets her (*Bereishit* 29:11); *Lavan* kisses his children and grandchildren before they leave with *Yaakov* (*Bereishit* 31:55); *Yosef* who kisses his brothers when he finally reveals himself to them (*Bereishit* 45:15); *Moshe* is kissed by *Aharon* when they meet on *Moshe's* return from *Midian* (*Shemot* 4:27); and *Yitro* kissed by his son-in-law *Moshe* when *Yitro* arrives at the camp of *Bnai Yisrael* in the desert (*Shemot* 18:7).

14. The instruction to protect *Shimi ben Geirah* appears in *Haftarat Veyechi* (*Melachim* 1:2:8). The *gemara* explains that one of his descendants was *Mordechai Hayehudi* (*Megilla* 13a).

15. *Yaakov* and *Eisav. Targum Yonatan* (*Bereishit* 50:13) explains that when the sons of *Yaakov* arrived at *Me'arat Hamachpela* to bury their father, *Eisav* refused to allow them to enter, claiming that it was his right as the first-born to be buried there. *Naftali* who was the speediest of the *shevatim,* quickly ran back to *Mitzrayim* to get the document that proved that *Eisav* had sold his burial plot to *Yaakov.* Meanwhile, they motioned to *Chushim,* the son of *Dan,* who was deaf, and was unable to fully comprehend what was going on. All he knew from his observation, was that *Eisav* was holding up the burial of his grandfather *Yaakov.* Incensed, he drew his sword and decapitated *Eisav.* The head rolled into *Yitzchak's* grave and the rest of *Eisav's* body was buried in the *Machpela* field. Thus the twins, *Yaakov* and *Eisav* were buried on the same day, even though *Yaakov* had predeceased his brother *Eisav* by at least 70 days.

16. In *Yaakov's* blessing to *Binyamin,* he says *"v'la'erev yechalek shalal"* – "in the evening, he will divide the spoil" (*Bereishit* 49:27). *Rashi* explains that this is a reference to *Mordechai* and *Esther,* descendants of *Binyamin,* who, in the "evening," the darker period of history when *Bnai Yisrael* are in *galut,* will

divide the spoils of *Haman*. *Rashi* quotes the *Midrash Tanchuma* who references the *pasuk* in the *megillah*, as it is said, (*Megillat Esther* 3:7) "behold, I have given *Esther* the house of *Haman*" (*Midrash Tanchuma, Vayechi* 14).

17. Both *Yitzchak* and *Yaakov* had weakened eyesight in their old age (*Bereishit* 27:1; 48:10).

18. When *Yosef* went to visit his ailing father *Yaakov*, *Yaakov* said that *Efraim* and *Menashe* were as precious to him as *Reuven* and *Shimon*. Both sets of brothers are mentioned in the same *pasuk* (*Bereishit* 48:5).

19. The person is *Yaakov*, who was also known as *Yisrael*. This occurs once in *Bereishit* 49:2 and again in *Shemot* 19:3.

20. When the *Bnai Yisrael* went to *Mitzrayim*, it was 2238 years after creation. Since we know that they were exiled in *Mitzrayim* for 210 years and since we know that the exodus took place in the year 2448, therefore 2448 - 210 = 2238.

PARSHAT SHEMOT QUESTIONS

1. Give three instances in Jewish history where a fire burned but its fuel source miraculously was not used up?
2. What did *Moshe* uproot from *Yitro's* garden?
3. From the time that it was created, who had possession of *Moshe's* "*mateh*" – "staff," that he used to perform all the miracles?
4. Why do we say "*hodu l'Hashem ki tov*" at a "*brit*" – "circumcision"?
5. What two "*issurim*" – "prohibitions" would *Amram* and *Yocheved* have transgressed, had they married after *Matan Torah*?
6. Which four people in the *Torah* had letters added to their names and what is the significance of the added letters?
7. On what day of what month did *Yocheved* place baby *Moshe* in the water?
8. How old was *Yocheved* when she gave birth to *Moshe*?
9. The Egyptian who was killed by *Moshe* (*Shemot* 2:11) in *Parshat Shemot* is mentioned again in the *Torah*. Where is he mentioned?
10. *Shemot* 2:1 begins with the words "*vayelech ish…*" – "and a man went." Where else in *Tanach* are these words used and what is the connection?
11. Where is there a hint in *Parshat Shemot* to the tradition of reading each *parshah* "*shnayim mikra v'echad targum*" – "read the portion of the week twice in the original text and once in the translation of *Onkelos*" on a weekly basis?
12. By what two names is the daughter of *Paroh* known?
13. Where is there a reference to the daughter of *Paroh* in our daily prayers?
14. What reference do we make to the daughter of *Paroh* every Friday night in our homes?
15. Who danced at the wedding of their parents?
16. Without looking, how does *Targum Onkelos* translate the word "*mateh*" – "staff," and in which song is this word sung during the course of the Jewish year?
17. How many people mentioned in *Parshat Shemot* had "*tzara'at*" – "leprosy" at one time or another during their lifetimes?
18. How many times does the word "*u'ri'eetem*" or "*u'ri'eeten*" – "and you will see" appear in the *Torah* and what is the connection between them?
19. Which three people mentioned in *Sefer Shemot* were considered part of *Bnai Yisrael* and traveled through the *midbar* with *Bnai Yisrael*, but were not physically present at the time of the actual *Exodus* from *Mitzrayim*?
20. How many times does the word "*vayira*" – "and he feared" appear in the *Torah*?

PARSHAT SHEMOT ANSWERS

1. The three instances in Jewish history where a fire burned but its fuel source miraculously was not used up, are:
   1. The "*sneh*" – "burning bush" (*Shemot* 3:2).
   2. The pillar of fire in the desert.
   3. The miracle of the *Chanukah* oil.

2. *Moshe* uprooted the "*mateh*" – "staff" which he later used to perform all the miracles. It is one of the 10 items that is highlighted in "*Pirkei Avot*" – "Ethics of our Fathers" (*Avot* 5:8) as having been created on "*Erev Shabbat Bein Hashmashot*" – "Friday afternoon at twilight" at the time of creation. *Yitro* planted it and no one was able to uproot it until *Moshe* came along. (*Pirkei D'Rebbi Eliezer* 40).

3. The *Baal Haturim* states that we have a tradition to place four "*tagin*" – "crown-like strokes" on top of the "*heh*" in the word "*hamateh*" – "staff" (*Shemot* 4:17), to indicate that there were nine righteous people since creation who had control of the staff. They were: *Adam, Chanoch, Noach, Shem, Avraham, Yitzchak, Yaakov, Yosef* and *Moshe*. The *Hagaot Haradal* indicates however that it would be impossible for *Chanoch* to have given it to *Noach*, as their lives did not overlap. He therefore inserts an extra person "*Metushelach*" in the chain, and says that there should be five "*tagin*" on the "*heh*" for a total of ten. *Yitro* is not included (even though he had possession between *Yosef* and *Moshe*), because at that time he worshipped idols, and therefore cannot be enumerated in the list of righteous people. At first, this poses some difficulty, because the *Baal Haturim* himself says that the staff that *Yehuda* gave *Tamar* was this very staff. This seeming contradiction is answered by the fact that *Yehuda* took the staff from *Yosef* and then returned it to *Yaakov*, and therefore *Yehuda* is not a direct link in the chain.

4. Two of the reasons we recite "*hodu l'Hashem ki tov*" at a *brit* are:
   1. It is a hint to the fact that *Moshe* had been born circumcised (*Chizkuni Shemot* 2:2 *citing the gemara Sotah* 12a).
   2. *Tehillim* 107 is the psalm of *Hodu Lashem Ki Tov* and lists four individuals who must give special thanks to *Hashem*, among whom is one who has been released from captivity. Thanks is therefore offered for the baby who has been released from nine months of captivity (*Chochmat Adam 149:21*).

5. The two *mitzvot* that *Amram* and *Yocheved* would have transgressed had they married after the giving of the *Torah* are:
   1. Marrying one's aunt; as *Yocheved* was *Amram*'s aunt (*Shemot* 6:20).
   2. "*machzir gerushato*" – "remarrying the wife that one has divorced after she had marital relations with another." The *Targum Yonatan*

(*Bamidbar* 11:26) explains that *Eldad* and *Meidad* were sons of *Elitzafan ben Parnach* who was married to *Yocheved* while she was divorced from *Amram*. The *midrash* tells us that as a result of the edict of *Paroh* to kill all the Jewish males, *Amram* separated from his wife until *Miriam* convinced him that by doing so, he was worse than *Paroh*, as *Paroh*'s edict only affected male births, but *Amram*'s separation would affect the birth of both males and females.

6. The four individuals were *Yehoshua*, who had a *yud* added to his name *Hoshea*; *Avraham*, who had a *heh* added to his name *Avram*; *Yitro*, who had a *vav* added to his name *Yeter*; and *Sarah*, who had a *heh* replacing the *yud* in *Sarai*. The added letters, *yud, heh, vav* and *heh* spell *Hashem*'s name.

7. The *gemara* in *Sotah* cites two opinions. The first is that since we know he was born on *Adar* 7 and was placed in the water when he was three months old, the date must have been the 6th of *Sivan*, the date of "*matan Torah*" – "the giving of the *Torah* on *Mount Sinai*" (*Rashi Shemot* 2:2). The other opinion is that he was placed there on the 21st of *Nisan*, the date of the splitting of the *Red Sea* (*Talelei Orot* on the *Megillah*). According to this opinion, the "three month" problem is solved by stating that it was a leap year. One should not take the *Torah*'s term "three months" literally; but rather it is to be understood as most of three months. That is, most of *Adar Rishon*, all of *Adar Sheni* and most of *Nisan*.

8. Since she was born as *Yaakov*'s family entered the walls of *Mitzrayim* (*Rashi Bereishit* 46:15), and since *Moshe* was 80 years old when he left *Mitzrayim* 210 years later, *Yocheved* must have been 130 years old when she gave birth to *Moshe* (*Ibn Ezra*).

9. He surfaces again in *Vayikra* 24:10 in the story about the one who curses *Hashem*. He is called "*ben ish Mitzri*" – "the son of an Egyptian." *Rashi* identifies him as the son of the Egyptian killed by *Moshe*.

10. The first time the phrase "*vayelech ish...*" appears, it refers to *Amram* who went and married *Yocheved*. Their union produced *Moshe*, the first redeemer of the Jews. The second reference is in *Megillat Rut* (1:1), which will result in the ultimate redeemer, *Mashiach ben David*. The *Shemen Hatov* says that the use of the word "*ish*" indicates that anyone is capable of producing the Redeemer. He need not be an *Amram* or an *Elimelech*, both of whom were the leaders of their generation.

11. The *Baal Haturim* (*Shemot* 1:1) quotes the *gemara* (*Berachot* 8b) and says that the letters of the first four words of *Sefer Shemot* spell "*ve-adam asher lomed haseder, shnayim mikra ve-echad targum, b'kol na'im yashir, yichyeh shanim rabot aruchim l'olam*" – "and he who reads the weekly *parshah* twice in the text and once in the *targum*, singing it pleasantly, will merit many long years."

12. In *Divrei Hayamim* (1:4:18), the daughter of *Paroh* is called *Bitya* as well as *Yehudiya*. Some *mefarshim* indicate that *Yehudiya* was in fact a description of her Jewishness, as she was present at the Nile because she was preparing to cleanse herself of her father's idolatry, as it is written: "and the daughter of *Paroh* came down to wash herself in the river" (*Shemot* 2:5), and *Rabbi Yochanan* said: she went down to wash and purify herself from the idols of her father's house. Others including *Rashi* (based on a *gemara* in *Megilla* 13a) indicate that *Yehudiya* was her real name.

13. Each day in *shacharit*, we recite the *pasuk* "*va'yaar Yisrael et hayad hag'dolah...vayaaminu b'Hashem u'veMoshe avdo*" – "and the Children of *Israel* saw the great Hand....and they had faith in *Hashem* and His servant *Moshe*" (*Shemot* 14:31). The *Lev Aryeh* explains that "*hayad hagdolah*" – "the great Hand" refers to the daughter of *Paroh* miraculously stretching out her hand to substantially more than its natural length to fetch the little cradle which held *Moshe*. *Rashi* (*Shemot* 2:5) comments on the word "*amata*" – "her handmaiden" and quotes a *gemara* (*Sotah* 12b) that the use of the word "*amata*" refers cryptically to the fact that her hand stretched many "*amot*" – "cubits." When *Bnai Yisrael* heard about this miracle, the nation had faith in *Hashem* and His servant *Moshe*. (*Hagada Ki Yishalcha Bincha, Rabbi Moshe Bogomilsky*)

14. In the song "*Eishet Chayil*" (*Mishlei* 31:10–31) which is sung in the home every Friday night before *Kiddush*, we say the *pasuk* "*ta'ama ki tov sachra...*" (*Mishlei* 31:18). The *Minchat Shai* points out that when the plague of *makat bechorot* was decreed, *Moshe* realized the daughter of *Paroh* was a firstborn and would therefore be killed during the tenth plague. He then pleaded to *Hashem* to make an exception for her, as she had saved his life. *Hashem* granted *Moshe*'s request. The *Minchat Shai* therefore interprets the *pasuk* in *Mishlei* to mean the following: because she involved herself with the one who was known as "*ki tov*" (i.e., *Moshe*), her "*neirah*" – "soul" was not extinguished that night. The *Minchat Shai* notes that the word for night is written here without the final "*heh*" which spells "*leil*," the word for night in the *Pesach* story – "*leil shimurim*."

15. When *Paroh* decreed the deaths of all newborn male children of *Bnai Yisrael*, *Amram* divorced *Yocheved*. The *gemara* (*Sotah* 12a) tells us that *Miriam* admonished her father *Amram*, telling him that by divorcing his wife *Yocheved*, he was worse than *Paroh*. For *Paroh*'s edict affected only males, while *Amram*'s divorce of *Yocheved* would affect the birth of both males and females. When *Amram* and *Yocheved* subsequently decided to remarry, *Aharon* and *Miriam* danced at the wedding of their own parents.

16. *Targum Onkelos* translates *"mateh"* – "staff" as *"chutra"* (*Shemot* 4:2). This word is found in the famous *Chad Gadya* song, which is sung at the very end of the *Pesach Seder*.

17. Four people in *Parshat Shemot* who had *"tzara'at"* – "leprosy," were *Paroh* (*Rashi Shemot* 2:23); *Paroh*'s daughter *Bitya* (*Midrash Shemot* 1:27); *Moshe* (*Shemot* 4:6); and *Miriam* (*Bamidbar* 12:10).

18. *Rav Shmuel Shmelke Halevi of Nikolsburg*, the *Chassidic rebbe* and mentor of *Rav Levi Yitzchak of Berditchev*, connects the four instances where the *Torah* uses the word *"u're'eetem"* or *"u're'eeten"* with the *Mishnah* in *Pirkei Avot* – "Ethics of our Fathers" (*Avot* 3:1) that advises: "pay attention to three things and you will not come to sin." Those three things are:

    1. "Know from whence you have come."
    2. "Know where you are headed."
    3. "Know before Whom you will eventually have to account for all your deeds."

    "Know from whence you have come" is hinted by the words in *Parshat Shemot* *"u're'eeten al ha'avna'im"* – "and you will see on the birthing stone" (*Shemot* 1:16); "know where you are headed" is hinted by the words *"u're'eetem et ha'aretz"* – "and you will see the Land of Israel" (*Bamidbar* 13:18); and "know before Whom you will eventually have to account for all your deeds" is hinted at in two *pesukim*, first, *"u're'eetem oto"* – "and you will see the blue strand of the *tzitzit* and remember the *mitzvot* of *Hashem*" (*Bamidbar* 15:39) and second, *"boker u're'eetem et kvod Hashem"* – "in the morning, you will see the glory of *Hashem* when he provides you with *mann* to eat" (*Shemot* 16:7) (*V'Dibarta Bam*, Rabbi Moshe Bogomilsky).

19. The following three people, *Tzippora*, *Moshe*'s wife; *Gershom* and *Eliezer*, *Moshe*'s two sons; were all in *Midian* at the time of the Exodus and joined *Bnai Yisrael* with *Yitro* at *Har Sinai* (*Shemot* 18:2–3).

20. The word *"vayira"* – "and he feared" appears three times in the *Torah*, two of those times regarding *Yaakov*:

    1. When *Yaakov* awoke from his dream (*Bereishit* 28:17).
    2. When *Yaakov* heard that *Eisav* was approaching with a huge army (*Bereishit* 32:7).
    3. It appears once in reference to *Moshe* when he realized that he had been seen killing the *Egyptian* (*Shemot* 2:14).

PARSHAT VA'ERA QUESTIONS

1. How old was *Yaakov* when he finished having children?
2. Which person who later had a book of *Tanach* named for him, is alluded to in both *Parshat Shemot* and *Parshat Va'era*?
3. At what point in history did light, sound and gravity all travel at the same speed?
4. Which *kohanim* were not born to a *kohen* father?
5. Which *Levi*'s father was a *Yisrael*?
6. Name the only two *pesukim* in the *Torah* that begin with the words *"lachen emor"* – "therefore you shall say" and their connection to each other?
7. What type of meat was *Paroh* compared to?
8. Whose beard was equal to his height?
9. How many people in the *Torah* lived 137 years?
10. Besides being his uncle, how else was *Moshe* related to *Elazar ben Aharon*?
11. My husband was the *kohen gadol*, my father was a *kohen*, my father-in-law was the *kohen gadol*, my son was the "*kohen mashuach milchama*" – "*kohen* anointed to go out to war" and I am nameless. Who am I?
12. What does "*Shovavim Tat*" (shin-vav-bet-bet-yud-mem tav-tav) stand for?
13. Name eleven couples in *Tanach* where the names of both the husband and wife begin with the same Hebrew letter.
14. What was *Levi*'s wife's name?
15. Name three human body parts that are used to describe *Hashem* in *Parshat Va'era*?
16. Who in *Parshat Va'era* had a grandfather and a great-grandfather who was the same person?
17. What happened tomorrow in *Parshat Va'era*?
18. Can you name two of *Aharon*'s brothers-in-law?
19. Who am I? I married two women. One saved my brother-in-law's life and one watched her do it?
20. Who am I? My husband was a *kohen*; my brother-in-law was a king; my brother was a prince; my son was a *kohen* and my grandson never died.

PARSHAT VA'ERA ANSWERS

1. In *Shemot* 6:6–7, the *pesukim* promise the salvation of *Bnai Yisrael*, with the four expressions of redemption that correlate to the four cups of wine drunk at the *Pesach seder*. It begins with the word "*lachen*" – "therefore" which equals 100 in *gematriya*. The *Baal Haturim* explains that in the "*zechut*" – "merit" of Judaism's three "*avot*" – patriarchs; *Avraham* who gave birth at 100; *Yitzchak* who found "*meah shearim*" – "one hundred gates"; and *Yaakov* who had all his children by age 100, we were redeemed. The calculation is based on *Yaakov* being 63 years old when blessed by *Yitzchak*, 14 years at *Yeshivat Shem v'Ever*, 20 years in *Lavan*'s home and two years delay on the road, which is when his youngest son *Binyamin* is born, and *Rachel* dies in childbirth. That would place *Yaakov* at 99 years old at the birth of his youngest child.

2. *Iyov* is alluded to in both *Shemot* and *Va'era*. The *gemara* (*Sotah* 11a) identifies the advisors of *Paroh* (*Parshat Shemot*) at the time of his decree to drown all male children, as *Yitro*, *Bilam* and *Iyov*. *Bilam* met the fate of death for agreeing with *Paroh*'s decree; *Iyov* suffered for remaining silent; and *Yitro*'s descendants sat in the courtyard of the *Temple* because he fled from *Paroh*'s palace. In *Parshat Va'era*, the *Torah* speaks about those who feared and those who did not fear *Hashem* during the plague of "*barad*" – "hail." The *Targum Yonatan* identifies the one who feared *Hashem* as *Iyov* and the one who did not fear *Hashem* as *Bilam*.

3. We know that the speed of gravity is 32 feet per second; the speed of sound is 1100 feet per second and the speed of light is 186,000 miles per second. When the plague of "*barad*" – "hail" was brought upon the Egyptians, the *pasuk* (*Shemot* 9:23) tells us that thunder, hail and fire, (interpreted by the *Malbim* as lightning), all transpired at the exact same second. This was a miraculous event.

4. *Aharon*, the first *kohen*, was the son of *Amram*, the son of *Kehat*, the son of *Levi*. Therefore *Aharon*'s father, grandfather and great-grandfather were all "*levi'im*" – "Levites." *Aharon*'s four sons, were likewise born as *levi'im* and all five, *Aharon*, *Nadav*, *Avihu*, *Elazar* and *Itamar* were appointed and anointed as "*kohanim*" – "priests." This ensured that all their offspring for eternity would also be *kohanim*. However, *Pinchas*, *Elazar*'s son, was already born by this time, before his father *Elazar* had been anointed as a *kohen*. He therefore had to be specially appointed as a *kohen* when he saved the nation from a plague (*Bamidbar* 25:12–13). Therefore in total, six individuals were *kohanim*, born to *levi'im*.

5. The capital letters in the names *Levi* and *Yisrael* in the question should have given away the answer. *Levi* was the third son of *Yaakov* and *Leah* and *Yaakov's* other name was *Yisrael*.

6. *Shemot* 6:6 deals with the four expressions of redemption leading up to the *Exodus,* that form the basis for the four cups of wine at the *Pesach Seder.* The second *pasuk* beginning with "*lachen emor*" (*Bamidbar* 25:12), is where *Hashem* promises *Pinchas* the everlasting covenant of peace. *Chazal* connects the two by teaching that *Pinchas* is *Eliyahu Hanavi,* who will usher in the ultimate redemption and the arrival of *Mashiach.* This connects the concept of redemption (via the *Exodus*) in the first *pasuk,* with the ultimate redemption and everlasting peace on earth as expressed in the second *pasuk* (*Baal Haturim Shemot* 6:6).

7. *Paroh* was compared to liver. The *pasuk* says "*kaveid lev Paroh*" – "and *Paroh's* heart was hardened" (*Shemot* 7:14). The hardening of *Paroh's* heart is mentioned ten times as *Hashem* introduces the 10 plagues in *Mitzrayim.* The *midrash* (*Shemot Rabbah* 13:3) relates this to the word "*kaveid*" meaning liver. Liver is a unique type of meat. All other meats become softer the longer they are cooked, whereas liver becomes tougher, the more it is cooked. Likewise, *Paroh,* the more punishment he received, the greater his stubbornness and defiance of *Hashem.*

8. The *gemara* (*Mo'ed Katan* 18a) states that *Paroh* was only an *amah* tall (biblical measurement, usually translated as a cubit, about 18–24 inches) and he possessed a beard equal to his height.

9. Three people are recorded by the *Torah* as having lived 137 years. They are *Levi* (*Shemot* 6:16); *Amram* (*Shemot* 6:20); and *Yishmael* (*Bereishit* 25:17).

10. Since it says in *Shemot* 6:25 that *Elazar* married one of the daughters of *Putiel* (another name for *Yitro*), and since we know that *Moshe's* wife, *Tzipora,* was *Yitro's* daughter, therefore *Moshe* was not only *Elazar's* uncle but also his brother-in-law.

11. I am the wife of *Elazar* who was a *kohen gadol* (*Bamidbar* 27:21). My father was *Yitro, kohen* of *Midian* (*Shemot* 2:16). My father-in-law was *Aharon,* also a *kohen gadol.* My son *Pinchas* was a *kohen mashuach milchama* (*Rashi Bamidbar* 31:6). My name is never mentioned in the *Torah.* I am simply referred to as the daughter of *Putiel* (*Shemot* 6:25).

12. It is an acronym for the first eight *parshiyot* in *Shemot: Shemot, Va'era, Bo, Beshalach, Yitro, Mishpatim, Terumah* and *Tetzaveh.* The Hebrew word *Shovavim* means "mischief makers" which is found in *Yirmiyahu* (3:22) which begins: "*shuvu banim shovavim*" – "return oh mischief makers." These eight weeks are a special time for *teshuva* and some have the custom to fast on the Monday and Thursday of each of these eight weeks. The earliest

mention of this custom is from *Rav Yeshaya Halevi Horowitz,* also known as the *Shelah Hakadosh.*

13. Eleven couples in *Tanach* where both husband and wife's name begin with the same letter of the Hebrew alphabet are: *Noach* and *Naama* (*Rabbeinu Bachya Bereishit* 4:22); *Eisav* and *Adah* (*Bereishit* 36:2); *Aharon* and *Elisheva* (*Shemot* 6:23); *Otniel Ben Knaz* and *Achsah bat Kalev* (*Yehoshua* 15:16); *Achav* and *Izevel* (*Melachim* 2:16:31); *Yehoyada* and *Yehosheva* (*Chomat Anach Melachim* 2:11:2); *Esther* and *Achashveirosh* (*Esther* 2:16); *Yoash* and *Yoadan* (*Melachim* 2:14:2); *Achaz* and *Aviya* (*Divrei Hayamim* 2:29:1); *Chizkiyahu* and *Cheftzibah* (*Melachim* 2:21:1); and *Menashe* and *Meshulemet* (*Melachim* 2:21:19).

14. *Levi's* wife's name was *Otah.* This is derived from the *pasuk* in *Pinchas* (*Daat Zekeinim Bamidbar* 26:59) "*asher yalda Otah l'Levi b'Mitzrayim*" and brings a proof from *Parshat Bo* (*Shemot* 10:11) "*ki Otah atem mevakshim.*" *Paroh* was telling *Moshe* that if they go to serve *Hashem* in the desert, they should leave *Otah,* his grandmother, and the matriarch of the Jewish people, behind as security.

15. The three body parts that are used in *Parshat Va'era* as anthropomorphic expressions of *Hashem* are the "*zeroah*" – "arm" (*Shemot* 6:6); "*yad*" – "hand" (*Shemot* 7:5); and "*etzbah*" – "finger" (*Shemot* 8:15).

16. *Moshe, Aharon* and *Miriam.* Since *Amram* married his aunt *Yocheved* (the sister of *Kehat* and daughter of *Levi*), *Levi* was grandfather (through *Yocheved*) and great-grandfather (through *Amram*) to *Moshe, Aharon* and *Miriam.*

17. The plague of frogs ended (*Shemot* 8:6); the plague of pestilence began (*Shemot* 9:5) and *Hashem* created a distinction between His people Israel and the Egyptians (*Shemot* 8:19). In each case, the word "*machar*" – "tomorrow" is used.

18. *Nachshon* and *Kalev* were both brothers-in-law to *Aharon. Aharon* married *Elisheva bat Aminadav,* the sister of *Nachshon* (*Shemot* 6:23). *Miriam* married *Kalev* (*Daat Zekeinim Shemot* 17:10; *Gemara Megillah* 13a).

19. I am *Kalev ben Yefuneh.* The *gemara* (*Megilla* 13a) says that I married two women. One was *Bitya,* daughter of *Paroh,* who saved *Moshe* in the basket in the Nile; and one was *Moshe's* sister *Miriam* who watched *Bitya* save *Moshe's* life.

20. I am *Elisheva bat Aminadav.* My husband was *Aharon Hakohen;* my brother-in-law was *Moshe Rabbeinu* (who was the king of *Kush* for 40 years) (*Yalkut Shimoni,* 1:168; *Sefer HaYashar, Parshat Shemot*); my brother was *Nachshon ben Aminadav,* who was the prince of the Tribe of *Yehuda;* my son *Elazar* became the *Kohen Gadol* after his father *Aharon* died; and my grandson was *Pinchas* who according to the *Targum Yonatan* (*Bamidbar* 25:12) lived forever.

PARSHAT BO QUESTIONS

1. From where do we learn the concept of *"schar halichah"* – "that credit is given not just for doing the *mitzvah*, but also for the travelling time to perform the *mitzvah*"?

2. From where do we learn the concept of *"shlucho shel adam k'moto"* – "if you assign someone to perform a *mitzvah* for you, it is as though you did the *mitzvah* yourself"?

3. From the *pasuk* *"ushemartem et hamatzot"* – "and you shall guard the *matzot*" (*Shemot* 12:17), *Rashi* deduces that *"mitzvah habaah leyadcha al tachmitzenah"* – "a play on words of *matzah* and *mitzvah*, one should not allow the performance of a *mitzvah* to become sour or delayed." Who is the example of a person who performed a *mitzvah* with *"zerizut"* – "at the earliest possible opportunity" and what practical application is there *halachically*?

4. A *"Midrash Pliah"* – "amazing and seemingly puzzling *midrash*": *"Ayn manichin tefillin elah b'Shabbat"* – literally, "one should only put on *tefillin* on *Shabbat*." Explain?

5. What three historical events occurred on the 15th of *Nisan*, prior to the first *Pesach*?

6. Besides being commanded to take the lamb and begin preparations for the *"korban Pesach"* – "the *Pesach* sacrifice," what other events occurred on the 10th of *Nisan*?

7. Which plague did not occur on a *Shabbat* and what is the proof from *Parshat Bo*?

8. Failure to do these two *"mitzvot asei"* – "positive commandments" is punishable by death. What are they?

9. Two of the laws of the *korban Pesach* are found in *Shemot* 12:46; namely, that one must eat the *Pesach* sacrifice in one place and one is not permitted to break any of the *Paschal* lamb's bones. If you examine that *pasuk*, you will notice that the first law is said in the singular and the second is said in the plural. Why?

10. What custom do we derive from the phrase *"ugot matzot"* (*Shemot* 12:39)?

11. The Hebrew word for cakes appears three times in the *Torah*. In two of the instances, the baking is quite normal and in the third instance, it is not normal at all. Where are the three instances and what is different about the third occurrence?

12. Which fruits produce honey?

13. What are the only two things in the *Torah* described as *"chazak me'od"* – "very strong"?

14. Who was the only eyewitness to the entire Egyptian exile?

15. What food item mentioned in the *Torah* before the advent of *mann*, tasted like *mann*?

16. This is a riddle for those who speak Hebrew with "*havarah Ashkenazis*": In *Parshat Bo*, there are two words mentioned in the same *perek*, three letters each, that are homonyms: one over, one under. What are the two words?

17. The origin of the *Pesach Seder* is in *Parshat Bo* and the four questions are a highlight of the *Pesach Seder*. Who was the first person in the *Torah* to be asked four questions?

18. The plague of "*makkat choshech*" – "darkness" lasted six days and six nights (*Rashi Shemot* 10:22). Where in the *Torah* was it dark for a full year? And where in the *Torah* was it light continuously for more than 24 hours?

19. How many people in the *Torah* admitted to sinning by making the statement "*chatati*" – "I have sinned"?

20. What is the connection between *Shabbat Hagadol* and the day *Bnai Yisrael* crossed the *Yarden*?

PARSHAT BO ANSWERS

1. The *Torah* says *"vayelchu vayaasu"* – "they went and they did" (*Shemot* 12:28). *Rashi*, quoting the *mechilta* (*Mekhilta d'Rabbi Yishmael* 12:25) says that the *Torah* enumerates their going also, to give them a unique reward for going and a unique reward for doing.

2. The *Torah* says *"veshochatu oto kol kehal adat Yisrael"* – "and all of Israel will slaughter the *korban Pesach*" (*Shemot* 12:6). *Rashi* points out that not everyone personally slaughtered the *Korban Pesach* and therefore the concept of receiving credit for *mitzvot* performed by others on your behalf, is deduced from this *pasuk*. (*Kiddushin* 41b).

3. The *Torah* tells us *"vayashkeim Avraham baboker"* – "and *Avraham* arose early in the morning to perform *Hashem's* commandment" (*Bereishit* 22:3). The practical application is that while a *"brit"* – "circumcision" may be done any time on the eighth day, it is preferable and recommended that it be done at the first opportunity in the morning (*Pesachim* 4a).

4. The *Aderet Eliyahu* (*Parshat Bo* 27) quotes a *midrash pliah* that says: *"Ayn manichin tefillin elah b'Shabbat,"* and cites *Rav Akiva Eiger* who explains the word *b'Shabbat* is an acronym for *"bemakom sayor, basar tapuach"* – literally, "in the place of the hair, in the meat of the apple." The *tefillin* of the *"rosh"* – "head" should be worn at the *"makom sayor"* – "hairline" and the *tefillin* of the *"yad"* – "hand" should be worn on the *"basar tapuach"* – "the meaty part of the bicep, which looks like the shape of an apple." Another possible explanation for this puzzling *midrash* is that on all days when we say the *"shir shel yom"* – "psalm of the day," we say for Sunday "today is the first day in reference *b'shabbat"*; for Monday, "today is the second day in reference *b'shabbat,"* and so on. Every day we mention the day in reference *"b'Shabbat."* The only psalm of the day where we do not insert the word *"b'Shabbat"* is *Shabbat* itself, when we say *"hayom yom Shabbat kodesh."* Therefore, *"Ayn manichin tefillin elah b'Shabbat,"* literally means "we only put on *tefillin* on those days when we insert the word *"b'Shabbat"* in the daily psalm."

5. *Rashi* (*Shemot* 12:41) identifies the three historical events as:
   1. The angels visiting *Sarah* to advise her of the impending birth of *Yitzchak*.
   2. *Yitzchak's* birth date.
   3. The *"brit bein habetarim"* – "covenant between the pieces."

6. It was the date of the first *Shabbat Hagadol* in *Mitzraim*; it was the day that *Miriam* died (*Shulchan Aruch Orach Chaim* 580:2); and the day *Bnai Yisrael* crossed the *Yarden* (*Yehoshua* 4:19).

7. The *Baal Haturim* says that the plague of locusts did not occur on *Shabbat* and brings as proof, the use of the word *"vayanach"* – "and it rested" in relation to the plague of locusts (*Shemot* 10:14). The *Baal Haturim* points out that this word is used in only two places in the *Torah*, one here and the other regarding *Hashem* resting from creating on *Shabbat* (*Shemot* 20:11).

8. The two *mitzvot asei* – "positive commandments" that are punishable by death if one fails to do them are *"korban Pesach"* – "the *Paschal* sacrifice" and *"brit milah"* – "circumcision."

9. According to the *Rambam*, if you move a piece of the lamb from one house to another and then someone else moves it again to another place, the second person has not transgressed any law (*Korban Pesach* 9:1). However, if one person breaks a bone of the *Korban Pesach* and then someone else breaks the same bone, both have transgressed the law (*Rambam, Korban Pesach* 10:4). Therefore, explains the *Haktav Vehakabalah* (*Shemot* 12:46), in the first case, the *Torah* cites the law in the singular and then changes to the plural for the second law.

10. The *Otzar Taamei Haminhagim* states that the custom of baking round *matzot* is derived from the word *"ugot"* – "cakes." Proof that the word *"ugah"* indicates something round comes from the *gemara* (*Taanit* 23a) which relates a story about *Choni Hamaagel* who made an *"ugah"* – "translated as a circle" and promised *Hashem* that he would remain in the circle until his prayers for rain were answered. They promptly were.

11. The Hebrew word for cakes is *"ugot."* The first occurrence is at the beginning of *Parshat Vayera*, where *Avraham* asks *Sarah* to prepare cakes for the three *"anashim"* – literally "men" but in fact angels who appear at his tent (*Bereishit* 18:6). The second time that the word *"ugot"* appears is regarding the baking of *matzot* in *Parshat Bo* (*Shemot* 12:39). The third time the word *"ugot"* appears is regarding the method used by *Bnai Yisrael* to prepare the *mann*. This third time is not the normal procedure for baking, as there was no flour with which to bake (*Bamidbar* 11:8); just *mann*.

12. *Rashi* (*Shemot* 13:5) states that figs and dates both produce honey.

13. The only two things that are described by the *Torah* as *"chazak me'od"* are the wind that removed the *"arbeh"* – "locusts" (*Shemot* 10:19) and the sound of the *Shofar* at *Matan Torah* (*Shemot* 19:16).

14. *Serach bat Asher* was listed among those *"shivim nefesh"* – "seventy souls" who came down to *Mitzraim* and she was the oldest person to leave (*Gemara Sotah* 13a). The *gemara* explains: How did *Moshe* know where *Yosef* was buried? He knew that *Serach bat Asher* remained from that generation who entered with *Yaakov*. *Moshe* went to her and said: "Do you know where *Yosef* is buried?" She said: "The Egyptians buried him in an iron casket and placed it in the Nile so that its waters become blessed." *Moshe* went to the banks

of the Nile and said: "*Yosef*, the time has come when Hashem will redeem us, and it is time for the fulfillment of *Bnai Yisrael*'s oath to bury you in the Israel." Immediately, *Yosef*'s casket floated to the surface, an *Moshe* carried *Yosef*'s bones to *Eretz Yisrael*, for burial in *Shechem*.

15. The *matzot* that *Bnai Yisrael* took with them when they left *Mitzraim* tasted like *mann*. The *Torah* tells us that *Bnai Yisrael* ate the *mann* for 40 years (*Shemot* 16:35) but the *mann* actually began falling on the 16th of *Iyar*, making the calculation 30 days short of 40 years. The *gemara* (*Kiddushin* 38a) says that the *matzot* that *Bnai Yisrael* brought with them at the time of the *Exodus* also tasted like *mann*. The *gemara* explains that even though the *mann* stopped falling on the day that *Moshe* died (7th of *Adar*), there was enough *mann* to last until the 16th of *Nisan* to complete the 40 years (*Torah Temimah Shemot* 16:35).

16. *Pesach* with a '*samech*' (*Shemot* 12:11) and *pesach* with a '*tav*' (*Shemot* 12:22). The first word, *pesach*, means to pass over and the second word, *pesach*, means doorway, something you pass under.

17. *Kayin* was asked four questions by *Hashem*; namely:
    1. "Why are you distressed?" (*Bereishit* 4:6).
    2. "Why is your face fallen?" (*Bereishit* 4:6).
    3. "Where is your brother *Hevel*?" (*Bereishit* 4:9).
    4. "What have you done?" (*Bereishit* 4:10).

18. There was one time when there was darkness for a year and that was during the year of the "*mabul*" – "flood of Noach" (*Siftei Chachamim Bereishit* 8:22). There are two possible answers for when there was light for more than 24 hours:
    1. When *Yehoshua* made the sun stand still in his fight against the *Emori*, daylight lasted 24 hours, according to *Rav Yehoshua ben Levi*, 36 hours according to *Rav Elazar*; or 48 hours according to *Rav Shmuel bar Nachmani* (*Gemara Avoda Zara* 25a).
    2. During the first week of creation, the light lasted for the 12 hours of Friday and all 24 hours of *Shabbat* (*Bereishit Rabba* 12:6).

19. There are only two people in the *Torah* who used the expression "*chatati*" – "I have sinned." *Paroh* (*Shemot* 9:27) and *Bilaam* (*Bamidbar* 22:34. It is interesting to note that both are non-Jews.

20. The same day that the *Exodus* from *Mitzrayim* officially began, is the exact date when *Bnai Yisrael* crossed the Jordan River and entered *Eretz Yisrael*. Both events occurred on the 10th day of *Nisan* (*Yehoshua* 4:19 and *Shemot* 12:1).

PARSHAT BESHALACH QUESTIONS

1. From where do we learn that one of the elements of *"Oneg Shabbat"* – "enjoyment of the *Shabbat*" is having three meals?

2. What is the origin of the custom of feeding birds on *erev Shabbat Shira* – *Parshat Beshalach*?

3. From where do we derive the requirement to read the *Torah* on Monday and Thursday?

4. Did non-Jews ever experience the taste of *"mann"* – "the heavenly food"?

5. What other parts of *Tanach* are scribed in the same form as *Az Yashir* (see also *Haazinu* question #1)?

6. What happened to *Paroh* after *"Kriat Yam Suf"* – "Splitting of the Reed Sea"?

7. Who was the first tribe to enter the sea after *Nachshon Ben Aminadav*?

8. What three roles are attributed to *Nachshon* in *Tanach*?

9. Who was the last person to enter the sea?

10. Which tribe had the shortest route to cross the sea?

11. How many different expressions of *Hashem*'s name are found in *Az Yashir*?

12. On what day did the *mann* begin to fall from heaven?

13. What *beracha rishona* would one make on *mann*?

14. Where is there a hint to *Haman*'s connection with *Amalek* in *Parshat Beshalach*?

15. To what three inanimate objects are the Egyptians compared?

16. How many *"erev rav"* came out of *Mitzrayim* with *Bnai Yisrael*?

17. Members of which tribe left *Mitzrayim* first?

18. Which non-*Jew* in the *Torah* caused the entire *Bnai Yisrael* to do *teshuva*?

19. *Moshe* is younger than me. Why should I listen to him? Who wanted to defy *Moshe* because of his age?

20. How many times is the word *"v'cham"* found in *Tanach*?

PARSHAT BESHALACH ANSWERS

1. The *pasuk* (*Shemot* 16:25) which states that the *"mann"* – "the special food that rained down from heaven" would not appear on *Shabbat*, has the word *"hayom"* – "today" mentioned three times; *"ichluha hayom, ki Shabbat hayom l'hashem, hayom lo timtzaena basadeh"* – "eat it today, for today is *Shabbat* to *Hashem*, today, you will not find it in the fields." From here, the *gemara* (*Shabbat* 117b) deduces the *mitzvah* of three *"seudot"* – "meals" on *Shabbat*; namely, Friday night, *Shabbat morning* and *seudah shlishit* on *Shabbat* afternoon.

2. There are numerous reasons given for feeding birds on *Erev Shabbat Shira*:
    1. In *Parshat Beshalach*, in the *Torah* reading of *Shabbat Shira*, we read that a double portion of *"mann"* would fall every Friday; however, *"mann"* would not fall on *Shabbat*. Despite that, there were those who went out to collect on *Shabbat* but did not find any *"mann"* (*Shemot* 16:27). The *midrash* (*Shemot Rabbah* 25:10) tells us that these rebellious individuals were none other than *Datan* and *Aviram*. The *Taamei Haminhagim* quotes the *Chozeh of Lublin* (*Taamei Haminhagim Addendum* 98) who relates that *Datan* and *Aviram* decided to spread *"mann"* around the camp on Friday night to discredit *Moshe* in the eyes of the nation. The birds came at night and ate all the *"mann."* The *pasuk* says "they went out to look for the *"mann"* and did not find any" (*Shemot* 16:27). It should have said "and there wasn't any." The term "did not find any" indicates that something had been there but was removed. To show our *"hakarat hatov"* – "appreciation" to the birds, we feed them specially on *Erev Shabbat Shira*.
    2. A second reason given is that the concept of song is learned from birds and we therefore pay "royalties" to birds this *erev Shabbat Shira* for teaching us how to sing praises to *Hashem*.
    3. On *Shabbat Shirah*, the *Maharal of Prague*, would bring the children of Prague to the *shul* courtyard. He would relate the story of *"kriat Yam Suf"* – "the splitting of the Reed Sea" and how the birds sang and danced while *Moshe* and the *Bnai Yisrael* sang *Az Yashir*, and that the children crossing *Yam Suf* took fruits from trees growing there and afterward fed them to the birds that sang (*Kaf Hachaim on Shulchan Aruch Orach Chaim* 324:11). The *Midrash* (*Shemot Rabbah* 21:10) relates that at the time of the splitting of the *Yam Suf*, fruit-bearing trees sprouted forth from the sea bed. The children picked the fruit from the trees, and gave them to the birds who joined the Jews in their song of praise to *Hashem*.

3. The *Torah* says that *Bnai Yisrael* went three days without water (*Shemot* 15:22). Water is often used as a metaphor for *Torah* as it says "*ain mayim elah Torah*" – paraphrased as "water for the Jewish people is *Torah*." Therefore, in order that three days should not pass by without the *Torah* being read, the *Neviim* enacted the requirement for reading the *Torah* on Monday, Thursday and *Shabbat* (*Rambam, Hilchot Tefillah* 12:1).

4. *Rashi* (*Shemot* 16:21) quotes the *mechilta* (*Mechilta d'Rabbi Yishmael* 16:21) and relates that when the sun melted all of the "*mann*" that remained in the fields, the resulting liquid flowed into streams from which animals drank. When a non-*Jew* ate the meat of one of those animals, he experienced the taste of "*mann*."

5. *Az Yashir* (*Shemot* 15:1–19), is written in a brick pattern. There are five regular lines at the top of the column, followed by a blank line. The lines of the *shira* follow for a total of 30 lines. These 30 lines are followed by another blank line and then by five regular lines. This creates a perfectly balanced column. This brick pattern is repeated in the song of *Devorah* (*Shoftim* 5:1–31) and the song of *David* (*Shmuel* 2:22:1–51).

6. He became the *king of Ninveh*. The *Baal Haturim* (*Shemot* 14:31) notes that the word "*vaya'aminu*" – "and they believed" appears in two places in *Tanach*. Once at the splitting of the sea and once more where it testifies to the people of *Ninveh*'s belief in *Hashem* at the time of *Yonah* (*Yonah* 3:5). When the threat of destruction was presented to the people of *Ninveh*, we are told that *Paroh* tore his garments and exhorted the people to repent, using his previous experience with the G-d of *Israel* as evidence of the truth of *Hashem*'s word.

7. There is a *machloket* in the *gemara* (*Sotah* 37a): *Rabbi Meir* says it was the tribe of *Binyamin* and *Rabbi Yehuda* says it was the tribe of *Yehuda*.

8. The answer does not include being the first into the sea, as this is never mentioned specifically in the *Torah*. Rather, the three roles attributed to *Nachshon ben Aminadav* are:
   1. As the brother of *Elisheva*, who married *Aharon* (*Shemot* 6:23).
   2. As the leader of the tribe of *Yehuda* (*Bamidbar* 1:7 and other places in *Bamidbar*).
   3. As the great-great-great-grandfather of King David (*Ruth* 4:20 and in *Divrei Hayamim* 1:2:10).

9. *Moshe Rabbeinu* was the last to enter. The *Ralbag* says that had *Moshe* entered before all the tribes had completed their entry into the sea, they might have feared that only *Moshe* would be saved and they would be afraid to follow. *Moshe* showed that he had ultimate faith in *Hashem*, by remaining at the rear of those entering the sea, with nothing separating him from

Paroh and his armies and therefore most vulnerable to the impending danger (*Ralbag Shemot* 14:19).

10. *Tosafot* in *Gemara Erechin* 15a says that they never really crossed from one side to the other; rather they entered the sea and took a semi-circular route to emerge on the same side of the river farther downstream. Since there were 12 paths; one for each tribe; the tribe with the inside path had the shortest route. It seems from a diagram in *Meam Loez*, that the paths were in order of the birth of the tribes. Therefore, *Binyamin* had the shortest route and *Reuven* had the longest.

11. There are five obvious expressions and two unique expressions of *Hashem's* name found in *Az Yashir*. The five obvious are (i) *yud-heh-vav* and *heh*, (ii) *yud* and *heh*, (iii) *alef-lamed* and *yud*, (iv) *alef-lamed-heh* and *yud*, and (v) *alef-daled-nun* and *yud*. The two unique expressions are the word "*zeh*" as one of *Hashem's* names (*Gemara Menachot* 53b) and the word "*ish*" as one of *Hashem's* names (*Gemara Sotah* 42b).

12. According to the *Chatam Sofer*, the supply of *matzah* which sustained the *Bnai Yisrael* from the time they left *Mitzrayim*, lasted until the 14th *of Iyar* (*Pesach Sheni*). The people went hungry for three days and then on the fourth, the *mann* began to fall. This would place the date as the 18th *of Iyar* which we know as *Lag BaOmer*, thus adding to our sense of joy on this day.

13. The *gemara* (*Berachot* 48b) tells us that with the advent of the falling of heavenly bread or "*mann*," *Moshe Rabbeinu* composed "*hazan et haolam*," the first *beracha* of "*birkat hamazon*" – "grace after meals." However, the *gemara* never discusses the blessing that might have been said prior to eating the "*mann*." One might surmise that since "*birchot hanehenin*" – "blessings of enjoyment" (blessings for tasting, seeing and smelling) were established by the *Rabbis*, no initial *beracha* would have been said when the *Bnai Yisrael* ate the "*mann*" in the desert. Nevertheless, since the *gemara* says that we will eventually partake of the "*mann*" that was hidden by *Yoshiyahu* (*Gemara Yoma* 52b), when we participate in the "*Seudat Livyatan*" – "the special meal at the advent of *Mashiach*," we should therefore be prepared with the correct *beracha*. There are a number of opinions. One is that no *beracha* is said, as *berachot* are only said on food which comes naturally; not food that comes miraculously. Another opinion (*Sefer Chassidim* and *Ramah miFano* in his *Asara Ma'amarot*) is that a special *beracha* would be established in the form of "*hamotzi lechem min hashamayim*" – "He who extracts bread from the heavens," as contrasted with the current... "bread from the earth." The *Chayei Adam* (51:17) rules that bread made from grains grown in a pot with no connection to the earth requires the *beracha* of "*boreh minei mezonot*" – "the one who created types of sustenance," and that "*mann*" would be similar (*Nishmat Adam* 152:1). *Rav Chaim Pelagi* (*Nefesh Chaim*

40:106) suggests a blessing of "*boreh minei mezonot*" as well, because "*mann*" tasted like wafers from honey; but clarified that since they were "*koveah seudah*" – "made this their full meal," they would have to make the blessing of "*hamotzi*." The *Bnai Yissaschar* (*Maamar Shabbatot* 3) suggests that if it were not for the opinion of the *Ramah miFano*, he would have ruled that no *beracha* would be said over the "*mann*" during the week; however, a special *beracha* of "*le'echol seudat Shabbat*" would be said upon eating the "*mann*" on *Shabbat*. A very interesting opinion is that of *Rav Eliezer Deutsch of Hungary* who said that since "*mann*" had the taste desired by the one who was eating the "*mann*," he would therefore make the correct corresponding *beracha* to its desired taste. We should all have the *zechut* to soon eat from the "*mann*" at the festive meal announcing the coming of *Mashiach*.

14. The *Baal Haturim* (*Shemot* 17:14), quoting the *mechilta*, states that the *gematriya* of "*macho emche*" – "I will surely erase…the memory of *Amalek*" is the same as "*zeh Haman*" – "this is *Haman*." Both are equal to 107. The *Rokeach* is quoted by the *Baal Haturim* as saying that the *gematria* of "*emche*" is 54, which is exactly the number of times that *Haman* is named in the *Megillah*.

15. In the "*shira*" – "the Song of *Moshe* at the Reed Sea," the Egyptians are compared to stone (*Shemot* 15:5), lead (*Shemot* 15:10) and straw (*Shemot* 15:7). *Rashi* quoting the *Mechilta d'Rabbi Yishmael* (*Shemot* 15:5) explains that the most wicked among the Egyptians sank slowly like straw, therefore suffering the longest; the average Egyptian sank like stone, therefore suffering less; and the most righteous drowned like lead, very quickly with the least amount of suffering.

16. The *Targum Yonatan* (*Shemot* 12:38) says that there were 2,400,000 "*erev rav*" – "mixed multitude" of non-Israelite people who left *Mitzrayim* with *Bnai Yisrael*. This *Targum Yonatan* is cited as a possible explanation for the word "*chamushim*" (*Shemot* 13:18). The *Bnai Yisrael* were one fifth (600,000) of those who left. If we add the 2,400,000 "*erev rav*" to the 600,000 *Bnai Yisrael* we have a grand total of 3,000,000 and 600,000 is one fifth of that.

17. The *Targum Yonatan* (*Shemot* 13:17) states that members of the tribe of *Efraim* left *Mitzrayim* 30 years prior to the *Exodus,* and were fatally attacked by the *Plishtim*. Their bodies were not buried and these were then the "dry bones" referred to in *Yechezkel*. As a result, at the time of the *Exodus, Hashem* led the rest of *Bnai Yisrael* on a circuitous route so that they would not see the bones and return to *Mitzrayim* in fear.

18. The *midrash* (*Shemot Rabbah* 21:5) comments on the causative form of the verb "*hikriv*" – "brought close," to mean that *Paroh* caused *Bnai Yisrael* to do *teshuva* by chasing after them. *Rabbi Berechia* is quoted in the *midrash*

as saying that *Paroh's* coming closer, did more for *Bnai Yisrael* than 100 fast days and many prayers, in prodding them to repent and return to *Hashem*.

19. The *midrash* (*Shemot Rabbah* 21:6) tells us that the "*Yam Suf*" – "The Sea of Reeds" claimed that it had been created on the third day of creation, whereas man was only created on the sixth day of creation. And therefore, why should the sea listen to *Moshe's* commands? *Moshe* related this to *Hashem*, and *Hashem* placed His "right hand" on *Moshe's* right hand. When the sea saw who was supporting *Moshe*, it split. And that is why the *pasuk* says "*hayam ra'ah vayanos*" – "the sea saw (*Hashem* together with *Moshe*) and fled" (*Tehillim* 114:3).

20. The word "*v'cham*" – literally, "and it became warm" is mentioned four times in the *Torah*. The *Baal HaTurim* (*Shemot* 16:21) connects these four *pesukim*. He quotes the *gemara* (*Yoma* 75a) which states that the "*mann*" was described as a "*zera gad lavan*" – "a white coriander seed." The *gemara* says that it was called "*gad*" because it was "*maggid*" – "told" or clarified for the Jewish people the answers to unclear situations in the *midbar*. The *pasuk* relating to the "*mann*" says "*v'cham hashemesh v'namas*" – "and the sun became warm and it melted" (*Shemot* 16:21), hinting at the fact that the "*mann*" would make things as clear as daylight. The three cases it clarified were:

    1. If a woman got remarried less than three months after being married to her previous husband and gave birth to a baby seven months later, and there was a doubt as to whether the baby was full term from the first husband or a premature baby from the second husband, the child's portion of "*mann*" would fall at the door of the correct father's tent; this is hinted at by another *pasuk* with the word "*v'cham*" – "*im yishkevu shnayim v'cham lahem*" – "if two lie together and they have warmth" (*Kohelet* 4:11).

    2. If a man threw the "*kiddushin*" – "marriage contract" or a "*get*" – "divorce contract" at a woman and it was a "*safek*" – "doubt" if it fell closer to him, in which case the *kiddushin/get* are invalid, or if they were closer to her, in which case they are valid, then if the "*mann*" would fall at the door to his tent, it is proof that the *kiddushin/get* were closer to her, and if the "*mann*" fell at the door to her father's tent, then it is proof that the *kiddushin* were closer to him. This is hinted to by a third *pasuk* containing the word "*v'cham*": "*v'cham la'adoni hamelech*" (*Melachim* 1:1:2) which is a *pasuk* that references *kiddushin*.

    3. If there was a disagreement over who owned an *eved canaani*, the "*mann*" would fall at the door of the correct owner's tent. This is hinted to by the fourth *pasuk* with the word "*v'cham*": "*v'Cham hu avi Canaan*" (*Bereishit* 9:18).

PARSHAT YITRO QUESTIONS

1. Where is there a reference in *Parshat Yitro* to always announcing yourself, even before entering your own home?

2. What was the origin of the *Shofar* that was blown at *Har Sinai* and was it ever used after *Har Sinai*?

3. Of the mountains mentioned in the *Torah*, one is identified by three different names and another is identified by four different names. Name the two mountains?

4. Name three places in the *Torah* where the word '*im*' – 'if' actually means 'when'?

5. One group of people was ordered to remain apart from the other, yet it was more for the benefit of the latter than the former. Who was ordered to remain apart from whom and why?

6. If there had been a blind man at *Har Sinai*, what would he have missed seeing?

7. By what eight names was *Har Sinai* known and why?

8. Every child learns that *Hashem* went to *Eisav* and *Yishmael*, among others, to offer them the *Torah*. They asked, "what is written in the *Torah*?" When they heard that the *Torah* forbade killing and theft, they rejected the offer, saying that the *Torah* did not match their lifestyle. Where in the *Torah* is there a *pasuk* which alludes to that *Midrash*?

9. How many times is the phrase "*lo tov*" found in the *Torah* and what is the connection between them?

10. When *Bnai Yisrael* heard the giving of the *Torah* at *Har Sinai*, how far back did they retreat in fear?

11. Who takes on the role of waiter in *Parshat Yitro*?

12. From where do we derive the custom of swaying during the study of *Torah* and prayer?

13. How many of the sons of *Yaakov* were born in *Eretz Yisrael*?

14. Where is *Midian* first mentioned in the *Torah*?

15. They share a common name. One was the most famous convert in the *Torah* and the other was one of *Yitzchak*'s grandchildren. Who are the two individuals?

16. What were the four other names for *Midbar Sinai*?

17. Who in the *Torah* sent a message by arrow?

18. How many people in the *Torah* bowed down to another person?

19. How long were *Bnai Yisrael* at *Har Sinai*?

20. How many letters are there in the *Aseret Hadibrot* and what is the significance of the number?

PARSHAT YITRO ANSWERS

1. When *Yitro, Moshe's* father-in-law, came with his daughter and grandchildren to *Har Sinai*, where *Bnai Yisrael* were encamped, the *pasuk* relates that *Yitro* announced to *Moshe "ani Yitro chotencha ba eilecha"* – "I, *Yitro* your father-in-law have arrived" (*Shemot* 18:6). The *Sforno* explains that *Yitro* sent this message as a matter of courtesy, so that *Moshe* would not be taken unawares by his sudden arrival, thereby complying with the warning in the *gemara* "do not enter your own house without advance notice" (*Pesachim* 112a). The *Rashbam* comments on that *gemara* that we deduce this courtesy from the *pasuk "v'nishma kolo b'vo'oh el haKodesh"* – "his voice would be heard as he entered the Holy place," referring to the bells that hung at the bottom of *Aharon Hakohen's* robe (*Shemot* 28:35).

2. *Rashi* (*Shemot* 19:13) indicates that this ram's horn was from the ram at the *akeidah* of *Yitzchak*. The *Pirkei D'Rebbi Eliezer* indicates that this was the left horn, while the right horn would be reserved to herald the coming of the *Mashiach*. The *Baal Haturim* deduces from the use of the phrase *"bimshoch hayovel"* – "the extended blast of the *shofar"* here and again at the fall of *Yericho* (*Yehoshua* 6:5), that this was, in fact, the same *shofar*.

3. The name of the two mountains are:
   1. *Har Sinai* (*Vayikra* 25:1) is also known in the *Torah* by two other names; *Chorev* and *Har HaElokim* (*Shemot* 3:1).
   2. *Har Chermon* is also known in the *Torah* by three other names; *Har Siyon* (*Devarim* 4:48), *Siryon* and *Snir* (*Devarim* 3:9).

   While *Yitro* answer 7 indicates that *Har Sinai* has eight names, only three names, *Sinai, Chorev* and *Ha-Elokim*, are identified in the *Torah* as the location of the giving of the *Torah*. Even though some commentators identify *Har Moriah*, which is specifically mentioned in the *Torah*, as another name for *Sinai, Moriah* is never identified in the *Torah* as the name of the place where the *Torah* was given.

4. The three places are:
   1. The *Torah* instructs us as to how we are to build an altar of stone; *"v'im mizbach avanim"* (*Shemot* 20:22).
   2. The *Torah* speaks about the requirement to lend money to a poor person; *"im kesef talveh et ami"* (*Shemot* 22:24).
   3. The *Torah* speaks about the *"bikkurim"* – "first fruits" offering; *"v'im takriv minchat bikkurim"* (*Vayikra* 2:14).

   In each case, the word *"im"* – literally "if" is used implying an optional action but in each case, the action is required and is not optional, as in "when" you do this.

5. *Hashem* gave instructions that the men separate from the women three days before the giving of the *Torah*. It was for the benefit of the women that this occurred so that the women would be ritually pure in honour of the occasion. (*Gemara Shabbat* 86a).

6. He might have missed seeing many things. However, one spectacular thing which he would have missed seeing was the thunder as the *Torah* says (*Shemot* 20:15) "And the whole nation saw the thunder," the only time in history when it was possible to see thunder.

7. According to the *midrash* (*Shemot Rabbah* 2; *Bamidbar Rabbah* 1; *Shir Hashirim Rabbah* 8), "*Har Sinai*" – "*Mount Sinai*" is known by the following eight names and for the following reasons:

   1. "*Har Sinai*" – from the word "*sneh*" – "bush." This refers to the burning bush on *Har Sinai*. Also, *Sinai* is related to the word "*sinah*" – "hatred," a mountain upon which hatred for the nations of the world descended because they did not accept the *Torah* (*Gemara Shabbat* 89a).

   2. "*Har Ha-Elokim*" – "*Hashem's* Mountain," because it was there that *Hashem* revealed His *Torah* to the Jewish people.

   3. "*Bet Imi*" – "my mother's house." By accepting the *Torah*, the Jews were born as a nation.

   4. "*Har Chorev*," from the word "*cherev*" – "sword." This alludes to the fact that the *Sanhedrin* received its right to implement capital punishment from the *Torah* received at *Sinai*.

   5. "*Har Chemed*" – "desirable mountain." G-d desired Mount *Sinai* as the place from which to give the most desirable of treasures, the *Torah*.

   6. "*Har Bashan*" from the word "*shen*" – "tooth." Sustenance and blessing come to the world on the merit of *Torah* study and observance. Just as teeth prepare the food for digestion, so too, the *Torah* brings nourishment to the world. Alternatively, *Bashan* is similar to "*ba sham*" – "He (*Hashem*) came there" to reveal *Himself* to the Jewish people.

   7. "*Har Gavnunim*," from the word "*gevina*" – "cheese." Cheese is a metaphor for purity, probably because it's made from pure white milk, and just as cheese is made by separating curds of milk from any impurities, *Chazal* tell us that the Jewish people at *Mount Sinai* were cured from all diseases and ailments.

   8. "*Har Moriah*" – "mountain of teaching," where *Hashem* taught *Moshe* the *Torah*. As well, the *Zohar* explains that it is called *Mount Moriah* because of the abundance of sweet-smelling myrrh, one of the ingredients in the "*ketoret*" – "incense offered in the *Beit Hamikdash*," that is found there.

8. The *pasuk* (*Devarim* 33:2) says "*Hashem* came from *Sinai*, having shone from *Mount Seir* and having appeared from *Mount Paran*." *Rashi* quotes

the *gemara* (*Avoda Zara* 2b) where *Rabbi Yochanan* says: This teaches that *Hashem* took the *Torah* to every nation and to those who speak every language, such as the children of *Eisav* in *Seir* and the children of *Yishmael* in *Paran*, but they did not accept it. *Hashem* then came to the Jewish people and they accepted it. The *gemara* (*Avoda Zara* 2b) then points out that if the other nations of the world all rejected the *Torah*, they can never complain that it was never offered to them.

9. The phrase "*lo tov*" – "it is not good" is found twice. The first is when *Hashem* says that it is not good for man to be alone and He therefore creates woman (*Bereishit* 2:18). The other occurrence of this phrase is when *Yitro* tells *Moshe* that it is not good for him to carry the weight of the nation's problems alone (*Shemot* 18:17). Both times, the *Torah* is speaking about being alone. The message that the *Torah* is trying to teach, is that being alone is not what *Hashem* wants for all of us. Being alone without interaction with society severely impedes our creativity and our growth. It is quite interesting that the word for life "*chayim*" – "life" is in the plural, indicating that life is meant to be lived with others.

10. *Rashi* (*Shemot* 20:15) says that they fell back 12 *mil*. Each *mil* is 2000 "*amot*" – "cubits" and an "*amah*" is approximately 1.5–2 feet. They therefore fell back between 6.8 and 9.1 miles.

11. *Rashi* (*Shemot* 18:12) quotes the *Mechilta d'Rabbi Yishmael* which tells us that *Moshe Rabbeinu* was a waiter to *Aharon*, the elders and *Yitro*. The *Midrash* comments that *Moshe* was showing gratitude to his father-in-law for giving him his wife and for giving him the opportunity to have children.

12. After receiving the *Torah* on *Har Sinai*, the *Torah* tells us that the people "trembled" (*Shemot* 20:15). The *Baal Haturim* comments that since the *Torah* was given with the emotion of fear and trembling, it is for this reason that we sway during *Torah* study. Another *pasuk* which is quoted as the source for this custom is from *Tehillim* 35:10; "*kol atzmotai tomarna*" – "all my bones will proclaim." Various commentaries differ as to whether one should sway during prayer as well as *Torah* study and the *Mishnah Berurah* (48:1:5) quotes the *Magen Avraham* who says that all opinions are valid and that it is all according to one's nature and method of concentration. If one can concentrate better while swaying, then one should do so. If it helps to be rigid, then that is what one should do. The *Zohar* points out that it seems to be a Jewish trait to sway and he explains that the soul of the Jew is compared to a flame; "*ner Hashem nishmat adam*" – "the flame of *Hashem* is the soul of man" and since a flame is constantly flickering, so too, the Jewish soul is in constant motion when it is close to *Hashem*; i.e; during *Torah* study.

13. Only *Binyamin* was born in *Eretz Yisrael*. It was for this reason that the *Beit Hamikdash* was in the portion of the Tribe of *Binyamin* (*Mechilta Yitro* 4:18).

14. *Midian* is mentioned in *Parshat Yitro* as the area where *Yitro* lived and served as the *kohen* or priest (*Shemot* 18:1). *Midian* is first mentioned in the *Torah*, not as a name of a place, but rather as the name of one of the sons of *Avraham* in his union with *Ketura* (*Bereishit* 25:2).

15. The answer is *Reuel*. *Reuel* was one of *Yitro's* seven names (*Shemot Rashi* 18:1) and *Reuel* was also the name of one of the sons of *Eisav* through his wife *Basmat* (*Bereishit* 36:4).

16. The *gemara* (*Shabbat* 89) lists *Midbar Tzin* (*Bamidbar* 20:1) as related to the word "*tzav*" because *Bnai Yisrael* were commanded to keep the *mitzvot* there; *Midbar Kadesh* (*Tehillim* 29:8) because *Bnai Yisrael were* made "*kadosh*" – "holy" there; *Midbar Kedeimot* (*Devarim* 2:26) because the *Torah* which was "*kadma*" – "preceded" the world, was given there; *Midbar Paran* (*Bamidbar* 13:3) because *Bnai Yisrael* "*paru*" – "increased and multiplied" there.

17. The *midrash* (*Midrash Aggadah Shemot* 18:6) relates that when *Yitro* arrived at the place where *Bnai Yisrael* were encamped, he was unable to enter because the "clouds of glory" that surrounded the camp were impenetrable ands were as solid as the wall of a boat. *Yitro* wrote the message "*ani chotencha Yitro ba eilecha*" – "I, *Yitro*, your father-in-law am coming to you" (*Shemot* 18:6) and shot it through the clouds with an arrow. Immediately upon receiving the arrow, *Moshe* came out to meet and greet his father-in-law.

18. There are six occurrences in the *Torah* where people bowed to other people:
    1. In *Parshat Yitro*, *Moshe* bows to *Yitro* (*Shemot* 18:7).
    2. *Avraham* bowed to the three angels thinking they were human visitors (*Bereishit* 18:2).
    3. *Avraham* also bowed to the *Bnai Cheit* when purchasing the *Me'arat Hamachpela* from them (*Bereishit* 23:7 and 23:12).
    4. *Yaakov* and his family bowed to *Eisav* (*Bereishit* 42:6).
    5. *Yaakov* bowed to *Yosef* (*Bereishit* 47:31).
    6. *Yosef* bowed to *Yaakov* (*Bereishit* 48:12).

19. *Bnai Yisrael* arrived at *Har Sinai* on *Rosh Chodesh Sivan* (*Rashi Shemot* 19:1) and left 11 months and 20 days later on the 20th of *Iyar* the following year (*Bamidbar* 10:11).

20. There are 620 letters in the "*Aseret Hadibrot*" – "The Ten Commandments." The *Baal Haturim* comments that this number is the sum of the 613 *mitzvot* plus the *Seven Noachide Laws*. The *gematriya* of the word "*keter*" – "crown" is 620 indicating that one who studies *Torah* diligently earns the crown of *Torah*. On the other hand, one who neglects *Torah* study risks "*karet*" – "excommunication" which is composed of the same three letters as "*keter*" and likewise has the *gematriya* of 620.

PARSHAT MISHPATIM QUESTIONS

1. How were *Kalev ben Yefuneh* and *Moshe Rabbeinu* related?
2. By what other names was *Miriam* known?
3. Who were *Chur*'s parents?
4. Compared to the other participants, I play a very small role in the performance of this forbidden act and yet I am considered to be the only guilty party. What have I done?
5. How many times does the phrase "*shalosh regalim*" appear in *Tanach*?
6. What *halacha* in the *Torah* teaches the concept of "*hakarat hatov*" – "an expression of appreciation" to animals?
7. *Chametz* and *Matzah* are sometimes permitted, sometimes forbidden and sometimes obligatory and sometimes optional. There are instances when:
    1. Both *chametz* and *matzah* are forbidden.
    2. When both are required.
    3. When *chametz* is forbidden and *matzah* is obligatory (give four instances).
    4. When *chametz* is forbidden and *matzah* is permitted but not required.
    5. When *chametz* is forbidden (nothing to do with *Pesach*).
    6. Where *chametz* is obligatory.
    7. When *matzah* is optional.
    What are they?
8. I am running in "*reshut harabim*" – "public domain," and bump into someone who is walking. I am "*chayav*" – "responsible for the damages." I am running in "*reshut harabim*" – "public domain," and bump into someone who is walking. I am "*patur*" – "excused from responsibility for the damages." Sounds like the exact same case, but there is a difference. What is the difference between the two cases from a *halachic* standpoint?
9. Which individual has to go to an "*ir miklat*" – "city of refuge" even though he never killed anyone?
10. Which group of people must go to an "*ir miklat*" – "city of refuge" even though they never killed anyone?
11. Who can never leave an "*ir miklat*" – "a city of refuge"?
12. Can one be freed from an "*ir miklat*" – "city of refuge" even though the active *kohen gadol* is still alive?
13. I have a mixture of meat and dairy that is *halachically pareve* – How is that possible?
14. We know that despite the fact that the *Torah* says "*ayin tachat ayin*" – "an eye for an eye," Jewish law dictates that we do not actually punish in that manner; but rather we extract monetary payment for the value of that eye,

based on the court's evaluation of the value of sight. Where is this hinted in the *Torah*'s words?

15. There is a reference in *Parshat Beshalach* to healing and there is a reference in *Parshat Mishpatim* to healing. What is the difference between the two and what can we learn from this?

16. How many people or places in the *Tanach* are referred to as "barren"; i.e., unable to bear children?

17. *Mishpatim* discusses the laws of an "*eved ivri*," a Hebrew slave. Which person in the *Torah* is specifically referred to as "the Hebrew slave"?

18. There is a law in the giving of charity called "*aniyei ircha kodmim*" – "the poor of your own city takes precedence over the poor of another city." From which verse do we learn this *halacha*?

19. From where in *Parshat Mishpatim*, is there a hint, that before meting out judgement, the judge has to attempt compromise through negotiation?

20. What two things are permitted when separated and forbidden when mixed?

PARSHAT MISHPATIM ANSWERS

1. *Calev* was *Miriam*'s husband (*Divrei Hayamim* 1:2:9) and therefore *Calev* was *Moshe*'s brother-in-law (*Rashi Shemot* 24:14).

2. *Miriam* was also known as *Puah* (*Shemot* 1:15) and *Efrat* (*Rashi Shemot* 24:14 and *Sotah* 11b).

3. *Chur*'s father was *Calev* and his mother was *Miriam* (*Rashi Shemot* 24:14).

4. The prohibition of digging a pit in the *"reshut harabim"* – "the public domain" is defined as a pit of at least 10 *"tefachim"* – "handbreadths" in depth. The *gemara* (*Bava Kama* 51a) explains that if one digs nine *tefachim* and another extends it by only one *tefach* to a total of ten *tefachim*, the second party bears the full guilt, even though he has done only a minor part of the forbidden act.

5. We normally refer to *"shalosh regalim"* as the three festivals of *Pesach*, *Shavuot* and *Sukkot*. However, despite the fact that this phrase appears in the *Torah* four times, the only time that it is used to describe the three festivals, is in *Parshat Mishpatim* (*Shemot* 23:14). The phrase is found in the *Torah* three additional times (*Bamidbar* 22:28; *Bamidbar* 22:32; and *Bamidbar* 22:33). For each of these occurrences, the phrase means "three times."

6. In *Parshat Bo*, the *Torah* says that during the plague of the firstborn, there was utter tranquillity and *"lo yecheratz kelev leshono"* – "no dogs barked" (*Shemot* 11:7). Because the dogs were silent and *Bnai Yisrael* were able to focus on the special, miraculous events of the night of the *Exodus*, we are told to repay the kindness of the dogs, by feeding them portions of meat that are forbidden to us – *"neveila"* and *"tereifa"* (*Rashi Shemot* 22:30).

7. *Chametz* and *Matzah* are sometimes permitted, sometimes forbidden and sometimes obligatory and sometimes optional. Here are the various categories:
    1. After the fourth *halachic* hour on *Erev Pesach*, both *chametz* and *matzah* are forbidden.
    2. The *korban todah* offering had to be accompanied by both *chametz* (loaves of bread) and three types of *matzah*; hence both *chametz* and *matzah* are obligatory (*Vayikra* 7:13).
    3. The *korban* offering of the *nazir* (*Bamidbar* 6:15) and the *miluim* offering (*Shemot* 29:2) had to be accompanied by *matzah* and could not contain *chametz*; hence *chametz* forbidden and *matzah* obligatory. As well, on the first night of *Pesach* (and the second night of *Pesach* in *Chutz Laaretz*), eating *chametz* is forbidden and eating *matzah* is obligatory (*Shemot* 12:15, 18).

4. For the remaining days of *Pesach, chametz* is forbidden and *matzah* is permitted but not required.

5. *Parshat Mishpatim* contains the general rule that *chametz* cannot be offered on the *mizbeach* or altar (*Shemot* 23:18), and the *korban minchah* could not be made of *chametz* (*Vayikra* 2:11); hence these are cases where *chametz* is forbidden.

6. The *shtei halechem* (the two loaves offered on *Shavuot*) had to be made of *chametz* (*Vayikra* 23:17) which is a case of *chametz* being required.

7. *Pesach Sheini*, the custom is to eat *matzah*, but is optional.

8. The first case took place during the week when the runner is doing something abnormal and therefore he has to pay extra special attention to ensure that he does not bump into anyone. The second case took place on *Erev Shabbat bein hashmashot* when running is considered part of general *Shabbat* preparations (*Bava Kama* 32; *Shulchan Aruch Choshen Mishpat* 378:8). The *Ran* comments that in the second case, the person is only *"patur"* – "excused from responsibility for the damages" when he is running to complete his *Shabbat* needs; if, however, he was hurrying to complete *non-Shabbat* needs, he would be *"chayav"* – "responsible for damages" done to the walker.

9. A *"rebbe"* – "religious studies teacher" must go with his student to an *"ir miklat"* – "city of refuge" (*Gemara Makot* 10a). This is derived from the *pasuk* (*Devarim* 19:5), which states: "he shall flee to one of these cities, and he shall live." Implied, is that everything necessary for his life must be provided for him. Therefore, a scholar must be provided with his teacher, for the life of one who is exiled without the possibility of *Torah* study is considered to be a death sentence.

10. If a *rebbe* kills accidentally and goes to the city of refuge, his whole *yeshiva* must accompany him for the same reason stated above (*Gemara Makot* 10a).

11. A *"kohen gadol"* – "high priest" who accidentally kills, has to flee to an *"ir miklat"* and cannot leave until the death of the *kohen gadol* (i.e., his own death) and is therefore doomed to remain there until his last day on earth (*Mishneh Makot* 2:7).

12. If a *kohen gadol* developed a *"mum"* – "a disqualifying flaw," he may be deposed. If the flaw subsequently disappears, he may be reinstated. Additionally, during the late 2nd *Beit Hamikdash* period, the Roman governors would sell the position of *kohen gadol* to the highest bidder. Therefore, there were times when there could have been more than one *kohen gadol*; one active and one not. The *Rambam* (*Hilchot Rotzeiach* 7:9) quotes a *Mishnah* (*Megillah* 1:9), which states that a resident of an *"ir miklat"* would be freed if any of the current or former *kohanim gedolim* would pass away.

13. I have a mixture with 59 parts *pareve*. One part of dairy and one part of meat accidentally fall into the mixture. The mixture cannot be deemed to be meat, because it is nullified based on the ratio of less than one sixtieth meat to the rest of the pot. Similarly, it cannot be deemed to be dairy because the ratio of dairy to the rest is likewise less than one sixtieth. Therefore the entire mixture is considered *pareve* (*Shulchan Aruch Yoreh Deah* 98:9).

14. The *Vilna Gaon* explains as follows: The *Torah* should have said "*ayin b'ayin*" – literally, "an eye for an eye," but instead uses the phrase "*ayin tachat ayin*" – literally, "an eye under an eye" (*Shemot* 21:24). Therefore, the *Gaon* explains that if you look at the letters under or following the letters of the word "*ayin*" which are *ayin, yud, nun*, you will find the letters *peh, kaf,* and *samech*, which spell the word "*kesef*" – "money."

15. In *Parshat Beshalach*, it says "*ki ani Hashem rofecha*" – "for I am *Hashem* who heals you" (*Shemot* 15:26). In *Parshat Mishpatim*, it says "*v'rapoh yerapeh*" – "and he should provide for the cost of healing" (*Shemot* 21:19). The *Baal Haturim* (*Shemot* 15:26) comments that in *Beshalach, Hashem* is identified as the healer, whilst in *Mishpatim*, it is man who is the healer. Therefore, says the *Baal Haturim*, the letter "*peh*" in *Beshalach* is soft (read as "*feh*"), without a "*dagesh*" – "dot in the letter," while the letter "*peh*" in *Mishpatim* is harsh (read as "*peh*"), with a "*dagesh*" – "dot in the letter." This indicates that *Hashem's* method of healing is precise, with no errors, and is administered with a soft touch. However, doctors are human, and while having the best intentions, at times can make errors, and can have a rough manner, causing pain, while providing medical attention.

16. There are seven references to "barren" in *Tanach*; six women and one place. They are:
    1. *Sarah Imeinu* (*Bereishit* 11:30)
    2. *Rivka Imeinu* (*Bereishit* 25:21)
    3. *Rachel Imeinu* (*Bereishit* 29:31)
    4. *Eshet Manoach* (*Shoftim* 13:3)
    5. *Chana* (*Shmuel* 1:1:5)
    6. The *Shunamit* woman (*Melachim* 2:4:14)
    7. The city of *Jerusalem* (*Yishayahu* 54:1)

17. In *Parshat Vayeshev*, the wife of *Potiphar* refers to *Yosef* as "the Hebrew slave" (*Bereishit* 39:17).

18. In *Parshat Mishpatim*, we read: "If you lend money to My people, to the poor among you, do not act toward them as a creditor; exact no interest from them (*Shemot* 22:24). *Rashi* quotes a *mechilta*, cited in the *gemara* (*Bava Metzia* 71a) which says that because the *Torah* specifies that the poor person has to be "*imach*" – "among you," therefore the poor of your own city take precedence over the poor of another city.

19. The *Baal Haturim* points out that the letters of the title of our *parshah* "*hamishpatim*" are a mnemonic for the first letters of the phrase "*hadayan metzuveh sheya'aseh peshara terem ya'aseh mishpat*"; "the judge is required to effect a compromise prior to issuing his ruling" (*Baal Haturim* 21:1).

20. There are a number of possible answers:
    1. Milk and meat are both permissible when eaten separately but forbidden when mixed (*Shemot* 23:20).
    2. Wool and linen are permitted when separate but when mixed are considered *shaatnez* (*Devarim* 22:11).
    3. An ox and a donkey or any two animals, one pure and the other impure, are individually permissible for work, but may not plow together (*Devarim* 22:10).
    4. Eating two different fruits is permissible but they may not be grafted together (*Devarim* 22:9).

PARSHAT TERUMAH-TETZAVEH QUESTIONS

1. From which *pasuk* do we learn that at least two persons should go together to collect for "*tzedakah*" – "*charity*"?

2. Where is there a hint in *Parshat Terumah* to every day in the year when one can read from the *Torah*?

3. Which animal mentioned in *Parshat Terumah* has the same name as a person mentioned in *Sefer Bereishit*?

4. In which two *parshiyot* do we have a *pasuk* containing three identical repetitions of the same five words?

5. Which word in *Parshat Terumah* hints at the length of time that the two *Batei Mikdash* would stand?

6. How did the donation of silver differ from the donation of all other items used in the construction of the *Mishkan*?

7. From where in *Parshat Terumah* do we derive the concept of an "*atara*" – "a special piece of material or silver sewn onto the collar of a *talit*"?

8. Did unicorns ever exist?

9. We have a concept of "*kol hamosif gore'a*" – "whoever adds to or embellishes the truth actually diminishes from it." Bring two examples of this principle from *Parshat Terumah*?

10. Where is there a reference in one *pasuk* to both the five "*sefarim*" – "books" of the *Torah* and the six "*sedarim*" – "orders" of the *Mishnah*?

11. Which *mitzvah* was only fulfilled seven times in history and will hopefully be fulfilled one more time in the future?

12. Which "*mitzvat asei*" – "positive commandment" was performed only nine times in history?

13. Why is *Moshe's* name not in *Parshat Tetzaveh*, and where is his name hinted at in *Parshat Tetzaveh*?

14. In what order were the names of the tribes inscribed on the "*ephod*" – "breastplate of the *Kohen Gadol*"?

15. Where were the "*avnei shoham*" stones previously mentioned?

16. Who in the *Torah* has a name that is one of the *Kohen Gadol's* articles of clothing?

17. Only three items in the *midbar* were required to be "*mikshah*" – "hammered and formed" from the same ingot, with nothing welded or mechanically attached. What were they?

18. Which word in *Parshat Tetzaveh* hints at the number of *kohanim* that were involved with the "*korban tamid shel Shacharit*" – "the daily morning offering"?

19. Connect *Nahar Pishon* that flowed from *Gan Eden* to the *bigdei kehuna*?

20. What did *Aharon* and *Achashverosh* have in common?

PARSHAT TERUMAH-TETZAVEH ANSWERS

1. The *Baal Haturim* says that from the plural language in the *pasuk*, "*tikchu et terumati*" – "they shall take My portion" (*Shemot* 25:2), we learn that two people should collect for *tzedakah* together.

2. The *Chatam Sofer* writes that there is a hint to the days that one can read from the *Torah* during the course of a year, from the words "*zahav*" – "gold," "*kesef*" – "silver," and "*nechoshet*" – "copper" (*Shemot* 25:3). The letters of the word "*zahav*," *zayin, heh* and *bet,* stand for the seventh day (*Shabbat*), the fifth day (Thursday) and the second day (Monday). The letters of the word "*kesef*," *kaf, samech* and *peh,* stand for *Kippurim* (*Yom Kippur*), *Sukkot* and *Purim/Pesach.* The letters of the word "*nechoshet*," *nun, chet, shin* and *tav,* stand for *neirot* (*Chanukah*), *chodesh* (*Rosh Chodesh/Rosh Hashana*), *Shavuot/Simchat Torah/Shemini Atzeret,* and *Taanit.*

3. The animal *tachash* (*Shemot* 25:5) has the same name as one of *Nachor's* sons (*Bereishit* 22:24). *Tachash* is translated by *Rashi* as a multi-coloured animal that is now extinct.

4. The *pasuk* is in *Parshat Terumah* (*Shemot* 25:35) and repeats "*v'chaftor tachat shney hakanim mimenah*" three times. The exact same phrase occurs again in *Parshat Vayakhel* (*Shemot* 37:21) repeated three times.

5. The first *Beit Hamikdash* existed for 410 years and the second *Beit Hamikdash* existed for 420 years. The *Baal Haturim* says the length of time during which each *Beit Hamikdash* existed, is hinted in the word "*v'shachanti*" (*Shemot* 25:8). The first *Beit Hamikdash* stood for 410 years and the letters of the word "*v'shachanti*" can be repositioned as "*v'shachan tav yud*" – "stood for 410." The second *Beit Hamikdash* stood for 420 years and the letters of the word "*shachanti*" can be repositioned as "*v'sheini tav kaf*" – "the second 420."

6. *Rashi* explains (*Shemot* 25:3) that silver was donated as a fixed amount of exactly one-half *shekel* per person. For all other items, there was no fixed amount; one could give as much or as little as one desired.

7. The "*kerashim*" – "planks that formed the walls" (*Shemot* 26:15) of the *mishkan* were marked so that they were always used on the same side of the *mishkan* each time it was erected. The *Mishnah Berurah* (*Shulchan Aruch Orach Chaim* 8:4) comments that from this *pasuk,* we derive the custom of placing a "silk piece of material" on one side of the *tallit* so that we will always be able to keep the front *tzitzit* in front and the back *tzitzit* in back. The *Mishnah Berurah* adds that the *Arizal* did not insist that we be so particular about the direction of the *tzitzit* and therefore some followers of the *Arizal,* like members of *Chabad,* do not have the custom to place an *atara* at the neck area of the *tallit.*

8. The *gemara* (*Shabbat* 28b) says that the *tachash* mentioned in *Parshat Terumah* (*Shemot* 25:5) was an animal that existed only in the time of *Moshe Rabbeinu* and it had one horn on its forehead, similar to what we know as the unicorn. Additionally, the *Midrash Tanchumah* states that the *tachash*, like *Yosef Hatzaddik* possessed a coat of many colours; specifically six colours.

9. The *gemara* (*Sanhedrin* 29a) gives two examples from *Parshat Terumah*. First, "*amatayim vachetzi orkah*" – "its length was two and a half *amot*" (*Shemot* 25:10). If you take away the "*alef*" from "*amatayim*," you are left with "*matayim*" – "two hundred." Therefore by adding an *alef*, you are diminishing the value from two hundred to two. The *Vilna Gaon* offers an alternate explanation. He says, taking away the "*vav*" from "*vachetzi*," changes the meaning from "its length is two and a half *amot*," to 'half its length is two *amot*" (i.e., its full length is four *amot*), and therefore by adding the "*vav*," you diminish its value. The second example from *Parshat Terumah* given in the *gemara*, is "*ashtay esray yeriot*" – "eleven curtains" (*Shemot* 26:7). By taking away the first letter "*ayin*," what remains is "*shtay esray.*" Hence, by adding the "*ayin*," you have diminished the number from twelve to eleven. Another example given by the *gemara* is also quoted in *Rashi* (*Bereishit* 3:3) where *Chava*, although commanded by *Hashem* to refrain from eating from the "*etz hadaat*" – "tree of knowledge," expands the commandment to also not touch the tree. By expanding the truth, the snake pushes her against the tree and since she did not die, convinces her to also eat its fruit.

10. The *pasuk* says: "join five of the curtains as one and the other six curtains as one" (*Shemot* 26:9). The *Targum Yonatan* says that the five curtains are symbolic of the "*Chamisha Chumshay Torah*" – "the five books of the *Torah*" and the other six curtains are symbolic of the "*Shisha Sidray Mishnah*" – "the six orders of the *Mishnah*."

11. In our *parshah*, we read "*v'asu li mikdash*," "and they shall make a sanctuary for Me" (*Shemot* 25:8). The *Sefer Hachinuch* lists this as *Mitzvah* 95. The *Baal Haturim* (*Bereishit* 24:67) comments on the word "*ha-ohelah*" – "to her tent" and says that this word appears in all of *Tanach* only seven times to reflect on the seven "official" sanctuaries to *Hashem* since the creation of the world. They include the *Mishkan* in the desert; *Mishkan* in *Gilgal* (*Yehoshua* 4:19); *Mishkan Shiloh* (*Yehoshua* 18:1); *Mikdash Nov* (*Gemara Zevachim* 118b, *Rambam*, *Hilchot Beit Habechirah* 1:2); *Mishkan Givon* (*Divrei Hayamim* 1:16:39); the *First Beit Hamikdash* and the *Second Beit Hamikdash*. *Yehi Ratzon* that we should merit seeing this *Mitzvah* performed an eighth and final time, when the Third *Beit Hamikdash* is built speedily in our time in *Yerushalayim Ir Hakodesh*.

12. The *Mishnah* (*Yoma* 3:5) cites a difference of opinion between *Rabbi Meir* and the *Chachamim* regarding the number of times the *mitzvah* of *parah*

adumah was performed in history. *Rabbi Meir* says seven and the *chachamim* say nine times. The tenth time will be performed when *Mashiach* arrives and the *Beit Hamikdash* is rebuilt, speedily in our days.

13. The *Vilna Gaon* says that the reason why *Moshe's* name does not appear in *Parshat Tetzaveh*, is because *Moshe* died on *Adar* 7, which occurs (except on rare occasions) during the week that we read *Parshat Tetzaveh*. Since *Moshe Rabbeinu* died during this week, he is physically hidden, and not being mentioned in *Parshat Tetzaveh*, is indicative of this fact. The *Gaon* says further that *Moshe's* name is spelled *mem, shin, heh*. *Mem* is spelled *mem-mem*; *shin* is spelled *shin-yud-nun* and *heh* is spelled *heh-alef*. If we take the hidden parts of the letters (i.e., *mem-yud-nun-alef*), the *gematriya* is 40 + 10 + 50 + 1 = 101, which is the exact number of *pesukim* in *Parshat Tetzaveh*.

14. There were six names on each "*shoham*" stone. According to *Rashi* quoting the *gemara* (*Sotah* 36a), they were listed in the order in which they were born. *Reuven, Shimon, Levi, Yehuda, Dan* and *Naftali* were on the first stone; *Gad, Asher, Yissachar, Zevulun, Yosef* and *Binyamin* were on the other. *Rashi,* quoting the *gemara* (*Sotah* 36a), points out that there were an equal number of letters on each stone; 25 letters on each, with *Binyamin* being written with two *yuds*. (*Rashi Shemot* 28:10). There is another opinion in the *gemara* that divides the names according to the way they were divided in *Sefer Bamidbar* (*Shemot* 1:2–4); namely: the sons of *Leah* on one stone; *Reuven, Shimon, Levi, Yehuda, Yissachar* and *Zevulun*; and the sons of *Rachel, Bilhah* and *Zilpah* on the other: *Yosef, Dan, Naftali, Gad, Asher* and *Binyamin*. According to this opinion; the number of letters are not equal in each column.

15. In *Bereishit* 2:12, the *Torah* describes various characteristics of the locations where the waters of *Gan Eden* reached. One of the characteristics of the land of *Chavila* is the presence of "*shoham*" stones.

16. The article of clothing to which we refer in the question was the "*ephod*." The leaders of the tribes who would lead *Bnai Yisrael* into Israel are mentioned in *Parshat Masei*. The "*Nasi*" – "prince" of *Menashe* was *Chaniel ben Ephod* (*Bamidbar* 34:23).

17. The three *mishkan* items that were required to be *miksha* were the *keruvim* (*Shemot* 25:18), the *menorah* (*Shemot* 25:31), and the *chatzotzrot* (*Bamidbar* 10:2).

18. The *pasuk* says "*et hakeves ha'echad ta'aseh*" (*Shemot* 29:39). The *Baal Haturim* quotes a *gemara* (*Yoma* 26b) and says that the letters of "*ta'aseh*" are the same letters that form the word "*tisha*" which means nine. No coincidence, as the number of *kohanim* required to perform the daily morning sacrifice was nine.

19. *Targum Yonatan* (*Shemot* 35:27) says that the *"avnei shoham"* – "the *shoham* stones" and the *"avnei miluim"* – "the precious stones," for the *ephod* and the *choshen* all come from *Nahar Pishon*, a river that flows from *Gan Eden*.

20. Their names both began with *"alef"* and they both married women whose names begin with *"alef,"* *Elisheva* and *Esther*. They both wore the *bigdei kehuna* – the priestly vestments that were worn exclusively by the *kohen gadol* and used the vessels of the *mishkan/beit hamikdash*. As well, both *Aharon* and *Achashveirosh* married women with connections to royalty; *Aharon* married *Elisheva bat Aminadav* who was from the tribe of *Yehuda*, whose descendants would form the *Kingdom of David*; and *Achashverosh* married *Vashti*, who was the granddaughter of *Nevuchadnetzar*.

PARSHAT KI TISA QUESTIONS

1. Who coined the phrase *"Yiyasher Kochachah"* – or colloquially, *"Yasher Koach"*?

2. How do we know that men wore earrings in the time of *Moshe Rabbeinu*?

3. How can two brothers belong to two different tribes?

4. How do we know that whatever money you give to *"tzedakah"* – "charity" will come back to you?

5. *Reuven* is obligated to give *Shimon* charity. But as soon as the money changes hands, *Shimon* is now obligated to return it to *Reuven*. Describe the case?

6. What monthly *minhag* has its source in *Parshat Ki Tisa*?

7. How was *Betzalel* related to *Moshe Rabbeinu*?

8. Where is there a hint to *Mordechai* in the *Torah*?

9. Why is the *Kriat HaTorah* of *Parshat Ki Tisa* divided so disproportionately; 92 *pesukim* making up the first two *aliyot* and only 47 for the other five?

10. I own a sheep and yet cannot benefit from it in any way; I cannot use its wool, drink its milk or slaughter it for its meat and skin. Who am I?

11. From where do we learn that one must assume the prevailing custom of the locale wherein one finds oneself?

12. Most years, we read from *Parshat Ki Tisa* seven times in less than a month, and none of those days are *Yom Tov*. Explain?

13. These four *Torah* words *"v'hikahu"*(*Devarim* 25:2); *"hamayma"* (*Shemot* 7:15); *"halailah"* (*Bereishit* 1:15) and *"v'natnu"* (*Shemot* 30:12) have something in common besides all being five letters long. What is common?

14. The *pasuk* *"v'shamru v'nei yisrael"* (*Shemot* 31:16) discusses how the Jewish people have kept all aspects of the *Shabbat* for generations, including the prohibition of travelling outside the *"techum Shabbat"* – "a limited physical area in which a *Jew* is permitted to walk on foot on *Shabbat* and Jewish holidays." Where do the words *"v'shamru v'nei yisrael"* refer to a prohibition of travelling on weekdays?

15. Which three words in *Parshat Ki Tisa* are palindromes (can be read forwards and backwards)?

16. Which service in the *mishkan* was a *segula* to become rich?

17. Name a person mentioned in the *Torah*, who had a *rebbe*, also mentioned in the *Torah*, who received prophecy, and who also had a child, not mentioned in the *Torah*, who received prophecy.

18. What is common between the rainbow, *Shabbat*, the *lechem hapanim*, *brit milah*, and the connection between *Hashem* and *Bnai Yisrael*?

19. Two adult males, both Jewish, find themselves together in the same place for a couple of days. On the first night, the first person is obligated to make *kiddush* over wine to welcome the *Shabbat*, and the other has no such obliga-

tion. The next night, the second person has his obligation to make *kiddush* to welcome the *Shabbat* and the first has no such obligation. Describe the case?

20. Why was the *Machatzit HaShekel* collected in the month of *Adar*, during the time of the *Beit HaMikdash*?

PARSHAT KI TISA ANSWERS

1. The *gemara* (*Shabbat* 87a) based on the *pasuk* of "*haluchot harishonim asher shibarta*" – "the first tablets that you broke" (*Shemot* 34:1) deduces from the usage of the word "*asher*," that this alludes to *Hashem* saying to *Moshe*: "*yishar kochacha*" – "may your strength be true" when *Moshe* broke the "*luchot*" – "the tablets of stone."

2. *Aharon* originally asked for the earrings of the women and children, thinking that they would not part with these precious possessions. However, the men took off their own earrings and gave them to *Aharon* to make the Golden Calf (*Rashi Shemot* 32:2)

3. Two brothers can belong to two different tribes when they are half-brothers, sharing the same mother (*Rashi Shemot* 32:27)

4. The *pasuk* says "*v'natnu*" – "and you should give" (*Shemot* 30:12) in the *parshah* dealing with the "*machatzit hashekel*" – "each person donating a half *shekel* to support the upkeep of the *mishkan*." The word "*v'natnu*" is a palindrome; that is, it can be read both forwards and backwards, indicating that whatever you give, you will get back (*Vilna Gaon*). Additionally, the *Toldot Aharon* points out that the word "*tzedakah*" using the *gematriya* method of "*at bash*" – "where you substitute the first letter of the *alef bet* with the last; the second with the second last, etc; hence it is called "*at* (*alef-tav*) *bash* (*bais-shin*)" equals "*tzedakah*," hence indicating that *tzedakah* is returned to you in full.

5. The *halacha* tells us that an "*ani*" – "poor person" is one whose total possessions equal less than two hundred *zuz*, a measure of currency in those times. Suppose *Shimon* has only 199 *zuz* and *Reuven* has 200 *zuz*. *Reuven* now must give charity to *Shimon*. But as soon as he does, the status of the two individuals changes as well, and *Shimon* ceases to be an *ani* and instead becomes a *halakhic* man of means. *Reuven* now becomes the pauper. *Shimon* is now obligated to give charity to *Reuven*. Curiously, the *gematriya* of "*tzedakah*" equals 199.

6. The *Shulchan Aruch* (*Orach Chaim* 417:1) cites that there is a *minhag* for women to refrain from "*melachah*" – "creative activity" on *Rosh Chodesh*. The *Mishnah Berurah* (417:3) gives as the reason for this *minhag*, the fact that women did not contribute from their gold for the construction of the golden calf.

7. *Betzalel* was the grandson of *Chur* (*Shemot* 31:2). We know that *Chur's* parents were *Calev* and *Miriam* (*Rashi Shemot* 24:14) and *Miriam* was *Moshe's* sister. Therefore *Moshe* was *Betzalel's* great-grandmother's brother.

8. The *gemara* (*Chullin* 139b) cites the hint to *Mordechai* from the *Torah* as the words "*mor dror*" (*Shemot* 30:23), which is translated by *Targum Onkelos* as

"mira dachia," which sounds a lot like *Mordechai. Parshat Ki Tisa* is always read during the month of *Adar,* the month of *Purim.*

9. The portion dealing with the golden calf appears in the second *aliyah.* Since the *yisraelim* were involved in the construction of the *"eigel hazahav"* – "the golden calf," it would be embarrassing if a *yisrael* received that *aliyah.* Likewise, because of *Aharon's* involvement, it would be inappropriate to give the honour of this *aliyah* to a *kohen.* As the *leviyim* had nothing to do with the sin of the *"eigel,"* we give this *aliyah* to a *levi.* Therefore, by the time that we reach the second *aliyah,* we have to be at the story of the *"eigel."* This serves to sensitize us not to discuss in the presence of others, matters that may evoke feelings of embarrassment in them.

10. If a firstborn male lamb is born to a sheep, its owner must raise it for 30 days and then give it to a *kohen.* The *kohen* must care for it and bring it as a *"korban"* – "sacrifice" sometime within the lamb's first year of life. Therefore the *kohen* owns the animal, but cannot use it or benefit from it in any way. We are told this law in *Shemot* 34:19. This law applies even today when there is no *Beit Hamikdash.* Therefore, a *kohen* when given such a firstborn male lamb, must care for it and feed it for its entire life. Since this would create an onerous burden on any *kohen,* he is provided with a legal loophole, which is to sell a share in the pregnant mother sheep to a non-*Jew.* The firstborn then has no *kedushah* as a *"b'chor,"* and the Jewish owner can then buy out the non-Jewish partner and the problem is solved.

11. The *gemara (Bava Metzia* 86b) notes that when *Moshe* went to heaven to receive the *"aseret hadibrot"* – "the ten commandments," he refrained from eating as he was now in the territory of angels (*Shemot* 34:28). Similarly, when the angels came to *Avraham,* they ate, or appeared to eat, as they were now in man's territory (*Bereishit* 18:8). The *gemara* quotes *Rabbi Tanchum bar Chanilai* who says: a person should never deviate from the local custom, as *Moshe* ascended to heaven and did not eat bread while he was there, whereas the three angels descended to this world, as guests visiting *Avraham,* and they ate bread.

12. The actual reading of the *Torah* portion of *Ki Tisa* generally falls within the same month as *Parshat Shekalim* and *Purim.* As a result:
    1. The first part of the *parshah* is read at *Shabbat minchah* the week before *Parshat Ki Tisa,* then the subsequent
    2. Monday and
    3. Thursday leading to
    4. *Shabbat Ki Tisa;*
    5. The *maftir* for *Parshat Shekalim,* and
    6. *Taanit Esther shacharit,* and
    7. *Taanit Esther mincha,* for a total of seven times.

13. They are all palindromes, i.e., if read forwards or backwards, they are spelled the same.

14. The only other place in *Tanach* where we find the words *"v'shamru Bnai Yisrael"* is *Bamidbar* 9:19. In that context, it is discussing the Pillar of Clouds that travelled with *Bnai Yisrael* through the desert. The *pasuk* tells us that *Bnai Yisrael* was only permitted to travel when the Pillar of Clouds began its journey. Therefore, in that case, *"v'shamru v'nei Yisrael"* mandated staying in one place during the week.

15. The three words are *"mayim"* (*Shemot* 30:18), *"v'natnu"* (*Shemot* 30:12), and *"shalosh"* (*Shemot* 34:23).

16. A *"segula"* is defined as a protective or benevolent charm or ritual. Offering the *"ketoret"* – "the incense offering in the Temple" is considered a *segula* to become wealthy (*Gemara Yoma* 26a). The custom of reading the *"ketoret"* daily as a *segula* for wealth, is cited in the *Kaf Hachaim* (*Orach Chaim* 132:23). He states that some have the custom of having the *"parshat ketoret"* written on parchment in *"ktav ashurit"* – "the *Torah* scroll font," and that one should read it slowly, being careful not to skip words, as the *"parshat ketoret"* warns makers of the *"ketoret"* not to omit any ingredients under penalty of death. Based on this, *Ashkenazim* generally omit this section on weekdays, for fear that one will omit parts while hurrying to complete their prayers.

17. *Yehoshua*'s *rebbe* was *Moshe Rabbeinu*. *Yehoshua* and *Rachav* had a daughter named *Chulda*. She is named in *Rabbinic* literature as one of the female prophetesses (*Gemara Megillah* 14a). *Moshe* and *Chulda* were both prophets.

18. They are all named as a *"brit olam"* – an everlasting covenant (*Bereishit* 9:16; *Shemot* 31:16; *Vayikra* 24:8; and *Bereishit* 17:7).

19. This is the classic case quoted in the *gemara* (*Shabbat* 69b) where two individuals are lost in the desert and have lost track of time. The *halacha* is that in order to determine which day is *Shabbat*, you begin by counting seven days from the day when you realized that you had lost track of time (*Shulchan Aruch Orach Chaim* 344:1). In our case, the two individuals lost track of the day of the week on two consecutive days, then met up just before the first was to mark his first *Shabbat*. For the second individual, it is still Friday.

20. The *gemara* (*Gemara Megilla* 13b) says it was divinely established for half *shekalim* to be collected in the month of *Adar* as an antidote to *Haman*'s *shekalim*, which he gave to *Achashveirosh* in *Adar*. The *gemara* quotes *Reish Lakish* "it is revealed in advance to *Hashem*, that in the future *Haman* would weigh *shekalim* against the Jewish people; therefore, *Hashem* mandated that the Jewish people's *shekalim* given to the Temple would precede *Haman*'s *shekalim*."

PARSHAT VAYAKHEL-PEKUDEI QUESTIONS

1. How old was *Betzalel* when he built the *Mishkan*?
2. On which day of which month was the *Mishkan* completed?
3. How many times does *Parshat Pekudei* contain the phrase "*ka'asher/k'chol asher tziva Hashem et Moshe*" and what practice was instituted by *Chazal* that corresponds to this number?
4. What is the connection between the completion of the *mishkan*, the *tefillah* of *Chana* (*Shmuel Hanavi's* mother) and our daily *tefillah*?
5. Someone steals an object. For this sin he is put to death. Why?
6. Name three completely different words in *Vayakhel* that have exactly the same letters arranged in different order.
7. When did *Moshe* and *Aharon* ever serve together as *kohanim*?
8. What was unique about the method of weaving the goat's hair that was used in the *mishkan*?
9. How many different body parts can be found in the *mishkan*?
10. How many gold bells were on the "*me'il*" – "robe" of the *Kohen Gadol*?
11. Which "*kli*" – "vessel" in the *mishkan* was built from the donations made by women only?
12. If one is praying facing south, what is he praying for?
13. What kind of question would the *Urim V'tumim* not answer?
14. Who was a great-grandfather at age 26?
15. Which of the *bigdei kehuna* reminds us of a daily feature in the newspaper?
16. May a *kohen* wear *tefillin* while doing the *avoda*?
17. In *Parshat Vayakhel,* we find the word "*chach*" (*Shemot* 35:22). This is a two letter Hebrew word made up of the same two letters, in this case two *chets*. In all of *Tanach,* of all the letters in the Hebrew alphabet, how many can be paired with themselves to form a two-letter word?
18. Where in the *Torah* is "*tumim*" listed before "*urim*"?
19. What is the only *mishkan* item that is specifically cited as having been built by *Betzalel*?
20. In *Parshat Pekudei*, it says that *Moshe* blessed *Bnai Yisrael* upon completion of the *mishkan* (*Shemot* 39:43). What did he say?

PARSHAT VAYAKHEL-PEKUDEI ANSWERS

1. He was 13 years old. *Gemara Sanhedrin* (69b) deduces this from the use of the word *"ish"* (*Shemot* 36:4). There is a similar analysis of the age of *Shimon* and *Levi* in the story of *Dina* and *Shechem* (*Bereishit* 34:25). *Rashi* (*Gemara Nazir* 29b) says that the *Torah's* use of the word *"ish"* always refers to age thirteen.

2. The *Baal Haturim* says that the *gematriya* of *"vateichel kol avodat hamishkan"* – "all the work of the *Mishkan* was completed" equals the *gematriya* of *"b'esrim vachamisha b'kislev nigmar"* – "it was completed on the 25th of *Kislev"* (*Shemot* 39:32).

3. The phrase *"ka'asher/k'chol asher tziva Hashem et Moshe"* is mentioned 18 times in *Parshat Pekudei*. Additionally, *"ka'asher tzivah Hashem kain ahsoo"* is found once. The *Baal Haturim* (*Shemot* 40:21) says that the above was the basis for the 18 *berachot* of *Shemoneh Esrei* and the one additional *beracha* that was added later, *"v'lamalshinim."*

4. The *Baal Haturim* (*Shemot* 40:21) points out that the total number of words in the phrases *"ka'asher/k'chol-asher tzivah Hashem et Moshe"* – "all that which *Hashem* commanded *Moshe"* indicating the completion of the various parts of the *mishkan*, is 113 which is equal to the number of words in the *tefillah* of *Chana* and is equal as well to the endings of the *berachot* of *Shemoneh Esrei* (e.g., *baruch ata Hashem magayn Avraham, etc.*). He points out that the word *"lev"* – "heart" also appears 113 times in the *Torah* indicating the level of *"kavanah"* – "concentration" that one must have during the *Shemoneh Esrei*. He quotes the *Baal Rokeach* (*Shulchan Aruch Orach Chaim* 101) who says that at the very least, one should attempt to have proper concentration at the endings of each of the *berachot* of *Shemoneh Esrei*, as these endings refer to the praise of *Hashem*, while the body of the *Shemoneh Esrei*, deals mainly with our personal requests.

5. If he steals one of the *"klei sharet"* – "the service vessels" that were used in the *mishkan* or in the *Beit Hamikdash*, the *halacha* is *"kanaim pogim bo"* – "a zealous person who witnesses the theft can kill him without any consequence" (*Gemara Sanhedrin* 81b). Although the *Torah* does not sentence one who steals these vessels to death, the *Mishnah* in *Sanhedrin* states that it is permitted for anyone who zealously witnesses the theft, to take appropriate action.

6. The three words are:
   1. *kaftor*
   2. *kaporet*
   3. *parochet*

Each contains the same four letters of *chaf, peh, reish* and *tav* (*Shemot* 35:12 contains both *kaporet* and *parochet* and *Shemot* 37:21 has the word *kaftor*).

7. *Rashi Shemot* 40:31 says that on the eighth day of the consecration of the *mishkan, Moshe* and *Aharon* served together as *kohanim*.

8. *Rashi Shemot* 35:26 quotes a *gemara* (*Shabbat* 74b) that the goat's hair was woven while still on the backs of the goats. This was a unique talent that the women at that time possessed.

9. The following is a pretty complete (but perhaps not totally exhaustive) list of the body parts that can be found in the *mishkan*:
   1. "*tzela*" – "ribs" describes the side of the *aron, mishkan* and *mizbeach*.
   2. "*panim*" – "face" describe the show breads and the faces of the *keruvim*.
   3. "*pe'ot*" – "sideburns" describe the corners of the *shulchan*.
   4. "*yerach*" – "thigh" describes the base of the *menorah*.
   5. "*kaneh*" – "esophagus" describes the branches of the *menorah*.
   6. "*safah*" – "lips" describes the edge of the covering of the *mishkan*.
   7. "*raglayim*" – "feet" describe the legs of the *shulchan*.
   8. "*rosh*" – "head" describes the top of the wall planks.
   9. "*kapot*" – "palms" describe the spoons used in the *mishkan*.
   10. "*katef*" – "shoulder" describes the sides of the *mishkan*.
   11. "*taba'ot*" – "cartilage rings around the windpipe" describes the rings for inserting the poles to carry the *mishkan* and its vessels.
   12. "*kenafayim*" – "wings" describes the raised corners of the *mizbeach*.

10. There is a *machloket* in the *gemara* (*Zevachim* 88b) as to whether there were 36 or 72 pure gold bells suspended at the bottom of the *Kohen Gadol's* "*me'il*" – robe. I guess you could call these "bell bottoms."

11. The "*kiyor*" – "basin" was made from the copper mirrors that the women donated. At first, *Moshe* did not want to accept mirrors, which are associated with vanity. However, *Hashem* explained that these mirrors were used by Jewish women, to make themselves physically attractive to their husbands, while enslaved in *Mitzrayim*. *Chazal* explains that this was one of the things that ensured the continuation of the Jewish people (*Rashi Shemot* 38:8).

12. He is praying for wisdom. The *gemara* (*Bava Batra* 25b) deduces from the position of the *keilim* – "vessels" in the *mishkan*, that if one desires wisdom, represented by the *menorah* which was on the south side of the *mishkan*, he should face south. On the other hand, if one desired wealth, represented by the *shulchan* which was on the north side, then he should pray facing north.

13. The *gemara* talks about *King David* seeking advice about whether he would be successful in the war against the *Pilishtim*. *Rashi* comments that not all questions could be answered by the "*urim v'tumim*" – "elements of the breastplate worn by the *Kohen Gadol* and used to answer a question or reveal

the will of *Hashem*," as it would not answer questions of "*issur v'heter*" – "items that are permissible or forbidden" (*Rashi Gemara Eruvin* 45a).

14. *Kalev* was 26 when his great-grandson, *Betzalel,* was born. We know that *Kalev* was 40 years old at the time of the *meraglim* which was in the second year after leaving *Mitzrayim* (*Yehoshua* 14:7). We also know that *Betzalel* was 13 when he built the *mishkan,* which occurred in the first year after leaving *Mitzrayim*, from the *Torah*'s description of him as "*ish*" (*Shemot* 36:4; *Sanhedrin* 69b). Therefore he was 14 years old when the *meraglim* went to spy out the *Land of Israel. Betzalel* is identified as the son of *Uri* and the grandson of *Chur. Chur* was the son of *Kalev* and *Miriam. Rashi* comments (*Shemot* 17:12) that *Chur* was *Miriam*'s son (this is derived from *Gemara Sotah* 11b). In his commentary, *Rashi* (*Shemot* 24:14) mentions that *Chur* was *Miriam*'s son and adds that his father was *Kalev ben Yefuneh* as it says in *Divrei HaYamim* (1: 2:19), "*Kalev* took *Efrat*, as a wife, and she gave birth to *Chur*." In *Sotah* 11b we learn that *Efrat* is *Miriam*. This indicates that there was a 26 year difference in age between *Kalev* and *Betzalel*.

15. The *ketonet* – "tunic" worn by the *kohen* is called "*ketonet tashbetz*" (*Shemot* 28:4). The word "*tashbetz*" is translated as checkered or quilted. The modern Hebrew word for crossword puzzle is "*tashbetz*" and is a daily feature in most newspapers.

16. A *kohen* cannot wear *tefillin* while doing the *avoda* because it would be a "*chatzitza*" – "separation." The *gemara* (*Zevachim* 19a) deduces from the words "*al besaro*" – "on his skin" that the *kohen*'s priestly garments should be directly on his skin (*Vayikra Rashi* 6:3). Therefore he could not wear *tefillin* under his clothes. As well, he may not wear *tefillin* on top of his clothing as *tefillin*, likewise, cannot have a *chatzitza* between the leather and the person's skin (*Shulchan Aruch Orach Chaim* 27:4).

17. The following two letter words composed of like letters, can be found somewhere in *Tanach* (only one example of each case is presented):
    1. "*gag*" (*gimel – gimel*) (*Tehillim* 102:8)
    2. "*dod*" (*daled – daled*) (*Vayikra* 10:4)
    3. "*hah*" (*heh – heh*) (*Yechezkel* 30:2)
    4. "*chach*" (*chet – chet*) (*Shemot* 35:22)
    5. "*sas*" (*samech – samech*) (*Yeshayahu* 51:8)
    6. "*rar*" (*reish – relish*) (*Vayikra* 15:3)
    7. "*sheish*" (*shin – shin*) (*Bereishit* 7:6)
    8. "*teit*" (*tav – tav*) (*Bereishit* 4:12)

18. In *Devarim* 33:8, part of *Moshe*'s final blessing to the tribe of *Levi* is "*tumecha v'urecha*," referring to the "*Urim v'Tumim*."

19. The *pasuk* says "*vaya'as Betzalel et ha-aron*" – "and *Betzalel* made the *aron*" (*Shemot* 37:1). *Rashi* comments that his name is mentioned specifically,

because he dedicated himself to the work more whole-heartedly than the other wise men.

20. *Rashi* on *Shemot* 39:43, quotes the *Mechilta* and says that *Moshe* blessed them with the following words: "May it be the will of *Hashem* that His *Shechinah* rest upon the work of your hands"; and *Moshe* then continued: "and let the beauty of *Hashem* be upon us and may You establish the work of our hands upon us" (*Tehillim* 90:17). This, from "let the beauty of *Hashem*" onward, is part of one of the eleven chapters of *Tehillim* (90–100) that are in the section beginning with *Tefillah L'Moshe*.

PARSHAT VAYIKRA QUESTIONS

1. Why were "se'or" – "leaven or *chametz*" and "*dvash*" – "honey" specifically excluded from being offered on the *mizbeach* – "altar"?

2. How is it possible to *halachically* eat "*terumah*" – "the priestly offering" "*bizman hazeh*" – "in current times"?

3. Name a person and his father-in-law who are both mentioned in the *Torah*, who shared the same name?

4. We both appear in *Tanach* in the first. But he is the first of the first of the last, and I am the last of the first of the third. We are identical in one respect, yet different in another respect. Neither of us is normal and he is much bigger than me. To clarify, we are not people. Who are we?

5. *Vayikra*, called "*Torat Kohanim*" – "the priestly Laws," highlights details of many "*korbanot*" – "offerings and sacrifices." Who in the *Torah* brought the first "*korban*" – "offering or sacrifice"?

6. When in the *Torah* was the first "*mizbeach*" – "altar" built?

7. From which word in *Parshat Vayikra* do we learn that one may not bring an offering to *Hashem* that has been stolen; that does not belong to you?

8. What is the saltiest *pasuk* in the *Torah*?

9. Grown ups may be offered but never young ones; young ones may be offered but never grown ups. To what are we referring?

10. The *gemara* (*Menachot* 104b) states that *Hashem* considers a poor person's offering to be as though he had offered his very soul to *Hashem*. From where in *Parshat Vayikra* does the *gemara* deduce this concept?

11. What living creatures are permitted to be used as sacrifices?

12. How do we know that "*shechita*" – "ritual slaughtering" can only be done specifically with a knife and not with a sharp stone?

13. There were specific "*klei sharet*" – "service utensils" used in the service in the *Mishkan*. One of these was the knives used for ritual slaughter. Were these the only knives permitted?

14. *Parshat Vayikra* begins with the *pasuk* "*vayikra el Moshe, vayedaber eilav*" – "and He called to *Moshe*, and *Hashem* spoke unto him" (*Vayikra* 1:1). What *halacha* do the *Rabbis* derive from *Hashem* calling out to *Moshe* before speaking to him?

15. The same *pasuk* (*Vayikra* 1:1) says "*vayedaber Hashem ailav me'ohel mo'ed laymor*" – "and *Hashem* spoke to him from the *ohel mo'ed*, saying." What *halacha* do we learn from the seemingly redundant "spoke" and "saying"?

16. It is customary to add salt when partaking of bread at a meal. It is also customary to dip the bread into salt rather than pouring the salt over the bread. Why?

17. *"Melach"* – salt, is paired in a couple of places in the *Torah* with the word *"brit"* – covenant. What is the connection between these two words?
18. *Sefer Vayikra* in eight weeks, nine weeks, 11 weeks or just 30 days? Explain.
19. In describing the parts of the animal that are offered as a sacrifice, *Parshat Vayikra* includes the *"kelayot"* – "kidneys." Where do kidneys sing?
20. Which wildlife specimens mentioned in *Parshat Vayikra* make their appearance in *Sefer Bereishit*?

PARSHAT VAYIKRA ANSWERS

1. The *Baal Haturim* says that the *"yetzer hara"* – "evil inclination" is compared to sourdough, and in order to seduce us to sin, the ideas of the *yetzer hara* are presented to be as sweet as honey (*Vayikra* 2:11). Both are therefore excluded from being offered on the *mizbeach*.

2. *Terumah* may not be eaten in our days, even by *kohanim*, as everyone today is considered impure. However, *halacha* permits the animals of *kohanim* to eat *terumah*. It has been reported that rather than destroy the massive amounts of fruits and vegetables separated daily as *terumah* in Jerusalem markets and subsequently destroyed, the Jerusalem Zoo "sold" its animals to a local *kohen* and therefore the separated *terumah* can now be *halachically* delivered as feed to the zoo. Obviously, this produce had to be supervised when transported from market to zoo.

3. The *Medrash* tells us that *Moshe* had ten names (*Midrash Vayikra* 1:3). One of his names was *Chever*, which was also one of the seven names of *Yitro*, *Moshe*'s father-in-law.

4. I am the small *"alef"* in the word *"vayikra"* (*Vayikra* 1:1) and he is the large *"alef"* in the word (*"Adam"*) (*Divrei Hayamim* 1:1:1). We both appear in the first word but he is in the first letter of the first word of the last book in *Tanach* (*Divrei Hayamim*) and I am the last letter of the first word of the third book of *Tanach* (*Vayikra*). We are both identical in one respect; i.e., both *"alephs,"* but different in that neither of us is the same size font as other letters in *Tanach*. Finally, neither of us is normal; he is a larger than normal *alef* and I am a smaller than normal *alef*. Neither of us are people.

5. The first person mentioned in the *Torah* to bring an offering was *Kayin* (*Bereishit* 4:3); an offering to *Hashem* from the fruit of the soil. The *gemara* (*Avoda Zara* 8a) says that *Adam Harishon* actually brought a sacrifice on the second day of his existence. The *gemara* says: "On the day that *Adam* was created, when the sun set, he said: Woe is me, as because I sinned, the world is becoming dark around me. This is the death that was sentenced upon me from Heaven. He spent all night fasting and crying, and *Chava* was crying opposite him. Once dawn broke, he said: Evidently, the sun sets and night arrives, and this is the order of the world. *Adam* arose and sacrificed a bull." The *Midrash Hagadol* (*Bereishit* 4:3) says that *Adam* told *Kayin* and *Hevel* on *erev Pesach*, the 14th of *Nisan*, that their offspring would bring the *Korban Pesach*, and they should also bring a *korban*.

6. Immediately after the flood, *Noach* builds a *"mizbeach"* – "altar" and then he sacrifices burnt offerings to *Hashem* from every clean animal and bird (*Bereishit* 8:20).

7. *Rashi* (*Vayikra* 1:2) in quoting the *Midrash Vayikra* explains that when the *Torah* states "*Adam ki yakriv mikem*" – "when any of you present an offering" using the word "*Adam*," this is a direct reference to the first man, *Adam*. Since *Adam* did not offer sacrifice of anything acquired by way of robbery, since everything in the world belonged to him, so too, you, shall not offer anything acquired by way of robbery (*Vayikra Rabbah* 2:7).

8. *Vayikra* 2:13 contains four words that have to do with "*melach*" – "salt," and hence is the saltiest *pasuk* in the *Torah*.

9. The *pasuk* (*Vayikra* 1:14) tells us "if his offering to *Hashem* is a burnt offering of birds, he shall choose his offering from "*torim*" – "turtle doves" or "*b'nai hayonah*" – "young doves." *Rashi* quotes the *gemara* (*Chullin* 22a) that when offering "*torim*," only adult turtle doves may be utilized; and when offering "*b'nai hayonah*," only young doves may be offered.

10. *Rashi* (*Vayikra* 2:1) explains that nowhere is the word "*nefesh*" – "soul" employed in connection with free-will offerings except in connection with the "*korban mincha*" – "meal-offering." *Rashi* asks rhetorically: who usually brings a meal-offering? The poor person! *Hashem* therefore regards it so highly, as though he offered his very "*nefesh*" – "soul" as an offering (*Gemara Menachot* 104b).

11. The *Rambam* (*Hilchot Maasei Hakorbanot* 1:1 – Laws of Sacrificial Procedures) states that three animals, cattle, sheep and goats; and two birds, turtle doves and young doves; are the only live beings that are permitted to be used for ritual sacrifices.

12. The *gemara* (*Menachot* 82b) deduces this from the *pasuk* in *Bereishit* where *Hashem* commanded *Avraham* to offer his son *Yitzchak* on the altar, in the historical event that we know as the "*akeida*." The *pasuk* states: "And *Avraham* stretched forth his hand, and took the knife to slaughter his son" (*Bereishit* 22:10). Three *pesukim* later, we are told that *Avraham* was sacrificing a burnt offering, as it says: "and offered it up for a burnt offering instead of his son" (*Bereishit* 22:13). We therefore deduce from here that one can only use a knife for "*shechita*" – "ritual sacrifice."

13. The *Rambam* states (*Hilchot Maasei Hakorbanot* 4:7) that "*lechatchila*" – "a priori," a special knife of the "*klei sharet*" – "service utensils" should be used. But where none was available, one may "*bediavad*" – "as a reluctantly acceptable standard," use any utensil which is permitted for "*shechita*" – "ritual slaughtering," including a sharpened stalk of a reed (*Chullin* 3a).

14. The *Torah* is teaching etiquette: *Rabbi Chanina* says: A person should not say anything to another person unless he calls him first (*Gemara Yoma* 4b).

15. The *gemara* (*Yoma* 4b) quotes *Rabbi Musya* who says that from the addition of the word "saying," it is derived that when one tells another some matter, it is incumbent upon the latter not to repeat it to others, until the former

explicitly says to him: go and tell others. As it is stated: "And *Hashem* spoke to him from within the *"ohel moed"* – "tent of meeting," saying *"laymor."* *Rav Steinsaltz* states that *"laymor"* is a contraction of *"lo emor,"* meaning: Do not say. One must be given permission before transmitting information.

16. According to *Kaf Hachaim* (*Shulchan Aruch Orach Chaim* 167), salt, which is bitter, represents severity; and bread, which is synonymous with life, represents kindness. These two words in Hebrew are anagrams, *"melach"* – "salt" and *"lechem"* – "bread" are composed of the same three letters, *lamed, chet* and *mem*. We wish to show that kindness overcomes severity and therefore it is the custom to dip the bread into the salt, rather than pouring the salt over the bread.

17. Salt is a mineral that neither spoils nor decays; it is wholesome and lasting. As a preservative, it prevents spoilage in other foods. These properties make salt the perfect metaphor for *Hashem*'s eternal relationship and *"brit"* – "covenant" with the Jewish people (*Rashi Bamidbar* 18:19).

18. Depending on the calendar, the book of *Vayikra* is completed during the weekly *Torah* readings in anywhere between eight and 11 weeks. The number of weeks depends on whether we double up the *sidrot* of *Tazriya* and *Metzora*, *Acharei Mot* and *Kedoshim*, and *Behar* and *Bechukotai*; as well as whether there is one *shabbat* during the holiday of *Pesach* (which always occurs during the reading of *Sefer Vayikra*) or two *shabbatot*. The riddle, though, also speaks about *Vayikra* occurring in 30 days. What this means is that the end of *Sefer Shemot* coincided with the completion of the *mishkan* which was *Rosh Chodesh Nisan*. The beginning of *Sefer Bamidbar* happens on the first day of *Chodesh Iyar* in the same year. Therefore the actual time span of *Sefer Vayikra* was one month or thirty days!

19. In *"nishmat*, at the end of *Shabbat Pesukei D'Zimra*, we say *"v'chol kerev u'kelayot yezamru lishmecha"* – "and all of our innermost feelings and kidneys, will sing praises to Your Name."

20. There are a number of wildlife specimens mentioned in *Parshat Vayikra* that are also mentioned in *Sefer Bereishit*, including, *"tzon"* – "sheep," where *Hevel* is described as a shepherd (*Bereishit* 4:2); *"yona"* – "doves," sent by *Noach* to determine whether the flood had ended (*Bereishit* 8:8); *"bakar"* – "cattle" where *Paroh* presents gifts of cattle to *Avraham* because of the incident with *Sarah* (*Bereishit* 12:16); *"gedayei-izim"* – "young goats," where *Rivka* tells *Yaakov* to put on sleeves of goatskin so that *Yitzchak* would assume that he was *Esav* (*Bereishit* 27:16); and *"seir izim"* – "goats," where *Yosef*'s brothers dipped his coat of many colours into the blood of a dead goat, so that *Yaakov* would assume that *Yosef* had been eaten alive (*Bereishit* 37:31).

PARSHAT TZAV QUESTIONS

1. How many types of *"korban asham"* do we find in the *"Parshat asham"*?
2. From where do we know that *"chavrutas"* – *"Torah* study partners" are like brothers?
3. What separated the *kohen's* skin from his priestly garments?
4. Which part of the *"bigdei kehuna"* (the priestly garments) was the same size for every *kohen*?
5. In Jewish life, normally day follows night. Name two *mitzvot* where night follows day?
6. Name the number of instances when a *kohen* or a *Kohen Gadol* was placed in 7-day isolation.
7. In which four instances was a *korban todah* required?
8. How many *parshiyot* have only two letters in their title?
9. Sandy Koufax was perhaps the most famous Jewish left-handed pitcher in professional baseball history. He was the youngest player ever elected to the Baseball Hall of Fame. But if he was a *kohen*, he would have a serious handicap. Explain?
10. Why were *korban olah* and *korban chatat* both slaughtered in the same area of the *mishkan*?
11. The fifth chapter of *Masechet Zevachim, Eizehu Mekoman,* offers an overview of all the different sacrifices that were brought in the *Beit Hamikdash,* with the exception of sacrifices brought from fowl. This entire chapter has been added to our *siddur* as an introduction to *"shacharit"* – the daily morning service. Present reasons why this lengthy portion has been added to our prayers?
12. In *Parshat Vayikra,* we learn about the details of the *"korban olah"* – "the burnt offering." The *Mishnah* (*Tamid* 4:3) specifies how and when the heart of an animal is taken out from a *korban olah*. Where does the *Torah* explicitly state that the heart of certain people came out?
13. Until now, commandments regarding offerings were instructed using *"daber"* – "speak" or *"emor"* – "tell." Here the *Torah* uses the more emphatic *"tzav"* – "instruct" or "command." Why?
14. Where does the *Torah* describe French Toast Bagels?
15. For any of these four occurrences, you would be required to offer ten of each of these four varieties. Explain.
16. Who utilized the first *mitzvah* in *Parshat Tzav* as the title of his book of *"she'elot u'teshuvot"* – "responsa," and what is the significance of the name of the *sefer* and the number of responsa contained therein?

17. If one used a *"kli cheres"* – "an earthenware vessel," to cook the *"korban chatat"* – "the sin offering," the *Torah* instructs us to break the earthenware vessel after it had been used. Why?

18. What miracle is connected to the breaking of earthenware vessels in the *Beit Hamikdash*?

19. Name the 18 miracles which occurred regularly in connection with the *Beit Hamikdash*?

20. At the end of every *parshah* in most *chumashim*, there is a *"siman"* mnemonic which connects the number of *pesukim* in the *parshah* to a highlight or concept presented in that *parshah*. Which *parshah* is described as having the same number of *pesukim* as the title of that *parshah*? And why is this problematic?

PARSHAT TZAV ANSWERS

1. The *Baal Haturim* (*Vayikra* 7:1) explains that *"asham"* appears five times in the seventh *perek* of *Vayikra* (the *parshah* of *"asham"*) as there are five different types of *"asham"* sacrifices that were brought as atonement for sins: *asham gezeilot, asham meilot, asham shifcha charufa, asham nazir* and *asham metzora*. The word *"asham"* appears in *pesukim* 1, 2, 5, 7 and 37.

2. The *Baal Haturim* says that we learn the concept of studying *"b'chavruta"* – "learning in pairs," from the proximity of the *pesukim* *"tihiyeh ish k'achiv"* – "every man like his brother" (*Vayikra* 7:10) and *"vezot Torat"* – "and this is the teaching" (*Vayikra* 7:11).

3. Nothing separated the *kohen's* skin from his garments. The *gemara* (*Zevachim* 19a) deduces from the words *"al besoro"* – "on his skin," that the *kohen's* priestly garments should be directly on his skin (*Vayikra Rashi* 6:3).

4. The *"avnet"* – "belt" was exactly 32 *"amot"* long and 23 *"etzba'ot"* – "fingers" wide for every *kohen*. *"Avnet"* is almost always found in the singular (*Vayikra* 8:13). The one exception is in *Parshat Tetzave* (*Shemot* 28:40). *"Migbaot"* – "turbans," on the other hand, is always in the plural, to teach us that these were made to fit each person's head (*Meshech Chochma Tzav* 51).

5. The *gemara* (*Chullin* 83a) notes that in matters that are related to the *mitzvah* of *"kodashim"* – "holy things," the night follows the preceding day. This is derived from the *pasuk* "it shall be eaten on the day that it is sacrificed; nothing should be left over for the next morning" (*Vayikra* 7:15). The *Torah Temimah* (*Vayikra* 7, *Torah Temimah* 48) points out that the only other *mitzvah* where night follows day is *"Birkat HaTorah"* – "the blessings that one is required to make before studying *Torah*." Most *mitzvot* are related to the *pasuk* in the story of creation where it says, "and it was evening, and it was day" (*Bereishit* 1:5), which indicates that day follows night. The study of *Torah* is related to the *pasuk*, *"v'hagita bo yomam valailah"* – "and you should delve in it day and night" (*Yehoshua* 1:8), indicating that night belongs to the preceding day. One proof for this exception would be that if one recited the blessings for the study of *Torah* in the morning and did not study all day but only began studying after nightfall, he would not have to repeat the *Birkat HaTorah* (*Shulchan Aruch Orach Chaim* 47:12).

6. *Rashi* (*Vayikra* 8:34) quotes a *gemara* (*Yoma* 3b) which indicates that there are three times when a *kohen* or *kohen gadol* is placed in seven day isolation. The first was the seven days of inauguration of *Aharon Hakohen* and his sons; the second was for the *kohen gadol* the week before *Yom Kippur*, and the third was for a *kohen* who was preparing the *"para adumah"* – "red heifer."

7. The four instances where a *korban todah* is required are:

1. Deliverance from captivity.
2. Recovery from painful illness.
3. Successful travel over the ocean.
4. Successful travel across a desert.

These four examples are highlighted in *Tehillim perek* 107, which begins with the words "*hodu l'Hashem*" – "give thanks to *Hashem*." In every *Shemoneh Esrei*, we say the words "*v'chol hachaim yoducha selah*" – "and all living beings give thanks to you." The word "*chayim*" is spelled *chet, yud, yud,* and *mem*. These four letters stand for "*chavush*" – "captive," "*yisurim*" – "affliction or illness," "*yam*" – "ocean or sea," and "*midbar*" – "desert" (*Shulchan Aruch Orach Chaim* 219:1). There is much discussion and difference of opinion whether crossing the ocean or desert in a plane requires this level of expression of thanks.

8. There are three *parshiyot* that consist of only two letters:
   1. *Noach*
   2. *Bo*
   3. *Tzav*

9. The *gemara* (*Bechorot* 43b) speaks about two categories of *kohanim* who are excluded from performing the service in the *Beit Hamikdash*; namely, someone who is a "*baal mum*" – "individual with a physical deformity," and someone who is "*aino shaveh bzaro shel Aharon*" – "dissimilar to the rest of the offspring of *Aharon*." The *Rambam* (*Hilchot Bi'at Mikdash* 8:11) classifies a left handed person as one who is "dissimilar to the rest of the offspring of *Aharon*" and as such he is excluded from performing the "*avodah*" – "service" in the *Beit Hamikdash*. The difference between a "*baal mum*" and one who is "dissimilar" is that if both went ahead anyway and performed the *avodah*, only the *avodah* of the one who is dissimilar would be accepted. The *Rambam* adds that an ambidextrous *kohen* may perform the *avodah*; only a lefty is excluded.

10. The "*olah*" – "burnt offering" was brought by one who is guilty of sinful thoughts but which did not result in any action. The "*chatat*" – "sin offering" was a sacrifice brought to atone for someone who actually sinned but accidentally. By bringing both sacrifices in the same place, no one would know the difference between the person who sinned in thought and the one who actually sinned in deed, thereby circumventing embarrassment to the one who is offering the *chatat*. The last thing a person needs at this difficult time is to have others witness him bringing a sacrifice and beginning to spread gossip about him (*Kli Yakar Vayikra* 6:18).

11. The *Shulchan Aruch* (*Orach Chaim* 50:1) states that every day, one should recite parts of *Torah, Mishnah* and *Gemara*. By reciting the section of the *Torah* dealing with the "*tamid*" – "daily" sacrifice, reading the *Mishnah* of

Eizehu Mekoman, and reading the *baraita/gemara* of *Rabbi Yishmael,* we are fulfilling this three part requirement. The *Mishnah Berurah* (*Orach Chaim* 50:2) adds that since *tefillah* has taken the place of sacrifice, we read the *Mishnah* detailing the sacrificial requirements of *Eizehu Mekoman.* Additionally, the *Mishnah Berurah* points out that we do not find any differences or *machlokes* in the entire chapter, which would indicate that this chapter is in its original form, as orally transmitted to *Moshe,* and passed on to the Jewish people over the generations.

12. The brothers of *Yosef* were instructed to go to *Mitzrayim* to purchase food during the famine. When they brought the food to their father *Yaakov,* one of them opened his bag and found his money inside the bag. The *pasuk* tells us that the brothers trembled and *"vayetzay libam"* – "their hearts came out!" (*Bereishit* 42:28).

13. *Rashi* quotes *Rabbi Shimon* (*Rashi Vayikra* 6:2) who says that there needed to be a more emphatic command because the offering of a *korban olah* involved monetary loss to the *kohanim.* The *kohanim* normally received a share of every sacrifice. However, the *"olah"* – "burnt offering" was totally consumed on the *mizbeach.* This might have been perceived by the *kohanim* as a waste of their time and effort. Therefore the *Torah* instructs them that despite the apparent monetary loss to them, they still needed to meticulously follow the instructions.

14. On the day of their inauguration, *Aharon* and his sons are instructed to bring a meal offering. The *Torah* tells us that this offering would be made on a pan with oil, scalded and repeatedly baked. *Rashi* comments, quoting the *gemara* (*Menachot* 50b) that the offering was first scalded in boiling water, then baked in an oven and finally fried in a pan. Anyone who has made bagels knows that the dough is first boiled and then baked. If we took that bagel and then fried it in oil, we would have a French Toast Bagel.

15. As previously stated, the *"Korban Todah"* – "Thanksgiving offering" was brought for any of the following reasons: deliverance from captivity, recovery from painful illness, successful travel over the ocean, and successful travel across a desert. The *Korban Todah* consisted of 40 loaves of bread; ten loaves of each of these four types of bread: unleavened cakes, unleavened wafers, unleavened cakes of flour saturated with oil and leavened bread (*Rashi Vayikra* 7:12). Hence four varieties for four reasons.

16. The first *mitzvah* in *Tzav* is *Terumat Hadeshen,* the removal of the previous day's *"deshen"* – "ashes" from the *mizbeach.* Rabbi Israel Isserlin ben Petachia (1390–1460) was best known for his *sefer Terumat HaDeshen,* which was used by *Rabbi Moshe Isserles* (the *Ramah*) as one basis for his comments on the *Shulchan Aruch* which specifies the differences between *Sephardi*

and *Ashkenazi* practice. The *sefer* was a collection of 354 responsa by *Rabbi Isserlein*; 354 being the *gematriya* of "*deshen.*"

17. There is a prescribed time for eating any "*korban*" – "sacrifice." After that time, it becomes known as "*notar*" – "left over" and may not be eaten. Because earthenware is a porous material which does not release what it has once absorbed, the remains of the meat cooked in it would be considered "*notar*" on the day following the offering of that sacrifice. Therefore they must be broken after each use.

18. *Rabbeinu Bachya ben Asher ibn Halawa* (Spain 1255–1340) in his *Torah* commentary (*Vayikra* 6:21) quotes a *gemara* (*Yoma* 21) that states that the shards of the broken earthenware vessels that had absorbed food and had become "*notar,*" were miraculously absorbed by the floor of the courtyard of the *Mishkan* and *Beit Hamikdash*. Had this miracle not occurred, the floor would have become covered with these shards and it would have been hazardous to walk there.

19. Here is a list of all the eighteen miracles as enumerated in *Rabbeinu Bachya* in his commentary (*Vayikra* 6:21); the first ten are also listed in the fifth chapter of *Pirkei Avot*:

1. No pregnant woman ever lost her fetus prematurely on account of the smell of burning sacrificial meat.
2. This sacrificial meat never exuded an unpleasant odour.
3. The *kohen gadol* was never incapacitated on *Yom Kippur* due to involuntary emissions.
4. No flies were found in the area designated for slaughtering and dressing the animals.
5. No blemish which would disqualify the offering of the "*omer*" or "*shtey halechem*" loaves of bread ever occurred; the same applied to the "*lechem hapanim*" – "show-breads" offering presented in the *Beit Hamikdash* every *Shabbat*. These three offerings were considered as one miracle in the count of the miracles which occurred.
6. The rains never extinguished the flames on the woodpile of the *mizbeach* (which had no roof cover).
7. Even the strongest wind would never deflect the column of smoke rising from the offerings being burned.
8. Although people stood very close together so that they had to touch one another (during the festivals), when the ritual called for them to prostrate themselves on the ground, they miraculously found adequate room for this.
9. No scorpion or snake ever bit anybody within *Yerushalayim*.
10. No one was ever heard to complain that there were no lodgings in *Yerushalayim* so that he had to spend the night outside the city.

11. The shards of earthenware vessels which served as pots to boil the remains of the *korban chatat* and which had to be burned or destroyed as the tiny fraction absorbed by the walls became *"notar"* – "left over," and as such forbidden, were absorbed by the floor of the courtyard of the *Beit Hamikdash*.

12. The *mizbeach* for the burnt-offering (the one in the courtyard) which had a woodpile on it which was kept aflame and which stood on a thin copper overlay, never melted the copper nor damaged the wooden beams underneath it (*Midrash Tanchuma Terumah* 11).

13. All seven *menorah* lights maintained the same level of oil, all burning at the same rate; none extinguishing before dawn (*Gemara Shabbat* 22); whether it was a long winter night or a short summer night, there was always just enough oil. The centre light, the first to be lit in the evenings and the last to be cleaned in the morning, had the same level of oil as the others. It would be the first one to be lit in the evenings and the last one to be cleaned in the morning.

14. A tongue of red coloured wool would be hung at the entrance of the Sanctuary at the beginning of *Yom Kippur*; this would turn white by evening (*Gemara Yoma* 67).

15. The scapegoat which was thrown off a cliff would break up in innumerable pieces before it ever hit the bottom of the valley into which it was thrown. Not a single of its limbs would remain intact by that time.

16. *Midrash Tanchuma* (*Tetzaveh* 3) concerning the *menorah* procedure, says: when the lights of the *Menorah* in the Sanctuary were kindled in the evening, every courtyard in *Yerushalayim* made use of its illumination provided by it. This is mystically hinted by "they shall take for you pure olive oil, pressed to provide illumination (*Shemot* 27:20)."

17. As soon as *Shlomo Hamelech* had built the *Beit Hamikdash*, he planted in it all kinds of confections made of gold which would produce fruit at the appropriate seasons. This is what we have been told in *Gemara Yoma* 21.

18. Another miracle related there is that the show-breads which were placed on the *Shulchan* in the Temple every *Shabbat* retained their warmth at the same level as when they had come from the oven for the entire week. This is based on *Shmuel I:21:7*, "to place bread which was still hot on the day it was shared out" (8 days after it had been baked).

20. At the end of *Parshat Tzav*, the commentaries write that there are 96 *pesukim* in *Tzav* and they use as the *siman* or mnemonic, the title of the *parshah*, "tzav," which is 96 numerically. The only difficulty with this riddle is that if you tally up the actual number of *pesukim* in *Tzav*, you will find that they total 97, not 96. See General Torah, beginning at question 143 for more on *parshah* mnemonics.

PARSHAT SHEMINI QUESTIONS

1. Name the non-Jewish king whose wife's name was the same as a non-*kosher* animal mentioned in *Parshat Shemini*?

2. If science could genetically produce a horse that chews its cud and has split hooves, would this horse meat be *kosher*?

3. From where in *Parshat Shemini* do we have a hint that the *kohen* blesses the people with his two hands held together as one?

4. From where do we know that the *kohen* must be standing when he blesses the people?

5. Name a "*tzadik*" – "righteous person" and a "*rasha*" – "wicked person," whose mothers had the same name and explain the connection to *Parshat Shemini*. (Note: The mothers of the *tzadik* and *rasha* are different people. Hence, *Yaakov* and *Eisav* would not be a valid answer!)

6. This *parshah* divides various animals, fish and fowl into *kosher* and *non-kosher* categories. We know that both animals and fowl require "*shechita*" – "ritual slaughtering." From which *pasuk* do we learn that fish do not require *shechita*? (Hint: It is not in this week's *Parshat Shemini*).

7. In what instance can a person eat an animal that does not undergo normal *shechita*?

8. Who were the first individuals to request a ruling from *Moshe Rabbeinu* to institute a special day to bring the *korban Pesach* (*Pesach Sheini*), if one was unable to bring it in its proper time??

9. The unintentional action of a non-*Jew* makes it forbidden to the *Jew*; however, the intentional action of the non-*Jew* to make it forbidden to the *Jew*, will now make it permissible to the *Jew*; however, the knowledge by the non-*Jew* that his intentional action makes it permissible, will once again make it forbidden to the *Jew*. Explain?

10. There are three consecutive *pesukim* in *Parshat Shemini* that discuss the same *halacha*; one is in the past, one is in the present, one is in the future. What are they?

11. Which *pasuk* in *Parshat Shemini* alludes to *Yosef*'s brothers, to *Aharon Hakohen* and to *Yitzchak Avinu*?

12. What is the danger of eating fish and meat together according to the *Shulchan Aruch*?

13. Which creature's meat is forbidden but its milk is permissible?

14. Name four sets of brothers who appear in *Parshat Shemini*?

15. The *Torah* tells us (*Vayikra* 10:4) that *Uziel* was an uncle of *Aharon*. But certainly we knew the relationship from an earlier *pasuk* (*Shemot* 6:18). Why does the *Torah* have to specify the relationship?

16. What *Torah* prohibitions relate to the drinking of *"yayin v'shechar"* – "intoxicating wine"?

17. Where does the *Torah* clearly describe an audio visual experience in *Parshat Shemini*?

18. From where do we derive the custom that an *"aveil"* – "mourner" may not cut his hair for thirty days?

19. The two physical signs that render an animal *kosher* are split hooves and chewing the cud (*Vayikra* 11:3). How many animals have split hooves but do not chew their cud?

20. In which book or books of the *Torah* does the camel not appear?

PARSHAT SHEMINI ANSWERS

1. The king's name was Ptolemy or *Talmei* in Hebrew. The *gemara* (*Megilla* 9a) relates that King Ptolemy of *Mitzrayim*, assembled seventy-two elders from the Sages of Israel, and put them into seventy-two separate rooms, and did not reveal to them for what purpose he assembled them, so that they would not coordinate their responses. He said to each of them: "Write a translation of the *Torah* of *Moshe* your teacher." *Hashem* placed wisdom in the heart of each and every one, and they all agreed to one common understanding. Not only did they all translate the text correctly, they all introduced the same changes into the translated text. The *gemara* enumerates some of the changes that they made, so that the king and his followers would not be able to twist the correct meaning. In the list of unclean animals, they translated the Hebrew word *"arnevet"* (*Vayikra* 11:6), not by its correct translation *"hare,"* but rather as *"tze'irat haraglayim"* – "the short-legged animal." This was done especially for the benefit of the king, since the name of Ptolemy's wife was *Arnevet* and rather than be blamed for mocking his wife, they translated the Hebrew word for hare into one of the hare's physical features.

2. The *Mishnah* (*Bechorot* 5b) rules on this exact case. The *Mishnah* quotes two cases. First, a *non-kosher* animal that gives birth to an apparently *kosher* animal, is ruled not *kosher*; and second, a *kosher* animal that gives birth to an apparently *non-kosher* animal, is ruled *kosher*. These rulings are based on the premise that the offspring is deemed to be the same as the parent. Therefore a horse that gives birth to offspring that apparently has been genetically modified to appear to be *kosher*, is still in fact not *kosher*.

3. In *Vayikra* 9:22, the *pasuk* says "and *Aharon* raised his hands" and the word "his hands" is spelled *"yud, daled, vav,"* which is the way you would normally spell the singular *"yado"* – "his hand." When a *Kohen* blesses the Jewish people and recites the *"birkat kohanim"* – "the priestly blessing," he is required to raise both hands and put them together. Thus, the two hands look like one, hence the spelling of *"yadav"* without the second *yud* as *"yud, daled, vav."* The *Kohen* is also required to place the right hand a bit higher than the left (*Shulchan Aruch Orach Chaim* 128:12.)

4. *Torah Temimah* (*Vayikra* 9:22) cites the *Torat Kohanim* who connects the reference to blessing the people in this *pasuk* with another *pasuk* (*Devarim* 10:8) which instructs the tribe of *Levi* *"laamod lifnei Hashem lesharto ulevarech bishmo"* – "to stand before *Hashem* while serving Him, and to bless the people in His Name." Just as they must stand while blessing there, so too, when the *kohanim* bless the people, they must do so standing.

5. The mother of *Avraham* was *Amatlai bat Karnevo* and the mother of *Haman* was *Amatlai bat Urvasi* (*Gemara Bava Batra* 91a). The *gemara* cites a "*siman*" – "sign or hint" as to why they had the same name and yet were mothers of individuals at opposite extremes. The "*siman*" is "*tamei, tamei, tahor, tahor.*" The *Rashbam* explains the "*siman*" as follows: the mother of *Avraham* was "*bat karnevo*" and there is a "*tahor*" – "*kosher*" animal called a "*karim*" which is close to "*karnevo.*" The mother of *Haman* was "*bat Urvasi*" and there is a "*tamei*" – "non-*kosher*" bird called the "*oreiv*" – "raven" which is close to "*Urvasi.*" The connection to *Parshat Shemini* is that the source for the "*oreiv*" being non-*kosher* is in *Parshat Shemini*.

6. When the *Bnai Yisrael* complained to *Moshe* that they had no meat to eat, and *Hashem* performed the miracle of the quail, the *pasuk* reads (*Bamidbar* 11:22) "can sheep and cattle be slaughtered for them and suffice for them or if all the fish of the sea will be gathered for them?" The *gemara* (*Chullin* 27b) deduces from the fact that the word "*yishochet*" – "slaughtered" is used only by sheep and cattle and not by fish, that fish do not require "*shechita*" – "ritual slaughtering."

7. A "*ben pekua*" – "unborn calf found in the womb of a cow that has just been slaughtered in a *kosher* manner" can be eaten without the traditional slaughter or *shechita* (*Gemara Chullin* 69a). In an article published by *Zomet* in 2015, we are told that the meat of a *Ben Pekua* can be eaten in any manner, (*Shulchan Aruch Yoreh Deah* 13), even many years later, and there is no need to check if it has one of the faults that would render a normal animal unkosher. Its meat is considered to be *pareve*. And surprisingly, the offspring of a male and female "*ben pekua*" (i.e. both parents are of this type) will never require *kosher* slaughtering; this includes subsequent generations. However, if only one parent is a "*ben pekua*," the offspring cannot be made *kosher*, even with ritual slaughtering. There appears to be a *machloket* as to whether the milk of a "*ben pekua*" is dairy or *pareve*.

8. When *Nadav* and *Avihu* died, *Misha'el* and *Eltzafan* were asked to attend to the dead bodies. They therefore became "*tamei*" – "ritually impure." According to the opinion that "*yom hashemini*" was the eighth day of *Nisan*, they would have remained impure until the first day of *Pesach* and they therefore were the first individuals who approached *Moshe* to establish *Pesach Sheini* as a second opportunity to bring the *Korban Pesach* (*Sukkah* 25b).

9. This is a very interesting *halacha*. The concept is that of "*stam yeinam*" – "a non-Jew touching the wine of a Jew." The *Shulchan Aruch* (*Yoreh Deah* 124:27) explains that if the *non-Jew* knows that his touching the wine will make it forbidden, and he intentionally touches it so as to make it forbidden, then the wine is permissible and the *Jew* should even drink it in front of the *non-*

Jew, so as to ensure that the *non-Jew* will no longer feel that he has anything to gain by touching the *Jew*'s wine. The *Shulchan Aruch* explains, however, that if the *non-Jew* is aware that his intentional touching of the wine will not make it forbidden to the *Jew*, and he declares that knowledge to the *Jew* by saying, for example, "go ask your *Rabbi* and you will see that it is still permissible," then, in that case, the wine once again becomes forbidden.

10. The three *pesukim* in *Vayikra* 11:4–6 discuss the *halacha* that an animal cannot just chew its cud; it must also have split hooves, in order to be considered *kosher*. In the first *pasuk*, referring to the camel, it phrases it in the present, "*mafris parsah*" – "it does not split its hooves"; in the second *pasuk*, concerning the hydrax, it phrases it in the future, ""*yafris parsah*" – "it will not split its hooves"; and in the third *pasuk*, it phrases it in the past, "*uparsah lo hifrisa*" – "it did not split its hooves." *Mafris, yafris, hifrisa* – present, future, past. *Rabbi Yisrael Salanter* explains that we can learn an important lesson from this law pertaining to the *kashrut* of animals, when interacting with our fellow human beings. Before declaring a person to be "*tamei*" – or not *kosher*, we must carefully analyze his present, past, and future. When we can be convinced that the past and present are not good and there is no chance for improvement in the future, only then may we declare a person unfit. Until that time, we must make every effort to involve and include that individual in our communal activities and affairs.

11. *Vayikra* 9:3 says that *Bnai Yisrael* should offer a "*se'ir izim*" – "goat" as a sin offering and an "*egel*" – "calf" and a "*keves*" – "sheep" as a burnt offering. *Targum Yonatan* explains that the goat alludes to the goat that the brothers killed into which they dipped *Yosef*'s coat; the *egel* alludes to the golden calf that *Aharon* built and which *Bnai Yisrael* worshipped, and the *keves* alludes to the ram from *Akeidat Yitzchak* that should atone for the sin of the *egel*.

12. The *Shulchan Aruch* (*Yoreh Deah* 116:2) says that cooking meat and fish together causes bad breath and is forbidden because it is connected to *tzaraat*, commonly translated as leprosy (*Rashi Gemara Pesachim* 76b).

13. A human being's meat is forbidden, but its milk is permissible.

14. Four sets of brothers mentioned in *Parshat Shemini* are *Moshe* and *Aharon* (*Vayikra* 9:1); *Nadav* and *Avihu* (*Vayikra* 10:1); *Mishael* and *Eltzafon* (*Vayikra* 10:4); and *Elazar* and *Itamar* (*Vayikra* 10:6).

15. There are many reasons given by the commentaries. *Rabbeinu Bachye* says: *Rashi* explains that *Uziel* was the brother of *Amram*, as it is written (*Shemot* 6,18): "and the sons of *Kehat* were *Amram, Yitzhar, Chevron*, and *Uziel*." Seeing that we were aware of this genealogy, we also knew that *Uziel* was an uncle of *Aharon*. The reason the *Torah* added these words was to teach us that the Uncle *Uziel* and Nephew *Aharon* were connected not only through their familial genes but also in their acquired characteristics. Just as *Aharon*

was known as a lover of peace and harmony, so his uncle before him had been known for these qualities.

16. There are two areas where the *Torah* prohibits the drinking of "*yayin v'shechar*" – "intoxicating wine." First in *Parshat Shemini* (*Vayikra* 10:9) where *kohanim* are prohibited from drinking intoxicating wine when entering the *Mishkan*; and secondly, in the description of the lifestyle restrictions of the *Nazir* where he is prohibited from drinking intoxicating wine (*Bamidbar* 6:3).

17. The *pasuk* says (*Vayikra* 10:20): *Vayishma Moshe, vayitav b'einav*" – And *Moshe* heard and it was good in his eyes (i,e,; he approved), hence an audio visual experience.

18. In *Parshat Shemini, Moshe* instructs *Aharon* and his sons, *Elazar* and *Itamar,* to not let their hair grow long while mourning the death of *Nadav* and *Avihu,* due to the timing that coincided with the joyous atmosphere of the dedication of the *mishkan.* The *gemara* (*Moed Katan* 14b) compares the wording used by the *Torah* "*rasheichem al tifra'u*" – "do not let your hair grow long" with the wording used in the instructions to the *nazir,* allowing him to cut his hair after a thirty day period of "*perah*" – "wild hair growth." Growth of the hair of less than thirty days duration, does not come under the term "*perah,*" and from here we derive the custom that an "*avel*" does not cut his hair for 30 days after the death of a close relative (*Sifrei Bamidbar* 25; *Sanhedrin* 22b).

19. The *gemara* (*Chullin* 59a) quotes the school of *Rabbi Yishmael* who said that the only animal that possesses split hooves but does not chew its cud is the pig.

20. The camel appears numerous times in the book of *Bereishit*; only once in each of *Shemot, Vayikra,* and *Devarim.* It does not appear in *Bamidbar.* In *Bereishit,* the camel is mentioned as follows:

    1. It appears as part of the gifts that *Paroh* gave *Avram* when *Paroh* took *Sarah* into his palace (*Bereishit* 12:16).
    2. In the story of *Eliezer* travelling to the home of *Betuel* and *Lavan* in trying to find a wife for *Yitzchak,* the camel is mentioned numerous times (*Bereishit* 24).
    3. In the story of *Yaakov* working for *Lavan,* we are told that *Yaakov* prospered immensely, and had many sheep, maidservants and menservants, camels and donkeys (*Bereishit* 30:43).
    4. When fleeing *Lavan, Yaakov* travels with his wives and children by camel (*Bereishit* 31:17) and *Rachel* hides *Lavan's* idols in the saddle of her camel (*Bereishit* 31:34).

5. When preparing for his meeting with his brother *Eisav, Yaakov* stra-tegically divides his camp which includes his family and livestock (including his camels) (*Bereishit* 32:7).

6. When bringing gifts for his reunion with his brother *Eisav, Yaakov* includes camels (*Bereishit* 32:16).

7. *Yosef*'s brothers sell him to a band of *Yishmaeilim*, who are travelling by camel (*Bereishit* 37:25). In *Shemot*, camels are mentioned once, in the plague of "*dever*" – "pestilence"; when *Hashem* warns *Paroh* that all of his livestock, including camels, will be smitten (*Shemot* 9:3). In *Vayikra*, camels are also only mentioned once, in *Parshat Shemini*, when *Hashem* enumerates *non-kosher* animals (*Vayikra* 11:4). And in *Devarim*, camels are mentioned only once, when *Hashem* repeats the list of *non-kosher* animals (*Devarim* 14:7).

PARSHAT TAZRIA-METZORA QUESTIONS

1. From where in *Parshat Tazria* is there a hint that one may get a haircut on *Lag BaOmer,* and on the "*Shloshet Yemei Hagbala*" – "the three days before *Shavuot*"?

2. Where is there a hint in *Parshat Metzora* to *Sefira, Lag BaOmer* and *Pesach Sheni*?

3. How many cases of "*tzara'at*" – "leprosy" are there in *Tanach*?

4. Which three groups or individuals were required to shave all hair off their bodies in fulfillment of a *mitzvah*?

5. The *pasuk* says: "*Bechol kodesh lo tigah*" – "she may not touch anything sacred" (*Vayikra* 12:4). What does touch mean here?

6. What disqualifies a *kohen* from ruling in the matters of leprosy?

7. Who cannot serve as a *Mohel* on *Shabbat*?

8. What is the connection between *Yehoshua Bin Nun* and the laws of the *metzora*?

9. Name three words in the *Torah* that each have four "*patach*" vowel sounds in a row?

10. Name one word in the *Torah* that has four "*kamatz*" vowel sounds in a row?

11. Name two words in the *Torah* that each have four "*segol*" vowel sounds in a row?

12. Why is a leper placed in isolation?

13. Why are birds such an integral part of the purification process of the *metzora*?

14. Where is there a hint in the rite of circumcision, to the 180 years *Yitzchak* lived?

15. In all instances, where one has an obligation to offer doves and pigeons, the *Torah* almost always mentions pigeons before doves. Why in the case of the mother's offering following purification after birth, is the dove mentioned prior to the pigeon?

16. It can be an affliction or it could be a delight…it all depends on where you place your eye. Explain.

17. What is a "*kvater*"?

18. There are thirteen three-word *pesukim* in the *Torah*. Two of these *pesukim* are back to back. Where are they?

19. Food items can become "*tameh*" – "impure" when they come in contact with seven types of liquids. What are the seven types?

20. How could a cured *metzora* know that he would contract *tzaraat* again?

PARSHAT TAZRIA-METZORA ANSWERS

1. Other than during a leap year, *Parshat Tazria* is almost always read during the *Sefira* period. The *Pardes Yosef* says that the *pasuk* reads "*v'hitgalach*" – "and he shall shave" (*Vayikro* 13:33). The word is written in the *Torah* with a large *gimel* indicating the three days before *Shavuot*. Additionally, it is the 33rd *pasuk* in *perek* 13 of *Vayikra*, which hints to *Lag BaOmer*, the 33rd day of the Counting of the *Omer*. The word "*v'hitgalach*" is equal in gematriya to "*lag yamim BaOmer*" (using the *kollel* rule of *gematriya*) which equals 452. In Hebrew 452 is *taf-nun-bet* which are the first letters of the phrase "*tisaper b'erev nun*" or "take a haircut on the eve of the 50th day," which is the eve of *Shavuot*.

2. The *Radziner Rebbe* points out that the three *pesukim* beginning with the words "*v'chi yit'har hazav mizovo*" (*Vayikra* 15:13–15) contain 49 words. The phrase "*v'safar lo*" – "and he should count," connects the 49 words to the concept of the counting of the 49 days of the *Omer*. *Bnai Yisrael* had to undergo 49 days of purification to reach the level of purity required for the acceptance of the *Torah* and this parallels the theme of purity in these three *pesukim*. The 33rd word is "*mo'ed*" which alludes to the festive theme of *Lag BaOmer*, the 33rd day of the *Omer*. The *Pardes Yosef* adds that the 29th word is *Hashem* and the 29th day of the *Omer* is *Pesach Sheini*. The commandment of *Pesach Sheini* evolved from the request of those who were travelling or impure at the time of *Pesach*. The response to the request was "*imdu v'eshmh'ah ma yetzaveh Hashem*" – "stand and hear what *Hashem* commands you" (*Bamidbar* 9:8).

3. The cases of *tzaraat* in *Tanach* include: *Bitya Bat Paroh* (*Shemot Rabbah* 1:23); *Moshe* (*Shemot* 4:1–7); *Miriam* (*Bamidbar* 12:1–15); *Gechazi & Naaman* (*Melachim II*:5); the four kings and *Aram* (*Melachim II*:7); *Azaryahu* (*Melachim II*:15) and *Uziyahu* (*Divrei Hayamim II*:26). Some say that *Azaryahu* and *Uziyahu* were one and the same.

4. The *Mishnah* (*Negaim* 14:4) lists three categories of people for whom it was a *mitzvah* to shave all their hair from their bodies. They are the *nazir*, the leper and the *levi* (only during the period when chosen for service in the desert). The *Baal Haturim* says that the large *gimel* in the word "*v'hitgalach*" is a hint to the three categories.

5. *Rashi* (*Vayikra* 12:4) quotes a *baraita* (*Yevamot* 75a) and comments that touch refers to eating, and that this prohibition addresses anyone who would eat holy things while "*tamei*" – "unclean."

6. *Rashi* (*Vayikra* 13:12) quotes a *Sifra* (*Tazria Parshat Nega'im, perek* 4) that says that the only thing that disqualifies a *kohen in* the area of leprosy is poor vision.

7. If it is his first time performing a *"milah"* – "circumcision," he may not do it on a *Shabbat* (*Shulchan Aruch Yoreh Deah* 266:7) for fear that he might err because of his inexperience, and thereby would come to be *"mechalel Shabbat"* – "transgress the *Shabbat* laws."

8. Someone who was afflicted with *"tzaraat,"* commonly translated as leprosy, was required to go "outside the camp" for a period of seven days. When *Bnai Yisrael* crossed over the Jordan to Israel, a *metzora* in a city surrounded by a wall from the time of *Yehoshua Bin Nun,* would be similarly sent from the city for seven days, as a walled city had the same status as "the camp" in the desert (*Mishnah Keilim* 1:7; *see Bartenura*).

9. Two of the three instances of four consecutive *patachs* in a word, are found in *Parshat Tazriya* and *Parshat Metzora*; *"hagabachat"* (*Vayikra* 13:42) and *"v'lasapachat"* (*Vayikra* 14:56). The remaining word appears twice, in each of the *"tochacha"* readings. The word is *"hakadachat"* (*Vayikra* 26:16; *Devarim* 28:22).

10. The only four consecutive *"kametz"* vowel sounds appearing in one word are found in the word *"harachama"* (*Devarim* 14:17).

11. The two four consecutive *"segol"* vowel sounds appearing in one word are found in the words *"hane'echelet"* (*Vayikra* 11:47) and *"necherefet"* (*Vayikra* 19:20).

12. *Rashi* (*Vayikra* 13:46) quotes the *gemara* in *Erechin* 16b and explains that since *tzaraat* is an affliction brought about by the sin of *lashon hara* and since the afflicted one attempted, through his gossip, to separate husband and wife, or man and his fellow man, he is separated from the Community of *Israel*.

13. The *gemara* (*Erechin* 16b) explains that since *tzaraat* is an affliction brought on by the sin of chattering gossip and slander, the purification process involves chattering and chirping birds.

14. The *Chida* (*Rabbi Chayim Yosef David Azulai, Israel-Italy,* 1724–1806) points out that there are a total of seven complete days and one night from birth to circumcision (we try to circumcise at the earliest moment on the 8th day after the birth of a male child, in line with the concept of *"zerizim makdimin l'mitzvot"*). Therefore, the total number of hours is $(7 \times 24) + (1 \times 12) = 180$, corresponding to the 180 years of *Yitzchak Avinu,* the first Jew to be circumcised on the 8th day after birth. The *Chida* maintains that the concern for *zerizut,* supersedes the value of a large crowd, and he therefore rules that a *brit milah* should not be delayed for guests.

15. The *Baal Haturim* (*Vayikra* 12:6) points out that in all the other cases, pigeons and doves are brought in pairs. In this case, only one pigeon or dove is brought. He explains that the pigeon has a special affinity for its mate, and when separated, literally mourns and is depressed by the sep-

aration, and will not mate with any other pigeon. Hence, the *Torah* places the pigeon second to teach us that it should only be offered as a last resort (i.e., when a dove cannot be found), out of concern and compassion for the pigeon's feelings.

16. According to the *gemara* (*Erechin* 15b), "*lashon hara*" – "gossip" causes "*nega tzara'at*" – "plague of leprosy." The word "*nega*" has the same three letters as "*oneg*." "*Nega*" is spelled "*nun-gimel-ayin*" and "*oneg*" is spelled "*ayin-nun-gimel*." If the "*ayin*" (i.e., "eye") moves from the end of the word to the beginning of the word, the meaning changes from plague to delight. That could be the intent of the *pasuk* "*lo hafach hanegah et eino*" – "the affliction did not change its appearance" (*Vayikra* 13:55). The *Chiddushei HaRim* (*Gerrer Rebbe*), explains that whether something is a "*nega*" – "plague" or is an "*oneg*" – "pleasure," all depends on where one places the "*ayin*" – "the eye"; it depends on a person's perspective. One of the earliest *Kabbalistic* texts says "there is nothing in good, higher than "*oneg*" – "delight" and there is nothing in evil, lower than "*nega*" – "plague"" (*Sefer Yetzirah* 2:4). *Kohelet* says "the wise man's eyes are in his head and the fool walks in darkness" (*Kohelet* 2:14). The eye represents your perspective on life, and where one places their eye or their perspective determines whether they are wise or not.

17. A "*kvater*" is the person honoured with carrying the baby, who is about to be circumcised, from the door of the room, to the "*mohel*." Generally, the mother gives the child to a woman, who takes the child to the entrance of the room where the circumcision is to take place. She then transfers the child to a man, who carries the baby to the "*mohel*" and "*sandek*" – "the person who holds the baby during the circumcision." We are not 100% sure where the term "*kvater*" originated but here are a few options. According to *Rabbi Chaim Lieberman* in his work "*Ohel Rachel*," the word *kvater* results from the combination of the words "*kavod*" – "honour," and "*teer*" – "door," i.e., an honour given at the door; and according to Philologos, it comes from the medieval German word Gottvater or "godfather." This honour is generally given to a couple or couples who have not yet been blessed with children of their own.

18. The two back-to-back three word *pesukim* are found in the listing of "*tzaraat*" categories (*Vayikra* 14:55, 56).

19. Wine, honey, oil, milk, dew, blood and water are the seven liquids which render foodstuffs susceptible to "*tumah*" – "impurity" (*Rambam Hilchot Tumat Ochlin* 1:2).

20. A cured *metzora* would know that he would contact *tzaraat* again, if the bird that was sent away, returned to the same house that day (*Targum Yonatan Vayikra* 14:7).

PARSHAT ACHAREI MOT-KEDOSHIM QUESTIONS

1. How many times does the "*kohen gadol*" – "the high priest" wash his hands and feet during the *Yom Kippur* service?

2. How many times did the *kohen gadol* immerse himself in the *mikvah* during *Yom Kippur*?

3. How many changes of clothing did the *kohen gadol* wear on *Yom Kippur*?

4. Is one permitted to marry his sister-in-law?

5. After the *Yom Kippur* service each year, what is done with the clothing of the *kohen gadol*?

6. How is it possible to do something to your fellow man after he has died, with the punishment for the perpetrator being death?

7. Which *mitzvah*, for which there is no formal *beracha*, can begin only from a sitting position?

8. The *Torah* says "you shall separate between clean and unclean animals and unclean and clean birds" (*Vayikra* 20:25). Why is the order of clean and unclean reversed for animals and birds?

9. Who was *Rabbi Yehoshua ben Korcha*'s father?

10. Name four times that one would have to stand when a minor, below *Bar Mitzvah*, enters the room?

11. This *parshah* is called "*Kedoshim*" – "holy," and in fact, most of the book of *Vayikra* involves itself with holiness. Where is the first mention of holiness in the *Torah*?

12. Name two words in *Tanach* for a lottery? Where are they found?

13. How many instances of lottery are mentioned in the *Torah*?

14. A child says to the teacher: "I studied my *Chumash* and I learned two laws. First, the law that one must glorify the beard on one's face, and second, that one may not cut in line in front of an elderly person." The teacher said: "Go back and study the concept of heteronyms and vowels." What is going on here?

15. Where is there a hint in *Parshat Achrei Mot* to the length of time that the first *Beit Hamikdash* existed?

16. What is the connection between the *kohen gadol* on *Yom Kippur* and *Binyamin* in the palace of *Paroh*?

17. Which of the priestly garments are explained by *Rashi* using the story of *Yosef* and *Potifar*'s wife?

18. Where does *Rashi* speak about theatres and stadiums?

19. Eight words that begin a *pasuk*, with every second word, (four of them), being the identical word. Note: the word is not "*et*" or "*v'et*."

20. Two people curse another person, the same person, at the same moment. One has transgressed and the other has not. Explain?

1. The *kohen gadol* washed his hands and feet ten times on *Yom Kippur* (*Rashi Vayikra* 16:4).

2. The *kohen gadol* immersed in a *mikvah* five times during *Yom Kippur* (*Rashi Vayikra* 16:4)

3. The *Kohen Gadol* wore five sets of garments, three golden and two white linen, during *Yom Kippur* (*Rashi Vayikra* 16:4).

4. There are three categories of sister-in-law. They are (a) his wife's sister; (b) his brother's wife and (c) his wife's brother's wife. Each has unique status in Jewish law:

   1. His wife's sister is forbidden to him while his wife is alive. If his wife dies, he may then marry her sister. If they divorce, however, and his wife is still alive, he may not marry her sister.

   2. He may not marry his brother's wife if they divorced or if his brother died with offspring. The only way in which this second category of sister-in-law would be permitted to him is the famous case of "*yibum*"; that is, his brother died and had no offspring. He is then obligated to marry his dead brother's wife and can only be released from that obligation via marriage or the "*chalitzah*" ceremony. Today, there is a *rabbinic* injunction against *Ashkenazim* following the "*yibum*" requirement; rather, "*chalitzah*" is always performed.

   3. The third sister-in-law is his wife's brother's wife and she only becomes permitted for marriage to her brother-in-law, if she becomes unattached from his brother through death or divorce.

5. At the end of *Yom Kippur* every year, the clothing of the *kohen gadol* is put into the "*geniza*" – "protected storage area for holy articles" and never used again (*Rashi Vayikra* 16:23).

6. *Vayikra* 20:9 contains the prohibition against cursing one's parents. The *pasuk*, however, seems to be repeating itself for no reason: "If anyone curses his father or his mother, he shall be put to death; he has cursed his father and his mother, his guilt is upon him." *Rashi* quotes a *gemara* (*Sanhedrin* 85b) and comments that the reason why this prohibition is repeated in the same *pasuk*, is to include the prohibition against cursing one's parents after they have already died. Such a sin is punishable by death through stoning.

7. The *mitzvah* of rising in the presence of an elderly person (*Vayikra* 19:32) must begin while you are seated.

8. The *gemara* (*Chullin* 63b) explains that the reason why the wording of "clean" and "unclean" is reversed for birds vs. animals, is because *Hashem* is teaching us an important lesson in pedagogy: to be clear and concise when teaching, just as the *Torah* is concise in its language. Since there are more

"tamei" – "unclean" animals than *"tahor"* – "clean" ones, and more clean birds than unclean ones, *Hashem* emphasized the concept of being clear and concise, by showing *Moshe* all the clean animals (thereby by elimination, indicating that all the others are unclean) and all the unclean birds (thereby by elimination, indicating that all the rest are clean).

9. I truly hope that no one guessed *"Korcha."* The *gemara* (*Bechorot* 58a) cites *Ben Azzai's* statement describing all the sages as inferior to the *"korcha"* – "bald headed one." *Rashi* explains that the "bald headed one" was *Rabbi Akiva* and that *Rabbi Yehoshua Ben Korcha* was *Rabbi Akiva's* son.

10. The four times that one would be required to stand for a minor are:
    1. At a *brit* when the eight day old baby enters the room (*Yoreh De'ah* 265:1).
    2. At a *pidyon haben* when the 30 day old baby enters the room (*Pidyon Haben K'Hilchato* 8:7 Footnote 22).
    3. If the minor is a scholar (*Yoreh De'ah* 246:1).
    4. If the minor is a king, such as *Shlomo Hamelech* who was 12 years old when he assumed the throne (*Rambam Hilchot Melachim* 2:5).

11. The first mention of holiness in the *Torah* is at the end of creation in *Bereishit* when the *Torah* tells us that *Hashem* rested on the 7th day; *"vayekadesh oto"* – "and he made the *Shabbat* day holy" (*Bereishit* 2:3). It is the only mention of holiness in the entire book of *Bereishit*.

12. The word used in the *Torah* is *"goral"* – "lottery" (*Vayikra* 16:8, *Bamidbar* 26:56; *Bamidbar* 33:54; *Bamidbar* 36:3) and it is repeated in many places in *Tanach*. In *Megillat Esther* (*Esther* 3:7), the word used is *"pur"* – "lottery."

13. There are three instances in the *Torah* where the concept of a lottery is mentioned:
    1. In the service for *Yom Kippur,* a lottery of goats is performed to decide which is the goat that is sacrificed and which is the *"Azazel goat"* (*Vayikra* 16:8).
    2. In *Bamidbar* (26:56 and 33:54), the division of *Eretz Yisrael* between the tribes is decided by lottery.
    3. In the discussion between the daughters of *Tzelaphchad* and *Moshe,* regarding their inheritance as women, they discuss the lottery that established their portion (*Bamidbar* 36:3).

14. There are two similar Hebrew words, *"zaken"* – "an elderly person" and *"zakan"* – "a beard." They are composed of the same three Hebrew letters (heteronyms) with different vowels or pronunciation. Since a *Torah* is written without vowels, one could easily mistake one word for the other. There are two *halachot* in *Parshat Kedoshim*, separated by five *pesukim*, one dealing with the beard and one dealing with the elderly. The *halachot* pertaining to the two, that caused confusion to the child in our riddle, are:

1. *"lo tashchit peat zekanecha"* – "do not destroy the corners of your beard" (*Vayikra* 19:27) which he mistakenly read as "do not cut corners in front of an elderly person."

2. *"vehadarta pnei zaken"* – "and you should respect or glorify seniors" (*Vayikra* 19:32) which he mistakenly read as "and you should glorify the beard on one's face."

15. In the beginning of *Acharei Mot*, the *Torah* says *"b'zot yavoh Aharon el hakodesh"* – "with this shall *Aharon* and only *Aharon* enter the *Kodesh*" (*Vayikra* 16:3). *Rashi* comments that the *gematriya* of *"b'zot"* is 410, which is the number of years that the first *Beit Hamikdash* stood. The *Siftei Chachamim* asks why *Rashi* only connects this concept to the first *Beit Hamikdash*? Were there no *kohanim gedolim* in the second *Beit Hamikdash*? The *Siftei Chachamim* answers: The *gematriya* of *"b'zot"* tells you for how many years there would be *kohanim* like *Aharon* (i.e., *kohanim gedolim*) who were anointed with the *"shemen hamishcha"* – "anointing oil." After the first *Beit Hamikdash*, they no longer anointed them with anointing oil like *Aharon*, because at the end of the first *Beit Hamikdash* era, the anointing oil was no longer available, having been hidden away from the time of *King Yoshia* onwards (*Rashi Vayikra* 16:32 and *Gemara Horayot* 12a).

16. The *kohen gadol* changes his clothing five times on *Yom Kippur* (*Vayikra Rashi* 16:4) and when *Binyamin* came to meet *Yosef* for the first time in *Mitzrayim*, he was given five changes of clothing (*Bereishit* 45:22).

17. *Rashi,* in translating the word *"yitznof"* – "he shall wear" (*Vayikra* 16:4) describing the wearing of the *"mitznefet"* – "turban," refers us to the *Targum Onkelos* who translates *"yitznof"* as *"yachet b'reishei,"* which means "he shall place on his head." *Rashi* comments that the word *"yachet"* is of the same root as the word *"va'achatetai"* which is how *Onkelos* translates the word *"vatanach"* used in describing the action of *Potifar*'s wife: *"vatanach bigdo"* – "and she placed his garment" (*Bereishit* 39:16).

18. *Rashi* (*Vayikra* 18:3) comments on the words *"uvechukoteihem lo teileichu"* – "and you shall not follow their customs," and quotes a number of sources (*Shabbat* 67a; *Sifra Acharei Mot Chapter* 13, *Section* 8) which indicate that attending theatres and sports arenas (specifically mentioned) are examples of following in the "customs" of the nations of the world.

19. In *Parshat Kedoshim* (*Vayikra* 19:36) we have instruction regarding honest weights. The *pasuk* says: *"moznei tzedek, avnei tzedek, eiphat tzedek, v'hin tzedek yihiye lachem"* – "you should have honest balances, honest weights, honest dry measures and honest liquid measures." The word *"tzedek"* – "honest" appears every second word in eight words in the same *pasuk*.

20. Two people are cursing a dead person. However one of the people doing the cursing is the dead person's son. The person who is not related to the

deceased has not transgressed any *Torah* laws. The dead person's son, however, has transgressed a *Torah* law. *Rashi* (*Vayikra* 19:14) on the *pasuk* "*lo tekalel chereish*" – "one shall not curse a deaf person" comments that there is another *pasuk* in *Shemot* (22:27) that speaks about cursing people, and there it includes the word "*b'amcha*" – "among your people," teaching us that you may not curse anyone among your people. *Rashi* explains that one might think that a deaf person is an exception, because he cannot hear the curse. But a deaf person is alive, and therefore is included "among your people," and as such, we need a special *pasuk* to indicate his inclusion. However, this law only applies to living beings. If one is dead, there is no transgression by cursing the one who passed away, even though it is a reprehensible thing to do. However, there is another *pasuk* later in our *Parshat Kedoshim* (*Vayikra* 20:9) which forbids the cursing of parents: "If anyone curses his father or his mother, he shall be put to death; he has insulted his father and his mother – his bloodguilt is upon him." *Rashi* points out that the words in that *pasuk* "he has insulted his father and his mother" seem to be superfluous. *Rashi* quotes a *gemara* (*Sanhedrin* 85b) which says that this phrase was added to teach us that cursing a parent even after death, is a *Torah* transgression, and is punishable by death.

PARSHAT EMOR QUESTIONS

1. From where does the *gemara* learn the concept of "*tosefet Shabbat*" – "adding from the weekday to the sanctity of *Shabbat* and *Yom Tov*," i.e., keeping extra minutes at the beginning and end of *Shabbat* and *Yom Tov*, from sunset to stars out, for a total of approximately 25 hours?

2. How does one honor a *kohen*?

3. If a *kohen* cannot defile himself for a dead human body (*Vayikra* 21:1), how was *Eliyahu,* who was a *kohen*, permitted to resuscitate the dead son of the *Isha Hatzarfatit* (*Melachim* 1:17:21)?

4. Which sect always observed *Shavuot* on a Sunday, and why?

5. Who was required to eat *matzah* every *Shabbat*?

6. In *halacha,* what is the connection between "*Sefirat HaOmer*" – "counting of the *Omer*" and the *mitzvah* of "*tzitzit*" – "putting on a four cornered garment with fringes in the corners"?

7. Why do we not recite a "*shehechiyanu*" on the *mitzvah* of *Sefirat HaOmer*?

8. What is the connection between *Purim* and *Lag BaOmer*?

9. In Jewish law, the day normally belongs to the previous night. In *Parshat Emor,* there occurs in the space of four *pesukim,* three separate *halachot* that seem to indicate that the principle of the day belonging to the previous night is not without some exceptions. What are the three *halachot*?

10. Name three *halachot* that are limited by the measurements of 20 "*amot*" – "cubits" and ten "*tefachim*" – "handbreadths."

11. Two widows are presented to a "*kohen hedyot*" – "regular *kohen*" as potential wives. One he can marry and the other he cannot. Why?

12. How many people were imprisoned in the *Torah*?

13. The *Birkei Yosef* (*Shulchan Aruch Orach Chaim* 489:20) says that one who converts during *Sefirat HaOmer* would count the remainder of the days of the *omer* without a *beracha*. How would it be possible for someone who converts during *Sefirat HaOmer* to complete the counting with a *beracha*?

14. I have not missed counting any days of the *Omer,* on time and with a *beracha*. Yet, I must count one day without a *beracha,* and then may continue with a *beracha*. Who am I?

15. Who is equated to the *kohen gadol* in "*kedusha*" – "holiness"?

16. There is a *kohen* in *shul*. He is not in the middle of *davening* and has equal status in the study of *Torah,* as all the other participants in the *minyan*. Yet, when it is time to call the first person up for an *aliya,* it is a *Yisrael* who is called and not the *kohen*. Why?

17. Where is there a *remez* in *Parshat Emor* that a man should get married at eighteen?

18. Where is there a *remez* in *Parshat Emor* that the *shofar* is not blown on *Shabbat*?
19. Was *Shlomit* a girl or a boy?
20. I have already accepted *Shabbat,* yet I may personally involve myself in a religious precept that belongs to Friday. What is that religious precept?

PARSHAT EMOR ANSWERS

1. The *gemara* (*Rosh Hashana* 9a) learns a number of lessons regarding extending the time of *Shabbat* and *Yom Tov,* both the beginning time and the ending time, from the unusual phrasing of the *pasuk* in *Vayikra* 23:32. First, because it says *"v'initem et nafshoteichem b'tisha lachodesh baerev"* – "And you shall afflict your souls on the ninth of the month in the evening," one might have thought that one must begin to fast the entire day on the ninth of the month of *Tishrei.* But because the *pasuk* says *"baerev"* – "in the evening," the *gemara* concludes that one should be *"mosif michol al hakodesh"* – "add from part of the weekday to the beginning of *Yom Kippur.*" The *gemara* then deduces from the phrase *"me'erev ad erev"* – "from evening to evening," that not only do we add time to the beginning of *Yom Kippur,* but we also extend the end of *Yom Kippur* past sunset. From this *gemara,* we have only derived that an extension is added to *Yom Kippur.* From where is it derived that one must also extend *Shabbat*? The *pasuk* states: *"tishbetu"* – "you shall rest," which is referring to *Yom Kippur* but from its root, alludes to *Shabbat* as well. Now, we have established extensions for both *Yom Kippur* and *Shabbat,* but from where do we know that the same applies to the *"chagim"* – "festivals"? Therefore the *pasuk* states *"shabbatchem"* – "Your *Shabbat,* your day of rest." Concludes the *gemara,* wherever there is a *mitzvah* of resting, be it *Shabbat* or a *"chag"* – "festival," one adds from the mundane to the sacred, extending the sacred time at both ends.

2. *Rashi* quotes the *gemara* (*Gittin* 59b) which derives from the *pasuk* (*Vayikra* 21:8) *"kadosh yihiye lach"* – "the *kohen* should be holy to you," that the *kohen* receives the first *aliyah* to the *Torah* and is honoured with leading the *"birkat hamazon"* – "grace after meals."

3. *Tosafot* answers that *Eliyahu* was permitted to defile himself for a dead body, even though he was a *kohen,* because he was certain that he would be successful in bringing the child back to life and therefore, even as a *kohen,* was permitted to resuscitate the child under the rule of *"pikuach nefesh"* – "saving one's life" (*Tosafot Bava Metzia* 113b).

4. The *"Tzidukim"* – "Sadducees" explained the *Torah* literally. They therefore always began *Sefirat HaOmer* on a Sunday, according to the literal meaning of the *pasuk* *"mimacharat haShabbat"* – literally, "the day after *Shabbat*" (*Vayikra* 23:15); which meant to them that *Shavuot* would always occur on a Sunday.

5. The *"lechem hapanim"* – "showbread" were baked as *matzah* and placed on the *Shulchan* in the *"mishkan"* – "tabernacle." The *matzah* of the previous week miraculously remained fresh and they were eaten by the *kohanim* on *Shabbat* (*Gemara Menachot* 29a).

6. In both *halachot*, we are told to stand to make the blessing. We derive this requirement to stand for the blessing of *tzitzit* from the *mitzvah* of *Sefirat HaOmer*. Regarding the counting of the *Omer*, the *Torah* says "*bakoma*" – "the standing crop" (*Devarim* 16:9). Because it comes from the same root as "*komah*" – "standing," we deduce that one should stand while making this *beracha*. And because the word "*lachem*" – "for you" is used by both *mitzvot*, we also stand for the *beracha* of *tzitzit*. The *Shulchan Aruch Orach Chaim*, (*Hilchot Tzitzit* 3b) points out that the word "*lachem*" appears in the instructions for six *mitzvot* and therefore, one should stand while making the *beracha* for all six *mitzvot*. They are *tzitzit, omer, milah, lulav, kiddush levana*, and *shofar*. The *Avudraham* coined the acronym "*alatz shalem*" to remember these six *mitzvot*; the acronym stands for "*omer, levana, tzitzit, shofar, lulav* and *milah*" (*Mishnah Berurah* 8:2; 585:1).

7. There are a number of reasons cited as to why we do not recite a *beracha* of "*shehechiyanu*" for the *mitzvah* of *Sefirat HaOmer*:
   1. Because the time period during which the *mitzvah* is performed is connected to the death of the students of *Rabbi Akiva*.
   2. The *Levush* (*Rabbi Mordechai Yaffe*, 1530–1612) (*Shulchan Aruch Orach Chaim* 489:1) writes: it is part of *Yom Tov* so it is included in the *shehechiyanu* of *Yom Tov*.
   3. The *Levush* adds: since *Sefirat HaOmer* was in anticipation of "*matan Torah*" – "the giving of the *Torah*" which is the main *simcha*, or reason for rejoicing, it doesn't make sense to say *shehechiyanu* on something we are anticipating before that day actually arrives!

8. *Purim* and *Lag BaOmer* both fall on the same day of the week. The days of the week of *Pesach* provide a hint for the days of the week upon which many of the festivals occur during the course of the year (*Shulchan Aruch Orach Chaim* 428:3). Using the tool of "*A-T, B-SH*" (*A-T* stands for the first and last letters of the Hebrew alphabet, *alef* and *tav*; *B-SH* stands for the second and second last letters, *bet* and *shin*, etc), the day of the week of the first day of *Pesach* (*alef*) corresponds to the day of the week of *Tisha B'Av* (*tav*); the day of the week of the second day of *Pesach* (*bet*) corresponds to the day of the week of *Shavuot* (*shin*); the day of the week of the third day of *Pesach* (*gimel*) corresponds to the day of the week of *Rosh Hashanah* (*reish*); the day of the week of the fourth day of *Pesach* (*daled*) corresponds to the day of the week of *Simchat Torah* (*kuf* for "*Kriat HaTorah*" – reading of the *Torah*); the day of the week of the fifth day of *Pesach* (*heh*) corresponds to the day of the week of *Yom Kippur* (*tzadi* for "*tzom*" – fast day); the day of the week for the sixth day of *Pesach* (*vav*) corresponds to the day of the week of the *Purim* (*peh*) holiday that occurred the month before that *Pesach*; the day of the week for the seventh day of *Pesach* (*zayin*) corresponds to the

day of the week of *Yom Ha-Atzmaut* (*ayin* for *atzmaut*). We also know that the day of the week upon which *Purim* occurs is the same day of the week as *Lag BaOmer* (*Shulchan Aruch Orach Chaim* 428:1).

9. These four *pesukim* containing *halachot*, where it seems that the day does not necessarily always belong to the previous night, occur in *Vayikra* 22:27–30. The first *halacha* is the requirement to wait until a newborn calf, sheep or goat reaches the age of eight days before offering it as a sacrifice. The *halacha* stipulates that it can only be slaughtered beginning the morning of the eighth day, thus indicating that the day is not connected to the previous night. The second *halacha* stipulates that one cannot slaughter an animal and its calf on the same day. This second *halacha* stipulates that the same day includes the night before, thus indicating that the day is, in fact, connected to the previous night. The third *halacha* deals with eating the meat of a sacrifice and stipulates that one cannot leave any over until morning, which is interpreted as allowing one to eat of the sacrifice until morning, thus indicating that the day is not connected to the previous night.

10. The *halacha* most obvious to our *Parshat Emor* is the *halacha* of *sukkah*, whereby the height of the walls of a *sukkah* may not exceed 20 *amot*, and the minimum height for a *sukkah* is 10 *tefachim* (*Gemara Sukkah* 2a). The second *halacha* governed by these two measurements is the halacha of carrying on *Shabbat* in a "*mavoy*" – "alleyway." A beam extending across the entryway to an alley may not exceed 20 *amot* in height and the height from the ground to the top of the wall at the entrance to the alley cannot be less than ten *tefachim* (*Gemara Shabbat* 22a). The third *halacha* governed by these two measurements is the *halacha* of the *Chanukah menorah*. The *menorah* cannot be placed higher than 20 *amot* and it should ideally be placed lower than ten *tefachim* from the ground (*Shulchan Aruch Orach Chaim* 671:6).

11. A "*kohen gadol*" – "high priest" may not marry a widow or a divorcée. A "*kohen hedyot*" – "regular *kohen*" is permitted to marry a widow but is not permitted to marry a divorcée. However, if a widow was previously divorced (or if she was previously in the category of women forbidden to a *kohen*, e.g., a prostitute or a *chalala* – see *Vayikra* 21:7), then her current status of widow is superseded by her previous status. Therefore in our question, one woman is purely a widow and the other, while a widow from her most recent marriage, was previously a divorcée or some other forbidden category.

12. There were 16 people imprisoned in the *Torah*: *Yosef* (*Bereishit* 39:20); the butler and the baker in *Paroh*'s court (*Bereishit* 40:30); all the brothers of *Yosef*, other than *Binyamin* (*Bereishit* 42:17); *Shimon*, the brother of *Yosef* (*Bereishit* 42:24) was detained while the other brothers went to get *Binyamin*; the "*mekalel*" – "the one who cursed" (*Vayikra* 24:12); and the "*mekoshesh aytzim*" – "the gatherer of wood on *Shabbat*" (*Bamidbar* 15:34).

13. If one converted on the afternoon of the second day of *Pesach* (in Israel, when it is *Chol Hamoed*), then he would count the first day of the *omer* without a *beracha* and then continue to count the remainder of the days with a *beracha* (*Shulchan Aruch Orach Chaim Shaarei Teshuva* 489:20).

14. We are referring to an *"onayn"* – "someone whose immediate relative has died and has not yet been buried." Such a person is *halachically* considered to be in a state of suspension and may not observe any of the *mitzvot*. The *Noda B'Yehuda* (*Rabbi Yechezkel ben Yehuda HaLevi Landau* – 1713–1793) is quoted by the *Shaarei Teshuva* (*Shulchan Aruch Orach Chaim* 489:20) as ruling that in such an instance, the *"onayn"* should count that night without a *beracha* and then resume counting with a *beracha* after his close relative is buried.

15. The *Nazir*. Both may not defile themselves, even for their closest seven relatives (*Bamidbar* 6:7; *Vayikra* 21:11). Both are described as having *"nezer Elokim"* – "Hashem's crown" upon them (*Bamidbar* 6:7; *Vayikra* 21:11).

16. It is a *minyan* composed of all *kohanim* and one *yisrael*. The *yisrael* is called for the first *aliyah* for the reason of *"darkei shalom"* – "so that no one *kohen* will be made to feel superior to his fellow *kohanim*" (*Shulchan Aruch Orach Chaim* 135:12).

17. *Vayikra* 21:13 states: *"v'hu isha bivtuleha yikach"* – "and he shall marry a woman who has never been married before." The *Baal Haturim* points out that the word *"v'hu"* is equal to 18 in *gematriya*. As well, the last letter of each word in the *pasuk* also equals 18. Additionally, the *pasuk* that first discusses the idea of marriage (*Bereishit* 2:21) contains the phrase *"ish et aviv v'et imo v'davak b'ishto"* – "man will leave his father and mother and cleave to his wife," the first letter of which also totals 18. Another *pasuk* with the same idea and also incorporating the word *v'hu*, is *Tehillim* 19:6: *"v'hu k'chatan yotzei meichupato"* – "and he is like a bridegroom emerging from the wedding canopy."

18. The *pasuk* about *Rosh Hashanah* (*Vayikra* 23:24) *"yihiye lachem shabbaton, zichron teruah"* – "it should be a time of complete rest, commemorated with loud blasts," utilizes the term *"shabbaton"* hinting that when *Rosh Hashanah* occurs on *Shabbat*, there is only a *"zichron"* – "a remembrance" of the *shofar* blast, but it is not actually blown. In *Parshat Pinchas* (*Bamidbar* 29:1), *Rosh Hashanah* is called *"yom teruah"* – "the day of the *Shofar* blast." The *gemara* (*Rosh Hashanah* 29b) explains that the first *pasuk* is referring to a *Yom Tov* that occurs on a *Shabbat* and the *mitzvah* of *Shofar* is derived from the second *pasuk*.

19. Trick question: In *Parshat Emor*, *Shlomit* is the mother of the *"mekalel"* – "the blasphemer." *Shlomit* was also the name of the daughter of *Zerubavel* (*Divrei Hayamim* 1:3:19). In *Divrei Hayamim* and in *Ezra*, *Shlomit* is the

name of various men (*Ezra* 8:10; *Divrei Hayamim* 1:23:9; 26:28; 26:25; *Divrei Hayamim* 2:11:20).

20. If I accepted *Shabbat* early and then realized that I forgot to count *Sefirat HaOmer* on Thursday night, I may count without a *beracha* and then resume with a *beracha* after nightfall on Friday night (*Iggrot Moshe, Vol. 6; Shulchan Aruch Orach Chayim*, 99:3).

PARSHAT BEHAR-BECHUKOTAI QUESTIONS

1. Why does the *pasuk* that discusses *"shemitah"* – "the agricultural sabbatical year" say *"v'shavta ha'aretz Shabbat"*? The word *Shabbat* seems out of place.

2. Where is there a hint in *Parshat Behar* to the number of *"yovel"* – "jubilee" periods that were observed during the time that the *Bnai Yisrael* spent in Israel until the exile?

3. My animal does not walk in a straight line which is very beneficial for me but costly for my friend. Explain.

4. There is a word which appears in *Parshat Bechukotai* that is recited at least four times every *Shabbat*. What is that word?

5. *Bnai Yisrael* are referred to as *"avadai"* – "my servants" in *Parshat Behar* (*Vayikra* 25:55). Who are the only individuals in the *Torah* referred to by *Hashem* as *"avdi"* – "my servant"?

6. It resembles *Shavuot* in the way we find it, *Rosh Hashanah* in what we do, *Yom Kippur* in when we do it, *Pesach* in what happens and is connected to Philadelphia? What is it?

7. The *Torah* (*Vayikra* 27) lists the values for different categories of people for a person who donates his worth to the *Beit Hamikdash*. What is the total (in *shekels*) of all categories and what is its significance?

8. The *minhag* is that the *"baal kriah"* – "individual reading the *Torah"* receives the *aliyah* that contains the *tochacha*. What if the *baal kriah* is a *kohen*?

9. When do 100 + 100 not equal 200?

10. What *minhag* practiced universally today, at the end of a particular day in the calendar, was a *Torah* commandment at the time that the *Beit Hamikdash* stood, was practiced twice in a century, at the very beginning of the same particular day?

11. From where do we learn, that where possible, your customers and your suppliers should preferably be Jewish?

12. Cite as many instances as you can either from *Tanach* or from *halacha* when the *shofar* is sounded?

13. The name of the *parshah* is "Behar" from the Hebrew phrase in the first *pasuk* "behar Sinai" – "on *Mount Sinai*" (*Vayikra* 25:1). How many different names did *Mount Sinai* have?

14. The *Torah* prohibition that forbids Jews to charge interest on a loan (*Vayikra* 25:36) is very clear. Why then does the *Torah* have to add the words *"veyareita mei'elokecha"* – "and you should fear *Hashem"* immediately following the prohibition?

15. What two places in the *Torah* have six words in a row, each beginning with the same letter?

16. Find as many references as possible in the *Torah* to the number 50?

17. How many times did *Bnai Yisrael* observe the *yovel*?
18. What was different about the *Amidah tefillah* on the *Yom Kippur* of *yovel* from the *Amidah tefillah* of *Yom Kippur* of a non-*yovel* year?
19. What is the connection of *Behar-Bechukotai* to the holiday of *Shavuot*?
20. What is the connection between one of the first Jewish settlements to observe "*Shemittah*" – "Agricultural Sabbatical Year" following the establishment of the State of Israel, and *Behar-Bechukotai*?

PARSHAT BEHAR-BECHUKOTAI ANSWERS

1. The *Matteh Moshe* (473) explains the addition of the word *"shabbat"* in a fascinating way. In a regular non-*Shemittah* year, the farmer cannot work his field on *Shabbat*. But the crops planted during the week continue to grow on *Shabbat*, and therefore the *"aretz"* – "land" does not rest on *Shabbat* during the course of a year. There are 52 *shabbatot* per solar year and over a period of seven years, there are 7 × 52 = 364 *shabbat* days when the land was "passively" working. As a result, the *Mateh Moshe* says that the *Torah* instituted *shemittah* once in seven years, when the land lies fallow in order to compensate for all of the *shabbatot* when it worked during those seven years. Therefore the *Torah* utilizes the phrase *"v'shavta haaretz shabbat l'Hashem."*

2. The *Baal Haturim* points out that the word *yovel* appears 14 times, six times with a *vav*, which is called *"malei"* – "complete" and eight times without the *vav*, which is called *"chaser"* – "lacking." He quotes a *gemara* (*Erechin* 12b) which states that there were 14 *yovel* periods during this entire time; six (with the *vav*) while the *Beit Hamikdash* was standing (i.e., complete) and eight (without the *vav*) without the presence of the *Beit Hamikdash* (i.e., lacking).

3. First allow me to explain the laws and processes of *"maaser beheima"* – "tithing of livestock." This *halacha* required every 10th newly born calf or lamb in a herd to be consecrated to the *kohen,* as explained in the *pasuk* "the tenth will be holy to *Hashem*" (*Vayikra* 27:32). Three times a year, the farmer would separately gather all his newly-born sheep and cattle into a corral. An opening wide enough for only one animal to pass through at a time, would be designed and as the young animals walked through, he would count from one to ten, marking each tenth one with a red streak. Those were designated as *"maaser beheima"* – "the livestock tithe." They were brought to *Jerusalem,* the only place where it was permitted to be eaten, and the meat was shared by its owner with whomever he pleased. In our case, after being counted, one of the animals in the secondary enclosure manages to get free and mingle with the as yet uncounted calves. The result is that the already counted animals do not have to be subjected to a recount and the uncounted animals are likewise exempt, as the *Torah* mandates that the tithed animal be a definite tenth (*Gemara Bava Metzia* 7a) and in this case, that is no longer possible. I have therefore profited by retaining my rights to the animals, while the *kohen* has been denied the receipt of the tenth of my newborn flock.

4. The word is *"komemiyut"* (*Vayikra* 26:13). We say it on *Shabbat* in the *birkat hamazon* three times (once for each recitation at each of the three required

Shabbat meals), and once in the *beracha* of *ahava rabba* before *kriat shema* in *shacharit*.

5. The three people who are referred to as *"avdi"* – "my servant" in the *Torah,* are *Avraham* (*Bereishit* 26:24), *Moshe* (*Bamidbar* 12:7), and *Kalev* (*Bamidbar* 14:24).

6. *Yovel* – the 50ᵗʰ year or the Jubilee Year. Just as we count seven weeks of seven days until *Shavuot,* we count seven – seven year *shemitah* cycles until the *yovel.* We blow the *shofar* at the *yovel* just as we do on *Rosh Hashanah.* The *shofar* is actually blown at *Yom Kippur* in the *yovel* year. Slaves are freed at the *yovel* year, just as we were freed from slavery on *Pesach.* The *pasuk* related to *yovel* (*Vayikra* 25:10) "and proclaim liberty throughout all the land to all its inhabitants" is written on the Liberty Bell in Philadelphia.

7. The values vary based on age and gender. They are 50 *shekels* (male ages 20–60) + 30 *shekels* (female ages 20–60) + 20 *shekels* (male ages 5–20) + 10 *shekels* (female ages 5–20) + 5 *shekels* (male ages one month – 5 years) + 3 *shekels* (female ages one month – 5 years) + 15 *shekels* (male ages 60 years and up) + 10 *shekels* (female ages 60 years and up) = a total of 143 *shekels.* The *Baal Haturim* (*Vayikra* 27:3) explains that this is an antidote for the 143 curses recorded in the *Torah* (45 in the *tochacha* of *Bechukotai* + 98 in the *tochacha* of *Ki Tavo*) because *"tzedakah tatzil mimavet"* – "charity saves one from death" (*Mishlei* 10:2).

8. If the *"baal kriah"* – *"Torah* reader" is a *kohen,* and if the reading of the *tochacha* is *Parshat Bechukotai* (where the *tochacha* is close to the beginning of the *parshah*), he receives the first *aliyah,* and reads until the end of the *tochacha* and the rest of *Parshat Bechukotai* is divided among the next six *aliyot.* On the other hand, if the reading of the *tochacha* is *Parshat Ki Tavo* (where the *tochacha* is close to the end of the *parshah*), then the *baal kriah/kohen* receives the *aliyah* of *"acharon"* – the final *aliyah* before *maftir*) and reads from the *tochacha* until the end of *Parshat Ki Tavo* (*Mishnah Berurah* 428:17).

9. The *Torah* promises that if we keep the *mitzvot, "v'radfu mikem chamisha meah, u'meah mikem revava yirdofu"* – "and five of you will chase one hundred, and one hundred of you will put ten thousand to flight" (*Vayikra* 26:8). The words *"meah u'meah"* – "one hundred and one hundred" are separated by a pause in the *Torah* reading and therefore if one did not punctuate correctly and read the *Torah* as *"me'ah, u'me'ah"* – "one hundred and one hundred" with no pause, we would have the source of our riddle.

10. At the end of every *Yom Kippur,* we have the *minhag* of blowing the *shofar.* This *minhag* developed as a remembrance of the *shofar* that was blown at the beginning of the *yovel* year, which occurred every 50 years, or twice in a century. The only explicit commandment that we have to blow the *shofar*

is the *shofar* ushering in the *yovel* year. In *Parshat Behar* that deals with the Jubilee year, *yovel*, the *Torah* says: "Then you shall sound the *shofar* loud; in the seventh month, on the tenth day of the month; on *Yom Kippur*, you shall have the horn sounded throughout your land" (*Vayikra* 25:9). Now that there is no *yovel*, we blow the *shofar* every *Yom Kippur* to commemorate what once was, and to express our hopes for the future. Hence we have a *minhag* annually at the end of *Yom Kippur* to recall a twice in a century *Torah* obligation at the beginning of *Yom Kippur*. The *Rambam* comments: "From *Rosh Hashanah* until *Yom Kippur*, the slaves, who were to be freed on the occasion of the jubilee year, neither left for their homes nor were they still subjected to their masters, nor were the fields restored to their original owners. The slaves would eat and drink and rejoice as they were wearing wreaths on their heads. As soon as *Yom Kippur* arrived, the court sounded the *shofar*. Thereupon the slaves left for their homes and the fields returned to their original owners" (*Rambam, Laws of Shmita* and *Yovel* 10:14).

11. *Rashi* quotes the *Sifra* on *Behar* and comments on the *pasuk* "when you sell property to your neighbour, or buy any from your neighbour, you shall not wrong one another" (*Vayikra* 25:14). *Rashi* interprets "*amitecha*" – "neighbour" as one associated with you by nationality, and hence if you intend to buy or sell anything, you should buy it from your fellow *Jew* or sell it to your fellow *Jew*.

12. We can cite at least 14 instances in Jewish history when the *shofar* was sounded; though I am sure that there are many more:
    1. On *Rosh Hashanah*.
    2. Every day during the month of *Elul*, except for *Erev Rosh Hashanah*.
    3. At the conclusion of the *neilah* service on the afternoon of *Yom Kippur*.
    4. The *shofar* was blown to warn *Bnai Yisrael* of imminent danger (*Amos* 3:6).
    5. The *shofar* was sounded at *Mount Sinai* (*Shemot* 19:16).
    6. After *Yehoshua* and the Jewish people marched around the city of *Yericho* while carrying the *Holy Ark*, the *shofar* was sounded. This was repeated for seven days and at the end of seven days, the walls came crumbling down (*Yehoshua* 6).
    7. Following *Hashem*'s instructions, *Gidyon* together with 300 men, carrying a torch, a clay pitcher and a *shofar*, fought the *Midyan* army. Their victory was ensured when they broke the pitchers and blew their *shofars*, frightening and subsequently defeating the *Midyan* army (*Shoftim* 7).
    8. Following *King David*'s capture of *Yerushalayim*, there was much celebration and *shofar* blowing (*Shmuel* 2:6).

9. When *King Shlomo* was crowned king and anointed by *Tzadok Hakohen*, the *shofar* was blown, followed by the sounds of many other musical instruments (*Melachim* 1:1).

10. In announcing the *yovel* year every 50 years (*Vayikra* 25:9).

11. The *rabbis* instituted that every *Erev Shabbat*, close to the onset of *Shabbat*, the *shofar* should be sounded as a reminder to everyone to complete their last minute preparations for *Shabbat* (*Gemara Shabbat* 32b).

12. The *shofar* was sounded to announce the new month when the first viewing of the moon was witnessed (*Rashi Tehillim* 81:4).

13. After the Six-Day War, *Rabbi Shlomo Goren* famously approached the *Kotel* and sounded the *shofar*. This fact inspired *Naomi Shemer* to add an additional line to her song "*Yerushalayim shel Zahav*" – "Jerusalem of Gold," saying, "a *shofar* calls out from the Temple Mount in the Old City."

14. The *shofar* will be sounded when *Mashiach* will arrive (*Yeshayahu* 27:13).

13. There are seven alternate names for *Har Sinai* listed in *Chazal*. They are:
    1. *Har Sinai* (*Vayikra* 25:1)
    2. *Har HaElokim* (*Shemot* 3:1)
    3. *Har Bashan* (*Tehillim* 68:16)
    4. *Har Gavnunim* (*Tehillim* 68:16)
    5. *Har Chorev* (*Shemot* 33:6)
    6. *Beit Imi* (*Shir Hashirim Rabbah* 2:3:4)
    7. *Har Chemed* (*Tehillim* 68:17)

    Some also include the name *Har Moriah*, (which most scholars identify as the "*Har Habayit*" – "The Temple Mount" where the *Beit Hamikdash* stood) based on the *Kabbalistic* notion that when *Hashem* gave the *Torah* in "*Midbar Sinai*" – "the *Sinai* Wilderness," He uprooted the mountain from its regular place in *Yerushalayim* and brought it to the wilderness, only to return it afterwards (*Rabbi Naftali Katz, Smichat Chachamim*).

14. *Rashi* (*Vayikra* 25:36) quotes a *gemara* (*Bava Metzia* 61b) which explains that it is a law of nature that man does not want his money to be inactive, rather he wants his money to be invested to earn more money. Therefore man will naturally try to talk himself into charging interest as a legitimate and permissible act, and may seek a legal loophole such as pretending that his money belongs to a *non-Jew* and therefore there will be no prohibition in charging interest. Thus the *Torah* had to add the words "*veyareita mei'elokecha*" – "and you should fear *Hashem*," to remind man that this is prohibited by *Torah* law.

15. There are two places in the *Torah* where six consecutive words all begin with the same letter:

1. In the story of the sons of *Yaakov* standing before their brother *Yosef* in *Mitzrayim*: "*ish el achiv aval asheimim anachnu*" – "They said to one another: Alas, we are being punished" (*Bereishit* 42:21); here we have six consecutive words all beginning with the letter "*alef.*"

2. In *Parshat Behar,* where the *mitzvah* of *yovel* is being commanded, it says: "*sheva shabbtot shanim sheva shanim sheva*" (*Vayikra* 25:8): here we have six consecutive words all beginning with the letter "*shin.*"

16. The number 50 appears in *Parshat Behar* in connection to *yovel*. Including *yovel*, I have found at least ten references to the number 50 in the *Torah*:

    1. The width of *Noach*'s ark was 50 *amot* (*Bereishit* 6:15).

    2. *Avraham* asked *Hashem* to save *Sedom* if he could find 50 righteous individuals there (*Bereishit* 18:24).

    3. *Yitro* suggested certain numbers of judges to deal with legislative issues in the desert and one level was 50 (*Shemot* 18:21).

    4. The coverings at the top of the *Mishkan* were connected by 50 loops and hooks (*Shemot* 26:5).

    5. The width of the *chatzer* of the *Mishkan* was 50 *amot* (*Shemot* 27:18).

    6. *Shavuot* is the 50th day after we begin to count the *Omer* (*Vayikra* 23:16).

    7. This is *yovel* in *Parshat Behar* (*Vayikra* 25:11).

    8. The *levi'im* were to work until age 50 (*Bamidbar* 4:3).

    9. The *Bnai Yisrael* donated 50% of the spoils of the war with *Midyan* to the *levi'im* (*Bamidbar* 31:30).

    10. If a man violates a young maiden, he must marry her and give her father reparations of 50 coins (*Devarim* 22:29).

17. The *Rambam* states that *Bnai Yisrael* counted 17 *yovels*. *Rashi* comments (*Gemara Erechin* 12b) that this is derived from a *pasuk* in *Melachim* (*Melachim* 1:6:1) "And it was in the 480th year…" Subtract the forty years that the *Bnai Yisrael* wandered in the desert, and therefore they entered the Land 440 years before the building of the first *Beit Hamikdash* which stood for 410 years, thereby totalling 850 years, which are seventeen *yovels* of fifty years each."

18. On a normal *Yom Kippur,* there are seven *berachot* in the *mussaf amidah*. On the *Yom Kippur* of a *yovel* year, there are nine *berachot* in the *mussaf amidah* similar to the *mussaf* of *Rosh Hashanah* (*Rambam, Hilchot tefillah* 2:8).

19. There are a number of possible answers. You could have answered that *Behar* is talking about *Har Sinai* and there could be no better connection to *Shavuot*. But that answer would involve only *Behar* and not *Bechukotai*. Or you could have answered that the entire description of *yovel* as counting seven years seven times and that the year following is *yovel*, is very similar to the counting of the *omer* from *Pesach* to *Shavuot* with the 50th day being *Shavuot*. But that too, is only a connection to *Behar*. You could also have

said that the word "*dror*" – "freedom" is a connection because the Jews' journey to *Mount Sinai* for *Shavuot* was all about being a free nation after the exodus. Again only *Behar*. The answer that I was looking for was the fact that there are four rules regarding the distribution of *parshiyot* in the *Torah* reading cycle of the year. They are:

1. The *Shabbat* before *Pesach* has to be *Tzav* in a regular year or *Metzora* in a leap year.
2. The *Shabbat* before *Shavuot* has to be *Bamidbar*.
3. The *Shabbat* after *Tisha B'Av* has to be *Va'etchanan* (*Shabbat Nachamu*).
4. The *Shabbat* before *Rosh Hashanah* has to be *Nitzavim*.

Since *Tzav* is the 25ᵗʰ *parshah* in the *Torah* and *Bamidbar* is the 34ᵗʰ, and since in most regular years there are only six *Shabbatot* between *Pesach* and *Shavuot*, there will be three double *parshiyot* during the month of *Iyar* in a regular year. So the answer to the riddle is that *Behar-Bechukotai* can never occur on the *Shabbat* before *Shavuot*. The *Biur Halacha* (*Shulchan Aruch Orach Chaim* 428:4) explains that since *Bechukotai* has the "*tochacha*" – "rebukes" and since *Shavuot* is the time that *Hashem* judges nature and fruit for the coming year, the calendar and *Torah* readings have been arranged such that *Bechukotai* can never occur the same week as *Shavuot*.

20. In *Parshat Behar*, we have the instructions for *Shemitah*. In *Bechukotai*, we have the only occurrence in the entire *Torah* of the word "*komemiyut*" – "upright" (*Vayikra* 26:13). One of the first settlements to observe the very first *shemittah* year after the establishment of the State of Israel (and every subsequent *shemittah* since) is the *Chassidic Moshav* of *Komemiyut* in southern Israel.

PARSHAT BAMIDBAR QUESTIONS

1. *Bamidbar* is the largest of seventeen what?
2. His father was the leader of a tribe; his son was a spy. Who was he?
3. From where can we deduce that there were no handicapped members of *Bnai Yisrael* in the desert?
4. Why did the Tribe of *Levi* have fewer members than the other Tribes? They all went down to *Mitzrayim* together and should have increased at a rate proportional to the rest of *Bnai Yisrael*.
5. Besides all being "*nesi'im*" – "princes," what was unique about *Netanel*, *Shlumiel*, *Gamliel* and *Pagiel*?
6. *Parshat Bamidbar* is always read immediately before the holiday of *Shavuot*, which occurs in the month of *Sivan*. However, *Sivan* is not mentioned by name in the *Torah*. Where is it specifically mentioned in *Tanach*?
7. Besides *Yom Yerushalayim*, what else happened on the 28th day of *Iyar*?
8. Which tribe had more females than males?
9. What was the colour of the flag of each tribe?
10. Where is *Megilat Esther* referred to in *Parshat Bamidbar*?
11. Two different words appear in *Parshat Bamidbar*. Each word has two different meanings. Each of the two meanings of one word is synonymous with the two meanings of the other word. What are the two words?
12. Who was *Nadav's* oldest son?
13. Which two people from *Megilat Esther* are mentioned in *Rashi* in *Parshat Bamidbar*?
14. Which camp's flag had a picture of a child on it?
15. Which camp's flag had the *pasuk* of *Shema* on it?
16. From where do we learn that a man only attains his full strength once he reaches age thirty?
17. Did *Bnai Yisrael* require boats in the desert?
18. By how many names is *Sefer Bamidbar* known?
19. *Aharon Hakohen* was related to one of the "*nesi'im*" – "princes" mentioned in the first *aliyah* of *Bamidbar*. Who was the *nasi* and how were they related?
20. Name as many places mentioned in the *Torah* that are also names of people who appear in the *Torah* (Names of places that contain the complete name of a person will also be accepted; example: the place called *Rimon Peretz* for the person *Peretz*)?

PARSHAT BAMIDBAR ANSWERS

1. There are 17 *parshiyot* that contain no *mitzvot*. *Bamidbar* is the largest of these seventeen.

2. There are two possible answers. One answer is *Elazar*. His father was *Aharon*, the leader of *Shevet Levi* and his son was *Pinchas*, who was one of the spies sent to spy on *Yericho* (*Yehoshua* 2:1). The second answer is *Nun*. His father was *Elishama ben Amihud* (*Divrei Hayamim* 1:7:26–27), the prince of the Tribe of *Efraim*, and his son was *Yehoshua*, one of the twelve "*meraglim*" sent by *Moshe* to spy on the land of *Canaan*.

3. The *pasuk* says "*kol yotzai tzava*" (*Bamidbar* 1:20). The *Ohr Hachaim Hakadosh* says that this means that every person was capable of going out to war and hence, he deduces from this *pasuk* that there were no handicapped members of *Bnai Yisrael*.

4. A few possible answers as to why the tribe of *Levi* had fewer members than the other tribes. The Rabbis teach us that the *pasuk* "as they were oppressed, so did they multiply" (*Shemot* 1:12), teaches us that the population increase was supernatural and proportional to the degree of oppression. The *Ramban* says that only the Tribe of *Levi* experienced a natural population increase, as they were not enslaved in *Mitzrayim*. Another answer is that since the rest of Israel was given the responsibility of supporting the *levi'im*, through the giving of tithes etc., *Hashem* had mercy and kept the proportion of *levi'im* small as compared to the rest of *Bnai Yisrael*.

5. *Rabbeinu Bechaye* comments that these four "*nesi'im*" – "tribal princes," *Netanel, Shlumiel, Gamliel* and *Pagiel,* were the only ones whose names included *Hashem's* name "*keil,*" and they "coincidentally" were the heads of tribes that travelled in the middle of their camps. For example, the *Yehuda* camp was made of three tribes, *Yehuda, Yissachar* and *Zevulun* and the *nasi* for *Yissachar* was *Netanel Ben Tzuar*. This gives credence to the phrase that appears throughout *Tanach* indicating that *Hashem* dwells "*b'toch*" – "in the midst of" the *Bnai Yisrael*. If you examine when each of these *nesi'im* brought their offering at the "*Chanukat Hamishkan*" – "the dedication of the *Mishkan*," you will notice that *Netanel* brought his on the second day; *Shlumiel* brought his on the fifth day; *Gamliel* on the eighth day; and *Pagiel* on the eleventh day. Add up 2 + 5 + 8 + 11 = 26, the *gematriya* of "*yud* and *heh* and *vav* and *heh*," the four letter name of *Hashem*, furthering the concept of *Hashem* dwelling in the midst of the *Bnai Yisrael* (*Rabbenu Bachaye Bamidbar* 2:2).

6. *Sivan* is found only once by name in *Tanach* in *Megillat Esther* (*Esther* 8:9).

7. Two other events occurred on the 28th *of Iyar*. According to the *Shulchan Aruch Orach Chaim* 580:2, the *yahrtzeit* of *Shmuel Hanavi* is on the 28th of

Iyar. The war with *Amalek,* as described in *Parshat Beshalach* also occurred on the 28th *of Iyar.* In the year of the *Exodus* from *Mitzrayim, Rosh Chodesh Iyar* was on a Sunday (*Gemara Shabbat* 87b) and the first *Shabbat* that the *Bnai Yisrael* observed was on the 22nd of *Iyar.* The *Bnai Yisrael* then travelled to *Refidim,* where they fought *Amalek.* When the *Torah* says that *Moshe* "remained with his hands in faithful prayer until sunset" (*Shemot* 17:12), the *Midrash Tanchuma* (*Beshalach Siman* 28) explains that *Moshe* stopped the revolution of the sun, the moon, and the coming of nightfall in their tracks, and as such, caused time and the sun to stand still. The *Amalek* were waiting for the onset of *Shabbat* so that *Bnai Yisrael* would be defeated by not wishing to wage war on *Shabbat. Moshe* stopped time so that *Shabbat* would not begin. Therefore the battle with *Amalek* was on a Friday, the 28th *of Iyar.*

8. The *Baal Haturim* (*Bamidbar* 1:42) notes that in the listing of the tribes in the first chapter of *Bamidbar,* each tribe listing begins with the word "*livnei*" except for the tribe of *Naftali* whose listing begins with the word "*bnai.*" The *Baal Haturim* explains that the tribe of *Naftali* was the only tribe with a greater number of females than males. He brings a hint from the blessing received by *Naftali* at the end of *Bereishit* (49:21). Part of the blessing contains the words "*ayala shelucha hanotein.*" The first letters of these three words spell "*isha*" – "woman." The *Baal Haturim* points out additionally that when the tribes are counted once again in *Pinchas,* all of the listings begin with the word "*bnai,*" because by this time, many of the males who had left *Mitzrayim* at the time of the *Exodus* had died, and all tribes now had more females than males.

9. The colour of the flag of each tribe matched the colour of its stone in the *kohen gadol's* breastplate (*Rashi Bamidbar* 2:2).

10. *Rashi* (*Bamidbar* 3:7) in commenting on the words "*v'shamru et mishmarto*" – "and they should perform duties for him," quotes a *gemara* (*Megillah* 13b), which says that when one is appointed to an official duty, it is called a "*mishmeret.*" *Rashi* cites as an example, the story of *Bigtan* and *Teresh,* when they were conspiring against *Achashverosh,* one said to the other, as related by the *gemara*: "but surely my "*mishmarti*" – "official duty" is not the same as "*mishmartecha*" – "your official duty" and therefore, we can never meet to put our plans into execution!"

11. The two words are *shevet* and *mateh.* Each word means tribe and each word means staff.

12. Trick question: *Nadav* had no children (*Bamidbar* 3:4).

13. *Bigtan* and *Teresh* are mentioned in *Rashi* (*Bamidbar* 3:7) when *Rashi* is defining the word "*mishmeret*" (see question 10 above).

14. The flag of *Machaneh Efraim* had a picture of a child on it (*Targum Yonatan Bamidbar* 2:18).

15. The flag of *Machaneh Reuven* had the words of the *pasuk "Shema Yisrael"* on it (*Targum Yonatan Bamidbar* 2:10).

16. The *Bartenura* comments (*Mishnah Avot* 5:21) that *Yehudah ben Teimah* wrote *"ben shloshim lekoach"* – "at thirty years of age, one reaches the peak of their strength" from the fact that the *levi'im* were allowed to participate in the work dismantling and transporting the *mishkan* starting at age 30 (*Bamidbar* 4:3).

17. The source of water that sustained *Bnai Yisrael* in the desert was the "*Be'er Miriam*" – "the well of *Miriam*." The *rabbis* explain that it was not a normal well with a rope, pulley and bucket, but rather was more like a flowing river that travelled with the entire community of Israel. The *midrash* (*Bamidbar Rabbah* 19:26) comments on the *pasuk* in *Chukat "be'er chafaruha sarim"* – "the well that the princes dug" (*Bamidbar* 21:18) that when *Bnai Yisrael* camped, the "*nasi*" – "prince" of each tribe, would place his staff at the edge of the encampment and the well/river of *Miriam* would know where to stop flowing and would know the boundaries of the encampment. The *midrash* continues to relate and provides proof from *pesukim* in *Tehillim* and elsewhere, that when someone from one "*shevet*" – "tribe" would want to visit a friend in another *shevet,* he or she would do so by boat, and therefore boats were needed in this desert!

18. Besides *Bamidbar*, the 4th book of the *Torah* is known by two other names: *Chumash Hapekudim* (*Gemara Yoma* 3a) and *Sefer Vayedaber* (*Gemara Shabbat* 116a). A brief explanation for the three names is as follows:

    1. *Bamidbar*, the fifth word in the book, is the location where all of the events in the *Sefer* take place.
    2. *Pekudim*, says *Rav Aharon Lichtenstein, zt"l,* has three meanings and all three connect to what is happening in this book. First, *Pekuda* is enumeration, as this is the book which begins with the census of the Jewish people. Second, it also means a charge or a command. *Pekudim* are those who are commanded, as in the Hebrew word *mefaked*, which means commander. And third, it connotes concern and relationship, as in the *pasuk "v'Hashem pakad et Sarah"* – "and *Hashem* took note of *Sarah* as He had promised" (*Bereishit* 21:1). *Rav Lichtenstein* explains that the counting of *Bnai Yisrael* was not a simple census for the sake of knowing how many people were part of the community. But rather, *Hashem* counted us because He was concerned for us and wanted all of us to fulfill the missions that He would charge us with as our Commander In Chief.
    3. The third name of the book is *Sefer Vayedaber* which is taken from the first word of the book.

19. *Aharon Hakohen* was married to *Elisheva bat Aminadav* and the *pasuk* there tells us that she was the sister of *Nachshon* (*Shemot* 6:23). The *nasi* for the tribe of *Yehuda* was the very same *Nachshon ben Aminadav* (*Bamidbar* 1:7) and therefore *Aharon* and *Nachshon* were brothers-in-law.

20. There are many examples of places mentioned in the *Torah* that are also names of people who appear in the *Torah*. The following are presented in no particular order. The references given for each will first have the reference for the name and secondly for the place.

    1. *Chevron* (*Shemot* 6:18; *Bereishit* 13:18)
    2. *Shechem* (*Bereishit* 34:2; *Bereishit* 12:6)
    3. *Chanoch* (*Bereishit* 4:17; *Bereishit* 4:17)
    4. *Terach* (*Bereishit* 11:32; *Bamidbar* 33:27)
    5. *Amon* (*Bereishit* 19:38; *Bamidbar* 21:24)
    6. *Moav* (*Bereishit* 19:37, *Bereishit* 19:37)
    7. *Canaan* (*Bereishit* 9:18; *Bereishit* 12:6)
    8. *Teiman* (*Bereishit* 36:11; *Bereishit* 36:34)
    9. *Sichon* (*Bamidbar* 21:21; *Bamidbar* 21:28)
    10. *Peretz* (*Bereishit* 38:29; *Bamidbar* 33:19)
    11. *Gad* (*Bereishit* 30:11; *Bamidbar* 33:45)
    12. *Mitzraim* (*Bereishit* 10:6; *Bereishit* 12:10)
    13. *Ashur* (*Bereishit* 10:22; *Bereishit* 25:18)
    14. *Haran* (*Bereishit* 11:26; *Bamidbar* 32:36)
    15. *Eshkol* (*Bereishit* 14:13; *Bamidbar* 13:23)
    16. *Mamre* (*Bereishit* 14:24; *Bereishit* 13:18)
    17. *Gilad* (*Bamidbar* 27:1; *Bamidbar* 31:1)
    18. *Lavan* (*Bereishit* 24:29; *Devarim* 1:1)
    19. *Midian* (*Bereishit* 25:2; *Bereishit* 36:35)
    20. *Edom* (*Bereishit* 25:30; *Bereishit* 36:16)
    21. *Se'ir* (*Bereishit* 36:20; *Bereishit* 36:30)
    22. *Timna* (*Bereishit* 36:12; *Bereishit* 38:14)
    23. *Efraim* *Bereishit* 41:52; *Devarim* 34:2)
    24. *Menashe* (*Bereishit* 41:51; *Devarim* 34:2)
    25. *Naftali* (*Bereishit* 30:8; *Devarim* 34:2)
    26. *Yair* (*Bamidbar* 32:41; *Bamidbar* 32:41)
    27. *Novach* (*Bamidbar* 32:42; *Bamidbar* 32:42).

Interestingly, while the names *Yisrael*, *Yehuda* and *Amalek* all appear in the *Torah*, there do not seem to be any places in the *Torah* called *Yisrael*, *Yehuda* or *Amalek*.

PARSHAT NASO QUESTIONS

1. One person took poison, two people died of its effects. Explain?
2. Name the three camps in the "*midbar*" – "desert."
3. Who was expelled from each of the three camps?
4. What is the connection between *Parshat Naso, Gemara Bava Batra* and Chapter 119 in *Tehillim*?
5. If the 12 tribes brought their offerings on 12 consecutive days, it would follow that at least one of them brought his offering on *Shabbat*. We know however that only a "*korban tzibbur*" – "a public offering" could be brought on *Shabbat*. How then could a "*nasi*" – "prince" have brought his "*korban yachid*" – "his private or individual offering" on the *Shabbat*?
6. Why was the *nasi* for the tribe of *Efraim* honoured with the *Shabbat* offering?
7. May a *nazir* drink a Budweiser Beer?
8. Why does a *kohen* remove his shoes when he blesses the congregation during the repetition of the *shemoneh esrei*?
9. Today, pregnant women are warned of potential birth defects caused by drinking alcoholic beverages. Find the earliest *pasuk* in *Tanach* warning pregnant women to refrain from drinking alcoholic beverages?

10. How do we know that the "*mei hamarim ham'ararim*" – "the bitter waters of the *sotah*" were never used or needed in the desert?
11. In what way is a *nazir* even more restricted than the *kohen gadol*?
12. For what positive *mitzvah* that is performed in the *beit knesset* may one be permitted to interrupt his *shemoneh esrei*?
13. How many fifteens can you find in Judaism?
14. How many people are listed in the *Tanach* as having been a "*nazir*"?
15. I am a *kohen* with no reason to be excluded from performing the "*birkat kohanim*" – "the priestly blessings" in the *shul*. And yet, I find myself, not on the *bimah*, but in the midst of the congregation, answering "*amein*" to the other *kohanim* who are performing the "*birkat kohanim*" on the *bimah*. What happened?

16. If the only *kohen* in *shul* is a minor, may he perform the "*birkat kohanim*" for the congregation?
17. According to the *Ashkenazi* custom in "*chutz la'aretz*" – "outside of *Eretz Yisrael*," why is there "*birkat kohanim*" only on *Yom Tov* and then, only during the *mussaf* service?

18. In the "*birkat kohanim*," what does the word "*koh*" – "like this" come to teach us?
19. Did *Yaakov Avinu* know his grandfather *Avraham Avinu*?
20. What is the connection of *Parshat Naso* to the holiday of *Chanukah*?

PARSHAT NASO ANSWERS

1. The *gemara* (*Sota* 28a) says that upon drinking the bitter waters, an unfaithful woman accurately accused of being a *"sota"* – "woman accused of infidelity" would die. The man with whom she had the affair, would suffer the same punishment.

2. The innermost camp was *"Machaneh Shechinah"* – "the Divine Camp," surrounded by the *"Machaneh Leviyah"* – "Camp of the *Levi'im*" which was encircled by the *"Machaneh Yisrael"* – "the Camp of the *Israelites*" (*Rashi Bamidbar* 5:2).

3. The *"metzora"* – "leper" was sent out of all three camps; the *"zav"* – "one who has seminal emissions" was sent out of the two inner camps but was permitted in the *Machaneh Yisrael*; and the *"tamei"* – "one who was defiled because of contact with a dead body" was only excluded from the *Machaneh Shechinah* (*Rashi Bamidbar* 5:2).

4. *Naso* has 176 *pesukim*. Gemara *Bava Batra* has 176 *blatt* (two sided pages). Chapter 119 in *Tehillim* has 176 *pesukim*. Each is the longest in its category. *Naso* is the longest *parshah* in the *Torah*. *Bava Batra* is the longest *"mesechta"* – "tractate" in the *gemara*. Chapter 119 is the longest chapter in *Tehillim*. The number 176 represents the multiple of two important numbers, 22 and 8. Twenty-two represents perfection, as it is the number of letters in the Hebrew alphabet, the same alphabet used to write the words of the *Torah*. As well, 8 represents a level of perfection, above and beyond the physical world, symbolizing the supernatural. The *mitzvah* of *"mila"* – "circumcision" happens on the eighth day, where *Hashem* proclaims to *Avraham* "walk before Me and become complete" (*Bereishit* 17:1) and represents the supernatural perfection of the human body. *Chanukah* is eight days as it recalls the supernatural and miraculous event of the oil lasting longer than physically possible. Therefore, the number 176, the product of these two perfect numbers, 8 and 22, represents completeness and perfection. The three examples of 176 mentioned above emphasize the concept of perfection. We read *Naso* on the *Shabbat* after *Shavuot* which commemorates our total commitment to the written law, *Torah*. Chapter 119 of *Tehillim* is seen as *David Hamelech's* love song to *Torah* and his perfect and total commitment to it. And the section of *Bava Batra* having 176 *blatt* indicates that *"Torah shebaal peh"* – "the oral *Torah*" is an equally perfect component in our Jewish life.

5. There is a rule that *"korban tzibbur docheh shabbat"* – "a communal offering" can override *Shabbat* prohibitions, but a *"korban yachid"* – "private offering" cannot. No individual offering is ever brought on *Shabbat*. But it is clear from the offerings of the *nesi'im* at the dedication of the *mishkan*,

which stretched for 12 days, that at least one of these individual offerings would have to be brought on *Shabbat*. As the second *"nasi"* – "tribal prince" to bring his offering, *Netanel ben Tzuar* could have outdone *Nachshon,* the prince of *Yehuda,* by offering a larger portion. However, he reasoned, says the *midrash,* that by doing so, the amount offered would have steadily spiralled, until it would become too costly and unaffordable. He showed sensitivity to his fellow princes and minimized the jealousy and hatred between the tribes. The *midrash* tells us that for this reason, the *korban yachid* of the *nasi* could be brought on a *Shabbat,* as this was an individual offering that maintained the sense of the *"tzibur"* – "the community." Each of the offerings, perfectly identical, expressing a sense of unity, was a *korban yachid* infused with the spirit of a *korban tzibur.*

6. The *midrash* (*Tanchuma Bereishit* 43:16) states that *Yosef* kept *Shabbat,* even in *Paroh*'s palace, and for this reason his descendant *Elishama ben Amihud* was honoured with bringing the *Shabbat* offering. The *midrash* deduces this from the words *"utevoach tevach v'hachein"* (*Bereishit* 43:16) and states that in the palace, food would be normally prepared fresh every day. The only reason why they would need to prepare something in advance would be because of *Shabbat.*

7. Not a trick question at all. A *"nazir"* may drink any brand of beer. Many people err in translating *"sheichar"* (*Bamidbar* 6:3) as "alcoholic beverages." However, a *"nazir"* is only forbidden to partake of wine and wine by-products. Other non-wine based alcoholic beverages would be permitted to a *"nazir."* A more accurate translation of *"sheichar"* would be "wine based brandy."

8. The *Shulchan Aruch* (*Orach Chaim* 128:5) states that a *kohen* may not *"duchan"* or perform *"birkat kohanim"* – "perform the priestly blessings in the synagogue" until he has removed his shoes. The *Mishnah Berurah* (128:15) explains that if the laces of a *kohen*'s shoes became undone while he was in the midst of *duchaning,* he might sit down to tie his shoes. Members of the congregation might therefore assume that he is a disqualified *kohen* as a result of being the son of a divorcée who had married a *kohen,* or some other case of disqualification, thereby causing the *kohen,* busy tying his shoes, much embarrassment. Therefore *Chazal* suggested that *kohanim* not wear shoes while *duchaning.* The *Mishnah Berurah* explains that this is a *"lo plug"* – "one does not make exceptions to a general rule because of fear of misinterpretation of the particular part of the rule"; i.e., if one saw *kohanim* wearing loafers, they might assume that all shoes are permissible.

9. The *haftarah* of *Parshat Naso* begins with the story of the wife of *Manoach,* mother of *Shimshon,* being visited by an angel. The angel advises her that

even though she is barren, she will conceive and give birth (*Shoftim* 13:4). He then warns her not to drink wine or intoxicants while pregnant.

10. The *parshah* of *Sotah* begins (*Bamidbar* 5:11) with the standard *pasuk* "*vayedaber Hashem el Moshe leimor*" – "and *Hashem* spoke to *Moshe* saying." The *Medrash* (*Bamidbar Rabbah* 9) says that the use of the word "*leimor*" (which traditionally means that what *Hashem* tells *Moshe* should now be repeated to others) indicates that the laws of *Sotah* are meant "*l'dorot*" – "for all generations." *Rabbi Yonatan Eybeschitz* comments that this *Midrash* is teaching us that the laws of *Sotah* are only for future generations and were not meant for the period of time when the *Bnai Yisrael* were travelling through the desert. He brings a proof for his view by quoting a *gemara* (*Yoma* 75a) relating that in the desert, if a woman was unfaithful, her portion of *mann* would cease falling at the door to her tent, and would instead fall at the door of her father's tent. Her infidelity would now be exposed and would necessitate that she cease living with her husband and move back to her parents' home. Therefore, as long as the *mann* fell (i.e., the period of time that they were travelling through the desert), there was no need for the bitter waters of the *sotah*.

11. The *kohen gadol* could not perform the "*avoda*" – "service in the Temple" after drinking wine but could do so after eating grapes. The *nazir*, however, cannot drink wine or eat grapes.

12. If a *kohen* happens to be the only *kohen* in *shul* and he is in the middle of "*shemoneh esrei*" – "the silent *amidah* prayer" when the *chazzan* reaches "*birkat kohanim*" – "the priestly blessings," the *kohen* would be permitted to interrupt his *shemoneh esrei* to "*duchan*" – "perform the priestly blessings" (*Mishnah Berurah Orach Chaim* 128:106).

13. The number 15 appears prominently in Judaism. Eleven of them are:
    1. The obvious one for *Parshat Naso* is the *Birkat Kohanim* (*Bamidbar* 6:24–26) which consists of fifteen words.
    2. There are 15 parts to the *Pesach Seder*.
    3. Fifteen in Hebrew can be written as a "*yud*" and a "*heh*," which is one of the names of *Hashem*.
    4. The Hebrew words for man and woman are "*ish*" and "*isha*." The common letters to both words are "*alef*" and "*shin*." The two uncommon letters are "*yud*" and "*heh*," indicating that the presence of *Hashem* in their union will ensure success (*Gemara Sotah* 17a).
    5. Fifteen or multiples of fifteen appear throughout the story of the flood in the time of *Noach*. The waters rose 15 *amot* above the highest mountains (*Bereishit* 7:20). The water covered the earth for 150 days (*Bereishit* 7:24). The ark measured 300 *amot* by 50 *amot* which results in an area of 15,000 sq. *amot* and with each level of the ark having a height of 10

amot (30 amot total divided by three), there were 150,000 cubic amot on each level (*Kli Yakar Bereishit* 6:15).

6. The number of steps from the *Ezrat Nashim* (the women's courtyard) in the *Beit Hamikdash* to the *Ezrat Yisrael* (the *Israelite* courtyard) was 15 (*Mishnah Sukkah* 5:4).

7. The *gemara* (*Yevamot* 2a) lists fifteen categories of women with whom familial relations are forbidden as incestuous.

8. There are fifteen *berachot* that begin the "*tefillat shacharit*" – "the morning prayers."

9. The moon is always fullest at the 15th of the Hebrew month.

10. A number of special days in the calendar fall on the 15th of the month, including *Pesach, Sukkot, Tu B'Shvat, Tu B'Av, Shushan Purim*.

11. There are fifteen stages in the *dayenu* section of the *Haggadah*.

14. There were three people mentioned in *Tanach* as having accepted the oath of being a *nazir*: *Shimshon* (*Shoftim* 13:5), *Shmuel* (*Shmuel* 1:1;11) and *Avshalom* (*Nazir* 4b). However, *Shimshon* is the only one identified specifically as a *nazir*.

15. The *Shulchan Aruch* (*Orach Chaim* 128:25) says that if there are more than 10 people in *shul* and all of them are *kohanim*, then ten *kohanim* stay in the congregation and the rest go up to the *bimah* to perform the "*birkat kohanim*."

16. The *Shulchan Aruch* (*Orach Chaim* 128:34) rules that if the only *kohen* in the *shul* is a minor, he may not perform the "*birkat kohanim*." However, if there are other *kohanim* who are adults, the minor may go up with them to perform "*birkat kohanim*" as a form of education and training.

17. The *Ramah* (*Shulchan Aruch Orach Chaim* 128:44) explains that since the priestly blessings have to be done in a spirit of "*ahavah*" – "love" and "*simcha*" – "joy," it should only be done on *Yom Tov*, because on all other days, one is not filled with love and joy, due to worry over financial matters and being absent from work; and even then, it may only be performed at *mussaf*, as one can then begin to feel close to enjoying the *simcha* of *yom tov* and the impending *yom tov* meal. It would be different in *Eretz Yisrael*, as there, one is always filled with additional *simcha* from being in our homeland.

18. The *midrash* (*Bereishit Rabbah* 43:8) states that *Bnai Yisrael* merited receiving the priestly blessings from the three patriarchs, *Avraham, Yitzchak* and *Yaakov*. The word "*koh*" appears in the *Torah* referring to each of the patriarchs. Regarding *Avraham* it is written "*koh yihiye zaracha*" – "like this should your offspring be" (*Bereishit* 15:5); regarding *Yitzchak* at the *akeidah*, it is written "*vaani vehanaar neilchah ad koh*" – "and I and the lad will proceed until here" (*Bereishit* 22:5); and regarding *Yaakov* it is written

at the giving of the *Torah* on *Har Sinai* "*koh tamar l'bet Yaakov*" – "so shall you say to the house of *Yaakov*" (*Shemot* 19:3).

19. The *Baal Haturim* (*Bamidbar* 6:24) quotes the *Seder Olam, perek* 1 and connects the 15 words of the *birkat kohanim* to the 15 years when all three of the patriarchs were alive. It is in their "*zechut*" – "merit" that the Jewish people receive blessings. *Avraham* was 100 years old at the birth of *Yitzchak* and *Yitzchak* was 60 years old at the birth of *Yaakov*. Since *Avraham* lived to 175, it follows that *Yaakov* was 15 years old when *Avraham* passed away.

20. The *Baal Haturim* (*Bamidbar* 7:1) points out that the section dealing with the "*chanukat hamishkan*" – "dedication of the *mishkan*" is situated between the "*birkat kohanim*" and the beginning of the next *parshah, Behaalotcha*, which speaks about the kindling of the *menorah*, as a hint to the *Chashmonaim*, the priestly family in the *Chanukah* story who will kindle the *menorah* in the future. The *Baal Haturim* refers us to the commentary of the *Ramban* (*Bamidbar* 8:2). The *Ramban* points out that when the twelve tribes brought their offerings in the *mishkan*, and the tribe of *Levi* was excluded, *Hashem* spoke to *Moshe* and said "speak to *Aharon* and tell him" (*Bamidbar* 8:2) do not worry, there will be yet another *Chanukah* in the future which will incorporate the kindling of "*neirot*" on the *menorah*; a time when the *Chashmonaim*, your priestly descendants, will be victorious with great miracles, and that *Chanukah* and the accompanying kindling of lights will endure forever, long after the destruction of the temples.

PARSHAT BEHAALOTCHA QUESTIONS

1. Why are there two inverted "*nuns*" before and after the *parshah* of "*vayehi binsoa*" (*Bamidbar* 10:35–36)?
2. What did the *mann* not taste like and why?
3. Where else in *Tanach* do we find reversed "*nuns*"?
4. How were *Eldad* and *Meidad* (*Bamidbar* 11:26) related to *Moshe Rabbeinu*?
5. Where do we find a *pasuk* in the *Torah* containing the words "*Bnai Yisrael*" five times and why is there such a concentration of "*Bnai Yisrael*" in one *pasuk*?
6. I was first on *Nisan* 21, 2448, I was first on *Nisan* 1, 2449, and I was first on *Iyar* 20, 2449 – who am I?

7. The "*na'ar*" – "lad" mentioned in *Bamidbar* 11:27 is identified by *Rashi* as *Gershom*, the son of *Moshe*. Which other people in the *Torah* are identified by the term "*na'ar*"?
8. We have a number of *mitzvot* with the concept of *tashlumin*; i.e., if you neglect to perform the *mitzvah* at the first and correct opportunity, you are given another chance to do it. Name a *mitzvah* where one who was obligated to perform the *mitzvah* in its correct time neglected to do it and when given the opportunity for *tashlumin*, is now forbidden from performing the *mitzvah*? (Note: nothing has changed in terms of the person's status, spiritually or physically, between the two opportunities).

9. Give two examples of "*tashlumim*" (a second chance to fulfill a missed *mitzvah*) and the major difference between the two examples.
10. Many times *Hashem* is compared to a Father. Where in *Parshat Behaalotcha* is *Hashem* actually compared to a Mother?
11. What ultimately happened to the "*chatzotzrot*" – "trumpets"?
12. In which chapter in the *Torah* do we find *Eldad* and *Meidad* referred to by different names and in the same chapter, we find the name of their father *Elitzafan ben Parnach*?

13. From where in *Parshat Behaalotcha* do we deduce that fish do not require *shechita*?
14. *Travel & Leisure* is a popular travel magazine. Where do we find two consecutive *pesukim*; the first *pasuk* embodying the concept of Travel and the second embodying the concept of Leisure?
15. From which *pasuk* do we derive the custom of incorporating phrases like "*baruch Hashem*," "*im yirtzeh Hashem*" etc., in our everyday language?
16. Name at least two cases where someone who was not obligated to bring the *korban pesach* in *Nisan* and who was not impure at the time nor was travelling at the time, is nevertheless required to bring the *pesach sheni*.

17. Name two things that were unique about the first time the *menorah* was lit in the *mishkan*.

18. What is the minimum number of letters necessary for a *Sefer Torah* to be considered a *davar "sheb'kedushah"* – "a holy article"?

19. If *Moshe* made one *menorah*, who made ten *menorahs*?

20. Three women, one Jewish, one Egyptian and one Persian, all connected by the same ailment?

PARSHAT BEHAALOTCHA ANSWERS

1. *Rashi* explains that these letters serve to divide these *pesukim* from the negative behaviour of *Bnai Yisrael* before these *pesukim,* and their negative behaviour after the *pesukim. Hashem* strategically placed the *"nuns"* in this section of the *Torah,* to separate the story, before these *pesukim,* of the *"eirev rav"* – "a group of outcasts who journeyed from *Mitzrayim* with *Bnai Yisrael"* and who complained about the lack of meat in the desert (*Bamidbar* 10:33); from the story, after these *pesukim,* about the *"mitonenim"* – "members of *Bnai Yisrael* who complained about their exhaustion from the constant travelling" (*Bamidbar* 11:1). *Rabbi Yonatan Eybeschutz* in his work, *Tiferet Yonatan,* points out that the inverted *"nun"* letters predict a time in the future, when the *"aron"* – "holy ark" would be hidden and *Bnai Yisrael* would no longer have its protection. This would be a time of *"nefila"* – "downfall" for the Jewish people. The *gemara* (*Berachot* 60b) adds: "why don't we say a phrase starting with *"nun"* in *ashrei*? Since it represents the errors of *Bnai Yisrael,* their *nefillah,* in the desert, when our actions caused the *"aron"* to travel from the camp and abandon us.

2. *Rashi* comments that *"mann"* – "heavenly food" tasted like all foods except for cucumber, melon, leek, onion and garlic, as they are harmful to nursing women (*Rashi Bamidbar* 11:5).

3. In total, there are nine inverted '*nuns*' in the *Tanach;* two in *Parshat Behaalotcha;* and the other seven appear in *perek* 107 of *Tehillim.*

4. The *Targum Yonatan* (*Bamidbar* 11:26) identifies the parents of *Eldad* and *Meidad* as *Elitzafan,* the son of *Parnach,* and *Yocheved,* the daughter of *Levi.* Therefore *Moshe* was their half-brother, through their common mother, *Yocheved.*

5. The *pasuk* is obviously in *Parshat Behaalotcha.* In *Bamidbar* 8:19, we find the words *"Bnai Yisrael"* five times. *Rashi* comments that as a demonstration of *Hashem's* love of *Bnai Yisrael,* he repeated the words *"Bnai Yisrael"* five times in one *pasuk,* the same number as the *Five Books of the Torah. Rav Aharon Adler* is quoted in the *Torah Tidbits* with a beautiful explanation of this rather cryptic *Rashi.* If you examine the *pasuk* closely, you will see the entire narrative of the *Five Books of the Torah.* The first mention of *Bnai Yisrael* in the *pasuk* is connected twice to the verb "to give" which epitomizes *Bereishit,* the book of giving the world to man and giving *Eretz Yisrael* to *Bnai Yisrael;* the second *Bnai Yisrael* in the *pasuk* is connected to the concept of *avoda,* which mirrors *Shemot,* the book of *"avdut"* – "servitude" and *"avoda"* – "service to *Hashem* in the *mishkan";* the third reference to *Bnai Yisrael* in the *pasuk* is connected to *"kapara"* – "atonement" and most of the book of *Vayikra* deals with atonement and sacrificial offerings; the

fourth *Bnai Yisrael* is connected to *"negef"* – "plagues" and indeed the Book of *Bamidbar* deals extensively with the trials and tribulations of *Bnai Yisrael* and the numerous plagues that befell them as they journeyed through the desert; and the finally, the fifth *Bnai Yisrael* in the *pasuk* is connected to the word *"b'geshet"* – "approaching or coming closer," and the book of *Devarim* talks about the final days in the desert, as they approached *Eretz Yisrael*.

6. *Nachshon ben Aminadav*, the prince of the tribe of *Yehudah*, was the first to jump into the *"yam suf"* – "Reed Sea" on *Nisan 21, 2448*; the first to bring the sacrifice of the *"nesi'im"* – "tribal princes" on *Nisan 1, 2449*; and the first in the travel formation on *Iyar 20, 2449*.

7. The following individuals are called *"na'ar"* in the *Torah* (only one reference is provided for each name; some of the following people are called *"na'ar"* numerous times throughout *Torah*): *Yishmael (Bereishit 18:7; Bereishit 21:12); Yitzchak (Bereishit 22:5); Shechem (Bereishit 34:19); Yosef (Bereishit 37:2); Binyamin (Bereishit 43:8); Moshe (Shemot 2:6); Yehoshua (Shemot 33:11);* and *Gershom (Bamidbar 11:27)*. We also find three pairs of individuals who are called *"nearim"* – "lads"; namely; *Yishmael* and *Eliezer (Bereishit 22:3); Yaakov* and *Eisav (Bereishit 25:27);* and *Menashe* and *Efraim (Bereishit 48:16)*.

8. A woman is obligated to bring the *"korban Pesach"* – "the Passover sacrifice" *(Rambam, Hilchot Korban Pesach 1:1)*. If one is unable to offer the *korban Pesach* on its correct date, by virtue of being away from home or impure, one is then given the opportunity of offering the sacrifice one month later on the 14th day of *Iyar (Bamidbar 9:11)*. This is called the *"Pesach Sheini"* – "the second *Pesach*." In terms of *Pesach Sheini*, a woman only has an optional obligation, because offering the sacrifice on *Pesach Sheini* is a *"mitzvat asei shehazman grama"* – "a time bound *mitzvah*," and women are not obligated in that category of *mitzvot (Rambam, Hilchot Korban Pesach 5:8)*. The original *Korban Pesach* is also a *mitzvat asei shehazman grama*; but women have an additional special obligation in that *mitzvah*, because they were also a part of the historical, miraculous exodus from *Mitzrayim*. However, if the evening of the 14th of *Iyar*, the time for the *Pesach Sheini*, were to occur on a *Shabbat*, then a woman would not even be permitted to optionally offer this sacrifice, because an optional sacrifice cannot override the obligations of *Shabbat*. Therefore, this is a case where one who was obligated to perform the *mitzvah* in its correct time, and neglected to do it, is forbidden from performing the *mitzvah* when given the opportunity for *"tashlumin"* – "an additional opportunity to perform the *mitzvah*."

9. Two examples of *tashlumim* are *Pesach Sheini* (in *Parshat Behaalotcha*) and making up missed *tefillot*. The difference is that even though the *Torah* only itemizes travel and impurity as reasons for *Pesach Sheini*, in actual fact, *Pesach Sheini* can be brought even in a case where one intentionally

did not participate in the initial *Korban Pesach*. However, if one intentionally missed *tefillah*, he may no longer make up the missed prayers (*Gemara Berachot* 26a). While *Halacha* gives one the opportunity to voluntarily add an additional prayer to compensate for an intentionally missed prayer, this is not considered "*tashlumim*" – "making up" the missed prayer, but rather a "*nedava*"; a voluntary contribution of a *tefillah*.

10. In *Bamidbar* 11:8, the taste of "*mann*" is compared, in the *Torah*'s words, to "*l'shad hashemen*." The *gemara* (*Yoma* 75a) explains that "*shad*" is a woman's breast. Hence, *mann* is compared to mother's milk. It is the only food that a baby wants or needs; similarly, *mann* was the only food desired and needed by *Bnai Yisrael*. A baby is completely dependent on its mother for nourishment. Likewise, *Bnai Yisrael,* in the desert, were completely dependent on *Hashem* for sustenance. As well, breast milk has the property of tasting like whatever the mother has recently eaten, similar to *mann*, which had the taste that one desired, other than the five foods, cucumber, melon, leek, onion and garlic, mentioned in the *Torah*. Just as mother's milk is a complete food and creates a closeness between mother and child; so, too, *mann* was a complete food and created a closeness between *Hashem* and *Bnai Yisrael*.

11. *Rashi* (*Bamidbar* 10:2) quotes the *Midrash Tanchuma* that says that the wording "*asay lecha*" – "make for yourself" indicates that only *Moshe Rabbeinu* was permitted to use the two silver trumpets. Ultimately, they were hidden before *Moshe* died (*Rashi Devarim* 31:28).

12. *Bamidbar* 34:19–28 lists the names of those who would lead their tribes into *Eretz Yisrael*. The head of the tribe of *Binyamin* was *Elidad ben Kislon* and the head of the tribe of *Efraim* was *Kemuel ben Shiftan*. These two individuals are identified by the *Midrash Rabba* (15:15) as *Eldad* and *Meidad*. (See also *Baal Haturim* on *Bamidbar* 34:21). Their father is mentioned in *Bamidbar* 34:25 as the head of the tribe of *Zevulun*. (See also *Parshat Behaalotcha* riddle #4).

13. The *Torah Temimah* (*Bamidbar* 11:22) quotes the *gemara* (*Chulin* 27b) that we deduce the *halacha* that fish do not require "*shechita*" – "ritual slaughtering" from the *pasuk* "Could enough sheep and cattle be slaughtered to feed all of Israel? Could all the fish in the sea be gathered to feed all of Israel"? By referring to sheep and cattle as "slaughtered" and fish as "gathered," we deduce the law that fish do not require *shechita*.

14. The *pesukim* are "*vayehi binsoa*" (*Bamidbar* 9:18) which speaks about Travel and the following *pasuk* "*uvenucho yomar*" (*Bamidbar* 10:36) which deals with resting or Leisure. Hence "Travel & Leisure."

15. The *Shlah Hakadosh* (*Rabbi Yeshaya Halevi Horowitz*, author of *Shnei Luchot Habrit*) points out that in just six *pesukim*, the words "*al pi Hashem*" – "according to the word of *Hashem*" is repeated seven times (*Bamidbar* 9:18–23), in describing the journeys of the *Bnai Yisrael* in the desert. Why

is it so necessary to repeat that every travel and every journey that was done was based on the word of *Hashem*? The *Shlah* deduces from these *pesukim* that we have to include *Hashem* in our daily conversation, and that this is the source for Jews, no matter where they go or wherever they arrive, to always say that they have arrived with *Hashem*'s help. We are all here because *Hashem* has a path and journey that all of us are meant to take and wherever we go and whatever we do, should always be "*al pi Hashem*."

16. The two cases would be:
    1. A convert who converted within the 30 days after *Pesach*.
    2. The minor who became *Bar Mitzvah* within the 30 days after *Pesach* (*Rambam Hilchot Korban Pesach* 5:7).

    Both would be required to bring the *Pesach Sheini*. The *Rambam* clarifies that in the case of a minor, if someone was required to bring the *Korban Pesach* and included the minor in his *korban*, then the minor would be exempt from bringing the *Pesach Sheini*.

17. First, because the *pasuk* says "*yaaroch oto*" – "he should arrange it" (*Shemot* 27:21), only the cleaning and preparation of the *menorah* had to be done by a *kohen*, but the actual lighting of the *menorah* need not be done by a *kohen* (*Rambam Hilchot Beit Hamikdash* 9:7). However, the very first lighting of the *menorah* was unique in that it had to be done by *Aharon Hakohen*. Second, the first time that the *menorah* was to be lit, was obviously not preceded by cleaning; however, each subsequent lighting had to be preceded by "*hatava*" – "cleaning."

18. The minimum number of letters required by a "*Sefer Torah*" – "a Torah scroll" in order for it to be considered a "*davar shebikedusha*" – "a holy object" is 85. This corresponds to the number of letters in the two sentence "*sefer*" of "*vayehi binsoa*" (*Bamidbar* 10:35–36), which is considered to be a "*sefer bifnei atzmo*" – "a unique and separate book of the *Torah*." The *Baal Haturim* (*Bamidbar* 11:1) quotes a *gemara* (*Shabbat* 116a) which says that a Torah scroll is considered a *davar shebikedusha* and should be saved from fire on *Shabbat* if it still has 85 letters intact, for the "smallest book" in the *Torah* is the two *pasuk* book of "*vayehi binsoa*" which consists of 85 letters. To carry the significance of the number 85 even further, the *Baal Haturim* cites a source which says that the book of *Rut* is considered a holy book because it has 85 sentences, which is equal to the *gematriya* of *Boaz*, one of the leading characters in *Megillat Rut*. The *Torah Temima* on the same *pasuk* cites a *Mishnah* (*Yadayim* 3:5) which also deals with the holiness of a scroll containing at least 85 letters; namely: "a scroll on which the writing has become erased and eighty-five letters remain, as many as are in the section beginning, "And it came to pass when the ark set forward" (*Bamidbar* 10:35–36) defiles the hands."

19. *Shlomo Hamelech* made 10 *menorahs* (*Divrei Hayamim* 2:4:7). The *Baal Haturim* says that the "*remez*" – "hint" in *Parshat Behaalotcha* is from the words "*kain asa et hamenorah*" – "thus did he make the *menorah*" (*Bamidbar* 8:4). The *Baal Haturim* points out that the word "*kain*" has a *gematriya* of 70 (i.e., 10 *menorahs* × 7 wicks), and the *gematriya* of the word "*asa*" is equal to *Shlomo*.

20. They are *Bitya,* daughter of *Paroh*; *Miriam*; and *Vashti*. They all had "*tzaraat*" – "leprosy" (*Shemot Rabbah* 1:23; *Bamidbar* 12:10; *Rashi Megillat Esther* 1:12).

PARSHAT SHLACH QUESTIONS

1. Where is there a hint to *Purim* in *Parshat Shlach*?
2. What is the connection between the sin of the *"meraglim"* – "spies" and the date the Jews were exiled from *Eretz Yisrael* after the destruction of the first *Beit Hamikdash*?
3. How many other times in *Tanach* were *"meraglim"* – "spies" sent?
4. Who built *Chevron*?
5. Which two sins kept the *Bnai Yisrael* in the desert for 40 years?
6. Who/What/Where are *"kruspedin"*?
7. In *Bamidbar* 13:23, it says that the spies came to *Nachal Eshkol* and they then cut down a branch with a cluster of grapes. The next *pasuk* (13:24) tells us that they called the place *"Nachal Eshkol"* – "the valley of the cluster of grapes" because it was there that they cut the cluster of grapes. Was it not already called *Nachal Eshkol* in *Bamidbar* 13:23?
8. Who was the *"mekoshesh"* – "the gatherer of wood" in *Bamidbar* 15:32?
9. From where in *Parshat Shlach* can we learn that doing something *"l'shem shamayim"* – "for the sake of heaven" can be deathly?
10. On which *Shabbat* did the *"mekoshesh"* desecrate the *Shabbat*?
11. How many people carried the cluster of grapes?
12. From where do we derive the principle that a congregation requires a minimum of ten individuals?
13. Wearing *"tzitzit"* is supposed to remind one of all the other *mitzvot* in the *Torah*. How is this concept connected to the word and construction of the *"tzitzit"*?
14. Wearing *"tzitzit"* is supposed to remind one of all the other *mitzvot* in the *Torah*. Where do we find a *gematriya* hint to this concept in the *parshah* of *"tzitzit"*?
15. Where is one not permitted to have the strings of his *"tzitzit"* exposed?
16. From where in *Parshat Shlach* do we learn that a lie must contain some element of truth in order for it to be believed?
17. How does the *mitzvah* of *"challah"* – "setting aside one piece of dough from each batch of bread that we make," differ from all other *"mitzvot Hateluyot Ba'aretz"* – "mitzvot that are connected to *Eretz Yisrael*"?
18. In the *Torah*, *Yehoshua* is referred to as *Yehoshua* *"bin"* Nun. Almost everyone else in the *Torah* is referred to as *"ben"* someone. Why the difference in respect to *Yehoshua*?
19. *Moshe Rabbeinu* was known as the most humble man on the face of the earth. *Yehoshua* also possessed this trait. How was *Moshe*'s humility connected to *Yehoshua*'s humility?
20. Who was *Kalev*'s wife?

PARSHAT SHLACH ANSWERS

1. There are two possible hints to *Purim* in *Parshat Shlach*:
   1. When *Moshe* instructed the spies, he gave them certain guidelines. One of these was to see whether the cities were fortified. *Rashi* (*Bamidbar* 13:19) explains that *Moshe* wanted to know whether these were walled cities or not. Since *Yehoshua* was one of the spies, this would have relevance in terms of the laws concerning *Purim* that depend on whether the city had a wall from the "time of *Yehoshua Bin Nun*."
   2. One of the punishments for the incident with the spies was an attack by *Amalek*, the same nation from which *Haman* descended (*Rashi Bamidbar* 14:43).

2. The *Baal Haturim* (*Bamidbar* 13:2) says that the *gematriya* of the title word of the *parshah* "*shlach*" is 338, and he quotes the *gemara* (*Avodah Zara* 9a) which states that the destruction of the *Beit Hamikdash* and the exile began in the year 3338, thereby connecting the sin of the *meraglim* to the eventual exile of our people.

3. There are a six occurrences of spies in *Tanach*:
   1. *Moshe* sent spies to scout out *Yazer* (*Bamidbar* 21:32).
   2. *Yehoshua* sent spies before entering *Eretz Canaan* (*Yehoshua* 2:1).
   3. *Yehoshua* sent spies to *Ai* (*Yehoshua* 7:2).
   4. *Bnai Dan* sent spies to scout out their "*nachala*" – "portion in the land" (*Shoftim* 18:2).
   5. *David* sent spies to verify that *Shaul* was chasing him (*Shmuel* 1:26:4).
   6. *Avshalom* sent spies to gather support for his rebellion (*Shmuel* 2:15:10).

4. *Cham* the son of *Noach* (*Rashi* 13:22). *Rashi* relates that *Cham* was the father of *Canaan* and *Mitzrayim*, and that he built cities for both; *Chevron* for *Canaan* and *Tzoan* for *Mitzrayim*.

5. The sins of the golden calf and the *meraglim* (*Rashi* 14:33). From the moment they made the golden calf, the decree of exclusion from entering the *Land of Israel* entered the mind of *Hashem*, but He waited for them and postponed their punishment until their measure of sin was full at the time of the sin of the *meraglim*.

6. "*Kruspedin*" are "*tzitzit*" in *Aramaic* (*Targum Onkelos, Bamidbar* 15:38).

7. The *Vilna Gaon* (*Peninim Mishulchan Hagra*) says that the place was already called *Nachal Eshkol* because of the person *Eshkol* mentioned in *Bereishit* 14:24. There, his name, *Eshkol*, is spelled without a *vav*, as in the name of the place *Nachal Eshkol* in *Bamidbar* 13:23. The next *pasuk* (*Bamidbar* 13:24) spells *Nachal Eshkol* with a *vav*, to reflect the additional reason for the name of the place; namely, the cutting of the grape cluster. The *Gaon* brings proof for his theory of "*chaser – malay*" – "the presence and absence of a *vav* in

the word" from two *gemarot* (*Sukkah 6b* and *Zevachim 37b*) where similar lessons are derived from the words *"sukkot"* and *"karnot."*

8. The *Gemara* (*Shabbat 96b*) quotes *Rabbi Akiva* as saying that the *"mekoshesh"* – "wood gatherer" was *Tzelaphchad. Rabbi Akiva* deduces this from the fact that the *pasuk* (*Bamidbar 15:32*) says that the *Bnai Yisrael* were in the *"midbar"* – "the desert" and they found a man gathering wood on *Shabbat.* Later on, when the daughters of *Tzelaphchad* were claiming their inheritance rights, they began with the statement "our father died in the desert" (*Bamidbar 27:3*). From the location "in the desert" common to both incidents, *Rabbi Akiva* deduces that this was *Tzelaphchad.* The *Daat Zekeinim* (*Bamidbar 15:32*) says that the words *"eitzim b'yom"* have the same *gematriya* as *Tzelaphchad.*

9. The *Targum Yonatan* (*Bamidbar 15:32*) says that the *"mekoshesh,"* the one who gathered wood on *Shabbat,* did so intentionally, in order to teach a lesson to *Bnai Yisrael.* Since the generation of the desert knew that as a result of the sin of the spies, they were destined to perish in the desert, they assumed that the laws of the *Torah* were no longer relevant, and would only be re-activated when the people would enter *Eretz Yisrael.* The *"mekoshesh"* therefore openly desecrated the Laws of *Shabbat,* so that he would be publicly punished, and the people would therefore understand that the laws were still relevant.

10. When the *mekoshesh* gathered wood and thereby desecrated *Shabbat,* it was the second *Shabbat* after receiving the commandment to observe the laws of *Shabbat.* The *Bnai Yisrael,* as a community, only kept one *Shabbat.* The *Daat Zekeinim* (*Bamidbar 15:32*) quotes a *gemara* (*Shabbat 118*) that had they kept two consecutive *Shabbatot,* no nation would have ever been able to rule over them.

11. *Rashi* (*Bamidbar 13:23*) says that there were two parallel poles supported by 4 men and two additional poles at right angles to the first two poles, supported by an additional 4 men; 8 men in total carrying the cluster of grapes.

12. *Rashi* (*Bamidbar 14:27*) in explaining how we arrive at the concept of a *"minyan"* – "a quorum of ten men needed to recite certain parts of Jewish communal prayer" quotes the *gemara* (*Megillah 23b*) where it is derived from the use of the phrase *"eidah hara'ah"* – "evil congregation" in our *pasuk.* Since there were 12 spies and two of them, *Yehoshua* and *Calev* were righteous, 10 would have been considered evil or *"ra'ah."* Therefore 10 equals an *"eidah"* or congregation.

13. *Rashi* (*Bamidbar 15:39*) points out that the *gematriya* of the word *"tzitzit"* is 600 and adding the 8 strings and 5 knots equals 613, the number of *mitzvot* in the *Torah.*

14. In the section of the *Torah* that speaks about "*tzitzit*" – "the fringed four corner garment" that is an integral part of the *Kriat Shema* prayer that we say three times daily, the *pasuk* says "*u'zechartem et kol mitzvot Hashem*" – "and you will remember all the commandments of *Hashem*" (*Bamidbar* 15:39). The *gematriyah* of "*kol mitzvot Hashem*" is 612 (*Gerrer Rebbe Gemara Nedarim* 32a). Therefore by doing the one *mitzvah* of *tzitzit*, you are remembering the other 612 *mitzvot*. As well, 612 is the *gematriyah* of "*brit*" – "covenant" and by observing *Shabbat*, which is also referred to as a "*brit*" (*Shemot* 31:16), its merit is equal to observing the other 612 *mitzvot*.

15. When one visits a "*beit hakvorot*" – "cemetery," one should keep his "*tzitzit*" covered so as not to appear to be mocking the dead, who are not able to perform this *mitzvah* (*Mishnah Berurah* 23:3).

16. *Rashi* (*Bamidbar* 13:27) says that the spies began their report by stating the truth that Israel is a land flowing with milk and honey. This truth helped validate the many untruths that they spoke concerning the *Land of Israel* and helped sway the "public opinion" of the entire nation regarding the decision to continue to the *Land of Israel*.

17. All the commandments that are dependent on being in *Eretz Yisrael* were only applicable after the possession and division of the land (14 years after entering), except for the *mitzvah* of *challah* which was incumbent upon the *Bnai Yisrael* immediately upon entry into the land. This is stated by *Rashi* (*Bamidbar* 15:18) and he quotes the *Sifrei* (*Bamidbar* 110:1) who derives this from the strange use of the word "*b'voachem*" – "when you enter," rather than the more common phrase "*ki tavo'u*."

18. *Talelei Orot* quotes a fascinating *midrash* (*Bereishit Rabbah Lech Lecha* 47) which relates that when *Hashem* changed *Sarai*'s name to *Sarah*, the displaced *yud* complained that it was being removed from the name of one of our matriarchs. *Hashem* replied and comforted the *yud* by telling it that previously it had been the last letter of *Sarai*, but that it would now be the first letter of a future leader of Israel, *Yehoshua*, whose name was changed from *Hoshea* by the addition of this *yud*. The *Steipler Rav* noted that when the *yud* occupied the last letter position of *Sarai*'s name, it had no vowels. When it moved to the front of *Yehoshua*'s name, it now had a *shva* or two dots beneath it. The *Steipler Rav* indicated that these two dots came from the *segol* or three dots under the *bet* of *ben* and therefore what was left under the *bet* of *ben* was just one dot or a *chirik*. Hence the pronunciation of the word as *bin*.

19. The *Targum Yonatan* (*Bamidbar* 13:16) tells us that *Moshe* changed *Hoshea bin Nun*'s name to *Yehoshua* because *Moshe* recognized that *Yehoshua* was humble. In explaining the comment by the *Targum Yonatan*, Rabbi Moshe Bogomilsky in the *sefer*, *Vedibarta Bam*, notes that when the *Torah* tells us

about *Moshe's* humility (*Bamidbar* 12:3), the *Torah* spells the word "*anav*" – "humble" without a "*yud*." When *Moshe Rabbeinu* was instructed to write that he was the humblest of all men, he was uncomfortable writing praises about himself, and while he had to fulfill *Hashem's* request, he left out the *yud* from the word *anav* as a testament to his humility. Upon seeing the humility of *Hoshea, Moshe Rabbeinu* gifted him with the humble *yud*, the smallest letter of the "*alef bet*" – "the Hebrew alphabet," that *Moshe* had left out of the word *anav.*

20. There are two sources in the *gemara.* According to *Sotah* 12a, it was *Miriam.* According to *Megillah* 13a, it was *Bitya Bat Paroh.* It is unclear whether these are two conflicting opinions, or whether *Kalev* was in fact married to both of them.

PARSHAT KORACH QUESTIONS

1. Three consecutive *parshiyot*. There is a 'p' in *Parshat Korach*; there is a 'p' in *Parshat Chukat*; and there is a 'p' in *Parshat Balak*. What are these three 'p's and what is the common thread that connects them?

2. Find a *pasuk* in the *Torah*, where, among its 17 words, are one verb, 10 names and the remaining six words are all from the same root word?

3. How many people in the *Torah* "fell on their faces?"

4. How did *Korach* become wealthy?

5. Why did *Korach* need three hundred mules?

6. What six *parshiyot* are named for people?

7. What did *Yitzhar* have in common with *Eisav*?

8. Who was *Korach*'s most famous descendant?

9. There are four categories of males; namely, *kohen, levi, yisrael* and non-*Jew*, and four categories of females; namely, *bat kohen, bat levi, bat yisrael* and non-*Jewess*. Which combinations of males and females would produce firstborns that would require a *pidyon haben* (redemption of the firstborn ceremony)?

10. *Datan*'s wife is featured in one of the stories in *Shemot*. Which story and what was her involvement?

11. Who was *Korach*'s grandfather?

12. "A land flowing with milk and honey" describes which country?

13. The law of "*pidyon haben*" – "redemption of the firstborn" appears in *Parshat Korach* (*Bamidbar* 18:15). Attendance at a *pidyon haben* is quite rare because of the fact that only males can be redeemed, a firstborn's parents who are *kohanim* or *levi'im* are exempt, and other exemptions that apply to this *mitzvah*. How is it possible for a father to attend at the *pidyon haben* of two of his children?

14. *Hashem*'s covenant with the *kohanim* is described as a "*brit melach*" – "a covenant of salt." Why is this covenant compared to salt?

15. From where do we derive the principle that we should seek good neighbours?

16. *Vayikra* 7:23 prohibits eating "*cheilev*" – "animal fat or suet." Where does the *Torah* allow eating "*cheilev*"?

17. *Yitzhar*, the best and the worst? Explain.

18. There are four ways to die expressed in *Parshat Korach*. What are they?

19. *Yekev* is a pit in front of the wine press; all juice squeezed from the grapes flow into the *yekev* (*Bamidbar* 18:27). What are "*yikvei hamelech*"?

20. Where do we find the following:
    1. An inanimate object that exhibits human characteristics.
    2. An inanimate object that exhibits plant-like characteristics.

PARSHAT KORACH ANSWERS

1. The "p" in this week's *Parshat Korach* is *"pi ha'aretz"* – "the mouth of the earth that opened to swallow *Korach*"; the "p" in next week's *Parshat Chukat* is the *"pi habe'er"* – "the mouth of *Miriam's* well, that provided water until her death"; and the "p" in *Parshat Balak* is the *"pi ha'aton"* – "the mouth of the donkey of *Bilaam*." All are connected by the fact that they were all created on the first Friday evening, *"bain hashmashot"* – "at twilight" (*Mishnah Pirkei Avot* 5:7).

2. The first *pasuk* in *Korach* (*Bamidbar* 16:1) has one verb *"vayikach"* – "and he took"; 10 names (*Korach, Yitzhar, Kehat, Levi, Datan, Aviram, Eliav, On, Pelet, Reuven*); the remaining six words are all derivatives of the root *"ben"* – "son of."

3. Three people are mentioned in the *Torah* as having "fallen on their faces." The phrase *"vayipol al panav"* – "and he fell on his face" is found twice by *Avraham* (*Bereishit* 17:3 and *Bereishit* 17:7); by *Moshe* and *Aharon* (*Bamidbar* 14:5); and by *Moshe* (*Bamidbar* 16:4).

4. The *Targum Yonatan* (*Bamidbar* 16:19) says that *Korach* found two of *Yosef's* hidden treasures and used the wealth to finance the revolt.

5. The *gemara* (*Pesachim* 119a) says that *Korach* was so wealthy that he needed three hundred mules to carry the keys to his treasure houses.

6. The six *parshiyot* named for people are *Noach, Chayei Sarah, Yitro, Korach, Balak,* and *Pinchas*. Interestingly, four of these were named for non-Jews.

7. Both *Eisav* and *Yitzhar* had sons named *Korach* (*Bereishit* 36:5 and *Bamidbar* 16:1).

8. *Korach's* most famous descendant was *Shmuel Hanavi* (*Divrei Hayamim* 1:6:13).

9. There are three possible male – female combinations that would require a *pidyon haben* of the firstborn male from that union: a *yisrael* to a *bat yisrael*; a non-Jew to a *bat yisrael*; and a non-Jew to a *bat kohen*. The surprise combination is obviously the non-*Jew* to the *bat kohen*. The *halacha* states that in this situation, because the *bat kohen* "married" a non-*Jew*, she has irrevocably denounced her special priestly status. Not so for the *bat levi* situation, as her initial status is nowhere near that of a *bat kohen* (*Shulchan Aruch Yoreh Deah* 305:18).

10. In the beginning of *Shemot* (2:11), *Moshe* goes out and sees the suffering of the Jewish people at the hands of their Egyptian taskmasters. He sees an Egyptian beating an *Israelite*; *Moshe* kills the Egyptian, and buries him in the sand. The *midrash* (*Shemot Rabbah* 1:28) comments on this story and says that this Egyptian had noticed the very beautiful wife of *Datan*. The Egyptian waited until *Datan* went out to work and then the Egyptian

entered her home and raped her. This Egyptian was seen by *Datan* leaving his home and this Egyptian was aware that he had been seen. He feared that *Datan* knew that he had raped his wife and he began to treat *Datan* cruelly in the fields. *Moshe* understood all that had transpired through his *"ruach hakodesh"* – "divine inspiration" and therefore knew that this Egyptian deserved the punishment of death, for raping another man's wife.

11. Trick question: It depends on which *Korach* we are speaking about. There are two people named *Korach* in the *Torah*. In *Parshat Korach, Korach*'s grandfather would be *Kehat* (*Bamidbar* 16:1). *Eisav* also had a son, *Korach*, from his wife *Ahalivama*, and therefore this *Korach*'s grandfather would be *Yitzchak* (*Bereishit* 36:5).

12. The easiest answer would be *Eretz Yisrael* (*Shemot* 3:8), but in *Parshat Korach*, we also have reference to *Mitzrayim* as *"eretz zavat chalav udevash"* – "a land flowing with milk and honey" (*Bamidbar* 16:13).

13. Because the *Torah* specifies *"peter rechem"* – "the firstborn of the womb" (*Bamidbar* 18:15), the *mitzvah* applies to the firstborn of the mother. If a man marries twice and the firstborn from each wife is a male and there are no other restrictions that apply, both firstborn sons of the two wives would be required to be redeemed.

14. *Rashi* (*Bamidbar* 18:19) explains that *Hashem*'s covenant with the *kohanim* is compared to salt, because salt is something which is wholesome and lasting and acts as a preservative to keep other things wholesome (*Sifrei Bamidbar* 118). *Rashi* presents an additional explanation that salt has the quality that it does not spoil or decay.

15. The *Torah* tells us (*Bamidbar* 3:29) that the *Levite* family of *Kehat* camped in the south, adjacent to the Tribe of *Reuven*, who also camped in the south. *Rashi* (*Bamidbar* 16:1) explains that all the leaders of the *Korach* rebellion, *Korach, Datan, Aviram* and *On* were neighbours. *Rashi* quotes the saying *"oy larasha, oy lishcheinav"* – "woe to the wicked, woe to his neighbour" (*Nega'im* 2:6). From here we learn the principle of seeking good neighbours.

16. In *Korach* we have the *pasuk* (*Bamidbar* 18:12): *"kol cheilev yitzhar, v'chol cheilev tirosh v'dagan"* – "all the best of the new oil, wine and grain" represent part of the *"terumah gedola"* – "gifts given to the *kohanim*." Here, the word *"cheilev"* does not mean "fat," but rather, means the choicest parts of the harvest.

17. The word *"Yitzhar"* appears in two different contexts in *Parshat Korach*. First, as the father of *Korach* (*Bamidbar* 16:1), and second, as the word for fine olive oil (*Bamidbar* 18:12). The *Midrash* (*Bamidbar Rabbah* 18:16) relates a fascinating idea connecting *Korach*, his father *Yitzhar*, and oil. Since *Korach*'s father's name was related to oil, and *Moshe*'s name was related to water, having been "drawn from the water" (*Shemot* 2:11), and just as water

and oil do not mix, but rather oil always rises to the top, *Korach* believed that he would be successful in his rebellion against *Moshe*. He was mistaken. Perhaps the connection to *"yitzhar"* – "oil," is the connection to *Korach's* descendant *Shmuel*, who would ultimately use the *"shemen hamishcha"* – "the anointing oil" as he anointed *David* as king of Israel which will lead *"bimheira b'yameinu"* to *Mashiach*.

18. There are four unique expressions of death in *Parshat Korach*:
    1. *"pen tisafu"* – "lest you be wiped out" (*Bamidbar* 16:26).
    2. *"kol ha'adam yemutun eileh"* – "die as all men do" (*Bamidbar* 16:29).
    3. *"va'achaleh otam k'rega"* – "and I will annihilate them in an instant" (*Bamidbar* 17:10).
    4. *"hein gavanu"* – "we have perished" (*Bamidbar* 17:29).

19. *Rashi* (*Bamidbar* 18:27) refers us to a *pasuk* (*Zechariah* 14:10) which defines *"yikvei hamelech"* – literally "the king's pits" as the oceans of the world. *Hashem* dug these enormous pits into which He placed water and we know them as *"okyanus"* – "oceans."

20. The inanimate object that exhibits human characteristics is the earth as it says "and the earth opened its mouth" (*Bamidbar* 17:32). The inanimate object that exhibits plant-like characteristics is the staff of *Aharon* that sprouted flowers which became almonds (*Bamidbar* 17:23).

PARSHAT CHUKAT-BALAK QUESTIONS

1. The "pen is mightier than the sword." Where are the pen and sword mentioned in the same *pasuk* in *Parshat Chukat*? (Warning – trick question!)

2. Besides *Parshat Chukat*, what is the only other occurrence of the phrase "*zot chukat haTorah*" in the *Torah,* and what is its connection to the one in *Parshat Chukat*?

3. Where is *Rashi's* first hint to New York City in the *Torah*?

4. During the 40-year trek through the desert, how many mountains did *Bnai Yisrael* have to cross?

5. How do we know that in every rock, there is water?

6. From where do we learn that one should patronize their hosts by purchasing local provisions?

7. By how many names is *Miriam* known in *Tanach*?

8. Two phrases composed by non-Jews have found their way into Jewish liturgy or Jewish ceremonial life. What are they and who composed these phrases?

9. Where is there a "*remez*" – "hint," from a specific word in *Parshat Balak*, to the prohibition against intermarriage?

10. What two anagrams (English words containing exactly the same letters) describe the two methods used by our enemies in their attempts to destroy us?

11. *Bilaam* and *Balak* should have had much gratitude ("*hakarat hatov*") to *Avraham*, *Yitzchak* and *Yaakov* and should never have cursed them. In fact, they owed their existence to the "*avot*" – "patriarchs." Explain?

12. Name two distinguished people in the *Torah* who saddled their own donkeys?

13. How many different animals are mentioned in *Parshat Balak*?

14. How many people in *Tanach* saw an angel holding a drawn sword?

15. Who was the only person in the *Torah* to clap his hands?

16. Who lifted two grown adults with one hand?

17. What happened to the "*Nechash Hanechoshet*" – "the copper snake"?

18. Who was able to receive messages from birds?

19. In what three ways did *Bilaam* resemble *Moshe Rabbeinu*?

20. A number of people in *Tanach* rode on a "*chamor*" – "donkey." Who rode an "*aton*" – "female donkey"?

PARSHAT CHUKAT-BALAK ANSWERS

1. The *pasuk* says *"pen bacherev aitzay likratecha"* – "lest I come to meet you with the sword" (*Bamidbar* 20:18). The Hebrew word *"pen"* means "lest" and the Hebrew word *"cherev"* means "sword." So in the same phrase we have the *"pen"* and the "sword."

2. The potion that was formed with the ashes of the *"parah adumah"* – "red heifer" is referred to as *"mei nidah"* – "waters of sprinkling" and is used to purify one who was in contact with a corpse. The only other use of the phrase *"zot chukat haTorah"* is regarding the laws of purifications of certain metallic vessels captured during a war (*Bamidbar* 31:22). There, too, the medium for purification is the *"mei nidah"*; the potion that was formed with the ashes of the *"parah adumah."*

3. *Rashi* (*Bamidbar* 20:22) comments on the words *"Hor Hahar"* – "the name of the mountain upon which *Aharon* died" as "a mountain on top of another mountain, similar to a small apple upon a big apple." As we know the nickname for New York City is "the Big Apple!"

4. *Bnai Yisrael* had to cross only three mountains during their 40 year journey. *Rashi* (*Bamidbar* 20:22) tells us that the *"amud ha'anan"* – "the pillar of clouds" that accompanied the *Bnai Yisrael* through the desert, smoothed out all mountains in their path, other than three mountains that played important roles in their relationship with *Bnai Yisrael.* Those three mountains were *Har Sinai*, upon which the *Torah* was given); *Hor Hahar*, upon which *Aharon* died; and *Har Nevo*, upon which *Moshe* died.

5. *Rabbi Chaim* of *Chernovitz*, author of *Be'er Mayim Chaim*, (*Bamidbar* 20:8) quotes *Rav Avraham Yehoshua Heschel*, the *Apter Rav*, also known as the *Ohaiv Yisrael* who notes that in *Parshat Chukat*, the word *"selah"* – "rock" from which *Moshe* was supposed to extract water, is spelled *"samech, lamed, ayin."* If you spell each letter in its "full form," the letters are *"samech, mem, chof"* for *"samech"*; *"lamed, mem, daled"* for *"lamed"*; and *"ayin, yud, nun"* for *"ayin."* Therefore the three middle letters are *"mem, mem, yud"* which spell *"mayim"* – "water." Hence, in every *"selah"* – "rock," there is *"mayim"* – "water."

6. *Rashi*, quoting a *midrash* (*Tanchuma, Siman* 12:1), comments on the words *"v'lo nishteh mei be'er"* – "and we will not drink the water from the well" (*Bamidbar* 20:17) that the well that is referred to here, is the well that travelled with *Bnai Yisrael* through the desert. This teaches us, *Rashi* says, that when one is a guest, even if he has enough of his own provisions, he should still purchase goods from local merchants to support local commerce, so that the local population can benefit from non-locals who visit.

7. *Miriam* is known by eight different names in *Tanach*. *Miriam*; *Puah* (*Shemot* 1:15); *Azuva* (*Divrei Hayamim* 1:2:18; *Gemara Sotah* 12a); *Yeriot* (*Divrei Hayamim* 1:2:18; *Gemara Sotah* 12a); *Efrat* (*Divrei Hayamim* 1:2:19; *Gemara Sotah* 12a); *Chelah* (*Divrei Hayamim* 1:4:5; *Gemara Sotah* 12a); *Naarah* (*Divrei Hayamim* 1:4:5; *Gemara Sotah* 12a); and *Acharchel* (*Divrei Hayamim* 1:4:8; *Midrash Shemot* 1:21).

8. Two commonly used phrases in Jewish life composed by non-Jews and appearing in the text of the *Torah* are:
   1. *"ma tovu ohalecha Yaakov"* (*Bamidbar* 24:5), composed by *Bilam* and recited every day at the beginning of *davening*.
   2. *"achoteinu at hayi l'alphey revava"* (*Bereishit* 24:60), composed by *Lavan* and recited by a father to his daughter at the "*badeken*" – "veil covering ceremony" before she marries.

9. The "*romach*" – "spear" that *Pinchas* used to kill *Zimri* and *Kazbi* is spelled "*reish, mem, chet*" which is equal in *gematriya* to 248. The 248th "*mitzvah lo taaseh*" – "negative commandment" is the prohibition against intermarriage with non-Jews.

10. The two anagram words that describe how our enemies have attempted to annihilate the Jewish people are "sword" and "words."

11. The *Baal Haturim* comments (*Bamidbar* 23:7) that both *Balak* and *Bilam* owed their very existence to the *Avot*. *Balak* was king and head of the nation of *Moav*. *Moav* was the child of a relationship between *Lot* and his daughters, because they mistakenly assumed that there were no more possible suitors existing on the earth. *Lot* was saved by *Avraham* in *Sedom* and therefore *Balak* owed his existence to *Avraham*. *Bilam* was a descendant of *Lavan*. *Lavan* only merited to have male descendants because of *Yaakov* marrying his two daughters. The *Baal Haturim* derives this from a *midrash* which points out that when *Yaakov* first came to *Lavan*, *Rachel* came to the well with the sheep. If *Rachel* had brothers, they would surely have been responsible for the caring of the flock. However, when *Yaakov* was ready to leave *Lavan*'s house, the *Torah* refers to *Lavan*'s sons (*Bereishit* 31:1). Had *Lavan* only had daughters, *Bilam* would not have descended from *Lavan*. Additionally, the *Baal Haturim* points out that immediately after the *Akeidah*, the *Torah* (*Bereishit* 22:20) tells us that *Milka* and *Nachor* had children. *Avraham* was concerned, now that *Yitzchak* had survived, whether he would be able to find a wife from a proper family. The *Torah* therefore tells us that in *Yitzchak*'s merit, *Milka* and *Nachor* had children, among whom was *Betuel*, the father of *Lavan* and *Rivka*. Thus, *Bilam*'s existence was due to *Yitzchak*.

12. Both *Avraham* (*Bereishit* 22:3) and *Bilaam* (*Bamidbar* 20:12) saddled their own donkeys. The word "*vayachavosh*" – "and he saddled" is used by both

Avraham and *Bilam*. While they both arose early, *Rashi* says that the use of the word *"vayashkeim"* – "and he arose very early" by *Avraham* and the word *"vayakam"* – "and he got up" by *Bilam*, indicates that *Avraham* got up earlier than *Bilam*. The *Kotzker Rebbe* says that because *Avraham* got up earlier to do *Hashem's* will and was nevertheless not able to succeed, *Bilam* who rose later to defy *Hashem's* will, would certainly not succeed.

13. There are 12 names of animals in *Parshat Balak*. They are:
    1. *tzipor* (bird – *Bamidbar* 22:2)
    2. *shor* (ox – *Bamidbar* 22:4)
    3. *aton* (donkey – *Bamidbar* 22:21)
    4. *bakar* (cattle – *Bamidbar* 22:40)
    5. *tzon* (sheep – *Bamidbar* 22:40)
    6. *par* (bull – *Bamidbar* 23:1)
    7. *ayil* (ram – *Bamidbar* 23:1)
    8. *re'em* (buffalo – *Bamidbar* 23:22)
    9. *nachash* (snake – *Bamidbar* 23:23)
    10. *lavi* (young lion – *Bamidbar* 23:24)
    11. *ari* (lion – *Bamidbar* 23:24)
    12. *se'ir* (billy goat – *Bamidbar* 24:18)

14. *Tanach* records three instances of people seeing an angel with their sword drawn. If you thought the answer was 4, the question specifically asked for "people," not animals! In the *Torah*, there is only one person (and one animal); obviously *Bilaam* and his donkey (*Bamidbar* 22:23). In *Nach*, there are two more people, *Yehoshua* (*Yehoshua* 5:13) and *David Hamelech* (*Divrei Hayamim* 1:21:16).

15. *Balak* clapped his hands out of frustration with *Bilam* for blessing *Bnai Yisrael* instead of cursing them (*Bamidbar* 24:10).

16. The *midrash* (*Bamidbar Rabbah* 20:25) says that *Pinchas* plunged his spear through the bodies of *Zimri* and *Kazbi* in one motion, and then with both bodies still pierced by the spear, he lifted the spear into the air.

17. *Rashi* says (*Bamidbar* 21:8) that the copper snake that *Moshe* built had no healing powers. However, because it was mounted on a tall staff, those who would look at the snake would glance heavenward and thereby express their faith in *Hashem*. The *Mishnah* (*Pesachim* 4:9) reveals that *King Chizkiyahu* destroyed the *Nechash Hanechoshet* because the people began to put their faith in the copper snake itself and ceased using it merely as a vehicle to face heavenward to *Hashem*. The copper snake had itself become an idol and therefore needed to be destroyed.

18. The *Zohar* (3:184b) states that *Balak's* father had the name *Tzipor* (literally "bird") because he practiced witchcraft with birds and was able to receive messages from birds.

19. *Moshe* and *Bilam* were similar in three ways: Both were prophets. Both had disabilities; *Moshe* had a speech defect (*Shemot* 4:10) and *Bilam* was lame and was partially blind (*Sanhedrin* 105b). Both were born circumcised (*Gemara Sotah* 12a and *Avot d'Rabbi Natan* 2:5).

20. *Bilam* (*Bamidbar* 22:21) and the *Isha Hashunamit* (*Melachin* 2:4:24) both rode on an *"aton"* – "female donkey."

PARSHAT PINCHAS QUESTIONS

1. Who gave a letter of his name to one of his sons?
2. Who in *Parshat Pinchas* had the same name as his uncle?
3. Why does *Bamidbar* 26:39 contain the letter 'peh' in every word that appears in the *pasuk*?
4. Were there ever any *kohanim* not born to *kohanim*?
5. Besides the letter 'heh' and the letter 'kuf,' what other letter in the *Torah* is made up of two parts?
6. Which word in the opening *pesukim* of *Parshat Pinchas* describes the life and death decisions that faced *Pinchas*?
7. How many "*kohanim gedolim*" – "high priests" descended from *Pinchas*, and where is this indicated in *Parshat Pinchas*?
8. What are the only two *mitzvot* referred to as "*chukat mishpat*" – "decree of justice"?
9. For how many years did *Yehoshua* lead *Bnai Yisrael*?
10. Which family had its name change from one part of the body to another?
11. Who was granted eternal life by *Yaakov Avinu*?
12. What do *Yocheved, Ard* and *Naaman* have in common, besides being related to one another?
13. We are told the names of *Pinchas*'s father and grandfather. What was his son's name?
14. I am a firstborn son. Yet, when I receive my inheritance upon the passing of my father, I do not receive a double portion. Why not?
15. Which family received a portion of *Eretz Yisrael* equal to itself?
16. There are five words that comprise a complete *pasuk* and appear in a specific order throughout *Torah* over 70 times. In *Parshat Pinchas*, the same five words, also comprising a complete *pasuk*, appear in a different order, the only such occurrence in the *Torah*. What is the *pasuk*?
17. Name a *halacha* whereby an attempt to transgress the *mitzvah* is a violation of the *mitzvah*, but the actual transgression of the *mitzvah* is frowned upon, but is not considered to be a real violation?
18. By what other name was *Zimri* known?
19. Which of the five daughters of *Tzelafchad* ranked second in wisdom?
20. Find a *pasuk* in *Parshat Pinchas* where every word ends in a "*mem sofit*." Then find another *pasuk* in the *Torah* with the same number of words and the "*mem sofit*" at the end of every word. What is the connection?

PARSHAT PINCHAS ANSWERS

1. *The Daat Zekeinim* (*Bereishit* 30:18) says that *Yissachar* had a son, who in *Bereishit* was called *Yov* (*Bereishit* 46:13) and who later in *Bamidbar* (*Bamidbar* 26:24) was called *Yashuv*. He explains that *Yov* was also the name of an idol and *Yissachar*, which is spelled in the *Torah* with two "*sins*" as "*Yissaschar*," gave one of the "*sins*" from his name to *Yov* to save him the embarrassment of having an idol's name. The *Baal Haturim* (*Bamidbar* 26:24) also cites a number of other authorities, who say that for this reason, we pronounce the two *sins* of "*Yissaschar*" in all *Torah* readings up to *Parshat Pinchas,* until the point when *Yashuv* appears for the first time, and from then on, it is pronounced *Yissachar*. He also presents the alternate custom (which appears to be the prevalent one) of using the *Yissaschar* pronunciation only the first time it appears (*Bereishit* 30:18), and from then on, using the pronunciation of *Yissachar*. The *Yalkut Shimoni* (*Naso* 715) states that *Yov*'s name was changed to *Yashuv* because he was involved in establishing a court system and he was "*yoshev*" – "sat" in judgement (*Divrei Hayamim* 1:12:33).

2. *Bamidbar* 26:40 lists *Binyamin*'s son *Belah,* and *Belah*'s two sons, *Ard* and *Naaman*. *Bereishit* 46:21 says that *Binyamin* himself had two sons, *Ard* and *Naaman*. So were *Ard* and *Naaman* sons of *Binyamin,* or grandsons? The *Tur Haaroch* (*Bamidbar* 26:40) tells us that *Binyamin*'s sons *Ard* and *Naaman* both died childless, and that *Belah* married their wives, fulfilling the *mitzvah* of *Yibum*. He then named the firstborn son from each of these unions after their dead father. Hence, *Belah* was a father and uncle to each of his sons, *Ard* and *Naaman*. Also *Ard* and *Naaman* each carried the name of their uncle, who just happened to be their respective mothers' first husband.

3. The *Baal Haturim* (*Bamidbar* 26:39) quotes a *midrash* (*Bereishit Rabbah* 71:5) which says that *Binyamin* knew "*b'ruach hakodesh*" – "with divine inspiration" about the sale of his brother *Yosef,* and that *Yosef* was still alive. However, he did not reveal this to his father, *Yaakov,* because *Hashem* did not want that fact revealed at that time. Hence this *pasuk,* which lists the offspring of *Binyamin,* has the letter "*peh*" – "meaning mouth" in each word. The *midrash* says that *Binyamin* inherited this trait from his mother *Rachel,* who did not reveal *Lavan*'s plan to substitute Leah as the prospective bride to *Yaakov*. The *Baal Haturim* also points out that the stone in the "*choshen*" – "breastplate of the *kohen gadol*" that corresponds to the Tribe of *Binyamin* was the "*yashfeh*" stone. The word "*yashfeh*" can be divided into the two words "*yesh peh*"; he has a mouth; but did not use it to reveal what his brothers had done.

4. *Aharon* was born a *Levi*. His children, likewise, were born as *levi'im* and all five, *Aharon, Nadav, Avihu, Elazar* and *Itamar* were appointed and anointed as *kohanim*. This ensured that all their offspring for eternity would also be *kohanim*. However, *Pinchas, Elazar's* son, was already born by this time. He therefore had to be specially appointed as a *kohen* when he saved the nation from a plague (*Bamidbar* 25:12–13). Therefore, in total, six individuals were *kohanim*, born to *levi'im*. A very interesting *gematriya* on this topic. The *gematriya* of *Bamidbar* 3:2 which lists *Aharon* and his sons, and the *gematriya* of the *pasuk* in *Pinchas* (*Bamidbar* 25:12) when he is awarded the *kehuna*, both equal 2391.

5. The "*vav*" in the word "*shalom*" (*Bamidbar* 25:12) is written with a separation in the "spine" of the letter. The *gemara* (*Kiddushin* 66b) refers to this as a "*vav ketia*" – "a cut *vav*." *Chazal* tell us that *Pinchas* was *Eliyahu Hanavi*. The *Baal Haturim* quotes the *Avudraham* (*Seder Motzaei Shabbat, d.h. "Eliyahu Hanavi"*) based on *Rashi* (*Vayikra* 26:42) which says that there are five instances in *Tanach* where *Yaakov* is spelled with a "*vav*," "*malei*" – "spelled in full," and there are, similarly, five places in *Tanach* where *Eliyahu* is spelled without a "*vav*," "*chaser*" – "diminished." *Yaakov* "took" the "*vav*" from *Eliyahu* and is holding it as security until the day when *Eliyahu* will herald the coming of *Mashiach* ("*bimheira b'yameinu*" – "speedily in our days"). He will then return the "*vav*" to *Eliyahu* and his name will again be "*shalem*" – "complete." The *Baal Haturim* adds that the "*vav*" (with numerical value of 6) is indicative of six noble characteristics of the *Mashiach* as described by the *pasuk* in *Yeshayahu* 11:2. These traits include wisdom, understanding, ability to advise, strength, knowledge and fear of *Hashem*. In *Shemot* 8:19, the *Baal Haturim* comments on the word "*f'dut*" – "distinct" (indicating *Bnai Yisrael* as a distinct nation) which is also written without a "*vav*"; "*chaser*" – "diminished." The same word is found in *Tehillim* 130:7 referring to the ultimate redemption. There it is written with a "*vav*" and the commentary on the *Baal Haturim* quotes the "*Ateret Paz*" who says that the "*vav*" is the "key to redemption." Additionally, the reason for our continued exile is because of "*sinat chinam*" – "baseless hatred." The word "*vav*" in Hebrew means hook, an item that connects two distinct objects; and the letter "*vav*" grammatically is used to connect ("*vav hachibur*") two words together. Therefore, if we wish to witness *Eliyahu/Pinchas* heralding the arrival of *Mashiach*, we have to improve in our ability to connect and love our fellow *Jew*.

6. The *Vilna Gaon* offers a fascinating explanation on the phrase "*heishiv et chamati*" – "he reversed my anger" (*Bamidbar* 25:11), by connecting it to an explanation he gave on the words "*machatzit hashekel*" – "half *shekel*" (*Shemot* 30:13). In *Shemot*, the *parshah* dealing with the "*machatzit hashekel*"

forms the basis for the concept of charitable donations or "*tzedakah.*" We read (*Mishlei* 10:2), that charity saves one from death, and the *Gaon* quotes the *pasuk* (*Mishlei* 12:28) "the road of righteousness leads to life; by way of its path there is no death." The Hebrew word for "righteousness" is "*tzedakah.*" From here, *Chazal* tell us that charity brings us closer to life and keeps death far away. The *Vilna Gaon* comments that the word "*machatzit*" is composed of a central letter "*tzadi*" which represents "*tzedakah*" – "charity"; the two adjacent letters "*chet*" and "*yud*" spell "*chai*" – "life"; and two outer letters "*mem*" and "*taf*" spell "*met*" – "death." And therefore charity is close to life, and removed from death. Similarly, *Hashem* praises *Pinchas* for performing the greatest charitable act of removing *Hashem*'s anger from His nation, Israel, by taking decisive action against *Zimri* and *Kozbi*. However, the *Torah* refers to *Pinchas*'s act as having "reversed" rather than having "removed" *Hashem*'s anger. The *Vilna Gaon* comments that the word "*chamati*" – "my anger" is composed of four letters. The middle adjacent letters are "*mem*" and "*taf*" which spell "*met*" – "death," while the outer two separated letters are "*chet*" and "*yud*" which spell "*chai*" – "life." Hence, comments the *Vilna Gaon*, the charitable act of *Pinchas* "reversed" these letters in the word "*chamati*" and once again joined the "*chet*" and "*yud*" together to give life, while separating the "*mem*" and "*tav*" to push off death.

7. As a result of *Pinchas*'s heroic and dramatic act, *Hashem* confers priesthood upon *Pinchas* and his descendants (*Bamidbar* 25:13). *Tosafot* in the *gemara* (*Zevachim* 101b) declares that all high priests that served in the First and Second Temples in *Yerushalayim* descended from *Pinchas*. There were 80 in the "*Bayit Rishon*" – "First Temple" and 300 in the "*Bayit Sheni*" – "Second Temple," for a total of 380 *Kohanim Gedolim*. The *Baal Haturim* comments that since the "*vav*" in "*shalom*" (*Bamidbar* 25:12) is cut into two parts, the letter now becomes a "*yud*" and therefore the word is now composed of the letters "*shin,*" "*lamed,*" "*yud,*" and "*mem sofit*" with a *gematriya* of 380, hinting at the 380 descendants of *Pinchas* who served as High Priests in both Temples. (Note: The number 380 as quoted in *Tosafot* is only one opinion. Certain commentaries to *Divrei Hayomim* 1:5 enumerate "*kohanim gedolim*" who descended from *Pinchas* and arrive at a much smaller number who served until the destruction of the "*bayit rishon,*" and there are other *gemarot* that contradict this number of *Tosafot*.)

8. The only two laws in the *Torah* that are called "*chukat mishpat*" – "decrees of justice" are the laws of inheritance (*Bamidbar* 27:11) and the laws of the cities of refuge (*Bamidbar* 35:29).

9. *Yehoshua* led *Bnai Yisrael* for 28 years (*Seder Olam*, Chapter 12). The *Baal Haturim* says that *Moshe*'s prayer to *Hashem* to find an appropriate leader as his replacement contains exactly 28 words. This prayer, found in *Bamidbar*

27:16–17, contains a clear description of the required qualifications for leadership. Immediately thereafter, *Yehoshua* is appointed as the future leader of *Israel*. The *Baal Haturim* connects the 28 year reign of *Yehoshua* with the *pasuk* "*ki hu hanotain lecha koach laasot chayil*" – "for He is the one who gives you strength to lead in battle" (*Devarim* 8:18). Thee s *Baal Haturim* points out that the word "*koach*" – "strength" is numerically equivalent to 28.

10. *Rashi* identifies the family of *Ozni* (*Bamidbar* 26:16) as the family formerly referred to as *Etzbon* (*Bereishit* 46:16), and then *Rashi* comments that "I do not know why his family was not called directly by his name." The *Chatam Sofer* quotes the *Shelah Hakadosh* who cites a *gemara* (*Gemara Ketubot* 5a) which connects the "*ozen*" – "ear" to the "*etzba*" – "finger." The *gemara* says that the reason for tapered fingers is to give one the ability to stuff their ears with their fingers, to guard against hearing improper or inappropriate speech. The *Chatam Sofer* then comments that perhaps what the *Torah* is teaching us, is that the tribe of *Gad* (to whom the family of *Ozni/Ezboni* belonged) were neighbours of *Reuven* and *Shimon*, which was the tribe of *Datan, Aviram,* the 250 men of the *Korach* rebellion, as well as *Zimri* and the 24,000 people, who perished in the plague as a result of the *Zimri* affair. Until they had all died out, the family was known as "*Etzboni*," having "their fingers in their ears," so to speak, not wishing to be influenced by the wickedness of their neighbours. However, after they were no longer subject to the evil influence of these members of *Reuven* and *Shimon,* they could "remove their fingers" and once again be known as "*Ozni.*"

11. The *Targum Yonatan* (26:46) explains why *Serach,* the daughter of *Asher,* is included in the census enumerated in *Parshat Pinchas.* He says that when the brothers of *Yosef* discovered that he was still alive, they were afraid to tell their elderly father, *Yaakov,* the good news, for fear that the shock would be too much to bear. They therefore asked *Serach* to sing to her grandfather and include in her sweet song the fact that *Yosef* was still alive. When *Serach* sang to *Yaakov* and revealed through her soothing lyrics that *Yosef* was alive, *Yaakov* blessed her and said that if this news was in fact true, he would bless her with eternal life. She was therefore still alive at the end of the 40 years in the desert and was eventually taken to *Gan Eden* by angels.

12. *Rashi* identifies three people who entered *Mitzrayim* with *Yaakov,* as fetuses; *Ard, Naaman* and *Yocheved* (*Bamidbar* 26:24, 59).

13. *Pinchas'* father was *Elazar* and grandfather was *Aharon Hakohen. Avishua* is named as *Pinchas's* son in *Divrei Hayamim* 1:5:30. Although the *Tanach* does not mention any other sons of *Pinchas, Josephus' Antiquities* (*Chapter* 11:5) does mention a son called *Aviezer,* and *Artscroll* suggests that perhaps *Aviezer* and *Avishua* were in fact the same person.

14. I was delivered by Cesarean section, and as such, I do not receive a double portion (*Rambam, Hilchot Nachalot* 2:11).

15. One of the families receiving a portion of *Eretz Yisrael* was called *Cheilek ben Gilad*. Therefore its portion or *"cheilek"* was equal to itself (*Bamidbar* 26:30)!

16. The *Baal Haturim* (*Bamidbar* 27:15) *points out that the pasuk "vayedaber Moshe el Hashem leimor"* – "and *Moshe* spoke to *Hashem*, saying" is unique and only occurs this one time in the *Torah*. Of course, the similar *pasuk* that appears over 70 times throughout *Torah*, is *"vayedaber Hashem el Moshe leimor"* – "and *Hashem* spoke to *Moshe*, saying."

17. In the laws of inheritance in *Parshat Pinchas*, the *halacha* states that one must leave his assets to his children. In actual fact, if one leaves a will stating that nothing goes to the children, the *Beit Din* will not accept it. In such a case, one is in violation of attempting to transgress a *Torah* law. Actual transgression of the law, can however be accomplished, if one gives away all their assets before death. This is an action that is frowned upon but yet permissible.

18. *Zimri* was *Shlumiel ben Tzurishadai*, the *"nasi"* – "prince" of the tribe of *Shimon* (*Bamidbar* 1:6). The *Baal Haturim* comments that the word *"kruay"* – "the appointed ones" is spelled with a diminished *"vav,"* because among the princes, there was one who was flawed; namely *"Shlumiel,"* who was *Zimri*. The *Baal Haturim* further explains that the word *"kriay"* (*Bamidbar* 16:2) is spelled with the *"yud"* completely missing, because it appears in the story of *Korach*, and we are thereby being told that *Korach* and his entire entourage were flawed, as opposed to the recounting of the princes (*Bamidbar* 1:5–15) where the *"vav"* is only shortened, but not completely missing, because only one *nasi, Shlumiel* aka *Zimri*, was flawed.

19. According to *Rashi* (*Bamidbar* 36:11), the listing of the daughters of *Tzelafchad* at the very end of *Sefer Bamidbar* has them ranked according to age, for they were married in the order in which they were born. But the listing in *Parshat Pinchas* (*Bamidbar* 27:1) has them ranked according to wisdom. Hence *Noa* would be the second wisest of the five daughters.

20. The two *pesukim* are *Bereishit* 32:15 enumerating the gifts that *Yaakov* sent to *Eisav*; and *Bamidbar* 29:33 which describes the *"musaf"* – "additional" sacrifices on *Sukkot*. The *Baal Haturim* explains that the gifts sent by *Yaakov* indicated a lack of *"bitachon"* – "trust" in *Hashem*, and therefore we bring 550 communal offerings per year (excluding the *"korban tamid"* – "daily sacrifice" and the *"korbanot"* – "sacrifices" for *Shemini Atzeret*, which are recorded after this *pasuk*), which match the total number of animals sent as gifts to *Eisav*.

PARSHAT MATOT-MAS'EI QUESTIONS

1. Which incident in *Parshat Matot* avenged the selling of *Yosef*?
2. *Bamidbar* 32:32 begins and ends with the letter "*nun*." How many such *pesukim* are there in the *Torah* and are they connected?
3. What is unique about the first *pasuk* in both *Matot* and *Mas'ei*?
4. Which tribes were on the front line in the conquest of *Eretz Yisrael*?
5. Which *pasuk* in *Parshat Matot* indicates the unity of the Jewish people?
6. Where in *Parshat Matot* is there a hint that *Moshe Rabbeinu*, and *David Hamelech* all required soldiers to present divorce documents to their wives before leaving for war?
7. How wide was the *Yarden* River?
8. Which *pasuk* in *Parshat Matot* is singled out for special mention in the *halachot* of "*shnayim mikra v'echad targum*" (the law requiring one to read weekly every *pasuk* of the *Torah* twice and its translation once)?
9. By what other name is *Balak* referred to in this week's *parshah*?
10. The *Torah* only explicitly mentions *Paroh*'s birthday in *Bereishit*. Whose birthday is hinted at in *Parshat Mas'ei*?
11. Where is there a hint to *Chanukah* in this week's *Torah* reading?
12. How do the first four words of *Parshat Mas'ei* allude to future exiles of the Jewish people?
13. How is it possible for a person to be forbidden to leave the city he is in, for as long as he lives?
14. What *mitzvah* applicable today, do we learn from the layout of the "*aray halevi'im*" – "*levite* cities"?
15. I have never lived in an "*ir miklat*" – "city of refuge" and yet I am buried in one. Describe the case?
16. How many times did the *Bnai Yisrael* travel from the date of the Exodus until the end of *Sivan* the following year?
17. Logically, one would think that since there were three "*aray miklat*" – "cities of refuge" on the western side of the Jordan serving 9 tribes, the eastern side would require only about one such city of refuge to serve the 2 ½ tribes there. Yet, the *Torah* prescribes three such cities on the eastern side of the Jordan. Why the imbalance?
18. In which of the 42 encampments listed in *Parshat Mas'ei* did *Bnai Yisrael* receive the *mann*?
19. What were the four instances in the *Torah* where *Moshe* had to check the *halacha* with *Hashem*?
20. Who is referred to in the same *pasuk* in the *Torah* together with his father and stepfather?

PARSHAT MATOT-MAS'EI ANSWERS

1. *Rashi* (*Bamidbar* 31:6) tells us that *Pinchas* led the battle against the *Midyanim* to avenge the sale, by the *Midyanim,* of *Yosef,* his maternal ancestor. *Pinchas* is described by the *gemara* (*Sotah* 43a) as being a descendant of both *Yitro* and *Yosef.*

2. *Rav Avraham Saba* (1440–1508, Spain, Portugal, Morocco) in his *sefer Tzror Hamor* (*Vayikra* 13:9) comments on the *haftarah* of *Tazria.* In the *haftarah, Elisha* suggests that *Naaman* immerse himself in the *Jordan River* in order to cure his *"tzaraat"* – "leprosy" (*Melachim* 2:5:10). But as we know in *Parshat Tazria,* the *Torah* tells us that if you have such an affliction, you are to go to a *kohen.* Instead, *Naaman* comes to consult with a *"navi"* – "prophet." The *Tzror Hamor* comments that the obligation to take this type of affliction to a *kohen,* is only incumbent on a *Jew*; a non-*Jew* can request advice from any wise person or prophet. *Elisha* noticed that *Naaman'*s name begins with a regular *"nun"* and ends with a "final *nun.*" *Elisha* learned the cure from the *pesukim* in the *Torah* that begin with a regular *"nun"* and end with a "final *nun.*" There are three such *pesukim* in the *Torah.* From the first such *pasuk,* he came to the conclusion that when one has *tzora'at* (*Naaman*), he should come to the *kohen* or *navi* (*Elisha*) as in the *pasuk* "*nega…v'huva el hakohen*" (*Vayikra* 13:9). From the third such *pasuk,* it is clear that when hearing the advice as to what the individual should do, he must listen to the prophet as the *pasuk* says in *Devarim* 18:15, "*navi…eilav tishma'un.*" And from the second double *nun pasuk* in the *Torah* (*Bamidbar* 32:32) "*nachnu…layarden,*" we are presented with the solution of immersing in the *Jordan River.* Perhaps this is why this *pasuk* does not say *"anachnu"* but rather says *"nachnu"* without the *alef* so that this can be a double *nun pasuk.* The *Tzror Hamor* states that there are many hidden secrets in the wording of the *Torah* if you are able to identify them.

3. Amazingly, they are equal in *gematriyot.* These two *parshiyot* are most often read together compared to all double *parshiyot.*

4. *Rashi* deduces from the wording "*lifnei Bnai Yisrael*" – "at the forefront of the *Bnai Yisrael,*" that the *Bnai Gad* and *Bnai Reuven* were the front line soldiers (*Rashi* 32:17).

5. The *Baal Haturim* points out that *Bamidbar* 31:4 begins and ends with an "*alef.*" The *pasuk* discusses the number of soldiers required for the battle against *Midyan.* The letter *alef* which appears at the beginning and end of the *pasuk* indicates that they were unified in purpose and were intent together to do the will of *Hashem.*

6. The *Baal Haturim* says that the two places in the *Torah* where one can find the word "*chalutz*" is in *Bamidbar* 32:21 and in *Devarim* 25:10. Since in the

first instance, this week's *Parshat Matot*, it is used regarding armed warfare, and in the *Devarim* reference, it is regarding *"yibum"* and *"chalitza,"* the *Baal Haturim* deduces that *Moshe*, in not wanting *"yibum"* situations, required soldiers to give *"gittin"* – "divorce papers" to their wives prior to leaving for battle. The *Baal Haturim* also quotes a number of sources to show that *David Hamelech* learned this from *Moshe Rabbeinu* and did likewise.

7. The *Baal Haturim* notes that since the *pasuk* (*Bamidbar* 32:32) begins and ends with the letter *"nun"* (*gematriya* value of 50) and since the *pasuk* speaks about crossing the *Jordan River*, the width of the river was 50 *"amot'"* – "cubits" wide.

8. The *pasuk* is *"Atarot v'Divon…"* (*Bamidbar* 32:3). The *gemara* (*Berachot* 8a) cites the requirement to read weekly every *pasuk* of the *Torah* twice and its translation once. The *gemara* adds that one should follow this custom for all *pesukim*, "even the *pasuk* of *Atarot v'Divon* etc.," as this practice will ensure long life. There are numerous reasons for the singling out of this *pasuk*, among which is the fact that the *pasuk* consists of nine names of places, and hence the translation is the same as the *pasuk*.

9. The *Targum Yonatan* (*Bamidbar* 31:8) identifies *Tzur*, king of *Midyan* as *Balak*.

10. In *Bamidbar* 33:38, we are told that on *Rosh Chodesh Av*, *Aharon* went up to Mount *Hor Hahar* to die. In the next *pasuk*, we are told that *Aharon* was 123 years old when he died "on *Hor Hahar*." *Rabbi Pinchas HaLevi Horowitz* (1731–1805) in his commentary *Haflaah* tells us that the repetition of "on *Hor Hahar*" hints to the fact that *Tzaddikim* end their years in complete fashion. Therefore we know that *Aharon* must have died on his birthday, on *Rosh Chodesh Av*.

11. In the travels mentioned in *Parshat Mas'ei*, the 25th encampment was *Chashmonah* (*Bamidbar* 33:29). This is an allusion to *Chanukah*, the 25th day of *Kislev*. The leaders of the Jewish people at the time of *Chanukah* were the family known as the *Chashmonaim*.

12. The *Chida* (*Rabbi Chaim Yosef Dovid Azulai*, 1724–1806) writes in his work *Nachal Kedumim* that the first letters of the opening four words of *Parshat Mas'ei* – *"eileh mas'ei Bnai Yisrael"* – "these are the journeys of *Bnai Yisrael*" allude to the four periods of Jewish exile. The initials of the first four words of our *Parshat Mas'ei* are *alef*, which stands for *Edom*; *mem*, which stands for *Madai*; *bet*, which stands for *Bavel*; and *yud*, which stands for *Yavan*.

13. If someone kills someone accidentally, he has to run to an *"ir miklat"* – "city of refuge" and remain there until the *"Kohen Gadol"* – "the High Priest" dies. If someone accidentally kills the *Kohen Gadol*, or if the *Kohen Gadol* accidentally kills someone; in each case, the murderer is stuck in the City of Refuge forever. Since the only way he can leave is upon the death of the *Kohen Godol* and since there was no *Kohen Godol* in active service when

he committed the act, he is unfortunately permanently attached to the "*ir miklat*" (*Rashi Gemara Sanhedrin* 18b).

14. The open space surrounding the *Levite* city had to measure 2000 by 2000 *amot*. The *gemara* (*Eruvin* 51a) derives from here the *mitzvah* of "*t'chum Shabbat*" – the 2000 *amot* maximum distance that one is permitted to walk outside the boundaries of a city on *Shabbat*.

15. The *Rambam* (*Hilchot Rotzeach* 7:3) says that if one has been sentenced to an "*ir miklat*" – "city of refuge" for killing "*b'shogeg*" – "accidentally" and on the way there, he dies, he is buried there and has to stay there until the death of the *Kohen Gadol*, at which time he would be re-interred in his family burial plot. This is based on the three times that the word "*shama*" – "there" is used when the *Torah* says where one should run if he kills unintentionally. *Chazal* explain that the three "*shamas*" – "there should be his dwelling place; there should he die; there should he be buried," that even though he never dwelt there, he still has to be buried there.

16. They traveled 14 times from the 15ᵗʰ of *Nisan*, 2448 to the 29ᵗʰ of *Sivan* 2449. The *Yalkut Me'am Loez* says that the *Bnai Yisrael* arrived in *Chatzerot* on the 22ⁿᵈ of *Sivan* after a month of eating meat at *Kivrot Hataavah*. Since the spies returned from their 40 day mission on *Tisha B'av*, it follows that they were dispatched on the 29ᵗʰ day of *Sivan*. Therefore the stay in *Chatzerot* only lasted seven days and in that short time span, *Miriam* was stricken with "*tzara'at*" – "leprosy," was quarantined, and *Korach*'s rebellion took place.

17. *Rashi* (*Bamidbar* 35:14) quotes a *gemara* (*Makkot* 9b–10a) which tells us that murders were more prevalent on the east side of the *Jordan*.

18. The *Baal Haturim* identifies "*Alush*" as the place where the *mann* began to fall. *Alush* is similar to the word "*lushi*" (*Bereishit* 18:6). He points out that *Sara Imeinu* baked bread for the angels and in the merit of *Avraham* and *Sara*'s hospitality, their children were provided with "heavenly" bread during their sojourn through the desert.

19. The four instances are the "*mekalel*" – "the blasphemer" (*Vayikra* 24:10); *Pesach Sheini* (*Bamidbar* 9:1); the "*mekoshesh*" – "the woodchopper who desecrated the *Shabbat*" (*Bamidbar* 15:32); and the laws of inheritance as requested by the daughters of *Tzelafchad* (*Bamidbar* 36:1). There was a fifth instance where *Moshe* was unsure of the *halacha*, the incident involving *Zimri* and *Kazbi*, but there, *Pinchas* stepped forward and acted.

20. The *pasuk* (*Bamidbar* 32:12) says "*Kalev ben Yefuneh Hakenizi*." *Rashi* quotes a *gemara* (*Sotah* 11b) and the *Siftei Chachamim* explains that the reason for the addition of the title "*hakenizi*," is because after *Kalev*'s father, *Yefuneh*, died, his mother remarried to *Kenaz*. They subsequently had a son named *Otniel*. So there is one *pasuk* that mentions a person, *Kalev*; his father, *Yefuneh*; and stepfather, *Kenaz*.

PARSHAT DEVARIM QUESTIONS

1. Name one word in *Sefer Devarim* that describes both a sin and a sinner?

2. How tall was *Moshe Rabbeinu* and where is the *"remez"* – "hint" to his height in *Parshat Devarim*?

3. How many times in Jewish history did the sun stop its revolution around the earth?

4. *Har Sinai* is known by many names, though some of them are not explicitly mentioned in the *Torah* (e.g. *Gavnunim, Beit Imi, Har Chemed*). Of the eight names mentioned in various *midrashim*, only four of them are explicitly referred to in the *Torah*; namely, *Har Sinai, Har HaElokim, Har Chorev,* and *Har Moriah* (see *Yitro* question 7). What other mountain is known by four different names, all explicitly mentioned in the *Torah*?

5. Where is the actual inheritance of *Kalev* in Israel alluded to in *Parshat Devarim*?

6. What was the difference in *Hashem's* instructions as to how we were to treat the nations of *Amon* and *Moav*?

7. Where is the *Tur Talga*?

8. In *Sefer Devarim*, what is the connection between the following five words; *"et, Hashem, atah, atem, hayom"*?

9. In the *haftarah* of *Parshat Devarim* (*Yeshayahu* 1:2) we read the phrase *"banim gidalti v'romamti."* Who was the father?

10. Which museum is referred to in the *Torah*?

11. What is another name for *Sefer Devarim*?

12. Where is there a reference in *Rashi* to the ski resort in Israel?

13. Find all the names of books of *Tanach* that are mentioned in *Parshat Devarim*?

14. Why does *Hashem* give *Moshe* encouragement in the form of the words *"al tirah oto"* – "do not fear him" (*Devarim* 3:2) when it speaks about *Og*, and does not give *Moshe* the same encouragement when meeting *Sichon*?

15. The name *Yehoshua* appears 31 times in the *Torah*. It is spelled *yud, heh, vav, shin*, and *ayin* in 30 instances. In one instance, it is spelled *maleh* with an extra *vav* (*Devarim* 3:21), as *yud, heh, vav, shin, vav* and *ayin*. Why is this instance different from all the rest?

16. *Devarim* 2:20 speaks about *Refaim* and *Zamzumim*. Have these people ever appeared in the *Torah* before?

17. In the first chapter in *Devarim, Moshe* recounts some of the history of the 40 years in the desert and rebukes the people for their lack of *"emunah"* – "faith" in *Hashem*. And yet in the middle of the story of the spies sent to scout out *Eretz Yisrael, Moshe* states *"vayitav b'einai hadavar"* – "the suggestion to send spies to scout the land met with favour in my eyes." If so,

why did *Moshe* complain about the *"meraglim"* – "spies," if he thought it was a good idea?

18. Two kings get to share *"maftir"* – "the last *aliyah* every *Shabbat"* three times in the *Torah*. Explain?

19. Why does the *Torah* need to tell us that *Og*'s bed was made of iron?

20. Where can you find a *pasuk* in *Parshat Devarim* with ten words, eight of them consecutive words ending with a *"mem sofit"*?

PARSHAT DEVARIM ANSWERS

1. The word is "*lavan*" (*Devarim* 1:1). *Lavan* was the name of *Yaakov's* father-in-law and *Rashi* explains here that the word "*lavan*" does not describe an actual place but rather the place where the sin over the *mann* took place. Since *mann* was white, hence the identification of the place by the word "*lavan*" – "white."

2. The *gemara* (*Berachot* 54b) lists *Moshe's* height as 10 *amot* (between 15 and 20 feet). The *gemara* says that *Moshe* was 10 *amot* tall, his staff was 10 *amot* long, and he jumped 10 *amot* and only reached *Og's* ankle. He hit him on the ankle and killed him. In *Devarim* 3:11, in describing the size of *Og's* bed, the *Torah* uses the word "*halo!*" – "behold." Usually in Hebrew, this word is spelled "*heh, lamed, alef.*" Here it is spelled "*heh, lamed, heh.*" The *Baal Haturim* says that the two "*hehs*" equalling 10, refer to *Moshe's* height and the "*lamed*" – "thirty" in the centre, indicates the total of thirty *amot* that are referred to in the *gemara*.

3. The *gemara* (*Avodah Zara* 25a) says that there were three instances where the sun stopped. Once for *Moshe* in his war with *Amalek*; once for *Yehoshua* when he defended the people of *Givon*; and once for *Nakdimon ben Gurion*, when he negotiated water supply for the Jewish people who came up to *Jerusalem* on one of the festivals. The two scriptural references to the stopping of the sun's orbit by *Moshe* and *Yehoshua* are tied together by the *gemara* because of the similar usage of the term "*hayom hazeh achel...*" – "on this day, I will begin" (*Devarim* 2:25; *Yehoshua* 3:7). The *gemara* references the source of *Nakdimon* from a story in another *gemara* (*Taanit* 20a).

4. In one *pasuk* (*Devarim* 3:9) we have three names for the same mountain; *Chermon, Siryon* and *Snir*. *Rashi* says that it is called by yet one additional name; *Har Si'on* (*Devarim* 4:48); and quotes a *sifrei* (*Sifrei Devarim* 37:10), explaining that the four names are a result of four kings priding themselves in this – one saying, "After me shall it be named," and another saying, "After me shall it be named." It is an indication of how much each nation coveted *Eretz Yisrael*.

5. *Rav Noach Mindes Lipshutz* (the *mechutan* of the *Vilna Gaon, died* 1797) in his work *Parpera'ot la-Hokhmah* noted that the inheritance of *Kalev* in *Eretz Yisrael* was *Chevron* (*Yehoshua* 14:13). The *gematriya* of *Chevron* is equal to the *gematriya* of "*yirena*" – "will see" (*Devarim* 1:36). The *pasuk* states that only *Kalev* "will see" the land and that is precisely the land that *Hashem* will give to him.

6. In the case of *Moav*, *Hashem* commanded us not to provoke them to war. However, we were permitted to harass them generally. In the case of *Amon* we were not permitted to provoke them in any way at all. *Rashi* (*Devarim*

2:9) explains that *Amon* was treated with greater respect because the daughter of *Lot* in naming him *Amon*, was more sensitive in naming her child, by not referring to her father's incestuous act. However, the other daughter who named her child *Moav*; literally "from my father," had little sensitivity and named her child with direct reference to the actions of her father.

7. *Tur Talga* is the way *Targum Onkelos* translates *Snir* which was one of the names given to *Har Chermon*, a mountain on the border of Israel & Syria.

8. The phrase "*Shema Yisrael*" appears five times in *Sefer Devarim*. These are the five words that follow the words "*Shema Yisrael*" in *Sefer Devarim* (*Devarim* 5:1; *Devarim* 6:4; *Devarim* 9:1; *Devarim* 20:3; *Devarim* 27:9).

9. The simple explanation is that *Hashem* is speaking about His children, *Bnai Yisrael*. However, in *Divrei Hayamim* (1:25:4), we have the names of 14 of the 17 children (14 sons and three daughters) of *Heman,* advisor to *King David*. Two of his children were named "*Gadalti*" and "*Romamti Ezer*." So to answer the question, *Heman* is the father.

10. *Parshat Devarim* (3:11) speaks about the giant king of *Bashan, Og,* and describes his huge bed. The *Torah* then says that the bed is now in the city of *Rabbah* which is in the area of *Bnai Amon*. *Targum Yonatan* (*Devarim* 3:11) states more specifically that it is housed in "*bet archeivan*" – "the archive house" which is another word for a museum; hence the only museum mentioned in the *Torah*.

11. There are three possible names for the fifth book of the *Torah*:
    1. *Sefer Devarim,* (*Devarim* 1:1) taken from the second word in the first *pasuk.*
    2. *Mishneh Torah* (*Devarim* 17:18), literally, repetition of the *Torah* as *Moshe*, before his death, recounts his life history.
    3. According to one opinion in the *Gemara* (*Avoda Zara* 25a), *Sefer Hayashar,* the book of the righteous, from the *pasuk* "And you shall do that which is "*yashar*" – "right" and good in the eyes of *Hashem*" (*Devarim* 6:18).

12. The *pasuk* (*Devarim* 3:9) tells us that *Mount Chermon* in Israel is known by three names, *Chermon, Sirion* and *Snir. Rashi* points out that it is also known by a fourth name, *Sion* (*Devarim* 4:48). *Rashi* then points out that the name *snir,* is from the Canaanite word *snih*, and is similar to the German word *schnee*, which means snow. It is quite interesting that the only ski resort in Israel is on *Mount Chermon,* one of the few places in Israel that is snow covered on an annual basis.

13. In *Parshat Devarim*, the following books of the *Tanach* are named: *Devarim* (*Devarim* 1:1), *Bamidbar* (*Devarim* 1:1), *Eicha* (*Devarim* 1:12), *Yehoshua* (*Devarim* 1:38), *Vayikra* (*Devarim* 3:14), and *Melachim* (*Devarim* 3:21).

14. *Rashi* (*Devarim* 3:2) explains that *Hashem* said this concerning *Og* but not about *Sichon*, because *Moshe* was hesitant to go to war against *Og*. In *Bereishit* (14:13), *Lot*, *Avraham*'s nephew, and family are captured and all their possessions are taken by the invading armies. The *pasuk* says that the *"palit"* – "fugitive" from the battle came and told *Avraham*, who then gathered his forces and saved *Lot* and his family. *Rashi* tells us that the *"palit"* was *Og*. Therefore *Moshe* was worried that *Og* would be protected in the merit of having assisted *Avraham* and his family. For this reason, *Hashem* tells *Moshe* not to fear *Og*.

15. The *Otzar Midrashim* (dealing with missing and extra letters in *Tanach*, *perek* 2) says that it was at this moment (*Devarim* 3:21) that *Yehoshua* was adorned with six crowns; the crowns of beauty, strength, wealth, wisdom, leadership and prophesy. And because there are six characteristics, there is an extra *vav* which has the value of six.

16. *Refaim* appears in *Bereishit* 15:20. *Rashi* on that *pasuk* identifies the land of the *Refaim* as the land of *Og*, king of *Bashan*, and references *Devarim* 3:13. At the end of *Devarim* 2:20, the *Torah* tells us that the *Amonim* called the *Refaim*, *Zamzumim*. In *Bereishit* 14:5, the *Torah* tells us that *King Kedarlaomer* and his allies struck the *Zuzim* in *Ham*. *Rashi*, in that *pasuk*, identifies the *Zuzim* as the *Zamzumim*.

17. *Rashi* (*Devarim* 1:23) explains this apparent contradiction with a very interesting parable. Someone was selling a donkey. The buyer wanted to test the man to see whether the animal was in good health. He asked him for a test drive. The seller agreed, and now the buyer knew that it was in good health, but he wanted to really make sure. He then asked "How about the mountains? Can I take it there?" The seller quickly answered "Yes." The buyer now understood that if the seller was willing to allow the donkey to be tested in such a strenuous manner, it must be a healthy animal, so he bought it. This should also have been the response of *Klal Yisrael*. You want to know about the land? Fine, *Hashem* will allow you to spy it out. This was good in *Moshe*'s eyes: now take his word, and make the purchase. However, they did not. They wanted to see it for themselves. And hence *Moshe* complained and chastised them.

18. *Sichon* and *Og* get *maftir* three times. In *Parshat Chukat*, *Sichon* and *Og* are mentioned in the *aliyah* for *maftir* (*Bamidbar* 21:32–35); as well, they are mentioned in the *maftir* portion for *Parshat Ki Tavo* (*Devarim* 29:6–8); and the third time is in our *parshah* of *Devarim* (*Devarim* 3:21) where they are not mentioned by name but are referred to as *"shnei hamelachim ha'eileh"* – "these two kings."

19. The *Ramban* (*Devarim* 3:11) explains that *Og* was so huge and heavy that no wooden bed would be able to hold him. The *Rashbam* explains further that

the word "*arso*" – "commonly translated as his bed" really refers to his crib and that as a child, *Og* was so big and rambunctious that no wooden crib would last. So they built him a crib of iron. This continued into adulthood.

20. *Devarim* 1:13 has the following words, all of which end in a "*mem sofit*": *lachem anashim, chachamim, unevonim vidu'im l'shivteichem va'asimem berosheichem.*

PARSHAT VA'ETCHANAN QUESTIONS

1. Name as many ways possible to read from *Parshat Va'etchanan* on *Tisha B'Av*?
2. What is the unique Hebrew name for each of the five fingers on one's hand and what is the connection to the first *pasuk* in *kriat shema*?
3. How many times in a normal week would one say the *pasuk* "*Shema Yisrael*"?
4. Name two *pesukim* in the *Torah* that contain all the letters of the Hebrew alphabet?
5. *Parshat Va'etchanan* begins with the prayer of *Moshe*. In Yiddish, to pray is to "*daven*." What is the origin of the word "*daven*"?
6. How is the entire *Torah* contained in the *haftarah* of *Va'etchanan*?
7. What *aliyah* begins and ends with the same *pasuk*?
8. The *haftarah* of *Va'etchanan* begins with a duplicated word "*nachamu, nachamu*." Which *haftarah* has four sets of duplicated words?
9. How does loving *Hashem* remind us of *Avraham, Yitzchak* and *Yaakov*?
10. Where in *Parshat Va'etchanan* do we have a *pasuk* that is said before opening, a *pasuk* that is said before reading and *pasuk* that is said after reading?
11. Where is there a hint in *Parshat Va'etchanan* that a person should marry off his children at a young age?
12. What are the two instances when a person could wear *tefillin* on *Shabbat*?
13. When is it a *mitzvah* to taste a meal the day before it is eaten?
14. Which inanimate object in the *Torah* sweats like a human?
15. When the *Torah* describes *Eretz Yisrael* as "a land flowing with milk and honey," what do "milk" and "honey" mean?
16. There are eight instances every week when we say the *pasuk* "*Shema Yisrael Hashem Elokeinu Hashem Echad*," only because of past persecution of the Jewish people. What are those eight instances?
17. Which woman in *Tanach* wore *Tefillin*?
18. How are *Tefillin* compared to the wings of a dove?
19. Prayer and song are valued together and equally in *Va'etchanan*. Explain?
20. Three times in the *Torah*, requests are made to royalty with almost the same wording. Two of these are addressed to flesh and blood kings and one is addressed to *Hashem*, the King of Kings. All involve access. What is the wording of the requests and to whom are they directed?

PARSHAT VA'ETCHANAN ANSWERS

1. Three possible answers as to how one could read *Parshat Va'etchanan* from the *Torah* on *Tisha B'Av*, and a number of ways that one could read parts of *Parshat Va'etchanan* but not from the *Torah*. First, three ways from the *Torah*:

   1. *Tisha B'Av* falls on *Shabbat* and therefore the fast day is pushed off until the Sunday which is the tenth of *Av*. On that *Shabbat* (the ninth of *Av*; i.e., *Tisha B'Av*) we would read *Parshat Devarim* and at *minchah* we would read from *Parshat Vaetchanan*.
   2. The regular *Torah* reading for *Tisha B'Av shacharit* is in fact from *Parshat Va'etchanan* "ki tolid banim."
   3. If *Tisha B'Av* falls on a Thursday and there are less than six people fasting, you would read the regular Thursday morning *Torah* reading from *Parshat Va'etchanan* (*Mishnah Berurah* 566:14–15).

   And now a number of ways to read from *Parshat Va'etchanan* on *Tisha B'Av* but not from the *Torah*:

   1. The first paragraph of "*kriat shema*."
   2. In certain *nuschaot*, one would say the *pasuk* "*ata horaita la'daat*" before taking out the *Torah*.
   3. The *pasuk* "*v'yadaata hayom*" is found in "*aleinu*."
   4. When lifting the *Torah* during *hagba'at haTorah*, we say the *pasuk* "*V'zot HaTorah*."
   5. "*V'atem hadveikim*" is recited each time we read the *Torah* before the *baal kriah* reads the first *aliyah*.

   All of these are found in *Parshat Va'etchanan*.

2. Hebrew for thumb is "*bohen*"; for index finger "*etzba*"; for middle finger "*ama*"; for ring finger "*kemitza*"; and for baby finger "*zeret*." Total *gematriya* of the Hebrew names of the five fingers is 1118; equalling the *gematriya* of the first *pasuk* in *kriat shema*. This is significant because of the role of our hand when reciting the *shema*. *Ashkenazim* cover their eyes with the right hand when reciting the first *pasuk* of *shema*, and *Sephardim*, place their thumb and baby finger in the corners of each of the eyes with the three middle fingers on the forehead, to form the letter *shin*. *Rav Yitzchak Ginsburgh* notes that the *gematriya* of the four letter name of *Hashem* (*yud – heh – vav* and *heh*) is 26 and the *gematriya* of *Elokim* is 86. The first and lowest common multiple of these two numbers is 1118. In the first *pasuk* of *shema* written in the *Torah*, the "*ayin*" of the word *shema* and the "*dalet*" of the word *echad* are written in a larger font, spelling the word "*eid*" – "witness" to signify that when we recite the *shema*, we are witness to *Hashem*'s kingship over mankind. Another *pasuk* with the same *gematriya* of 1118 is "*Hashem hoshiah*

hamelech yaaneinu beyom kareinu" – *"Hashem,* grant victory! May the King answer our call" (Tehillim 20:10), indicating that when we recite *shema's* first *pasuk* with a *gematriya* of 1118, we merit *Hashem's* protection as in the second *pasuk* of *Hashem hoshiah* with the same *gematrya* of 1118.

3. The *pasuk "Shema Yisrael" (Devarim* 6:4) is said by most people 32 times a week. It is said once a day in *"korbanot"* (7 times a week); once a day in *kriat shema* of *shacharit* (7 times a week); once a day in *kriat shema* of *maariv* (7 times a week); once a day in *kriat shema* when going to sleep (7 times a week); at the end of *tachanun* on Monday and Thursday (twice a week); when we take out the *Torah* on *Shabbat* morning (once a week) and in the *Kedusha* of *musaf shel Shabbat* (once a week). Total number of times is 32. Some also say the *pasuk Shema Yisrael* at the end of *az yashir* daily which would take the total up to 39 times a week. However, the most prevalent *minhag* is that which is cited above which would total 32 times a week. The *gematriya* of the Hebrew word *"lev"* – "heart" is 32. Perhaps, that is connected to the *pasuk* at the beginning of *"kriat shema"* which says that the words of this important *tefillah* should be *"al levavecha"* – "upon your hearts" (*Devarim* 6:6).

4. The *Baal Haturim* points out that there are two *pesukim* which contain all letters of the *alef bet.* One is in our *parshah, Va'etchanan (Devarim* 4:34) and the other is in *Beshalach (Shemot* 16:16).

5. The *Taamei Haminhagim* (161) explains that since the three daily prayers were established by *Avraham (shacharit), Yitzchak (mincha)* and *Yaakov (maariv),* they are considered *"d'avuhon"* – "from our fathers," and this sounds like the word *"davening."*

6. The letters of the title of the *haftarah (Nachamu)* are *nun, chet, mem* and *vav. Nun* and *chet* are 58. *Mem* and *vav* are 46. Juxtapose them and you get 5846, which is precisely the number of *pesukim* in the entire *Torah.*

7. Trick question: The first *aliya* in *Va'etchanan* ends with the *pasuk "V'atem had'veikim…" (Devarim* 4:4). When a *kohen* is called to the *Torah,* the *gabbai* calls him by name and then concludes the formal text of calling him up, with the *pasuk "V'atem had'veikim…" (Devarim* 4:4). Hence this *aliya* begins and ends with the same *pasuk!*

8. The *haftarah* of *Shoftim* has four sets of duplicated words; namely, *"anochi"* (*Yeshayahu* 51:12); *"hitoreri"* (*Yeshayahu* 51:17); *"uri"* (*Yeshayahu* 52:1); and *"suru"* (*Yeshayahu* 52:11).

9. The word *"v'ahavta"* – "and you shall love" at the beginning of the first *pasuk* of *Shema,* is composed of the same letters as the word *"ha'avot"* – "the patriarchs," i.e. *Avraham, Yitzchak* and *Yaakov.*

10. The *pasuk "ata horeita" (Devarim* 4:35) is said before opening the *"aron hakodesh"* – "the holy ark" every *Shabbat* in the *Sefard nusach* and by all on

Simchat Torah; the *pasuk* "*v'atem had'veikim*" (*Devarim* 4:4) is said before the first *aliyah* is read; the *pasuk* "*v'zot haTorah*" (*Devarim* 4:44) is said after the *Torah* reading when the *Torah* is raised.

11. The *pasuk* says (*Devarim* 4:9) "*v'hodatam l'vanecha v'livnei vanecha*" – "and you will let the events that you witnessed at *Har Sinai* be known to your children and grandchildren." The *Yerushalmi* (*Kiddushin* 1:7) says that the only way a person will be able to teach his grandchildren is if he is able to marry off his children when they are young. At first glance, this *pasuk* seems to be a curse, because if the grandfather is the one educating the grandchildren, it indicates that his children are incapable of doing so. The *Torah Temima* explains that the *Torah* is describing a case where the father marries off his children young, and then merits teaching his grandchildren because his children are still not educated enough themselves to educate their children.

12. The two cases where one would be permitted to wear *tefillin* on *Shabbat* are:
    1. If a person finds *tefillin* in an unsafe or disrespectful spot on *Shabbat* and there is no *eiruv* allowing him to carry, he must put them on and take them home (*Shulchan Aruch Orach Chaim* 301:42).
    2. If a person is lost in the desert and has lost track of time, he begins counting days from that point on and keeps *Shabbat* on the seventh day. Nevertheless, he should still *daven Shacharit* with *tefillin* except for the *Shemoneh Esrei* of *Shabbat* as that would be performing two contradictory *mitzvot* at the same time – the *tefillah* of *Shabbat* while wearing *tefillin* (*Biur Halacha Shulchan Aruch Orach Chaim* 344:1).

13. It is a *mitzvah* on "*Erev Shabbat*" – "Friday before sunset" to taste the food that will be eaten on *Shabbat* (*Mishnah Berurah* 250:2).

14. In *tanach* (*Shoftim* 5:5), the *pasuk* says "*harim nazlu mipnei Hashem, zeh Sinai*" – "the mountains quaked before *Hashem*; this is *Sinai*," indicating that at the time of the giving of the *Torah*, *Har Sinai* shook as though in an earthquake. *Rabbi David Altschuler* (1740–1780) in his commentary *Metzudat David,* comments that sweat poured from the mountain (*Metzudat David Shoftim* 5:5).

15. *Rashi* (*Shemot* 13:5) explains that the milk is goat's milk and the honey is derived from figs and dates.

16. The eight instances where *shema* is recited because of past persecution of the Jewish people are the daily recitation of the *pasuk* of *Shema* right after *Birkat Hashachar* beginning with "*l'olam yeheh adam*" (7 times a week) and the one time when we recite the *pasuk* in the *Shabbat musaf kedusha*. In the 5th century, the Persian king, Yezdegerd the 2nd, considered the recitation of the *Shema* as treasonous, and he placed guards outside the shuls to ensure that Jews would not say *Shema*. In order to fulfill the *mitzvah* of saying the *Shema* in its proper time, the *Rabbis* instituted a daily recitation

of the *Shema* at home before coming to *shul* (daily, following "*l'olam yeheh adam*"), and a special *Shabbat* insertion during *Mussaf*, by which time the guards had left their posts. After Yezdegerd was overthrown and killed, these two insertions became a permanent part of our *Siddur* (*Rav Tzidkiyah ben Avraham Anaw* 1210–1280 in his work *Shibolei Haleket* 45).

17. *Michal*, the daughter of *Shaul*, the wife of *King David*, wore *Tefillin* (*Gemara Eruvin* 96a).

18. The *Magen Avraham* (*Shulchan Aruch Orach Chaim* 28:4) states that when one removes their *tefillin*, one should wrap the straps on either side of the *tefillin* box in the form of wings of a dove. The *gemara* (*Shabbat* 49a) tells the story of *Elisha*, who, when faced with a Roman decree forbidding the wearing of *tefillin*, nevertheless wore his *tefillin* proudly in the streets. Upon seeing a Roman officer approaching him, *Elisha* took his *tefillin* and hid them in his hands. When the Roman officer asked him what he held in his hands, he replied "I am holding the wings of a dove." When he was ordered to open his hands, a miracle occurred and behold the *tefillin* had changed into a dove. *Elisha* became known as "*Elisha Baal Kenafayim*" – "*Elisha*, the one who possessed wings."

19. "*Va'etchanan el Hashem*" means "and I beseeched *Hashem*" (*Devarim* 3:23). The *Vilna Gaon* (1740–1800) in his work, *Aderet Eliyahu*, points out that *va'etchanan* is equal in *gematriya* to 515 and that *Moshe* prayed 515 different *tefillot* to *Hashem* so that He would allow him into *Eretz Yisrael*. The *Baal Haturim* comments that the *gematriya* of *vaetchanan* is equal to the *gematriya* of both "*tefillah*" – "prayer" and "*shira*" – "song" indicating that when turning to *Hashem*, one needs both the content of the prayers we recite, as well as the style of the prayers through musical songs that we use to adorn our prayers.

20. In *Parshat Chukat*, *Moshe* sent messengers to the king of *Edom* and asked "*naabra na b'artzecha*" – "please allow us to pass through your land" (*Bamidbar* 20:17). Later in the same *parshah*, *Chukat*, messengers were sent to *King Sichon* with the request "*e'ebra b'artzecha*" – "allow us to pass through your land" (*Bamidbar* 21:22). In our *parshah*, *Va'etchanan*, *Moshe* asks *Hashem*, "*e'ebrah na v'ereh*" – "please allow me to pass and see the good *Land of Israel*" (*Devarim* 3:25). So we have three similar requests, "please let me/us pass into/through your land." Two are directed to flesh and blood rulers, the king of *Edom* and *King Sichon*, and one is directed at the *King of Kings*, *Hashem*.

PARSHAT EIKEV QUESTIONS

1. From where do we derive the *halacha* that we must recite 100 *berachot* a day? Who instituted this practice?

2. From where do we derive the custom of holding bread with all ten fingers while reciting the *beracha*?

3. How many *mitzvot* are involved in the production of bread?

4. What is the origin of covering knives when reciting *"birkat hamazon"* – "grace after meals"?

5. What four items enumerated in the *gemara* are not included in the annual income allocated to an individual on *Rosh Hashanah*; (i.e., if you spend money on these items they are over and above your heavenly preset income allotment) and where is there a *remez* in *Parshat Eikev*?

6. Two Jewish men, over the age of thirteen sit at the same table at the same time and eat the exact same meal which would normally require *"birkat hamazon"* – "grace after meals" and when ready to get up from the table, both do not remember whether or not they had said *"birkat hamazon."* The *halacha* in this particular case, is that one has to say the grace again and the other doesn't. Why?

7. Three *rabbis* were sitting discussing a particular *halacha* based on a *pasuk* in *Eikev*. The first *rabbi* said, "45 + 1 = 100 and that's how I derive the *halacha*." The second *rabbi* said, "well, if you use the principle of *AZBY*, then 45 = 100 and that's how I derive the *halacha*." The third *rabbi* said, "for me, 99 is close enough to 100 and that's good enough for me; besides 99 + 1 = 100." Explain the *halacha* and what is the *pasuk* under discussion?

8. From which *pasuk* do we learn that one should answer *"amein"* to the *beracha* of a *non-Jew*?

9. Where is there a hint in *Parshat Eikev* to the *Mishnah*'s words *"ben arba'im shana l'bina"* – "a person at 40 has wisdom" (*Avot* 5:21)?

10. How many times does the command *"kum leich"* – "get up and go" appear in the *Torah*?

11. When is there a custom not to eat grapes? *Halacha* or just sour grapes?

12. If one has before him wine and cake, which *beracha* does he make first?

13. If one has before him a date and a fig, over which fruit does one make the initial *beracha*?

14. If one has before him grapes (*haetz* and one of the *sheva minim*) and bananas (*haadama*), which *beracha* is recited first?

15. If one has before him an apple and a date, over which fruit does one make the *haetz*?

16. How is it possible that I must say the *beracha* "*hamotzi*" twice and "*birkat hamazon*" once during the course of one meal, although I have never left the table and never took my mind off the delicious food?
17. Which letter does not appear in the *birkat hamazon*?
18. Who composed the *beracha* "*hatov v'hamaitiv*" – "the 4th *beracha* in *birkat hamazon*" and for what event was it composed?
19. Did *Bnai Yisrael* wear shoes in the desert?
20. In one *pasuk*, find four positive *mitzvot*, listed consecutively, in exactly the same order, by the *Rambam* in the *Sefer Hamitzvot*?

PARSHAT EIKEV ANSWERS

1. The *pasuk* says "*Mah Hashem...shoel may-imach*" – "what does *Hashem* ask of you" (*Devarim* 10:12). This *pasuk* is cited in *Gemara Menachot* 43*b* as the source of this *halacha*. *Rashi* comments that we should read the word as "*meah*" – "hundred" and not as "*mah*" – "what." The *Baer Heitev* says that *David Hamelech* instituted the 100 daily *berachot* to counter the 100 deaths per day occurring in his time (*Shulchan Aruch Orach Chayim* 46:3). He further states that on *Yom Kippur*, when one cannot recite *berachot* over food, some *poskim* have suggested that periodically during the day, one should smell spices and recite "*boreh minei besamim*," to help reach the goal of 100 *berachot*. *Rav Yosef ben Yitzchak Bechor Shor* (12th century, France) comments that in this *pasuk* there are exactly 99 letters. And therefore by changing the word from "*mah*" to "*meah*" you are adding one letter to equal 100 letters, referencing the 100 *berachot* to be said daily. It is also interesting to note that if you take the word "*mah*" which is spelled "*mem-heh*" and transpose it using the "*at – bash*" *gematriya* method (a basic "reflective" substitution, where the first and last letters of the *alef bet* are transposed for one another; hence the name *at-bash*; and similarly the second and second last, and so on), the "*mem*" becomes a "*yud*" with a numerical value of 10 and the "*heh*" becomes a "*tzadi*" with the numerical value of 90 for a total of 100. As well, there is a *pasuk* (*Tehillim* 128:4) which says "*hinei ki chein yevorach gever yerei Hashem*" – "So shall the man who fears *Hashem* be blessed," where the first two words of the *pasuk* "*ki chein*" have the gematriya of 100, as if to indicate that a person will bless and be blessed with 100 *berachot*.

2. The *Baal Haturim* points out that the *pasuk* in *Devarim* 8:8 which talks about the bountiful foods found in *Eretz Yisrael* has ten words, "*eretz chita u'seorah, v'gefen, u'te'enah v'rimon eretz zeit shemen u'devash*" – "a land of wheat and barley, of vines, figs, and pomegranates, a land of olive trees and honey." From here, he derives the custom of holding the bread with all ten fingers while reciting the *beracha* "*hamotzi*," which likewise has ten words. As well, it is connected to the ten *mitzvot* associated with the making of bread (see question 3).

3. Again, the *Baal Haturim* connects the 10 words in *Devarim* 8:8 to the ten *mitzvot* associated with the production of bread; namely:
   1. You may not plow with an ox and with a donkey together (*Devarim* 22:10).
   2. Do not plant in your vineyard mixed species (*Devarim* 22:9).
   3. Leave fallen sheaves for the poor (*Vayikra* 19:10).
   4. Leave forgotten sheaves for the poor (*Devarim* 24:19).
   5. Do not collect grain from the corners of the field (*Vayikra* 23:22).
   6. You may not muzzle an ox while it threshes (*Devarim* 25:4).

7. Remember to give *Terumah* to the *kohen* (*Bamidbar* 15:21).

8. Remember to give *Maaser Rishon* to the *levi* (*Bamidbar* 18:24).

9. Separate *Maaser Sheni* and take it to *Jerusalem* (*Devarim* 12:17).

10. Separate *Challah* and distribute it to the *kohen* (*Bamidbar* 15:20).

4. There are two reasons given in *Mishnah Berurah* 180:11.

   1. The first reason is that the table is compared to the "*mizbeach*" – "altar" in the Temple. The altar was built without the use of metal implements because metal is used at times to shorten life, whereas the altar was used to serve *Hashem* and hence lengthen life (*Rashi Shemot* 20:22). As such, knives are removed from the dining table.

   2. The second reason is quoted in the name of *Rabbeinu Simcha* who tells of a certain man who reached the part of *birkat hamazon* which speaks about rebuilding *Yerushalayim* and became so distraught that he plunged the knife that was on the table into his stomach. Hence, knives are removed before *birkat hamazon*. Some rule that this applies only on the weekdays and not on *Shabbat* or *Yom Tov*. *Rav Ovadia Yosef* explained that *Shabbat* is a taste of the world to come, where there will be no death and hence on *Shabbat*, knives do not express the potential for harm or violence.

5. The *gemara* (*Beitzah* 16a) says that while a person's income is preset on *Rosh Hashanah* for the coming year, what is spent for *Rosh Chodesh, Shabbat, Yom Tov* and *Talmud Torah* are not included in the total. *Rabbi Solomon David Sassoon* (1915–1985, England) in his work *Moshav Z'keinim al HaTorah* notes that the word "*meireishit*" – "from the first crop" (*Devarim* 11:12) is curiously spelled without an *alef*. This indicates two things:

   1. That the remaining letters can be scrambled to form the word *Tishrei*, which is the beginning of the year (i.e., *Rosh Hashanah*).

   2. That these letters are the first letters of the words, *Rosh Chodesh, Shabbat, Yom Tov* and *Talmud Torah*; precisely the items that are enumerated in the *gemara* as exceptions to the preset income rule.

6. The law requiring one to say the "*birkat hamazon*" is based on the *pasuk* (*Devarim* 8:10) which says "you will eat and you will be satisfied and bless *Hashem*." Therefore it is a "*mitzvah d'oraita*" – "a Torah law" requiring one to "*bench*" – "say grace" only when one is satisfied. However, the "*Rabbanan*" – "the Sages" enacted a law requiring one to *bench* in all circumstances where one has eaten bread, whether one is satiated or not. Therefore, if a person is unsure whether or not he remembered to bench, we have to know whether it is a *Torah* law or a *Rabbinic* law before requiring him to "*bench*" again. The difference is as follows: if it is a *Torah* law, then we enact the principle of "*safek d'oraita l'chumra*" – "in case of doubt regarding a *Torah* law, we tend to be more stringent." If it is a *Rabbinic* law, then we enact the prin-

ciple of "*safek d'rabbanan l'kula*" – "in case of doubt regarding a *Rabbinic law*, we tend to be more lenient." Hence, in the case where one ate but was not satiated, his obligation to "*bench*" is a *rabbinic* obligation and therefore since he was in doubt as to whether he had "*benched*," the law would side with the leniency of not repeating the "*birkat hamazon*." And likewise, in the case where one ate and was satiated, his obligation to "*bench*" is a *Torah* obligation, and therefore, since he was in doubt as to whether he had already "*benched*," the law would side with the stringency of repeating the "*birkat hamazon*." (*Mishnah Berurah* 184:13)

7. As stated above in question 1, during the reign of *King David,* 100 Jews were dying each day. To stem the catastrophe of this plague, *King David* instituted the requirement to recite 100 blessings each day. The *Shulchan Aruch* (*Orach Chaim* 46:14) explains how one can arrive at the number 100. The *gemara* (*Menachot* 43b) derives this law from the *pasuk* (*Devarim* 10:12), "*mah Hashem Elokecha shoel mayimach*" – "what does *Hashem* ask of you," by changing the spelling of the word "*mah*" – "what" to "*meah*" – "one hundred." So to answer the riddle, one *rabbi* stated that 45 (the numerical value of "*mah*") would equal 100 (the numerical value of "*meah*"), if you simply add an "*alef*" – "one." Therefore, according to the first rabbi, 45 (*mah*) plus 1 (*alef*) = 100 (*meah*). The second *rabbi* said that if you use the *gematriya* method of *AT* – *BASH*, (ie., substituting letters in a word that are counted from the beginning of the alphabet, with letters that are the same distance from the end of the alphabet), the "*mem*" (13th letter in the Hebrew alphabet) in "*mah*" becomes a "*yud*," and the "*heh*" (5th letter in the Hebrew alphabet) in "*mah*" becomes a "*tzadi*." Hence, using *AT* – *BASH*, the numerical value of the word "*mah*" becomes the numerical value of "*yud*" (10) plus "*tzadi*" (90) which equals 100. Hence 45 = 100. The third *rabbi* said that if you count the number of letters in that *pasuk* (*Devarim* 10:12), you will total 99 letters, which according to the rules of *gematriya* is close enough to 100 and by adding the letter "*alef*" to the word "*mah*," we will now have 100 letters in the *pasuk*.

8. The *pasuk* says "*baruch tihiye mikol ha'amim*" – "you should be singled out from all the nations to receive blessings" (*Devarim* 7:14). The *gemara* (*Yerushalmi Berachot* 5:5) deduces from here that if a *non-Jew* blesses a *Jew*, the *Jew* should answer *amein*. The *Mishnah Berurah* in his commentary on *Shulchan Aruch* (*Orach Chaim* 215:2) derives from here that a *Jew* should answer *amein* to any *beracha* made by a non-*Jew*. Some state that this is a requirement and others state that it is optional.

9. The *Baal Haturim* points out that the *pasuk* ends with the words "*zeh arbaim shana*" – "these 40 years" (*Devarim* 8:4); and the next *pasuk* begins with "*veyadata in levavecha*" – "you will know with your heart" (*Devarim* 8:5),

alluding to the fact that a person acquires wisdom after the age of 40. The *Baal Haturim* adds that the word "*levavo*" – "his heart" is equal in *gematriya* to 40 and that the letter "*mem*" with a value of 40 is located right at the midpoint of the "*alef bet*" – "the Hebrew alphabet."

10. Three times. *Yitzchak* says it to *Yaakov* (*Bereishit* 28:2); *Hashem* says it to *Bilaam* (*Bamidbar* 22:20); and *Hashem* says it to *Moshe* (*Devarim* 10:11).

11. It is customary not to eat grapes on *Rosh Hashanah*. The *Mishnah Berurah* quotes the *Vilna Gaon* who says that one should not eat grapes on *Rosh Hashanah* for mystical reasons. The *Chazon Ish* permits it and says that the *Gaon* forbade it because there were only sour grapes available in *Vilna* at that time of the year (*Mishnah Berurah* 600:4).

12. It depends; usually the *beracha* of "*mezonot*" – "blessing on cake" comes first. If, however, it is at *kiddush*, then obviously, wine comes first (*Shulchan Aruch Orach Chaim Rema* 211:4).

13. Both of these fruits are from the "*sheva minim*" – "fruits identified with *Eretz Yisrael*." The order of the *sheva minim* is based on their proximity in the *pasuk* (*Devarim* 8:8) to the word "*eretz*." The order then is olives, dates, grapes, figs and pomegranates and since dates precede figs in the hierarchy, we make that blessing first.

14. In this case only (i.e., *ha'etz* and *ha'adama*), the concept of "*chaviv*" – "personal preference" applies. Therefore, if one prefers bananas to grapes, one would make the *ha'adama* first. In all other cases, there is a priority order of:
    1. *Hamotzi*
    2. *Mezonot*
    3. *Hagefen* (excluding *kiddush*)
    4. *Haetz*
    5. *Haadama*
    6. *Shehakol*
    7. *Shehechiyanu*

15. Since the date is one of the *sheva minim*, it goes first, even though the apple is more "*chaviv*" – "preferred."

16. The *Mishnah Berurah* (271:17) explains that if one made *kiddush* over wine after he had already begun to eat the *Shabbat* or *Yom Tov* meal, he must make an additional *hamotzi* because the saying of *kiddush* is considered to be an interruption. However, he is only required to say *birkat hamazon* once.

17. The *Baer Heitev* (*Shulchan Aruch Orach Chaim* 185:1) points out that the letter "*peh sofit*" – "final *peh*" does not appear at all in the normal *birkat hamazon*. It does, however, appear in the *Al Hanisim* prayer that is added to the *birkat hamazon* on *Purim*. The reason is that *peh sofit* is the common final letter to the words "*af*" – "anger" and "*ketzef*" – "quarrel"; both expressions of disunity. The *Baer Heitev* quotes the *Bach* who states that in order

to escape the possible wrath of *Hashem*, one should always say the *birkat hamazon* with intense "*kavana*" – "concentration."

18. The *Turei Zahav* explains it as follows: The city of *Beitar* fell to the Romans on *Tisha B'Av*, 65 years after the destruction of the second temple. The Romans did not permit the Jews to bury their dead, as punishment for revolting against the Roman government. A number of years later, on "*Tu B'Av*" – "15th day of *Av*," a new emperor permitted the burial of bodies and it was found miraculously that none of the bodies had decomposed. The *Sanhedrin* of *Rabban Gamliel* in *Yavneh* decided to compose a special *tefillah*, "*hatov v'hameitiv*" to commemorate this miraculous event (*Shulchan Aruch Orach Chaim* 189).

19. It depends. The *pasuk* says "The clothes upon you did not wear out, nor did your feet swell these forty years" (*Devarim* 8:4). There is another *pasuk* in *Ki Tavo*: "I led you through the wilderness forty years; the clothes on your back did not wear out, nor did the sandals on your feet" (*Devarim* 29:4). From the second *pasuk*, it appears that they did wear shoes and those shoes did not wear out over the 40 years in the desert. However *Rashi* (*Devarim* 8:4) implies that they walked barefoot and the miracle of the forty years was that their feet did not swell, as would normally be the case if one were to go barefoot on hot sand for an extended period of time. The *Siftei Chachamim* (*Devarim* 8:4) attempts to clarify the seeming contradiction by suggesting that the Jews who left *Mitzrayim* had shoes and those shoes did not shred. *Rashi*'s explanation here refers to the Jews who were born in the desert who did not have shoes and their feet did not swell.

20. In *Devarim* 10:20, we have the *pasuk*, "*et Hashem Elokecha tirah, oto taavod, uvo tidbak, uvishmo tishaveiah*" – "You must fear *Hashem* your God: only Him shall you serve, to Him you should cleave, and by His name shall you swear." The *Rambam* in *Sefer Hamitzvot* lists the following commandments: Positive Commandment #4 – we are commanded to establish in our minds fear and dread of *Hashem*, as it says in the *pasuk* "You shall fear *Hashem* your Lord." (*Devarim* 6:13); Positive Commandment #5 – we are commanded to serve *Hashem*, as it says in the *pasuk* "And you shall serve Him" (*Devarim* 13:5); Positive Commandment #6 is that we are commanded to be close to the wise and to associate with *talmidei chachamim*, as it says in the *pasuk* "To Him you shall cleave," (*Devarim* 10:20); Positive Commandment #7 – we are commanded to swear in *Hashem*'s name because it exalts, glorifies, and magnifies *Hashem*, as it says in the *pasuk* "And swear in His name." (*Devarim* 10:20). So here in this one *pasuk* we have four positive *mitzvot* listed in exactly the same order as they are listed by the *Rambam*.

PARSHAT RE'EH QUESTIONS

1. Find one *pasuk* that contains eight *mitzvot*?

2. Name an animal mentioned in the *Torah* that chews its cud and has split hooves and is nevertheless not *kosher*?

3. When the *Torah* was translated into Greek during the time of *King Ptolmy*, the word for hare – *"arnevet"* was changed to *"tzeirat haraglayim"* – "short legged creature." Why?

4. One of the non-*kosher* fowl that is listed in our *Parshat Re'eh* is *"bat hayaanah"* – "the offspring of the *yaanah*." Why only the young of the species? What about the *yaanah* itself?

5. On the *pasuk* "aser te'aser," the *Midrash Pliah* says that these words are related to the *pasuk*, *"im hasmol v'ayminah, v'im hayamin v'asme'ilah"* (*Bereishit* 13:9). What is the relationship between the two *pesukim*?

6. From where do we know that one may not get married on *"Chol Hamoed"* – "Intermediate Days of *Pesach* or *Sukkot*"?

7. *"Ayloney Moreh"* – "the Plains of *Moreh*" are mentioned in *Parshat Re'eh* (*Devarim* 11:30). Where were the Plains of *Moreh* previously mentioned in the *Torah*?

8. How many other "Plains of…" are mentioned in the *Torah*?

9. Which member of the animal kingdom was musical?

10. Which member of the animal kingdom has the same name as a city in Northern Israel?

11. Which member of the animal kingdom has the same name as a brother-in-law of *Esav*?

12. The *gemara* (*Pesachim* 68b; *Beitzah* 15b) explains that the use of the same word *"atzeret"* in two different places, in one case, together with the word *"la'Hashem"* (*Devarim* 16:8) and in a second instance, together with the word *"lachem"* (*Bamidbar* 29:35), teaches us that on *"Yom Tov"* – "a Jewish festival," we have to experience both physical and spiritual enjoyment. The phrase used is *"chatzi la'Hashem v'chatzi lachem"* – "half for *Hashem* and half for you." Where is this concept indicated in the Hebrew words *"la'Hashem"* and *"lachem"*?

13. There is only one *mitzvah* in the *Torah* that has the heading *"rak chazak"* – "just be strong." Which *mitzvah*? How many other times in *Tanach* do we find the words *"rak chazak"*?

14. Can one test *Hashem*?

15. Which *pasuk* in *Parshat Re'eh* dictates the necessity for Jewish unity?

16. The *Torah* reading for the days when *yizkor* is recited on the *Shalosh Regalim* is taken from *Parshat Re'eh*. What custom is connected to *yizkor* and to *Parshat Re'eh*?

17. The same *mitzvah*, presented three times in the *Torah*, with the exact identical wording. What is the *mitzvah* and why the three time identical wording?
18. Find a 15 word *pasuk* with six verbs?
19. The name of a two word modern *Israeli* city is mentioned in *Parshat Re'eh* but the two words are not adjacent to each other? Name the city?
20. With all the markers that the *Torah* gives us to find this place, one would certainly not get lost and would not need help from Waze. What place am I referring to and what are the markers?

BEREISHIT

SHEMOT

VAYIKRA

BAMIDBAR

DEVARIM

PARSHAT RE'EH ANSWERS

1. There is a *pasuk* (*Devarim* 12:17) that contains eight different *mitzvot*. One may not eat *maaser sheni* outside of *Yerushalayim* whether it is from (1) grain, (2) wine, (3) or olive oil. One may (4) not eat sacred first born animals outside of *Yerushalayim*. One may (5) not eat sacred sacrificial meat outside of the Temple courtyard. One may (6) not eat the meat of a *Korban Olah* – "burnt offering." One may (7) not eat other sacrifices before their blood is properly sprinkled on the "*mizbeach*" – altar. One may (8) not eat first fruits before they are placed in front of the *mizbeach*.

2. The *pasuk* says (*Devorim* 14:7) "*ach es zeh lo sochlu...hashesuoh*" – literally; "but from those that chew their cud and have split hooves, you may not eat; the *shesuoh*." *Rashi* identifies this as a unique animal that had two spines and two backs and the *Targum Yonatan* says that this animal had two heads.

3. The *gemara* (*Megillo* 9b) tells us that King Ptolmy's wife's name was *Arnevet* and the elders who translated the *Torah* into Greek felt that it would not be politically correct to use the name of the queen as the name of a non-*kosher* animal.

4. *Chizkiyah bar Manoach* (13th century France) in his work, *Chizkuni* (*Devarim* 14:15) tells us that the *yaanah*'s meat was inedible and therefore the *Torah* had no need to prohibit eating its meat; however the meat of the young "*bat hayaanah*" was edible.

5. The *gemara* (*Shabbat* 119a) uses our *pasuk* "*aser te'aser*" (*Devarim* 14:22) to learn the lesson of "*aser bishvil shetitasher*" – "give tithes in order to become wealthy"; ie., if you distribute one tenth of your income to the needy, in the merit of helping those less fortunate, you will be blessed with wealth. The *gemara* utilizes the similarity of the letters "*sin*" in "*aser*" – "you should tithe" and the "*shin*" in "*titasher*" – "you will become wealthy." *Rav Nisan Markel* in his work *Binat Nevonim* connects this *gemara* regarding the connection of the "*sin*" and "*shin*" to a *pasuk* in *Bereishit* 13:9. The *pasuk*, speaking about *Avraham* separating from his nephew *Lot*, says: "*im hasmol v'ayminah, v'im hayamin v'asme'ilah*" – "if you go to the left, then I will go to the right and if you go right, then I will go left." The *Binat Nevonim* notes that the difference between the letters "*sin*" and "*shin*" is whether the dot above the letter is on the right or on the left. He therefore explains: the message is that, "*im hasemol*," if you read the word with the dot on the left side as "*aser*" – "share your wealth by giving a tenth to charity," then "*ve'eiminah*," I, *Hashem*, will read it as a "*shin*" and enable you to merit "*te'asheir*" – "to become wealthy." However, "*ve'im hayamin*," if you read the word with the dot on the right side as "*asheir*" – "I will stay with my riches and become even wealthier by not supporting others through charity," then, "*ve'asme'ilah*," *Hashem* will

move the dot to the left side and decree that "*te'aser*" you will lose your wealth and only retain one tenth of your riches.

6. The *gemara* (*Moed Katan* 8b) deduces this from the *pasuk* "*v'samachta b'chagecha*" – "and you shall rejoice on your festival days" (*Devarim* 16:14); "*b'chagecha v'lo b'ishtecha*" – "on your festive days but not with your wife." The *Rambam* (*Hilchot Yom Tov* 7:16) states that one's joy is so great on the day of one's marriage, specifically because of one's love of one's spouse, that this would create a case of "*ein me-arvin simcha b'simcha*" – "we do not schedule two joyous occasions at the same time" (*Rambam* Laws of Marriage 10:14).

7. The "*Ayloney Moreh*" – "Plains of *Moreh*" are mentioned as part of *Avram's* journey in *Parshat Lech Lecha* (*Bereishit* 12:6).

8. Three:
   1. The "*Ayloney Mamre*" – "Plains of *Mamre*" was the place where the three angels came to visit *Avraham* (*Bereishit* 18:1).
   2. The "*Alon Bachut*" – "the Plains of Weeping" was the burial place of *Devorah*, the wet nurse of *Rivka* (*Bereishit* 35:8). In the case of *Devorah*, some translate the word "*alon*" as "the oak tree."
   3. "*Ayloney Moreh*" – "the Plains of *Moreh*" mentioned in *Parshat Re'eh* (*Devarim* 11:30).

9. Trick question: The "*zemer*" – literally, "mountain sheep" but the word *zemer* also means song, so the *zemer* was musical (*Devarim* 14:5). Interestingly, the *zemer*, listed among the ten types of *kosher* animals in *Parshat Re'eh*, is identified as the giraffe by *Rav Saadia Gaon, Rabbenu Yona, Radak*, and others.

10. There is an animal called the "*akko*" – "wild goat" (*Devarim* 14:5). There is a city in northern Israel called *Akko* (Acre in English). However, the animal is spelled *alef-kuf-vav* while the city is spelled *ayin-kaf-vav*.

11. There is an animal mentioned in *Parshat Re'eh* called "*Dishon*" – "Ibex" (*Devarim* 14:5). *Eisav* had a brother-in-law called *Dishon* (*Bereishit* 36:25).

12. *Rabbi Eliyahu Kramer, known as Vilna Gaon* (1720–1797, *Lithuania*) points out in *Peninim Mishulchan Hagra* that the *gematriya* of the word "*la'Hashem*" is 56 and the *gematriya* of the word "*lachem*" is 90. If you apply the principle that half of *Yom Tov* is "*lachem*" – "for your personal enjoyment" and half is "*la'Hashem*" – "for your spiritual devotion" and therefore divide each word by 2, i.e., take half the *gematriya* of "*la'Hashem*" (56 divided by 2 = 28) and half the *gematriya* of "*lachem*" (90 divided by 2 = 45) and add them together (28 + 45 = 73), you get the *gematriya* of "*yom tov*" which is equal to 73.

13. The words "*rak chazak*" appear regarding the *mitzvah* forbidding the eating of blood (*Devarim* 12:23). *Rashi* quotes a *Sifri* that cites a "*machloket*" – "argument" between *Rabbi Yehuda* and *Ben Azzai*. *Rabbi Yehuda* says

that the reason for the use of the phrase *"rak chazak"* specifically with the *mitzvah* of not eating blood is because in those days, people were apt to eat blood, and hence a special warning was warranted. *Ben Azzai,* on the other hand, says that because it was totally uncommon for people to eat blood, this special warning acted like a *"kal vachomer."* If a special warning was given for such an easy *mitzvah,* just imagine how careful one must be when encountering a difficult *mitzvah.* The phrase *"rak chazak"* only appears in two other places in *Tanach* (*Yehoshua* 1:7; *Yehoshua* 1:18).

14. The *pasuk* says *"lo tenasu et Hashem"* – "One should not test *Hashem"* (*Devarim* 6:16). The *Torah Temima* (*Devarim* 14:22) on the *pasuk "aser te'aser"* quotes the *gemara* (*Taanit* 9a), *"aser bishvil shetitasher"* – "that one should give *tzedakah* in order to increase one's wealth." The *Torah Temima* continues to comment by saying that this *pasuk* proves that one cannot test *Hashem,* except in the area of giving *tzedakah* in order to increase one's wealth, and cites as proof the *gemara* (*Ketubot* 66b) which quotes *Nakdimon ben Gurion's* daughter who says that using your money for acts of *"chesed"* – "kindness" i.e., charity, will act like salt and preserve your wealth. Therefore, giving *tzedakah* can affect your *mazal. Rav Shlomo Levinstein* (*Bnei Braq, Israel*) writes in his *sefer Umatok Ha'or* that if you take the letters of the word *"te'aser"* and take 10% of each letter, you will be left with *"mazalcha"* – "your *mazal."* The *"tav"* (400) becomes a *"mem"* (40); the *"ayin"* (70) becomes a *"zayin"* (7); the *"sin"* (300) becomes a *"lamed"* (30); and the *"reish"* (200) becomes a *"chaf"* (20), spelling the word *"mazalcha."*

15. The *pasuk* says *"lo titgodedu"* – "do not gash yourselves" (*Devarim* 14:1). The *gemara* (*Yevamot* 14a) deduces from this *pasuk,* through a play on words, that communities should not divide themselves into small cliques; *"lo taasu agudot agudot"* – "do not make many groupings," and gives an example of the need for unity in a community such as having only one *beth din.*

16. There is a custom that when one says *yizkor* on a *chag* in memory of a departed relative, that one pledges *tzedakah* – charity in their memory. The *Torah* reading on the days of *Shalosh Regalim* ends with the words *"ish k'matnat ado"* – "each individual according to his means" (*Mishnah Berurah* 494:17).

17. The *Torah* says three times *"lo tevashel gedi bachalev imo"* – "You shall not boil a kid in its mother's milk" (*Devarim* 14:21; *Shemot* 23:19 and *Shemot* 34:26). The *Torah's* exact three time repetition of this *halacha* is to teach us that if one would do this to any of these three categories; namely, non-domesticated animal like a deer; fowl or fish; and non-kosher domesticated animal like a pig; one would only transgress a *rabbinic* law and not a *Torah* prohibition (*Gemara Chullin* 113a). The *Torah* or *d'oraita* prohibition applies

to all meat and all milk from animals similar to a goat, which is specifically mentioned in the verse, such as cows and sheep.

18. The 15 word *pasuk* containing six verbs is *Devarim* 13:5: "*acharei Hashem Elokeichem telechu, v'oto tira'u, v'et mitzvotav tishmoru, u'vekolo tishma'u, v'oto ta'avodu, uvo tidbakun*" – "after *Hashem* you should walk, and you should fear Him, and observe His *mitzvot*, and listen to His voice, and serve only Him, and cleave to Him."

19. In *Devarim* 13:17, we have the word "*Tel*" – "mound" and in *Devarim* 16:1, we have the word "*Aviv*" – "springtime." Together they are *Tel Aviv*, one of Israel's largest cities.

20. No need for Waze in finding *Har Gerizim* or *Har Eival*. In the *pasuk* (*Devarim* 11:30), we are given the following six geographic markers to *Mount Gerizim* and *Mount Eival*. Both are on the:
    1. Other side of the *Jordan*,
    2. beyond the west road, that is
    3. in the land of the *Canaanites*,
    4. who dwell in the *Aravah*,
    5. near *Gilgal*,
    6. by the oaks or plains of *Moreh*.

PARSHAT SHOFTIM QUESTIONS

1. How is it possible to kill someone who is already dead?
2. If *"yaaleh v'yavoh"* is an elevator, and if *"teitzay rucho yashuv l'admato"* is a flat tire, then where in the *Torah* do we find the name of the TV show "Law & Order"?
3. Which word is an acronym for the four types of leaders in Israel mentioned in *Parshat Shoftim*?
4. Someone is murdered…there are no witnesses. Yet, we are able to identify the murderer and execute him for his crime *k'halacha*. What is the case?
5. A person was slandered. The perpetrators were executed? Why?
6. Regarding this *mitzvah*, it truly is the thought that counts. Explain.
7. From which *pasuk* in *Parshat Shoftim* do we have a hint to the custom of *"upsheren"* – "the custom of not cutting a baby boy's hair until he is three years old"?
8. It is time for *Kriat HaTorah* in *shul*. The *baal kriah*, a male *Jew* over the age of 13, is totally prepared for the reading, He is a fine, upstanding *Jew,* and it would seem that there is no reason to preclude him from being the *baal kriah*. The *Torah* scroll is *kosher*, is in perfect shape and is open to the correct place for the day's reading. Yet, the *baal kriah* is told that he cannot read from the *Torah* that day. Why not?
9. *Parshat Shoftim* gives reasons for exemptions from army duty. The *Rambam* (*Hilchot Dei'ot* 5:11) deduces from the *parshah* that one has to first have a job, then a house and then he can get married. However, the order of the exemptions specified in *Parshat Shoftim* (*Devarim* 20:5–7) seem to indicate that the order is house, job and marriage. Explain.
10. How many times is the phrase *"shema yisrael"* found in the *Torah*?
11. How does the Hebrew language teach us that bribery leads to perversion of justice?
12. In *Parshat Shoftim* we are commanded to listen to our *Rabbis* (*Devarim* 17:11). For how many *"mitzvot d'rabbanan"* – "rabbinic commandments" do we recite a *beracha* *"asher kidshanu b'mitzvotav v'tzivanu"* – "who sanctified us with His *mitzvot* and commanded us," just like we would for a *"mitzvah d'oraita"* – "a *Torah* commandment"? How many and what are they?
13. Two two-letter words that are complete opposites appear next to each other in *Parshat Shoftim* and in three other places in the *Torah*. What are the two words and where else do they appear together?
14. From where in *Parshat Shoftim* does the *Rambam* derive the need to minimize and control socialization between the sexes?

15. I am a member of the *Sanhedrin* in a capital case and am the last member of the court to rule the defendant guilty. As a result the defendant is freed. What is the case?

16. Can a "*mitzvah d'rabbanan*" – "a *rabbinic* commandment" interrupt a "*mitzvah d'oraita*" – "a *Torah* commandment"?

17. *Torah* or *Nevi'im*? Explain.

18. Find the names of two major *halachic* texts that are mentioned in this *Parshat Shoftim*?

19. When it comes to wives, how many is too many?

20. The *Torah* lists a number of things of which a king should not have too many; namely silver, horses and wives. The *Torah* then says that whilst sitting on the throne of his kingdom, the king should write a *Sefer Torah* (*Devarim* 17:18). Why does the *Torah* say "*k'shivto al kisei mamlachto*" – "sitting on the throne of his kingdom," it should have more concisely have said "*vehaya kesheyimloch*" – "it shall be when he rules"? Is there special significance in the word "*kisei*"?

PARSHAT SHOFTIM ANSWERS

1. The *gemara* (*Berachot* 18b) quotes the verse (*Devarim* 17:6): "by the testimony of two or three witnesses shall the dead person be killed." The *Torah Temimah* references a *gemara* (*Berachot* 18b) that teaches that just as *tzadikim* are considered alive even after they pass on, so too, wicked persons in their lifetime are called dead. This teaches that those wicked persons who have committed crimes for which they will be executed by *Beit Din*, are already considered dead, even while they are alive.

2. The answer is in the first two words of *Parshat Shoftim* – "*shoftim v'shotrim*" – "Law and Order."

3. *Parshat Shoftim* describes the four types of leaders in Israel, as *Moshe* clarifies the qualifications and responsibilities of kings, judges, priests and prophets. In Hebrew, these four leaders are *melech, shofet, kohen* and *navi*. The first letters of these words spell *mishkan* – the central address for the governance of the community. While Hashem is the ultimate ruler and administrator of the world, responsibility and authority over the management of earth is through humans and this is shared by the four types of leaders.

4. The *Targum Yonatan* on the subject of "*egla arufa*" – "the ritual performed when a corpse is found between two cities" (*Devarim* 21:8), tells us that after the *Sanhedrin* would perform the required ceremony, a row of worms would emerge from the calf and trace a line to the home of the murderer, who would then be condemned to death for his crime.

5. The *pasuk* teaches us the law of "*eidim zomemim*" – "conspiring witnesses"; namely, "we should do to them what they had planned to do to their brethren" (*Devarim* 19:19). Two witnesses said that *Reuven* killed *Shimon*. A second pair testified that the first pair could not have seen *Reuven* kill *Shimon* because they were somewhere else with them at the time that they said it happened. The first pair said slander and the punishment is capital.

6. The *mitzvah* of "*eidim zomemim*" – "conspiring witnesses" relates to the intention of the witnesses and not their actions. The *Torah* says "and you should do to him that which he had planned to do to his brother" (*Devarim* 19:19). The *gemara* (*Makkot* 5b) deduces from the above *pasuk*, "that which he had planned and not that which he had done."

7. The *pasuk* says "*ki ha'adam eitz hasadeh*" – "man is compared to the tree in the field" (*Devarim* 20:19). Just as the *mitzvah* of "*orlah*" forbids the eating of the fruit of the tree for the first three years, so too, we have the *minhag* of not cutting a male child's hair for the first three years. Additionally, just as it is forbidden to cut the "*peyot*" – literally "corners," of facial hair in certain areas of the face and temple with a straight razor, so too, we have the

mitzvah of "*peah*" which requires us to leave the produce of the corners of one's field to the poor. Many people travel to the grave of *Rabbi Shimon Bar Yochai* in *Meron*, Israel, on *Lag BaOmer* where there is a festive celebration and a communal hair cutting of those children who turned three that year. It is a celebration of a child reaching the age of *chinuch* and the ability to learn and absorb the words of *Torah*. See answer to *Nitzavim-Vayeilech* #18.

8. The *Torah* from which they were reading belonged to the king (*Devarim* 17:18). According to the *Rambam*, (*Hilchot Melachim* 3:1), a commoner may not read from the *Torah* of the king. The *pasuk* says: "*v'kara bo kol yemai chayav*" – "and the king should read from it all the days of his life" (*Devarim* 17:19). We deduce from this *pasuk*, that it is only the king who may read from the king's *Sefer Torah*.

9. Although the order of the *pesukim* is house, job/vineyard, and then marriage, the order in the *Rambam* is job, house and marriage (*Mishneh Torah Hilchot Dei'ot* 5:11). But if you read the *pesukim* carefully, perhaps there is no contradiction. *Rav Eliezer Rokeach* (1665–1742, Amsterdam) in his work *Maaseh Rokeah* explains the *Rambam* as follows: since the example of the vineyard is listed as "one who has planted a vineyard and not yet redeemed it" (*Devarim* 20:6), the vineyard must therefore be at least four years old, because of the laws of "*orlah*" and prior to the completion of four years, it would be impossible to redeem. Therefore, it is not inconceivable that the actual planting of the vineyard took place well before the actual building of the house.

10. The phrase *Shema Yisrael* is found in the *Torah* five times. All of the instances are in *Sefer Devarim* (*Devarim* 5:1; *Devarim* 6:4; *Devarim* 9:1; *Devarim* 20:3; *Devarim* 27:9).

11. The Hebrew word for perverting justice is "*tateh*," spelled *tav, tet, heh* (*Devarim* 16:19) and the Hebrew word for bribery is "*shochad*," spelled *shin, chet, daled* (*Devarim* 16:19). *Rav Yishayahu Halevi Horowitz* (1555–1630, Czech and Israel), known as the *Shlah Hakadosh*, explains the connection in his work *Shnei Luchot Habrit*, that the letters of "*tateh*" directly follow the letters of "*shochad*" in the Hebrew alphabet, with *tav* following *shin*; *tet* following *chet* and *heh* following *daled*. Hence, bribery leads to the perversion of justice.

12. There are six *mitzvot d'rabbanan* for which we make a *beracha* with the words "*asher kidshanu b'mitzvotav v'tzivanu*" – "He who sanctified us with His commandments and commanded us…" are:
    1. *Netilat yadayim* – washing hands before eating.
    2. Lighting *Shabbat* and *Yom Tov* candles.
    3. Lighting *Chanukah* candles.
    4. Reading the *Megillah* on *Purim*.

5. Reciting *Hallel*.

6. The three types of *eiruv*; *Eiruv Tavshilin*, *Eiruv Chatzerot* and *Eiruv Techumim*.

13. The two words are "*lo kain*" – literally "no yes." But in this context, it means "it is not so." It appears in *Parshat Shoftim* when *Moshe* tells *Bnai Yisrael* that they are not like the other nations of the world (*Devarim* 18:14). It also appears in *Bereishit* 48:18; *Shemot* 10:11 and *Bamidbar* 12:7.

14. The last topic in *Parshat Re'eh* was the *Shalosh Regalim* and the first topic in *Parshat Shoftim* was the need to appoint officers. The *Rambam* learns that *Beit Din* must appoint officers during the festivals "to go around and inspect gardens, orchards and riverbanks, so that men and women not gather there together, to eat and drink and possibly come to sin" (*Rambam Hilchot Yom Tov* 6:21).

15. The *halacha* states that in a capital case, if 13 out of the 23 judges in the *Sanhedrin* rule guilty, the defendant is guilty and receives the death penalty. In our case, I am the last to vote and all the other judges have already ruled guilty. If I rule innocent, he is still guilty because more than the minimum number of 13 have ruled guilty. However, if I rule guilty, then another *halacha* applies; namely, that a unanimous death penalty is suspect and the defendant must be freed (*Gemara Sanhedrin* 17a).

16. There are numerous cases where *halacha* specifies that a *mitzvah d'oraita* is interrupted in order to perform a *mitzvah d'rabbanan*. Here are some of them:

1. *Torah* study is interrupted for the reading of *Megillat Esther* (*Shulchan Aruch Orach Chaim* 687:2).

2. *Torah* study is interrupted for the lighting of *Chanukah candles* (*Mishnah Berurah* 672:2).

3. If one is in the middle of reciting *kriat shema* and suddenly the moon becomes visible, when one feels that there will not be another opportunity to say *kiddush levana*, one may interrupt the *shema* (*Biur Halacha Mishnah Berurah* 426:18).

The basic principle is that the study of *Torah* can always be interrupted by a *d'rabbanan* that can only be performed by an individual (*Shulchan Aruch Yoreh Deah* 246:18).

17. *Shoftim* is the only *parshah* in the *Torah* that has the same name as a book in *Nevi'im*.

18. In *Parshat Shoftim*, we find the phrase "*Mishneh Torah*" (*Devarim* 17:18), which is also a *sefer* written by the *Rambam*, and "*bayit chadash*" (*Devarim* 20:5), a *sefer* written by *Rav Yoel Sirkis*, known as the *Bach*, the acronym of his *sefer*.

19. *Rashi* (*Devarim* 17:17) quotes a *gemara* (*Sanhedrin* 21a) which states that since *King David* had six wives, and the *navi, Natan,* states "if that had been too little, I would add such and such as these" (i.e. an additional 12 wives) (*Shmuel* 2:12:8); and from here we deduce that 18 is the upper limit.

20. The *Torah* enumerates three things that can serve to distract him from ruling properly; namely, too much silver, too many horses and too many wives. *Rav Shlomo Ephraim Luntchitz* (1550–1619, Poland and Czech) comments in his *sefer Kli Yakar* that the Hebrew for these three categories is *kesef, sus,* and *isha.* The first letters of these three categories are *kaf, samech,* and *alef,* which spells *kisei.* The king must always focus on not allowing these three things to distract him from the duties of the throne, thereby ensuring that his kingdom will thrive.

PARSHAT KI TEITZEI QUESTIONS

1. You must not know you are doing this *mitzvah* while you are doing it. If you realize you are doing it, it ceases to be a *mitzvah*. Which *mitzvah* is it?
2. Forgetting this *mitzvah* results in a transgression. Which *mitzvah* is it?
3. Where is there a hint in the words *"zecher"* and *"amalek"* that would indicate that the eradication of *"amalek"* leads to the recognition of the unity of *Hashem*?
4. May one marry his sister-in-law?
5. For certain *mitzvot* enumerated in the *Torah,* we are promised a long life. Identify those *mitzvot*?
6. We know that 49 - 47 = 2. How can we explain 47 + 49 = 2?
7. Name two *mitzvot* in *Parshat Ki Teitzei* that appear in consecutive *pesukim*; both *mitzvot* involve pairs, however, one is a specific pair and the other is a general pair.
8. Where is there a hint in the spelling of the word *bechor* in *Parshat Ki Teitzei* to the fact that it is the firstborn who receives a double portion of inheritance?
9. Who in *Tanach* decided on a specific weapon of war because of a *mitzvah* in the *Torah*?
10. How many times do we find a phrase beginning with the words *"ki teitzei"* in the *Torah*?
11. What two kinds of *Torah* beef are low in cholesterol?
12. How could *tzitzit* and *tefillin* cause someone to transgress a *"mitzvah lo taaseh d'oraita"* – "a negative commandment in the *Torah*"?
13. Which is the only fruit that cannot be grafted?
14. The *kohanim* were permitted to wear their *"bigdei kehuna"* – "priestly garments" even when they were not working. However, one *"beged"* – "garment" was an exception to this rule because it was *"shaatnez"* – "a mixture of wool and linen." Identify the *"beged"* – "garment"?
15. What is the first allusion to *shaatnez* in the *Torah*?
16. Where do we make weekly reference to *shaatnez*?
17. The Aramaic translation of which *masechet* in *gemara*, results in the name of another *masechet*? The answer is found in *Parshat Ki Teitzei.*
18. Regarding the *mitzvah* of *"hashavat aveida"* – "returning a lost article," the *Torah* (*Devarim* 22:1–3) cites an inclusive rule ("for all lost objects") and specifies four cases: oxen, donkeys, sheep and clothing. What is the reason for singling out sheep?
19. Why did *Bnai Yisrael* merit the *mitzvot* of *tzitizit* and *tefillin*?
20. From where do we learn that one should put on the *tallit* before the *tefillin*?

PARSHAT KI TEITZEI ANSWERS

1. The *mitzvah* of *"shikchah"* – "forgetting a bundle, and leaving it for the poor" (*Devarim* 24:19) only applies when one actually forgot the bundle.
2. The *mitzvah* of "remembering that which *Amalek* did to us" is a positive commandment. Attached to it is the negative commandment "never to forget" (*Devarim* 25:19). Therefore forgetting will result in a transgression.
3. *Rav Klonimus Kalman Epstein* (1753–1825, Krakow) in his work *Maor V'Shemesh* points out that if you remove the *gematriya* of *"zecher"* – "memory," which equals 227, from the *gematriya* of *"amalek"* which equals 240, (*Devorim* 25:19), you are left with 13 which is the *gematriya* of *"echad"* – "one" and *"ahavah"* – "love." That is, when *Amalek* is eradicated, *achdut* will be achieved through unity and love.

4. It depends what kind of sister-in-law she is. There are three types of sisters-in-law:
   1. If it is your wife's sister, you may marry her only if your wife has died.
   2. If it is your brother's wife, then the laws of *"yibum"* and *"chalitza"* apply; if the brother died with no children, then there is a requirement from the *Torah* to marry his widow in order to "establish a name in Israel for his family." However, today, we are *rabbinically* required to conduct the ceremony of *"chalitza."*
   3. If it is your wife's brother's wife, then you may marry her, if she is widowed or divorced and if you are widowed or divorced.

5. There are three *mitzvot* for which we are promised long life; namely, honouring one's parents (*Shemot* 20:12); sending the mother bird from the nest (*Devarim* 22:6); and honest weights and measures (*Devarim* 25:13).
6. The 47th *parshah* in the *Torah* is Re'eh. The 49th *parshah* in the *Torah* is Ki Teitzei. The 2nd *parshah* in the *Torah* is Noach. The *haftarah* of Noach is the combination of the *haftarot* of Re'eh and Ki Teitzei. Therefore 47 + 49 = 2.

7. The *mitzvah* of *shaatnez* (*Devarim* 22:11) involves a specific pair; namely linen and wool. No substitution of any other material will render the garment as *shaatnez*. One *pasuk* earlier (*Devarim* 22:10) prohibits plowing fields with an ox and a donkey harnessed together. *Chazal* explain that this is a very general prohibition. *Sefer Hachinuch* says this *mitzvah* (*mitzvah* 550) applies not only with an ox and a donkey, but the same is true for any pair of animals, one of which is pure and the other is impure. And not only plowing is forbidden, but also any common labour, such as threshing, or pulling a wagon, and all other types of labour. These two *pesukim* highlight for us the necessity to explain and clarify *"Torah shebichtav"* – "the written law" with *"Torah shebaal peh"* – "the oral law."

8. The *Vilna Gaon* points out that the Hebrew word for first born, *bechor,* consists of three letters, *bet, kaf* and *reish.* The numerical values of these three letters are exactly double the value of the letters that precede them in the alphabet. *Bet* has a value of 2 and is double the value of the preceding letter *alef; kaf* has a value of 20 and is double the value of the preceding letter *yud*; and *reish* has a value of 200 which is double the value of the preceding letter *kuf.* These are the only three letters in the Hebrew alphabet with this characteristic, and therefore, says the *Vilna Gaon,* this is a proof from the text of the first born receiving a double portion of the inheritance.

9. The *pasuk* (*Devarim* 22:5) says: "*lo yihiye kli gever al ishah*" – "a woman should not wear a man's clothing." The *gemara* (*Nazir* 59a) deduces from this *pasuk* that a woman should not go to war dressed in armour. In the story of *Yael* and *Sisra*, the *Tanach* relates that *Yael* killed *Sisra* with a hammer blow to the head. The *Targum Yonatan* (*Shoftim* 5:26) explains that *Yael* did not use a sword to kill *Sisra* because of the admonition in *Parshat Ki Teitzei* forbidding a woman to use a man's clothing or tools. A sword would therefore be considered a man's tool.

10. There are four phrases that begin with the words "*ki teitzei.*" "*Ki teitzei lamilchama*" occurs twice (*Devarim* 20:1 and *Devarim* 21:10); "*ki teitzei machane*" (*Devarim* 23:10); and "*ki teitzei aish*" (*Shemot* 22:5). The two phrases of "*ki teitzei lamilchama,*" while in different weekly *Torah* readings, are located close to each other and it is important for the *Baal Kriah* to verify the correct spot, so that he does not show the incorrect spot to the *oleh.* There are differing opinions whether an *oleh,* shown the incorrect *Torah* reading spot, is required to repeat his *beracha* or not. (*Shulchan Aruch Orach Chaim* 140:3).

11. Another *Torah* joke! The two kinds of *Torah* beef that are low in cholesterol are the "*para aduma*" – "red heifer" (*Bamidbar* 19:1–22), and the "*egla arufa*" – the axed heifer" (*Devarim* 21:1–9). According to *Torah* law, neither of these heifers could have ever been pulled with a yoke (yolk)!

12. *Targum Yonatan* (*Devarim* 22:5) explains the words "*lo yihiye kli gever al ishah*" – "a woman should not wear a man's clothing" to mean that a woman may not wear *tzitzit* or *tefillin.*

13. *Rav Eliyahu Kitov* (1912–1976, Poland and Israel) in his *sefer, Ish Uveito* quotes the *gemara* (*Yerushalmi Kila'im* 1:7) which asks why children are compared to olive shoots? The *gemara* responds that unlike other fruit trees, the olive tree does not accept grafting and therefore all cuttings from the olive tree will be the same as the parent tree. So too, the children of righteous parents will be pure and righteous.

14. The *avnet* (*Rambam Hilchot Klei Hamikdash* 8:11). The "*avnet*" – "kohen's girdle," was constructed from fine white linen and was interwoven with

purple, blue, and scarlet material. According to the *rabbis*, the purple, blue, and scarlet were made from wool and interwoven with the fine linen.

15. The *midrash* (*Tanchuma Bereishit* 9:9) explains that *Kayin's korban* was flax, from which linen is made, and *Hevel's korban* was wool from sheep. The *midrash* says that *Hashem* decreed that we should not wear *shaatnez* because it is not fitting that a sinner's offering and the sacrifice of a worthy individual should be combined.

16. In *Eshet Chayil* which we sing every Friday night before *kiddush*, we say "*darshah tzemer u'phishtim*" – "she seeks wool and linen" (*Mishlei* 31:13). *Pirkei d'Rabbi Eliezer* explains that this alludes to *Sarah* who insisted on a separation between *Yitzchak* and *Yishmael*, because she realized that it was dangerous for them to be together.

17. The word "*kila'im*" means "a mixture of different species." It is also the title of one of the *masechtot* of *Mishnah*. *Onkelos'* translation of *kila'im* is the *aramaic* word "*eruvin*" (*Devarim* 22:9), which is also the name of one of the *masechtot*.

18. The *gemara* records many opinions and back and forth arguments trying to justify each of the four specified items. The conclusion at the end of this long exercise is that there is no specific reason for singling out sheep (*Bava Metzia* 27a).

19. *Avraham* refused to take any booty from the *King of Sedom* and said "I will not take even a thread or a shoe strap" (*Bereishit* 14:23). We therefore merited the thread of *tzitzit* and the leather straps of *tefillin* (*Gemara Chullin* 89a).

20. Here are a few answers:

    1. Because the word "thread" appears before "shoe strap" (*Bereishit* 14:23), we put on the *tallit* before the *tefillin*.

    2. We have a principle of "*tadir v'she'eino tadir, tadir kodem*" – "if you have two *mitzvot* to perform at the same time, the one which is more common, goes first." In the case of *tallit* and *tefillin*, we wear the *tallit* every day and the *tefillin* every day except for *Shabbat*, and therefore the *tallit* takes precedence.

    3. We have a principle of "*maalin b'kodesh*" – "we perform *mitzvot* in ascending order of holiness" and therefore we first don the *tallit* which is less holy than the *tefillin* (*Shulchan Aruch Orach Chaim* 25:1).

PARSHAT KI TAVO QUESTIONS

1. What word is found among the curses mentioned in *Parshat Ki Tavo*, the same number of times as its own numerical value?

2. The *Rambam* writes that the commandments of *Hashem* obligate all areas of human endeavour: action, speech and thought. What one *mitzvah* has *Torah* obligations in all these three areas of human endeavour?

3. Which *pasuk* in *Parshat Ki Tavo* is found inside *Hashem's tefillin*?

4. What word in the section dealing with the "*bikkurim*" – "first fruit offering" indicates that the amount to be offered as "*bikkurim*" be one part in sixty?

5. What is the only Hebrew letter missing from the section on "*bikkurim*" and why?

6. *Amein = Hashem* × 2. Explain.

7. Why were there specifically 11 curses given on *Har Eval*?

8. Identify one *pasuk* from the "*tochacha*" – "admonishments" in *Parshat Ki Tavo* which, when read as written in the *Torah*, is a curse, but when read backwards, word for word, is transformed into a *beracha*?

9. The *Arizal* states that the *mitzvah* of "*bikkurim*" – "first fruits," is a "*tikkun*" – "an atoning action," for the sin of the "*meraglim*" – "spies." List all connections between the two concepts of *bikkurim* and the *meraglim*?

10. *Rav Klonimus Kalman Epstein* (1753–1825, Krakow) states in his *sefer Maor vaShemesh* that the *mitzvah* of *bikkurim* atones for the sin of *Adam Harishon* eating from the *Etz Hadaat* – the tree of knowledge in *Gan Eden*. Explain the connection?

11. From which words in *Parshat Ki Tavo* do we learn that the person who lifts the *Torah* for *hagba* must lift it in all four directions so that everyone sees the writing?

12. When is it important for the *baal kriah* to be on good terms with the person receiving the *aliya*?

13. Give at least 15 references to "stones" in the *Torah*.

14. From where do we know that when it comes to tithing, a poor person and a *levi* must walk away from the table satisfied?

15. Where is there a requirement to feed *seudah shlishit* to a poor person?

16. Perhaps the *Breslov* "na – nach – nachma – nachman" was invented in *Parshat Ki Tavo*?

17. Most *parshiyot* have one word titles. How many have two word titles?

18. Where is there a reference to *tefillin shel rosh* in *Parshat Ki Tavo*?

19. In recent years, Israel has lent emergency support to countries around the world who have experienced natural disasters such as earthquakes, fires, floods, volcanoes, etc. Where is that predicted in the *Torah*?

20. Where do we find one of the "*simanim*" of *Rosh Hashanah* in *Parshat Ki Tavo*?

PARSHAT KI TAVO ANSWERS

1. The four-letter name of *Hashem* is found 26 times among the curses and its numerical value is 26.

2. The *mitzvah* of *bikkurim* contains all three areas of action, speech and thought. The *mitzvah* involves the action of bringing the fruit to the *Beit HaMikdash*, the reading through speech of the *parshah* of "*arami oveid avi*" and the thought process of being happy.

3. The *gemara* (*Berachot* 6a) cites the *pasuk* (*Devarim* 26:19) which states: "And He will make you high above all the nations" which is one of the four *pesukim* found in the *tefillin* which *Hashem* wears.

4. According to the *Baal Haturim*, the word "*tene*" – "basket" is equal to 60 in *gematriya*. The *Vilna Gaon* says that according to the *Torah* there is no minimum requirement for the *mitzvah* of *bikkurim*. The Rabbis, however, set this amount as ⅟₆₀th (*Rambam Hilchot Bikkurim* 2:17). The *Gaon* says that it is hinted by the use of the word "*tene*" – "basket."

5. The "*samech*" is the only letter missing. The *Baal Haturim* quotes the "*Ittur Bikkurim*" and says that the reason for the missing "*samech*" is that since *bikkurim* is in fact ⅟₆₀th, there is no need for this letter whose value is 60. An alternate explanation is that since one part in 60 has been separated, there are only 59 parts left and the "*samech*" (or 60) is missing. The *Ittur Bikkurim* adds that this is why the word "*tene*" is used for basket instead of "*sal*," which contains the letter "*samech*."

6. The *gemara* (*Berachot* 53b) says "He who answers *amein* is greater than the one who makes the *beracha*." The *Baal Haturim* explains (*Devarim* 27:26) that the *gematriya* of *Hashem*, as in the spelling "*yud-heh-vav* and-*heh*," is equal to 26. The *gematriya* of *Hashem* as in the spelling "*alef-daled-nun* and-*yud*," as it is pronounced, is equal to 65. The two added together equal 91 which is precisely the *gematriya* of *amein*. Therefore, the answering of *amein* is greater than the one who makes the *beracha* as it only contains one name of *Hashem*, while the word *amein* is equal to *Hashem*'s name times two.

7. *Rashi* (*Devarim* 27:24) answers that each curse spoken on *Har Eival* corresponds to one of the tribes of *Israel*. However, since *Moshe* did not intend to bless the tribe of *Shimon* before his death, he also did not want to curse the tribe of *Shimon*, and therefore there were only 11 curses.

8. *Rav Chaim Yosef David Azulai*, known as the *Chida* (1724–1806, *Israel*) in his work *Nachal Kedumim* says that he had learned from *chazal* that all the curses in the *tochacha* contained hidden messages of *beracha*. As an example, this particular *pasuk* found in *Devarim* 28:31, can be read reversed as follows: "*moshia lecha, v'ain l'oivecha n'tunot tzoncha; lecha yashuv, v'lo*

milfanecha gazul chamorcha; mimenu tochal, v'lo l'einecha tavuach shorcha."
Read this way, the *pasuk* turns from a curse into a blessing.

9. There are at least eight connections between the *mitzvah* of "*bikkurim*" – "first fruits" (*Devarim* 26:2) and the story of the "*meraglim*" – "spies" (*Bamidbar* 13:2). They are:

    1. The sin of the *meraglim* occurred at the time of "*bikkurei anavim*" – "the first fruits of the vine" (*Bamidbar* 13:20).

    2. The *meraglim* brought the largest fruits that they could find, as a sign that it would be difficult to conquer the land, and we therefore bring the finest fruits to the *Beit Hamikdash* as *bikkurim*.

    3. The *mitzvah* of *bikkurim* is the only *mitzvah* connected to *Eretz Yisrael* that requires a verbal pronouncement – "*arami oved avi*" (*Devarim* 26:5), which is an atonement for the verbal "*dibah*" – "evil report" (*Bamidbar* 13:32) of the *meraglim*.

    4. Wellsprings of Torah cites *Rav Menachem Ziemba, hy"d*, who quotes the *Arizal* who cites the *mishnah* (*Bikkurim* 3:1) which discusses the designation of the *bikkurim* fruit. The *Mishnah* says that if one sees a ripened fig or a ripened cluster of grapes or a ripened pomegranate, one should tie them with a ribbon and say that these are designated as *bikkurim*. Amazingly says the *Arizal*, the same specific fruits mentioned in the *Mishnah* are the only fruits mentioned in the story of the *meraglim* (*Bamidbar* 13:23).

    5. *Rashi* (*Devarim* 26:16) says that if you bring *bikkurim*, you will merit to bring them again the following year. Therefore the bringing of *bikkurim* guarantees long life, the exact opposite of the story of the *meraglim* which shortened the lifespan of an entire generation.

    6. In the story of the *meraglim*, *Moshe* tells the spies to "take from the fruit of the land" (*Bamidbar* 23:20), and in the *mitzvah* of *bikkurim*, similar words are used "and you shall take from the first of every fruit" (*Devarim* 26:2).

    7. In the story of the *meraglim*, it is stated "we arrived at the land to which you sent us (*Bamidbar* 13:27) and in the *mitzvah* of *bikkurim*, it is stated "when you arrive in the Land" (*Devarim* 26:3).

    8. The *meraglim* describe the land as "flowing with milk and honey (*Bamidbar* 13:27) and in the *mitzvah* of *bikkurim* we say "He gave us this land, a land flowing with milk and honey" (*Devarim* 26:9–10).

10. The *Mishnah* (*Bikkurim* 3:1) states "a man goes into his field and sees that a fig tree has bloomed." The *gemara* (*Berachot* 40a) quotes *Rabbi Nechemya* as saying that the fruit that *Adam* ate in the *Garden of Eden* was a fig tree. The *gemara* goes on to say that the very tree with which they sinned, pro-

vided the cover they required, once they realized their nakedness; namely the *"te'ena"* – "the fig tree" (*Bereishit* 3:7).

11. From the words *"arur asher lo yakim et divrei haTorah hazot"* – "cursed is he who does not uphold the words of this *Torah*" (*Devarim* 27:26), the *Torah Temimah,* based on a *gemara* (*Yerushalmi Sora* 7:4) learns that this refers to the person who lifts the *Torah* at the end of *Kriat HaTorah* (for *Ashkenazim;* However, *Sephardim* and *Chabad* lift the *Torah* at the beginning of the *Kriat HaTorah*). He must *"yakim"* – "uphold" the *Torah* in all directions so that the *"divrei haTorah"* – "the words of the *Torah*" can be seen. Seeing the *Torah*'s words during *hagba,* according to many authorities, applies equally to men and women.

12. The person receiving the *aliyah* (*oleh*) that contains the section of the *"tochacha"* – "the words of rebuke" (*Vayikra* 26:14–46; *Devarim* 28:15–69), must be on good terms with the person who reads it. If it were given to someone the *baal kriah* disliked, it would be possible to think that the *baal kriah* is directing all these curses specifically with the *oleh* in mind. Furthermore, a person cannot have personal thoughts when reading the *Torah* (*Ramah Shulchan Aruch Orach Chaim* 53:19; *Mishnah Berurah* 53:58; 138:5).

13. There are at least 15 references to stones in the *Torah:*

    1. *Yaakov* using the stones as a pillow (*Bereishit* 28:18).
    2. *Yaakov*'s covenant with *Lavan* called *"yegar sahaduta"* (*Bereishit* 31:45).
    3. *Moshe*'s chair in the war with *Amalek* (*Shemot* 17:12).
    4. The Ten Commandments – *Aseret Hadibrot* (*Shemot* 31:18).
    5. The commandment not to hew the stones of the alter with iron (*Shemot* 20:22).
    6. In the garments of the *kohanim, shoham* stones and setting stones were needed for the *ephod* and *choshen* (*Shemot* 25:7).
    7. Instructions on the removal of stones containing leprosy (*Vayikra* 14:40).
    8. The commandment of death by stoning for certain transgressions (*Vayikra* 20:27).
    9. The instruction to not erect an *"even maskit"* – "special flooring stone" used for idol worship (*Vayikra* 26:1).
    10. The *mitzvah* of accurate weights (*Devarim* 25:13).
    11. Giant stone monuments containing all the words of the *Torah* that were erected immediately upon entering Israel after crossing the *Yarden* (*Devarim* 27:2).
    12. The two stories of *Moshe* hitting the rock to get water (*Shemot* 17:6; *Bamidbar* 20:7).
    13. The Egyptians and their chariots sank like stones (*Shemot* 15:5).
    14. The stone removed from the well at the time of the meeting of *Yaakov* and the shepherds of *Lavan* (*Bereishit* 29:3).

15. The sharp stone used by *Tzippora* to circumcise her son (*Shemot* 4:25).

14. The *pasuk* says (*Devarim* 14:29) that when the *levi* or the poor come to partake of the tithes that were designated for them, "*v'achlu v'savei'u*" – "they shall eat their fill." *Rashi* quotes the *Sifri* who says that it is required to ensure that they are no longer hungry, but satisfied.

15. The *Mishnah* (*Peah* 8:7) outlines minimal requirements in the distribution of charity to a poor person. One of the parameters is that if you are hosting a poor person over *Shabbat*, you must provide three meals.

16. The *pasuk* states (*Devarim* 27:8) "*vekatavta al haluchot et kol divrei haTorah hazot ba'er heitev*" – "And on those stones, you shall inscribe every word of this *Torah* most distinctly." *Rashi* comments on the words "*ba'er heitev*," that the words were inscribed on the stones in 70 languages. The *Siftei Chachamim* quotes the *Nachalat Yaakov* and says that they were written in 70 languages to enable the nations of the world to copy it. He then directs us to read his commentary on *Devarim* 1:5 where the word "*heitev*" also appears. In it, he writes: "The numerical value of the word *heitev* is seventy, when calculated as follows: = היט"ב, 24 = הי"ט, 15 = י"ה, 5 = "ה 26; the numbers 5, 15, 24, and 26 add up to 70. Hence the concept of "*na – nach – nachma – nachman*" was invented in *Parshat Ki Tavo*.

17. There are six *parshiyot* with two word titles. They are *Lech Lecha, Chayei Sarah, Ki Tisa, Ki Teitzei, Ki Tavo* and *V'zot Haberacha*. Some *Chumashim* add a seventh which is *Acharei Mot*; but many *Chumashim* refer to this *parshah* simply as *Acharei*.

18. The *pasuk* says "*v'rau kol amei ha'aretz ki shem Hashem nikra alecha, v'yaru mimeka*" – "And all the nations of the world will see that the *Hashem*'s name is written on you, and they shall stand in fear of you" (*Devarim* 28:10). The *Chatam Sofer* cites two explanations for this *pasuk*. One, from the *gemara* (*Menachot* 35b) that this *pasuk* is referring to the "*tefillin shel rosh*" – "*tefillin* worn on the forehead.*" The second explanation quoted by the *Chatam Sofer* is from the *Ramban* explaining that Jews, by placing their faith in *Hashem* and not in happenstance or luck, will be recognized by the nations of the world as having a unique relationship with *Hashem*.

19. The *pasuk* says "*v'hilvita goyim rabbim*" – "you will lend support to many nations" (*Devarim* 28:12). The *Ibn Ezra* and the *Chizkuni*, among others, say that this prophecy will result in Israel assisting nations that have crop failures and other natural disasters. This prophecy is being fulfilled before our very eyes.

20. The *pasuk* says "*unetancha Hashem l'rosh v'lo l'zanav*" – "*Hashem* will make you the head, not the tail" (*Devarim* 28:13). This is the basis for the *minhag* to eat from the head of a fish or a lamb on the first night of *Rosh Hashanah*.

PARSHAT NITZAVIM-VAYEILECH QUESTIONS

1. Who were the only people mentioned in the *Torah* to discuss the *"acharit hayamim"* – "end of days"?

2. What does *Vayeilech* have in common with *Bereishit, Lech Lecha, Metzora, Pinchas* and *Chukat*?

3. Which *pasuk* in *Parshat Nitzavim* is a hint to the month of *Elul*?

4. How many times does the word *"mikeitz"* – "at the end of" appear in the *Torah*? What is common about all of them?

5. Which three kings in *Tanach* were the most prolific idol worshippers?

6. Some of the letters in a *Sefer Torah* are written with a stylized crown on top of the letter. Which letters have the crown?

7. How wide must a column be in a *Sefer Torah*? (i.e., how many letters at a minimum on each line)?

8. What is the widest column in a *Sefer Torah*?

9. How many rows must there be in every column?

10. *V'zot Haberacha* is the shortest *parshah* in four aspects. In one aspect, *Nitzavim* and *Vayelech* are each shorter. Which aspect?

11. How many times do we find the term *"nitzavim"* in the *Torah*?

12. Where is *Moshe* speaking directly to generations of Jews yet unborn and to future converts to Judaism?

13. What regular *Shabbat Torah* reading is sometimes read once a year, sometimes read twice a year and in some years is not read at all?

14. In the same vein, what fast day is sometimes observed once a year, sometimes observed twice a year and in some years is not observed at all?

15. In *Parshat Nitzavim*, we find a scribal oddity; namely, the insertion of dots over 11 consecutive letters in a *Torah* scroll, spread over two words *"lanu ulevaneinu"* and the first letter *"ayin"* of the next word *"ad"* (*Devarim* 29:28). Where else in the *Torah* do we find the scribal *"mesorah"* – "tradition" to insert dots over letters?

16. In *Parshat Ki Tavo*, the *pasuk* says *"b'sefer haTorah hazot"* – "in this *Sefer Torah"* (*Devarim* 28:61). In *Parshat Nitzavim*, the *pasuk* says *"b'sefer haTorah hazeh"* – "in this *Sefer Torah"* (*Devarim* 29:20). One uses the feminine *"zot"* and one uses the masculine *"zeh."* Which is it?

17. On the *pasuk "vayelech Moshe"* (*Devarim* 31:1), the *Baal Haturim* comments *"bet-gimel Hamelech peh-tav vayelech."* What does this cryptic comment mean?

18. From where do we have a guarantee that *Torah* will never be forgotten?

19. How are the *pesukim* of *Shemot* 23:26 and *Devarim* 31:2 connected?

20. How are the numbers 13 and 24 connected to the last, very busy day of *Moshe*'s life?

PARSHAT NITZAVIM-VAYELECH ANSWERS

1. The only people in the *Torah* to use the phrase *"acharit hayamim"* – "the end of days" were *Yaakov* (*Bereishit* 49:1); *Moshe Rabbeinu* (*Devarim* 4:30; 31:29); and *Bilam* (*Bamidbar* 24:14).

2. These six *parshiyot* are the only ones that have only positive *mitzvot*. *Bereishit* and *Lech Lecha* have one each; *Metzora* has eleven, *Chukat* has three; *Pinchas* has six and *Vayeilech* has two.

3. The *Baal Haturim* points out that the first letters of the words *"et levavcha v'et levav"* – "your hearts and the hearts of" (*Devarim* 30:6) spell *Elul*. This *pasuk* speaks about *"teshuva"* – "repentance," hinting at the special power of the month of *Elul* for repentance and the *minhag* to say *"selichot"* – "penitential prayers" during this time.

4. The word *"mikeitz"* appears nine times in the *Torah* and in each instance, it is followed by a specified amount of time:
   1. *"vayehi mikeitz yamim rabbim"* – "it was after many days that *Kayin* brought his offering" (*Bereishit* 4:3).
   2. *"vayehi mikeitz arba'im yom,"* 40 days after the ark settles on *Mount Ararat, Noach* sends the raven (*Bereishit* 8:6).
   3. *"mikeitz eser shanim l'shevet"* – "10 years after settling in *Eretz Canaan, Sara* gives *Hagar* to *Avraham"* (*Bereishit* 16:3).
   4. *"vayehi mikeitz shnatayim yamim"* – "two years after the butler is released, *Paroh* has his two dreams" (*Bereishit* 41:1).
   5. *"vayehi mikeitz shloshim shana v'arba meot shana"* – "and 430 years after the *Brit Bein Habetarim,* the *Bnai Yisrael* leave *Mitzrayim"* (*Shemot* 12:41).
   6. *"mikeitz arbaim yom"* – "40 days after they are sent, the *meraglim* return" (*Bamidbar* 13:25).
   7. *"mikeitz arbaim yom"* – "after being on *Har Sinai* for 40 days, *Moshe* receives the first set of *luchot"* (*Devarim* 9:11).
   8. *"mikeitz sheva shanim"* – "after seven years, *shemita* is observed" (*Devarim* 15:1).
   9. *"mikeitz sheva shanim"* – "after seven years, the *mitzvah* of *hakhel* is performed" (*Devarim* 31:10).

5. *Achav, Yeravam,* and *Menashe.* The *Baal Haturim* sees this hinted in the words *"asher yakumu meiachareichem"* (*Devarim* 29:21) which begin with the same letters as *Achav, Yeravam,* and *Menashe.*

6. The letters are identified by the acronym *"SHATNEZ GATZ."* The letters are *shin, ayin, tet, nun, zayin, gimel,* and *tzadi.*

7. The *Shulchan Aruch* (*Yoreh Deah* 272:2) specifies that the minimum number of letters that must be able to appear on a line of the *Torah* is 30, as denoted by the word "*l'mishpchoteichem*" (a word of ten letters) written three times.

8. The column where one can find the *Shirat Hayam* ("*az yashir*") is unique as it is wider than all other columns in a *Sefer Torah*.

9. The general standard today is 42 lines in a column of a *Sefer Torah*. *Masechet Sofrim*, a minor tractate of the *gemara* dealing with the rules of the writing and reading of a *Sefer Torah*, says that each "*amud*" – "column" of a *Torah* should have at least 42 lines, like the number of travels of *Bnai Yisrael* in the desert. However, the *Rambam, Tur* and *Rosh* all say, based on the same source, that ideally the *amud* should have no less than 48 lines and *Rav Shlomo Ganzfried* (1804–1886, Ukraine and Slovenia), author of the *Kitzur Shulchan Aruch*, says in his work on scribal writings, *Keset Hasofer* concludes that they must have had a different version of this *Masechet Sofrim*. The *Rambam* also reveals that when he wrote his own *Sefer Torah*, he wrote in *amudim* of 51 lines, similar to the *Yemenite* Jews to this day, who write their *Torah* with 51 lines per *amud*, in line with their custom of following all of the *Rambam*'s rulings.

10. *V'zot Haberacha* is the shortest *parshah* in number of words (512), number of letters (1969), number of lines (70), and value in *gematriya* (134008). But *Nitzavim* and *Vayeilech* are shorter in the number of *pesukim*. *V'zot Haberacha* has 41 *pesukim*, while *Nitzavim* has 30 and *Vayeilech* has 40.

11. There are four other places in the *Torah* where the word "*nitzavim*" is used:

   1. When the angels came to *Avraham*'s tent, "*shlosha anashim nitzavim*" – "there were three angels standing" (*Bereishit* 18:2).

   2. When *Yosef* felt he could not longer control his emotions in front of his brothers, "*lechol hanitzavim alav*" (*Bereishit* 45:1).

   3. When *Moshe* and *Aharon* leave *Paroh*, they found protesters standing and waiting for them "*nitzavim likratam*" (*Shemot* 5:20).

   4. When *Datan* and *Aviram* confront *Moshe*, "*v'Datan v'Aviram yatzu nitzavim*" (*Bamidbar* 16:27).

   In each case, *nitzavim* connotes standing firmly and confronting. There is a mission and purpose in being there. It is totally unlike the Hebrew word for standing, "*omdim*," which connotes passive standing. There are a number of other places where we find the word "*nitzav*," but these are the only places with "*nitzavim*."

12. In *Parshat Nitzavim* (*Devarim* 29:14), *Moshe* directs his comments to "both with those who are standing here with us this day…and with those who are not with us here this day." *Rashi* comments that you may think that some people were absent, and it is that to which the *pasuk* refers. But *Rashi* rejects that explanation, because we had just read "you stand this day, all of you,

before *Hashem*" (*Devarim* 29:9). And therefore *Rashi* concludes that this must mean that *Moshe* is referring to generations to be born in the future. The *gemara* (*Shevuot* 39a) quotes a *baraita* which says that the words "those who are not with us here this day" refers to "subsequent generations, and the converts who will convert in the future."

13. It is *Parshat Vayelech,* and we are obviously speaking about the Jewish calendar year. Because *Vayelech* is always read around *Rosh Hashanah,* there are years when it is read just before *Rosh Hashanah,* and years when it is read just after *Rosh Hashanah.* If *Rosh Hashanah* occurs on either a *Shabbat* or a Thursday (i.e., in the case of a Thursday, *Yom Kippur* will be on a *Shabbat*), then there will be only one possible *Shabbat Torah* reading between *Rosh Hashanah* and *Simchat Torah,* and that will be the reading of *Haazinu,* so that we can read *V'zot Haberacha* on *Simchat Torah.* In those calendar years, *Vayelech* would be read on the *Shabbat* before *Rosh Hashanah.* Therefore, if you had two consecutive years when *Rosh Hashanah* is on a *Shabbat,* you would read *Vayelech* once in each of those years. However, if *Rosh Hashanah* in Year 1 occurred on either Thursday or *Shabbat,* and in Year 2 occurred on one of the two other possible days, then *Vayelech* would fall before *Rosh Hashanah* 1 and after *Rosh Hashanah* 2; hence, we would not read *Vayelech* at all that year. The third possibility is that *Rosh Hashanah* 1 was either Monday or Tuesday, and *Rosh Hashanah* 2 was either Thursday or *Shabbat,* and with that combination, *Vayelech* would be read after *Rosh Hashanah* 1 and before *Rosh Hashanah* 2; hence, *Vayelech* would be read twice in that Hebrew calendar year.

14. The answer is *Asara b'Tevet* and we are now speaking about the secular calendar year. Hope I did not throw you off, but this riddle has nothing to do with *Nitzavim – Vayelech.* It is inserted here because of its similarity to the previous riddle. *Asara B'Tevet* sometimes occurs in December and sometimes occurs in January. There are cases when *Asara B'Tevet* will be in January and again in December and hence we have *Asara B'Tevet* twice in that secular calendar year, and there are cases when *Asara B'Tevet* will be in December and not again until the following January and hence there is no *Asara B'Tevet* in that calendar year at all.

15. In *Bamidbar* 3:39, we have a similar occurrence of scribal dots above the word "*v'Aharon*" in the *Torah* scroll. The *Minchat Shai* comments that there are ten locations in the *Torah* where dots are inserted by the "*sofer*" – "scribe" according to a "*mesorah*" – "tradition." *Rashi* refers us in that same location (*Bamidbar* 3:39) to the *Sifri Bamidbar* 69:2, commenting on the dots above the word "*rechokah*" – "from a distant way" (*Bamidbar* 9:10), where the *Sifri* enumerates the other locations of this oddity. The *Sifri* (*Sifri Bamidbar* 69:2) explains each of the occurrences of scribal dots. The ten occurrences are:

1. *Bereishit* 16:5 – "May Hashem judge between me (*Sarah*) and between you (*Abraham*), "*uveinecha*": There is a dot above the *yud* in "*uveinecha*."

2. *Bereishit* 18:9 – "And they said to him – "*eilav*": Where is *Sarah*, your wife?" There are dots above the *alef, yud* and *vav* in "*eilav*."

3. *Bereishit* 19:33 – "and he did not know in her laying down and in her rising – "*uvekumah*." There is a dot above the *vav* in "*uvekumah*."

4. *Bereishit* 33:4 – "And he (*Eisav*) kissed him (*Jacob*)," "*vayishakehu*." There are dots above all the letters in "*vayishakehu*."

5. *Bereishit* 37:12 – "And his brothers went to graze their father's flock in *Shchem*," "*et*." There are dots above "*et*."

6. *Bamidbar* 21:30 – "We have laid it waste until *Nofach* which reaches unto *Medva*," "*asher*." There is a dot above the *resh* in "*asher*."

7. *Bamidbar* 3:39 – "All the numbered of the *levi'im*, whom *Moshe* and *Aharon* numbered," "*Aharon*." There are dots above "*Aharon*."

8. *Bamidbar* 3:29 – "And *issaron, issaron*, for the one lamb," "*v'issaron*." There is a dot above the second *vav* in "*v'issaron*."

9. *Devarim* 29:28 – "The hidden things are for *Hashem* and the revealed ones are for us and our children forever," "*lanu ulevanenu ad*." There are dots above "*lanu ulevanenu*" and the *ayin* in "*ad*."

10. *Bamidbar* 9:10 – "from a distant way," "*rechokah*." There is a dot above the *heh* in "*rechokah*."

16. *Rashi* (*Devarim* 29:20) explains that the word "*hazot*" refers to "*Torah*" which is a feminine noun, while the word "*hazeh*" refers to the word "*sefer*" which is a masculine noun. *Rashi* explains that one can determine whether the emphasis of the *pasuk* is speaking about the noun *Torah*, or the compound noun *Sefer Torah*, by the position of the "*tipcha*" which is the "*trop*" – "musical note."

17. The *Baal Haturim* refers us to the *Shulchan Aruch* (*Orach Chaim* 428), which states that *Nitzavim* always occurs before *Rosh Hashanah*, and therefore, when *Rosh Hashanah* (which cannot occur on Sunday, Wednesday or Friday), occurs on Monday or Tuesday, there will then be two *Shabbatot* between *Rosh Hashanah* and *Sukkot*, requiring us to split *Nitzavim* and *Vayelech*; reading *Nitzavim* before *Rosh Hashanah*; *Vayelech* between *Rosh Hashanah* and *Yom Kippur*; and *Haazinu* between *Yom Kippur* and *Sukkot*. The "*siman*" – "hint" to this rule is provided to us by the *Baal Haturim* based on a *pasuk* (*Daniel* 1:5) "*mipat bag hamelech*." The *Baal Haturim* says: "*bag haMelech*," i.e., "*bet-gimel*" – if *Rosh Hashanah* (*haMelech*) occurs on a Monday or Tuesday, then "*pat Vayelech*" – "*pat*" from the word "*patot*" – "break into parts" (*Vayikra* 2:6), then *Nitzavim* and *Vayelech* are broken in two and we read *Vayelech* by itself but not as part of a double *parshah*. But if *Rosh Hashanah* occurs on a Thursday or *Shabbat*, then there will be only

one *Shabbat* between *Rosh Hashanah* and *Sukkoth* and on that *Shabbat* we will read *Haazinu*, resulting in *Nitzavim* and *Vayelech* being read together before *Rosh Hashanah*.

18. The *pasuk* says "*ki lo tishakach mipi zaro*" – "since it will never be lost from the mouth of their offspring" (*Devarim* 31:21). *Rashi* comments that this is an assurance to Israel that the *Torah* will never be entirely forgotten by their descendants, and as proof, references a statement by *Rabbi Shimon Bar Yochai* in the *gemara* (Shabbat 138b). It is fitting therefore that annually on *Lag BaOmer*, young male children reaching the age of three, the age when they formally begin *Torah* studies, are taken for their first haircut to the burial place of *Rabbi Shimon Bar Yochai*, connecting him perpetually to the future generations of our people.

19. In *Devarim* 31:2, *Moshe* proclaims that today he reached the age of 120 years. *Rashi* comments that this was the 7th day of *Adar*, *Moshe*'s birthday and also the day that he would die. In *Shemot* 23:26, the *pasuk* says *Hashem* will "let you know the full count of your days." The *gemara* (*Sotah* 13b) connects these two *pesukim* with the lesson that *Hashem* completes the years of *tzaddikim* from day to day and from month to month, indicating that the righteous will live out their years fully; resulting in their passing on their birthday.

20. The *Daat Zekeinim*, quoting the *midrash*, (*Devarim* 31:26) says that on this date, the seventh day of *Adar*, *Moshe* personally wrote 13 *Torah* scrolls. He read 12 of them, one for each of the tribes, urging them to observe the *Torah* meticulously. He read to the men and women separately, warning them to treasure their *Torah* scroll and protect it from all hazards. He took the 13th *Torah* scroll and deposited it in the *Aron Hakodesh* next to the second set of "*luchot*" – "tablets" that he brought down from *Har Sinai*. Hence, 13 is the number of scrolls that *Moshe* wrote and 24 is the number of times that he read from the *Torah* on the last day of his life, 12 times for men and 12 times for women.

1. What other parts of *Tanach* are scribed in the same form as *Parshat Haazinu*?

2. From which *pasuk* do we learn the *halacha* of "*zimun*" – "the formal invitation to "*bench*" – "say grace after meals" that is required when at least three adult males eat together"?

3. Three Jewish males over *Bar Mitzvah* are beginning *birkat hamazon* at the same time, at the same table, and yet are not required to do "*zimun*." Why not?

4. I am about to say *birkat hamazon*. I am the only male over *Bar Mitzvah* at the table and therefore there is no "*zimun*." Yet I am required to *bench* "*al hakos*" – "with a full cup of wine." Why?

5. Three Jewish males over *Bar Mitzvah* are beginning *birkat hamazon* at the same time, at the same table, and yet only one is permitted to lead the "*zimun*." They all washed, all ate bread, all ate their meal and all finished at the same time. None are mourners; they are all of the same status; i.e., there is no *kohen*, no exceptional *Torah* scholar, no king etc. Explain the case?

6. Name two *Torah* phrases concerning wine which describe the finest wines by using adjectives that literally describe non *kosher* substances?

7. Why is *Yehoshua* called *Hoshea* in *Parshat Haazinu* (*Devarim* 32:44)?

8. It's a name in a song in the *Torah*, it's part of a name of a song on *Shabbat* and part of a name of a song on *Chanukah*? What is the word?

9. *Hashem* is described as "*tzadik v'yashar hu*" in *Shirat Haazinu*. Who is hinted to in the *pasuk* "*Or zarua la'tzadik u'liyishrei lev simcha*"?

10. What is the one *mitzvah* that the *Rambam* includes as a *mitzvah* and the *Sefer Hachinuch* doesn't?

11. How many songs are there in *Tanach*? What are they?

12. How many rows are there in *Shirat Haazinu*?

13. The letters *alef-nun-yud* can be combined to form the word *ani* and the word *ayin*. How is the spelling of these two words connected to the *teshuva* process?

14. What is the meaning of the mnemonic "*heh-zayin-yud-vav-lamed-kaf*"?

15. There are four types of heavenly moisture, all occurring in one *pasuk* of *Parshat Haazinu*. Identify the four types?

16. What new name for *Bnai Yisrael,* that has never been used in the *Torah* until this point, is introduced in *Parshat Haazinu*, and appears twice more in *Parshat V'zot Haberacha*?

17. Find five words in a row in *Parshat Haazinu*, all beginning with the same letter?

18. Bring proof of *Rashi*'s knowledge of ornithology?

19. *Rashi* (*Devarim* 32:26) quotes the *Sifri* (*Sifri Devarim* 322:1) which breaks the word "*afeihem*" into three syllables "*af*" "*ei*" "*hem*" meaning: "*af*," I said in

My anger; "*ei*" "*hem*," that those who are looking for them would ask about them, "Where are they?" Where else in *Rashi's* commentary on *Torah* does he break down a word into three parts in order to clarify its definition?

20. Two words in the first *pasuk* in the *Torah* have been asked to be witnesses three times in *Sefer Devarim*. Now they are asked to come and testify. Who are the witnesses and what are the four references in the *Torah*?

PARSHAT HAAZINU ANSWERS

1. The song of *Haazinu* (*Devarim* 32:1–43) is written in a *Torah* scroll as two columns with a blank space in between. This form is also found in the *Shirah* of *Yehoshua* (12:9–24); in *Megillat Esther* (9:7–9) when the sons of *Haman* are listed; and in *Megillat Kohelet* (3:2–8) following the introductory passage of "to everything there is a time and a time to every purpose under *Heaven*."

2. In *Haazinu* (*Devarim* 32:3), we read, "*ki shem Hashem ekra, havu godel laylokaynu*" – "When I (singular) call *Hashem*'s name, you (plural) praise *Hashem* for His Greatness." This teaches us that when three eat together, one calls the other two to bless *Hashem*.

3. If three adult males ate together at one of the first two *Shabbat* meals and all forgot to say the special *Shabbat* addition of "*r'tzei*," they have to repeat the *birkat hamazon* in its entirety. However, since they had already performed the "*zimun*" the first time around, they are not required to do that again (*Shulchan Aruch Orach Chaim* 188:9).

4. It must be the *Pesach Seder* night, for then, everyone is required to recite *birkat hamazon* with a full "*revi'it*" – "specific quantity" of wine.

5. The case is where three males sat together, one was eating dairy and the other two were eating meat. In order for "*zimun*" to take place, there has to be the possibility of eating together; i.e. sharing bread together. Since those eating meat cannot eat dairy for a considerable amount of time (one to six hours depending on custom), and since the one eating dairy is permitted to eat meat simply by washing his mouth, the one eating dairy is therefore the only one who makes "*zimun*" possible; the only one capable of sharing bread together. Therefore he must lead the "*zimun*" (*Mishnah Berurah* 196:9).

6. The first phrase is found in *Parshat Korach* (*Bamidbar* 18:12); "*cheilev tirosh*" – literally, "the fat of the wine." The second phrase is found in *Parshat Haazinu* (*Devarim* 32:14) "*dam einav*" – literally "the blood of the vine." Both fat ("suet") and blood are non *kosher* items.

7. The *Kli Yakar* says that *Moshe* gave *Yehoshua* this name for the sole purpose of *Hashem* protecting him from the "*atzat meraglim*" – "the plan of the *meraglim*" (*Bamidbar* 13:16). Accordingly, the name *Yehoshua* was to be used as protection for as long as people from that generation were alive. Once that generation died out, *Yehoshua* had no need for the name and as such would once again be called *Hoshea*. The *yud* given to *Hoshea* was taken from *Sarai*'s name when her name was changed to *Sarah*, at age 89, a year before she gave birth to *Yitzchak*. We also know that *Sarah* died at the age of 127 meaning that *Sarai* was called *Sarah* (without a *yud*) for 38 years. *Yehoshua* had the *yud* added to his name at the incident of the spies,

in the second year after *Yetziat Mitzrayim.* The Jews traveled in the desert for 40 years before entering *Eretz Yisrael,* meaning that *Yeshoshua* had the letter *yud* for 38 years, the exact amount of time that *Sarah* didn't. Now that the 38 years were up (this being the exact end of the 40 years in the desert), *Yehoshua's* name reverted back to *Hoshea.*

8. The word is "*tzur*" – "rock." It is the name of *Hashem* in the song *Haazinu* (*Devarim* 32:4). It is the first word of the song *Tzur Mishelo* sung at the *Shabbat* meal on Friday night. It is the second word in the song *Maoz Tzur* sung on *Chanukah.*

9. *Rav Yitzchak ben Moshe of Vienna* (1200–1270, Bohemia and Vienna) in his introduction to his *sefer, Or Zarua,* says that the last letter of each word of the *pasuk* "*or zarua la'tzadik u'liyishrei lev simcha*" (*Tehillim* 97:11) spell *R' Akiva,* who was a *tzadik* and a *yashar.*

10. "*Yayin Nesech*" – literally "poured wine" indicating wine poured and presented to a deity in the service of idolatry. The *Sefer Hachinuch* includes it under the general ban against benefiting from food consecrated to a deity.

11. The *Baal Haturim* quotes the *Mechilta* on the *pasuk* "*az yashir*" in *Parshat Beshalach* (*Shemot* 15:1). The word "*yashir*" is composed of the letter "*yud*" (*gematriya* of 10) and the word "*shir*" (song) implying that there are 10 songs in *Tanach.* They are enumerated by the *Baal Haturim* as:

    1. *Shirat hayam* (the song at the Red Sea, *Shemot* 15:1)
    2. *Shir habe'er* (the song at the well, *Bamidbar* 21:17)
    3. *Shirat haazinu* (*Devarim* 32:1)
    4. The song of *Yehoshua* (*Yehoshua* 10:12)
    5. The song of *Devorah* (*Shoftim* 5:1)
    6. The song of *Chanah* (*Shmuel I:2:1*)
    7. The song of *David* (*Tehillim* 18:1)
    8. The song of *Shlomo* (*Tehillim* 30:1)
    9. The song of *Chizkiyahu* (*Yeshaya* 38:10)
    10. The song of *Mashiach* (*Yeshaya* 42:10)

12. In our *Ashkenazi* tradition, here are 70 rows in *Shirat Haazinu;* although the *Rambam* says that *Haazinu* should be written on 67 lines in a *Sefer Torah* (*Hilchot Sefer Torah* 8). Based on the most popular tradition today, the two columns in which *Haazinu* is arranged, appear as mirror images to each other. The first begins with the word "*v'a'ida,*" one of the six columns in the *Torah* whose first word is set by tradition (see *Vayechi* riddle #7), followed by the last six lines of *Parshat Vayelech.* There is then one line left blank and the first 35 lines of the song *Haazinu.* The next column begins with the final 35 lines of the song *Haazinu,* followed by a blank line and then six more lines from the non-song part of *Haazinu,* making the two adjacent 42 line *Torah* columns look like mirror images.

13. In order for one to be successful in *"teshuva"* – "the act of repentance," one must reach a level of *"ayin"* – "selflessness." One has to feel that *Hashem* is everything while man is nothing. A person who thinks highly of himself uses the word *"ani"* – "I am." The word *"ani"* is spelled *alef* – *nun* – *yud*. The *gematriya* of the letter *nun* is 50, the same *gematriya* as the word *"ha'adam"* – "man." Such a person places the *"nun"* – "the man" before the *"yud"* – "symbolizing *Hashem*." A person striving to do *teshuva* sees the greatness of *Hashem* and his own nothingness. Such a person is in a state of *"ayin"* – "selflessness" spelled *"alef – yud – nun"* and places the *"yud"* – i.e., "*Hashem*" before the *"nun"* – *"ha'adam"* – "man" (based on a concept by *Rav Aryeh Kaplan* in *Jewish Meditation*).

14. The *gemara* (*Rosh Hashanah* 31a) tells us that the *Shirat Haazinu* (*Devarim* 32) was sung weekly in the *Beit Hamikdash* and was divided into six segments. The mnemonic is *"haziv lach"*; *"heh-zayin-yud-vav-lamed-kaf."* This division by segment is also the way we read the *aliyot* in *shul*. The *Shulchan Aruch* rules this way (*Orach Chaim* 528:5) and explains the mnemonic. The *"heh"* stands for *"haazinu"* which is the beginning of the first *aliyah, kohen* (*Devarim* 32:1). The *"zayin"* stands for *"zechor"* and the *levi aliyah* (*Devarim* 32:7). The *"yud"* stands for *"yarkiveihu,"* the *shlishi aliyah* (*Devarim* 32:13). There is a difference of opinion as to whether the *"revi'i"* *aliyah* should begin with the *"vav"* of *"vayar"* (*Devarim* 32:19) or *"vayishman"* (*Devarim* 32:15). The latter is based on a *Tosafot* (*Sofrim* 12:7) but is suspect, because that would mean an *aliyah* of only two *pesukim*, and therefore most authorities rule with the reading proceeding until *"vayar"* (*Devarim* 32:19). There is considerable difference of opinion on the last two stops; the *"lamed"* and the *"kaf"* of the mnemonic *"haziv lach."* Some hold that it is *"lulei"* (*Devarim* 32:27) for the *"lamed"* or *chamishi aliyah* and *"ki yadin"* (*Devarim* 32:36) for the *shishi aliyah*. Others hold that it is *"loo"* (*Devarim* 32:29) for the *"lamed"* or *chamishi aliyah* and *"ki esa"* (*Devarim* 32:40) for the *shishi aliyah*. The *Beit Yosef* says the custom is the latter, which is what most *Sephardi* synagogues follow and the former is documented by the *Bach* as the *Ashkenazi* custom as followed in Krakow.

15. In *Haazinu* (*Devarim* 32:2) the following four types of heavenly moisture all appear in the same *pasuk*: *"matar"* – "rain," *"tal"* – "dew," *"se'irim"* – "showers," and *"revivim"* – "droplets."

16. The name *"yeshurun"* is a name by which *Bnai Yisrael* is called for the first time in *Haazinu* (*Devarim* 32:15) and twice in *V'zot Haberacha* (*Devarim* 33:5 and 33:26). *Ibn Ezra* says that the name is derived from the word *"yashar"* – "upright" which defines *Bnai Yisrael*.

17. In *Haazinu* (*Devarim* 32:10) we have the following five words *"y'leil yeshimon yesovivenhu yevonineihu yitzrenu"* all beginning with the letter *"yud."*

18. *Rashi's* knowledge of the nature of birds is clear in his commentary to the *pasuk* in *Haazinu* dealing with the "*nesher*" – "eagle" (*Devarim* 32:11). *Rashi* comments as follows: "When it comes to moving the young from one place to another, the eagle does not take them with its claws, as other birds do, because other birds are afraid of the eagle that soars so high and flies above them. Therefore, the other birds transport their young holding them by their claws for fear of the eagle. But the eagle is afraid only of an arrow, therefore it carries their young on its wings, saying, "It is better that the arrow pierce me than that it should pierce my young." *Rashi* then quotes the *pasuk* in *Yitro* (*Shemot* 19:4) which describes *Hashem* protecting the *Bnai Yisrael* like an eagle protects its young.

19. In *Vayikra* 19:19, *Rashi* defines the word "*shaatnez*" – "mingled linen and wool" and says, again quoting the *Sifri* (*Kedoshim* 4:18) that the word is composed of three syllables and means a material that is "*shua*" – "pressed"; or "*tevi*" – "woven" or "*nez*" – "twisted" together, thereby arriving at the word "*shaatnez*."

20. In *Bereishit* 1:1, *Hashem* creates "*shamayim*" – "heaven" and "*aretz*" – "earth." In three places in *Devarim* (*Devarim* 4:26; *Devarim* 30:19; *Devarim* 31:28), heaven and earth are asked to be witnesses. In *Parshat Haazinu*, they are finally summoned to give testimony "Listen, heavens, let me speak; let the earth hear my words" (*Devarim* 32:1).

PARSHAT V'ZOT HABERACHA QUESTIONS

1. In which tribe's geographic portion was *Moshe Rabbeinu* buried?
2. How many people other than *Moshe Rabbeinu* have been called *"Ish Ha-Elokim"* in the *Torah*? How many people in *Tanach* are referred to by this title?
3. What are the only two things that are called *"morasha"* – "our heritage"?
4. If "Sunkist" is a trade name for an orange, what would be an appropriate trade name for a melon?
5. Who buried himself?
6. How many people died with a "divine kiss," a kiss from *Hashem*?
7. Name the people mentioned in the *Torah* whose bodies did not decompose after death?
8. Where is there a hint to *Moshe's* body not decomposing after death?
9. Which *"tzadik"* – "righteous person" was buried close to an idol?
10. Which two people in *Tanach* are referred to as *"eved Hashem"*?
11. Who was *Yehoshua's* wife?
12. How many chapters of *Tehillim* were written by *Moshe*?
13. Who was the first person to study *Chumash* with *Rashi*?

14. Two men, one was blessed, one was cursed. The blessing and the curse were both directed at the same thing and for the same reason. Who were they?
15. The *Chatam Sofer* said: "From the first word of *Torah* to the last – there is much happiness." Explain.
16. Which part of the *Torah* can be read with less than a *minyan*?
17. Where is the *pasuk* "Chazak, chazak, v'nitzchazek" from?
18. Did *Moshe Rabbeinu* ever see *Chevron*?
19. Where does *Moshe Rabbeinu* predict the war between the Greeks and the *Chashmonaim*?

20. In *Devarim* 34:6, we are told that *Moshe* was buried in the valley in the land of *Moab*, near *Bet-peor*; and no one knows his burial place to this day. Where in the *"berachot"* – "blessings" that *Moshe* gave to *Bnai Yisrael* is there a hint to the fact that *Moshe's* burial place was hidden?

PARSHAT V'ZOT HABERACHA ANSWERS

1. *Moshe* was buried in the tribal portion of *Gad* (*Rashi* on *Devarim* 33:21; *Gemara Sotah* 13b).

2. In the *Torah*, there is only one, *Moshe*, and it occurs only in one place (*Devarim* 33:1). In *Tanach*, *Moshe* is called *Ish Ha-Elokim* five additional times. At least ten others are given this lofty title in *Tanach*. They are: *Elkanah* (*Shmuel* 1:2:27); *Shmuel* (*Shmuel* 1:9:6); *David Hamelech* (*Nechemiah* 12:24); *Shemayahu* (*Melachim* 1:12:2); *Iddo* (*Melachim* 1:13:1); *Eliyahu* (*Melachim* 2:1:13); *Elisha* (*Melachim* 2:4:9); *Michah* (*Melachim* 1:20:28); *Amotz* (*Divrei Hayamim* 2:25:7). There are others who are called *Ish Ha-Elokim* in the *Tanach*, but who are not identified by name.

3. The *Baal Haturim* (*Devarim* 33:4) points out that only the *Torah* and "*Eretz Yisrael*" – "The Land of Israel" are honoured with the appellation "*morasha*" – "heritage." The Artscroll Stone *Chumash* quotes *Rabbi Mordechai Gifter* who explains the difference between "*nachala*" – "inheritance" and "*morasha*" – "heritage." An inheritance becomes the property of the heir, who can do as he wishes with the inherited item. He could preserve and protect it or alternatively, he could reject and discard it. On the other hand, heritage implies transferring and transmitting from one generation to the next. The heirs must preserve the heritage intact so that it can remain in the family forever. In this vein, both *Torah* and *Eretz Yisrael* fit the description of heritage.

4. *Rashi* (*Devarim* 33:14) quotes a *Sifri* (*Sifri Devarim* 353:3) and tells us that while most fruits require sunlight in order to ripen, there are two exceptions based on the phrase "*geresh yerachim*" – "the yield of the moon," which require moonlight to ripen. These are melons and cucumbers. Hence, melons would be called "moonkist"!

5. *Moshe Rabbeinu* (*Rashi* 33:14) buried himself. *Rashi* offers two opinions: one, that *Hashem* buried *Moshe*, and the second, that *Moshe* buried himself. *Rashi* quotes *Rabbi Yishmael* who cites this *pasuk* as one of three occurrences in the *Torah*, where, although the *pasuk* does not seem reflexive, the meaning of the *pasuk* is, in fact, reflexive (i.e., "and he buried him" really means "and he buried himself"). The other two are:
   1. Regarding a *nazir* ("and he should bring him" meaning "and he should bring himself" – *Bamidbar* 6:13).
   2. Regarding the sanctity of sacrifices and *terumah* ("and they will bear for them" meaning "and they will cause themselves to bear" – *Vayikra* 22:16).

6. The *gemara* (*Bava Batra* 17a) names six people who died with a divine kiss. They are *Avraham, Yitzchak, Yaakov, Moshe, Aharon* and *Miriam*.

7. The *gemara* (*Bava Batra* 17a) names seven people whose bodies did not decompose after death. They are *Avraham, Yitzchak, Yaakov, Moshe, Aharon, Miriam* and *Binyamin*.

8. The *pasuk* (*Devarim* 34:7) says "*Moshe* was a hundred and twenty years old when he died; his eyes were undimmed and his vigour unabated." *Rashi*, quoting the *Sifri* (*Sifri Devarim* 357:34), apparently deduces from the fact that the *pasuk* only refers to *Moshe's* eyes and vigour, after the words "when he died," that his body did not decompose.

9. The *gemara* (*Sotah* 14a) states that *Moshe Rabbeinu* was buried in close proximity to the idol *Baal Peor*, in order to atone for the sin that *Bnai Yisrael* did with *Baal Peor* (*Bamidbar* 25). *Tosafot* explains that on each anniversary of the sin of *Baal Peor*, the idol would rise and attempt to prosecute and denigrate *Bnai Yisrael*. *Tosafot* continues to explain that when *Baal Peor* would see the grave of *Moshe*, it would sink back to the level of its nose and be quiet.

10. *Moshe* and *Yehoshua*. In *Devarim* 34:5, *Moshe* is referred to as "*eved Hashem*" – "servant of *Hashem*." *Yehoshua* is also referred to as "*eved Hashem*" in a couple of places (*Yehoshua* 24:29; *Shoftim* 2:8).

11. *Yehoshua's* wife was *Rachav*. The *gemara* (*Megillah* 14b) says that *Rachav* converted and then married *Yehoshua*.

12. Eleven chapters of *Tehillim* (*Tehillim* 90–100) were written by *Moshe* corresponding to the 11 blessings that he gave the "*shevatim*" – "tribes" before he died (*Rashi Tehillim* 90:1).

13. Trick question: *Rashi's* father studied *chumash* with *Rashi* from *Rashi's* earliest years; hence *Rashi's* father was the first to study *chumash* with *Rashi*.

14. The *Chizkuni* (*Devarim* 33:13) explains that both *Adam* and *Yosef* were enticed by a woman. When *Adam*, the first human being, had sinned by allowing himself to be seduced by his wife, the land on which he lived afterwards was cursed, "*arura ha'adama*" (*Bereishit* 3:17) as a result, and his livelihood became one that required hard toil. *Yosef*, on the other hand, who had withstood the seduction by the wife of *Potiphar*, was rewarded, in that the land his descendants dwelled on, was especially blessed "*mevorechet Hashem artzo*" (*Devarim* 33:13).

15. The first word in the *Torah* is "*Bereishit*" and the last word is "*Yisrael*." Both words contain the letters "*alef*," "*shin*," "*reish*," and "*yud*," which spells "*ashrei*," indicating, says the *Chatam Sofer*, that study of *Torah* brings happiness (*Chatam Sofer Devarim* 34:12).

16. The *Rambam* (*Hilchot Tefillah* 13:6) states that the eight verses which conclude the *Torah* (*Devarim* 34:5–12) may be read in *shul* even when there is less than a *minyan*. Though it is all *Torah* and *Moshe* uttered these verses as received from the mouth of *Hashem*; still, as they convey the thought that they were composed after *Moshe's* death, they have clearly been altered

(from the text as it stood originally). An individual may therefore read them (without a *minyan*).

17. In *Shmuel* (*Shmuel* 2:10:12) *Yoav* states "*chazak, chazak, v'nitzchazek*" to encourage *Avishai* during a war against *Amon*.

18. Trick question: Certainly, *Moshe Rabbeinu* never saw the place *Chevron*, as he never entered *Eretz Yisrael*. But he most certainly saw his uncle (*Amram's* brother) *Chevron* (*Bamidbar* 3:19).

19. On the *pasuk* (*Devarim* 33:11), in the blessing that *Moshe* confers on *Levi*, "smite the loins of his enemies; let those who hate him, rise no more," *Rashi* quotes a *midrash* (*Bereishit Rabbah* 99:2) that says that *Moshe* was referring to the impending war that would take place eleven centuries later between the Greeks and the *Chashmonaim*. The *Chashmonaim* were *kohanim* and hence were descendants of the tribe of *Levi*. Even though they were outnumbered, they were able to defeat the mightiest army in the world, assisted by the blessing that *Moshe* conferred on the tribe of *Levi*.

20. In the blessing given to the tribe of *Gad*, *Moshe* says "*ki sham chelkat mechokek safun*" – "for there, is the portion of the covered legislator" (*Devarim* 33:21). *Rashi* points out that *Moshe* was buried in the portion of the tribe of *Gad*, who remained on the other side of the *Jordan* river together with the tribe of *Reuven* and half the tribe of *Menashe*. The word "*mechokek*" is derived from the word "*chok*" or "law," and curiously is the same *gematriya* as the number of positive commandments, 248. The word "*safun*" is similar to the word "*tzafun*" – "hidden" and *Rashi* quotes the *Sifri* who says that the field where *Moshe* was buried, was hidden and concealed from every creature (*Sifrei Devarim* 355:6).

GENERAL
TORAH

GENERAL TORAH QUESTIONS

1. How many pairs of letters in the alphabet are never found adjacent to each other in *Tanach*?

2. Is there in *Tanach* a "*mem sofit*'" – "final *mem*" that occurs in the middle of a word?

3. Is there in *Tanach* a regular "*mem*" that appears at the end of a word?

4. Name two words in the *Tanach*, each containing three consecutive "*mems*."

5. Name a *pasuk* in the *Torah* with eight consecutive words all ending in the letter "*mem sofit*"?

6. At the end of *Megillat Eichah*, there is an abbreviated code that reads: "*Siman Yud, Tav, Kuf, Kuf.*" What is the meaning of this code?

7. Most of the *parshiyot* in the *Torah* are named by their first or second word (33 out of 54). Which *parshah* waits the longest for its name?

8. Four words, "*echad ani v'hu ish*" that seemingly do not follow one another, but they actually do, all in one *pasuk*. Where is the *pasuk*?

9. What is the only *parshah* that is not separated from the *parshah* that preceded it?

10. Where in *Tanach* do we have two brothers born to the same mother and father, yet one is a *kohen* and one is a *levi*?

11. Two kings in *Tanach*, one Jewish, one not, plus a grandson of *Yaakov*, all with the same name? Identify them all?

12. What *mesechta* begins on "*amud bet*" – "page two"?

13. Who was the "king of the accountants" in the *Torah*?

14. Which letter appears the latest in the *Torah*?

15. Which letter is missing both from the *parshah* speaking about the creation of the *menorah* as well as the *parshah* in the beginning of the *Torah* describing the creation of the world?

16. The *menorah* was kindled in the first and second "*Batei Mikdash*" – "holy temples" for a total of 830 years; 410 years in the first and 420 years in the second. Where is there a hint to this in the *Torah*?

17. Is it "if" or "maybe" or "but" or "because"? What is the key to understanding the real meaning? Read the question again for the hint to the answer?

18. Where do we find a word in *Tanach* with three consecutive "*nuns*"?

19. Find two words in *Tanach*, one of which is said in our daily *tefillah* and the other in our *Shabbat tefillah*; each word consists of six letters, three different letters repeated twice?

20. Who gave birth twice on the same day; once to twins and once to triplets?

21. On which *Shabbat* is it possible to read from four consecutive *parshiyot*?

22. Three consecutive *parshiyot* contain a total of 170 *mitzvot*, over 25% of the 613 *mitzvot*. What are these three *parshiyot*?

23. How many times in the *Torah* do we find reference to the first day of *Nisan*?

24. Who is the only "*ben Yisrael*" mentioned in the *Torah*?

25. Which two *parshiyot* are read combined more than any other pair?

26. What is unique about *Revi'i* (the fourth *aliyah*) in a two *parshah Torah* reading?

27. Which is the only two *parshah Torah* reading, that is evenly split into two regular *aliyot* per *aliya*?

28. Besides Fast Days, is there ever a time when we read a special *haftarah* without reading from a second *Sefer Torah*?

29. How many *pesukim* in *Tanach* begin and end with the letter *nun*?

30. If we always read a special *maftir* to coincide with a *musaf* offering, why do we not read a special *maftir* every *Shabbat*?

31. Where in the *Torah* can we find 10 consecutive words, where 50% of them are from the same root?

32. Two places in the *Torah* where there is a command to "get up and leave"! One is spoken to individuals and one is spoken to a group. Who said it to whom and what are the circumstances?

33. I am mentioned only once in the *Torah* and then only after I have died. Who am I?

34. For whom is the term "*zaken ba bayamim*" – "old, well on in years" used in *Tanach*?

35. Which of the children of *Yaakov* lived the longest?

36. In how many books of *Tanach* is *Hashem*'s name missing?

37. What is the only "*yartzheit*" mentioned in the *Torah*?

38. What is the only birthday party mentioned in the *Torah*?

39. Who was *Yehoshua Bin Nun*'s grandfather?

40. At the time of the "*eigel*" – "golden calf," the *Torah* refers to *Yehoshua* as a "*na'ar*" – "youth." Do we know how old *Yehoshua* was at this point?

41. Which of *Noach*'s sons was grandfather to grandmother?

42. The *Torah* enumerates the ten generations from *Noach* to *Avraham*. Surprisingly, their lives overlapped. Where is there a hint in the first *pasuk* of *Noach* to the number of years by which their lives overlapped?

43. We are told that *Yitzchak* physically resembled his father *Avraham* (*Rashi Bereishit* 25:19). Name five other similarities in the lives of *Avraham* and *Yitzchak*?

44. Who referred to his son as "he is my father"?

45. How is it possible to have the same *Shabbat Kriat HaTorah* in Israel and *Chutz La'aretz*, and yet be required to read different *haftarot*?

46. How is it possible to have different *Shabbat Kriat HaTorah* in Israel and *Chutz La'aretz* and yet be required to read the same *haftarah*?

47. Which *parshah* is never read on *Shabbat* in *Chutz La'aretz*?

48. How did *Antiochus* of *Chanukah* fame affect our *Shabbat* for all time?

49. What unique and similar occurrence happened to *Avraham* in *Elonei Mamrei*, and to *Yitzchak* in *Gerar* and *Be'er Sheva*?

50. The king of *Bashan, Og,* appears in many places in the *Torah*. How did he get the name *Og*?

51. Who in the *Torah* had their names changed and were later called again by their original name?

52. The word "*teivah*" can be translated as "word" or "ark/container." Name as many different stories as you can, where this word is found in the *Torah* or its commentaries, when it means "ark/container"?

53. Who converted at the age of 50, married a former spy and among her descendants were nine prophets?

54. The *gemara* identifies the four most beautiful women in the world. Who are they?

55. The *Torah* lists 10 generations between *Adam* and *Noach* and another ten generations between *Noach* and *Avraham*. Add in *Yitzchak, Yaakov* and the *shevatim* and you will see that there are at least 23 generations in *Sefer Bereishit*. The question is how many generations can you list from *Sefer Shemot*?

56. How were *Adam* and *Chava*'s great-great-great-great-great-great-great-grandson and their great-great-great-great-great-granddaughter related?

57. How many times during the course of a year do we read books of the *Tanach* in their entirety in a public gathering?

58. One *Shabbat*, there are more people in *shul* who are "*chiyuvim*" – "individuals who would ordinarily be entitled to receive an *aliyah* on that *Shabbat*," than available *aliyot*. And yet, we are not permitted to make any "*hosafot*" – "extra stops to create additional *aliyot*" during this *Torah* reading? What are we reading that week?

59. Which name is shared by the greatest number of different individuals in the *Torah*? There are two answers?

60. *Chevron* is the name of a place mentioned in the *Torah* (*Bereishit* 13:18) as well as the name of a person mentioned in the *Torah* (*Shemot* 6:18). How many times are names shared by people and places in the *Torah*?

61. Where is *Shaul* first mentioned in *Tanach*?

62. Where is *Shmuel* first mentioned in *Tanach*?

63. What tribe was *Yosef* from?

64. What tribe was *Yair ben Menashe* from?

65. In what *sefer* of the *Torah* does *Yosef*'s name last appear?

66. What does ZM"N NK"T (*Zayin, Mem, Nun, Nun, Kuf, Tet*) stand for?

67. Where is the name *Yitzchak* spelled with a "*sin*" instead of the more common "*tzadi*" and when is this read before large groups of people?

68. How many individuals died without sin?

69. Who was the first person to have braided hair?

70. Most *parshiyot* are named for a word that appears somewhere in the first few *pesukim*. Many titles of *parshiyot* in the *Torah* are similar to a word in the *parshah* but without the "*heh hayediah*" – "the definite article, *heh*" that is attached to the actual word in the *parshah*. Name them?

71. What is the most common *pasuk* in the *Torah* (i.e., the identical *pasuk* is found in many different places in the *Torah*)?

72. In the course of one year, which *pasuk* is read most often in the *Torah*? (As opposed to the previous question, which asks for the same *pasuk* found in many different places in the *Torah*, this is one *pasuk* that is read numerous times)?

73. How many *mitzvot* in the *Torah* have a concept of "*hiddur*"?

74. Where do we have an indication in *Rashi* in *Tanach* that Venice is man-made?

75. Where in *Tanach* is the first reference to glass?

76. Who knows 40? Name as many references as possible in Jewish life to the number 40.

77. Name a person in *Tanach* whose second half of his Hebrew name is the English translation of the first half of his name?

78. How many times during the course of a year do we read from the same *parshah* both at *Shacharit* and at *Mincha*?

79. Normally the *Torah* reading is the same on Monday and Thursday. How is it possible to read one part of the *parshah* on Monday and a different part of the same *parshah* on Thursday?

80. There are times, such as the *Shabbat* before a *Yom Tov*, when we read from the next regularly scheduled *parshah* even though that *parshah* will not be read for a couple of weeks because of *Yom Tov* occurring in the middle of that period. Give one instance where *Kriat HaTorah* for *minchah l'Shabbat* is not from the next regularly scheduled *parshah* at all?

81. Where do we find two consecutive *pesukim* in the *Torah*, the first *pasuk* ending with the very word that begins the second *pasuk*?

82. We are familiar with the *rabbinic* dictum "*derech eretz kadma laTorah*" – "ethical behaviour precedes the *Torah*." Our question is: what else does "*derech eretz*" precede?

83. How is it possible that as a result of one person consuming something, another person is physically affected, even when the second person is located in another country, thousands of miles away?

84. Name the only time in the year, when we actually call someone up for an *aliyah* to the *Torah* and then interrupt him by inserting another part of the liturgy?

85. Name a father and son mentioned in *Tanach* whose names are both palindromes (i.e., if read forwards or backwards, they are spelled the same)?
86. *Reish* is a letter that never has a *dagesh* (a dot used as a grammatical symbol) in it. There is one place in the *Torah* where we find a *reish* with a *dagesh* above it. Where is that place?
87. Which *parshah* has no *haftarah*?
88. Which *parshah* is the single largest "*Parshah petucha*" in the *Torah*?
89. Why do we read the *Torah* after *shemoneh esrei* in *shacharit* but before the *shemoneh esrei* at *minchah* time?
90. When is it possible to read the same *haftarah* on two consecutive *Shabbatot*?
91. How is it possible for four people to be called to the *Torah* consecutively and to read the identical *Torah* portion for each of them?
92. Find a phrase in the *Torah* which speaks in general terms about four generations in descending order?
93. Who were *Chulda*'s parents?
94. In which *parshah* do we find the "*meraglim*" – "spies"?
95. In the 40 years in the desert, in what three ways did the *leviim* set themselves apart from all the other tribes?
96. Whose name appears in *Tanach* the exact number of years that he lived?
97. In the *Torah*, *Hashem* appeared to a number of non-Jews at night. How many and who were they?
98. Which books in *Tanach* have chapters where the verses are written in alphabetical order?
99. How many times does the phrase "*Eretz Yisrael*" appear in the *Torah*? In *Tanach*?
100. Which *haftarah* begins and ends with the same word (besides the prefix "*vav*" in front of one of them)?
101. Two people in the *Torah*, both from the same town, both donkey riders, both early risers. Who were they?
102. Which two *masechtot* begin with the same *Mishnah*?
103. Which *masechet* is the opposite of the *seder* in which it is found?
104. If 14 carat gold is used in Israel, where would 11 carat gold be used?
105. Was the thickness of the wicks used in the *menorah* in the mishkan consistent throughout the year?
106. We have a general principle of "*haosek b'mitzvah patur min hamitzvah*" – "if one is busy doing one *mitzvah*, he is exempt from doing other *mitzvot*." From where do we derive this principle?
107. Where does the *Torah* mention honey and oil that are not derived from their usual sources?
108. Name two brothers, mentioned in the *Torah*, whose paternal grandfather and maternal great-grandfather were the same person?

109. And following this question, name two brothers, mentioned in the *Torah*, whose paternal great-grandfather and maternal grandfather were the same person?

110. The combined number of *pesukim* that I read from this *parshah* on the *Shabbat mincha,* Monday and Thursday *Torah* readings total 1.5 times the number of *pesukim* in the *parshah*. To which *parshah* am I referring?

111. There is a certain religious sect who observed *Shabbat* in Israel and in *chutz la'aretz* in non-*shemitah* years but during the year of *shemitah* observed *Shabbat* only in *chutz la'aretz*. Why?

112. Other than *Moshe*, how many other people in *Tanach* assembled the people as their leadership reached its end?

113. Which three non-Jews said the phrase *"baruch Hashem"* – "blessed is *Hashem*" in the *Torah*?

114. How many names did *Yitro* have?

115. There is a popular saying "tie a string around your finger in order to remember something." What two *mitzvot* that have knots are connected to remembrance? And where in *Bereishit* did someone tie knots in order to recall a commitment he had made?

116. When my *Shabbat* table is filled with guests, I am told that I am blessed with peace, goodness, salvation and forgiveness. From what material must such a *Shabbat* table be built and to what is it compared?

117. How many people in the *Torah* are recorded as having torn *"keriah"* – "torn their garments in grief," and who were they?

118. How many times in his commentary on *Torah*, does *Rashi* reference *"taryag mitzvot"* – "the 613 *mitzvot*"?

119. Who was *Petachya*?

120. How is the United Nations World Health Organization connected to a story in *Bamidbar*?

121. Which army was chosen based on the birthday of its soldiers?

122. Who was the greatest sorcerer in *Mitzrayim* during the time of *Moshe* and *Aharon*?

123. There are four instructions in the *Torah* where *Hashem* provided a deeper explanation to *Moshe*, in order to enable him to enact the directive. The four are connected by one two letter word. What is the word and what are the four instructions?

124. *Nimrod* and *Avraham* were connected by a date in the calendar. Explain?

125. In *Yaakov's berachot* to his children, before he passed away at the end of *Bereishit*, the individual blessings all begin with the name of the son being blessed, except for one. Which one, and why?

126. Which two kings mentioned in *Tanach* assumed the throne at the same age, and ruled for the same number of years, and whose names refer to *Moshe's* instruction to his successor?

127. Name two words in the *Torah* that each have two "*trop*" – "musical notes," and yet the second note is sung before the first?

128. Sometimes the *Torah* uses a double expression for emphasis; as in "*pakod yifkod*" – "will surely remember" (*Bereishit* 50:24). Where is there one *pasuk* in the *Torah*, which utilizes three double expressions for emphasis?

129. The seventh prime minister of Israel, a popular herb, and used in the construction of the "*ephod*" – "the breastplate" of the *Kohen Gadol*. What is common?

130. What is the connection between *Yaakov* and his family leaving *Lavan's* home; *Bnai Yisrael* fleeing *Mitzrayim*, *Amalek*, and the *mitzvah* of "*bikkurim*" – "the first fruits"?

131. What number connects *Mitzrayim*, *Ephron* and *Eisav*?

132. What connects *Aravna*, *Chamor* and *Ephron*?

133. How many people in *Tanach* left Israel because of famine, seeking food elsewhere?

134. Name two siblings in the *Torah* who each had twins?

135. Who got married because his son got married?

136. What connects the 18th *of Tammuz*; the blossoming of *Aharon's* staff with almonds; the daughters of *Lot*; and *Yitro's* advice to *Moshe* to delegate responsibility?

137. How many instances do we have in *Tanach* where people hid in caves?

138. There are a number of people in the *Torah* referred to as "*adoni*" – "my master." Name as many as you can, and indicate who was referred to as "*adoni*" the greatest number of times in the *Torah*?

139. Name two reasons why *Rosh Hashanah* was an important date in *Yosef's* life?

140. Name two incidents in the *Torah* where we have worms pointing the finger at the guilty party?

141. Most of the "*taamei hamikra*" – "musical cantillation notes" appear in every *parshah* in the *Torah*. Some appear infrequently, like the "*shalshelet*" which occurs only four times in the *Torah* and the *meircha ch'fula* which appears five times in the *Torah*. In which *parshah* can we find two "*taamei hamikra*" – "musical cantillation notes" which do not appear anywhere else in the *Torah*? What are they?

142. Name a *sefer* in *Tanach* where all the chapters except for one, have the exact same number of *pesukim*?

143. In question 20 in *Parshat Tzav*, we discussed the concept of the "*siman*" or mnemonic that appears at the end of almost all the *parshiyot* of the *Torah*, that is numerically equivalent to the number of the *pesukim* in that *parshah*.

The next few questions will deal with these simanim. Which *parshah*'s *siman* is the very last word in the *parshah* and equivalent to the number of *pesukim* in that *parshah*?

144. Which two *parshiyot* have an equal number of *pesukim* and utilize as their *siman*, the names of two kings of Israel, whose names are numerically equivalent?

145. Which *parshah* featuring a builder, has the number of *pesukim* equivalent to the name of another builder, who appears elsewhere in the *Torah*?

146. Which *parshah* has the number of *pesukim* equivalent to the name of someone who appears in that *parshah*'s *maftir*?

147. Which *parshah* has no *siman* at all?

148. Which *parshah* has as its *siman* the number of *pesukim* in the *parshah* plus the number of *pesukim* in the previous *parshah*?

149. As we said in question 20 in *Parshat Tzav*, the *siman* "*tzav*" seems incorrect as there are actually 97 *pesukim* in the *parshah*. Two parts to this question:
    1. Which other *parshah* could use the *siman* "*tzav*"?
    2. Which other *parshah* also has 97 *pesukim*?

150. Which other *parshiyot* have a *siman* that seems incorrect?

151. Which *parshah* has the same number of *pesukim* as the number of years lived by one of the *nevi'im* and has as its *siman* the name of a famous *Torah* spy?

152. The *gemara* (*Gemara Sotah* 42a) says "those who are in the class of liars will not stand in the presence of *Hashem*." Where is this hinted in the *Torah*?

153. Which *parshah* has, as its *siman*, the name of a nephew of *David Hamelech*, and whose second part of his name is the English translation of the first part of his name?

154. I began life as a vegetarian but after six centuries began eating meat. Who am I?

155. In the *Torah*, two daughters of *Paroh* married Jews. Who are the daughters and who did they marry?

156. What connects the marriage of *Yitzchak*, the marriage of *Eisav*, *David Hamelech*'s reign, *Shlomo Hamelech*'s reign, the wandering in the desert, and the silver sockets?

157. We are told that *Moshe Rabbeinu* lived for 120 years (*Devarim* 34:7). There are three "*tannaim*" – "*rabbinic* sage authors of the *Mishnah*" who are recorded as also living for 120 years. Who are they?

158. Find three consecutive words in the *Torah* that are different expressions of anger?

159. How do the final three words in the *Torah* hint at the inclusion of all sections of the Jewish people?

160. Who or what swallowed whom or what in *Tanach*?

161. Buildings of stone are as strong as iron and it all relates to our mothers. Explain?

162. How many *"kal v'chomer"* – "a fortiori" statements are found in *Tanach*? And how many of those are in the *Torah*? How many of the *Torah* based ones can you list?

163. Who was the first of *Yaakov's* family to go from *Canaan* to *Mitzrayim*?

164. The *midrash* lists *"nashim chasidot giyorot"* – "righteous female converts" who are all mentioned in *Tanach*. How many can you name?

165. Where in the *Torah* is the same word repeated 11 times, each time separated by another word?

166. Which three women in *Tanach* died during childbirth?

167. I lived before the flood and was later the king of a nation, enemy to *Israel*. Who am I, how did I survive the flood and where is there a hint to my surviving the flood in *Sefer Bereishit*?

168. We are told that *Bnai Yisrael* were redeemed from the slavery of *Mitzrayim* because they did not change their Jewish names, their Jewish language, or their unique mode of dress. Where in *Sefer Bereishit* do we have a reference to these three expressions of uniqueness as constituting perfection in man?

169. There are three categories of double word phrases in the *Torah*:

    1. Two consecutive identical words, spelled and pronounced the same. Example – *"Avraham Avraham"* (*Bereishit* 22:11).

    2. Two consecutive words that are spelled the same, derived from the same root, but pronounced differently. Example: *"haremes haromeis"* – "creeping insects" (*Bereishit* 1:26). The two words with the same root derivation are spelled with the same four letters in the same order, but the vowels or Hebrew sounds are different.

    3. Where the two consecutive words are derived from the same root word but are different forms of the root and therefore spelled differently. Example: In *Parshat Bereishit* (2:17), *Adam* is warned not to eat from the tree of knowledge, for "on the day that you eat from it, *"mot tamut"* – "you shall surely die." The words *"mot"* and *"tamut"* are variations of the same root word, related but spelled differently.

    For the purpose of the following questions, we have not considered a fourth category of double word phrases; two consecutive identically spelled words that are unrelated. Example: In *Parshat Lech Lecha* (*Bereishit* 12:1), we find two identically spelled but otherwise unrelated words *"lech lecha"* meaning "go for yourself."

    a. How many "category one" and "category two" words are found in the *Torah* and where is there a hint to this phenomenon?

    b. Which *parsha* has the greatest number of "category one" words; i.e., two consecutive identical words, spelled and pronounced the same?

GENERAL TORAH ANSWERS

1. There are five pairs. *Gimel-tet, gimel-kuf, zayin-tet, zayin-tzadi, samech-tzadi. Chazal* explain one of these pairs. *Gimel* and *tet* never appear together as they spell "*get*" – "divorce" which separates two people from each other. The numerical value of "*get*" is 12 which is the exact number of lines in a "*get*."

2. Yes. A "*mem sofit*" appears in the word "*l'marbeh*" (*Yeshayahu* 9:6) which is also found as the last *pasuk* in the *haftarah* of *Yitro*.

3. Yes. A regular "*mem*" is found at the end of the word "*hem*" (*Nechemya* 2:13).

4. The two words with three consecutive "*mems*" are "*umimamlacha*" (*Divrei Hayamim* 1:16:20) and "*hamamam*" (*Divrei Hayamim* 2:15:6).

5. There are two *pesukim* with eight consecutive words all ending in a *mem sofit*. They are:
   1. *Devarim* 1:13 which reads: "*lachem anashim, chachamim unevonim viduim leshivteichem, vaasimem berosheichem.*"
   2. *Bereishit* 32:15 which reads "*izim matayim, uteyashim esrim, recheilim matayim v'eilim esrim.*"

6. The code identifies the four places where we end the reading by reverting back to the second last *pasuk*, because the last *pasuk* does not contain a happy message. These four places are *Megillat Eichah, Megillat Kohelet, haftarah* for *Shabbat Rosh Chodesh* (from *Yeshayahu*) and the *haftarah* for *Shabbat Hagadol* (from *Trei Asar*). So the code stands for *Yeshayahu, Trei Asar, Kohelet* and *Kinot* (for *Eichah*). As a matter of interest, we also do not stop at "*sheini*" in *Parshat Devarim*, because that would force us to start the next section with the word "*eichah*" and therefore, many shuls have the *minhag* to end "*rishon*" at the *pasuk* before *rishon* and to begin "*sheini*" from the *pasuk* before. There was also a custom cited in the *Sefer Haminhag* that was adopted by Jews in Provence, France, Spain, Corfu and Persia concerning the words that conclude *Parshat Balak*. The last *pasuk* documents the fact that 24,000 people perished in the plague. As a result, these communities would continue to read the beginning of *Parshat Pinchas* until the words "*briti shalom*" in order to conclude with a "*davar tov*." A similar custom was recorded in the *sefer "Al HaTorah"* concerning the concluding *pasuk* of *Parshat Vayikra* which ends with the words "*mikol asher yaaseh l'ashma va*" – "of all that he has done to trespass thereby." In various communities, when the *baal kriah* would complete this verse, the congregation would stand up and recite "*Lakeil asher shovat mikol melachto bayom hashevii*" – "they praise *Hashem* who rested from all work on the seventh day." No one really understood why this was said, until it was explained by *Rabbi Mendel MiRiminov* who pointed out that the first letters of the

phrase "*lokeil asher...*" form the words "*l'ashma va,*" thus providing a more positive slant on the words that end the *parshah*.

7. The title of *Parshat Kedoshim* appears as the 14th word in the *parshah*; the latest in all of *Torah*.

8. The *pasuk* is found in *Bereishit* 41:11, when the butler tells *Paroh* about his encounter with *Yosef* in jail. "*Vanachalma chalom b'lailah echad ani v'hu, ish kachalomo chalamnu.*"

9. There is no extra space between *Vayechi* and *Vayigash*. Every other *parshah* in the *Torah* either begins on a new line or is separated from the previous *parshah* by at least a nine letter space. This type of *parshah* is called a "*parshah stuma*" – "a closed *parshah*." One explanation in *Rashi* is that *Yaakov* wanted to reveal when the "*acharit hayamim*" – "the end of days" would be, but it was "closed" (concealed) from him (*Bereishit* 47:28).

10. *Moshe* and *Aharon*. *Moshe* was a *levi* and *Aharon* was a *kohen*.

11. The name is *Shaul*. We have two *Shauls* in *Bereishit,* one is one of the kings of *Edom* (*Bereishit* 36:37), the other is mentioned as one of the sons of *Shimon* (*Bereishit* 46:10). *Rashi* comments that he was in fact the product of the union of *Dinah* and *Shechem*, and *Shimon* in an act of selflessness raised the son as his own. The other *Shaul* is the most famous of the three, *King Shaul*, who was anointed by *Shmuel Hanavi* (*Shmuel* 1:15:1).

12. *Mesechta Tamid* begins on "*amud bet.*"

13. Trick question: In Israel today, an accountant is a "*roeh cheshbon*" – literally "the one who observes bills." In the *Torah* (*Devarim* 2:30), we are introduced to "*Sichon Melech Cheshbon*" – "*Sichon* the king of accountants."

14. The letter *samech* first appears in the 42nd *pasuk*, the 575th word and the 2210th letter in the *Torah,* as part of the word "*hasovev.*"

15. There is no *samech* in either the *Torah* section dealing with the construction of the *menorah* or in the section dealing with the creation of the world. The *Baal Haturim* (*Shemot* 25:31) comments that both the *menorah* and creation indicate the presence of light in this world and therefore the *samech* is missing as it signifies the "*sotem*" – "sealing" of the mouth of the *Satan* from prosecuting the Jewish people.

16. The *pasuk* at the beginning of *Parshat Tetzaveh* says "*v'yikchu eilecha shemen zayit zach katit lamaor*" – "and bring clear oil of beaten olives for lighting" (*Shemot* 27:20). The *Baal Haturim* comments that the word "*katit*" – "beaten" has a *gematriya* of 830, which is precisely the number of years that the *menorah* was lit in the first and second *Beit Hamikdash* combined.

17. The answer to the riddle is the Hebrew word "*ki.*" It appears in many places in the *Torah.* The *gemara* (*Rosh Hashanah* 3a) explains that the word "*ki*" has four meanings; namely, if, perhaps, but or because. The hint to the solution

was right in the question: the "key" to understanding the real meaning of this riddle is found in the word "*ki*"!

18. The word with three consecutive "*nuns*" is "*chanenayni*" and it appears in *Tehillim* 9:14.

19. The two words are *haleluhu*" (*Tehillim* 150) and "*vayatzitzu*" (*Tehillim* 92). *Haleluhu* has the letters *heh, lamed* and *vav*. *Vayatzitzu* has the letters *vav, yud* and *tzadi*.

20. *Chava* gave birth to five children in one day. The *gemara* (*Sanhedrin* 38b) tells us that on the eighth hour of her first day on earth, *Chava* gave birth to *Kayin* and *Hevel*. While you might assume that they were twins, the *midrash* (*Bereishit Rabbah* 22:7) relates that *Kayin* had a twin sister and *Hevel* was part of a triplet; the other two being girls. Therefore from the *midrash*, it appears that these were two separate births. *Kayin* then married one of the girls born with *Hevel* and *Hevel* married the twin born with *Kayin*.

21. On *Shabbat Rosh Chodesh Av*, when the regular *Torah* reading happens to be the double *parshah* of *Matot Mas'ei*, we would read the *maftir* from *Pinchas* and the reading for *Shabbat minchah* would be from *Parshat Devarim*. Hence, we would have read on that *Shabbat* from the four consecutive *parshiyot* of *Pinchas, Matot, Mas'ei* and *Devarim*.

22. *Re'eh, Shoftim* and *Ki Teitzei* contain 170 *mitzvot*; almost 28% of all the *mitzvot* in the *Torah* in three *parshiyot*.

23. *Rosh Chodesh Nisan* is either mentioned or alluded to in four places in the *Torah*. First when the concept of the Jewish calendar is mentioned (*Rashi Shemot* 12:3); second, when the *mitzvah* is given to assemble all the components of the *Mishkan* (*Shemot* 40: 1–35); third, when *Aharon* and his sons were inaugurated to do the priestly service (*Vayikra* 9:1 – *Rashi*); and fourth, the day that the *Mishkan* was completed (*Bamidbar* 7:1 – *Rashi*). However, the actual name of the month, *Nisan*, is not mentioned by name in the *Torah* at all!

24. Trick question: The only "*ben Yisrael*" is *Binyamin*. All the others were "*bnai Yaakov*" as they were all born before *Yaakov* was given the added name of *Yisrael*.

25. *Matot – Mas'ei* are read combined 89.5% of the time. They are separated only in 13 month years that begin on Thursday. In Israel, they are also separated (another 10% of the time) in 13 month years when the first day of *Pesach* is on *Shabbat*.

26. The fourth *aliyah* in a double *parshah Torah* reading is always the bridge *aliyah*; i.e., it always has the end of the first *parshah* and the beginning of the second *parshah*.

27. *Acharei Mot-Kedoshim* is the only double *parshah Torah* reading, evenly split into two *aliyot* per *aliya*.

28. *Shabbat Hagadol* (the *Shabbat* before *Pesach*) is the only regularly scheduled *Shabbat* that has a special *haftarah* without a special *maftir*. Occasionally, when *Rosh Chodesh* falls on a Sunday, we read the special *haftarah* of "*machar chodesh*" without any special *maftir*.

29. The *Rabbeinu Bachya* (*Parshat Matot* 32:32) comments on the word "*nachnu*" and says that the actual spelling of this word in Hebrew should be "*anachnu*." However, says the *Rabbeinu Bachya*, in our *pasuk*, the need for the verse to commence with the letter "*nun*" is dictated by the fact that this *pasuk* is one of the eleven *pesukim* in *tanach* beginning and ending with the letter "*nun*." These eleven *pesukim* contain the 13 letter "*Shem Hameforash*" (*Hashem's* Holy Name) and there is a tradition that saying these eleven *pesukim* will protect one from *ayin hara*. A number of *siddurim* include these 11 *pesukim* as part of the liturgy for *Motzaei Shabbat*. (*Tefillat Kol Peh Kol Bo* and the *Siddur Hashaleim*).

30. There is a minimum requirement of three *pesukim* in order to take out a *Sefer Torah* from the "*aron hakodesh*" – "the holy ark." Since the *Torah* reading for the *musaf* of *Shabbat* is only two *pesukim*, *chazal* did not institute a weekly *maftir* reading relating to the *musaf* offering for *Shabbat*. The only time that we do read this section is on *Shabbat Rosh Chodesh*, when it is followed by the five *pasuk Rosh Chodesh musaf* reading (*Shulchan Aruch Orach Chaim* 137:2).

31. In the beginning of *Parshat Lech Lecha*, we have the following 10 words "*va'avarechecha va'agadlah shemecha veheyei beracha, va'avarcha mevorachecha umekalelecha a'or, venivrechu*" (*Bereishit* 12:2–3) where five of them are from the root "*bet-reish-chaf*" – "to bless."

32. The first time that the *Torah* says "*kumu tze'u*" – "get up and leave" is *Lot* speaking to his sons-in-law and urging them to leave because *Hashem* is about to destroy the city of *Sedom* (*Bereishit* 19:14); and the second time is *Paroh* urging *Moshe* and *Aharon* to please leave *Mitzrayim* with the entire *Bnai Yisrael*, because *Paroh* is now admitting defeat at the hands of *Hashem* (*Shemot* 12:31).

33. I am *Devorah* the nursemaid of *Rivka* (*Bereishit* 35:8). The *Torah* simply states that I died and that I was buried not far from *Betel*.

34. The phrase "*zakein ba bayamim*" is used for three individuals in *Tanach*. *Avraham* (*Bereishit* 24:1), *Yehoshua* (*Yehoshua* 13:1 and *Yehoshua* 23:1) and *David* (*Melachim* 1:1:1).

35. *Rabbeinu Bahaye* (*Shemot* 1:6) lists the birthdates of all the sons of *Yaakov* and how many years they lived. *Levi* lived the longest at 137 years.

36. *Hashem's* name does not appear in *Megillat Esther* or in *Shir Hashirim*.

37. The only *yahrtzeit* is that of *Aharon Hakohen*, who died on *Rosh Chodesh Av*, in the 40th year after the *Bnai Yisrael* left *Mitzrayim* (*Devarim* 33:38).

38. The only birthday party mentioned in the *Torah* is that of *Paroh* when he dealt with the butler and the baker (*Bereishit* 40:20).

39. *Yehoshua Bin Nun*'s grandfather was *Elishama ben Amihud*, the prince of the tribe of *Efraim* (*Divrei Hayamim* 1:7:26).

40. When the *Torah* refers to *Yehoshua* as a "*na'ar*," it was in the first year of the *Bnai Yisrael*'s sojourn in the desert. *Rashi* explains (*Divrei Hayamim* 1:22:5) that *Yehoshua* lived for 110 years, and led *Bnai Yisrael* after *Moshe*'s death for 28 years. Therefore 110 - 28 - 40 = 42. Some adults answer 39 whenever they are asked their age, but the *Torah* considers *Yehoshua* youthful and young at the age of 42!

41. Trick question: *Noach* had three sons, *Shem, Cham* and *Yafet. Cham* had a son called *Kush*, and *Kush* had a son called *Savta*, which is Hebrew for grandmother (*Bereishit* 10:7).

42. In the first *pasuk* of *Noach*, the *Torah* states that *Noach* was a *tzadik* in his generation. *Rashi* quotes the *gemara* (*Sanhedrin* 108a) where the rabbis debate whether *Noach* was considered righteous in his generation only because he was righteous in comparison to the rest of his generation who were corrupt, or rather, because he was righteous in a corrupt environment, *Noach* would have certainly measured up even in the generation of *Avraham*. The *Chatam Sofer* offers a different slant on the *pasuk* and says that *Noach* and *Avraham* overlapped by 58 years, which is the *gematriya* of *Noach*. And therefore the *pasuk* is translated as: "*eileh toldot Noach*" – "these are the generations of *Noach*"; "*tzadik tamim hayah b'dorotov*" – "there was a perfect *tzadik* who lived in *Noach*'s generation" i.e., in the "*noach* years" – "in the 58 years that they overlapped," and that was *Avraham*.

43. In addition to being physically similar, there are at least five other similarities in the lives of *Avraham* and *Yitzchak*. They are:
    1. They both married family, *Avraham* marrying his niece *Sarah* and *Yitzchak* marrying his cousin *Rivkah*.
    2. Both their wives, *Sarah* and *Rivkah* were unable to have children, without divine intervention.
    3. They each had two sons, with one son being righteous and one being evil.
    4. Each lied about his wife to *Avimelech*, each telling him that she was his sister.
    5. Each was involved in digging wells.

44. Trick question: *Aharon Hakohen* had a son called *Avihu. Avihu* means "he is my father" (*Vayikra* 10:1).

45. It is possible to read a combined *Matot-Massei* in *Chutz La'aretz* and yet have to read them separately in Israel. When this occurs, both communities read *Pinchas* (although on different weeks) but the *haftarah* that we read

for *Pinchas* is different. In Israel, where *Matot* and *Massei* are separate, we read the actual *haftarah* of *Pinchas*. In *Chutz La'Aretz,* we read the *haftarah* of *Massei* for the week of *Pinchas.* This is because *Pinchas* would then be the first of the Three Weeks when we read the "*t'lat d'puranutah*" – "three *haftarot* of affliction."

46. If *Shavuot* is on Friday and *Shabbat,* in *Chutz La'Aretz,* (therefore, only on Friday in Israel), the *Torah* readings will be "out of sync" between Israel and the Diaspora. A number of weeks later, uniformity is returned when *Balak* is read in Israel and *Chukat-Balak* is read in *Chutz La'Aretz.* When that occurs, the *Torah* reading is different between *Chutz La'Aretz* and Israel and yet the *haftarah* of *Balak* is read in both places.

47. *Parshat V'zot Haberacha* is never read on *Shabbat* in *Chutz La'aretz* as *Simchat Torah* never falls on *Shabbat* outside of *Eretz Yisrael.*

48. *Tosafot Yom Tov* on *Mishnah Megillah* (*Megillah* 3:4) comments that the reason why we read a weekly *haftarah* is that *Antiochus* forbade the public reading of the *Torah.* As a result, the sages decreed that we should have a public weekly reading of a section of "*nevi'im*" that has a similar message as the scheduled *Torah* reading. When the decree of *Antiochus* was rescinded, the custom continued until today.

49. These are the only three times in the *Torah* where it says "*vayeira eilav Hashem*" (*Bereishit* 18:1; *Bereishit* 26:2 and *Bereishit* 26:24).

50. The *Midrash* says that *Og* was alive in the generation of the flood and was still alive when the *Bnai Yisrael* were in the desert. It was *Og,* identified as "*hapalit*" – "the survivor," who came to tell *Avraham* that his cousin *Lot* was taken captive (*Bereishit* 14:13). *Tosafot* (*Niddah* 61a) says that when *Og* came to *Avraham* to deliver the news, *Avraham* was busy baking "*ugot*" – "cakes" for *Pesach.* It was because of those "*ugot*" that *Og* acquired his name.

51. The two individuals were *Yaakov* (whose name was changed to *Yisrael* and who was subsequently called *Yaakov* again) and *Hoshea bin Nun,* whose name was changed to *Yehoshua* (and who was subsequently called *Hoshea* again).

52. There are two places in the *Torah* where we find a "*teivah*" meaning "ark/container"; namely, by *Noach*'s ark (*Bereishit* 6:14); and when they placed *Moshe* in the ark (*Shemot* 2:3) to hide him from *Paroh*'s decree. There are two additional places where there is a reference to "*teivah*" meaning "ark/container" in the commentaries; namely, when *Avraham* wanted to hide his wife *Sarah* from *Paroh* (*Rashi Bereishit* 12:14); and when *Yaakov* wanted to hide *Dinah* from his brother *Eisav* (*Rashi Bereishit* 32:23).

53. The answer is *Rachav* from *Sefer Yehoshua.* The *gemara* (*Zevachim* 116b) relates that *Rachav* was 10 years old when *Bnai Yisrael* left *Mitzrayim.* She engaged in prostitution during the 40 years that *Bnai Yisrael* were in the

desert. When the spies came to scout out *Yericho*, she was 50 years old and based on that experience, she converted. She then married *Yehoshua* (*Gemara Megillah* 14b) who was a former spy, and among her descendants were nine prophets: *Neriah, Baruch, Seraiah, Machsiyah, Yirmiyahu, Chilkiyah, Chanamel, Shalum* and *Chuldah*.

54. The *gemara* (*Megillah* 15a) lists *Sarah, Avigayil, Rachav* and *Esther* as the four women possessing the most extraordinary beauty in the world. Another opinion in the *gemara* substitutes *Vashti* for *Esther* in the list.

55. There are ten generations listed in *Sefer Shemot*. *Avraham, Yitzchak, Yaakov, Levi, Kehat, Amram, Miriam, Chur, Uri* and *Bezalel*.

56. They were husband and wife. The great-great-great-great-great-great-great-grandson was *Noach* and the great-great-great-great-great-granddaughter was *Naama*.

57. There are at least nine books of *Tanach* that are read in their entirety at a single public gathering in the course of a year. We read *Esther* on *Purim* twice, *Eicha* on *Tisha B'av, Shir Hashirim* on *Pesach, Rut* on *Shavuot* and *Kohelet* on *Sukkot*. We read *Yonah* at *minchah* on *Yom Kippur,* and the Book of *Ovadia* (all 21 *pesukim* in one chapter) as the *haftarah* for *Shabbat Vayishlach*. Many also have the custom of staying up all night on *Hoshana Rabbah* to read the entire book of *Devarim*. That is nine. According to the *gemara* (*Shabbat* 115b), the two *pasuk* section beginning with "*vayehi binsoa ha'aron*" is a "*sefer bifnei atzmo*" – "a self contained book of the *Torah*" and therefore that would be number ten. As well, Jews of Morocco and Aleppo and many other *Sephardic* communities say *Shir Hashirim* every *Erev Shabbat*, some before *minchah* and some before *Kabbalat Shabbat*. That would add over 50 occurrences in the course of a year!

58. We are reading *Parshat Haazinu*. The *gemara* (*Rosh Hashanah* 31a) says that the special song that the *levi'im* sang in the *Beit Hamikdash* for the *musaf* offering on *Shabbat* was the *Shirat Haazinu* and it was divided into six sections; the same six sections into which the first six *aliyot* of *Haazinu* are divided. The *Mishnah Berurah* (428:5:11) states the opinion of the *Magen Avraham* that even if there are "*chiyuvim,*" we should not insert additional stops in the reading of *Haazinu*.

59. When I asked this question in the Youth *Minyan*, someone answered *Paroh*. However, I believe that *Paroh* was simply a title like 'king' and each of the *parohs* had a specific name like *Rameses* etc. The two answers are *Chanoch* and *Reuel*. *Chanoch* was shared by four people, and they are all in *Bereishit*. In *Bereishit* 4:17, *Chanoch* is the son of *Kayin*; in *Bereishit* 5:18, *Chanoch* is the son of *Yered*; in *Bereishit* 25:4, *Chanoch* is the son of *Midyan*; and in *Bereishit* 46:9, *Chanoch* is the son of *Reuven*. The name *Reuel,* likewise, is shared by four people; in *Bereishit* 36:10, *Reuel* is a son of *Eisav*; in *Shemot* 2:18, *Reuel*

is one of the seven names of *Yitro*; in *Bamidbar* 2:14, *Reuel* is the father of *Elyasaf,* the prince of the tribe of *Gad*; and in *Bamidbar* 10:29, *Reuel* is identified as the father of *Yitro.* The commentaries explain that *Yitro* was called *Reuel,* as was his father.

60. There are numerous such occurrences in the *Torah* besides *Chevron.* They are:
    1. *Chanoch* (name *Bereishit* 4:17; place *Bereishit* 4:17)
    2. *Kush* (*Bereishit* 10:6; *Bereishit* 2:13)
    3. *Mitzrayim* (*Bereishit* 10:6; *Bereishit* 37:36)
    4. *K'naan* (*Bereishit* 10:6; *Bereishit* 16:3)
    5. *Ashur* (*Bereishit* 10:11; *Bereishit* 2:14)
    6. *Aram/Padan Aram* (*Bereishit* 10:22; *Bereishit* 25:30)
    7. *Haran/Bet Haran* (*Bereishit* 11:26; *Bamidbar* 32:36)
    8. *Shechem* (*Bereishit* 34:2; *Bereishit* 12:6)
    9. *Mamre* (*Bereishit* 14:24; *Bereishit* 13:18)
    10. *Eshkol/Nachal Eshkol* (*Bereishit* 14:13; *Bamidbar* 13:23)
    11. *Moav* (*Bereishit* 19:37; *Bamidbar* 21:11)
    12. *Lavan* (*Bereishit* 24:29; *Devarim* 1:2)
    13. *Midyan* (*Bereishit* 25:2; *Shemot* 2:15)
    14. *Gilad/Har Hagilad* (*Bamidbar* 26:29; *Bereishit* 31:21)
    15. *Edom* (*Bereishit* 36:1; *Bereishit* 36:16)
    16. *Seyir/Har Seyir* (*Bereishit* 36:30; *Bereishit* 36:8).
    17. *Yair/Chavot Yair* (*Bamidbar* 32:41; *Bamidbar* 32:41)
    18. *Novach* (*Bamidbar* 32:42; *Bamidbar* 32:42)
    19. *Dan* (*Bereishit* 30:6; *Devarim* 34:1)
    An answer "with an asterisk" would be *Damesek*; in *Bereishit* 15:2, we meet *Avraham's* servant *Eliezer* and he is called by the *Torah* "*Damesek Eliezer*," which could be translated as *Eliezer* of *Damascus* (the place), or perhaps he became known as *Damesek Eliezer* (the name) because he was named for the place from where he came. There is also the person *Teiman* (*Bereishit* 36:15) and the phrase *Eretz Hateimani* (*Bereishit* 36:34). If we include *Rashi,* we also have the place *Kiryat Arba* (*Bereishit* 23:2) and the name *Arba* (*Rashi Bereishit* 23:2); and the place *Efrat* (*Bereishit* 48:7) and the name *Efrat* (*Rashi Shemot* 24:14). As well, if we extended the question to include all of *Tanach,* there would be many more name/place combinations. Curiously, there is no *Eretz Yisrael* or *Eretz Yehuda* in the *Torah.*

61. *Shaul* from *Rechovot Hanahar* was one of the kings of *Edom* (*Bereishit* 36:37).

62. *Shmuel ben Amihud* was the leader of the Tribe of *Shmuel* when *Bnai Yisrael* took possession of *Eretz Yisrael* (*Bamidbar* 34:20).

63. Trick question: The answer will depend on which *Yosef* we are speaking about. Obviously, *Yosef HaTzaddik* was the originator of the tribes of *Menashe* and *Efraim.* But there is another *Yosef* mentioned in the *Torah.* In

the section that deals with the 12 *meraglim* (*Bamidbar* 13:7), *Yigal ben Yosef* was the representative of the tribe of *Yissachar*.

64. Trick question: *Ibn Ezra* (*Bamidbar* 32:41) says that *Chetzron*, the son of *Peretz* and the grandson of *Yehuda* married the granddaughter of *Menashe*. Their grandson was *Yair*, and therefore he was from the tribe of *Yehuda* even though his name was aligned to his maternal family by the *Torah* referring to him as "*ben Menashe*" – "the son (i.e., descendant) of *Menashe*."

65. *Yosef*'s name last appears in *Sefer Devarim*, in the final *parshah* of *V'zot Haberacha*.

66. ZM"N NK"T is a short form for the six sections of the *Mishnah* (*Shisha Sidrei Mishnah*); *Zera'im, Moed, Nashim, Nezikin, Kodashim* and *Taharot*.

67. We find *Yitzchak* with a "*sin*" in *Tehillim* 105:9. This *pasuk* is part of the *brit milah* text when the baby is given his name. *Chazah Tziyon* explains that the exile to *Mitzrayim* was supposed to last for 400 years, calculated from the birth of *Yitzchak*, but really lasted only 210 years, calculated from *Yaakov*'s descent to *Mitzrayim*. For this *chesed* from *Hashem*, we derive great joy as shown from the numerical difference between *Yitzchak* with a "*tzadi*" and *Yischak* with a "*sin*." The difference between a "*sin*" (*gematriya* 300) and a "*tzadi*" (*gematriya* 90) is 210. The *Shelah* explains that the use of this *pasuk* at a *brit* (rather than a similar *pasuk* in *Divrei Hayamim*) is because we can divide this unique spelling into "*yesh chok*" – "there is a statute"; and that statute is the rite of circumcision (quoted in the *sefer*, *Brit Milah, Rabbi Paysach J. Krohn*, Artscroll p.134). There are three other places where *Yitzchak* is spelled with a "*sin*" (*Yirmiyahu* 33:26 and *Amos* 7:9 and *Amos* 7:16).

68. The *gemara* (*Shabbat* 55b) discusses whether death is possible without sin and concludes that it is possible, naming four people who died without sin; namely, *Yishai*, father of *David*; *Binyamin*, son of *Yaakov*; *Amram*, father of *Moshe*; and *Kilav*, son of *David*. Some add *Moshe* and *Aharon* to the list.

69. The *gemara* (*Berachot* 61a) quotes *Rabbi Shimon ben Menasya* who says that the use of the word "*vayiven*" – "and He built" instead of the more correct "*vayitzar*" – "and He created," referring to the creation of *Chava*, indicates that *Hashem* braided *Chava*'s hair and brought her to *Adam*.

70. There are five titles of *parshiyot* that actually have a "*heh*" at the beginning of the word in the actual text; they are: *Mishpatim, Shemini, Metzora, Matot* and *Devarim*.

71. The most common *pasuk* in the *Torah* is "*vay'daber Hashem el Moshe laymor*" – "And *Hashem* spoke unto *Moshe*, saying." This *pasuk* is found 69 times in the *Torah*. In fact, if one were to include all *pesukim* with those exact five words, the number of times that this occurs grows by just one to 70, for the

one time that we find the pasuk "vay' daber Moshe el Hashem laymor" – "And Moshe spoke unto Hashem, saying" (Bamidbar 27:15).

72. The one pasuk that is read most often from the Torah over the course of a year is the third pasuk read on Rosh Chodesh (Bamidbar 28:3). In a normal Rosh Chodesh Torah reading, this pasuk is read twice (once as the last pasuk for the first aliyah and once as the first pasuk of the second aliyah). The maximum number of times that this pasuk could be read in one year is 31, including all Rosh Chodesh days when this pasuk would be repeated. The Rosh Chodesh days when this pasuk would only be read once, include any Shabbat Rosh Chodesh and the day when Rosh Chodesh and Chanukah coincide. On Rosh Chodesh Tishrei (i.e., Rosh Hashanah), this pasuk would not be read at all. The only other time when this pasuk would be read would be during the regular Torah reading of Parshat Pinchas. Therefore, the number of times that this pasuk is read during the course of a year will vary from year to year. Suffice it to say that the total number can be over thirty times in one year.

73. There are only two positive commandments that involve the concept of "hiddur"; the obligation to specifically beautify a mitzvah. They are etrog (Vayikra 23:40) and showing honour to the elderly (Vayikra 19:32). Rabbi Shlomo Riskin related a fascinating story about Rabbi Arye Levin, the Tzadik of Yerushalayim. He was once observed entering the etrog market in Yerushalayim just before the chag of Sukkot. He quickly made his choice, without, it seemed, much regard for the necessity of choosing one which embodied the qualities of "hiddur." Everyone present assumed that he must have had some important emergency to attend to, and it was for that reason, that he spent so little time carefully making his choice. They followed him as he made his way to a nearby nursing home and were amazed when he made what seemed to be a regular bikkur cholim call. When he was questioned why he rushed to this mitzvah, in apparent disregard for the mitzvah of hiddur etrog, he explained that the Torah only applies the concept of hiddur to two mitzvot; namely, etrog and giving honor to the elderly. And given the fact that both of these mitzvot were literally "staring him in the face," he would rather beautify the elderly than beautify one of the four species.

74. Rashi (Yeshayahu 42:10) on the phrase "those who go down to sea and those who fill it…," comments that this refers to those who fill the sea with enough earth to support their house. When joined together with others nearby, who do the same, the result is the formation of an island community and the islanders then travel from one house to another by small boats. Rashi then says that this is similar to the city of Venice.

75. The one and only reference to glass in Tanach is found in Iyov (28:17) where it is stated that glass and gold cannot begin to approximate the value of

wisdom. This would indicate that glass at that time was a most valuable commodity.

76. There are many references to 40 in Jewish life. Some are:
    1. The flood lasted for 40 days and nights (*Bereishit* 7:17).
    2. *Noach* waited 40 days before sending out the raven, after the ark came to rest on *Harei Ararat* (*Bereishit* 8:6).
    3. *Moshe Rabbeinu* spent 40 days and nights on *Har Sinai* (*Shemot* 34:28).
    4. He then spent an additional 40 days and nights receiving the second set of tablets after the incident of the *eigel hazahav* – the golden calf (*Devarim* 9:18).
    5. The *meraglim* spied out the land of *Canaan* for 40 days (*Bamidbar* 13:25).
    6. The *Bnai Yisrael* travelled through the desert for 40 years (*Bamidbar* 8:2).
    7. *Yitzchak* was 40 years old when he got married (*Bereishit* 25:20).
    8. *Eisav* was 40 years old when he got married (*Bereishit* 36:24).
    9. *Yehoshua* was 40 years old when he went to spy *Eretz Canaan* (*Yehoshua* 14:7).
    10. *David Hamelech* ruled for 40 years (*Shmuel* 2:5:4).
    11. *Shlomo Hamelech* ruled for 40 years (*Melachim* 1:11:42)
    12. A *mikvah* contains 40 *seah* of water (*Gemara Eruvin* 4b).
    13. The punishment for certain transgressions is (up to) 40 lashes (i.e. 39 lashes) (*Devarim* 25:3).
    14. Age 40 is the time for acquiring wisdom (*Pirkei Avot* 5:21).
    15. In the Friday evening *tefillah* of *Kabbalat Shabbat* we say *arba'im shanah akut b'dor* (*Tehillim* 95:10).
    16. Forty days before a child is born, a *bat kol* is heard revealing their mate (*Gemara Sotah* 2a).
    17. *Yona* prophesied that in forty days, Nineveh would be overthrown (*Yona* 3:4).
    18. *Eliyahu* fasted 40 days and nights (*Melachim* 1:19:8).
    19. The *korban todah* consisted of 40 loaves of bread (*Rambam Mishnah Torah Hilchot Maaseh Hakorbanot* 9:17).
    20. *Avdon*, one of the *shoftim*, had 40 sons and 30 grandsons (*Shoftim* 12:14).
    21. The *Plishtim* ruled over Israel for 40 years (*Shoftim* 13:1).
    22. Rabbi *Eliezer* says that each plague that *Hashem* inflicted on the *Mitzriyim* was equivalent to four plagues for a total of 40 plagues (*Haggadah Shel Pesach Magid*).
    23. *Shlomo Hamelech* had 40,000 stalls for his horses (*Melachim* 1:5:6).
    24. The *melachot* of *Shabbat* are referred to as 40 less 1 which is thirty nine (*Mishnah Shabbat* 7:2).
    25. The period of embalming *Yaakov* by the *Mitzriyim* took 40 days (*Bereishit* 50:3).

26. The land was tranquil for forty years in *Gidon's* time (*Shoftim* 8:28).

27. *Yehoash Hamelech* ruled in *Yerushalayim* for 40 years (*Melachim* 2:12:2).

28. *Avraham Avinu* recognized *Hashem* at age 40 (*Rambam Mishnah Torah Hilchot Avodah Zara* 1:3).

I am sure there are other references to 40 in Jewish life, but this is a pretty good start.

77. The answer is *Yonadav*. The name *Yonadav*, has "dove" as the ending, which is the English translation of "*Yonah*" at the beginning of the name. There were two *Yonadavs* in *Tanach*. One was the nephew of *David* (*Shmuel* 2:13:3) and the other was the son of *Reichav* (*Yirmiyahu* 35:19).

78. There are three possible answers to when we read from the same *parshah* at *shacharit* and *mincha*. On every public fast day (except *Yom Kippur* and *Tisha B'Av*), we read the identical reading from *Parshat Ki Tisa* during *shacharit* and *mincha*. On *Yom Kippur*, we read different readings for *shacharit* and *minchah* but both from *Parshat Acharei Mot*. In Israel, when *Shemini Atzeret/Simchat Torah* falls on *Shabbat* (it can never fall on *Shabbat* in *Chutz La'aretz*), one would read from *Parshat Bereishit* for *Chatan Bereishit* during *shacharit*; and at *mincha*, one would read again from *Parshat Bereishit* (i.e., the following week's regularly scheduled *Torah* reading). Two additional suggestions were offered in the *Youth Minyan*. Both seemed plausible, but neither is possible because the calendar does not allow either to occur. The first suggestion was when *Parshat Tetzave* coincides with *Parshat Shekalim*. In that case, during *shacharit*, we would read from *Parshat Ki Tisa* for *Shekalim*, and then at *mincha*, we would read again from *Parshat Ki Tisa*, the following week's regularly scheduled *Torah* reading. However, *Parshat Shekalim* never falls on *Shabbat Parshat Tetzave*. The second suggestion was *Rosh Chodesh* which occurs during *Parshat Balak*. During *Shacharit*, we would read *Parshat Pinchas* for the *Rosh Chodesh maftir*, and during *minchah* we would again read from *Parshat Pinchas*, the following week's regularly scheduled *Torah* reading. However, *Shabbat Parshat Balak* never coincides with *Rosh Chodesh*.

79. There are two possible answers. If *Tisha B'Av* falls on a Thursday, then the Monday reading would be the first *aliyah* in *Vaetchanan* and the Thursday reading would be the special *Tisha B'Av* reading from another section of *Vaetchanan*. If *Taanit Esther* falls on either Monday or Thursday, and that week's *Torah* reading happens to be *Ki Tisa*, then one day (Monday or Thursday) would be from one part of *Ki Tisa* (e.g., the following week's regularly scheduled *Torah* reading) and the other day would be from another part of *Ki Tisa* (reading for a fast day). Since *Purim* never falls during the week of *Beshalach*, and *Chanukah* never falls during the week

of *Naso,* and *Rosh Chodesh Av* never falls during the week of *Pinchas,* none of those suggestions would be correct.

80. The case of when *Kriat HaTorah* for *minchah* on *Shabbat* will differ from the next regularly scheduled *parshah's Torah* reading, can only occur when *Yom Kippur* falls on *Shabbat.* In that case, at *mincha,* we do not read from the next regularly scheduled *parshah,* but rather we read from the special *Torah* reading for *minchah* of *Yom Kippur.*

81. In *Parshat Va'era* (*Shemot* 7:16, 17), the first *pasuk* ends with the phrase *"v'hinei lo shamata ad koh"* – "and behold, you have not listened until now." The second *pasuk* begins with the phrase *"koh amar Hashem"* – "thus says *Hashem.*" The first *pasuk* ends with the word *"koh"* and the second *pasuk* begins with the word *"koh."*

82. This is a bit of a trick question: Normally, when one hears the phrase "*derech eretz,*" one thinks of "good conduct" or "respect." However, the phrase appears only once in the *Torah* and refers to a direction. The *Torah* says that *Hashem* did not lead the Jews out of *Mitzrayim "derech eretz plishtim"* – "by way of the land of the *Plishtim*" (*Shemot* 13:17). Therefore, in the *Torah,* "*derech eretz*" precedes the word "*plishtim.*"

83. The *Rambam* (*Hilchot Sota* 3:17) states that upon drinking the bitter waters, an unfaithful woman, accurately accused of being a "*sota,*" would die. At the very same time, the man with whom she had an affair, would suffer the same punishment, no matter where he was in the world at that particular moment.

84. On the first day of *Shavuot* (in *Ashkenazi* shuls) we call the *kohen* for the first *aliyah.* Before he begins his *beracha,* we read the special *Shavuot* poem of *Akdamut.*

85. *David Hamelech* and his father *Yishai* both have names that are palindromes; that is, they read the same forwards and backwards. *David* is *daled – vav – daled. Yishai* is *yud – shin – yud.*

86. It is the "*reish*" in the word "*asher*" (*Bamidbar* 21:30). The *Baal Haturim* explains that the name *asher* has the same letters as the word *rosh.* The "*reish*" is earmarked with a "*dagesh*" – "dot" to indicate that the *pasuk* is discussing the destruction of *Moav* and that its "*rosh*" – "head" was destroyed; leaving only the *alef* and *shin* which spell "*aish*" or fire.

87. *Parshat V'zot Haberacha* is the only *parshah* with no *haftarah.* It is always read on *Shemini Atzeret/Simchat Torah* and therefore is never read on a regular *Shabbat.*

88. *Parshat Mikeitz* is the single largest *parshah petucha.*

89. The *amida* or *shemoneh esrei* is the substitute for the "*korban tamid*" – "daily sacrifices" that were offered in the *Beit Hamikdash.* Because nothing preceded the daily morning *korban tamid,* and because the *shemoneh esrei*

is "today's" *korban*, the reading of the *Torah* in the morning follows the *shemoneh esrei*. Similarly, because nothing followed the daily afternoon *korban tamid*, we read the *Torah* at *minchah* before we say the *shemoneh esrei*.

90. This can never happen in *"chutz la'aretz"* – "outside Israel." If *Purim* in *Jerusalem* occurs on *Shabbat*, then the *haftarah* that is read, is the very same *haftarah* that we would have read the previous *Shabbat* on *Parshat Zachor*.

91. In *"chutz la'aretz"* – "outside Israel" on *Chol Hamoed Sukkot*, we daily take out one *Sefer Torah* for *Kriat HaTorah*. Four individuals are called to the *Torah*. Because of the issue of *"sfeika d'yoma,"* we read the *Sukkot* offering for each of three different days for the first three *aliyot*; and then for the fourth *aliyah*, we read the offerings of all three days. In *Eretz Yisrael*, however, where there is no issue of *"sfeika d'yoma,"* the same *Sukkot* offering for the day on which the *Torah* reading takes place, is read for each of the four *aliyot*, each day of *Chol Hamoed Sukkot*.

92. In *Parshat Yitro* (*Shemot* 20:5), in the portion of the *"aseret hadibrot"* – "the ten commandments," the *Torah* speaks of "visiting the guilt of the parents upon the children, upon the third and upon the fourth generations."

93. *Chulda's* parents were *Yehoshua* and *Rachav* (*Gemara Megillah* 14b).

94. Trick question: *Parshat Mikeitz*. The only people called *meraglim* in the *Torah* are the brothers of *Yosef*, when he accuses them of being spies (*Bereishit* 42:9). The *meraglim* that *Moshe* sent to scout the land are called *"anashim"* and never referred to as *"meraglim."*

95. There were three areas where the *leviim* set themselves apart from the other tribes:
    1. When the other tribes murmured against *Moshe* and *Hashem*, the *leviim* did not join in (*Rashi Devarim* 33:8).
    2. They did not sin with the *"eigel hazahav"* – "golden calf."
    3. And they continued to circumcise their sons throughout the 40 years in the desert (*Rashi Devarim* 33:9).

96. *Avraham* lived 175 years and his name appears in *Tanach* 175 times.

97. In the *Torah*, *Hashem* appeared to three non-Jews at night. They were *Avimelech* (*Bereishit* 20:3); *Lavan* (*Bereishit* 31:24); and *Bilam* (*Bamidbar* 22:20).

98. Certain chapters of *Tehillim* and *Megillat Eicha* are alphabetically arranged according to the Hebrew alphabet.

99. Curiously *Eretz Yisrael* never appears in the *Torah*. However, in *Nevi'im* and *Ketuvim*, it appears 11 times (*Shmuel* 2:13:7; *Melachim* 2:5:2, *Melachim* 2:5:4, *Melachim* 2:6:32; *Yechezkel* 27:17, *Yechezkel* 40:2 and *Yechezkel* 47:18; *Divrei Hayamim* 1:22:2; *Divrei Hayamim* 2:2:16, *Divrei Hayamim* 2:30:25, and *Divrei Hayamim* 2:34:7)

100. The *haftarah* of *Emor* begins with the word *"v'hakohanim"* and ends with the word *"hakohanim"* (*Yechezkel* 44:15; *Yechezkel* 44:31).

101. *Avraham* and *Bilam* were both from *Aram Naharayim* (*Bereishit* 24:2 and *Bereishit* 24:10; *Devarim* 23:5). They both rose early and personally saddled their donkeys (*Bereishit* 22:3; *Bamidbar* 22:21).

102. *Masechet Nidda* and *Masechet Eduyot* both begin with the same *Mishnah*, since *Eduyot* is not about a specific topic, but rather a collection of topics.

103. *Masechet Chullin* is found in the section of *Mishnah* called *Kodshim*. *Chullin* means ordinary or mundane and yet is found in the section called *Kodshim*, which means sacred or holy things.

104. This was a riddle in the *Torah Tidbits*. The Hebrew word for gold is *"zahav,"* which has as its *gematriya* 14. The *Aramaic* word for gold is *"dahav"* (*Shemot* 28:14), which has as its *gematriya* 11. And therefore 14 carat gold is used in Israel, 11 carat gold would be found in *Bavel* or in a place where one would speak *Aramaic*.

105. Since there could not be any oil left over from one day to the next, based on the *pasuk* which tells us that the *menorah* had to burn *"mei'erev ad boker"* – "from evening until morning" (*Shemot* 27:21), and since the length of the night varies from season to season, the *Daat Zekeinim* suggests that the wicks used in the summer were thicker than those in the winter months so that all the oil would be burned up, such that no oil was left over from day to day (*Daat Zekeinim* 27:21).

106. In *Parshat Shemini*, we are told that *Mishael* and *Eltzafan* took care of the burial of *Nadav* and *Avihu* (*Vayikra* 10:4) even though by doing so, they would become impure and unable to bring the *Korban Pesach,* given that *Nadav* and *Avihu* died on *Rosh Chodesh Nisan*. *Rashi* comments (*Gemara Sukkah* 25b) that from here we learn the concept of *"haosek b'mitzvah patur min hamitzvah."* *Rashi* further comments that we can also deduce that one cannot put off a "lower category" *mitzvah* (such as burial) available immediately, for a "higher category" *mitzvah* opportunity (*korban Pesach* with the punishment of *karet*) in the near future.

107. In *Parshat Haazinu*, the *Torah* reads *"dvash miselah v'shemen meichalmish tzur"* (*Devarim* 32:13). Honey and oil coming from rocks and stones.

108. *Menashe* and *Ephraim*. Their father was *Yosef* and hence their paternal grandfather was *Yaakov*. *Yosef*'s wife was *Osnat*. *Rabbeinu Behaye* (*Bereishit* 41:45) quotes the *Pirkei d'Rabbi Eliezer* who says that *Osnat* was the daughter of *Dinah*, the result of her rape by *Shechem*. Therefore their maternal great-grandfather was *Yaakov*. The *Torah* states that she was the daughter of *Potifera*, and the *gemara* (*Sanhedrin* 19) explains that he was called her father, because "anyone who raises an orphan in his home is deemed to have given birth to that person."

109. *Moshe* and *Aharon*. Their father was *Amram* and hence their paternal grandfather was *Kehat*, and their paternal great-grandfather was *Levi*. Their mother was *Yocheved* and therefore their maternal grandfather was *Levi*.

110. The *parshah* is *Nitzavim*. There are 40 *pesukim* in the *parshah* and on each of *Shabbat mincha*, Monday and Thursday, I read 20 *pesukim* from the *parshah*, for a total of 60 *pesukim*, or 1.5 times the number of *pesukim* in the *parshah*.

111. There is a *pasuk* "*Shabbat hi l'Hashem b'chol moshvoteichem*" – "it is *Shabbat* for *Hashem* wherever you settle" (*Vayikra* 23:3). The *Chizkuni* and *Ibn Ezra* both comment on this *pasuk,* that *Shabbat* is observed whether you are in Israel or in *chutz la'aretz*. This commentary is quite strange, for who would have thought differently? What was their point? The *Meshech Chochmah* (*Vayikra* 23:3; *Meshech Chochmah Parshat Emor* 66) explains this seemingly difficult commentary by *Chizkuni* and *Ibn Ezra* by quoting a *gemara* (*Horayot* 4b) which speaks about the *pasuk* (*Shemot* 34:21) which states "six days shall you work and on the seventh, you shall rest; you shall rest from plowing and harvesting." *Rashi* explains that the latter half of the *pasuk* refers to the "*shemitah*" – "sabbatical" year. However, the *Meshech Chochmah* explains that the *Tziddukim*, who interpreted the written *Torah* literally, explained this *pasuk* to mean that in a year when there is no plowing or harvesting, in a *shemitah* year, there will likewise be no observance of *Shabbat*. As a result, the *Tziddukim* suspended observance of *Shabbat* every seven years, but only in *Eretz Yisrael*. In *Chutz La'aretz*, where there was no observance of *shemitah*, *Shabbat* would still be observed. Therefore *Chizkuni* and *Ibn Ezra,* commenting on "*Shabbat hi l'Hashem b'chol moshvoteichem*" – "it is *Shabbat* for *Hashem* wherever you settle" clarify the mistake of the *Tziddukim* and say that *Shabbat* is always observed, whether one is in *chutz la'aretz* or in Israel.

112. *Rashi* in commenting on the phrase "*atem nitzavim*" (*Devarim* 29:12) tells us that *Yehoshua* (*Yehoshua* 24:1) and *Shmuel* (*Shmuel* 1:12:7) did the same in assembling and addressing the nation prior to their ending their rule of leadership and notes variations of the common use of the word "*nitzavim*" in each case.

113. In the *Torah*, the three non-Jews who said "*baruch Hashem*" are *Noach* (*Bereishit* 9:26); *Eliezer* (*Bereishit* 24:27); and *Yitro* (*Shemot* 18:10). In addition, *Avimelech* of *Gerrar* (*Bereishit* 26:29) and *Lavan* (*Bereishit* 24:31) said the similar phrase "*b'ruch Hashem*" with a "*shva*" sound beneath the *bet*. In fact, it appears that while this phrase is used ubiquitously by many Jews today, it is only recorded in the *Torah* as being said by non-Jews.

114. *Rashi* in *Parshat Yitro* (*Shemot* 18:1) says that *Yitro* had seven names; namely, *Reuel, Yeter, Yitro, Chovav, Chever, Keini* and *Putiel*. However, *Chizkuni* points out that *Yitro* had an eighth name, *Reichav* (*Yirmiyahu* 35:2), and

suggests that the reason why *Rashi* omitted this name from the list, is because *Rashi* only referred to the names that are explicitly mentioned in the *Torah* itself.

115. The two *mitzvot* are *tzitzit* and *tefillin*. In the *parshah* of *tzitzit*, the *pasuk* says *"ure'item oto uzechartem"* – "and you will see the *tzitzit* and you will remember the *mitzvot"* (*Bamidbar* 15:39). In the *parshah* of *tefillin*, the *pasuk* says *"ulezikaron bein einecha"* – *"tefillin* should be a sign on your arm and a remembrance between your eyes" (*Shemot* 13:9). Tying a knot around your finger is apparently a Jewish concept. In the *midrash* (*Bereishit Rabbah* 88:7), we are told that when *Yosef* had interpreted the butler's dream and had asked him to remember *Yosef* favourably to *Paroh*, the butler tied knots in order to remember his promise. Additionally the *Zohar* (*Zohar* II:190a) relates that *Rav Yossi* would make knots in his clothing in order to remember certain teachings of *Torah*. The *Shulchan Aruch Harav* (*Orach Chaim* 24:1) teaches that the connection of *tzitzit* to remembering the *mitzvot*, is similar to people who tie a knot in their belt as a reminder of a task or an event. He goes on to teach that there are five knots in the *tzitzit* corresponding to all the *mitzvot* in the five books of the *Torah* that you wish to remember and they are located on four corners of the garment so that you will remember the *mitzvot* wherever you may be in the four corners of the world.

116. My table must be composed of *"atzei shittim"* – "acacia wood." The word *"shittim"* is an acronym for *"shalom, tovah, yeshua,* and *mechila"* – "peace, goodness, salvation, and forgiveness" (*Daat Zekeinim Shemot* 25:5). The *gemara* (*Gemara Chagiga* 27a), in commenting on a *pasuk* (*Yechezkel* 41:22) which begins describing the *"mizbeach"* – "altar" and ends speaking about a *"shulchan"* – "table," states that whereas in the time of the *Beit Hamikdash*, the *mizbeach* atoned for our sins, today it is our table that atones for us through the merit of sharing our meals through welcoming guests.

117. There are 15 individuals mentioned in the *Torah* who tore *"keriah."* They are *Reuven*, who tore his garments when he returned to the pit to save *Yosef* and discovered that he was no longer there (*Bereishit* 37:29); *Yaakov*, upon hearing the news from his children that *Yosef* must have been devoured by a wild animal (*Bereishit* 37:34); the 11 brothers of *Yosef* upon discovering *Yosef*'s cup in *Binyamin*'s sack (*Bereishit* 44:13); and *Kalev* and *Yehoshua*, after the incident with the *meraglim*, upon hearing the complaints of the people against *Moshe* and *Aharon* (*Bamidbar* 14:6). There is also reference in the *Torah* to two groups of individuals who must rend their garments in grief; the *"avel"* – "mourner" (*Vayikra* 10:6); and the *metzora* (*Vayikra* 13:45).

118. *Rashi* mentions the *"taryag mitzvot"* in three places in the *Torah*:
    1. On the words *"im Lavan garti"* – "I lived with *Lavan"* (*Bereishit* 32:5) where *Rashi* comments "and I kept the 613 *mitzvot."*

2. On the word *"ketoret"* (*Bamidbar* 7:20), which *Rashi* says is numerically equivalent to *"taryag"* using the *gematriya* "method of permutation."

3. On the *mitzvah* of wearing *tzitzit* (*Bamidbar* 15:39), which, based on the construction if the fringes recalls the 613 *mitzvot* in the *Torah*.

119. *Petachya* was *Mordechai* of the *Purim* story (*Menachot* 65a). He was called *"Petachya"* – "*Hashem* will open" because he was able to speak all 70 languages known in that region of the world and he was therefore able to elucidate and open the explanation of difficult topics and interpret them for the people.

120. The United Nations World Health Organization as well as the American Medical Association, and numerous other medical associations worldwide, utilize, as part of their organization symbol, the Rod of Asclepius. This snake-entwined staff symbol, takes its name from the Greek deity associated with healing and medicinal arts in Greek mythology. Greek healing temples were called by the name "asclepion," and one such temple was found on the Greek island of Kos, where Hippocrates, the Greek father of medicine, may have begun his career. As we know, doctors are sworn to the Hippocratic Oath, to which physicians affirm that they will treat the ill to the best of their ability, to preserve a patient's privacy and to teach the secrets of medicine to the next generation. Many people believe that this symbol had its origin in the *Torah*'s recounting of *Hashem*'s instruction to *Moshe* to take a fiery serpent and place it on a staff of copper. Those who were suffering from the plague would look at this snake-entwined staff and would be cured (*Bamidbar* 21:9). *Rashi* comments that looking at this phenomenon, automatically would make such a person think of heaven, and that his only hope for surviving the plague would come from heaven. Interestingly, the next mention of this special pole occurs some 700 years later in *Tanach* (*Melachim* 2:18:4), where it is recounted that *Chizkiyahu*, king of *Yehudah*, shattered this symbol, because, over the years, the concept of looking heavenward for salvation, evolved into an actual worship of the snake entwined staff, which constituted *"avodah zara"* – "idolatry," one of Judaism's most serious transgressions.

121. When *Bnai Yisrael* first battled *Amalek* in *Refidim* (*Shemot* 17:8), *Moshe* instructed *Yehoshua* *"b'char lanu anashim"* – "choose some men" and do battle with *Amalek*. The *Chizkuni* (*Shemot* 17:9) comments on what seems to be the extra word "some," that the nation of *Amalek* were expert at sorcery and were able to utilize the negative influences of the zodiac to predict military outcomes. *Moshe* therefore instructed *Yehoshua* to choose soldiers that were all born in the month of *Adar Sheini*, which is not governed by any constellation, rendering the sorcerers powerless.

122. When *Moshe* and *Aharon* first came to *Paroh,* and *Aharon* threw down his staff which transformed into a snake, the *Torah* tells us *"vayikra gam Paroh"* – "and *Paroh* also called" on his sorcerers to do the same. The *Paneach Raza* comments on the seemingly extra word of *"gam"* – "also" and says that this includes calling *Paroh*'s wife, who was greater at sorcery than all the other Egyptian sorcerers combined.

123. There are four instances in the *Torah* where *Moshe* required assistance in focusing in on *Hashem*'s directive; they are:
    1. Understanding the stages of renewal of the moon, to thereby understand the concept of the calendar (*Shemot* 12:2).
    2. How to construct the *menorah* (*Bamidbar* 8:4).
    3. The concept of the *half shekel* (*Shemot* 30:13).
    4. The laws of purity pertaining to creeping animals (*Vayikra* 11:29).

    All four of these concepts are connected by the word *"zeh"* – "this is"; *"hachodesh hazeh"*; *"zeh maaseh hamenorah"*; *"zeh yitnu"*; *"v'zeh lachem hatamei."* The *gemara* (*Menachot* 29a) says that *Hashem* showed the moon, the menorah and the creeping animals, using His anthropomorphic "finger." In the case of the *half shekel, Hashem* showed *Moshe* a flaming coin (*Shemot Rashi* 30:13).

124. The *Torah* relates (*Bereishit* 25:29) that *Eisav* came home tired and found *Yaakov* preparing a pot of lentils. The commentaries (*Targum Yonatan* 25:29 and *Daat Zekeinim* 25:30) explain that *Yaakov* was making lentils as the meal of the mourners for his father *Yitzchak,* as that was the day when *Avraham* passed away; and that *Eisav* was tired because that was also the day when *Eisav* killed *Nimrod.* Therefore *Avraham* and *Nimrod* share the same *yahrtzeit.*

125. The only *beracha* that does not begin with the name of the son being blessed is that of *Yosef.* The *Baal Haturim* (*Bereishit* 49:22) notes that *Yaakov* was giving respect and recognition to his son *Yosef,* in his position as the viceroy of *Mitzrayim,* and the fact that one should not address a royal highness directly by name.

126. The two kings are *Yechizkiyahu* and *Amatzyahu.* Both assumed the throne at age 25 and both ruled for 29 years (*Divrei Hayamim* 2:29:1, *Divrei Hayamim* 2:25:1); both were cited for doing what was good and proper in the eyes of *Hashem* (*Divrei Hayamim* 2:31:20, *Divrei Hayamim* 2:26:4) and the *gematriya* of *Yechizkiyahu* and *Amatzya* are equivalent. Their names evoke the instruction of *Moshe* to *Yehoshua "chazak ve'ematz"* (*Devarim* 31:1).

127. The two words are *"zeh"* (*Bereishit* 5:29) and *"kirvu"* (*Vayikra* 10:4).

128. In *Parshat Mishpatim,* the *pasuk,* in speaking about how to treat the widow and orphan with sensitivity, the *Torah* says "if you will surely mistreat them, as they will surely cry out to Me, I will surely heed their outcry" (*Shemot*

22:22); utilizing the three double expressions of "*anei t'anei,*" "*tza'ok yitzak*" and "*shamoa eshma*" in the same *pasuk*.

129. It is the "*shamir.*" *Yitzchak Shamir* was the seventh prime minister of Israel, *shamir* is the Hebrew word for dill and the *shamir* was the type of worm, created at twilight on *erev shabbat,* the sixth day of creation, that was used to carve the stones of the *ephod* (*Bartenura, Avot* 5:6).

130. The *Baal Haturim* (*Devarim* 26:1) points out that when *Yaakov* and his family fled *Lavan's* home, the *Torah* describes it as "*vayugad l'Lavan ki barach Yaakov*" – "and *Lavan* was told that *Yaakov* had fled" (*Bereishit* 31:22); and that when *Bnai Yisrael* left *Mitzrayim,* the *Torah* describes it as "*vayugad l'melech Mitzrayim ki barach ha'am*" – "and the king of *Mitzrayim* was told that the nation had fled" (*Shemot* 14:5). In both places, says the *Baal Haturim,* the informer was *Amalek* and in both places the phrase "*ki barach*" is used. Therefore, says the *Baal Haturim,* now that we have been commanded to erase the name of *Amalek,* the *Torah* begins the *parshah* of *Bikkurim,* which speaks about our early history with *Lavan,* and begins with the words "*ki tavoh,*" the antidote to "*ki barach.*" The *Baal Haturim* further explains that the *gematriya* of the word "*ki*" is 30 which refers to the constant presence of 30 *tzaddikim* in Israel (*Gemara Chullin* 92a) who are like "*avot*" – "fathers" to *Bnai Yisrael*; "*avot*" being an "anagram" of the word "*tavoh.*"

131. The number that connects *Mitzrayim, Ephron* and *Eisav* is 400. *Hashem* told *Avraham* that his descendants would be enslaved in *Mitzrayim* for 400 years (*Bereishit* 15:13); *Avraham* purchased the *Mearat Hamachpela* for 400 silver coins (*Bereishit* 23:16); and *Eisav* came to meet *Yaakov* and his family with an army of 400 men (*Bereishit* 33:1).

132. The three individuals *Aravna, Chamor* and *Ephron* each sold a significant portion of land to the Jewish people and these three geographic locations support our eternal claim to the *Land of Israel* as not only binding because *Eretz Yisrael* was promised to the Jewish people by *Hashem,* but legally binding in terms of a formal purchase agreement. *Ephron* sold the *Maarat Hamachpela* in *Chevron* to *Avraham* (*Bereishit* 23:16); *Chamor* sold *Shechem* to *Yaakov* (*Bereishit* 33:19); and *Aravna* sold the "*Har Habayit*" – "the *Temple Mount*" in *Jerusalem* to *David Hamelech* (*Shmuel* 2:24:24).

133. In *Tanach,* we find four people who left Israel because of a famine, to seek food elsewhere. They are:
    1. *Avraham* (*Bereishit* 12:10)
    2. *Yitzchak* (*Bereishit* 26:1)
    3. *Yaakov* and his sons (*Bereishit* 42:5)
    4. *Elimelech,* the husband of *Naomi* (*Megillat Rut* 1:1)

134. *Rivka* and *Lavan* were brother and sister. *Rivka* had twin sons, *Yaakov* and *Eisav* (*Bereishit* 25:23) and *Lavan* had twin daughters, *Leah* and *Rachel* (*Ishei Hatanach* quoting *Seder Olam Rabbah* 2).

135. The *gemara* (*Baba Kama* 92b) explains the juxtaposition of the account of the marriage of *Yitzchak* and *Rivka,* with the account of *Avraham* remarrying with *Keturah,* by telling us that the two are connected; and that in fact, after seeing his son marry, *Avraham* was troubled by the fact that he was not married.

136. The 18th of *Tammuz* is the day after the *"eigel hazahav"* – "the golden calf." That event and the other three mentioned in the question are the only four places in the *Torah* referred to as *"vayehi mimochorat"* – "and it was on the morrow" (*Bereishit* 19:34); *Shemot* 18:13; *Shemot* 32:30; *Bamidbar* 17:23).

137. The first people to hide in caves for safety were *Lot* and his daughters after the destruction of *Sedom* (*Bereishit* 19:30). In the rest of *Tanach,* we find the following individuals or groups who hid in caves:
    1. *David Hamelech* (*Tehillim* 57:1).
    2. *Eliyahu* (*Melachim* 1:19:9).
    3. 5 kings in the time of *Yehoshua* (*Yehoshua* 10:17).
    4. The people of Israel (*Shmuel* 1:13:6).
    5. 50 sons of prophets hidden by *Ovadiah* (*Melachim* 1:18:4).

138. *Sarah* refers to *Avraham* as *"adoni"* – "my master" (*Bereishit* 18:12); in the story of *Rivkah* and *Eliezer* at the well, there are numerous references by *Eliezer* about his master *"adoni,"* *Avraham* (*Bereishit* 24:27); *Yehuda* calls *Yosef* *"adoni"* when he comes to plead for his brothers, after the goblet was found in *Binyamin*'s sack. But by far, the use of *"adoni"* is greatest when *Yaakov* meets *Eisav* after returning from *Lavan.* Five times *Yaakov* calls *Eisav* *"adoni"* – "my master" and in the previous chapter *Yaakov* tells his servants three times to use the same word when referring to *Eisav.*

139. The *gemara* (*Rosh Hashanah* 10b) tells us that on *Rosh Hashanah, Yosef* was conceived, and on *Rosh Hashanah,* he was also released from prison.

140. There are two times where the commentaries indicate that worms identified the guilty party in the *Torah.* First, in the recounting of the *mann,* the *Torah* says that one was not permitted to leave over excess *mann* from one day to another. The *Torah* says that some people defied the instruction and left over excess *mann,* and *Rashi* identifies them as *Datan* and *Aviram.* The *midrash* (*Midrash Tanchuma Tetzaveh* 11) says that worms made their way from the tent of *Datan* and *Aviram* to the surrounding tents, pointing the finger at the perpetrators. Secondly, *Targum Yonatan* on the subject of *"egla arufa"* – "the ritual performed when a corpse is found between two cities" (*Devarim* 21:8), tells us that after the *Sanhedrin* would perform the required ceremony, a row of worms would emerge from the calf and trace a line to

the home of the murderer, pointing the finger at the one who would then be condemned to death for his crime.

141. In *Parshat Masei* (*Bamidbar* 35:5), we have two musical cantillation notes that appear only here in the *Torah*. They are the "*karnei fara*" and the "*yerach ben yomo*." The rule is that the "*yerach ben yomo*" always precedes a "*karnei fara*." While they do appear more frequently in the rest of *Tanach*, they only appear once in the *Torah*.

142. In *Megillat Eichah*, the first, second, fourth and fifth chapters all have 22 *pesukim*. The third chapter, while not having 22 *pesukim*, nevertheless has 66 *pesukim*, a multiple of 22.

143. The last word in *Parshat Vayeitzei* is "*machanaim*" which has as its *gematriya* 148 which is the number of *pesukim* in *Vayeitzei*. Hence the *siman* is "*machanaim*."

144. *Parshat Bereishit* and *Parshat Mikeitz* both have 146 *pesukim*. They both utilize the names of two kings of Israel, *Yechizkiyahu* and *Amatzya* as their "*simanim*," both names being equal in *gematriya* to 146.

145. *Parshat Noach* features *Noach* as the builder of the ark. The *parshah* has 153 *pesukim*. There is another famous builder in the *Torah*, *Betzalel*, who built the *Mishkan*. The *gematriya* of his name is 153 and his name is used as the *siman* for *Noach*.

146. *Parshat Masei* has 132 *pesukim* and has as its *siman* the name of one of *Tzelafchad*'s daughters, *Machla*. Her name appears in the *maftir* of *Masei*.

147. *Parshat Pekudei* has no *siman* cited.

148. *Parshat Vayeilech*, with 30 *pesukim*, has as the cited *siman* the name "*Adoniya*" – "*Hashem* is my *Lord*," which has the *gematriya* of 70, the number of *pesukim* in both *Nitzavim* and *Vayeilech* combined.

149. They are:
    1. The other *parshah* that could use the *siman* "*tzav*"; i.e., has exactly 96 *pesukim*, is *Parshat Terumah*.
    2. *Parshat Shoftim* has 97 *pesukim*.

150. There are three other *parshiyot* where the stated number of *pesukim* matches the *siman* given, but if you count the *pesukim*, the stated number is incorrect. *Parshat Yitro* has as its *siman* "*yonadav*," which has a *gematriya* of 72, indicating that there are 72 *pesukim* in the *parshah*. If you count the number of *pesukim* in *Yitro*, there are actually 75 *pesukim*. *Parshat Vayishlach* has as its *siman* "*kelita*," which has a *gematriya* of 154, indicating that there are 154 *pesukim* in the *parshah*. If you count the number of *pesukim* in *Vayishlach*, there are actually 153 *pesukim*. *Parshat Bo* has as its *siman* "*yimaneh*," which has a *gematriya* of 105, indicating that there are 105 *pesukim* in the *parshah*. If you count the number of *pesukim* in *Bo*, there are actually 106 *pesukim*.

151. *Parshat Haazinu* has 52 *pesukim* and its *siman* is "*Kalev*," the name of one of only two spies who brought back a positive report. *Shmuel Hanavi* lived for 52 years (*Gemara Moed Katan* 28a).

152. The first *pasuk* in *Parshat Nitzavim* (*Devarim* 29:9) says "*atem nitzavim hayom*" – "you are standing this day." The *Chida* points out that the word "*atem*" is an anagram for the word "*emet*" – "truth," indicating that only those who speak the truth will merit to stand in *Hashem*'s presence.

153. *Parshat Yitro*, with 72 *pesukim*, has as its *siman* "*yonadav*" who was a nephew of *David Hamelech* (*Shmuel* 2:13:3). The first part of the name "*yona*" is Hebrew for the last part of the name "*dove*."

154. Up until the "*mabul*" – "flood," man was not permitted to eat meat. But once the flood was over, meat became permissible. Therefore *Noach*, for six centuries, was a vegetarian; and for the last 350 years of his life was permitted meat (*Bereishit* 9:3 and *Gemara Sanhedrin* 59b).

155. *Hagar* married *Avraham* (*Bereishit* 16:1) and *Bitya* married *Kalev* (*Gemara Megillah* 13a). Both were daughters of *Paroh*.

156. They are all connected by the number 40. *Yitzchak* got married at 40, *Eisav* married at 40, *David Hamelech* ruled for 40 years, as did *Shlomo Hamelech*, the *Bnai Yisrael* wandered in the desert for 40 years, and there were 40 silver sockets used in the *mishkan*.

157. The three *tannaim* who lived, like *Moshe*, for 120 years, are: *Rabbi Akiva*, *Rabbi Yochanan ben Zakkai* and *Hillel* (*Sifri Devarim* 357:33). In each case, the *Sifri* breaks their 120 years down to three periods of 40 years. *Moshe* was in *Mitzrayim* for 40 years, in *Midian* for 40 years and led *Bnai Yisrael* for 40 years in the desert. *Rabbi Akiva* was a shepherd for 40 years, learned in the *yeshiva* for 40 years and led the Jewish people for 40 years. *Hillel* went from *Bavel* to Israel at the age of 40, studied *Torah* for 40 years and led the Jewish people for 40 years. *Rav Yochanan ben Zakkai* was in business for 40 years, studied *Torah* for 40 years and led the Jewish people for 40 years.

158. The *Torah* tells us "*b'af uv'cheimah uv'ketzef gadol*" – "in anger, fury, and great wrath" (*Devarim* 29:27), three consecutive words that are expressions of anger.

159. The last three words of the *Torah* are "*l'einei kol Yisrael*" – "before all of Israel" (*Devarim* 34:12). The words themselves are inclusive; however, the last three words begin with the letters "*lamed*," "*kaf*," and "*yud*"; hinting at the three sections of the Jewish people, the *kohen, levi* and *yisrael*.

160. The thin stalks swallowed the healthy stalks in *Paroh*'s dream (*Bereishit* 41:24); the staff of *Aharon* swallowed the staffs of *Paroh*'s sorcerers when *Moshe* first appeared before *Paroh* (*Shemot* 7:12); the earth swallowed *Korach* and his congregation (*Bamidbar* 26:10) and the whale swallowed *Yona* (*Yona* 2:1).

161. The *Torah* states: *"eretz asher avaneha barzel"* – "Israel is a land whose stones are like iron" (*Devarim* 8:9). The *gemara* (*Taanit* 4a) says; "read not *"avaneha"* – "stones"; but rather *"boneha"* – "her builders." The *Torah* scholars of *Israel*, who are spiritually as strong as iron, are its real builders. And from where do they derive their strength? The *Arizal* says that the letters of the word *"barzel"* – "iron" spell the four mothers of the 12 tribes, *"Bilhah, Rachel, Zilpah* and *Leah."*

162. In *Parshat Mikeitz* (*Bereishit* 44:8), *Rashi* comments that here is found the first of 10 *"kal vachomer"* statements in *Tanach* and he refers us to the *midrash* (*Bereishit Rabbah* 92:7) for a listing of all ten; four of which are in the *Torah*. Others enumerate many more than the *midrash*. First, a definition of *kal vachomer*: Assume there are two connected cases, one is lenient and one is stringent. If the lenient case has certain restrictions, then it would logically follow that the stringent case would certainly have these restrictions. Conversely, if the stringent case has areas of permissibility, then it would follow that the lenient case would similarly have that area of permissibility. The *beraita* of *Rabbi Yishmael* found at the end of the *korbanot* section in the *Siddur* lists thirteen principles of logic used to determine Jewish law and one of these is the *kal vachomer*. The four *Torah* based examples listed in the *midrash* are:

   1. "Indeed we returned the silver, obviously we wouldn't steal!" (*Bereishit* 44:8).
   2. "The *Bnai Yisrael* did not listen to me, certainly it is doubtful that *Paroh* would!" (*Shemot* 6:12).
   3. "And *Hashem* said to *Moshe*, 'If her father would spit in her face, she would hide from sight for seven days; surely then, if the *Hashem* rebukes her, she should hide for fourteen days!" (*Bamidbar* 12:14).
   4. "Indeed while I, *Moshe*, still live among you, you were rebellious, how much more so after my death!" (*Devarim* 31:27).

163. According to the *midrash*, the first of *Yaakov*'s family to go from *Canaan* to *Mitzrayim* was *Osnat*. The *midrash* (*Pirkei d'Rabbi Eliezer* 38:1) relates the following: When *Dina*, *Yaakov*'s daughter, ventures out of her home, the *Torah* relates the story of *Shechem*, son of *Chamor*, who takes *Dina*, and rapes her (*Bereishit* 34:1). *Osnat* is born as a result of this rape and is rejected by her uncles, the sons of *Yaakov*, who are embarrassed that there is an illegitimate child in the house of *Yaakov*. *Yaakov*, seeing that his family was deeply ashamed, takes steps to protect her. The little girl was banished from the camp and placed under a thorn bush. They called her *Osnat*, a derivative of *sneh*, the Hebrew word for thorn bush. *Yaakov* brought a golden plate with *Hashem*'s name inscribed upon it and hung it on her neck. According to some, *Yaakov* wrote, "Whoever meets you, meets

the seed of *Jacob*." *Hashem* sends the angel *Michael* who took her down to *Mitzrayim*, the home of *Potiphera*. *Potiphera's* wife was barren, and *Osnat* was raised as her daughter. When *Yoseph* took charge of *Mitzrayim*, all were taken by his extraordinary beauty and showered him with gifts to gain his favour. *Osnat* had nothing to offer, other than the golden plate bearing the inscription that *Yaakov*, her grandfather, had made her. When *Yoseph* saw what was written on it, he knew that she was his relative, and he married her.

164. The *Yalkut Shimoni* (*Tanach* 9:1) lists nine women that are described as "*nashim chasidot giyorot*" – "righteous female converts." They are *Hagar, Osnat, Tzipporah, Shifra, Puah, Bitya, Rachav, Rut* and *Yael*.

165. When enumerating the names of the sons of *Eisav*, each name is separated from the next by the word "*aluph*" – "clan," a total of 11 times. (*Bereishit* 36:40 to 36:43).

166. The three women mentioned in *Tanach* who died during childbirth are *Rachel* while giving birth to *Binyamin* (*Bereishit* 35:18); the wife of *Pinchas ben Eli* while giving birth to *Ichavod* (*Shmuel* 1:4:20); *Michal bat Shaul* (*Shmuel* 2:6:23; see *Radak*). Even though the *pasuk* says that *Michal* had no children "until her dying day," the *Radak* deduces from the added words "until her dying day" that "however, on her dying day, she gave birth and died in childbirth."

167. I am *Og*, the giant and the King of *Bashan*. The *midrash* indicates that prior to the flood *Og* asked Noach to save him and *Og* pledged that he would be *Noach's* servant for the remainder of his life. *Pirkei d'Rabbi Eliezer* 23 states that *Noach* added an outer plank to the ark and *Og* held on throughout the flood. The *pasuk* (*Bereishit* 7:23) says: "*vayishaer ach Noach*" – "and only *Noach* and those with him in the flood survived." Both *Baal Haturim* and *Daat Zekeinim* indicate that the words "*ach Noach*" numerically equal 79 which is also the numerical value of *Og*, indicating that not only Noach's family survived, but *Og* as well.

168. In *Parshat Vayislach* (*Bereishit* 33:18), the *pasuk* tells us that *Yaakov* came to *Shechem* as a "*shaleim*" – "as a person of perfection." The *Chatam Sofer* notes that the letters of the word "*shaleim*"; "*shin*," "*lamed*" and "*mem*" are an acronym for "*shem*" – "name"; "*lashon*" – "language" and "*malbush*" – "mode of dress"; indicating that in all the years that *Yaakov* was away from the Jewish environment of his parents' home, he retained his unique identity and that is what protected him from the societal influences of the community of *Lavan*.

169. The answers are as follows:

   a. Rabbi Hillel Horovitz shared the following with me based on an essay by Professor Eli Merzbach of Bar Ilan University. There is a *gemara* (*Kiddushin* 30a) which explains "*sofrim*" from the root "to count" as the official Hebrew word for scribes as follows: They are thus called because they count all the letters in the *Torah*; their counting has revealed that the *"vav"* of the word *"gachon"* (*Vayikra* 11:42) marks the halfway point of letters in the *Torah*; the phrase *"darosh dorash"* (*Vayikra* 10:16) marks the halfway point of words in the *Torah*; and the *pasuk* beginning with the word *"v'hitgalach"* (*Vayikra* 10:33) marks the halfway point in *pesukim* in the *Torah*. This is a very troubling statement in the *gemara*, as the official count of words in the *Torah* is 79,980 making word 39,990 the halfway point in words; whereas the words *"darosh dorash"* are words 40,921 and 40,922 in the *Torah* and therefore do not represent the midway point of words in the *Torah*. Professor Merzbach then quotes *Rav Yitzchak Yosef Zilber* (1917-2004, Russia) who pointed out that the *gemara* was not referring to the midway point of all words in the *Torah*, but rather the midway point between all the category one and category two word phrases explained in the question. Professor Merzbach then enumerates 89 category one and category two word phrases, and the 45th such phrase is *"darosh dorash"* (*Vayikra* 10:16); indicating 44 such phrases before *"darosh dorash"* and 44 such word phrases following *"darosh dorash."* (For a fascinating discussion of this topic, visit https://www.biu.ac.il/JH/Parasha/shmini/mer.html).

b. *Parshat Noach* has eight "category one" double word phrases; *"Noach Noach"* (*Bereishit* 6:9); *"shiva shiva"* (twice; *Bereishit* 7:2; *Bereishit* 7:3); *"shnayim shnayim"* (twice; *Bereishit* 7:9; *Bereishit* 7:15); *"me'od me'od"* (*Bereishit* 7:19); *"Shem Shem"* (*Bereishit* 11:1); and *"Terach Terach"* (*Bereishit* 11:27).

BIGGEST/ SMALLEST, LONGEST/ SHORTEST, ETC.

BIGGEST/SMALLEST, LONGEST/SHORTEST, ETC. QUESTIONS

1. What is the shortest *pasuk* in the *Torah* in letters?
2. What is the shortest *pasuk* in the *Tanach* in letters?
3. What is the longest *pasuk* in the *Tanach* in words?
4. What is the longest word in the *Torah*?
5. What is the tallest letter in the *Torah*?
6. What is the longest word in *Tanach*?
7. Which word in *Tanach* has the largest value (in *gematriya*)?
8. Which word in *Tanach* has the smallest value (in *gematriya*)?
9. What is the shortest word in the *Torah*?
10. What is the shortest *amud* (page) in the *gemara*?
11. Which is the shortest *sefer* in the *Torah*?
12. Which is the shortest *sefer* in *Tanach*?
13. What is the longest *perek* in the *Torah*?
14. What is the shortest *perek* in the *Torah*?
15. What is the shortest *perek* in *Tanach*?
16. What is the longest regular *Shabbat* morning *Torah* reading?
17. What is the longest possible *Shabbat* morning *Torah* reading?
18. Which *sefer* has the most *mitzvot*?
19. Which single *parshah* has the most *mitzvot*?
20. On which *Shabbat* would we read the most *mitzvot* in the *Torah* reading?
21. What is the shortest *parshah* in the *Torah* (in *pesukim*)?
22. Which *parshah* has the longest *pesukim* (measured in average number of letters per *pasuk*)?
23. What is the longest *parshah* in the *Torah* (in *pesukim*)?
24. What is the longest possible *Torah* reading on a one-*parshah* *Shabbat* morning?
25. What is the smallest *parshah* in the *Torah* (in *gematriya*)?
26. What is the shortest *parshah* in the *Torah* (in lines)?
27. What is the longest "*masechta*" – "tractate" in the *gemara*?
28. What is the shortest *mesechta* in the *gemara*?
29. What is the longest chapter in *Tehillim*?
30. What is the longest *aliyah* in the *Torah*?
31. What is the longest regular *maftir* (a *maftir* of a regular *Torah* reading)?
32. Which word begins the greatest number of *Shabbat* morning *Torah* readings in the course of a year and how many begin with that word?
33. The vast majority of *pesukim* in *Tanach* begin with the letter *vav*. Which *sefer* in *Tanach* has only one *pasuk* beginning with the letter *vav*?

34. How many *parshiyot* are named for the first word in the *parshah*?
35. *Parshat Hachodesh* has a *maftir* of 20 *pesukim*. *Parshat Parah* is longer at 22 *pesukim*. But there is one *maftir* that is considerably longer. What is it?
36. What is the longest "Monday-Thursday-*Shabbat Mincha*" *Torah* reading?
37. *Sefer Bereishit* has the most, most, most, most and least. Explain.
38. Where in the *Torah* do we find the greatest number of different proper names in one *pasuk*?
39. Where in *Tanach* do we find the greatest number of different proper names in one *pasuk*?
40. Where do we find in the *Torah* five consecutive words that are all verbs, and all beginning with the same letter?
41. Where in the *Torah* do we find a *pasuk* with thirteen consecutive words all containing the letter "*lamed*"?
42. Where in the *Torah* do we find a *pasuk* with seven consecutive words, all beginning with the letter "*vav*"?
43. What is the greatest number of consecutive *pesukim* in the *Torah* that begin with the letter "*vav*"?
44. Where in the *Torah* do we find a *pasuk* with five consecutive words, all beginning with the letter "*bet*"?
45. What is the maximum number of consecutive days that a "*tzibbur*" – "congregation" can read from the *Torah*?
46. What is the longest possible *benching* in the year?
47. What is the longest *shemoneh esrei* (excluding *Rosh Hashana, Yom Kippur*, and *erev Yom Kippur*)?
48. Which *parshah* in the *Torah* has the greatest number of names of women?
49. Which *pasuk* in the *Torah* has the greatest number of names of places?
50. Which *pasuk* in the *Torah* has the greatest number of different vegetables?
51. Which *pasuk* in the *Torah* has the greatest number of different kinds of jewellery?
52. Which *pasuk* in the *Torah* has the greatest number of different types of metal?
53. Which *pasuk* in the *Torah* mentions the greatest number of generations of one family?
54. Which *pasuk* in the *Torah* has the greatest number of different consecutive words with the same "*shoresh*" – "root"?
55. Which *pasuk* in *Tanach* has the greatest number of different consecutive words with the same "*shoresh*" – "root"?
56. Which word in *Tanach* contains the greatest number of "*mems*"?
57. Which *pasuk* in *Tanach* contains all the letters of the *alef bet* including all the final *letters; chaf sofit, mem sofit, nun sofit, peh sofit, tzadi sofit*?
58. Find 12 *pesukim* in a row in the *Torah* that all begin with the same word?

59. People like good things. Find three consecutive *pesukim* in *Tanach* that begin with the word "*tov*" – "good"?

60. One *parshah* in the *Torah* contains ten different *tefillot* or *pesukim* that have made their way into our liturgy, by far the most of any *parshah* in the *Torah*. Which *parshah* is it and name as many of the ten as you can?

61. I hope you do not answer "*lo yadati*" to this question. How many times in the *Torah* do we find the phrase "*lo yadati*" – "I do not know."

62. Where do we find four consecutive words in the *Torah* that have the same "*trop*" – "musical note"; that of the note "*munach*"?

63. What is the least number of *pesukim* that we read from a *Sefer Torah* when calling up at least three *aliyot*?

64. The *braita* in the *gemara* (*Gemara Megilla* 21b) says that one should not read less than 10 *pesukim* in a regular *Torah* reading. As a result, the *Torah* readings for *Shabbat mincha,* Monday morning and Thursday morning, all have at least ten *pesukim* spread over the three *aliyot*. How many of these readings have exactly 10 *pesukim*?

65. Normally, a *pasuk* is divided into two segments, with the musical note "*etnachta*" dividing the first part from the second. An *etnachta*, therefore, never occurs more than once in a single *pasuk*. There are, however, some *pesukim* that do not contain any *etnachta* and hence the entire *pasuk* represents one single segment. What is the longest *pasuk* in the *Torah* that does not contain an *etnachta*?

66. There are a number of expressions of crying in the *Torah*, all with the *shoresh* "*bachah*" – "to cry," spelled *bet-chaf-heh*; "*vayeivch*"; "*vayivchu*"; "*bachah*," "*b'chi*," "*v'livkota*." There are ten occurrences of the word "*vayeivch*" in *Bereishit*. Who cried the most?

67. Name the largest number of consecutive letters in the *Torah* (not necessarily in the same word) to form a palindrome?

68. How many times does the word "*kasher*" appear in *Tanach*?

69. What is the shortest interval in days during which we read publicly from each of the five books of the *Torah*?

70. How many days are in the longest possible year in the Jewish calendar?

71. Who was the one in the *Torah* who rose early, most frequently?

72. Who was the one in *Tanach* who rose early, most frequently?

73. *Noach's* sons are always listed as *Shem, Cham* and *Yefet*. Do we assume from this that *Shem* was the oldest, next *Cham* and youngest *Yefet*?

74. In the 40 years of wandering in the desert, where and for how long was the shortest stay for *Bnai Yisrael*?

75. In the 40 years of wandering in the desert, where and for how long was the longest stay for *Bnai Yisrael*?

76. Which letter of the Hebrew alphabet begins the fewest *pesukim* in the *Torah*?

77. Find three words in a five word *pasuk* that are composed of the same three letters, all in the same order, but the vowel punctuation of each is different?

78. Where in *Tanach* do we find seven consecutive *pesukim* all beginning with the same two letter word? Hint: you may need time to figure out the answer to this riddle!

BIGGEST/SMALLEST, LONGEST/SHORTEST, ETC. ANSWERS

1. There are 13 *pesukim* in the *Torah* with only three words. The shortest of these in letters is found in *Parshat Vayigash* "*Uvnai Dan Chushim*" which has only 10 letters (*Bereishit* 46:23).

2. The shortest *pasuk* in all of *Tanach* in letters is the *pasuk* "*Adam Sheit Enosh*" (*Divrei Hayamim* 1:1:1) with just nine letters.

3. *Megillat Esther* 8:9 has 43 words, making it the longest *pasuk* in *Tanach* in words.

4. The word "*u'vemisharotecha*" – "and in your kneading bowls" has 10 letters (*Shemos* 7:28)

5. The tallest letter in the *Torah* is the "*nun sofit*" of the word "*mishpatan*" (*Bamidbar* 27:5). Some letters are written normally extending below the line (*kuf, nun sofit, tzadi sofit, peh sofit*) and one is written normally extending above the line (*lamed*). The "*nun sofit*" in "*mishpatan*" is the only letter that extends either above or below the line that is written extra large in the *Torah*. Hence, it is the tallest letter in the *Torah*.

6. There are a few eleven letter words in *Tanach*; namely,
    1. "*uvetoavoteihem*" (*Yechezkel* 16:47)
    2. "*v'ha'achashdarpanim*" (*Megillat Esther* 9:3)
    3. "*v'chealilotechem*" (*Yechezkel* 20:44)

7. In *Parshat Korach* (*Bamidbar* 16:13), we have the word "*tistarer*" (from the root "to rule over") which has a value of 1500.

8. The words "*bo*" and "*av*" appear in many locations in *Tanach*. With a *gematriya* of three, they are the words with the smallest *gematriya* value in the *Torah*.

9. One might think that the smallest words in the *Torah* would be "*bo*" and "*av*" (see above answer). However, while these are two of many two letter words in the *Torah*, they are not the shortest in terms of letters. In *Parshat Ha'azinu* (*Devarim* 32:6) we have a one letter word; "*ha*" – "is it". The notes in many *chumashim* indicate that this letter "*heh*" is written larger than typical letters in the *Torah* and that this letter is a word unto itself (*Minchat Shai*).

10. *Nazir* 33*b* is the shortest by far. It has no lines of *gemara* or *Rashi*. It is only *Tosafot*.

11. *Vayikra* is the shortest *sefer* in terms of *parshiyot, pesukim*, words and letters. However, according to those who contend that the two sentences beginning with "*vayehi binsoa*" (*Bamidbar* 10:35–36) are a "*sefer bifnei atzmo*" – "a separate book of the *Torah*," it is clear that this "*sefer*" would be the shortest in all categories.

12. The Book of *Ovadiah* has one chapter with 21 *pesukim*.
13. *Bamidbar* 7 is the longest chapter in the *Torah with* 89 *pesukim*.
14. *Vayikra* 12 is the shortest chapter in the *Torah,* a mere eight *pesukim*.
15. *Tehillim* 117 is the shortest chapter in *Tanach* with a grand total of two *pesukim*.
16. *Matot-Massei,* having a combined 244 *pesukim, is the longest regular Shabbat Torah* reading.
17. If *Matot-Massei* falls on a *Shabbat Rosh Chodesh Av,* the total with the *Rosh Chodesh maftir* would be 251 *pesukim*.
18. *Vayikra* is the leader with 247 of the 613 *mitzvot,* or over 40%.
19. There are 74 *mitzvot* in *Ki Teitzei,* the largest *mitzvah* count in any single *parshah.* They are divided into 27 positive and 47 negative *mitzvot*.
20. When we read the two *parshiyot* of *Acharei Mot – Kedoshim* together, we read 79 *mitzvot*.
21. *Vayeilech* has only 30 *pesukim*.
22. Curiously enough, the answer to this question is also *Vayeilech.* Even though it is the shortest *parshah* in the *Torah* in terms of *pesukim,* its *pesukim* have the largest average number of letters.
23. *Naso* is the longest *parshah* in the *Torah* with 176 *pesukim*.
24. If the eighth day of *Chanuka* falls on a *Shabbat,* a special *maftir* is added to *Parshat Mikeitz.* It is ironic that the *maftir* comes from *Parshat Naso,* the longest *parshah* in the *Torah. Mikeitz* has 146 *pesukim* and the *maftir* for the 8th day of *Chanukah* is 40 *pesukim* for a total of 186 *pesukim*.
25. *V'zot Haberacha* is the smallest *parshah* in the *Torah* in *gematriya* with a total of 134,008.
26. *V'zot Haberacha* is the shortest *parshah* in the *Torah* in lines with a total of 70 lines.
27. We define a full 2 sided page of the *"gemara"* – "Talmud" as either a *"blatt"* or a *"daf."* One side is called an *"amud."* *Bava Batra* which has 176 *blatt,* which makes it the longest *mesechet* in *gemara*.
28. *Masechet Horiot* is the shortest *masechet* in *gemara* with only 13 *"dafim"* – "pages."
29. Chapter 119 which has 176 *pesukim.* Curiously, the answer to this question and #23 and #27 above are the same. So, what is significant about the number 176? *Chazal* has suggested that the number 176 is the product of 22 and 8. Both these numbers are symbols of completeness; 22 as the total number of primary letters in the Hebrew alphabet, the same alphabet that has been used to transmit *Hashem*'s perfect *Torah;* and 8 being the *Maharal*'s symbol of a complete or perfect number; using 8 as the day of the *mitzvah* of circumcision, or the completion of man's creation, as embodied in the statement by *Hashem* to *Avraham* "walk before me and be complete." One

can therefore deduce that if the numbers 22 and 8 are complete, their product, 176, too, must be complete (See the answer to *Parshat Naso* #4).

30. The longest *aliyah* in the *Torah* is *revi'i* when *Matot* and *Massei* are combined; 72 *pesukim*.

31. The *maftir* for *Pinchas* and *Nitzavim* both have six *pesukim*.

32. The most common word beginning a *Shabbat* morning *Torah* reading is *"vayedabeir"*; this being common to 16 *parshiyot*.

33. The book of *Shir Hashirim* has only one *pasuk* beginning with the letter *vav* (*Shir Hashirim* 7:10).

34. There are 16 weekly *Torah* readings that are named for the first word in the *parshah*. We might have 17 but we are excluding *"V'zot Haberacha"* because it is a two word title and it is not read as a regular weekly *Shabbat* morning reading.

35. The *maftir* for the eighth day of *Chanukah* when it falls on *Shabbat* (*Bamidbar* 7:54–8:4) is the longest *maftir* of the year at 40 *pesukim*.

36. It is the reading for *Parshat Eikev* (25 *pesukim*). Even though both *Bereishit* (34 *pesukim*) and *Ki Tisa* (45 *pesukim*) have longer first *aliyot*, in each of those cases, the "Monday-Thursday-*Shabbat Mincha*" reading does not consist of the entire first *aliya*. Some have the custom of not breaking up the list of travels in *Parshat Massei* and they would therefore read a longer portion (49 *pesukim*). However, this is not a very widespread custom and most shuls do not follow it. There is an instance where the *Shabbat minchah Torah* reading could be considerably longer. In cases where residents of *chutz la'aretz* happen to be in Israel for a two-day *yom tov* that falls on a Friday and *Shabbat* in *chutz la'aretz*, and only as a one-day *yom tov* on a Friday in Israel, the subsequent *Shabbat* morning *Torah* readings would be different in Israel and the *Diaspora*. If the visitors return to *chutz la'aretz* before adjustments are made in order to synchronize both communities, some have the custom of reading the entire "missed" *parshah* as part of the *Shabbat minchah Torah* reading.

37. *Sefer Bereishit* has the most *parshiyot*, the most *pesukim*, the most words and the most letters of any *sefer* in the *Torah*, yet it has the least *mitzvot*; only three.

38. There are two *pesukim* in the *Torah*, each containing 11 different names; *Bereishit* 46:21 and *Bamidbar* 27:1.

39. In *Divrei Hayamim* 1:25:4, we have a listing of *Heman* and his 14 sons for a total of 15 proper names in one *pasuk*. A number of *pesukim* later, we are told that *Heman* also had three daughters for a total of 17 children. *Heman*, not to be confused with *Megillat Esther*'s *Haman*, was an important advisor to *David Hamelech*.

40. In *Bereishit* 25:34 we have the words "*vayochal, vayeisht, vayakam, vayelech, vayivez*" – "and he (*Eisav*) ate, and he drank, and he arose, and he left, and he spurned the birthright."

41. The *pasuk* is in *Bamidbar* 22:37 counting 13 words from the second word "*Balak*." Interestingly, the *pasuk* has a total of 18 words and 15 of them contain the letter "*lamed*." This may be the greatest concentration of "*lameds*" in one *pasuk*!

42. In *Parshat Noach*, we have the phrase "*v'katzir, v'kor, v'chom, v'kayitz, vachoref, v'yom, valailah*" – "seedtime and harvest, cold and heat, summer and winter, day and night" (*Bereishit* 8:22), seven consecutive words beginning with a *vav*.

43. From *Shemot* 1:11 to *Shemot* 3:15 inclusive, there are 52 consecutive *pesukim* that begin with the letter "*vav*."

44. In *Parshat Vaera*, the *pasuk* reads "*basadeh, basusim, bachamorim, bagemalim, babakar*" – "in the fields – the horses, the asses, the camels, the cattle" (*Shemot* 9:3), five consecutive words beginning with the letter "*bet*."

45. The maximum number of consecutive days that a *tzibbur* can read from the *Torah* occurs when the first day of *Sukkot* falls on a Monday night/Tuesday. In this case, you would read the regular *Torah* reading on Monday *Erev Sukkot*, then read for the nine days of *Sukkot/Shemini Atzeret* with *Sukkot/Shemini Atzeret* ending on Wednesday evening. This would be followed by another regular *Torah* reading on Thursday morning for an 11 day consecutive *Torah* reading. This obviously only works in *chutz la'aretz*.

46. *Shabbat Rosh Chodesh Chanukah* is the longest possible "*benching*" – "grace after meals" of the year, as we add the special insert for *Shabbat* of "*retzai*," the special insert for *Rosh Chodesh* of "*yaaleh v'yavo*," the special insert of "*al hanisim*" for *Chanukah*, and the two special "*harachamans*" for *Shabbat* and *Rosh Chodesh*.

47. The *maariv* prayer of *Motzaei Shabbat Rosh Chodesh Chanukah* is the longest possible *shemoneh esrei* as we add "*ata chonantanu*," "*yaaleh v'yavo'*, and "*al hanisim*." If one is praying according to *nusach Ari*, it is even longer because they say "*sim shalom*" instead of "*shalom rav*."

48. *Parshat Vayishlach* names 14 women, the largest number of women named in any *parshah* of the *Torah*. They are *Ada, Ahalivama, Ana, Basmat, Timna, Mehetavel, Matred, Rachel, Leah, Dina, Devorah, Rivka, Bilha* and *Zilpa*.

49. *Bamidbar* 32:3 mentions nine geographic places in the same *pasuk*.

50. The *Torah* relates how the *Bnai Yisrael* were complaining about missing the wonderful life that they had in *Mitzrayim*, where they enjoyed "cucumbers, melons, leek, onions and garlic" (*Bamidbar* 11:5); five different vegetables in one *pasuk*.

51. In *Bamidbar* 31:50, the *Torah* is relating details of an offering made by *Bnai Yisrael* to *Hashem* and among the donations brought were five types of jewellery; "armlets, bracelets, rings, earrings and pendants."

52. *Bamidbar* 31:22 speaks about the purification of vessels and lists six metals in one *pasuk*; gold, silver, copper, iron, tin and lead.

53. The daughters of *Tzelafchad* approached *Moshe* to clarify the laws of inheritance. The seven generations listed in one *pasuk* are the five daughters, *Tzelafchad, Chefer, Gilad, Machir, Menashe* and *Yosef* (*Bamidbar* 27:1).

54. In *Bamidbar* 4:47, we have four consecutive words with the same *shoresh* in the phrase "*laavod avodat avoda va'avodat...*"

55. In *Yishayahu* 24:16, we have five consecutive words with the same *shoresh* in the phrase "*bogdim bagadu uveged bogdim bogadu.*"

56. The word "*mimitkomemim*" has five "*mems*" (*Tehillim* 17:7).

57. *Tzefania* 3:8 contains all 22 letters and five final letters of the Hebrew alphabet (see question #4 in *Vaetchanan* for the two *pesukim* in the *Torah* containing all 22 letters, but not all final letters).

58. In *Parshat Ki Tavo* (*Devarim* 27:15–26), each of the 12 consecutive *pesukim* begin with the word "*arur*" – "cursed be."

59. In *Megillat Eichah*, there are three consecutive *pesukim* beginning with the word "*tov*" (*Eichah* 3:25–27).

60. The *parshah* is *Vaetchanan*. Here are the 10 different *tefillot/pesukim* that are found in *Vaetchanan* that have made their way into our liturgy:
    1. "*V'atem hadeveikim*" is recited immediately prior to *Kriat HaTorah* (*Devarim* 4:4).
    2. "*Atah hareita ladaat*" is recited by some when taking the *Torah* from the *Aron* and by everyone on *Shemini Atzeret/Simchat Torah* (*Devarim* 4:35).
    3. "*V'yadaata hayom*" (*Devarim* 4:39) concludes the first paragraph of *Aleinu*.
    4. "*V'zot haTorah*" (*Devarim* 4:44) is recited during the *hagbah* ritual.
    5. The *tefillah* of *Shema Yisrael* (*Devarim* 6:4–9) and the first of the *three* paragraphs of *Kriat Shema* are recited thrice daily.
    6. "*Uvikashtem misham*" (*Devarim* 4:29) is recited numerous times in the year as part of the *selichot*.
    7. "*Avadim hayinu*" (*Devarim* 6:21) is recited in the reading of the *Haggadah* on the *Seder* night.
    8. "*U'tzedakah tihiye lanu*" (*Devarim* 6:25) is recited during *Musaf* of *Rosh Hashanah*.
    9. Part of *Shabbat* morning *kiddush* (*Devarim* 5:13–14).
    10. Finally, one of the "*sheish zechirot*" – "six remembrances" said daily after *shacharit* (*Devarim* 4:9–10).

61. There are six places in the *Torah* where we find the phrase "*lo yadati.*" They are:

1. *Kayin* responding to *Hashem* (*Bereishit* 4:9).
2. *Avimelech* responding to *Avraham* (*Bereishit* 21:26).
3. *Yitzchak* to *Eisav* (*Bereishit* 27:2).
4. *Yaakov* waking up after his dream of the ladder (*Bereishit* 28:16).
5. *Paroh* responding to *Moshe* and *Aharon* (*Shemot* 5:2).
6. *Bilam* to the angel of *Hashem* (*Bamidbar* 22:34).

62. In *Parshat Bamidbar* (*Bamidbar* 3:4), the *pasuk* begins with the words "*vayamat Nadav v'Avihu lifnei*"; each word has the "*munach*" note beneath the word.

63. There is a *braita* quoted in the *gemara* (*Megillah* 21b) which says that one may not read less than ten *pesukim* during a public *Torah* reading. However, there is one exception to the rule of the *braita*, and that is the *Torah* reading of *Purim* morning when three people are called to the *Torah* and the total number of *pesukim* that are read are nine. The *gemara* explains that this is an exception because the reading of *Amalek* is the order of the day and the story and the chapter ends at the ninth *pasuk*.

64. The two *Torah* readings of *Shabbat mincha,* Monday and Thursday that are exactly ten *pesukim* are *Parshat Vayishlach* and *Parshat Masei*.

65. The longest *pasuk* in the *Torah* that contains no *etnachta* is in *Parshat Behaalotcha* (*Bamidbar* 9:1). The *pasuk* has 14 words.

66. Although there are more than ten cryings in *Bereishit*, there are only ten utilizing the word "*vayeivch.*" In the ten occurrences of "*vayeivch*" – "and he cried" in *Bereishit*, *Eisav* cried once (*Bereishit* 27:38); *Yaakov* cried twice (*Bereishit* 29:11; 37:35); and *Yosef* cried a total of seven times (*Bereishit* 42:24; 43:30; 45:14; 45:15; 46:29; 50:1; 50:17).

67. There are 11 letters spread over three words "*lemoadah miyamim yamima,*" taking the "*heh*" from "*lemoadah*" and the ten letters of "*miyamim yamima*" to form *Torah*'s longest palindrome.

68. The word "*kasher*" – "*kosher*" appears only once in the entire *Tanach*, in *Megillat Esther* (8:5) "*v'kasher hadavar lifnei hamelech*" – "and the matter is proper before the king."

69. It is possible for a congregation to read publicly from each of the five books of the *Torah* in as little as eight days. In Israel, this would be from the first day of *Sukkot* until and including *Shemini Atzeret*. In *Chutz Laaretz*, this would be from the second day of *Sukkot* until and including *Simchat Torah*. *Bereishit* (1:1–31 and 2:1–3) and *Devarim* (33: 1–29 and 34:1–12) are read on *Shemini Atzeret* in Israel and *Simchat Torah* in *Chutz Laaretz*. We read *Shemot* (33:12–23 and 34:1–26) on *Shabbat Chol Hamoed* (if there is one on that particular year). We read *Vayikra* (22:26–33 and 23:1–44) on the first and second day of *Sukkot*. And we read *maftir* each day from *Bamidbar* (Chapter 29, when we read about the *korban* of that day of *Sukkot*).

70. There are six possible configurations of the Jewish calendar. The variables are:
    1. The length of the months of *Cheshvan* and *Kislev,* both of which could have 29 or 30 days, and
    2. Whether the year is a leap year, in which case a month of 30 days is added. If both *Cheshvan* and *Kislev* have 29 days, the year is called *"chaseirah"* – "deficient" and there will be 353 days in that year. If *Cheshvan* has 29 days while *Kislev* has 30 days, the year is called *"kisidrah"* – "regular" and there will be 354 days in that year. And if both *Kislev* and *Cheshvan* have 30 days, the year is called *"sheleimah"* – "perfect" and there will be 355 days in that year. Add to each of those three cases the 30 days of an added month in a leap year and you then have the possibility of 383, 384 and 385 days in a year. Therefore the longest possible Jewish year in days is 385 days.
71. The *Torah* attributes the word *"vayashkeim"* – "and he rose early" to *Avraham* three times (*Bereishit* 19:27; *Bereishit* 21:14; *Bereishit* 22:3).
72. *Tanach* attributes the word *"vayashkeim"* – "and he rose early" to *Yehoshua* four times (*Yehoshua* 3:1; *Yehoshua* 6:12; *Yehoshua* 7:16; *Yehoshua* 8:10).
73. The *pasuk* says that *Shem* also had children and he was *"achi Yefet hagadol"* (*Bereishit* 10:21). The translation of *"achi Yefet hagadol"* is ambiguous. It could be read as "the brother of the older brother *Yefet,*" or as "the elder brother of *Yefet.*" At this point we have no indication where *Cham* fits in. We are told that *Noach* first had children when he was 500 years old (*Bereishit* 5:32). We also know that the flood began in *Noach's* 600th year, which means that *Noach's* eldest son was then 100 years old. And there is a *pasuk* (*Bereishit* 11:10) which tells us that *Shem's* eldest son, *Arpachshad,* was born when *Shem* was 100 years old, two years after the flood. Therefore, *Shem* could not have been the eldest, and therefore *"achi Yefet hagadol"* must mean that "*Shem* was the brother of the older brother *Yefet.*" There are differing opinions as to when *Cham* was born, however, there is a *gemara* (*Sanhedrin* 69b) which states that there was a one year gap between each of the three sons. And therefore if *Yefet* was the eldest and born when *Noach* was 500 years old, and *Shem* born two years later when *Noach* was 502 years old, it would then follow that *Cham* was born when *Noach* was 501 years old, making him the middle child.
74. Their shortest stay, according to *Yalkut Me'am Loez* (*Bamidbar* 12:16), was in *Chatzerot,* where they stopped over while *Miriam* was quarantined. *Me'am Loez* states that this was *"midah k'neged midah"* – "measure for measure," to reward *Miriam* for waiting by the *Nile* for four hours to see what would happen to baby *Moshe,* until the daughter of *Paroh* arrived and saved him. For a calculation on how *Me'am Loez* arrives at the seven day period, see the answer to question #16 on *Matot Mas'ei.*

75. Their longest stay, according to *Rashi* (*Devarim* 1:46) and *Yalkut Me'am Loez* (*Bamidbar* 33:2), was for a period of 19 years in *Kadesh*. *Me'am Loez* quotes *Rashi* (*Bamidbar* 33:1), who says that even though they traveled through the desert for 40 years, *Hashem*, through His love for *Bnai Yisrael*, decreed that they would only make 42 stops, and that the majority of these stops were in the first year, when they made 14 stops, and the last year, when they make eight stops. Therefore, in the interim 38 years, they made 20 stops. And since they remained in *Kadesh* for 19 years, they therefore were on the road only 19 times in 19 years, an average of one journey per year. We see this from the *pasuk* (*Devarim* 1:46) which says that they remained in *Kadesh* many years, "*kayamim asher yeshavtem*" – "equal to the days that you rested"; meaning that the 19 years of *Kadesh* were equal in length to the number of years that they travelled.

76. Only two *pesukim* in the *Torah* begin with the letter *samech*. They are "*saru maher*" (*Shemot* 32:8) and "*selach na*" (*Bamidbar* 14:19).

77. The *pasuk* says "*asham hu, ashom, asham l'Hashem*" (*Vayikra* 5:19). All three of the words have the letters *alef, shin, mem sofit*; the vowels of each of the three words are different.

78. In *Kohelet*, we find seven consecutive *pesukim* begging with the word "*eit*" – "there is a time" (*Kohelet* 3:2-8)

CALENDAR, HOLIDAYS & FAST DAYS

THE CALENDAR QUESTIONS

1. What holiday addition to the *"benching"* – "grace after meals" is it that most people don't say and hope they never have to?
2. Which *haftarah* for a regularly scheduled *Shabbat* reading is read least often?
3. On how many *Shabbatot Mevarchim* during the course of a year, is it possible to take out two *Sifrei Torah*?
4. Which *parshah* is always *Shabbat Mevarchim*?
5. What is the significance of the first day of *Shevat* in the *Torah*?
6. In the *Torah* reading for *Parshat Shekalim* we learn the *mitzvah* of "*tzedakah*" – "charity." Where in that reading do we learn the principle that money given to charity will return to us in due course, and from where do we learn that the giving of charity keeps one from death?
7. It is Tuesday morning. It is not *Rosh Chodesh*, not a fast day, not *Chanukah*, not *Purim*, not a *Yom Tov* and not *Chol Hamoed*. Yet, we take a *Sefer Torah* from the ark, call three men up for *aliyot* and read from the week's regular *Torah* portion. Why?
8. Proper names of the Jewish months are not mentioned in the *Torah*, but some are mentioned in *Tanach*. Which *sefer* in *Tanach* contains the greatest number of names of Jewish months?
9. The names we have for the Jewish months originated in *Bavel*. Which months are not mentioned by their Babylonian name anywhere in *Tanach*?
10. Cite two examples in the *Tanach* where people built *sukkot* that had nothing to do with the holiday of *Sukkot*?
11. Generally, because *Jerusalem* is in an earlier time zone, rituals are performed earlier there than in New York. What celebration occurs earlier in New York than in *Jerusalem*?
12. Disregarding the time zone differences, how many times would people in *Eretz Yisrael* begin saying something at least one day earlier than people in *chutz la'aretz*?
13. Many times we have a "*seudat mitzvah*" – "festive meal connected to a *mitzvah*" as a result of actions that preceded the *seudah*. For example, the *seudah* of a *brit* results from the *brit*, the *seudah* for a *siyum* results from the *siyum*. What *mitzvah* happens as a result of a *seudah* which will follow the performance of the *mitzvah*?
14. Which *beracha* can only be said on a Wednesday or Thursday?
15. Which *beracha* can only be said on a Wednesday?
16. Which *beracha* can only be said on a Sunday, Tuesday or Thursday?
17. On what day of what month did *Nadav* and *Avihu*, the sons of *Aharon*, die?
18. On what day of what month did *Miriam* die?
19. On what day of what month did *Yehoshua Bin Nun* die?

20. On what day of what month did *Shmuel Hanavi* die?

21. Which holidays are connected to roses?

22. On which two Friday nights would one not host a *Shalom Zachar*?

23. Besides *Sukkot/Shemini Atzeret* in *Chutz La'aretz*, give another instance where it is possible to say the complete *Hallel* nine days in a row?

24. Which Jewish months have 29 days?

25. On which days of the year can *Mashiach* not come?

26. In a normal week, we read the beginning of the *Shabbat Torah* reading three times before the actual *Shabbat* reading; namely, at *Shabbat mincha*, and on Monday and Thursday mornings. From which *Torah* reading do we read until *Sheni* seven times before the actual *Torah* reading, (a total of eight times including the regular *Shabbat* morning reading)?

27. Why can the first day of *Rosh Hashanah* never fall on a Sunday, Wednesday or Friday?

28. Which *beracha* can only be said on a Sunday, Tuesday, Thursday or Friday and is said every week of the year at least once?

29. In a standard "*luach*" – "calendar" that outlines the *tefillot* and customs of the day, one occasionally finds a short form of five *alephs* in a row. What does this instruction mean?

30. What is the greatest number of *berachot* that can be recited for *kiddush*?

31. Which day of the year was known as "*Yom Tavoach*" – "Day of Sacrifice"?

32. Which *parshah* is never read *Shabbat minchah* in *chutz la'aretz*?

33. It is *Shabbat Parshat Shekalim*. I am in *shul* and hear the special *Torah* reading for *Parshat Shekalim* and yet, when it comes time for the *haftarah*, the *Baal Maftir* reads a different *haftarah*. Why?

34. There is a general requirement to be "*b'simcha*" – "filled with joy" on *yom tov*. Psychologists will tell you that happiness is connected to your approach to life; do you think of the glass as half full or half empty? How does *lashon hakodesh* connect your thoughts to happiness?

35. Name a weekday *shemoneh esrei* that includes the names of five sets of grandparents and grandchildren?

36. When is *Yom Hameyuchas* – the day of distinction?

37. Usually we read from a *parshah* three times the week preceding it. When is it possible to read from a *parshah* four times, before reading it on *Shabbat* morning?

38. What connects the 17th of *Marcheshvan*, the 7th of *Adar*, the 15th and 16th of *Nisan*, and the 10th of *Tishrei*?

39. How is it possible to read from five different *parshiyot* on one *Shabbat*?

40. Occasionally, this particular *parshah* has only 13 of its *pesukim* read publicly in a Jewish calendar year. Which *parshah* and what is the circumstance?

41. Three of us are in *shul* one morning during the repetition of the *shemoneh esrei*. One of us responds *"amein"* 26 times; another 22 times and yet a third only three times. We are all active participants in the *minyan*. What day is it and where are we?

42. Name five countries mentioned in *Hallel*? (Bit of a trick question.)

43. How many holidays in the Jewish calendar are referred to by the word *"atzeret"*?

44. How is it possible to read from the *Torah* on five consecutive days, with none of these days being one when we would recite *Hallel*?

45. I look forward to the *seder* night(s) each year. Where would I have not wanted to be on the *seder* nights of the year 3404?

46. Besides the fact that they are both fast days, how are *Yom Kippur* and *Asara B'Tevet* similar?

47. What was unique about the *Birkat Hachodesh* for *Rosh Chodesh Cheshvan* 5765, which occurred on *Shabbat Bereishit, Tishrei* 24 (October 9, 2004)? And as a follow up, when was the previous time that this phenomenon occurred and when will it occur again in the future?

THE CALENDAR ANSWERS

1. Most people hope to never say *ya'aleh veyavo* for *Yom Kippur*. If a sick person needs to eat on *Yom Kippur*, he adds the *ya'aleh veyavo* insertion into the *benching* and mentions *Yom Kippur*. Even sick people rarely say this, because – if they can – they always try to eat small amounts which don't require *benching*.

2. Since *Shabbat Chanukah* generally falls on *Parshat Mikeitz*, the regular *haftarah* for *Mikeitz* is seldom read. In about 90% of the cases, it is preempted by the special *haftarah* for *Chanukah*. Only when *Chanukah* is Friday to Friday, is *Vayeishev* read on *Shabbat Chanukah* and *Mikeitz* read the day after *Chanukah*. When *Chanukah* is *Shabbat* to *Shabbat*, both *Vayeishev* and *Mikeitz* are the readings for the two *Shabbatot Chanukah*. The *haftarah* for *Mikeitz* was last read in 5761 (2000) and will be read again in 5781 (2020), again in 5784 (2023) but not again until 5801 (2040). Therefore in a span of 40 years it will be read four times or about 10% of the time.

3. It can occur up to three times during the year:
   1. The *Shabbat* preceding *Rosh Chodesh Tevet* is *Shabbat Chanukah*, except when the first candle is on *Motzaei Shabbat* or Sunday night, in which case *Birkat Hachodesh* is the *Shabbat* before *Chanukah*.
   2. The *Shabbat* preceding *Rosh Chodesh Adar* coincides with *Parshat Shekalim*, except when *Rosh Chodesh Adar* falls on *Shabbat*.
   3. The *Shabbat* preceding *Rosh Chodesh Nisan* is always a two *Torah Shabbat* as it coincides with either *Parshat Parah* (when *Rosh Chodesh Nisan* is on *Shabbat*) or *Parshat Hachodesh* (when *Rosh Chodesh Nisan* is on a weekday).

4. *Shabbat Bereishit* is always *Shabbat Mevarchim of Marcheshvan*.

5. The first day of *Shevat* was the day that *Bnai Yisrael* arrived at their final place of encampment before entering *Eretz Yisrael*. *Moshe* begins his last 37 days on earth and reviews with his people the *mitzvot* and their obligations. *Sefer Devarim* is recounted in these 37 days. As such, *Sefer Hatoda'ah* (The Book of our Heritage authored by *Rav Eliyahu KiTov zt"l*) compares *Rosh Chodesh Shevat* to *Yom Kippur* and *Shavuot*, in that it is a time of rededication to *Torah* and *Hashem*.

6. The word "*v'natnu*" – "and they shall give" (*Shemot* 30:12) is a Hebrew palindrome, i.e., it can be read forwards and backwards, indicating that money that is donated to charity will find its way back to the giver. The *Vilna Gaon* comments that the word "*machatzit*" – "half," a five letter word which was the denomination of the "*machatzit hashekel*" currency required by all to support the *Beit Hamikdash*, is formed with a central letter "*tzadi*" which stands for the word "*tzedakah*" – "charity." It is flanked on either side by a

"*chet*" and a "*yud*" which spell the Hebrew word "*chai*" – "life." The outer extremities of the word are "*mem*" and "*tav*" which spell the Hebrew word "*met*" – "death." Therefore, says the *Gaon, tzedakah* brings us closer to life and keeps us removed from death.

7. The *Ateret Zekeinim* commentary on the *Shulchan Aruch* (*Orach Chaim* 135) states that where *Torah* reading has been missed on a Monday because of some accident (war, major storm etc), then the Monday portion should be read on Tuesday, because the *Torah* says "*vayelchu shloshet yamim bamidbar v'lo matzu mayim*" – "And they went three days in the desert without finding water" (*Shemot* 15:22). From this *pasuk,* we deduce the *Torah* reading of Monday and Thursday, so that there will never be three days without reading from the Jews' wellspring of *Torah.* Therefore, if one misses on Monday, Tuesday will still keep us in the three day period. This is the only day in the week when this can occur. If for example one missed both Monday and Tuesday, we would not read on Wednesday, because it would already be the 4th day.

8. The Book of *Esther* contains the names *Nisan, Sivan, Tevet* and *Adar.*

9. *Iyar, Tamuz, Av, Tishrei* and *Marcheshvan* are not mentioned anywhere in *Tanach.*

10. In *Parshat Vayishlach* (*Bereishit* 33:17), *Yaakov* builds *sukkot* for his animals; and the prophet *Yona* builds a *sukkah* to provide shade for himself (*Yona* 4:5).

11. *Purim* always occurs one day earlier in New York than in *Jerusalem* because in most places *Purim* is celebrated on the 14th day of *Adar,* but in *Jerusalem,* a walled city from the time of *Yehoshua Bin Nun,* it is celebrated on the 15th day of *Adar.*

12. There are at least 15 answers to this question:
    1. When the last day of *Pesach* in *Eretz Yisrael* is a Friday, the *Torah* reading on the *Shabbat* following *Pesach* would be *Parshat Shemini* in a regular year or *Parshat Acharei Mot* or *Kedoshim* in a Leap Year. As that *Shabbat* would still be *Pesach* in *chutz la'aretz,* the regular *Torah* reading would not resume until the following *Shabbat.* Both communities would resume identical reading following the dual reading of *Parshat Matot-Massei* in *chutz la'aretz.*
    2. Similarly, when *Shavuot* in *Eretz Yisrael* is a Friday, the *Torah* reading on the *Shabbat* following *Shavuot* would be *Parshat Naso.* As that *Shabbat* would still be *Shavuot* in *chutz la'aretz,* the regular *Torah* reading would not resume until the following *Shabbat.* Both communities would resume identical reading following the dual reading of *Chukat-Balak* in *chutz la'aretz.*

3. In *Eretz Yisrael*, we begin saying *"v'tain tal u'matar"* on the 7th day of *Marcheshvan* about two weeks after *Sukkot*, while in *chutz la'aretz* we begin saying *"v'tain tal u'matar"* on either December 4th or 5th. Generally Jewish holidays and customs follow the Jewish calendar, linked to the phases of the moon. The starting time for *v'tain tal u'matar* in *chutz laaretz*, however, is linked to the civil or solar calendar.

4. In *Eretz Yisrael*, we begin saying *"v'tain beracha"* on the first day of *Chol Hamoed Pesach* (the second day of *Pesach*), while in *chutz la'aretz,* it is begun on the first day of *Chol Hamoed Pesach* (the third day of *Pesach*).

5. When the last day of *Pesach* in *Eretz Yisrael* is a Friday, the reading of *Pirkei Avot* – Ethics of our Fathers begins on the next day (the first *Shabbat* following *Pesach*), while in *chutz la'aretz,* it would not begin until the following *Shabbat*.

6. *Yizkor* is said in *Eretz Yisrael* on the 7th day of *Pesach* (last day there) while *Yizkor* is said in *chutz la'aretz,* on the 8th day of *Pesach* (last day there).

7. *Yizkor* is said in *Eretz Yisrael* on the 1st day of *Shavuot* (only day there) while *Yizkor* is said in *chutz la'aretz* on the 2nd day of *Shavuot* (last day there).

8. *Havdalah* is said in *Eretz Yisrael* at the end of the first and seventh days of *Pesach*, while in *chutz la'aretz, havdalah* is said at the end of the second and eighth days of *Pesach*.

9. *Havdalah* is said in *Eretz Yisrael* at the end of the first day of *Shavuot*, while in *chutz la'aretz, havdalah* is said at the end of the second day of *Shavuot*.

10. *Havdalah* is said in *Eretz Yisrael* at the end of the first and eighth (actually *Shemini Atzeret*) days of *Sukkot*, while in *Chutz La'Aretz, havdalah* is said at the end of the second and ninth (actually *Shemini Atzeret/Simchat Torah*) days of *Sukkot*.

11. The reading of *V'zot Haberacha* and the beginning of *Bereishit* occurs on *Shemini Atzeret* in *Eretz Yisrael* while those in *chutz la'aretz* do not begin until the following day (*Simchat Torah*).

12. If the first day of *Pesach* is a *Shabbat*, then *Shir Hashirim* is read in *Eretz Yisrael* on the first day of *Pesach*, while in *chutz la'aretz* it is not read until the last day of *Pesach* (the second *Shabbat* of *Pesach*).

13. *Rut* is read on the first (only) day of *Shavuot* while in *chutz la'aretz* it is not read until the second day.

14. If the first day of *Sukkot* is a *Shabbat*, then *Kohelet* is read in *Eretz Yisrael* on the first day of *Sukkot*, while in *chutz la'aretz* it is not read until *Shemini Atzeret*.

15. In the *musaf Shemonei Esrai* of *Sukkot,* the reading of the sacrificial offering of the day, is begun on the first day of *Chol Hamoed* and therefore it would be read one day ahead in *Eretz Yisrael* as compared to *chutz la'aretz.*

13. It is the custom in many places in *Eretz Yisrael* to "*duchen*" – "to say the priestly blessings" every day; and twice on *Shabbat* and *Yom Tov* at both *Shacharit* and *Mussaf.* However in *chutz la'aretz,* the *Ashkenazi* community only *duchens* on *Yom Tov* and then only at *mussaf.* The reason given is that in order to *duchen,* there must be joy or *simcha;* and in *chutz la'aretz,* there is an inherent lack of *simcha.* There is, however, *simcha* on *yom tov,* even in *chutz la'aretz.* However, the *Shulchan Aruch* (*Orach Chaim* 128:44) points out that the real element of *simcha* on *yom tov* is a result of the *seudat yom tov,* the holiday meal that we eat after the conclusion of *mussaf.* Therefore there is little or no *simcha* at *shacharit.* And therefore, we only *duchen* at *mussaf.* As a result, we have a *mitzvah* of *duchening* that occurs because of a *seudah* that follows the *mitzvah.*

14. The *beracha* of *Eiruv Tavshilin* which permits one to prepare food on *Yom Tov* for *Shabbat* is said on *Erev Yom Tov,* which can fall either on a Wednesday or Thursday in *chutz la'aretz* and on a Thursday for the *Shalosh Regalim* in *Eretz Yisrael* and either a Wednesday or Thursday for *Rosh Hashana* in *Eretz Yisrael.*

15. *Kiddush Hachamah,* the blessing of the sun, takes place every 28 years, when the sun is in the exact spot in relation to the earth, as it was at the time of creation. This always takes place on a Wednesday.

16. The *beracha* is "*menachem tzion u'bonei Yerushalayim,*" which is the *beracha* of "*nachem*" recited in the *mincha shemoneh esrei* of *Tisha B'Av,* since *Tisha B'Av* can only fall on Sunday, Tuesday or Thursday.

17. *Nadav* and *Avihu* died on the first day of *Nisan* (*Shulchan Aruch Orach Chaim* 580:2).

18. *Miriam* died on the 10th of *Nisan* and from that time on, her well no longer functioned (*Shulchan Aruch Orach Chaim* 580:2)

19. *Yehoshua Bin Nun* died on the 26th of *Nisan* (*Shulchan Aruch Orach Chaim* 580:2). Some differ however, and say that he died on the 28th of *Nisan* (*Mishnah Berurah* 580:2:4).

20. *Shmuel Hanavi* died on the 28th of *Iyar* (*Shulchan Aruch Orach Chaim* 580:2). The *Megillat Taanit* differs, however, and says that he died on the 29th of *Iyar* (*Mishnah Berurah* 580:2:5).

21. We mention roses in the specific liturgy for each of the holidays of:
    1. *Purim* ("*Shoshanat Yaakov*")
    2. *Chanukah* ("...*naaseh nes la'shoshanim*")
    3. *Pesach* (in *Shir Hashirim:* "...*k'shoshana bein hachochim*")

22. The two nights would be *Yom Kippur* and the *Pesach* Seder night. The *Shalom Zachor* should be held following the Friday night meal. On *Yom Kippur* night, one would obviously not have a festive gathering with food. On the *Pesach Seder* night, one should not eat after eating the *matzah* of the *afikoman*, and therefore on this night too, it would be inappropriate to schedule a *Shalom Zachor* (*Ohr Somayach Ask the Rabbi*).

23. If you were travelling eastbound from the Orient to North America during *Chanukah*, you would gain a day. Therefore, if you were travelling on the second day of *Chanukah*, you would *daven Shacharit* and recite *Hallel* before leaving and during the flight you would cross the dateline, experience sunset and sunrise and would therefore once again be required to *daven Shacharit* with *Hallel* for the same day. In total, one would therefore recite complete *Hallel* nine days in a row.

24. Trick question: They all do!

25. We are told (*Gemara Eruvin* 43b) that *Eliyahu Hanavi* will not come to herald the coming of *Mashiach* on either the day preceding *Shabbat* or the day preceding *Yom Tov*, in order that the community's preparation for *Shabbat* and *Yom Tov* not be disturbed. Since we know that *Eliyahu* will come one day before *Mashiach*, therefore *Mashiach* will not come on either a *Shabbat* or a *Yom Tov*.

26. If the first day of *Pesach* is on a *Shabbat*, then the last day is also on a *Shabbat*. In most years when this occurs, the *parshah* following *Pesach* will be *Shemini*. Therefore, one would have begun reading *Shemini* at *minchah* on *Shabbat Hagadol* and then again on that Monday and Thursday, once again at *minchah* on the first day of *Pesach*; at *minchah* on the last day of *Pesach* and again on the Monday and Thursday after *Pesach* before the actual *Torah* reading the *Shabbat* following *Pesach*. In the case of a leap year, when the first day of *Pesach* falls on *Shabbat*, the *parshah* following *Pesach* is *Acharei Mot*. So the two possible answers are *Acharei Mot* and *Shemini*. This riddle only works in *chutz la'aretz*, as in Israel, there would never be two *Shabbatot* on a *Pesach*, as *Pesach* can only be seven days long. This riddle has at times been called "*Shemini b'shemini, shemoneh shemini*" (i.e., we read *Shemini* when *Shabbat* is *b'shemini*, on the eighth day; then we read *shemoneh*, eight times, *Shemini*) when it deals with *Parshat Shemini*; not sure what it is called when it occurs on *Parshat Acharei Mot*.

27. This is known as the principle of "*lo adu rosh*." If *Rosh Hashanah* would begin on a Sunday, then *Sukkot* would also begin on a Sunday and therefore *Hoshanah Rabbah* would fall on a *Shabbat* which would make it impossible to wave the *Hoshanot*. If *Rosh Hashanah* would fall on a Wednesday, then *Yom Kippur* would fall on a Friday (*Erev Shabbat*) and two days in a row with the restrictions of *Shabbat* are impossible. If *Rosh Hashanah* would

fall on a Friday, then *Yom Kippur* would begin immediately upon the conclusion of *Shabbat,* and for the same reason, the two consecutive days with *Shabbat* restrictions being impossible, would apply.

28. We make a *beracha* of "*boray meorei ha'eish*" when viewing the *havdalah* candle at the conclusion of *Shabbat* or *Yom Kippur.* Since *Yom Kippur* can only fall on a *Shabbat,* Monday, Wednesday or Thursday (from the principle of "*lo adu Rosh*"; the first day of *Rosh Hashanah* can never fall on a Sunday, Wednesday or Friday); the only days when we would make *havdalah* (including a candle) would be Sunday, Tuesday, Thursday or Friday.

29. It means "*ain omrim kayl erech apayim*" – "we do not say the *tefillah* "*kayl erech apayim*" before the Monday or Thursday *Kriat HaTorah.*

30. *YaKNHaZ* is a symbol for the five *berachot* in the *kiddush* of *Yom Tov* which coincides with *Motzaei Shabbat.* In that case, the five *berachot* are "*boreh pri hagafen,*" "*mekadesh yisrael v'hazmanim,*" "*borei me'orei ha'aish,*" "*hamavdil*" and "*shehechiyanu.*" They are known by the acronym "*YaKNHaZ*" which stands for *yayin, kiddush, ner, havdala, zman.* The longest *kiddush* possible would be when the second night of *Sukkot* falls on *Motzaei Shabbat* in which case one would make six *berachot*; the five listed above and the *beracha* "*layshayv basukkah.*"

31. The day after *Shavuot,* besides being known as "*Isru Chag,*" was also known as "*Yom Tavoach.*" On a normal *Yom Tov,* those who pledged a sacrifice or offering to *Hashem* would be able to fulfil their obligation on *Chol Hamoed.* However, with *Shavuot* being only one day, the pledges of *Yom Tov* tended to be carried out on the day following *Yom Tov.* Hence the name *Yom Tavoach.*

32. *Parshat Bereishit* is only read *Shabbat minchah* when *Simchat Torah* falls on a *Shabbat,* and that can only occur in *Eretz Yisrael.* When that happens, the following *Shabbat* is *Shabbat Bereishit* and therefore we would read *Bereishit* on *Shabbat Simchat Torah* (*Shemini Atzeret*) at *minchah* time. Since *Simchat Torah* never coincides with *Shabbat* in *chutz la'aretz, Bereishit* will never be read at *Shabbat minchah* in *chutz la'aretz.*

33. It was *Shabbat, Rosh Chodesh, Parshat Shekalim,* and therefore three *Sifrei Torah* were taken from the ark for the three different *Torah* readings of the day. Based on the principle of "*tadir v'she'ayno tadir, tadir kodem*" – "if you have two acts before you, the order of which act is first is based on the frequency of the act," we would read from the weekly *Torah* reading from *Sefer Torah #1; Rosh Chodesh* from *Sefer Torah #2*; and *Parshat Shekalim* from *Sefer Torah #3.* An error was made and *Parshat Shekalim* was read from *Sefer Torah #2* and *Rosh Chodesh* from *Sefer Torah #3.* The rule is that the *haftarah* is always based on the last *Torah* reading of the day and therefore one would have to read the *haftarah* for *Shabbat Rosh Chodesh* which begins with "*Koh amar Hashem Hashomayim Kisi*" (*Mishnah Berurah* 685:5).

34. The *Tikunei Zohar* connects thought and happiness by noting that the word *"b'simcha"* – "with happiness" and the word *"machshava"* – "thought or intent" are spelled with the exact same letters, indicating that the key to happiness is often found through our thought process.

35. The *"shemoneh esrei"* for *Rosh Chodesh Chanukah* has the following five sets of grandparents and grandchildren: *Avraham* and *Yaakov* (first *beracha*); *Adam* and *Enosh* (*beracha* of *"ata chonein"*); *Yitzchak* and *Yehuda* (*Yitzchak* from the first *beracha* and *Yehuda* from the added phrase at the end of *shemoneh esrei "v'arva l'Hashem minchat Yehuda"*); *Yochanan* and *Yehuda* (*Yochanan* from the added *Chanukah* insert of *Al Hanissim* and *Yehuda* from the added phrase at the end of *shemoneh esrei*) and *Yaakov* and *Rosh* (*Yaakov* from the first *beracha* and *Rosh*, who was the son of *Binyamin*, from the *Rosh Chodesh* insert of *yaale v'yavo*).

36. *Yom Hameyuchas* is the second day of *Sivan*, the day before the beginning of the *"Shloshet Yemei Hagbalah"* – "the three days of restraint" when *Bnai Yisrael* were commanded to prepare for the giving of the *Torah* on *Mount Sinai*. The title is based on the *gemara* (*Shabbat* 86b–87a), which identifies the second of *Sivan* as the day when the Jewish people were charged by *Hashem* to be a *"mamlechet kohanim v'goy kadosh"* – "a priestly nation and a holy people" (*Shemot* 19:6). The *Aruch Hashulchan*, (*Orach Chaim* 494:7), notes that this is the reason why it is called *Yom Hameyuchas* – the day upon which we, as a Jewish people, emerged as a "holy nation," the day upon which we established our *"yichus"* for all time. Since this day occurs immediately before *Shavuot*, it is suggested that it reminds everyone prior to *Shavuot*, that success in the *Torah* or performance of *mitzvot* does not depend on *"yichus"* – "pedigree or family prestige," but rather, it is through one's dedication to *Torah* study and the observance of *mitzvot* that one creates one's own *yichus*. If we take the word *yachas*, spelled *yud, chet, samech* out of the word *meyuchas*, we are left with *mem* and *vav* or forty-six, as in the forty-sixth day of the *Omer*, the day of *Yom Hameyuchas*.

37. The week of *Shabbat Nachamu* we read from *Parshat Vaetchanan* which is always the *parshah* read on the *Shabbat* following *Tisha B'Av*. Besides reading from that *parshah* the previous *Shabbat minchah* and on *Monday* and *Thursday* of that week, we also read from *Parshat Vaetchanan* for the special *shacharit* reading for *Tisha B'av*.

38. The phrase *"b'etzem hayom hazeh"* – "on that very day" is mentioned in the *Torah* 11 times. The dates mentioned in our question are all connected to this phrase, namely; the 17th of *Marcheshvan* is the day that the *"mabul"* – "the flood of *Noah*" began (*Bereishit* 7:13); the 7th of *Adar* is the day *Moshe* died (as well as the day that he was born) (*Devarim* 32:48); the 15th of *Nisan* is the day the *Bnai Yisrael* left *Mitzrayim* (*Shemot* 12:41 and *Shemot*

12:51); the 16th *of Nisan* is the day the *Omer* offering was brought (*Vayikra* 23:21); and the 10th *of Tishrei* is *Yom Kippur* (*Vayikra* 23:28; *Vayikra* 23:29; *Vayikra* 23:30). The phrase of "*b'etzem hayom hazeh*" – "on that very day" also appears in the *Torah* in connection to *Avraham* circumcising his son *Yishmael* (*Bereishit* 17:23 and *Bereishit* 17:26); and to guarding the *matzot* (*Shemot* 12:17).

39. If *Parshat Tazria* coincides with *Parshat Hachodesh* and with *Rosh Chodesh*, (which will next occur on *Nisan* 1, 5782/April 2, 2022 and then not again until 5803/2043), then we take three *sifrei Torah* out in the morning and read six *aliyot* from *Tazria*, the 7th *aliyah* from *Parshat Bo* for *Parshat Hachodesh* and *maftir* for *Rosh Chodesh* from *Parshat Pinchas*. In many shuls during the month of *Nisan*, at the end of *Musaf*, there is a custom to read the recounting of the offerings of each tribe for the dedication of the *mishkan* from *Parshat Naso*; and then during *mincha*, you would read from *Parshat Metzora*. The result is reading from five different *parshiyot* on one *Shabbat*.

40. The *parshah* is *Vayeilech*. Because *Vayeilech* is always read around *Rosh Hashanah*, there are years in the Hebrew calendar when it is read just before *Rosh Hashanah* and years when it is read just after *Rosh Hashanah*. Therefore, in our case, in that particular year, *Haazinu* was the first regularly scheduled weekly *Torah* reading on the first *Shabbat* morning after *Rosh Hashanah*, and *Nitzavim* was the last regularly scheduled *Torah* reading on the last *Shabbat* morning preceding the following *Rosh Hashanah*. The 13 *pesukim* of *Vayeilech*, which are read at *Shabbat mincha* of *Parshat Nitzavim* and on Monday morning, were read that year just before *Rosh Hashanah*. Therefore only 13 *pesukim* of *Parshat Vayeilech* were publicly read that calendar year.

41. We are in Israel on *Rosh Chodesh* in a *shul* where they "*duchan*" – "recite the *birkat kohanim*" every day. The first individual, a regular participant in the *minyan*, responds "*amein*" to the nineteen *berachot* of *shemoneh esrei*, the three phrases in *yaale v'yavo*, the *beracha* of the *kohanim* as they begin their blessings, and the three sections of the *birkat kohanim* for a total of 26. The second individual is a *kohen* and therefore responds *amein* to the 19 *berachot* of *shemoneh esrei* and the three places in *yaale v'yavo*. The third individual is the *shaliach tzibbur* who only responds to the three sections of the *birkat kohanim* (*Mishnah Berurah* 128:17; *Shaar Tzion* 61).

42. The five countries mentioned in *Hallel* are:
   1. *Yarden* (Jordan)
   2. *Yisrael* (Israel)
   3. *Mitzrayim* (Egypt)
   4. *Hodu* (India)
   5. Malta ("*ana Hashem malta nafshi*")

43. One would assume that there would be two and that is correct. However, which two is kind of surprising. There are only three times that the word *atzeret* appears in the *Torah*. In the first two instances, *atzeret* refers to the holiday of *Shemini Atzeret* (*Vayikra* 23:36 and *Bamidbar* 29:35). The third instance refers to the seventh day of *Pesach* (*Devarim* 16:8). Curiously, nowhere in the *Torah* is *Shavuot* referred to as *atzeret*, even though In the *Mishnah*, (*Rosh Hashanah* 16a) and *gemara* (*Pesachim* 68b) it is called "*atzeret*" and the *Targum Onkelos* to *Bamidbar* 28:26, interprets the word "*beshavu'oteichem*" – "your festival of weeks" as "*be'atzrateichon.*"

44. If the first day of *Rosh Hashanah* is Thursday, then we would read on Thursday and Friday (*Rosh Hashono*), *Shabbat,* Sunday (a delayed *Tzom Gedalyah*) and then Monday (the regular Monday morning *Kriat HaTorah*); hence five consecutive days, with none of these days being one when we would recite *Hallel.*

45. The year 3404 was the year when *Haman* intended to wipe out the entire Jewish population of *Shushan* and the rest of *Achashverosh*'s provinces. *Esther* and *Mordechai* ordered the entire Jewish community to fast for three days and nights. The dates were *Nisan* 14–16 (*Gemara Megillah* 15a) and therefore in *Shushan* and the surrounding provinces there were no *Pesach sedarim* that year.

46. *Yom Kippur* and *Asara B'Tevet* are similar in that neither is ever pushed off. If *Yom Kippur* occurs on a *Shabbat*, we still fast, unlike other fast days that may fall on a *Shabbat*, which are delayed until Sunday. If *Asara B'Tevet* occurs on a Friday, we still fast on Friday. Like *Yom Kippur*, the expression "*b'etzem hayom hazeh*" – "on this specific day" (*Vayikra* 23:28) appears in reference to *Asara B'Tevet* (*Yechezkel* 24:2).

47. The *molad* for *Rosh Chodesh Cheshvan* 5765 which was announced on *Shabbat Bereishit*, *Tishrei* 24 (October 9, 2004) was on *Thursday, Tishrei* 29 (October 14, 2004) at exactly 2:00 a.m. No minutes and no *chalakim*. This "whole hour *molad*" occurs every 1080 months or every 87 years plus 3 or 4 months. The previous time the *molad* was on the hour was *Tammuz* 5677 (1917), when the *molad* was Wednesday at 1:00 a.m. The next time will be *Adar I* 5852 (2092), when the *molad* will be Friday at 3:00 a.m. (Thanks to Rabbi Eliezer Langer and to Professor Ari Brodsky for this riddle).

ROSH CHODESH & TAANIT TZIBUR QUESTIONS

1. Who authored the *musaf shemoneh esrei* of *Rosh Chodesh* and where is there a *"remez"* – "hint" to the author's name in the *musaf*?

2. Two people sit down to a meal on a Wednesday afternoon, which happens to be *Rosh Chodesh*. They begin at the same time, both wash and make *hamotzi*, eat exactly the same meal, finish at the same time, and now have to *bench*. However, when *benching*, one says *"yaale v'yavoh"* and the other doesn't. Why not?

3. When we announce the *molad*, what do we mean by *"chalakim"*?

4. I know what the *molad* was last month but do not have a calendar handy this month. How can I pinpoint the exact time of this month's *molad*?

5. On which *"Machar Chodesh" Shabbatot* – "*Shabbat* that occurs on the day before *Rosh Chodesh*" do we read a *haftarah* other than the *haftarah* designated for the *Shabbat* before *Rosh Chodesh* called *"Machar Chodesh"*?

6. Normally on *Shabbat Rosh Chodesh*, we recite the *haftarah* of "*Hashamayim Kisi*." In certain years, there can be three *Shabbat Rosh Chodesh* occurrences when we would not recite the normal *Shabbat Rosh Chodesh haftarah* of "*Hashamayim Kisi*." Explain.

7. What are the two times that *Rosh Chodesh* can not fall on a *Shabbat*?

8. What is the minimum number of times in a year that we can experience *Erev Rosh Chodesh* (i.e., *Machar Chodesh*) that falls on a *Shabbat*?

9. How is it possible for two shuls to recite different texts for the *Molad* on the same *Shabbat*?

10. On which *Rosh Chodesh* do we read the complete *Hallel*?

11. On which *Rosh Chodesh* do we not read *Hallel* at all?

12. What is the maximum number of *Rosh Chodesh* days in one year?

13. Which three people in *Tanach* were named in honour of the moon?

14. Which *perek* in *Tehillim*, that we recite daily, contains the reason for saying *Hallel* on *Rosh Chodesh*?

15. When was *Gedaliyah* assassinated?

16. It is a *Taanit Tzibbur*. There are two shuls in North America on the same street. During *Shacharit*, they both *lain*; however, they *lain* from different portions. When *minchah* comes around, one *shul lains* and the other doesn't. Explain the case.

17. The *"Korban Todah"* – "an individual's Thanksgiving offering" was not offered on *Shabbat* and *Yom Tov* and could only be eaten until *"chatzot"* – "midnight." Therefore, we do not say the prayer that appears in our *siddurim*, *"Mizmor L'todah"* – "A Song of Thanksgiving" on *Shabbat, Yom Tov, Erev*

Yom Kippur (because the fast begins at sundown and the *Todah* could be eaten until midnight) and *Erev Pesach* (because the *Todah* was *chametz* and the prohibition of eating *chametz* begins before noon on *Erev Pesach* and the *Todah* could be eaten until midnight). Why therefore do we say *Mizmor L'todah* on *Erev Tisha B'Av*?

18. Name a date when *Halacha* suggests that it is proper to fast every year on that day and on that same day many Jews recite *Hallel*?

19. The incident of the *"meraglim"* – "spies" occurred on *Tisha B'Av*. Where is there a hint in *Megillat Eicha,* that the *meraglim* did not accurately report on their mission after returning to the camp; but rather falsely related what they had actually observed?

20. We are aware of the six public fast days during the course of the year. What are the *Taaniyot Tzaddikim*?

21. Which is the only *Taanit,* which when it falls on a *Shabbat,* is pushed back to Thursday, instead of being pushed forward to Sunday?

22. When did the events commemorated by the *Fast of Asarah B'Tevet* occur?

23. When attending *shul* on *Tisha B'Av* morning, we have the *minhag* to sit on low chairs or on the floor when *davening* and when saying "*kinot*" – "lamentation prayers for *Tisha B'Av*." However, one person is required to sit on a chair. Who is that person?

24. The three weeks between the 17th of *Tammuz* and the 9th of *Av* are dangerous weeks, as historically many national calamities occurred to the Jewish people during this period. Why is it the safest time for a student?

25. Who in history, according to the *gemara,* fasted the longest?

26. An easy way to remember the Jewish fast days is through the following sentence: "the black one, the white one, the long one, the short one, his, hers, theirs or ours." Can you solve it?

27. Which fast day mentioned in *Chazal* is determined not by its Hebrew date, but rather by which *parshah* is being read that particular week?

ROSH CHODESH & TAANIT TZIBUR ANSWERS

1. The *Chida* writes (*Birkei Yoseif, Orach Chaim* 423:2) that *Rachel Imeinu* prophetically saw that women would not sin in the matter of the Golden Calf and would therefore be rewarded with *Rosh Chodesh* as a "women's holiday." She then authored the *musaf* prayer for *Rosh Chodesh*, and her name is alluded to in the "*roshei teivot*" – "first letter of each of the words" of "*Rashei Chadashim Leamcha*" which spells "*Rachel.*"

2. They began their meal while it was still day and finished their meal after nightfall when it was no longer *Rosh Chodesh*. One *davened Maariv* before *benching* and the other didn't. The one who already *davened*, can no longer can say "*yaale v'yavoh*," while the one who did not *daven Maariv* must still say "*yaale v'yavoh*." (*Mishnah Berurah* 188:34).

3. In the *halachic* calendar, there are 60 minutes to the hour, and 18 "*chalakim*" to the minute. Hence there are 1080 (60 × 18) "*chalakim*" to the hour.

4. The average time that it takes the moon to go through its phases is 29 days, 12 hours, 44 minutes and one *chelek*. If the *molad* in the first month is Sunday, 30 minutes and 8 *chalakim* after 3 in the afternoon, then you can figure out the next month's *molad* in the following manner. Jump ahead four weeks or 28 days and you now have to add 1 day 12 hours, 44 minutes and one *chelek* and you have the *molad*. Therefore the new *molad* will be Tuesday, 14 minutes and nine *chalakim* after four in the morning.

5. There are three occasions when "*machar chodesh*" – "the special *haftarah* for *Shabbat* that immediately precedes a *Rosh Chodesh*" would be preempted. When *Rosh Chodesh Adar* (or *Adar II*) falls on Sunday, the preceding *Shabbat* day is *Parshat Shekalim* and the *haftarah* of *Parshat Shekalim* preempts "*machar chodesh*." Likewise, when *Rosh Chodesh Nisan* falls on Sunday, the preceding *Shabbat* day is *Parshat Hachodesh* and the *haftarah* of *Parshat Hachodesh* preempts "*machar chodesh*." The third possibility is *Parshat Re'eh* which can be the day before *Rosh Chodesh Elul*. That *Shabbat* would be one of the "*shiva d'nechemta*" – "the seven special *haftarot* that follow *Tisha B'av*," and they cannot be preempted. Therefore, if *Rosh Chodesh Elul* falls on a Sunday, the regular *haftarah* for *Re'eh* would still be read. Some shuls will add the first and last *pesukim* of the *haftarah* of "*machar chodesh*."

6. In certain years, the *Rosh Chodesh* of the three months of *Tishrei*, *Adar* and *Av* can all fall on *Shabbat*. The *Rosh Chodesh* of *Tishrei* is obviously also *Rosh Hashana*, and it has its own special *haftarah*. The *Rosh Chodesh* of *Adar* in such a year will also be *Parshat Shekalim* and the *haftarah* for *Shekalim* supersedes the *haftarah* of *Shabbat Rosh Chodesh*. Finally, *Rosh*

Chodesh Av always falls in the sad period of the three weeks and its special *haftarah* also takes precedence over the *Shabbat Rosh Chodesh haftarah*.

7. *Rosh Chodesh Kislev* and *Rosh Chodesh Sivan* can never fall on a *Shabbat*.

8. It happens at least once a year but can occur up to three times in one year.

9. The *molad* that we use today is based on the average time (29 days, 12 hours, 44 minutes and one part) that it takes the moon to go around the earth, measured from one new moon to the next in *Jerusalem*. The actual *molad* would take into account the fact that the earth-moon system does not travel at exactly the same velocity at all times in its orbit around the sun. That actual *molad* would be used by the *Sanhedrin* to determine if and when the witnesses would be able to see the new moon of a particular month (*Torah Tidbits*). The custom today is that we use the average *molad* for *Rosh Chodesh* benching in all places around the world, irrespective of time zones and daylight savings times. Occasionally when *Rosh Chodesh* falls on Sunday, the average *molad* may occur early on *Shabbat* morning and that time would be announced in shuls around the world. Therefore, if one were to be *davening* in Australia, the *molad* would be occurring some hours later in Jerusalem and therefore the announcement would be "the *molad* will be later this morning..." However, if one were to be *davening* on that same *Shabbat* in Canada, the *molad* would have occurred some hours earlier in *Jerusalem* and therefore the announcement would be "the *molad* was earlier this morning..." Hence, two vastly different announcements for the same *molad*.

10. *Rosh Chodesh Tevet* always falls during *Chanukah* and we therefore recite the complete *Hallel*.

11. *Rosh Chodesh Tishrei* is *Rosh Hashanah* and we do not recite *Hallel* at all.

12. The maximum number is 20 days. *Cheshvan, Adar Rishon, Adar Sheni, Iyar, Tammuz* and *Elul* are when we would have a two-day *Rosh Chodesh. Shvat, Nisan, Sivan* and *Av* are when we would observe a one-day *Rosh Chodesh. Kislev* and *Tevet* can be either one- or two-day *Rosh Chodesh* and the first of *Tishrei* being *Rosh Hashana* does not have a *Rosh Chodesh* day at all. Therefore, in a leap year when both *Kislev* and *Tevet* are celebrated as two-day *Rosh Chodesh*, there can be 20 *Rosh Chodesh* days.

13. The *gemara* (*Chullin* 60b) relates the following: Initially the sun and the moon were created the same size. When *Hashem* diminished the size of the moon, He comforted the moon by telling it that three important individuals would be given the description "*hakatan*" – "the small one" in the moon's honour. The three individuals were *Yaakov Hakatan* (*Amos* 7:2), *Shmuel Hakatan* (the *tanna* in the *gemara*), and *David Hakatan* (*Shmuel* 1:17:14).

14. The *Taamei Haminhagim* (436) quotes the *Tanya Rabati* who says that *David Hamelech* alluded to the reciting of *Hallel* on *Rosh Chodesh* by incorporating

the word "*hallelu/halleluka*" – "praised be *Hashem*" 12 times in Chapter 150 of *Tehillim*. This corresponds to the 12 months of the year and the repeating of the last *pasuk* in our *tefillah* adds another "*halleluka*" which alludes to a two-day *Rosh Chodesh* as well as the extra *Rosh Chodesh* of a leap year. The *minhagim sefer* "Rite and Reason" adds that if we assume that the first mention of "*halleluka*" is for the month of *Nisan*, the 6th mention has the phrase "*hallelu b'teika shofar*" which would correspond to the month of *Elul* when we blow the *shofar* daily in anticipation of the "*Yamim Noraim*" – "Days of Awe" of *Rosh Hashanah* and *Yom Kippur*.

15. According to the *Mishnah Berurah* (549:1:2), he was killed on the 3rd of *Tishrei* which is the day that we commonly observe as *Tzom Gedaliyah*. However the *Ba'er Heiteiv* (549:1:1) says that he was in fact assassinated on *Rosh Hashanah*. The fast day, however, is set for the third of *Tishrei*, two days later, because we do not fast on *Rosh Hashanah*.

16. If there are less than six people fasting in one of the *minyanim*, then that *minyan* would not be allowed to read the special *Kriat HaTorah* for a public fast day (*Orach Chaim* 566:3/*Shaarei Teshuva* 4). If however, it was Monday or Thursday, then that *minyan* would be required to read the regular reading for *shacharit*. When the time for *minchah* comes, the *shul* with a *minyan* of people still fasting read the special *Torah* reading for a fast day and the other does not.

17. If we were able to offer the *korban todah* in the *Beit Hamikdash* today, there would not be a *Tisha B'Av*. Therefore, our ability to offer the sacrifice today has nothing to do with when *Tisha B'Av* begins, but rather it is the lack of the *Beit Hamikdash* that is the impediment, and it is for that reason that we still recite *Mizmor L'Todah* on *Erev Tisha B'Av*.

18. In our time, we celebrate *Yom Yerushalayim* on the 28th of *Iyar*. In order to commemorate the liberation and reunification of *Yerushalayim* in the 1967 Six Day War, many people give thanks to *Hashem* by reciting *Hallel*. At the same time, the 28th day of *Iyar* is noted by the *Shulchan Aruch* (*Orach Chaim* 580:2) as the *yahrtzeit* of *Shmuel Hanavi* and many people have the tradition of fasting in memory of the *Navi* and *Tzadik Shmuel*. So you have the dichotomy of some saying *Hallel*; others fasting; both are correct.

19. The first letters of each verse in the first four chapters of *Eichah* are arranged according to the order of the Hebrew alphabet. However, if you look at the second, third, and fourth chapters, you will notice that the letters *ayin* and *peh* are reversed, with *peh* appearing prior to *ayin*. In *Rashi's* commentary on the *megillah* (*Eichah* 2:16), he quotes the *gemara* (*Sanhedrin* 104b) where *Rava*, in the name of *Rav Yochanan*, explains that the letter *peh* refers to the mouth, and the letter *ayin* refers to the eye. This connects *Eichah* to the sins of the "*meraglim*" – "spies" who slandered *Eretz Yisrael*, or in other words,

uttered with their mouths what they did not see with their eyes. The incident of the *meraglim* is one of the reasons that we fast on *Tisha B'Av*. As well, this reversing of the order of the *peh* and the *ayin*, could refer to the destruction of both "*batei hamikdash*" – "both Temples in *Jerusalem*," which occurred because of "*sinat chinam*" – "baseless hatred," which happens when the "*peh*" – "mouth" speaks before the "*ayin*" – "eye" sees. Interestingly, the *Maharsha* says that the regular order of the *alef bet* was retained in the first chapter of *Eichah*, because otherwise we would think that *Yirmiyahu* simply had a different ordering of the Hebrew alphabet than we do. However, there have been a number of archaeological discoveries in Israel of manuscripts written in alphabetical order, where the *peh* precedes the *ayin*, including a text of *Eichah* where the *peh* precedes the *ayin* even in the first chapter.

20. On the 8th day of *Tevet*, the *Torah* was translated for the first time into Greek by the order of Egyptian King Ptolemy, whose intention was to deny the divine authorship of the Torah. However, the translation was miraculous, in that 72 elders who were sequestered into 72 separate rooms, all translated the *Torah* in an identical manner. Some say that there were only 70 elders, and that is the reason why this event was given the name "*Targum Shivim*" – "the translation of the 70." *Tevet* 8 is therefore considered a tragic day and designated as a "*taanit tzaddikim*" – "a fast day for righteous individuals." On the 9th of *Tevet*, both *Ezra* and *Nechemya*, two leaders during the Babylonian exile, died. This day, too, is part of the "*taanit tzaddikim*." Add these two days to a third day in the sequence, the tenth of *Tevet* and you have a very tragic period in Jewish history.

21. *Taanit Esther* is the only fast day pushed back instead of forward. Since *Purim*, in that case, would be on a Sunday, the fast day cannot be pushed forward. And since it is being pushed back already, we do not push it to Friday, as it would then interfere with our enjoyment of and preparation for *Shabbat*.

22. This question is a bit like "who is buried in Grant's Tomb"? The events commemorated by the Fast of the tenth of *Tevet* did not all occur on the tenth of *Tevet*. True, the siege of *Yerushalayim* did begin on the tenth of *Tevet*. But the fast also commemorates the tragedy of *Targum Shivim* (see answer 20 above), the deaths of *Ezra* and *Nechemya*, as well as a general day of mourning and fasting to remember those who died "*al kiddush Hashem*" in the "*Shoah*" – Holocaust," as for most victims of the *Shoah*, there is no burial location and no known *yahrtzeit*.

23. The one who is honoured with "*hagba*" – "lifting up the *Torah* after the *Torah* reading" will sit in a chair while the second person performs "*gelila*" – rolling the *Sefer Torah*." In a *Sephardi* congregation, *hagba* does not require sitting.

24. This time of the year is safest for a student because the *Shulchan Aruch* (*Orach Chaim* 551:18) states that one should not strike a student during this time.

25. According to the *gemara* (*Gemara Eruvin* 18b) *Adam Harishon* fasted for 130 years. The *Ben Ish Chai*, in his commentary *Ben Yehoyada*, comments that *Adam* fasted to atone for the sin of eating from the *"eitz hadaat"* – "tree of knowledge." The *Ben Ish Chai* explains that since the sin utilized the sense of sight, as it says "when the woman saw that the tree was good for eating and a delight to the eyes" (*Bereishit* 3:6), *Adam* fasted 130 years which is the *gematriya* of *"ayin"* – "eye."

26. Here is the solution to the key to the Jewish fast days: The Black One is *Tisha B'Av*, as it is the saddest day in the calendar; the White One is *Yom Kippur* as we wear white as a symbol of purity and the "cleaning of our slate"; the Long One is *Shiva Asar B'Tammuz* as it occurs at the height of the summer and is usually the longest fast in the daylight hours; the Short One is *Asara B'Tevet* as it occurs in the winter and is usually the shortest fast in the daylight hours; His is *Tzom Gedaliah*, the only fast day related to a male figure; and Hers is *Taanit Esther*, the only fast day related to a female figure and Theirs or Ours is the *Taanit Bechorim* or Fast of the Firstborn and it is Theirs or Ours because fasting on that day depends on whether you are a firstborn or not.

27. The *Magen Avraham* (*Shulchan Aruch Orach Chaim* 580) cites a fast day that was observed by certain individuals on the *Erev Shabbat* Friday of the reading of *Parshat Chukat*, in commemoration of the *Erev Shabbat Chukat* in 1242 when 20 wagonloads of Hebrew manuscripts of *Talmud* and *Baalei Tosafot* were burnt in Paris, France, under the rule of King Louis the 9th. The *Maharam MiRotenberg* witnessed this tragedy and wrote a poem of lamentation, which we refer to as *Kinah* 41, read annually on *Tisha B'Av*. The *Magen Avraham* adds that on or about the same day in the years of *Tach VeTat* (1648–1649) during the pogroms of the Chmielnicki Massacres, two towns with significant Jewish population were destroyed during *Parshat Chukat,* and as a result, the *Erev Shabbat* Friday of *Parshat Chukat* was designated as a fast day. Therefore, instead of a specific day established as a fast day, and different from every other fast on the Jewish calendar, this one, set annually on *Erev Shabbat* preceding *Parshat Chukat* is the only fast day other than *Asarah B'Tevet* that can occur on a Friday.

YAMIM NORAIM QUESTIONS

1. Name an instance where you could read the *Torah* on five consecutive days, but on none of those days would you recite *Hallel*?

2. The *pasuk* "*ki melech kol haaretz elokim zamru maskil*" is found in *Tehillim* (47:8). We are familiar with this *pasuk* because it is part of the special *tefillah* recited immediately prior to "*tekiat shofar*" – "the blowing of the *shofar*." The fellow next to me in *shul* recited this *pasuk* 22 times in a 48 hour period. When did this occur and what is his name?

3. Why do we use an apple as the fruit that is dipped into the honey on *Rosh Hashanah*?

4. What is the connection between *Rosh Hashanah* as an appropriate day for childless couples to pray for children and dipping apples into honey?

5. What is the greatest number of days that one can recite *selichot* before *Rosh Hashanah* in one year?

6. We read seven *pesukim* before hearing the *shofar*. The first is "*min hameitzar*" and the first letters of the other six *pesukim* spell the phrase "*kra Satan*" – "let the words of the accuser be torn." In which *tefillah* that is said every week, do we find first letters that form this very phrase?

7. It took 2085 years from my creation to my first appearance. Who am I, and what is my connection to *Rosh Hashanah*?

8. The *Torah* only refers to *Rosh Hashanah* as occurring in the 7th month of the year, as the name of the month *Tishrei* is not mentioned by name in the *Torah*. *Chazal* identifies that 7th month as *Tishrei*. Where in the *Torah* are there hints to the actual name of *Tishrei* as the month in which *Rosh Hashanah* occurs?

9. *Rosh Hashanah* is a time of "*zichronot*" – "remembrances." Which people were remembered on *Rosh Hashanah*?

10. What are the only three *pesukim* in the *Torah* that refer to *Hashem* with the word "*melech*" – "king" and what part of our *tefillah* connects these three occurrences?

11. How is *Yosef* connected to *Rosh Hashanah* in two ways?

12. Where was a *shofar* blown on *Shabbat*?

13. There is a general rule that *tachanun* is not recited at *minchah* preceding a day when *tachanun* is not said. What are the three exceptions to this rule?

14. The *Mishna Berurah* says that if *Rosh Hashana* occurs on *Shabbat*, when we do not blow the *shofar* at all, you may use the *shofar* for one specific purpose. However, you cannot use the *shofar* for that same purpose, if *Rosh Hashana* occurs on a weekday. What is this purpose?

15. The prohibition of eating *chametz* on *Pesach* and the prohibition of eating on *Yom Kippur* carry the same punishment of "*karet*" – "being cut off from

the Jewish people." Why then is it forbidden to touch *chametz* on *Pesach* while it is permissible to touch food on *Yom Kippur*?

16. In the *"avodah"* – "the section of the *tefillah* that deals with the service of the *Kohen Gadol* in the *Beit Hamikdash* on *Yom Kippur,*" we read the phrase, *"yotze mipi Kohen Gadol"* – "when they heard the name of *Hashem* emanate from the mouth of the *Kohen Gadol.*" Why does the *tefillah* not say the much simpler *"k'sheamar kohen hagadol"* – "when the *kohen gadol* said"?

17. Normally a *"brit"* – "circumcision" which is not on the eighth day after birth, would not occur on *Yom Kippur.* Whose *brit* occurred on *Yom Kippur,* even though he was more than eight days old?

18. My older brother is my twin. He is in perfect health and yet this *Yom Kippur* I will fast and he will not have to fast *halachically.* Why not?

19. What similarities can you think of between *Yom Kippur* and *Pesach*?

20. Which two *mitzvot* require the use of two identical animals?

YAMIM NORAIM ANSWERS

1. If *Rosh Hashanah* occurs on a Thursday, you will read from the *Torah* on five consecutive days, even though we do not recite *Hallel* on any of those days. We therefore read Thursday & Friday for *Rosh Hashana*, regular *Shabbat reading*, Sunday which is *Tzom Gedaliah* "*nidcha*" – "moved to Sunday because you cannot fast on *Shabbat*" and the regular Monday morning *Torah* reading.

2. One would normally say this *pasuk* (*Tehillim* 47:8) 14 times on the two days of *Rosh Hashanah*, as part of the verses that are recited seven times before blowing the *shofar*. There is also a custom, that appears to have its source in a *Rashi* (*Micha* 6:9) and quoted by the *Kaf Hachaim* (*Shulchan Aruch Orach Chaim* 122:11), that one should insert a personal *pasuk* at the end of *Shemoneh Esrei* that begins and ends with the same letter as one's name. Many *siddurim* have a list of these "personal *pesukim*" printed at the end of *shemoneh esrei* of *shacharit*. And therefore, if the name of the person reciting this *tefillah* was *Catriel*, then his "personal *pasuk*" which should be inserted at the end of *Shemoneh Esrei*, would be this same *pasuk* "*ki melech kol haaretz Elokim zamru maskil*," and hence he would recite this *pasuk*, in each of the four times that he would recite *Shemoneh Esrei*, for a total of eight times over the two days of *Rosh Hashanah*; plus the 14 times that he would say the *pasuk* before *tekiat shofar* on each of the two days of *Rosh Hashanah*, for a total of 22 times in the 48 hour period of *Rosh Hashanah*.

3. The earliest source of dipping apples in honey is from the *Avudraham* as quoted by the *Rema* (*Shulchan Aruch Orach Chaim* 583:1). The *Zohar* (*Bereishit* 27) says that *Yitzchak* gave *Yaakov* his blessing on *Rosh Hashanah*. In the blessing, *Yitzchak* refers to the sweet smell of *Yaakov*'s garments (*Bereishit* 27:27) and compares that smell to the "smell of the field blessed by *Hashem*." The *gemara* (*Taanit* 29b) refers to the "field of sacred apples" and the *midrash* points out that the fragrance smelled by *Yitzchak* was the fragrance of an apple orchard from *Gan Eden*. Since this took place on *Rosh Hashanah*, we have the *minhag* to use an apple as the fruit that is dipped into honey.

4. The *Nachalei Binah* says that "*pru u'revu*" – "be fruitful and multiply" is equal in *gematriya* to "*tapuach*" – "apple"; and "*isha*" – "woman" is equal in *gematriya* to "*dvash*" – "honey." Therefore, *Rosh Hashanah* is a special time for barren women to be remembered by *Hashem* and blessed with children and it is for this reason that we eat *tapuach b'dvash*.

5. When *Erev Pesach* is *Shabbat*, then *Rosh Hashanah* occurs on Tuesday. *Selichot* will then begin the previous Sunday for a total of eight days. *Selichot* are not said on *Shabbat*. We are obviously speaking about the *Ashkenazi*

community, as members of the *Sephardi* community recite *selichot* for the entire month of *Elul*.

6. The second line of the prayer *"ana b'koach,"* recited every Friday night immediately before *Lecha Dodi,* contains six words. The first letters of each of these words spell *"kra Satan"* – "destroy the accuser." *Kabbalistic* sources tell us that the prayer *"ana b'koach"* cryptically contains the 42 letter name of *Hashem*. It has 42 words (7 lines of six words each) and the first letters of each word unite to reveal the hidden name. This *kabbalistic* prayer also contains the concealed message to "destroy the accuser" or the Satan who is synonymous with evil in the world. The message of "destroy the accuser" is also contained in the verses recited immediately before the blowing of the *shofar* on *Rosh Hashana* to hammer home the message that the Jewish people are standing before *Hashem* on the *"yom hadin"* – "day of judgement" and need to bypass the accuser/Satan to have direct access to their creator in pleading their case for continued good life.

7. I am the *shofar*. I was created on the sixth day of creation at twilight (*Mishnah Avot* 5:6). But I made my first appearance as part of the ram tangled in the undergrowth at the *"akeida"* – "binding of *Yitzchak*." Since *Avraham* was born in the year 1948 and *Yitzchak* was born when *Avraham* was 100, and *Yitzchak* was 37 years old at the time of the *akeida*, we can arrive at the sum of 1948 + 100 + 37 = 2085 years from creation to the appearance of the *shofar* at the *akeida*.

8. There are two hints to *Tishrei* as the name of the first month of the year; namely:
   1. The *Baal Haturim* (*Devarim* 11:12) points out that the word *"mireishit"* – "from the first of the year" is spelled abnormally without an *"alef,"* and therefore the letters can be scrambled to form the word *"miTishrei"* – "from the month of *Tishrei*."
   2. The first word in the *Torah* "*Bereishit*" – "in the beginning" (*Bereishit* 1:1) can likewise be scrambled to form the phrase *"alef b' Tishrei"* – "on the first of *Tishrei*" (*Baal Haturim Bereishit* 1:1).

9. The *gemara* (*Berachot* 29a) states that *Sarah, Rachel* and *Chana* were all barren until *Hashem* remembered them on *Rosh Hashanah* and allowed them to conceive, and as we know *Yosef* was *Rachel's* firstborn child. Also *Yosef* was released from the Egyptian jail on *Rosh Hashanah*, when the butler finally remembered his promise to *Yosef*, made two years earlier (*Gemara Rosh Hashana* 10b).

10. The only three *pesukim* in the *Torah* that refer to *Hashem* as *"melech"* – "king," are found in the *Musaf* prayer of *Rosh Hashanah*. They are *Shemot* 15:18, *Bamidbar* 23:21, and *Devarim* 33:5.

11. *Yosef* was conceived on *Rosh Hashanah* (*Gemara Berachot* 29a) and he was released from jail on that date (*Gemara Rosh Hashanah* 10b).

12. In the *Beit Hamikdash,* the *shofar* was blown even on *Shabbat* because there was no fear of "*shema yaavirenu*" – "someone carrying it in the public domain on *Shabbat*" in the *Beit Hamikdash* (*Gemara Rosh Hashana* 29b). The *Baal Haturim* (*Vayikra* 23:24) says that the *pasuk* contains the phrase "*Shabbaton zichron teruah,*" to indicate that on *Shabbat,* there is only a "*zichron*" – "a remembrance of blowing the *shofar*" but no actual blowing of the *shofar.* However, says the *Baal Haturim,* there was blowing of the *shofar* in the *Beit Hamikdash.* He quotes a *pasuk* (*Yoel* 2:1) "*tiku shofar b'tzion*" – "the *shofar* should be sounded in *Tzion*" and points out that the first letter of each word, rearranged, spell "*Shabbat*" hinting that in *Tzion* (*Beit Hamikdash*), the *shofar* was blown even on *Shabbat.*

13. The three exceptions to the rule not reciting *tachanun* at *minchah* preceding a *non-tachanun* day are:
    1. *Erev Rosh Hashanah*
    2. *Erev Yom Kippur*
    3. *Pesach Sheini*

14. When *Rosh Hashanah* occurs mid-week, a *shofar* may only be used for the purpose of blowing. The *Mishnah Berurah* (588:15) states that on *Shabbat Rosh Hashanah,* if there is nothing else available, one may use the *shofar* as a scoop to draw water or for another similar activity. However, *Rav Shlomo Zalman Auerbach* in *Shemirat Shabbat K'Hilchato* (Chapter 28: footnote 80) says that the position of the *Mishnah Berurah* was only relevant to times when they used the *shofar* to hold water. Today it's not used to hold water and is therefore *muktzah machmat chisaron kis* (this position of *Rav Shlomo Zalman Auerbach* is not stated in the original edition of *Shemirat Shabbat* printed in 1965). *Rav Shlomo Zalman Auerbach* adds that during the month of *Elul,* when the *shofar* is used for practice in preparation of *Rosh Hashanah,* a *shofar* is considered a *kli she'melachto l'issur.*

15. The *Mishnah Berurah* (612:32) quotes the *Ran* who explains that all food is forbidden on *Yom Kippur* and since we are especially in awe of *Hashem*'s majesty on this day, we are not afraid that individuals will err and accidentally eat. However, on *Pesach,* since eating is permitted, we may forget, and while handling "*chametz*" – "leavened food," may inadvertently eat it.

16. The *Hon Ashir* quotes (*Mishnah Yoma* 6:2) the *Arizal* who says that the *Kohen Gadol* never actually said the name of *Hashem* during the *Avodah.* He merely opened his mouth and the name of *Hashem* miraculously came out and was heard.

17. The *Daat Zekeinim* (*Bereishit* 17:23) says that *Avraham Avinu* had his *brit* on *Yom Kippur*. He deduces this from the common word of "*b'etzem*" which occurs both by *Avraham's brit* and by the laws of *Yom Kippur*.

18. I am a girl who is 12 years old. My twin brother is still a minor *halachically*, and therefore is not required to fast until he is 13 years old. I am already considered to be an adult *halachically* and therefore will be required to fast this year.

19. The following are similarities between *Yom Kippur* and *Pesach*:
    1. Many men have the custom to wear a "*kittel*" – "white caftan" on *Yom Kippur* and at the *Pesach Seder*.
    2. We say "*l'shana ha'bah birushalayim habenuya*" – "next year in the rebuilt Jerusalem" at the end of *Yom Kippur* and the end of the *Pesach Seder*.
    3. The punishment for eating on *Yom Kippur* and for eating *chametz* on *Pesach* is identical, "*karet*" – "extinction of the soul and denial of a share in the world to come."
    4. There is a special sermon given on the *Shabbat* immediately preceding each, *Shabbat Hagadol drasha* before *Pesach* and *Shabbat Shuva drasha* before *Yom Kippur*.
    5. A cute answer, no *chametz* can be eaten on either day!

20. Two identical goats were needed for the *Yom Kippur avoda* (*Gemara Yoma* 62a) and two identical birds were needed to purify the "*metzora*" – "leper" (*Mishnah Negaim* 14:5).

SUKKOT, SHEMINI ATZERET & SIMCHAT TORAH QUESTIONS

1. We know the historical events that happened on *Pesach*, *Shavuot*, *Chanukah*, *Purim*, *Rosh Hashanah* and *Tisha B'Av*. But what happened on the 15th of *Tishrei*, the day we observe as the first day of *Sukkot*?

2. *Chutz Laaretz* question: Which food is forbidden on *Shemini Atzeret* but permitted on *Simchat Torah*?

3. How can a *Sukkah* which was *kosher* one year become invalid the next year even though it is in exactly the same position and condition as the previous year, and nothing external has changed either (i.e., no trees have grown over it etc.)?

4. In a year when the first day of *Sukkot* falls on *Shabbat*, there are at least five unique events that occur in Israel that do not occur in *Chutz La'aretz*. What are they?

5. How is it possible for the exact same *sukkah* (no internal or external changes) to be *kosher* only on *Chol Hamoed*, but not *kosher* on *Shabbat*, *Yom Tov* or *Shabbat Chol Hamoed*, when nothing has been done to change the state or location of that *Sukkah*?

6. How is it possible for the exact same *sukkah* (no internal or external changes) to be *kosher* only on *Shabbat* or *Shabbat Chol Hamoed*, but not *kosher* on *Yom Tov* or on *Chol Hamoed* (not *Shabbat*), when nothing has been done to change the state or location of that *sukkah*?

7. What are you supposed to do with your *aravot-hoshanot* after using them on *Hoshana Rabbah*?

8. What round objects are permissible on *Sukkot* and what round objects are forbidden on *Sukkot*?

9. There are seven individuals who we symbolically welcome into our *sukkah* as *"ushpizin"* – "guests." We know the *yartzeit* of three of the *"ushpizin"*; namely, *Moshe* (*Adar* 7), *Aharon* (*Av* 1) and *David* (*Sivan* 6). How can I know the day of the week of the *yartzeit* of the other *"ushpizin"*?

10. When was *Pesach* to *Sukkot* less than six months?

11. How many times a year are we obligated to eat?

12. When could one *shul* be required to read the *megillah* one day and another *shul* required to read it a week later?

13. How many times in *Tanach* does it discuss people sitting in *Sukkot*?

14. When can a person be considered an inanimate object according to *halacha*?

15. A number of important days in the Jewish calendar, like *Pesach* and *Sukkot*, start on the 15th of the month. Which 15th always falls on *Rosh Chodesh*?

16. On *Sukkot* we have the "*arbah minim*" – "the four species," consisting of the *lulav, etrog, hadassim* and *aravot*. What are the "*arbah minim*" of the sacrifice of the "*metzora*"?

17. Why is the *etrog* unique among all other fruits?

18. What is it that is "*assur*" – "forbidden" for you to do on *Shemini Atzeret*, but if someone else performs this "*issur*" – "prohibition," it then becomes "*mutar*" – "permissible" for you?

19. The *piyut* of *Simchat Torah* refers to *Torah* as "*paz u'peninim*" – "gold and pearls." What is the significance of this description?

20. The evenings of *Shemini Atzeret* in Israel and *Simchat Torah* in *chutz laaretz* are unique, in that in each locale, it is the only evening during the year when you would read from the *Torah* at the *Maariv* prayers. But not everyone reads from the same place in the *Torah*. Explain?

SUKKOT, SHEMINI ATZERET &
SIMCHAT TORAH ANSWERS

1. After the sin of the *"eigel hazahav"* – "the golden calf," the *"ananei hakavod"* – "clouds of glory" left the Jewish people. Only after *Moshe* returned on *Yom Kippur* with the second set of tablets and the message of *Hashem*'s forgiveness, and only after the command to build the *mishkan* and the collection of materials for the *mishkan*, did the clouds return. This according to the *Vilna Gaon* (*Kol Eliyahu* #84) was the 15th of *Tishrei*.

2. An *etrog*, which was used for the *mitzvah* of *"arba minim"* – "taking the four species; the *lulav, etrog, hadassim* and *aravot"* during the seven days of *Sukkot*, may not be eaten on *Shemini Atzeret* but is permitted on *Simchat Torah* (*Shulchan Aruch Orach Chaim* 665:1). However, if one had numerous *etrogim* to be used for the daily *mitzvah* of *arba minim* on *Sukkot*, and dedicated a particular *etrog* for a particular day of *Sukkot*, he may then eat that *etrog* the next day.

3. If nothing was done to prepare the *sukkah* for this year's holiday (i.e., it was untouched since last year), it is invalid. An essential requirement in constructing the *sukkah* is *"ta'aseh v'lo min he'asuy"* – "you must make it yourself and not merely utilize what is already there" (*Shulchan Aruch Orach Chaim* 629:15). Therefore, if a *sukkah* is untouched from last year and still has its walls and *schach*, it is not a *kosher sukkah* until you do a new action, like repositioning the *schach* to make it *kosher* for this year. Some positive action (putting on or repositioning the *schach*, etc.) must be done to properly prepare it for the *chag*.

4. The five unique events that occur only in *Eretz Yisrael* when the first day of *Sukkot* is on a *Shabbat*, are:
   1. We read seven *aliyot* for *V'zot Haberacha*.
   2. We read *Kohelet* on the first day of *Sukkot*.
   3. We only take the *lulav* and *etrog* on *Chol Hamoed*.
   4. We read *Bereishit* at *minchah* on *Shabbat*.
   5. We read the *Torah* on a Friday night (at the end of *hakafot* on *Shemini Atzeret* in Israel).

5. The *Shulchan Aruch* (*Orach Chaim* 528:3) speaks about a *sukkah* built on top of a camel where one uses the humps of the camel as part of the walls of the *sukkah*. Such a *sukkah* may not be used on *Shabbat* or *Yom Tov*.

6. The *Shulchan Aruch* (*Orach Chaim* 530:7) speaks about a *sukkah* built in an alleyway where there is a *"lechi"* – "pole-marker" that would be used for an *eruv*. In the laws of *eruv*, such a pole marker would "close" the space between the two walls of the alleyway as a third wall for the purposes of carrying,

hence creating the three walls required to validate a *sukkah*. Since the "*lechi*" has validity only in regards to the laws of *eruv*, which apply only on *Shabbat*, that "virtual" third wall disappears on *Yom Tov* or *Chol Hamoed* and therefore this would be a case of a *sukkah* that is *kosher* only on *Shabbat*.

7. The *Ramah* (*Shulchan Aruch Orach Chaim* 564:9) says that one should put them away and use them to help the fire of the oven used for the baking of *matzoh* based on the principle that once used for a *mitzvah*, an item should ideally, where possible, be used for another *mitzvah*.

8. A round *sukkah* can be used on *Sukkot* as long as a 7 × 7 *tefachim* square will fit within the circle (*Shulchan Aruch Orach Chaim* 634:2). A round *etrog* that resembles a ball is not permitted on *Sukkot* (*Shulchan Aruch Orach Chaim* 648:18). One is supposed to remove their rings from their fingers while reciting the *berachot* over the "*arbah minim*" – "the four species" (*Shulchan Aruch Orach Chaim* 651:6).

9. The *Taamei Haminhagim* in the section dealing with the "*Hilula*" – "*yahrtzeit*" of *Rabbi Shimon Bar Yochai*, quotes the *Minchat Elazar of Munkatch* in his *sefer Shaar Yissachar* who explains that the *yahrtzeit* of each of the seven *ushpizin* falls on the same day of the week as that upon which he will be the *ushpizin* the following *Sukkot*. We have two different *minhagim* for the order of the *ushpizin*. According to the *Arizal*, the order is *Avraham, Yitzchak, Yaakov, Moshe, Aharon, Yosef* and *David*. The other *minhag* places *Yosef* immediately after *Yaakov*. If you check the known *yartzeits* (i.e., *Moshe, Aharon* and *David*), it would appear that the *Minchat Elazar of Munkatch*'s claim regarding the days of the week upon which the *yahrtzeit* falls, follows the *minhag* of the *Arizal*.

10. Trick question: *Bnai Yisrael* left *Ramses* on *Pesach* and travelled from there to *Sukkot* (*Shemot* 13:20). *Rashi* comments that the journey from *Ramses* to *Sukkot* took one day, and therefore we have a case of *Pesach* to *Sukkot* in less time than the six months that it takes on the calendar!

11. We are required "*mid'oraita*" – "by *Torah* law" to eat a "*k'zayit matzah*" – "an olive sized piece of *matzah*" on the first night of *Pesach*; and to eat a "*k'zayit*" of bread in the *sukkah* on the first night of *Sukkot*. We are also required to eat on *Yom Tov*, to fulfill the requirement of "*v'samachta b'chagecha*" – "and you shall rejoice on your festivals" (*Devarim* 16:14). The *Shulchan Aruch* (*Orach Chaim* 604:1) rules that there is a *Torah* obligation on *Erev Yom Kippur* to eat, drink, and have a festive food-filled meal, and *Rashi* (*Rosh Hashanah* 9a) explains that the reason for this is on account of *Hashem*'s love for us, to enable us to tolerate the fasting. There is also a *mitzvah* to eat three *seudot* on *Shabbat* (*Gemara Shabbat* 118b).

12. There are two possible answers. If the first day of *Sukkot* occurred on a *Shabbat*, then there is no *Shabbat Chol Hamoed*. In that case, in Israel, one

would read *Kohelet* on the first day of *Sukkot*, and in *chutz la'aretz, it would* be read one week later on *Shemini Atzeret*. Similarly, if the first day of *Pesach* is a *Shabbat*, *Shir Hashirim* is read in Israel on the first day of *Pesach*, and in *chutz la'aretz* on the eighth day of *Pesach* which would be the second *Shabbat* of *Pesach*.

13. *Bnai Yisrael* lived in *Sukkot* while in the desert (*Vayikra* 23:43); *Yona* sat in a *sukkah* (*Yona* 4:3); in the time of *Nechemya*, the people built *sukkot* to observe the holiday (*Nechemya* 8:16); and *Ben Hadad*, the king of *Aram*, and his army camped in *sukkot* while laying siege to the city of *Shomron* (*Melachim* 1:20:12).

14. A person can be considered to be an inanimate object, according to *halacha*, when he is counted as a wall of a *sukkah* (*Shulchan Aruch Orach Chaim* 630:12). A *sukkah* needs 2 walls and part of a third wall in order for it to be a kosher *sukkah*. The *Shulchan Aruch* explains that should the third wall fall down on *Sukkot*, one can ask a friend to stand where the third wall previously stood and he would be constituted as a part of a third wall, thereby making the *sukkah* kosher.

15. The 15th day of the *Omer* always occurs on *Rosh Chodesh Iyar*.

16. The *arbah minim* consists of a *lulav, etrog, hadassim* and *aravot*. The "*korban*" – "sacrificial offering" of the *metzora* consists of a "*tzipor*" – "bird"; "*shni tolaat*" – "worm-dyed crimson wool"; "*eizov*" – "hyssop"; and "*etz erez*" – "a piece of cedar" (*Vayikra* 14:4).

17. *Rashi* (*Vayikra* 23:40) comments that the *etrog* is unique among all fruits, in that its bark and fruit have the same taste.

18. If the *gabbai* neglects to announce to the congregation to recite "*mashiv haruach*" in the silent *mussaf shemoneh esrei* of *Shemini Atzeret,* then the congregation is not permitted to add it at that time. However, if someone is reciting the silent *shemoneh esrei* and mistakenly proclaims loudly "*mashiv haruach umorid hageshem,*" it now becomes permissible for everyone else to say it (*Shulchan Aruch Orach Chaim* 114:2; *Mishneh Berurah* 114:4).

19. Rabbi *Yehoshua Leib Diskin,* the *Rav* of *Brisk* and *Yerushalayim*, explained that there is an essential difference between gold and pearls. The disadvantage of gold is that its value is only directly proportional to its weight. One ounce of gold is worth $1000; two ounces $2000 etc. Its major advantage, however, is that if one has a large nugget of pure gold and needs some money, he can break off a chunk, and the value of the gold will only be diminished by the value of the part that has been separated. On the other hand, the value of pearls or any precious stones is that its value increases geometrically with size. One karat is worth, for example, $1000, but two karats may be worth $3000 and so on. The disadvantage is that if you break off a part of the pearl or stone, it becomes flawed, is reduced in value enormously and

in fact could be worthless, no matter what size remains. *Torah*, says *Rav Diskin*, has the advantages of both gold and pearls. The reward for learning increasing amounts of *Torah* grows geometrically with the completion of every unit, every *sefer*, every *masechta*. However, should one just complete one fraction of the *sefer*, the value to the person is not flawed, but rather there is reward for every small portion of *Torah* that one learns.

20. The *Rema* (*Shulchan Aruch Orach Chaim* 669:1) says that on the evening of *Shemini Atzeret/Simchat Torah*, we should read the five *aliyot* that are called "*hanedarim shebaTorah*," which, the *Mishnah Berurah* explains, are the *parshiyot* that people traditionally purchased during the course of the year, for the honour of receiving that particular *aliyah*. These include the blessings of *Yitzchak* to *Yaakov*, "*Hamalach Hagoel*," "*Vayichulu*," "*Birkat Kohanim*," and "*Ma Tovu*." The *Mishnah Berurah* then goes on to say that in our day, we have the custom to read three *aliyot* from "*V'zot Haberacha*," which is the most prevalent custom in communities around the world.

CHANUKAH QUESTIONS

1. Give a number of hints from the *Torah* to the holiday of *Chanukah*?
2. Why is the *Chanukah menorah* placed on the south side of a *shul*?
3. How many times is *Chanukah* referred to in the *Mishnah*?
4. Find connections between *Pesach* and *Chanukah* in both directions; i.e. something from *Chanukah* that refers to *Pesach* and something from *Pesach* that refers to *Chanukah*.
5. Name a *Chanukah* situation where one would not make the *beracha* of "*l'hadlik ner shel Chanukah*," but would nevertheless make the other two *berachot* of "*she'asah nissim*" and "*shehecheyanu*"?
6. In 5781 (corresponding to the secular years of 2020–2021), *Purim* (14ᵗʰ *of Adar*) falls on a Friday in most of the world's Jewish communities. However, in *Yerushalayim*, given that it is a city surrounded by a wall since the time of *Yehoshua*, *Purim* is celebrated on the 15ᵗʰ *of Adar* which occurs on a *Shabbat*. What is interesting is that the *Shabbat Purim Torah* reading and the *Shabbat Chanukah Torah* reading are clear indications of the *Purim* concept of "*v'nahafoch hu*." Explain?
7. The first day of *Chanukah* is a Friday. What is the *Torah* reading the next day, *Shabbat Chanukah*?
8. How is it possible for one person to make five *berachot* in a 24 hour period, each *beracha* containing the words "*l'hadlik ner…*"?
9. What is the maximum number of *Chanukah* candles (not counting any *Shabbat* candles or any "*shamash*" candles) that can be lit on *Rosh Chodesh* which coincides with *Chanukah*?
10. Where in the *Torah* is there a *pasuk* that hints to the three *berachot* recited on the first night of *Chanukah*?
11. What laws of *Chanukah* can be learned from the *pasuk* "*kaf achat asara zahav meleah ketoret*" (*Bamidbar* 7:14)?
12. On which *Shabbat*, which does not coincide with *Rosh Chodesh*, do we read from four different *parshiyot*?
13. Who doesn't get the *aliyah* of *maftir* on *Chanukah*?
14. May one who is visually impaired light their own *Chanukah* candles?
15. From where in the *Chanukah* liturgy do we deduce that *Haman*'s ten sons in the *Purim* story, were decapitated before being hung?
16. A *Chanukah* equation: $44 = n(1 + n)/2 + n$. What is "n"?
17. On *Shabbat Chanukah* in the secular calendar year 1948, no one ate *seudah shlishit* on *Shabbat Chanukah*. Why not? When will this happen again?
18. In some years on this day, we recite *Hallel*; in other years on the same day, we recite *Tachanun*; and this has nothing to do with any controversy over *Yom Ha'atzmaut*. What is the date?

19. Besides the special *berachot* that we recite annually on *Chanukah*, what other *beracha*, said periodically, has its origins in the month of *Kislev*?

20. I am unable to light the *Chanukah* menorah and therefore I appoint a *shaliach* to light the *menorah* on my behalf. However, *halachically*, the agent should light the *menorah* but not recite any of the applicable *berachot*? Where am I?

CHANUKAH ANSWERS

1. Here are a few of the hints from the *Torah* to the holiday of *Chanukah*, which occurs on the 25th day of the Hebrew month of *Kislev*:

   1. Immediately following the listing of the Festival cycle (*Vayikra* 23), we are instructed regarding the lighting of the *menorah* in the *mishkan* with pure olive oil (*Vayikra* 24:1–4). The *Bnai Yissaschar* in the name of the *Rokeach* adds that the positioning of the *mitzvah* of kindling the *menorah* with pure olive oil right after the *mitzvah* of celebrating *Sukkot* and *Shemini Atzeret* for eight days, was a divine hint that *Chanukah* would be a miraculous eight day holiday involving olive oil.

   2. In the listings of the places where *Bnai Yisrael* camped during their 40 years in the desert, the 25th place is *Chashmonah* (*Bamidbar* 33:29).

   3. The 25th word in the *Torah* is "*ohr*" – "light" (*Bereishit* 1:3).

   4. The *Torah* reading on *Shabbat Chanukah* is generally (about 90% of the time) *Parshat Mikeitz*, which begins with the dreams of *Paroh*, highlighting the victory of the weak cows and sheaves over the strong ones, synonymous with the *Chanukah* story of the victory of the small band of *Chashmonaim* over the mighty Greek army.

   5. In *Parshat Mikeitz*, it says "*u'tvoach tevach v'hachein*" (*Bereishit* 43:16). The letters of *Chanukah* are found in this phrase beginning with the "*chet*" of the word "*tevach*" and all the letters of "*v'hachein*." The *gematriya* of "*u'tvoach tevach*" is 44 which is the number of candles lit during the entire festival.

   6. In *Parshat Shemot* (*Shemot* 3:4), the *Torah* says "*ki sar lirot vayikra.*" The "*roshei teivot*" – "first letter in each word of the phrase" spell *Kislev*. This is the only place in the *Torah* where the initial letters of consecutive words spell *Kislev*. The *midrash* (*Pirkei D'Rabbi Eliezer* 40) explains that the subject of this section of *Torah*, the burning bush, a fire that burned without using up its supply of fuel, was meant to symbolize the wicked (*Egyptian* oppressors) who cannot extinguish the flames (i.e., *yirat shomayim* and *maasim tovim*) of the righteous *Bnai Yisrael*. So too, the *menorah* (which also miraculously did not consume its source of fuel for eight days) symbolized the defiance of the Jews to the Greek decrees. Therefore it is noteworthy that the only occurrence of "*roshei teivot*" spelling *Kislev* should appear in the story of the burning bush. (*Niflaot MiToratecha*).

   7. The Rebbe, Rav Heschel, when he was a young boy, was asked how many lights we light in total on *Chanukah*. He quickly answered 44, and explained that there is a *pasuk* in *Tehillim* (124:7) that says "*hapach nishbar va'anachnu nimlatnu*" – "the flask is broken and we are saved."

The *gematriya* of *"pach"* is 88 and therefore when it is broken in two, half of 88 is 44, the number of lights that we kindle over the course of the eight days of *Chanukah*. This is a *remez* to the *"pach shemen"* – "the flask of oil."

8. The *Baal Haturim* states that the only two times that the word *"kaneh"* is found in the *Torah*, is to describe the stalks of wheat (*Bereishit* 41:5) and the main shaft (*Vayikra* 25:31) of the *menorah*, thus connecting *Chanukah*, whose symbol is the *menorah*, with *Parshat Mikeitz*, where we read of the weak stalks of wheat overpowering the strong stalks, which is generally the *parshah* read on *Chanukah*.

9. In *Parshat Vayigash* (one of three possible *Chanukah parshiyot*), when *Yehuda*, in speaking to *Yosef*, summarizes the events that had just transpired, he says *"ha-yesh lachem av oh ach...yesh lanu av zaken"* – "you asked us, do we have a father or a brother? And we answered, we have an elderly father..." (*Bereishit* 44:19,20). This could be explained as the *machloket* between *Beit Hillel* and *Beit Shammai* (*Gemara Shabbat* 21b) regarding the number of candles lit on each of the nights. Do we start with one and add one each night as embodied in the word *"av"* which is composed of the letters *alef* and *bet*; i.e., 1...2...etc. (*Bet Hillel*), or do we start with eight and reduce the number by one each night as embodied in the word *"ach"* which is composed of the letters *alef* and *chet*; i.e., the first is eight, the second is seven, etc...(*Bet Shammai*)? And he immediately gives the answer *"yesh lanu av zaken"* – "we have an old father." *Hillel* was known as *Hillel* the Elder (*Hillel Hazaken*). The answer given therefore indicates the adopted custom of beginning with one candle and adding one each night, according to the position of *"av zaken"*...*Bet Hillel*.

10. In *Parshat Vayigash*, one of the three *parshiyot* read on *Chanukah*, the word *"Goshnah"* ("to *Goshen*") appears a couple of times (*Bereishit* 46:28,29). It has four letters, *Gimel, Shin, Nun* and *Heh*, which are the four letters that appear on the *dreidel* (in *Chutz La'Aretz* only; in Israel, there is a *Peh* instead of the *Shin*).

11. After *Yaakov* was finished wrestling with the angel of *Eisav* (*Rashi* in *Bereishit* 32:25, says that *Yaakov* was alone as he returned to retrieve some earthenware flasks), the *Torah* says *"vayizrach lo Hashemesh* (*Bereishit* 32:32). One could translate this as "the *shamash* brought light to *"lo"* which is equal in *gematriya* to 36, the number of candles lit during the holiday of *Chanukah*.

2. The *Menorah* in the *Ohel Moed* was also positioned on the south side and therefore when we light the *menorah* in *shul*, it is placed near the south wall of the *shul*.

3. *Chanukah* is referenced six times in the *Mishnah,* namely; *Bikurim* 1:6; *Taanit* 2:10; *Rosh Hashana* 1:3; *Megillah* 3:4 and 3:6; *Bava Kama* 6:6. The only time that *'ner Chanukah'* is mentioned in *Mishnah* is in *Bava Kama* 6:6. Coincidentally, 6 × 6 = 36, the total number of *"Nerot Chanukah"* that are lit on *Chanukah.*

4. Two scriptural connections between *Pesach* and *Chanukah* are:
   1. The phrase *"mi chamocha ba'eilim Hashem"* which is part of the *Shira,* sung at the splitting of the sea, which occurred on *Pesach.* This phrase was the battle cry of the *Chashmonaim,* and its initials also spell *"maccabi."*
   2. The second stanza of *Maoz Tzur,* sung on *Chanukah,* contains the phrase *"chayl Paroh v'chol zaro"* referring to the drowning of *Paroh's* army in the sea.

5. The situation could be the following: It is the first night of *Chanukah* and that year, the first night falls on *Friday* night. A woman is alone and therefore lights both *Chanukah* and *Shabbat* candles. Even though, when we are faced with two *mitzvot,* we perform the more prevalent *mitzvah* first, in this case, the *halacha* is that she lights the *Chanukah* candles first and then the *Shabbat* candles. The reason is that if she lit the *Shabbat* candles first, it would already be *halachically Shabbat* for her, and she would no longer be permitted to light the *Chanukah* candles. However, on this particular night, she errs and lights the *Shabbat* candles first. The only way she can now fulfill the *mitzvah* of *Chanukah* is to have someone else light on her behalf. The *Mishnah Berurah* (679:1) rules that in a case like this, she is still able to make the second and third *berachot* of *"she'asah nissim"* and *"shehecheyanu."*

6. In 5781 (2020–2021), the *Shabbat Torah* reading on Purim is *Parshat Tetzaveh* which deals with such *Chanukah* concepts as *menorah, mizbeach,* and olive oil. The *Shabbat Chanukah Torah* reading, on the other hand, is *Parshat Vayeishev,* which deals with a butler, officers of a non-Jewish king, and the hanging of the baker, all of which are elements more in tune with a *Purim* story.

7. *Chanukah* taking place from Friday to Friday is quite a rare occurrence. When it happens, the *Torah* reading is always *Vayeishev,* and we have the rare instance of a non-*Mikeitz Chanukah.* We then have the rare reading of *Mikeitz* on the day following *Chanukah,* with the equally very rare reading of the *haftarah* of *Mikeitz,* which occurs about 10% of the time. Normally, *Mikeitz* is read on *Shabbat Chanukah* and the *haftarah* of *Mikeitz* is preempted by the *haftarah* of *Shabbat Chanukah.*

8. The case is of a single male who happens to be the *"shamash"* – *"salaried sexton or caretaker"* of the *shul.* On Thursday evening after dark, he lights the *Chanukah* candles in *shul* with a *beracha;* he then lights *Chanukah*

candles at home with a *beracha*; on Friday evening, he lights *Chanukah* and *Shabbat* candles at home, each with a *beracha*, and then proceeds to *shul*, where, before the onset of *Shabbat*, he lights one more time for the *shul*; a total of five *berachot*, each containing the words "*l'hadlik ner shel…*" (*Mishnah Berurah* 671:45, 49).

9. The maximum number is 21. If *Rosh Chodesh Tevet* is a two-day *Rosh Chodesh* that occurs on a Thursday and Friday, then 6 *Chanukah* candles are lit on Wednesday evening after nightfall, 7 *Chanukah* candles on Thursday evening, and since we would light the candles for Friday evening before nightfall (when it is still *Rosh Chodesh* and not yet *Shabbat*), another 8 candles would be lit for a grand total of 21 candles lit on a *Rosh Chodesh*.

10. In *Bamidbar* 21:8, *Hashem* commands *Moshe* to make a copper "*saraf*" – "snake," place it on a "*nes*" – "pole," so that anyone who sees it "*vachai*" – "will live." The *Ben Ish Chai* in his commentary on *Parshat Vayeshev* says that the word "*saraf*" has an alternate meaning of "burned," hinting to the first *beracha* of *Chanukah* "*l'hadlik*"; the word "*nes*" has an alternate meaning of "miracle," hinting to the second *beracha* of "*sheasah nissim*"; and the word "*vachai*" refers to the third *beracha* of "*shehechiyanu.*"

11. *Rav Tzvi Hirsh MiZidochov* is quoted in *Vidibarta Bam* by *Rav Moshe Bogomilsky* and points out that the *Torah* readings for *Chanukah* are the daily offerings of the "*nesi'im*" – "princes" during the dedication of the *Mishkan*. One of the *pesukim* hints at the laws of *Chanukah*, namely, "*kaf achat asara zahav meleah ketoret.*" Each word in the *pasuk* is an acronym for a *halacha* of *Chanukah*. "*Kaf*" stands for "*kaf pachot*" – "the menorah must be less than 20 *amot* in height"; "*achat*" stands for "*alef chet tadlik*" – "one should light one candle and add one more each night until the eighth night"; "*asara*" stands for "*ad shetichleh regal min hashuk*" – "because of the importance of highlighting the miracle of *Chanukah*, we can light as long as there is pedestrian traffic in the streets"; "*zahav*" stands for "*zemana hakochavim b'tzeitam*" – "the time for lighting is when the evening stars appear in the heavens; "*meleah*" stands for "*mitzvah l'hadlik etzel hapetach*" – "one should light near the doorway" so that passersby can see the light and appreciate the miracle; and "*ketoret*" stands for "*karov tefach rachov tadlik*" – "one should light within a handbreadth of the width of the doorway." These *halachot* are based on *Shulchan Aruch Orach Chaim* 671 and 672.

12. If the first day of *Chanukah* is *Shabbat*, then on the second *Shabbat Chanukah*, we will be reading in *shacharit* from *Parshat Mikeitz*, *maftir* from both *Parshat Naso* and *Parshat Behaalotcha* and *Shabbat minchah* from *Parshat Vayigash*.

13. *Shlumiel Ben Tzurishadai*. Since the first day of *Chanukah* can occur on any day of the week except Tuesday, it follows that the fifth day of *Chanukah*

can never be on *Shabbat*. Therefore the *"korban"* – "sacrificial offering" of the fifth *nasi, Shlumiel Ben Tzurishadai,* can never be read as the *maftir* on *Shabbat*. All the others can be read as *maftir* on *Shabbat*, including the ninth, tenth, eleventh and twelfth *nasi,* which are part of the *maftir* when there is a second *Shabbat Chanukah.*

14. One should attempt to be included in another's *mitzvah* of lighting *Chanukah* candles; but if this is impossible, a blind person may light *Chanukah* lights independently. (*Shulchan Aruch Orach Chaim Magen Avraham* 675:4)

15. In the *Chanukah* song *Maoz Tzur,* we have the phrase *"rov banav vkinyanav"* – literally "most of his sons." *Tosafot* (*Gemara Yoma* 31a) explain that *Haman's* sons were decapitated before hanging. Thus the verse can be explained to mean that "most" of each son was hung, ie, the body minus the head.

16. The total number of candles lit on *Chanukah* is 44. In math, to get the total number in a series 1 + 2 + 3 + ..., you use the equation $n(1 + n)/2$ where n = the last number in the series. Therefore on the eight days of *Chanukah,* you light $8(1 + 8)/2 = 36$ candles. Then add "n" (8) for the number of *"shamashim."*

17. Trick question: In the secular calendar year 1948, there was no *Shabbat Chanukah.* In 1947, *Chanukah* occurred entirely in the month of December. In 1948, much of *Chanukah* was in December but it spilled over to January 1949, such that *Shabbat Chanukah* coincided with New Year's Day, January 1st, 1949. And therefore no one ate *seudah shlishit* on *Shabbat Chanukah* 1948. This is a phenomena that rarely happens. The next occurrence of this rare phenomena will be in the calendar year 2043.

18. In years when *Kislev* has 30 days, the third of *Tevet* will be the day following *Chanukah,* when we would recite *Tachanun.* In years when *Kislev* has 29 days, the third of *Tevet* is the eighth day of *Chanukah* when we would recite *Hallel.*

19. It is the *beracha* of *"zocher habrit v'neeman bivrito"* that is recited whenever one witnesses the appearance of a rainbow. The *Sefer Hatodaah* writes that the first appearance of a rainbow occurred at the end of the great *"mabul"* – "flood" of *Noach. Noach* left the safety of the ark and re-entered the world on the 28th of *Cheshvan.* The *Torah* tells us that *Noach* built an altar and brought sacrifices of thanksgiving to *Hashem* from every *kosher* animal and bird. *Kislev* began and it was at that point that *Hashem* blessed *Noach,* permitted him to use meat as food, forbade him from shedding human blood, and established a *"brit"* – "covenant" with him to never again inflict a flood on mankind. To seal this covenant, *Hashem* showed *Noach* a rainbow. It is for this reason that the zodiac sign of the month of *Kislev* is a *"keshet"* – "rainbow."

20. I am in a plane travelling from east to west across the Pacific ocean and in the process of crossing the International Date Line. The *halacha* where I

am unable to light the *menorah* by myself, is that I should designate some-one as my "*shaliach*" – "agent" to light a *menorah* for me, preferably in my own home; it could be my spouse or any adult male or female. The *shaliach*, when lighting their own *menorah*, should have me in mind as he/she recites the *berachot*. However, if the *shaliach* has already lit their own *menorah*, he should recite an additional set of *berachot* when he lights the *menorah* on my behalf. In our case, however, if my flight will cross the dateline at such a time where I will not experience the 7th night of *Chanukah* at all, my *shaliach* should light my *menorah* without a *beracha*, because the *mitzvah* of lighting the *menorah* on that particular night did not apply to me at all.

PURIM QUESTIONS

1. From where do we learn that "one who properly gives credit to the originator of a quote brings redemption to the world"?

2. *Achashverosh* ruled 127 provinces. Some were on land and some were islands. How many land based provinces and how many island provinces did he have in his kingdom of 127?

3. How many kings and queens are mentioned in the *Megillah*?

4. Connect these three things: *Megillat Esther*; the two *parshiyot* in the *Torah* that deal with *Amalek*; and the psalm of *Hallel Hagadol*?

5. Who killed his wife because of his friend and his friend because of his wife?

6. The phrase "*Arur Haman*" – "cursed be *Haman*" is the opposite of "*Baruch Mordechai*" – "Blessed be *Mordechai*," but what is the one thing they have in common?

7. How many times does *Hashem*'s name appear in the *Megillah*?

8. The mother of one of the greatest *Tzaddikim* of the Jewish people and the mother of one of the most evil enemies of the Jewish people are related in name only. Explain?

9. Nine people were listening to *Megillat Esther*. Near the end of the *Megillah* reading, they realized that there were actually ten people in the room. They now realized that they would have to start the *Megillah* reading over again. Why?

10. What is the connection between *Purim* and *Bedikat Chametz*?

11. How many prophetesses were there?

12. Name as many people's names as possible that are mentioned in the *Torah* and also appear as names in *Megillat Esther*?

13. *Mordechai*'s name is found in the *Purim* song, *Shoshanat Yaakov*. In which other equally famous *non-Purim* song is the name *Mordechai* found?

14. Which four kings ruled over the entire world?

15. How many sons did *Haman* have?

16. How many years did *Esther* hide the fact that she was Jewish from *Acheshverosh*?

17. Present a good reason for special *simcha* on the second day of *Pesach* even in the *Land of Israel*?

18. Which *beracha* is not recited if the *megillah* is read in private?

19. In the *Purim* story, we are looking for two root words that are homophones; two or more words having the same pronunciation but different meanings, origins, or spelling. *Mordechai* refused to do one in front of *Haman* and the other, *Mordechai* did because of *Haman*'s evil decree. Name the two words?

20. Besides *Purim*, when do we eat something special to remember the story of *Purim*?

21. And what would a riddle book be like without a few *Purim Torah* riddles... questions 21 to 24 are all *Purim* jokes; first: It says in the *megillah,* "*v'noach meioiveihem*" (*Esther* 9:16). What in the world was *Noach* doing in the *megillah*?

22. What was *Achashveirosh*'s mother-in-law's name?

23. How do you know that *Esther* worked for the city?

24. If a woman has only one candle to light for *Shabbos* may she stand in front of a mirror and thereby have two candles?

PURIM ANSWERS

1. In *Mishnah* (*Pirkei Avot* 6:6), it is written "everyone who says a thing in the name of him who said it, brings deliverance into the world, as it is said: "*Vatomer Esther lamelech b'shaim Mordechai*" – "And *Esther* told the king in *Mordechai*'s name" (*Esther* 2:22).

2. The *Vilna Gaon* states that the hint for the answer to this riddle is in the first *pasuk* of the 10th and last chapter of *Esther*. The numerical value of the word "*mas*" – "taxes which were imposed on land," is equal to 100 and the word "*v'iyay*" – "and the islands" equals 27 for a total of 127.

3. There are five kings and queens mentioned in the *Megilla*. They are *Achashveirosh, Vashti, Esther, Nevuchadnetzar* and *Yechanya*.

4. The *Rokeach* points out that there are 166 *pesukim* in *Megillat Esther*; 166 words in the *parshiyot* that deal with *Amalek* (*Shemot* 17:8–16 & *Devarim* 25:17–19); and 166 words in *Hallel Hagadol*, which is the psalm that deals with *Hashem* saving *Bnai Yisrael* from their enemies. He adds that perhaps this is an allusion to the *gemara* (*Megillah* 14a) which explains that the reason that we do not recite *Hallel* on *Purim* is because the *megillah* itself is *Hallel*. In this numerical connection, we see that the *pesukim* of the *megillah* and the words of *Hallel Hagadol* both number 166.

5. *Achashverosh* killed his wife *Vashti* because of the advice of his friend and advisor *Haman* (*Memuchan*) (*Esther* 1:16) and then killed *Haman* because of the advice of his wife *Esther* (*Esther* 7:10).

6. The *gematriya* of each phrase of *arur Haman* and *baruch Mordechai* is 502.

7. *Hashem*'s name never appears in the *Megillah*.

8. The *Gemara* (*Bava Batra* 91a) identifies *Haman*'s mother as *Amatlai bat Urvasi*. The *Gemara* notes that she had the same name (*Amatlai*) as *Avraham*'s mother.

9. They were reading from a "*Megillah bein haKetuvim*," a *megillah* that was written on a greater scroll that included other parts of *ketuvim*, such as *Eichah, Tehillim, Mishlei* etc. The *halacha* (*Shulchan Aruch Orach Chaim* 691:8) says that when reading for individuals (i.e. less than a *minyan* of men), one can fulfil his obligation by reading from a "*Megillah bein haKetuvim*." However, once you are reading for a *minyan*, you have a special obligation of "*pirsumei nisah*" – "publicizing the miracle of *Purim*," and that can only be done with a special scroll that contains only "*Megillat Esther*" – the Book of *Esther*." Therefore, in our case, they were reading from a "*Megillah bein haKetuvim*" thinking that there were only nine people present. Once they realized that there were 10 people present, they knew that they needed an actual *Megillat Esther* and they had to find one and begin reading again.

10. *Otzar Taamei Haminhagim* points out that the decree for the annihilation of the Jews in Persia was written by *Achashverosh's* scribes on the 13th of *Nisan* (*Megillat Esther* 3:13). At nightfall of the 13th of *Nisan*, just as the 14th of *Nisan* commences, is the ideal time for *Bedikat Chametz*. We place 10 pieces of *chametz* throughout the house before the search to symbolize the 10 sons of *Haman*.

11. The *gemara* (*Megillah* 14a) names seven prophetesses: *Sarah, Miriam, Devorah, Chana, Avigayil, Chuldah,* and *Esther*.

12. There are four possible answers of names of people mentioned in the *Torah* that also appear in *Megillat Esther* either as a person or place. They are: *Kush* (*Bereishit* 10:6 as a person and *Esther* 1:3 as a place); *Madai* (*Bereishit* 10:2 as a name and *Esther* 1:3 as a place); *Yair* (*Bamidbar* 32:41 and *Esther* 2:5 both names of people); and *Yehuda* (*Bereishit* 29:35 as a person and *Esther* 2:6 as a place).

13. The author of the famous *Chanukah* song, *Maoz Tzur,* was another *Mordechai,* who probably lived in the mid 13th century. The song consists of six stanzas, and the first letter of the first five stanzas spell the name *Mordechai*.

14. The *gemara* (*Megillah* 11a) lists *Achashveirosh, Achav, Shlomo* and *Nevuchadnetzar* as the four kings whose kingdoms consisted of the entire world.

15. According to the *gemara* (*Megillah* 15b), *Haman* had many more than the 10 sons who are listed as hung in the *megillah*. *Pirkei d'Rabi Eliezer* 50 says that he had 40 sons; 10 were scribes for the king and the other 30 were spread throughout the provinces. One opinion in the *gemara* says that he had 30 sons, another opinion says that he had 90 sons and yet another opinion says that he had 208 sons, equal to the *gematriya* of "*rov*" in the *pasuk* "*vayesaper lahem Haman et kevod ashro v'rov banav*" – "and *Haman* recounted to them the glory of his riches and the multitude of his sons" (*Esther* 5:11).

16. *Esther* hid this fact from *Achashveirosh* for five years. *Esther* is appointed queen in the 7th year of *Achashveirosh's* reign (*Esther* 2:16). She keeps her identity secret until she is forced to reveal it to foil *Haman's* plans in the 12th year of *Achashveirosh's* reign (*Esther* 3:7).

17. *Haman* was hung on the evening of the 2nd day of *Pesach* (16th of *Nisan*). His evil decree was announced on the 13th day of *Nisan* (*Esther* 3:12). The Jews fasted for three days and on the third day *Esther* hosted the banquet with the king. The following evening, the 16th of *Nisan*, at a second banquet, *Esther* revealed her identity and *Achashveirosh* ordered the immediate hanging of *Haman* (*Rashi Gemara Megillah* 15a, 16a).

18. The *beracha* recited following the reading of the *Megillah* ("*harav et riveinu*") is only recited in the presence of ten or more men (*Shulchan Aruch Orach Chaim* 692:1).

19. The words are "*kore'a*" with a "*kuf*" meaning to rend one's garment in grief, and the other is "*kore'a*" with a "*kaf*," meaning to bow down. *Mordechai* refused to bow down to *Haman* (*Esther* 3:2) and *Mordechai* tore his garments in grief after hearing *Haman*'s decree (*Esther* 4:1).

20. The *Mishnah Berurah* (490:2) states that it is praiseworthy to have something special during the meal on the second day of *Pesach* to commemorate *Esther*'s banquet which led to the hanging of *Haman* on that day.

21. Obviously a joke. The phrase "*v'noach meioiveihem*" is properly translated as "and they rested from their enemies." But for the sake of *Purim Torah*, the answer to "what was *Noach* doing in the *Megillah*?" is that *Haman* wanted to build his gallows for *Mordechai* and was intent on building one that could reach a height of "*chamishim amot*" – "fifty cubits" (*Esther* 5:14), but could not find that length of lumber. He then remembered that *Noach*'s ark was 50 *amot* wide and so he consulted with *Noach* and that is what *Noach* is doing in the *Megillah*.

22. He had two mothers-in-law. Play on words; "*chamah*" is Hebrew for mother-in-law. The first was *Shachachah*, as it says "*V'chamat hamelech Shachachah*." The second was *Boara*, as it says "*Vechamoto boara*." How could he have two mothers-in-law? Because it says, "*gam Vashti hamalka asta m'shtei nashim*;" Another play on words. *Vashti* was made from two women.

23. Because after making the king and *Haman* come to a special feast, she then said that the king and *Haman* should come back tomorrow.

24. More *Purim Torah* jokes: The answer is no; because then you would have two women requiring four candles, not two.

PESACH QUESTIONS

1. We do not begin saying "*v'tayn tal u'matar*" – the special *tefillah* asking for rain after *Sukkot,* until those travelling from *Yerushalayim* have enough time to reach home before the onset of the rainy season. If so, why do we not ask for rain to stop early enough before *Pesach,* to allow those travelers to reach *Yerushalayim* without the threat of rain?

2. What is the earliest connection between *Pesach* and "*tal*" – "dew"?

3. How many times is *Moshe Rabbeinu's* name mentioned in the *Haggadah shel Pesach*?

4. Which word in the *Haggadah* is neither Hebrew nor Aramaic?

5. How many times was the "*Korban Pesach*" – "the Paschal Sacrifice" offered in the entire time that the *Children of Israel* were in the desert?

6. How is it possible for someone to be *halachically* required to have three meals on the first day of *Pesach* when it is not *Shabbat*?

7. How is it possible for someone to be *halachically* required to drink five cups of wine on the night of the *Seder,* and also be required to make a "*borei pri hagafen*" on each of them?

8. I begin the *Seder.* I complete "*magid*" and then make the *beracha* "*hamotzi*" followed by the *beracha* of "*al achilat maror*" and only later make the *beracha* of "*al achilat matzah.*" I was at all times conscious of what I was doing and was in keeping with *halacha* at all times. What was the specific case?

9. Give another case where one would make the *beracha* of "*maror*" before the *beracha* of "*al achilat matza*"?

10. Is the word "*magid*" found anywhere in the *Torah*?

11. I have fulfilled a "*d'rabbanan*" – "Rabbinic commandment" when I was not yet commanded to fulfill a "*d'oraita*" – "Torah commandment." And as a result, I can no longer fulfill the *Torah* commandment when I am finally commanded to fulfill it. How is this possible?

12. It's "*Isru Chag*" – "the day after *Pesach*" in Israel. Israeli *Reuven* says to Canadian *Shimon* "you had it…we read it." What was he talking about?

13. Which *Mitzvah* requires 30 participants at the same time?

14. At the *seder,* I am eaten. In *Tanach,* I am a colourful material. What am I, and what is the connection between the two references?

15. According to the *Targum Yonatan,* where was the first *korban pesach* sacrificed?

16. Name at least five differences between the *kiddush* of the *seder* and *kiddush* on any other *Shabbat* or *Yom Tov.*

17. This riddle is a *chutz laaretz* riddle only. When the first day of *Pesach* falls on a Sunday, the first day of *Chol Hamoed* is 1st, 2nd, and 3rd; the second

day of *Chol Hamoed* is 2nd, 3rd, and 4th; the third day of *Chol Hamoed* is 3rd, 4th and 5th; and the fourth day of *Chol Hamoed* is 4th, 5th and 6th. Explain.

18. On *Erev Pesach*, firstborns observe the Fast of the Firstborns. If, however, a firstborn is present at a *"siyum"* of a portion of *Torah*, he is permitted to participate in the feast that follows the *"siyum."* Where in the letters of the word *"siyum"* is there a hint that even those who did not learn the portion can participate fully with the one who did?

19. I am Jewish, male and have drunk the proper *"shiur"* – "quantity" of wine at the *seder* while reclining, and nonetheless I am still not *"yotzei"* – "fulfilled my obligation." Why?

20. In one place in *Tanach*, we are commanded not to eat something raw, and in the same wording in another place in *Tanach*, we are commanded not to eat at all. Find these two places in *Tanach* and determine the connection between the two?

PESACH ANSWERS

1. *Rav Moshe Carlebach* of *Ohr Sameach* offers four answers:
    1. The *mitzvah* of "*hachnasat orchim*" – "welcoming guests into your home" includes the element of "*leviyah*" – "escorting the visitor from one's home" at the conclusion of the visit, but does not include meeting him before he arrives.
    2. Visitors to *Yerushalayim* before the rainy season (i.e., *Sukkot*) will not have prepared by bringing rain gear with them, whereas those coming during the rainy season (i.e., *Pesach*) would be adequately prepared.
    3. Since rain is not needed before the 7th of *Marcheshvan*, we can put individual needs before national needs; however, Israel still needs rain until *Pesach*, and therefore we cannot put our personal comfort before national welfare.
    4. Leaving Israel after the *Chag* of *Sukkot* is a sad event and we do not wish to compound the sadness by adding rain, whereas coming up to *Yerushalayim* for the *Chag* of *Pesach* is itself a joyous event and even the onset of rain showers will not deter those who are coming.
2. *Yitzchak* gave the *berachot* to *Yaakov* on *Pesach* (*Rashi Bereshit* 27:9). The *berachot* began with the words "*v'yiten lecha ha'Elokim mital hashamayim*" – "and *Hashem* should give you from the dew of the heavens" (*Bereishit* 27:28). This connects "*tal*" to *Pesach*.
3. *Moshe's* name appears once in the *Haggadah*, in the phrase "*Vayaaminu baHashem u'veMoshe avdoh.*"
4. The word "*afikoman*" is based on the Greek word "*epikomon*" meaning "that which comes after" or "dessert."
5. Only twice. The first year, it was brought in *Mitzrayim*. In the second year, when *Bnai Yisrael* were already in the desert, it was brought once on *Pesach* (*Bamidbar* 9:1; see *Rashi* quoting a *Mechilta*) and once on *Pesach Sheni*. Following the second year, because there were numbers of *Israelites* who were uncircumcised, the *Pesach* sacrifice could not be brought. It was resumed once they entered Israel.
6. If one forgets to eat the *afikoman* and has already "*benched*" – "recited Grace after Meals" but has not yet drunk the third cup of wine, he must wash again, eat the *afikoman* and *bench* a second time. He therefore eats three meals on the first day of *Pesach* when it is not a *Shabbat*. (*Orach Chaim Mishnah Berurah* 477:2).
7. If one forgot to make *havdalah* and has already completed the *Seder*, he drinks a fifth cup and makes a "*borei pri hagafen*" on it, even though this will occur following the eating of the *afikoman* (*Orach Chaim Mishnah Berurah* 473:1:5).

8. If a person only had one *"kezayit"* of *matzah shemurah*, he should save it for the *afikoman* and only then make the *beracha* of *"al achilat matzah"* (*Orach Chaim Mishnah Berurah* 482:3). This therefore means that he would be reciting the *beracha* of *maror* before the *beracha* of *al achilat matzah*.

9. If a person only had *"maror"* as the vegetable at the *Seder*, one would also have to use that for *"karpas,"* and would therefore make two *berachot* on the *"karpas"*; namely *"boray pri ha'adama"* and *"al achilat maror"* and then when reaching the *mitzvah* of *maror*, one would dip it into the *charoset* and eat it without making a specific *beracha* (*Shulchan Aruch Orach Chaim* 475:2).

10. The word *"magid"* is found only once in the entire *Torah* and ironically, it is spoken by *Paroh* when he tells *Yosef* that he retold his dreams to his advisors and they were not able to *"magid"* – "explain the meaning of the dreams." (*Bereishit* 41:24).

11. In the time of the *Beit Hamikdash,* a minor who became an adult between *Pesach* and *Pesach Sheni*, was required to eat the *korban pesach* on *Pesach Sheni*. However, if he was included in the *Pesach* offering on *Pesach*, thereby fulfilling the commandment *rabbinically*, he is exempt from bringing or eating from the sacrifice on *Pesach Sheni*, even though he now has a *Torah* mandated requirement to fulfill the commandment.

12. On that year, the 7th day marked the last day of *Pesach* in Israel and it occurred on a Wednesday. Therefore *"isru chag"* occurred on a Thursday. Israeli *Reuven* says to Canadian *Shimon* "you had it…we read it." "You had it" refers to *Shimon*, a *Jew* of *"chutz laaretz"* who had observed the 8th day of *Pesach*. "We read it" refers to *Reuven*, a *Jew* of *Israel* who read the Thursday *Torah* reading of *Parshat Shemini* which means "the eighth day."

13. The *Mishnah* in *Pesachim* says that the *korban pesach* should be slaughtered with three groups of people, based on the *pasuk "khal adat Yisrael"* – "the congregation of the assembly of *Israel"* (*Shemot* 12:6). *Rashi* comments on the *gemara* (*Gemara Pesachim* 64b), which says that 30 people participate in each *korban pesach*, that each of the three descriptions, namely; congregation; assembly; Israel; indicate a group of ten for a total of 30.

14. The answer is *karpas*. At the *Seder*, *karpas* is eaten as the opening vegetable dish and is usually celery or potato. In *Megillat Esther*, *karpas* is a colourful material (*Esther* 1:6). *Rashi* (*Bereishit* 37:3) in describing the *"ketonet passim"* – "coat of many colors" refers to the *"karpas"* of the *Megillah* and it was this coat that resulted in the jealousy between *Yosef* and his brothers that eventually led to the exile in *Mitzrayim* and ultimately to the holiday of *Pesach*.

15. The *pasuk* says (*Shemot* 19:4), "…and I have carried you on wings of eagles and have brought you to me." Based on the seemingly superfluous words "and have brought you to me," the *Targum Yonatan* explains that on the night of the *Exodus*, *Hashem* miraculously transported *Bnai Yisrael* from

Ramses to *Har Hamoriah* (the future site of the *Beit Hamikdash*) where they brought the *Korban Pesach* and were then quickly returned to *Ramses* to continue their journey towards *Har Sinai*.

16. Here are some differences between the *kiddush* at the *Seder* and the *kiddush* recited on other *Yamim Tovim* or on *Shabbat*:

    1. *Kiddush* at the *seder* must be after nightfall, whereas *kiddush* on any other *Shabbat* and most *Yamim Tovim* can be before nightfall.

    2. At the *seder*, everyone has to drink their own wine, whereas one can fulfill their obligation for *kiddush* on any other *Shabbat* or *Yom Tov*, if wine is drunk by the one saying the *beracha*.

    3. At the *seder*, one has to lean while drinking, whereas one can drink the wine of *kiddush* on any other *Shabbat* or *Yom Tov* either leaning or sitting.

    4. *Kiddush* at the *seder* must be on wine whereas one can make *kiddush* on any other *Shabbat* or *Yom Tov* over bread.

    5. *Kiddush* on any other *Shabbat* or *Yom Tov* is immediately followed by washing over bread, but at the *seder* there is much time and a number of steps in the order of the *seder* between the actual *kiddush* and the *hamotzi*.

    6. And while this is not a universal difference, it is worth including; when one has the *minhag* of wearing a *kittel* at the *seder*, this would be the only time that one would make *kiddush* with a *kittel*.

17. When the first day of *Pesach* is Sunday, the first day of *Chol Hamoed* is the 1st day of *Chol Hamoed*, the 2nd day of the *Omer* and the 3rd day of the week; the second day of *Chol Hamoed* is the 2nd day of *Chol Hamoed*, the 3rd day of the *Omer* and the 4th day of the week; …etc.

18. The *Rema* (*Shulchan Aruch Yoreh Deah* 246:26) writes that there is a *mitzvah* to make a "*Seudah*" – "festive meal" upon the completion of a section of *Torah*, and this meal is considered a *seudat mitzvah*. The *Vilna Gaon* says that the revealed portion of letters of the word "*siyum*" are equal in numerical value to the hidden portion of the letters of the word "*siyum*." For example, the first letter is "*samech*." The word "*samech*" is spelled *samech, mem, kaf*. The revealed portion, i.e., the letter itself, has a value of 60. The hidden portion, i.e., the *mem* and the *kaf*, have a value of $40 + 20 = 60$. Each of the other letters of the word "*siyum*" have the same property. *Yud* is 10 and the hidden portion of *yud*, i.e., *vav* and *daled* are equal to $6 + 4 = 10$. The other two letters of *vav* and *mem* have the same property. Therefore, says the *Vilna Gaon*, at a "*siyum*," two kinds of participants have equal status – the active partners who have learned the material, and the inactive or hidden partners who only attend the celebration; and both can enjoy the meat and wine together.

19. There are two possible answers as to why I have not fulfilled my obligation even though I drank four cups on the Seder night; namely:

    1. I drank the correct "*shiur*" – "liquid amount" of wine, but instead of drinking it in four cups at various points in the *Seder*, I drank it from one large "*kos*" – "cup of wine" (*Mishnah Berurah* 472:25).

    2. I drank four separate cups of wine but I drank them in a row, without reciting the relevant parts of the *Haggadah* in between each cup (*Shulchan Aruch Orach Chaim* 472:8).

20. The first instance is a law regarding the "*Korban Pesach*": "*al tochlu mimenu na*" – "do not eat it raw" (*Shemot* 12:9). The second time is when *Esther* commands the Jews of *Shushan* to fast for three days and nights, with exactly the same wording "*al tochlu v'al tishtu*" – "do not eat or drink" (*Megillat Esther* 4:16). The connection is that both of these events were on *Pesach*; the same day of the calendar as the three day fast of *Esther* was from *Nisan* 14–16, including the *seder* night.

SHAVUOT QUESTIONS

1. What is the connection of *Megillat Rut* to *Shavuot*?
2. How long did *David Hamelech* live?
3. Which enemy of Israel mentioned in the *Torah* foresaw the birth of *David Hamelech*?
4. Two daily prayers composed by *David Hamelech* are not found in *Tehillim*, but are found in another *sefer* of *Tanach*. What are the prayers and where are they found?
5. Who was *Yoav ben Tzruya*, how was he related to *David Hamelech* and what was his father's name? (Be careful! This might be another "Grant's tomb" kind of question!)
6. What were *David*'s brothers' names? What were *David*'s sisters' names?
7. Who wrote *Tehillim*?
8. One shot removed a first cousin twice removed. Explain?
9. How did *Avraham Avinu*'s *tefillot* save *David Hamelech*?
10. What part of this famous musician's instrument had its roots on *Har HaMoriah*?
11. In the early days of clocks, you would need to do this to keep your clock going. Take the homograph of this action and identify the famous owner of this clock?
12. What is "*shatnez gatz*"?
13. *Hashamayim, Noach, Bnai Noach, Shem, Terach, Yishmael, Yitzchak, Esav, Yaakov, Aharon* and *Peretz*. What is common to all of the above?
14. This chapter in *Tanach* begins exactly as it ends. Where is it? Explain?
15. What was *Rut*'s name before she converted and why is *Rut* the traditional name given to female converts?
16. Barley on *Pesach* and barley on *Shavuot*? Explain?
17. How many ways is the number seven connected to *Shavuot*? Where else in the *Torah* do we find the number seven explicitly mentioned?
18. In the same section of the *Torah* dealing with the "*moadim*" – "holidays," and juxtaposed to the *Omer* and *Shavuot*, we find one sentence (*Vayikra* 23:22) that discusses the "*matnat aniyim*" – "the gifts given to the poor"? What is the connection? Connect this to "*Megillat Rut*"?
19. What four *halachot* do we learn from *Megillat Rut*?
20. Why do we eat dairy products on *Shavuot*?

SHAVUOT ANSWERS

1. There is no specific reference in *Megillat Rut* to the holiday of *Shavuot*. But *Chazal* have offered the following connections:
    1. *Shavuot* is the birthday and *yahrtzeit* of *David Hamelech* (*Midrash Rabbah Rut* 3:2) and at the end of *Megillat Rut* we are introduced to *David*, the great-grandson of *Rut*.
    2. The story of *Rut* takes place at the barley harvest time (*Rut* 1:22) and on *Shavuot* we read about the harvest. As well, *Rut*'s coming to Israel took place around the time of *Shavuot*, and her acceptance into the Jewish faith is reminiscent of the acceptance of the Jewish people of *Hashem's Torah*.
    3. To teach how great *Torah* is, that a *non-Jew, Rut*, left her society to become a *Jewess* and follow the *mitzvot* and to eventually become the "mother" of *malchut Beit David* and ultimately the *Mashiach*.
    4. To learn to treat converts with respect like *Boaz* did to *Rut*.
    5. To inspire us to give "presents" to the poor as the *Torah* requires us to do. The manner in which the poor were treated in the harvest season with sympathy and sensitivity should be an inspiration to all. A further connection from this instruction regarding sharing our wealth with the poor is that the *gemara* teaches us that before accepting a convert, the convert should be asked whether they are willing to accept the *mitzvot* of the *Torah* and one of the *mitzvot* specified is that of giving *tzedakah* and sharing the gleanings and corners of the agricultural fields with the less fortunate (*Gemara Yevamot* 47a). This concept has strong connections to *Rut*, who was a convert and who was subsisting off the grain she gathered in the field of *Boaz*.
2. *David Hamelech* lived for 70 years. (*Rashi Bereishit* 47:29). The *Zohar* (*Vayishlach* 168) attributes *David Hamelech*'s 70 years to two different calculations. On the one hand, the *Zohar* cites perhaps the most popular calculation by stating that *Adam Harishon* was originally supposed to live for 1000 years, but "donated" 70 years of his life to *David Hamelech*. But then the *Zohar* offers another calculation. He says that *Avraham* was supposed to live 180 years but had his life shortened by five years. *Yaakov* should have lived as long as *Avraham* but his life was shortened by 28 years to 147 years. And *Yosef* should have lived to 147 like his father *Yaakov* but had his life shortened by 37 years and lived 110 years. Take the total of 5 + 28 + 37 = 70. Hence *David Hamelech*'s years were donated by *Avraham, Yaakov* and *Yosef*. The *Chida* (*Yosef Tehillos* 42:9) says that if the *Zohar* is correct in both calculations, then *David Hamelech* should have lived 140 years. The *Chida* responds and quotes a *pasuk*: "by day, may *Hashem* grant

His faithful care, so that at night a song to Him may be with me" (*Tehillim* 42:9). The *gemara* (*Sukkah* 26b) says that *David Hamelech* was basically up all night, never sleeping more than "60 breaths." The *Chida* therefore says that *David Hamelech* lived for a total of 140 years; 70 years by day and 70 years by night.

3. Two possible answers. First, the *Zohar* says that *Balak*, the king of *Moav*, foresaw that one day, one of his descendants would rise up and defeat *Moav*. This is derived from the wording "*ki atzum hu mimeni*" – "for he is stronger than me" (*Bamidbar* 22:6). The use of the singular "*hu*" indicates one person, *David*, and the word "*mimeni*" may also indicate "from me," i.e., one of my offspring. The *Shlah* points out that the ultimate might of the Jewish people is *Mashiach*. And since *Mashiach* is a descendant of *David Hamelech* and therefore a descendant of *Rut*, he also is a descendant of *Balak*. And therefore, says the *Shlah*, *Balak* was saying that the might of the Jewish people comes "*mimeni*" – "from me." The second answer is *Bilaam*, who says "*v'yarom may'Agag malko, v'tinasay malchuto*" – "and his king, will be greater than *Agag* and his kingdom will be raised up." *Rashi* explains that "his king" refers to *Shaul* and "his kingdom" refers to *David* and *Shlomo* (*Rashi Bamidbar* 24:7).

4. *Hodu L'Hashem Kiru Bishmo* (*Divrei Hayamim* 1:16:8) and *Vayevarech David* (*Divrei Hayamim* 1:29:10) recited every day, are found in *Sefer Divrei Hayamim* and are part of *pesukei d'zimra*:

    1. *Hodu L'Hashem* – The first section of *Hodu* until "*V'halel la'Hashem*" (*Divrei Hayamim* 1:16:36) was written by *David HaMelech* to be recited by the *leviim* upon the *aron's* return to *Ir David*. Subsequently, the first half of these *pesukim* were sung every morning, during the morning "*korban tamid*" – "daily morning offering," whereas the second half were sung along with the "*korban tamid bein ha'arba'im*" – "daily afternoon offering."

    2. The four verses of *Vayevarech David* were composed by *David* at one of the most dramatic moments of his life, when he was denied the right to build the *Beit Hamikdash*, but was allowed to set aside resources for its construction by his son *Shlomo*.

5. *Yoav ben Tzruya* was the commander of *David's* armies and he was *David's* nephew, by way of *Tzruya*, *David's* sister (*Divrei Hayamim* 1:2:16). *Avshai*, *Yoav*, and *Asa-El* were the three sons of *Tzruya*. Their father is not identified by name in *Tanach*; *David's* three nephews are always connected by name to their mother *Tzruya*.

6. *David* had seven brothers; *Eliav, Avinadav, Shim'a, Netanel, Raddai, Otzem* and *Elihu* (*Divrei Hayamim* 1:2:13–15 & 27:18). *David* had two sisters; *Tzruya* and *Avigayil* (*Divrei Hayamim* 1:2:16).

7. Trick question: Although the bulk of *Tehillim* is attributed to *David Hamelech*, parts of *Tehillim* were written by *Adam, Malki Tzedek, Avraham, Moshe, Shlomo, Assaf* and the three sons of *Korach*, a total of ten people who collaborated to write the *sefer* of *Tehillim* (*Shir Hashirim Rabbah* 4:3).

8. *Rut* and *Orpah* were sisters; daughters of *Eglon*, king of *Moav* (*Shoftim* 3:19; *Gemara Nazir* 23b). *Golyat* was *Orpah*'s son. *David* was *Rut*'s great-grandson, making *David Hamelech* and *Golyat* first cousins twice removed. *David* took five smooth stones from the brook and only shot one of them to kill *Golyat* (*Shmuel* 1:17:40).

9. When *Avraham Avinu* prayed that *Lot* be delivered from the destruction of *Sedom*, he thereby saved all of *Lot*'s future offspring, including *David* who came from *Moav*, the son of *Lot*.

10. The ten strings of *David*'s harp were made from sinews that came from the ram at the *Akeida* (*Meam Loez Bereishit* 22:18).

11. Homographs are words that are spelled the same but have different meanings. Originally, one would "wind" the clock to keep it going. But this famous alarm clock worked with a homograph of "wind." A harp was suspended over *David*'s bed. At midnight, a north "wind" would blow through the strings of the harp and awaken *David* to learn *Torah* (*Eichah Rabbati* 2:27).

12. *Shavuot* is the holiday of "*matan Torah*"–the giving of the *Torah*." Some of the letters in a *Sefer Torah* are written with a stylized crown on top of the letter. The letters are identified by the acronym "*SHATNEZ GATZ.*" The letters are *shin, ayin, tet, nun, zayin, gimel, tzadi*.

13. All these words/names follow either "*eileh toldot*" or "*v'eileh toldot*" – "these are the generations of." Other than *Aharon* (from *Bamidbar*) and *Peretz* (from *Rut*), all are in *Bereishit*.

14. Chapter 118 in *Tehillim* begins with the *pasuk,* "*hodu l'Hashem ki tov, ki l'olam chasdo*" and it ends with exactly the same *pasuk*.

15. *Gilit.* (*Zohar Chadash, Midrash Rut* 182). Once she married *Machlon*, she changed her name to *Rut. Rut* is 606 in numerical value, indicating that by becoming *Rut,* she was adding 606 *mitzvot* to the seven that she already had, the seven *mitzvot* of "*Bnai Noach*" for a total of 613.

16. Barley on *Pesach* is connected to the *Omer* offering brought on the second day of *Pesach. Barley* on *Shavuot* is connected to *Megillat Rut* (*Rut* 1:22) as it is written "*b'techilat ketzir se'orim*" – "at the beginning of the barley harvest."

17. There are two ways that the number 7 is connected to *Shavuot*:
    1. The holiday of *Shavuot* is at the end of counting seven complete weeks from the second day of *Pesach* (*Vayikra* 23:15).

2. When bringing the *"shtei halechem"* – "the two loaves of bread offered on *Shavuot*," seven lambs, each one year old, were offered as well (*Vayikra* 23:18).

There are numerous places in the *Torah* where the number seven is explicitly referenced. Some of those (in no particular order) are the following:

1. Seven days of the week (*Bereishit* 2:2).
2. Concerning the rules of an *Eved Ivri* who does not want to go free in the seventh year (*Shemot* 21:5).
3. *Yaakov* worked for *Lavan* on two occasions for seven years each in order to marry *Rachel* and *Leah* (*Bereishit* 29:27).
4. The sons of *Yaakov* sat *shiva* for seven days (*Bereishit* 50:10)
5. *Noach* was commanded to bring seven male and seven female of each species of kosher animal and bird into the ark during the time of the flood and *Hashem* gave him seven days notice that the flood would begin (*Bereishit* 7:2–4).
6. The holiday of *Pesach* is seven days (*Shemot* 23:15).
7. The holiday of *Sukkot* is seven days (*Vayikra* 23:34).
8. When a woman gives birth to a male, she is *tamei* for seven days (*Vayikra* 12:1).
9. We are commanded to count the *Omer* for seven complete weeks (*Vayikra* 23:15).
10. Every seventh year, is an agricultural sabbatical year called *shemitah* (*Vayikra* 25:4).
11. *Rosh Hashanah* occurs on the first day of the seventh month (*Vayikra* 23:24).
12. *Yom Kippur* occurs on the tenth day of the seventh month (*Vayikra* 23:27).
13. The gold *menorah* in the *mishkan* had seven branches (*Shemot* 25:37).
14. The *yovel* or jubilee year occurred every 50 years after counting seven *shemitah* cycles (*Vayikra* 25:8).
15. *Yitro* had seven daughters (*Shemot* 2:16).
16. The seven days of consecrating the *mishkan* (*Vayikra* 8:33).
17. *Paroh's* dreams of seven cows and seven sheaves (*Bereishit* 41:2).
18. When discovering a *"tzara'at"* – "leprosy" contamination, one has to be quarantined for a seven day period (*Vayikra* 13:4).
19. *Noah* sent the dove and raven for periods of seven days (*Bereishit* 8:10).
20. There are seven nations that must be defeated when settling *Eretz Yisrael* (*Devarim* 7:1). There are many more examples.

18. This *pasuk* (*Vayikra* 23:22) deals with the *mitzvah* of leaving the corners of your agricultural land and the produce that drops from the harvesting machinery to the poor and the stranger. It is placed in the middle of the laws concerning the *"moadim"* – "holidays" to teach us that while we are

super involved in the festive celebration of our *chagim*, we should never forget to share our good fortune with those less fortunate.

19. We deduce four *halachot* from *Megillat Rut*; namely:

    1. The laws of the convert and specifically the *halacha* of *"amoni, v'lo amonit"* – "that while a male member of the people of *Amon* is not permitted to enter into the Jewish nation (*Devarim* 23:4); a female, like *Rut*, may in fact enter the Jewish nation" (*Gemara Ketubot* 7b).

    2. The law of *"kinyan sudar"* – "acquisition through the transfer of an article of value." This concept has its origin in *Rut* 4:7, where *Boaz* removed his shoe and transferred it to the *"goel"* – "redeemer" as a contractual acquisition.

    3. When *Boaz* greeted his workers by saying *"Hashem imachem"* (*Rut* 2:4), the *gemara* (*Berachot* 54a) learns that people should greet each other with the name of *Hashem*.

    4. When *Boaz* assembled 10 elders to be present at his marriage to *Rut*, the *gemara* (*Ketubot* 7b) deduces that the *sheva berachot* at a wedding need a *minyan* of men.

20. These are some of the many reasons given for the custom of eating dairy products on *Shavuot*; namely:

    1. Until receipt of the *Torah*, there was no requirement to keep *kosher*. After the revelation at *Har Sinai* on *Shavuot*, they had to slaughter *kosher* and had to make all their utensils *kosher*. And since *Matan Torah* was on *Shabbat*, they could not do any *kashering* or cooking. And so the simplest alternative was to eat dairy (*Mishnah Berurah* 494:12).

    2. *Torah* is compared to milk from the *pasuk* *"dvash v'chalav tachat leshonecha"* – "Like honey and milk, *Torah* is beneath your tongue" (*Shir Hashirim* 4:11). Just as a baby at birth subsists on a diet of its mother's milk, so too *Bnai Yisrael* were considered as newborns after receiving the *Torah* and therefore had a dairy diet.

    3. *Rabbi Isaac Tyrnau*, in his *Sefer HaMinhagim*, quotes the *pasuk* from the *parshah* dealing with *Shavuot*, *"chadasha l'Hashem b'shavuoteichem"* (*Bamidbar* 28:26), and points out that the first letters of this phrase spell *"chalav"* – "milk."

    4. *Rema* (*Shulchan Aruch Orach Chaim* 494:3) explains that as there were *"shtei halechem"* – "two loaves offered in the *Beit Hamikdash* on *Shavuot*," we therefore eat two loaves of bread at the meal, and since it is not permitted to use the same loaf of bread for both a dairy and meat meal, it is customary to eat two meals; one dairy, which is based on the reasons presented for eating dairy on *Shavuot*, and one meat, to fulfill the concept of *simcha* on *Yom Tov*, as we know that there is no *simcha* without meat.

5. *Magen Avraham* (*Shulchan Aruch Orach Chaim* 494:6) offers another reason, as follows: the *Zohar* compares the seven weeks between *Pesach* and *Shavuot* to the "*shivat neki'im*" – "seven clean days" that a woman counts before going to the *mikvah*. The level of purity reached by women after visiting the *mikvah*, is similar to the purity reached by *Bnai Yisrael* over the 50 days between the *exodus* from *Mitzrayim* and their arrival at *Har Sinai* for *Shavuot*. Milk or dairy is viewed as a pure food, for the first thing fed to babies for nourishment is the mother's milk and while nursing, women generally do not menstruate. And therefore we eat dairy on *Shavuot*.

6. One of the names for *Har Sinai* is *Har Gavnunim* (*Tehillim* 68:16), which is translated as peaks or heights. But the word *gavnunim* is similar sounding to the word for cheese, *gevina,* and hence we eat dairy on *Shavuot*.

HALACHOT, CUSTOMS & BLESSINGS

HALACHOT, CUSTOMS & BLESSINGS QUESTIONS

1. You have to be able "to see the difference" in order to make this *beracha*, which is recited once per week (on one occasion per year, it could be recited twice in a week). What is the *beracha* and what is the *halacha*?

2. This is a *beracha* made where the "sun does not shine," where we need monthly renewal, and where one of Vincent Van Gogh's famous paintings would definitely be the time to fulfill the *mitzvah*. What is the *beracha* and what is the *mitzvah*?

3. Where in this daily *tefillah* do you have three consecutive two letter words, the three words all having different meanings and each having the same two letters?

4. How is it possible for one fruit to be the source of nine *berachot*, eight of them unique? What is the fruit and what are the *berachot*?

5. One minute you make a certain *beracha* over a certain item. A minute later, you make a completely different *beracha* over exactly the same item, even though the item has undergone no change whatsoever. There is no grain in the item. Explain?

6. I am an adult. It is one hour before my birthday and I have a *mitzvah* that I am required to perform. Sixty one minutes later, I am no longer obligated to perform that *mitzvah*. Nothing has changed other than my age. How old am I turning and what is the *mitzvah* that I am now not obligated to perform?

7. Can a *Mitzvah D'rabbanan* (a *Rabbinical* Law) interrupt a *Mitzvah D'oraita* (a *Biblical* Law)?

8. I am having two types of food. If I have them one day, then I make the two *berachot* in a certain order. If I have them on another day, I reverse the order. Why?

9. If one is prepared to eat grapes (*beracha haetz* and one of the *shivat haminim*) and bananas (*beracha ha'adama*), which *beracha* is recited first?

10. If one is prepared to eat an apple and a date, over which fruit does one make the *haetz*?

11. If one is prepared to eat a date and a fig, over which fruit does one make the initial *beracha*?

12. I make a "*borei pri hagafen*" and then a "*shehakol*" and do not drink after either *beracha*. Where am I?

13. I state "*asher kidshanu*" and then do not say "*b'mitzvotav*." What *beracha* might I be reciting?

14. In a similar vein, where do we have two *berachot*, each containing the words "*asher kidshanu b'mitzvotav*" that are recited over the same *mitzvah*?

15. I forgot to say *retzei* in the *Shabbat benching*, do I have to repeat the *benching*?
16. Is it ever possible for a first born grandson of a *kohen* to have a *pidyon haben*?
17. Is it ever possible for a first born grandson of a *levi* to have a *pidyon haben*?
18. At what point are we told to prepare for the *chupah* at our child's wedding?
19. What actions can I do to alter my *"mazal"* – "fortune or destiny"?
20. Normally *halacha* requires that we recite a *beracha* before performing a *mitzvah*. This is called, in *halachic* terms, *"over l'asiatan."* The reason given is that one should not enjoy something before thanking *Hashem* for it. Therefore before we eat anything, we make a *beracha*. Before blowing the *shofar*, we make a *beracha*. On which *mitzvot* do we make the *beracha* after its performance?
21. I have ten Jewish males over the age of *bar mitzvah* in one place and yet cannot *daven* with a *minyan*?
22. Which divorced woman can never get married again?
23. I came to *shul* late and I left early. It had nothing to do with the *kiddush* club! In fact I was fulfilling an important *halacha*. Explain?
24. From which *pasuk* do we learn that all *devarim shebikdushah* (*kaddish, kedushah, barchu, Kriat haTorah, birkat kohanim*) require a *minyan*?
25. How is it possible over the course of nine weeks to alternately say and not say *tzidkatcha tzedek* from week to week? (i.e., week #1, not say; week #2, say; week #3, not say; etc.)
26. If *"boker"* – "morning," *"erev"* – "evening," and *"layla"* – "night" are all singular, why is *"tzaharayim"* – "noon" in the plural?
27. Why do we say *tzidkatcha tzedek* in the *tefillah* of *Shabbat Mincha*?
28. Why is the act of preparing one for burial called *"chesed shel emet,"* and where is there a hint in the word *"emet"* to the three essential components of a Jewish burial?
29. I am presented with the opportunity to do two *mitzvot* at precisely the same moment; they are:
    1. Visiting the sick.
    2. Attending to someone who just passed away.
    Which should I do first?
30. How many *berachot* do we say only once a year in *chutz la'aretz*? In addition to these, how many more do we say only once a year in *Eretz Yisrael*?
31. Which *beracha* is recited exactly 10 times per year, whether in *chutz laaretz* or in Israel?
32. In the *tefillah*, *"yoshev b'seiter elyon"* we repeat the last *pasuk*, even though in the original version (*Tehillim* 91) the last *pasuk* appears only once. Why do we repeat it?

33. There are eight instances every week, once a day and twice on *Shabbat*, when we add a very well known *pasuk* to our *tefillot*, only because of past persecution of the Jewish people. What are those eight instances?

34. From which *kosher* animal may we derive no material benefit today; i.e., we have to care for the animal, but may not sell it, drink its milk, use its wool etc.?

35. We repeat sentences in "*tefillah*" – "prayer" from time to time, such as "*kol haneshama tehallel…*"; "*orech yamim asbi'ayhu…*" What is the greatest number of consecutive sentences in *tefillah* that are recited once and then immediately repeated once?

36. When do we repeat an entire chapter of *tanach* seven times in succession?

37. What is the greatest number of consecutive sentences that are repeated thrice in *tefillah*?

38. Where in *halacha* do we have the concept that women's clothes are more expensive than women's shoes?

39. There are four male babies born within one hour of each other in the same time zone. All are born Jewish, all are healthy, and yet they have their *brit milahs* on four consecutive days. Why?

40. Similar case as above, except that we are now dealing with six babies, born in good health, within one hour of each other, in the same time zone. Their *brit milahs* now take place on six consecutive days. Explain?

41. I am a Jewish, healthy, first born male and was born uncircumcised to a Jewish father and mother with all my organs intact. Yet, I am exempt from ever requiring circumcision. Why?

42. Healthy twin boys are born to a Jewish father and Jewish mother. The first-born has his *brit milah* after his younger brother. Why?

43. Twin boys are born to a Jewish father and Jewish mother. Yet the younger boy becomes *Bar Mitzvah* before his older brother. Why?

44. When is a *mitzvah* delayed for more than 24 hours, because by performing that *mitzvah* one would enter into a state of "*simcha*" – "joy"?

45. What are the two events that a *kohen* and a *yisrael* sometimes see, but an adult *levi* never sees?

46. The *Baal Haturim* notes that there is a hint in the "*Birkat Kohanim*" – "Priestly Blessings" to the fact that one should greet everyone pleasantly and this applies to all humanity, even a *non-Jew*. From where does the *Baal Haturim* deduce this lesson?

47. How is it possible for one person to be called up for three consecutive *aliyot* on the same day?

48. Besides *Yerushalayim*, which modern day *Israeli* city is mentioned in the daily *davening*?

49. How is it possible that I must say *Hamotzi* twice and *birkat hamazon* once during the course of one meal, although I have never left the table and never took my mind off the delicious food?

50. Where was the *"birkat haminim,"* the 19th *beracha* of the *Shemoneh Esrei,* composed?

51. I recite the *beracha* "shehakol," then drink a can of soda, and this act triggers an additional 20 *berachot*? Why?

52. When would one not answer *"baruch (Elokeinu) she'achalnu mishelo u'vetuvo chayinu"* upon hearing the *zimun* leader pronounce *"...nevarech (Elokeinu) she'achalnu mishelo"*?

53. He is permitted to eat, but he must eat food that belongs to someone else; he may not eat food that he owns. What is the case?

54. I am not fasting. I am not a vegetarian or vegan. I am permitted to eat. But I am only permitted to eat *pareve*. What is the case?

55. I am saying *birkat hamazon* for one of the *Shabbat* meals. Yet, I am not required to add the special *Shabbat* addition of "*retzei.*" Why not?

56. I am about to say *birkat hamazon*. I am the only male over *bar mitzvah* at the table and therefore there is no *"zimun."* Yet I am required to *bench* "al hakos" – "with a full cup of wine." Why?

57. Name a *tefillah* which was originally to be recited only by minor children, but which today is recited by children and adults alike?

58. Which *tefillot* were originally placed in the *siddur* exclusively for latecomers but were eventually adopted by all?

59. Usually *Ashkenazim* follow the ruling of *Ashkenazi poskim* such as the *Ramah,* while *Sephardim* follow *Sephardi poskim* like *Rav Yosef Karo,* the *mechaber.* Where do we find a case in *halacha* where *Ashkenazim* follow the ruling of the *Rambam,* who was a *Sephardi,* and *Sephardim* follow the ruling of *Tosefot,* who were *Ashkenazim*?

60. At which *"maariv l'chol"* – "weekday evening prayer" is it customary to wear a *tallit*?

61. During which *"shacharit l'chol"* – "weekday morning prayer" do we not wear a *tallit*?

62. When do we not say *ashrei* at *mincha*?

63. You should not look for me, but once you see me, you are required to make a *beracha*. What am I?

64. Every *Shabbat* eve, we welcome *"malachim"* – "angels" into our home when we sing *"Shalom Aleichem."* Every day of the year, we directly speak to *"malachim"* with a certain sentence in *davening*. Most days, we say this sentence three times; some days four times and once a year five times. What is the sentence?

65. How is it possible to say "*shehakol*" as the "*beracha rishona*" when eating a certain food and yet be required to make an "*al haetz*" as the "*beracha achrona*"?

66. The word "*nu*" is sometimes used in a colloquial way, with a specific intonation, in order to prod someone to get the job done. But in our liturgy, we say seven consecutive words all ending in the suffix "*nu*" (*nun, vav*). Where is this?

67. Where in *davening* do we find 15 consecutive words beginning with the letter "*vav*"?

68. Where in *davening* do we find 24 consecutive words ending with the letter "*chaf sofit*"?

69. Which letter of the Hebrew alphabet is only found in the *birkat hamazon* one day a year?

70. Which woman in *Tanach* wore *Tefillin*?

71. From the end of the *tefillah* "*baruch sheamar*" in *pesukei d'zimra*, until the beginning of "*yishtabach*," every *pasuk* is a real *pasuk* in *Tanach*, except for one. Which *pasuk* is it?

72. I can be a witness at your wedding, but you cannot be a witness at mine. Explain?

73. The *tefillah* "*aleinu*," in addition to being the closing *tefillah* to our daily *tefillot* and a featured highlight *tefillah* on the High Holidays, is recited at the conclusion of two ceremonies. What are the ceremonies and why is "*aleinu*" specifically recited then?

74. The "*korbanot*" – "sacrifices" were traditionally our method of serving *Hashem*. With the destruction of the *Beit Hamikdash*, we now turn to prayer to serve *Hashem*. In the daily *tefillah*, we say a section from *Torah*, a section from *Mishnah*, and a section from *Gemara*, in order to connect our prayer to our primary sources. What section represents the *Mishnah* and why was it chosen?

75. Name four times that one would have to stand when a minor, below *Bar Mitzvah*, enters the room?

76. When is a man, who is not a *kohen*, required to wear a special pair of pants?

77. When would one be required to say the *beracha* "*hatov v'hameitiv*" – "the *beracha* said upon hearing good news" and the *beracha* "*dayan ha'emet*" – "the *beracha* said upon hearing bad news" at the same time?

78. What are the four reasons for "*benching gomel*" – "the special blessing to thank *Hashem* for delivering one from a dangerous situation" and where is there a daily hint to these four situations in *davening*?

79. I am invited to travel back in history and attend the *bar mitzvah* of the son of a very famous family. I am amazed when the *bar mitzvah* boy is called up as *kohen*; his father is called up as *levi* and his paternal great-great-grandfather receives the third *aliya* as the *yisrael*. Whose *bar mitzvah* am I attending?

80. How is it possible for one to recite the *birchat haTorah* "*asher bachar banu mikol ha'amim...*" twice, with nothing said in between the first *beracha* and the second?

81. Who composed the *beracha* "*hatov v'hamaitiv*," the 4th *beracha* in *birkat hamazon*, and for what event was it composed?

82. What is the biblical reference for reciting a blessing over sweet fragrances?

83. Why does "*tefillat shacharit*" – "the morning prayer," begin with the hymn "*Adon Olam*"?

84. When would one be required to hire and pay someone to participate in a *minyan*?

85. Two adult males, both Jewish, find themselves together in the same place for a couple of days. On the first night, the first person is obligated to make *kiddush* over wine to welcome the *Shabbat* and the other has no such obligation. On the very next night, the second person has his obligation to recite *kiddush* to welcome the *Shabbat* and the first has no such obligation. Describe the case?

86. What is the longest possible "*shemoneh esrei l'chol*" – "weekday *shemoneh esrei* prayer"?

87. How can one say a *beracha achrona* in place of a *beracha rishona* and then say a *beracha rishona* in place of a *beracha achrona*?

88. Which *berachot* can only be made once in a person's lifetime?

89. Often a *chatan* and *kallah* will schedule their wedding day for *Rosh Chodesh* to avoid fasting that day. On which *Rosh Chodesh* would a *chatan* and *kallah* nonetheless be required to fast?

90. Where does the *pasuk* "*ata hu ha'Elokim*" of the *tefillah* "*vayevarech David*" end?

91. It is Friday night and I am making *kiddush* on wine. I make the *beracha* "*mikadesh haShabbat*" but I do not recite a "*borei pri hagafen*." Why not?

92. What *beracha* was established on Sunday the 16th of *Iyar*?

93. Every day, we recite 19 *berachot* in *shemoneh esrei*. On *Shabbat*, we only recite seven *berachot* in the *shemoneh esrei*. Which *tefillah* was inserted into our *Shabbat tefillot* to make up for the missing 12 *berachot*?

94. When is a house *halachically* not a home?

95. What four *mitzvot* are not performed on *Shabbat* for fear that one will carry in the "*reshut harabim*" – "in the public domain"?

96. We generally do not give consecutive *aliyot* to a father and son, or to two brothers. When would this be permissible?

97. Generally, the first *mitzvah* in which a newborn male participates, is his "*brit milah*" – "circumcision." Where is there a hint in this *mitzvah* that this newborn male now has only 612 *mitzvot* left to perform?

98. A "*pikeach*" – "a perceptive, smart or insightful person" is one who carefully listens to and considers both sides of a discussion before deciding which position to support. Someone who is not perceptive does not wish to hear alternate opinions, hears one "*tzad*" – "side" and is unreasonable. Where is that hinted at in the Hebrew?

99. The word "*v'nishma*" appears in *Tanach* three times. How does the *Baal Haturim* connect these three occurrences and use them as support for a *halacha* cited in the *gemara*?

100. When we are saying *shemoneh esrei*, there are five times when we must bow, in praise of *Hashem*. One of these is at the *beracha* of *Modim*. The commentaries speak about our body bending like a snake and then returning to an upright position like a stick. To which element used in the erection of the *mishkan* is this similar, where a rigid rod miraculously becomes a malleable bendable bar?

101. We have learned that the *Avot* established the three daily prayers; *Avraham* established *Shacharit*, *Yitzchak* established *Mincha*, and *Yaakov* established *Maariv* (*Berachot* 26a). Besides these three daily prayers, each of the *Avot* is connected by the *Rambam* with one other *mitzvah*, that is observed until today. What are these three *mitzvot* and to which of the *Avot* is each credited?

102. Where is there a hint in the names *Avraham*, *Yitzchak* and *Yaakov* to the parts of the *tefillah* that each composed?

103. How is it possible to make a "*shehechiyanu*" on a *mitzvah*, even though it is the day before I am required to observe the *mitzvah*?

104. From which *pasuk* do we deduce the prohibition of counting people in the normal way; instead, utilizing a *pasuk* of 10 words to count people?

105. As a follow-up to the previous question, what two *pesukim* are we instructed to use in order to count participants in a *minyan*?

106. What Arabic word is used every day in our prayers before the section of "*pesukei d'zimrah*"?

107. It is *Motzaei Shabbat* and I am required to say *shemoneh esrei* for *maariv* twice. Why?

108. If I were to say that "7 and 28 were connected," how many examples of this can you find in Judaism?

109. The *halacha* mentions the phrases "*pikdu upischu*," "*minu v'atzru*," "*tzumu v'tzalu*," "*kumu v'tiku*." To what are these phrases referring?

110. What *halacha* stumped *Shlomo Hamelech*, the wisest of all men, to the extent that he wrote (*Kohelet* 7:23) "*amarti echkama, v'hi rechokah mimeni*" – "I thought I could understand it, but it eludes me"?

111. I am one of nine that existed in history over a period of about 1400 years from *Moshe Rabbeinu* until the destruction of the second *Beit Hamikdash*.

There have been none since and the next one will only make its appearance with the coming of *Mashiach*. What am I?

112. One sentence in *Kabbalat Shabbat* is connected to the deaths of two individuals; one mentioned in the *Torah* and one mentioned in *Nevi'im*. What is the *pasuk* and who are the two individuals?

113. In one of the *berachot* of *Shemoneh Esrei,* we find seven names of people. To which *beracha* am I referring?

114. Where in *tefillah* can you find seven consecutive words that are all numbers?

115. This chapter of *Tehillim* is recited every *Shabbat* morning and every *Motzaei Shabbat*. It is unique in that it contains just about every letter of the Hebrew alphabet including the "ending letters." The only letter that is missing is the letter *zayin*, which has a *gematriya* of seven. The chapter number, coincidentally, is a multiple of 7. Which chapter and why is it missing the *zayin*?

116. Where do we find a phrase of *Eliezer,* the servant of *Avraham*, cited in the *Torah*, making its way into the *musaf tefillah* of the "*yamim noraim*" – "the high holidays"?

117. The *etrog,* one of the four species taken on *Sukkot*, is required to be "*mehudar*" – "beautiful." The more beautiful it is, the more it personifies wholeness or perfection. What are the four areas of Jewish life where we seek perfection, hinted at by the letters of the word "*etrog*"?

118. How many blessings relate to smell and what are they?

119. There are two individuals mentioned in *Pirkei Avot*, both converts, whose names are pseudonyms, based on the number five. Who are they, why do we not use their correct names and what is their connection to the number five?

120. Normally, an "*aveil*" – "mourner" has the opportunity to recite the "*kaddish yatom*" – "the mourner's *kaddish*" at every *shacharit, mussaf, minchah* and *maariv* prayer. Name three consecutive prayer sections in the course of a year where there is no opportunity for a mourner to recite *kaddish*?

121. When is the only time that one could read from the *Torah* on Friday at *Mincha*?

122. We do not eat it, drink it, smell it, see it, or touch it, and yet when we personally experience it, we recite a *beracha*. What is it?

123. *Reuven* and *Shimon* are brothers. Their father passes away and yet only Reuven is permitted to attend the funeral. Explain?

124. A person walks into a room and is not a king, *kohen gadol*, parent or *talmud chacham*. Yet I am required to stand for that person. For whom am I standing?

125. I am edible. When I am not yet fully developed, I am *fleishig*. Once fully developed, I am *pareve*. What am I?

126. When reciting the "*mi shbeirach l'choleh*" – "the prayer for the recovery of a sick individual" on *Shabbat*, we add the words "*Shabbat hi milizok*" – "on

Shabbat we refrain from crying out," and then we also add "*u'refuah kerovah lavo*" – "and recovery is coming soon" (*Shulchan Aruch Orach Chaim* 288:14 – see *Magen Avraham*). What is the significance of this added phrase to our prayer?

HALACHOT, CUSTOMS & BLESSINGS ANSWERS

1. A blind person cannot make the *beracha* "*borey me'orei ha'aish*," one of the three *berachot* recited during *havdalah* (*Shulchan Aruch Orach Chaim* 298:13). One must be able to benefit from the light of *havdalah* and since *havdalah* is to show the difference between *Shabbat* and the rest of the week, you "have to be able to see the difference." Someone who is visually impaired cannot see the light, and is therefore not permitted to recite this *beracha*. However, a blind person may make the other *havdalah berachot* (*Mishnah Berurah* 298:34).

2. The *mitzvah* is *Kiddush Levana*, the blessing on the renewal of the moon's cycle, performed once a month. But this *mitzvah* requires it to be done at night, and when the moon is clearly visible, as in the name of one of Van Gogh's famous paintings "Starry Nights." There is a difference of opinion as to whether a blind person can say this *beracha*. Some say that just as a cloud covered moon exempts us from performing this *mitzvah*, so too, the inability of a visually impaired person to see the moon would likewise exempt him. But others feel that this blessing recognizes creation and its constant rejuvenation and is not dependent on the individual benefiting from it, and therefore a blind person would likewise be required to do the *mitzvah* and recite the blessing. In addition, while the blind person personally cannot benefit directly, he certainly benefits indirectly because others utilize the light to assist him. (*Mishnah Berurah* 426:1).

3. In the *tefillah* of *aleinu*, we recite the words "*umitpallelim el eil lo yoshia.*" The words "*el*" "*eil*" and "*lo*" are all two letter words with the identical letters of "*alef*" and "*lamed.*"

4. The fruit is an *etrog*. The *berachot* are:
   1. The *beracha* upon seeing the flowers of the *etrog* tree bloom in the spring ("*shelo chisar b'olamo davar...*").
   2. The *beracha* upon separating the tithes, *terumah* and *ma'aser* ("*l'hafrish terumot u'maasrot*").
   3. The *beracha* upon smelling the *etrog*, not in conjunction with the *havdalah* service ("*hanotain rayach tov bapeirot*").
   4. The *beracha* upon smelling the *etrog* in conjunction with the *havdalah* service ("*boray minay b'samim*").
   5. The *beracha* when waving the *lulav* and *etrog* on *Sukkot* ("*al netilat lulav*").
   6. The accompanying *beracha* on the first day of *Sukkot* ("*shehechiyanu*").
   7. The *beracha* upon eating the *etrog* after *Sukkot* ("*boray pri haetz*").

8. The accompanying *beracha* upon eating an *etrog* for the first time that year ("*shehechiyanu*").

9. The *beracha* after eating fruit ("*boray nefoshot*").

5. The case involves the *mitzvah* of "*besamim*" – "smelling fragrant spices after *Shabbat.*" There are different categories of fragrant spices. Each category requires a different blessing. For example, for spices that grow on trees, the blessing is "Blessed are You *Hashem* ...who creates fragrant trees." For spices derived from herbs which do not grow on trees, the blessing is "Blessed are You *Hashem* ... who creates fragrant herbs." However, at the *havdalah* ceremony after *Shabbat,* a different blessing is said. At *havdalah,* the blessing is always "Blessed are you *Hashem* "*borei minei besamim*" – "who creates various types of fragrances." In essence, this blessing is for a mixture of spices, or for spices of an unknown nature. But at *havdalah,* this is the standard blessing regardless of the type of spice. This avoids confusion, since often it's difficult to identify a given spice, its origins and proper blessing. This is according to the *Ashkenazi* custom. *Sephardic* Jews say the precise blessing (*Mishnah Berurah* 297:1).

6. The *mitzvah* of standing for your elders (*Vayikra* 19:32) is generally accepted as standing for one who is 70 years or older (*Kiddushin* 33a). However, if you are also 70, you do not have to stand for another 70 year old person (*Shulchan Aruch Yoreh Deah* 254). So in this riddle, I am 69 years old and it is one hour before I turn 70.

7. There are numerous cases where *halacha* dictates interruption of a "*d'oraitah*" – "a *Torah* mandated law" for the performance of a "*d'rabbanan*" – "a *rabbinically* mandated law." They include:

   1. *Torah* study, which is a "*d'oraita,*" is interrupted for the reading of *Megillat Esther* (*Shulchan Aruch Orach Chaim* 687:2).

   2. *Torah* study is interrupted for *Chanukah* candle lighting (*Mishnah Berurah* 672:2).

   3. If one is studying *Torah* and it was time for *bedikat chametz,* the *Torah* study should be interrupted (*Mishnah Berurah* 431:2).

   4. If one is saying *kriat shema,* which is a "*d'oraita,*" and the moon became visible and it was cloudy, such that one feels that there may not be another opportunity to say *kiddush levana,* the *kriat shema* should be interrupted (*Shaarei Teshuva Shulchan Aruch Orach Chaim* 426:3).

8. Here is the general principle: If one has two foods of different *berachot,* the order of the *berachot* is as follows: *hamotzi, mezonot, hagafen* (excluding *kiddush*), *haetz, ha'adama, shehakol.* This order doesn't change even if one of the foods is from the "*shivat haminim*" – "the seven special foods identified with Israel" or if one of the foods is preferred to the person making the *beracha* (*Mishnah Berurah* 211:35). In our question, the answer is "it

all depends." If it is at *kiddush* on *Shabbat*, then obviously the *beracha* on wine is made first. But if *kiddush* is not involved, the *beracha* of *mezonot* for cake comes first.

9. If one is ready to eat two foods, one has the *beracha* of *ha'etz* and one has the *beracha* of *ha'adama*, the rule of "*chaviv*" – "the usually preferred food to the diner" takes precedence. If they're both equally liked, then precedence is given to the presently preferred food. If both or neither are preferred, then if one is from the *shivat haminim*, it takes precedence. If neither are from the *shivat haminim* and are equally preferred, then *ha'etz* takes precedence over *ha'adama*. (*Mishnah Berurah* 211:18). Therefore in our case, if *bananas* are preferred, that *beracha* would be first. If grapes are preferred, then its *beracha* would go first. However, if neither are preferred or both are equally preferred, then grapes would be first because it is one of the *shivat haminim*.

10. The *berachot* for both of these fruits is *ha'etz*. But since the date is one of the *shivat haminim*, it goes first, even if the apple is more "*chaviv*" – "desired by the diner."

11. Both of these fruits are from the *shivat haminim*. The order of the *shivat haminim* is based on their proximity in the *pasuk* (*Devarim* 8:8) to the word "*eretz*" (*Shulchan Aruch Orach Chaim* 211:4). The order is olives, dates, grapes, figs and pomegranates, and therefore dates would precede figs.

12. Trick question: I am under the *chuppah*. The *sheva berachot* begin with the *berachot* "*borei pri hagafen*" and "*shehakol bara lichvodo*." Hence, we have a *beracha* of *hagafen* followed by a *shehakol* and nothing is drunk at this point!

13. I might be reciting one of two *berachot*; namely:
    1. I could be a *kohen* in *shul* and reciting *birkat kohanim*, where the *beracha* is "*asher kidshanu bikdushato shel Aharon*."
    2. I could be reciting *kiddush* of the *Shalosh Regalim* which reads "*asher kidshanu mikol am v'romemanu mikol lashon*."

14. At the "*brit*" – "circumcision" of a Jewish male, there are two consecutive *berachot* recited:
    1. By the *mohel*, who says "*asher kidshanu b'mitzvotav v'tzivanu al hamilah*."
    2. By the father of the baby, who says "*asher kidshanu b'mitzvotav v'tzivanu lehachniso bivrito shel Avraham Avinu*."

15. It depends. If one forgot to say *retzei* in the first two meals of *Shabbat*, one should repeat the *benching*, since bread is required for the first two meals, and therefore it is *Shabbat* that dictates the *benching*, rather than the eating of bread itself; therefore, omitting *retzei* invalidates the *benching*. "*Seudat shlishit*" – "the third *Shabbat* meal," however, can be fulfilled by eating foods other than bread, and therefore it is the bread and not *Shabbat* that dictates the reciting of the *benching*, and therefore the omission of *retzei* does not invalidate the *benching* (*Shulchan Aruch Orach Chaim* 188:7).

16. Yes. If the *kohen* grandfather married a person who was forbidden to him (e.g., a divorcée), then his children are "*chalalim.*" A "*chalal*" is a "defective" *kohen*, who loses the rights of honour that are given to the *kohen*, such as performing the "*birkat kohanim*" – "the blessing the congregation during the services," and receiving the first *aliyah* when reading the *Torah.* Therefore, in our case, if this *kohen chalal* had a son or daughter, who then had a firstborn son of their own, that boy would have to have a *pidyon haben* (*Rambam Hilchot Isurei Biah* 19:1)

17. No. The *halacha* explicitly forbids a *kohen* from marrying a divorcée or a convert, however, it does not speak about a *levi* or *yisrael.* Thus, the child of a male *levi* is a *levi* with no restrictions, regardless who the *levi* marries. Therefore if the male *levi* has a son or daughter, they would be considered a *levi* and a *bat levi,* and their first born male offspring would therefore be exempt from having a *pidyon haben.*

18. The *gemara* (*Gittin* 57a) relates to us the custom of planting a cedar tree when a male child was born, and a pine tree upon the birth of a female. The wood of those trees would be used to build the poles of the *chupah* at their wedding.

19. The word "*mazal*" in Hebrew is derived from the verb "*nozel*" – "to drip." Many people translate "*mazal tov*" as good luck, but since we believe that there is no coincidence in Jewish life, the concept of "good luck" seems to be incongruent with Jewish values. If we extrapolate on the connection of *mazal* and *nozel,* we can therefore consider *mazal* to be the trickling down of fortune, good or bad, from above; sort of our "destiny." The *gemara* (*Rosh Hashanah* 16b) lists five things that can help change a person's "*mazal,*" five actions that can influence the type of drip we receive from above. They are: giving charity, praying, changing one's name, doing *teshuva,* and changing one's place of living.

20. There are at least three *mitzvot* where the *beracha* is made after its performance; namely:

    1. When someone converts, they make the *beracha* after immersing in the *mikvah,* because before immersing, the person is not yet Jewish.

    2. When washing our hands for *netilat yadayim,* we say the *beracha* after washing, as then we are certain that our hands are clean.

    3. For *Ashkenazi* women, the *beracha* is recited after lighting candles for *Shabbat* (*Shulchan Aruch Orach Chaim* 263:5), because making the *beracha* first would indicate that you have already accepted *Shabbat* and then it would be problematic to light them. Therefore, in order for *Ashkenazi* women to not gain enjoyment from the candles before reciting the blessing, they are required to cover their eyes until after the *beracha* has been recited. *Sepharadi* women make the *beracha* before

lighting, and to avoid the problem mentioned above, they are required to say once a year that they do not accept *Shabbat* upon themselves until after the candles are lit.

21. One or more of the 10 males is an *"onayn"* – "pre-burial mourner" (*Mishnah Berurah* 55:24). *Halacha* dictates that an *"onayn"* – may not be counted to form a *minyan*.

22. The *Rambam* (*Hilchot Melachim* 2:2) says that a woman who is divorced from the king may never marry again.

23. The *Shulchan Aruch* (*Orach Chaim* 529:1), in describing the *halachic* concept of *"simchat yom tov"* – "being joyous on the holiday," says that part of the fulfillment of this precept is to arrive in *shul* a bit later than usual and leaving a bit earlier than usual. There is a concept in *halacha* that we should celebrate our *chag "chatzi l'Hashem v'chatzi lachem"* – "half in spiritual service of *Hashem* and half in physical enjoyment," such as a larger feast than normal. Being long in *shul* would interfere with the fulfillment of this *halachic* precept.

24. *Mishnah Berurah* (55:2) states that we derive this from the *pasuk* (*Vayikra* 22:32) "and I will be sanctified among the *Children of Israel*." The word "among" – *"betoch"* is the same as the word used in the story of the ten spies who brought back negative reports from the *Land of Israel*. There, they are referred to as a "congregation" and hence, we deduce that all congregations must be composed of a minimum of ten male adults.

25. If *Rosh Chodesh Shevat* occurs on a *Shabbat*, the *Shabbat* preceding *Rosh Chodesh* (week #1) we say *Tzidkatcha*; week #2 (*Rosh Chodesh*) we do not say it; week #3, we say it; week #4 (*Tu B'Shvat*) we do not say it; week #5, we say it; week #6, (*Erev Rosh Chodesh Adar*) we do not say it; week #7, we say it; week #8 (either *Erev Purim* or *Erev Purim Katan* in a leap year) we do not say it; week #9, we say it.

26. The *Ramban* (*Shemot* 12:6) explains that the singular of *tzaharayim* is *"tzohar"* – "light." In the morning, when the sun is in the east, my shadow would be cast to the west. In the afternoon, the opposite would be true; the area to the west would be light, but there are shadows to the east of my body. It is only at noon, when the sun is directly overhead, that there is light both to the east and west of my body. Since both sides have absolute light, the word for noon is plural.

27. Three famous *tzaddikim* died on *Shabbat* at *minchah* time (*Mishnah Berurah* 292:6). They were *Yosef Hatzaddik*, *Moshe Rabbeinu* and *David Hamelech*. That is why the *tefillah* consists of three *pesukim* containing the word *Tzidkatcha*. The *Mishnah Berurah* states that *tzidkatcha* is reminiscent of *"tziduk hadin,"* recited at every funeral accepting *Hashem*'s judgments and

decrees, and since *tziduk hadin* is recited standing, *tzidkatcha* should also be recited standing.

28. The term *"chesed shel emet,"* meaning "the truest act of kindness," applies to the final act of compassion to fellow Jews, the preparation of the body for burial and cemetery rites by members of the community. The phrase makes sense because it is the one act that is totally altruistic, since the recipient can never thank the burial society for this voluntary act. The *Baal Haturim* (*Bereishit* 47:29) notes that the letters of *"emet"* spell *"aron"* – "casket"; *"mitah"* – "the bed on which the deceased is lain"; and *"tachrichim"* – "shrouds in which the deceased is wrapped."

29. Accompanying the dead is a *mitzvah* that passes and if you do not grab the opportunity while you can, you will not get another chance; hence it should be done before visiting the sick.

30. In *chutz la'aretz*, there are five *berachot* that are only said one time a year:
    1. The *beracha* of *nacheim* on *Tisha B'av.*
    2. The *beracha* of lighting the candles on *Yom Kippur* eve.
    3. The *beracha* of *bedikat chametz.*
    4. The *beracha* immediately following *barchu* in *Shacharit* of *Yom Kippur,* "*hapoteach lanu shaar rachamim.*"
    5. The *beracha* when one sees the budding of a fruit tree the first time each year in the month of *Nisan.*

    In *Eretz Yisrael*, there are a few more *berachot* that we only say once annually:
    1. *"Al achilat matzah"*
    2. *"Al achilat maror"*
    3. The *beracha* at the end of *'magid'* in the *Haggadah* before the second cup of wine *"asher gealanu…"*

31. There is a *beracha* on *Rosh Hashanah* that is said 10 times a year. It is the *beracha* "*melech al kol haaretz mekadesh Yisrael v'yom hazikaron.*" This *beracha* is recited in *shemoneh esrei* of *maariv, shacharit, musaf* and *minchah* on both days of *Rosh Hashanah* for a total of eight times. It is also the closing words of the evening *kiddush* on both evenings of *Rosh Hashanah* for a total of ten times a year. This riddle works universally as *Rosh Hashanah* is two days whether in Israel or in *chutz laaretz*. It is possible that one individual in the *kehillah* could say this more than ten times a year and that would be the person honoured with the *aliyah* of *maftir*, as this is also the concluding *blessing* of the *haftarah* on both days of *Rosh Hashanah.*

32. On *Motzaei Shabbat* following the reciting of *shemoneh esrei*, we have an ancient custom that was mentioned in the *siddurim* of *Rav Amram Gaon* and *Rav Saadiah Gaon*, to recite Chapter 91 of *Tehillim* which begins with "*yosheiv b'seter.*" However, we precede reciting this *psalm* with the last *pasuk* of Chapter 90 which begins with the words *"vihi noam."* The *Avudraham*

in his commentary on the *tefillah* of *Motzaei Shabbat* states that if we total the number of words in *Tehillim* 90:17 plus *Tehillim* 91:1–16, we will arrive at a total of 124 words. If we would recite the entire *Tehillim* 91 plus the last *pasuk* of *Tehillim* 90 twice, the number of words would therefore equal (124 × 2) 248, the number of limbs in the human body. This would symbolize *Hashem*'s protection of the Jewish people, which is especially fitting at the conclusion of *Shabbat*, as we face the week ahead. And while we should repeat the entire chapter to arrive at that total, this would constitute a "*tirchah d'tzibburah*" – "an inconvenience for the entire congregation," and therefore the custom of repeating just the last verse was adopted.

33. The eight instances are the daily recitation of the *pasuk* of *Shema Yisrael* in the section of *Birchat Hashachar* beginning with "*l'olam yehay adam*" (7 times a week) and the one time that we recite *Shema Yisrael* in the weekly *Shabbat Musaf Kedushah*. In the 5th century, the Persian king, Yezdegerd II, considered the recitation of the *Shema* as treasonous, and placed guards outside shuls to ensure that Jews would not say *Shema*. In order to fulfill the *mitzvah* of saying the *Shema* in its proper time, the *Rabbis* instituted a daily recitation at home, before going to *shul*, and a special *Shabbat* insertion during *Musaf* in *shul*, by which time the guards had left their posts. After Yezdegerd was overthrown and killed, these two special insertions became a permanent part of our *Siddur*. The "*Otzar Hageonim*" (*Megillah* note 145) quotes *Rav Zidkiyah ben Avraham Harofeh* (13th Century Rome) in his *sefer*, *Shibbolei Haleket*, that this custom was instituted so that Jewish children would not forget the *nusach* of *Shema Yisrael*, one of the foundations of our faith.

34. A firstborn of a *kosher* animal, unlike a firstborn child, cannot be redeemed. It must be raised for 30 days and then given as a gift to the *kohen*. He must in turn, bring it as a sacrifice (assuming it has no blemishes) within its first year. However, since we have no *Beit Hamikdash* in our day, the *kohen* must care for it for its entire life without deriving any benefit from it. Since *Chazal* were worried that the *kohen* may be tempted to sell it or get rid of it in some other way, they created a legal loophole to avoid the difficulty of caring for it with no benefit to the *kohen*. They suggested that the farmer sell a minor share in the ownership of the pregnant mother to a *non-Jew* and then after the mother gives birth, you buy back the share. This eliminates any *halakhic* problem as the birth took place under non-Jewish ownership and the status of "*bechor*" – "firstborn" does not apply.

35. In *Hallel*, we repeat twice ten consecutive sentences beginning with "*odcho ki anitani*," and ending with "*hodu l'Hashem ki tov*."

36. Before the blowing of the *shofar* on *Rosh Hashanah*, we recite the entire Chapter 47 of *tehillim* seven times. Chapter 47 consists of ten *pesukim*.

37. In *Kiddush Levana*, we recite seven consecutive sentences three times each beginning with "*baruch yotzreich*" and ending with "*siman tov u'mazal tov.*"

38. In the laws of "*simchat Yom Tov*" – "rejoicing on Jewish holidays," the *Shulchan Aruch* (*Orach Chaim* 529:2) directs us to purchase candies and nuts for our children; and clothing and jewellery for our wives. He then adds the phrase "each according to his means." The *Maharil* is then quoted in the *Biur Halacha* (529:2) as saying that if one cannot afford clothing or jewellery, one should buy shoes for one's wife, indicating that shoes are a less expensive purchase than clothes.

39. It is one week before *Yom Tov*. *Yom Tov,* that year, was on *Shabbat* and Sunday in *chutz laaretz,* and only on *Shabbat* in Israel. Three babies are born in Israel; one on Friday, one "*bein hashmashot*" – "at twilight," and the third on *Shabbat* itself. At the same time, another baby is born in Egypt (same time zone), also "*bein hashmashot.*" The *halacha* is that one may perform a *brit* on *Shabbat* or on *Yom Tov,* but only if that is the actual eighth day. If, for example, a child cannot have his *brit* on the actual eighth day because he is ill, and the first delayed day when he is healthy is *Shabbat* or *Yom Tov,* you must then wait until the next non *Shabbat/Yom Tov* day to perform the *brit.* Therefore, the three that are born in Israel have their *britot* on Friday (the one actually born on Friday), *Shabbat* (the one actually born on *Shabbat*), and Sunday (the one born *bain hashmoshot*), which is no longer *yom tov* in Israel. The one born "twilight Friday evening," *bain hashmoshot,* in Egypt, must wait until Monday, as both *Shabbat* and Sunday are *yamim tovim.*

40. Babies 2, 3, 4 & 5 in this case are the same as the case above. However, we have now injected two additional *halachot.* First, the *halacha* of "*eved canaani.*" A Canaanite slave is bought by a *Jew* on Thursday. Even though the baby is less than eight days old, the *halacha* is that the baby's *brit milah* takes place on the day that he is purchased. Hence, he becomes *brit milah* number one (*Gemara Shabbat* 135b). The second *halacha* is that of a convert. If a woman converts to Judaism, her male child is given his *brit milah* on the day she converts (*Rashi Shabbat* 135a). Therefore in our case, she converts on Tuesday and hence her baby is *brit milah* number 6. Note that in our question, there is no criteria for the children to be Jewish because of baby number 1.

41. Triplets are born on *erev Shabbat;* the eldest is born 'bein hashmashot', and the other two are born when it is definitely *Shabbat.* Therefore, the last two are circumcised on the following *Shabbat* and the eldest is scheduled for his *brit* on Sunday. However, both who are circumcised on *Shabbat,* unfortunately die from the procedure and therefore the third is exempt from ever requiring a *brit* (*Gemara Yevamot* 64b; *Shulchan Aruch Yoreh Deah* 263:2).

42. If the older twin was born *"bein hashmashot"* – "twilight" on Friday and his younger brother was born when it was actually *Shabbat,* the younger boy will therefore have his *brit milah* on *Shabbat* and the older boy will have his *brit milah* on Sunday. He cannot have it on Friday (because maybe he was really born on *Shabbat,* and he would therefore be only seven days old) and he cannot have it on *Shabbat* (because if he was really born on Friday, he would now be nine days old on *Shabbat* and the only baby who can have a *Shabbat brit* is an eight day old baby). He therefore is pushed off until Sunday.

43. If it was a leap year and the first baby was born on the last day of *Adar I* and his twin was born on the first day of *Adar II.* When they reach the year of their *bar mitzvah,* it is not a leap year. Therefore the second boy celebrates his *bar mitzvah* on the first of *Adar* and the firstborn celebrates his *bar mitzvah* on the 29th of the month (*Shulchan Aruch Orach Chaim* 55:10).

44. The *Maharil* says that normally one would say *"kiddush levana"* – "sanctification of the New Moon" as early as three days after *Rosh Chodesh,* on the first available *Shabbat* night. However, the two exceptions to this rule are the *kiddush levana* of *Chodesh Av* and the *kiddush levana* of *Chodesh Tishrei.* In the first instance of *Chodesh Av,* he explains that since *kiddush levana* is like receiving the glory of *Hashem,* which naturally evokes an emotion of *"simcha,"* and since *"simcha"* is forbidden during the first nine days of *Av,* we delay *kiddush levana* until *Motzei Shabbat Nachamu* (*Magen Avraham, Shulchan Aruch Orach Chaim* 426:6). In the second instance, joy is impossible because of the feelings of awe experienced in the 10 Days of Repentance that begin on *Rosh Hashanah.* Therefore, *kiddush levana* for *Tishrei* is delayed until *Motzei Yom Kippur* (*Ramah, Shulchan Aruch Orach Chaim* 426:4).

45. An adult *levi* never sees the same *kohen* getting two *aliyot* in a row (which occurs when there is no *levi* in *shul* to get the second *aliyah*) and he never sees a non-*levi* *"bechor"* – "firstborn," washing a *kohen*'s hands for *birkat kohanim* (a firstborn substitutes to wash the *kohen*'s hands when there is no *levi* available) (*Mishnah Berurah* 128:22). There are a few cases where this would not apply; namely:
    1. On *Simchat Torah,* if the *levi* is scheduled to be honoured with *Chatan Torah* or *Chatan Bereishit,* he would not receive the regular *levi aliyah,* even if he was the only *levi* in *shul* (*Taamei Haminhagim* 831).
    2. If it was a fast day and the only *levi* in *shul* is not fasting, he would not receive an *aliyah.*
    3. If the only *levi* in a *"beit avel"* was the mourner.

As we are in the midst of the COVID-19 pandemic at this time, many authorities have ruled that in order to socially distance and prevent the spread of the virus, the *baal kriah* should receive all the *aliyot*, and as such, if the *baal kriah* was a *kohen*, the *levi* in the congregation would this year see the *kohen* receiving at least two *aliyot* in a row.

46. The *Baal Haturim* notes that the last word in the *Birkat Kohanim* is "*shalom*" – "peace or hello." He points out that the *gematriya* of the word "*shalom*" is the same as the word "*Eisav*" and deduces from here that you should be quick to greet all those you meet, including non-Jews (*Baal Haturim Shemot* 6:26).

47. If a *kohen* receives the *aliya* for *maftir* on *Shabbat* morning, is then called for *kohen* at *Shabbat minchah* and then "*bimkom levi*" – "in place of a *levi*" at *Shabbat mincha,* (as there was no *levi* present at *mincha*), you then have a case of the same person receiving three consecutive *aliyot* on the same day. See comment to answer #45 above regarding COVID-19.

48. The *parshah* of the *Akeida* appears immediately after the "*birchot hashachar*" and at the end of the *parshah* of the *Akeida*, the city of *Be'er Sheva* is mentioned.

49. The *Mishnah Berurah* (271:4:17) says that if one made *kiddush* over wine, after he had already begun to eat the *Shabbat* or *Yom Tov* meal, he must make an additional *Hamotzi* because the saying of *Kiddush* is considered to be an interruption. However, he is required to only say *birkat hamazon* once.

50. Unlike the other eighteen blessings which were composed by the *Anshei Knesset Hagedola*, the *beracha* "*v'lamalshinim*" was composed by *Rav Shmuel Hakatan* in the *Yeshiva* of *Rabban Gamliel* in *Yavne*, some five hundred years later, after the destruction of the second *Beit Hamikdash*. The *beracha* was composed in response to the heretics of the day who threatened tradition. The Hebrew letters of the name of the city, *Yavne*, are *yud, bet, nun* and *heh* which stand for the essential elements and *berachot* of the *havdalah* service; namely, *yayin, besamim, ner* and *havdalah*. This indicates that *Yavne* at the time separated itself from the rest of the world by being a unique geographical location for holiness and service to *Hashem*. The Hebrew word with the letters *yud, bet, nun* and *heh* can also be pronounced "*yibaneh*" – "it will be rebuilt," "it" referring to the *Beit Hamikdash*. The *Beit Hamikdash* was destroyed because of baseless hatred and this additional *beracha* asks us to not speak ill about our fellow man; the merit of which will be the rebuilding of the *Beit Hamikdash*.

51. If I forgot to say "*ata chonantanu*" in the *Maariv* prayers on *Motzei Shabbat*, the *halacha* is that I am not required to repeat the *Shemoneh Esrei*, as long as I do not eat or drink before saying *havdalah*. However, if I drank a can of soda prior to reciting *havdalah*, then I must repeat the entire *Shemoneh Esrei*. Therefore, not including the *beracha* on what I drank, I would now have to recite the *borei nefashot* after drinking and then would have to repeat

the 19 *berochot* of *Shemoneh Esrei* before saying *havdalah*, for a total of 20 *berachot* triggered by one can of soda (*Mishnah Berurah* 294:1:4).

52. If one did not eat, but is nevertheless present when the group begins to "*bench*" together, he does not respond with the traditional "*baruch (Elokeinu) she'achalnu mishelo u'vetuvo chayinu.*" However, he does not remain silent. He must respond with a special pronouncement of "*baruch (Elokeinu) u'mevoroch shmo tamid l'olam va'ed*" (*Shulchan Aruch Orach Chaim* 198:1).

53. The meal that the mourner eats when returning from the burial is called the *Seudat Havra'ah.* It must be from food which is not your own (*Gemara Moed Katan* 27, *Shulchan Aruch Yoreh Deah* 378).

54. The case revolves around the period of the *Nine Days* from *Rosh Chodesh Av* until *Tisha B'Av.* During this time, *Ashkenazim* are not permitted to eat meat. But they can eat meat on the *Shabbat* that coincides with this period. So if one eats meat for "*seudah shlishit*" – "the third *Shabbat* meal," he cannot eat dairy for 1, 3, or 6 hours (depending on his family custom). He also cannot eat meat once *Shabbat* ends because of the restriction of the Nine Days. He therefore cannot eat meat or dairy but can eat *pareve.* A similar case would be the final dinner meal on *Erev Rosh Chodesh Av,* if one ate meat for that meal, he would not be able to eat meat or dairy immediately after nightfall, but could eat *pareve.*

55. A person was eating *seudat shlishit* and before *benching,* he *davened Maariv.* When he subsequently says *birkat hamazon,* he should not add "*retzei*" (*Mishnah Berurah* 263:67). The *Ba'er Heiteiv* says that this applies most certainly if one has *davened Maariv* before *benching.* He however implies that if all one has done is proclaim "*baruch hamavdil bein kodesh l'chol,*" he should still add "*retzei*" to the *benching.*

56. It must be the *Seder* night, for then, everyone is required to recite *birkat hamazon* over a full "*revi'it*" – "*halachic* measure" of wine.

57. The *Kitzur Shulchan Aruch* (26:14) says that originally, "*kaddish yatom*" – "known as the mourner's *kaddish,*" (but literally "the orphan's *kaddish*"), was recited only by minor children. Today, all mourners recite *kaddish yatom.*

58. Certain *tefillot* were originally added to the liturgy to allow latecomers to "catch up." They are:

    1. The *tefillah* of "*baruch Hashem le'olam amein v'amein,*" established as part of the weekday "*maariv*" – "evening service," so that people working late who arrived late in *shul,* could catch up to the others. This would allow everyone to finish together, and that way, they would be able to return home safely in the dark together (*Gemara Berachot* 2a).

    2. The prayer "*bameh madlikin,*" was added to the Friday evening service, for a similar reason. Since one could be delayed getting to *shul* on Fri-

day night from the rush of leaving work, the saying of these *mishnayot* was added to the Friday evening *tefillah*. We do not say *bameh madlikin* on *Shabbat Chol Hamoed*, since one is not supposed to work on *Chol Hamoed* and therefore all should be able to arrive in *shul* early (*Shulchan Aruch Orach Chaim Mishnah Berurah* 270:1:2).

3. The *beracha* of "*magayn avot*," also called "*beracha may'ayn sheva*," was added after the Friday night *Maariv Shemoneh Esrei* for the same reason (*Shulchan Aruch Orach Chaim Mishnah Berurah* 268:8:20).

4. *Rav Gedaliah Felder*, in his *sefer*, *Yesodai Yeshurun*, explains that the reason for the saying of a second *barchu* just before *aleinu* at the end of the Friday night *Maariv* is to allow those who arrived late to answer to *barchu*. This appears to be for Friday night only, since we try to be "*mosif michol al hakodesh*" – "to extend the time of *Shabbat* by beginning *kabalat Shabbat* before nightfall," and therefore some people arrive late for *davening*.

59. There is a difference of opinion as to how many people in one household should light the *Chanukah* lights. According to *Tosofot*, only one person should light per household, and everyone else is "*yotzei*" – "fulfills their obligation" with his lighting. According to the *Rambam*, each person in a household should light for themselves. *Tosofot*, who were *Ashkenazi*, is quoted by *Rav Yosef Karo*, a *Sephardi*, in the *Shulchan Aruch*; while the *Ramah*, who was an *Ashkenazi*, cites the opinion of the *Rambam*, who was a *Sephardi* (*Shulchan Aruch Orach Chaim* 671:2).

60. On *Motzei Yom Kippur* (immediately after the fast of *Yom Kippur*), we *daven maariv l'chol*. Since we are still wearing a *tallit* from the day's prayers, it is customary to leave the *tallit* on, for the *maariv* service.

61. On *Tisha B'av* morning, we *daven shacharit l'chol*, but do not wear a *tallit* or *tefillin*.

62. We do not say *ashrei* at *minchah* on *Yom Kippur*.

63. A rainbow should not be looked for, but once seen, one is required to make the special *beracha*, "*zocher habrit*" (*Mishnah Berurah* 229:1). The *gemara* (*Ketuvot* 77b) relates that no rainbow was ever seen during the lifetime of the *Tanna Rabbi Shimon Bar Yohai*, which was interpreted to be a good thing because it meant that *Hashem* was not angry enough to have to display the rainbow.

64. In the silent *shemoneh esrei*, we end with the sentence "*oseh shalom...*" which concludes with the words "*...v'imru Amein*" – "...and they shall answer Amein." The *Mateh Moshe* as quoted by the *Magen Avraham* (*Shulchan Aruch Orach Chaim* 66:6) says that since this is said in the silent *shemoneh esrei*, it must be referring to the two angels who accompany you wherever you go.

65. The *Ramah* (*Shulchan Aruch Orach Chaim* 202) says that if fruit is ground to the point of no longer being recognizable as fruit, you would make a "*shehakol*" before eating the fruit. Therefore a fruit jelly made from one of the *Sheva Minim* (seven specific foods indigenous to *Eretz Yisrael*) would require a "*shehakol*." However, the *Mishnah Berurah* (202:42) explains that while one can substitute a "*shehakol*" for a "*borei pri haetz*," one cannot substitute a "*borei nefoshot*" for an "*al haeitz*" and if one ate a *k'zayit* of this fruit jelly, one would be required to make an "*al haeitz*" as the "*beracha acharona*." A classic example of a food that would fall into this category would be fruit leather made from grape or date jelly.

66. In *birkat hamazon*, we say "*Elokeinu, Avinu, Ro'einu, Zuneinu, Parneseinu, Vechalkileinu, Veharvicheinu…*"

67. We find 15 consecutive words beginning with the letter "*vav*" in the *Shacharit tefillah* of "*v'yatziv v'nachon…*" The *Daat Zekeinim* (*Shemot* 38:21) comments that these 15 adjectives describing *Hashem* as the paradigm of truth, recited immediately after the *kriat sh'ma*, all beginning with the letter "*vav*," hint at the 15 "*vavim*" – "hooks" in the hangings of the "*mishkan*" – "tabernacle" which were made from the excess silver that "appeared" to be missing in *Moshe*'s accounting of the inventory of donations for the *mishkan*.

68. In *kiddush levana*, the sentence "*baruch yotzrech…*" has eight words and we repeat the sentence three times. Each word in the sentence ends in a "*chaf sofit*" for a total of 24 consecutive words ending in *chaf sofit*.

69. The "*peh sofit*" generally does not appear in *birkat hamazon*. The *Baer Heitev* (*Shulchan Aruch Orach Chaim* 185:1) notes that the letter "*peh sofit*" is the final letter of many words that indicate anger and "*machloket*" – "arguments" and therefore never made it into the grace after meals. The *Baer Heitev* then proceeds to promise those who say *birkat hamazon* with intense concentration, a life free of anger and dispute, and filled with a good and honourable livelihood. However, on one day a year, on *Purim*, we add the section for "*al hanissim*" and one of the words is "*taf*." Some suggest that its shape resembles a gallows and noose, hinting at the noose that *Haman* had originally prepared for *Mordechai*, but which *Haman*, himself, was ultimately hanged from.

70. *Michal* the daughter of *King Shaul*, first wife of *David Hamelech*, wore *Tefillin* (*Gemara Eiruvin* 96a).

71. The following sentence in the prayer *yehi ch'vod* in *pesukei d'zimra* is made up of three components: "*Hashem melech*" is part of a *pasuk* in *Tehillim* 10:16; "*Hashem malach*" is part of a *pasuk* in *Tehillim* 93:1; and "*Hashem yimloch l'olam va'ed*" is a *pasuk* in *Shemot* 15:18.

72. Two possible answers. One is that I am male and you are female. Therefore I (the male) can be a witness at your wedding, but you (the female) are not

eligible to be the witness at mine. The second answer is that the second wedding is a union of a man and the sister of the wife in the first wedding. Therefore the groom in the second wedding can be a witness for the first wedding. However, the groom in the first wedding is now the brother-in-law of the groom in the second and can therefore not serve as a witness for his relative.

73. The two ceremonies are a "*brit milah*" – "circumcision" and "*kiddush levana*" – "sanctification of the moon." In the case of a *brit milah*, the *Sefer Kushyot* (written by a student of the *Maharam Mi'Rotenberg*) comments that it is fitting and logical that only after the ceremony, where the child has now entered the "covenant of *Avraham Avinu*," where he is now different than all non-Jews, should the *aleinu* prayer be recited, which states "*shelo asanu k'goyei ha'aratzot*" – "He, *Hashem*, has not made us like the nations of the earth." In the case of *kiddush levana*, the *Bi'ur Halacha* (*Mishnah Berurah* 426:2:13) states that lest it be perceived that we are worshipping the moon, we recite *aleinu*, wherein we say that others bow down to idols and we do not. The *gemara* (*Bava Batra* 75a) compares *Yehoshua*, the author of *aleinu*, to the moon.

74. The section that we say from the *Mishnah*, is "*eizehu mekoman shel zevachim*" (*Zevachim Perek* 5), which is recited every morning in the section called "*korbanot*" just before the beginning of *pesukei d'zimra*. This chapter, which contains no "*machloket*" – "disagreements," was specifically chosen to teach us the concept of unity, and furthermore, because there is unity of opinion in this *Mishnah*, it is a clear *Mishnah* handed down from *Moshe* from *Mount Sinai*.

75. The four times that one stands for a minor are:
    1. At a *brit* when the eight day old baby enters the room (*Yoreh De'ah* 265:1).
    2. At a *Pidyon Haben* when the 30 day old baby enters the room (*Pidyon Haben K'hilchato, Perek Chet, Halacha* 7; Footnote 22).
    3. If the minor is a scholar (*Yoreh De'ah* 246:1).
    4. If the minor is a king, such as *Shlomo Hamelech* who was 12 when assuming the throne (*Rambam Hilchot Melachim* 2:5).
    Note: In the case of a *Pidyon Haben*, it is not clear whether this is a requirement or merely an accepted custom.

76. The *Mishnah* in *Shekalim* 3:2 indicates that the person collecting the half *shekel* coins in support of the upkeep of the *Beit Hamikdash*, should be wearing pants that have no hems or pockets where one could hide any of the coins being collected. The *Mishnah* goes on to say that he also should be barefoot so as to reduce the places where he might be tempted to hide any collected coins.

77. The *Shulchan Aruch Orach Chaim* 223:2 says that if one's father passes away and leaves a large inheritance, the son would make the *beracha "dayan ha'emet"* because of the death of his father, and would also make the *beracha "shehecheyanu"* thanking *Hashem* for the inheritance. However, if there is more than one heir, then one would make the *beracha "dayan ha'emet"* and the *beracha "hatov v'hameitiv"* (i.e., it is good for him and for others also).

78. The four instances where one would have to *"bench gomel"* (Gemara *Berachot* 54b) are:

    1. One who has travelled at sea
    2. One who has crossed the desert
    3. One who recovered from a very serious illness
    4. One who was released from prison

    This is based on *Tehillim* 107 which describes the four instances when we cried out to *Hashem* at the time of *Yetziat Mitzrayim*. The *Shulchan Aruch* (*Orach Chaim* 219:1) provides for us a mnemonic to remember these four instances. In *shemoneh esrei* we say *"v'chol hachaim yoducha sela"* – "and all living beings give thanks to You." The word *"chaim"* – "living beings" is made up of four letters; *"chet"* which stands for *"choleh"* – "a sick person"; *"yud"* for *"yisurin"* – "jailed"; *"yud"* for *"yam"* – "ocean"; and *"mem"* for *"midbar"* – "desert."

79. I am attending *Aharon Hakohen's Bar Mitzvah*. He is a *kohen*; his father, *Amram*, is a *levi*; and his paternal great-great-grandfather, *Yaakov Avinu*, is a *yisrael* (coincidentally, his name is also *Yisrael*).

80. The case is where one arrived in *shul* late, around the time that they were beginning to read the *Torah*, and was reciting the *birchot haTorah* at the beginning of the *siddur* in the section called *"berachot."* Just then, he was called to the *Torah* for an *aliyah*. The *Tur* quotes his father, the *Rosh*, who says that even if he completes saying the *beracha* at the precise moment that he is called up, he should repeat the *beracha* again in front of the *Torah* as a sign of respect and reverence (*Tur Orach Chaim* 139).

81. The *gemara* (*Taanit* 31a) says that one of the events that we mourn on *Tisha B'Av* is the fall of *Beitar* in the year 135 and the massacre of its many defenders. *Beitar* was the stronghold of *Bar Kochba*, the leader of the Jewish revolt against *Hadrian*. *Hadrian* refused to allow their burial and so the dead bodies remained above ground for many years. Miraculously, none of them decomposed. Many years later on *Tu B'Av*, *Hadrian's* successor, *Antoninus*, allowed the dead to be buried. To commemorate this miracle and to express the nation's profound gratitude to *Hashem*, an additional *beracha* was added to the *birkat hamazon*, the *beracha* of *hatov v'hameitiv*, composed by *Rabban Gamliel* in *Yavne*. This fourth *beracha* of *birkat hamazon* is regarded as a *rabbinic* obligation, while the first three *berachot*

are *biblical* in nature. The first *beracha* was composed by *Moshe Rabbeinu,* (*Berachot* 48b); the second *beracha* was composed by *Yehoshua* (*Levush, Shulchan Aruch Orach Chaim* 187:2); and the third by *King David* (*Levush, Shulchan Aruch Orach Chaim* 188:1).

82. The *pasuk* (*Tehillim* 150:6) says "*kol haneshama tehallel kah*" which indicates that every soul will praise *Hashem.* The *gemara* (*Berachot* 43b) notes that fragrance is the only thing that provides nourishment to the soul and not the body. Therefore, we are required to recite a *beracha* when smelling sweet fragrances.

83. The *Vilna Gaon* states that since *Avraham Avinu* was the one who instituted the morning prayer, and since from the day *Hashem* created the world no one called *Hashem* by the term "*Adon*" – "Master" until *Avraham* came and referred to Him by the title "*alef, daled, nun, yud*" (*Gemara Berachot* 7b), we therefore begin *shacharit* with the hymn "*adon olam.*"

84. The *Shulchan Aruch Orach Chaim* 55:21 states that in a city that has only 10 Jewish residents, and one of them wants to leave for the *Yamim Noraim,* the leaders of the community may force him to remain or compel him to pay another to take his place.

85. The *gemara* (*Shabbat* 69b) records a case about a person who is lost in the desert, and because he has lost track of the days, is unsure when to observe *Shabbat.* The *halacha* follows the opinion of *Rav Huna* who argues that from the moment that he realizes he is lost, he should count six days and then observe the first *Shabbat* (*Shulchan Aruch Orach Chaim* 342:1). Our case is where two individuals are lost in the desert and one begins counting his six days, one day before the other. They then find themselves together toward the end of the week. When "lost person A" is ready to recite *kiddush* on his Friday night, it is only Thursday night for "lost person B." The next night, lost person B is making *kiddush* and lost person A is making *havdalah.*

86. The longest possible "*shemoneh esrei l'chol*" would occur on *Motzei Shabbat Chanukah Rosh Chodesh.* A person *davening* "*nusach sfard*" in Israel or "*nusach ha'ari*" anywhere in the world, would add "*ata chonantanu,*" "*yaaleh v'yavo,*" and "*al hanissim*"; and instead of "*shalom rav,*" would say "*sim shalom.*"

87. If one receives an *aliyah* and mistakenly recited the closing *beracha* "*asher natan lanu*" instead of the opening *beracha* "*asher bachar banu,*" then when the *kriah* ends for his *aliyah,* he should recite the opening *beracha* "*asher bachar banu*" instead of the closing *beracha* "*asher natan lanu*" (*Mishnah Berurah* 139:15).

88. There are four such *berachot*:
    1. The *Shach* comments that in situations where people (such as Jews who observed their Judaism in secret, as in the times of the Inquisition) circumcised themselves, they would make the *beracha* "*l'hikanes bibrito*

shel Avraham avinu" – "to enter into the covenant of *Avraham avinu*" (*Shulchan Aruch Yoreh Deah* 265:1).

2. A person who is a *bechor* and whose parents never arranged a *pidyon haben* for him at the age of 30 days, then arranges for his own first born redemption ceremony later in life. He would then make a special *beracha* "*lifdot habechor*" (*Shulchan Aruch Yoreh Deah* 305:10).

3. A male convert recites the *beracha* "*al hatevila*" when immersing in the *mikvah* in his conversion ceremony.

4. A person would recite the *beracha* "*lekadesh shmo barabim*" before dying "*al kiddush Hashem*" – "in a manner that sanctifies *Hashem*'s name."

89. Generally, a bride and groom do not fast on *Rosh Chodesh*. However, on *Rosh Chodesh Nisan*, they do fast (*Mishnah Berurah* 573:9). The *Mishnah Berurah* adds that if they married on *Rosh Chodesh Av*, they would also fast; although such an occurrence would be very rare, as this falls within the tragic period of the *Three Weeks* where we do not schedule weddings.

90. This is a very tricky question because the punctuation in the *siddur* differs dramatically from the actual text in *Tanach*. The *pasuk* which begins with the words "*ata hu Hashem HaElokim*" ends with the words "*shemo Avraham*" (*Nechemia* 9:7). The next *pasuk* begins with the words "*umatzata et levavo ne'eman*" and ends with the words "*ki tzadik ata*" (*Nechemia* 9:8).

91. If one began eating early on Friday and has wine with his meal and then the time for *kiddush* arrives, he does not repeat the *beracha* "*boreh pri hagafen*" but simply picks up the *kiddush* cup and recites the last *beracha* of "*mekadesh hashabbat*" (*Shulchan Aruch Orach Chaim* 271:4).

92. The *gemara* (*Berachot* 48b) says that *Moshe Rabbeinu* composed the first *beracha* of *birkat hamazon* ("*hazan et hakol*") on the day when the *mann* first fell. *Rashi* (*Shemot* 16:1) tells us that that date was Sunday, the 16th of *Iyar*, 2448.

93. The *Kol Bo* suggests that *ein kelokeinu* was added to the *tefillah* of *Shabbat* to make up for the twelve less *berachot* that we have on *Shabbat*. There are twelve lines in *ein kelokeinu*. One stanza begins with the letter *alef*; one begins with the letter *mem* and one begins with the letter *nun*, which spells *amein*. The last two stanzas begin with the words "*baruch*" and "*atah*" so it is analogous to reciting "*baruch atah, amein*" twelve times.

94. The *gemara* (*Sukkah* 3b) states that the minimum area for a house to be functional, such that people will live in it, is 4 *amot* by 4 *amot* or 16 square *amot* (roughly 36 square feet). Therefore a house is not a home when it does not meet these minimum sizes. To put things in perspective, the average size of a hotel room is about 300 square feet, with smaller hotel rooms measuring 150 square feet.

95. The four *mitzvot* that we refrain from performing on *Shabbat* for fear of carrying in the public domain, are:
   1. Blowing the *shofar* (*Gemara Rosh Hashanah* 29b)
   2. Reading *Megillat Esther* (*Gemara Rosh Hashanah* 29b)
   3. Making the *beracha* on the *Lulav* and *Arbah Minim* (*Gemara Sukkah* 43a)
   4. Sprinkling a person who is *tamei* with the waters of the *Parah Adumah* (*Gemara Pesachim* 69a)

96. The *Maharil* gives the reason of *"ayin hara"* for this custom (*Shulchan Aruch Orach Chaim* 141:6). The *Mishnah Berurah* cites an exception to this custom when the two consecutive *aliyot* are being read from two different *sifrei Torah* (*Mishnah Berurah* 141:6:20).

97. The *gematriya* of *"brit"* is 612; indicating that after performing the *mitzvah* of *milah*, there are now 612 of the 613 *mitzvot* remaining to perform.

98. *Rav Naftali MiRopshitz* explains that the *gematriya* of *"pikeach"* is 188 and *"tzad"* is exactly half of that at 94, indicating that the *pikeach* studies both *"tzedadim"* – "sides" of any issue before firming up his own opinion. Moreover, the *pikeach* is one who respects both sides of the discussion even when he is not in agreement.

99. The three occurrences of the word *"v'nishma"* are:
   1. *"kol asher diber Hashem na'ase v'nishma"* – "all that *Hashem* has spoken, we will faithfully do" (*Shemot* 24:7).
   2. *"v'nishma kolo b'vo'o el hakodesh"* – "and its sound would be heard when he comes into the holy sanctuary" (*Shemot* 38:35).
   3. *"v'nishma pitgam hamelech asher ya'aseh b'chol malchuto, ki raba hi"* – "the judgement executed by your majesty will be heard throughout the kingdom, as vast as it is" (*Esther* 1:20).

   The *Baal Haturim* (*Shemot* 28:35) cites these three locations of the word *"v'nishma"* and then quotes a *gemara* (*Megillah* 3b) which quotes *Rava* who says that if one must choose between Temple service and reading the *megillah*, reading the *megillah* takes precedence, and similarly if one must choose between *Torah* study and reading the *megillah*, reading the *megillah* takes precedence. Therefore, says the *Baal Haturim*, *"v'nishma pitgam hamelech"* – "hearing the word of the king in the *Purim* story" takes precedence over *"v'nishma kolo b'vo'o el hakodesh"* – "the service in the *Temple*" and *"na'ase v'nishma"* – "the study of *Torah*"; *"ki raba hi"* – "because these are the words of *Rava*" as he has ruled in the *gemara*.

100. The *briach hatichon* was the supporting bar inserted into the shaft that held the walls together in the *mishkan* (*Shemot* 26:28). The *gemara* (*Shabbat* 16a) says that when the planks that formed the walls of the *mishkan* were all erected around the three walls, there was a central interior rod that was inserted into the planks that connected and stabilized the walls. Since the

mishkan had three walls, and according to one opinion in the *gemara*, the central supporting bar was one piece, this element was in fact quite miraculous. The *Targum Yonatan* (*Shemot* 26:28) relates that this supporting bar was in fact from the tree planted by *Avraham* in *Beer Sheva* (*Bereishit* 21:33) and was the staff that *Yaakov* used to split and cross the *River Yarden* and that this supporting bar was stiff like a rod when being transported from camp to camp and miraculously became malleable and twistable like a snake, when it was needed to insert within the planks and traverse the 90 degree angles at each of the two wall corners. This description is the same as that used to describe our bowing at the *beracha* of *Modim*.

101. With *Avraham*, circumcision was also commanded; *Yitzchak* separated *maaser*; and *Yaakov* is connected with the prohibition against eating the sciatic nerve (*Rambam, Hilchot Melachim* 9:1).

102. The second letter of each of the names of the *avot* indicate the time of the *tefillah* that they composed. The "*beit*" in *Avraham* stands for "*boker*"; the "*tzadi*" in *Yitzchak* stands for "*tzahariym*"; and the "*ayin*" in *Yaakov* stands for "*erev.*"

103. If *Chanukah* begins on a *Shabbat*, then on Friday afternoon, the order of lighting the *Shabbat* and *Chanukah* candles, requires us to light the *Chanukah* candles first. This is because if we were to light the *Shabbat* candles first, we would have accepted *Shabbat* and would therefore no longer be permitted to light the *Chanukah* candles. And therefore, the result is that we make the *beracha* "*shehechiyanu*" on Friday, even though the holiday of *Chanukah* and the *mitzvah* of lighting the candles begins on *Shabbat*.

104. There is a *pasuk* (*Shmuel* 1:15:4) wherein *Shaul* wished to count his army. He gave each soldier a lamb and counted the lambs. *Rashi* comments that he did this because it is forbidden to count the Jewish people based on the *pasuk* "*asher lo yisapher meirov*" – "who are too numerous to count" (*Bereishit* 32:12).

105. We are told that it is an accepted Jewish custom (*Kitzur Shulchan Aruch* 15:3) to count 10 people for a *mitzvah*, by using the ten word *pasuk* "*Hoshiyah Et Amecha*" (*Tehillim* 28:9). *Piskei Teshuvot* (156:24) adds that it is also acceptable to use the ten word *pasuk* "*VeAni BeRov Chasdecha*" (*Tehillim* 5:8).

106. The *gemara* (*Rosh Hashanah* 26a) informs us that the word for rooster is normally "*tarnegol*" but in our daily *berachot* section of "*birchot hashachar*," we utilize the word "*sechvi*" for rooster. The *gemara* tells us that the origin of this word is Arabic and is from the Syrian city of Kan Nishraya.

107. There are at least four cases when I would have to recite *shemoneh esrei* twice in the *tefillat maariv* on *Motzaei Shabbat*. They are:
    1. I forgot to *daven minchah* on *Shabbat* afternoon (*Shulchan Aruch Orach Chaim* 108:1).

2. I am *davening* a *tefillat nedava* which means that in the Temple, one was permitted to add a *"tefillat nedava"* – "voluntary non-obligatory offering," so too, one can add a voluntary *shemoneh esrei* as long as one adds a special personal request (*Shulchan Aruch Orach Chaim* 107:1).

3. I ate before reciting *Havdalah* with wine and therefore must daven again and recite *havdalah* in *shemoneh esrei* (*Shulchan Aruch Orach Chaim* 294:1).

4. I forgot to say *"ata chonantanu"* in the first *shemoneh esrei* and did not say *havdalah* because of a lack of wine, and therefore must repeat *shemoneh esrei* with *"ata chonantanu"* (*Shulchan Aruch Orach Chaim* 294:2).

108. There are a number of significant elements in Judaism that connect the numbers 7 and 28. They are:

1. 7 words and 28 letters in the first *pasuk* in the *Torah* (*Bereishit* 1:1).

2. 7 words and 28 letters in the introductory *pasuk* to the *"Aseret Hadibrot"* – "Ten Commandments" (*Shemot* 20:1).

3. 7 words and 28 letters in the phrase in *kaddish* "*yehei shmei rabbah mevorach leolam uleolmei almaya.*" Coincidence?

Additionally, the number 28 is numerically equal to *"koach"* – "strength" and the *gemara* (*Gemara Shabbat* 119b) indicates that if one answers *"yehei shmei rabbah"* with all their strength, one's sins are forgiven. As well, this section of *kaddish*, beginning with the words *"yehei shmei rabbah"* until *"da'amiran b'almah"* (and not including *"v'imru amein"*) also totals 28 words and speaks about the praise of *Hashem* and all of His glory. These 28 words correspond to the 28 life experiences enumerated by *Shlomo Hamelech* (*Kohelet* 3:2) beginning with *"eit laledet, v'eit lamut"* – "a time to be born, a time to die," which highlights our need to serve *Hashem* in the best way possible at every stage of our life and in every life experience.

109. The *Shulchan Aruch* (*Orach Chaim* 428:4) discusses the setting of the *"chagim"* – "holidays" in the Jewish calendar and the organization of the *parshiyot* that we read before those *chagim*. The *Shulchan Aruch* presents us with special mnemonics or codes by which we are to recall the connection of *parshiyot* to specific *chagim*. In a regular year, *"pikdu u'pischu"* refers to *Parshat Tzav* being *Shabbat Hagadol* directly before *Pesach*. However, in a leap year, *"sigru u'pischu"* refers to *Parshat Metzora* right before *Pesach*. The other three are: *"minu v'atzru,"* *Parshat Bamidbar* directly before *Shavuot*; *"tzumu v'tzalu',* the fast of *Tisha B'Av* directly before *Parshat Va'etchanan*, which also sets *Parshat Devarim* as *Shabbos Chazon* and *Va'etchanan* as *Shabbat Nachamu*; and *"kumu v'tiku,"* as *Parshat Nitzavim* before *Rosh Hashanah*.

110. The *gemara* (*Gemara Yoma* 14a) quotes *Rav Akiva* who says that *Shlomo Hamelech*, when writing these words, was referring to the contradictory

nature of the sprinkling of purification water that purifies an impure person and renders a pure person impure. The process of purification is that the *kohanim* slaughter and burn a *"para aduma"* – "red heifer," then combine the ashes with water. When a person becomes *"tamei"* – "ritually impure" through contact with the dead, the priests sprinkle this water upon them, and the impurity is removed. Yet those involved with the preparation of this recipe become impure. Even someone with the wisdom of *Shlomo Hamelech* could not solve this paradox.

111. I am a *"para aduma"* – "red heifer." The *Rambam* writes that throughout history, nine red heifers were prepared in fulfillment of the *mitzvah* of *para aduma*. *Moshe* prepared the first, *Ezra* prepared the second, and there were seven more, prepared between *Ezra* and the destruction of the second *Beit Hamikdash*. The tenth will be prepared by *Mashiach* (*Mishneh Torah, Hilchot Parah Adumah* 3:4).

112. In *Kabbalat Shabbat*, we recite a *perek* of *Tehillim* where we read "*Moshe* and *Aharon* among His priests, and *Shmuel*, among those who call on His name" (*Tehillim* 99:6). From this *pasuk*, *Korach* saw he would have a descendant, *Shmuel*, who would be equal in stature to *Moshe* and *Aharon*, and as a result felt confident in arguing with them. That confidence ultimately led to his death. As well, *Shmuel*, realizing that he was equated with *Moshe* and *Aharon*, claimed that his choice as king, *Shaul*, could not be removed during his lifetime. Therefore, *Hashem* caused *Shmuel* to die at the relatively young age of 52, in order to be able to have *Shaul* die (*Taanis* 5b).

113. In the *beracha* of *Sim Shalom*, we find the names *Shalom, Tovah, Beracha, Chen, Rachamim, Chayim* and *Yisrael*.

114. In *Nishmat*, we have the phrase "*achat mei'alef eleph alphei alaphim v'ribei revavot*"–one of the thousand thousands and myriad myriads," seven consecutive numbers in one phrase of a prayer.

115. The chapter is *"yosheiv b'seter"*– Chapter 91 in *Tehillim*. The only letter missing from this chapter is the *zayin*. The *Avudraham* (*Tefillat Maariv Motzaei Shabbat*:9) explains that the chapter speaks about being protected by *Hashem* and points out that the Hebrew word *zayin* means weapon, and everyone who recites this chapter with *"kavana"* – "concentration" and proper intentions will be protected from harm and will not require weaponry of any sort. The *Avudraham* adds that *zayin*, which is numerically equivalent to seven, is a hint to the fact that there are seven *motzaei Shabbat* during the year when we omit saying this chapter, namely; the *Shabbat* preceding the holiday of *Pesach* and the *motzaei Shabbat* of *Pesach*; the *Shabbat* preceding the holiday of *Sukkot* and the *motzaei Shabbat* of *Sukkot*; the *Shabbatot* preceding the holidays of *Shavuot, Rosh Hashanah* and *Yom Kippur*. *Motzaei Shabbat* is the time when we leave the protection

of the sanctity of *Shabbat*, and therefore we recite this *tefillah*. However, a *Shabbat* that coincides with a *chag* or immediately preceding a *chag*, affords an extra measure of spiritual protection for the Jewish people, and we can therefore omit reciting this chapter of *Tehillim*.

116. As we begin the *musaf tefillah* of the *yamim noraim*, the *chazzan* says the *tefillah* "*hineni.*" In it, he beseeches *Hashem* to please "*mazliach darki asher anochi holech*" – "please grant success in the way upon which I am heading." These words were first uttered by *Eliezer* as he embarked on the mission to help find a wife for *Yitzchak* (*Bereishit* 24:42).

117. The letters of the word *etrog* hint at the following four areas in Jewish life where we seek perfection:
    1. "*emunah shleimah*" – "complete faith"
    2. "*teshuva shleimah*" – "complete repentance"
    3. "*refuah shleimah*" – "complete recovery from illness"
    4. "*geulah shleimah*" – "complete redemption"

118. There are five *berachot* for smelling. *Boreh Atzey Besamim* – for pleasant smells from a tree or its branches; *Boreh Isvei Besamim* – for grass smells; *Hanotein Rayach Tov Bapeirot* – for pleasant smells emanating from edible fruits; *Boreh Minei Besamim* for spices that are not trees, fruits or grass; and *Boreh Shemen Oreiv* for the smell of persimmon oil, a unique *beracha* for a fruit indigenous to *Eretz Yisrael*. The *beracha Boreh Minei Besamim* is similar to the *Shehakol* blessing on food items, in that, if one is unsure which of the above blessings apply, one should use the *Boreh Minei Besamim*.

119. At the end of the 5ᵗʰ *perek* of *Pirkei Avot* are two *Mishnahs*; one by a *Tanna* called *Ben Bag Bag* and the other *Tanna* known as *Ben Heh Heh*. *Tosafot* (*Gemara Chagigah* 9b) clarifies that both of these individuals were converts and because of the danger involved in converting to Judaism at the time, their names were actually codes for their real identities. The name "*Ben Heh Heh*" is indicative of the adoptive parents of all converts; *Avraham* and *Sarah*, both of whom are recognized as the first Jews and both of whom had a letter "*heh*" added to their names; *Avrom* becoming *Avraham* and *Sarai* becoming *Sarah*. Similarly, "*Ben Bag Bag*" is composed of a "*bet*" and a "*gimmel*" which, added together, equals five or a "*heh*"; that constituting his code as a convert.

120. There is no mourner's *kaddish* to be found in the three consecutive *Yom Kippur* prayers of *mussaf, minchah* or *neilah*.

121. We read the *Torah* at *mincha* only on three occasions:
    1. *Shabbat* afternoon
    2. *Mincha Yom Kippur*
    3. *Mincha* on all five other public fast days

From all these occasions, the only possibility of a Friday afternoon would be the fast day of *Asarah B'Tevet*, which is the only fast day that can fall on a Friday.

122. Here are a few answers:
    1. When one hears thunder, one recites the *beracha "shekocho ugevurato maleh olam."*
    2. When one hears particularly bad news, one recites the *beracha "dayan emet."*
    3. When one hears particularly good news, one recites the *beracha "hatov v'hameitiv."*

123. *Shimon* is either the *kohen gadol* or he is a *nazir*. Neither can attend any funeral, even the funeral of a very close relative.

124. I am standing for the wife of a *talmud chacham* (*Gemara Shevuot* 30b).

125. According to the *Shulchan Aruch* (*Yoreh Deah* 87:5), an undeveloped egg yolk, found inside a chicken, is deemed to be *fleishig* as it is considered part of the chicken. However, if it develops and now has both the yolk and the albumen, it is deemed to be *pareve* and can be eaten with either dairy or meat.

126. We know that on *Shabbat*, one does not make personal requests. Therefore the entire middle section of the *shemoneh esrei*, consisting of 13 personal request *berachot* is omitted on *Shabbat*. However, we do wish to request *Hashem*'s assistance for those who are ill and therefore we allow a *mi shebeirach* for a *choleh*. The *sefer Torat Emet* by *Rabbi Avraham Moshe Eidlitz* points out that the 13 *berachot* recited during the week in the middle of *shemoneh esrei* are replaced by one *berachah* that begins with the words *"yismach Moshe"* – "*Moshe* rejoiced." Therefore if someone wishes to pray for the recovery of a sick individual on *Shabbat*, when he says *"yismach Moshe,"* he should reflect on the fact that the word *Moshe* is an acronym for the words *"Shabbat hi milizok"* – "on Shabbat we refrain from crying out" and the result will be that *"refuah kerovah lavo"* – "recovery is coming soon." *Rabbi Eidlitz* adds that there is a hint to this process in the *Torah* (*Parshat Yitro* 19:19) in the pasuk *"Moshe* spoke and *Hashem* answered him loudly," with the acronym of *"Moshe"* being *"Shabbat hi milizok"* and the acronym of *"kol"* being *"u'refuah kerovah lavo."*

BRAINTEASERS

BRAINTEASERS QUESTIONS

1. Once upon a time, a young man came to a *rabbi* and asked, "*Rabbi*, please tell me what is the foundation upon which the entire *Torah* is based while I stand on one foot." The *Rabbi* answered "Whistle until the fish comes backwards." What did he mean?

2. How are the meanings of truth and falsehood reflected in their Hebrew construction?

3. How is water from the sea, Like atonement like a cow? (Say these clues in Hebrew And then you'll know just how!) How's an onion in the shade, Like three that he kneaded? (These clues, too, are much clearer, When in Hebrew they're repeated.) Explain?

4. When one of the *Chassidic Rebbes* was eight years old he was asked a riddle: "What verse in the *Torah* has the first three words the same as the last three words?" He replied, "The verse where *Moshe* did not say "*emet*" – "the truth." What did he mean?

5. Here is a phrase in Hebrew, "*Hechatan noten l'arusato meit v'raglav betocho.*" Explain.

6. *Rav Chaim Volozhin* once asked the *Vilna Gaon* where a hint to his name could be found in the *Torah*. What was his answer?

7. Who in *Tanach* has a name that makes him sound as if he is his own uncle?

8. Who in *Tanach* has a name that makes him sound as if he is his own grandmother?

9. Who in *Tanach* has a name that makes him sound as if he is his own grandfather?

10. What is unusual about the fifth of the first of the first of the first of the third?

11. What is three to a three through a third on the third in the third?

12. If you take it this way, it means it isn't important. But you must bring it this way, because it is important. What is it?

13. A boy is beginning to learn the *alef bet,* and knows all the letters but has not yet mastered the vowels or where the words begin and end. He says to his father, "I just read a very interesting passage in the *Torah*. When I translate it into English, it reads, 'who, who, who, who, what?'" His father was puzzled. What *parshah* was the boy reading in the *Torah*?

14. There is a popular legend about *Rashi, Rav Shlomo Yitzchaki,* who, while travelling, was accused of being a thief who had stolen someone's coat. *Rashi*, though innocent, was forced to pay for the coat. When *Rashi* left the house of his accuser, he wrote the letters of his name "*shin-lamed-mem-heh*" five times on the door. What was contained in this cryptic message?

15. Here is a very strange mathematical equation: 30 - 30 = 60. Solve this equation in two different ways? (Hint: remember that this book has something to do with Judaism so try to use Hebrew to solve the equation!)

16. What is the connection between *Avraham*, the human body, *Kriat Shema* and the planet Pluto?

17. *Reuven*, a member of the *Chevra Kadisha*, once approached the *Beit Din*. He said that some time earlier, he was involved in a "*machloket*" – "*dispute*" with *Shimon*, and *Reuven*, had made a promise to never again see *Shimon*. *Shimon* had now died and *Reuven* was responsible to do the "*tahara*" – "preparing the body for burial." He wanted to know, now that *Shimon* had died, whether his promise to never again see *Shimon*, was null and void. One of those sitting in the *Beit Din* was *Rabbi Baruch Halevi Epstein*, known as the *Torah Temima*. He immediately gave his *halachic* ruling, basing it on two *pesukim* in the *Torah*. What are the two *pesukim* and how do they apply to this case?

18. Name a specific chapter in *Tehillim* which, depending on how the calendar falls, should be recited as part of *tefillah*, one day only (i.e., it is said today, but not yesterday and not tomorrow), two days in a row, three days in a row, four days in a row, five days in a row, six days in a row, NEVER seven days in a row, eight days in a row, nine, ten, eleven, twelve or thirteen days in a row?

19. Name two common *Torah* words with a common root that are palindromes (words that are read the same backwards and forwards; e.g., "level" is a palindrome), and when translated, one is in the past tense and one is in the future tense. When a "*vav*" is added to each of the words, the past tense word becomes future tense and the future tense word becomes past tense.

20. Why do we give the blessing of "*yiddishe nachat*"? Is there any other kind?

21. Why can people in Israel eat more than people in *chutz la'aretz*?

22. At the circumcision of *Rabbi Yehoshua Yisrael Tronk* (1821–1893, Poland), later to be known by the name of his work, the *Yeshuot Malko*, he was given two names by his father; namely *Yehoshua Yisrael*. Right after naming his son, the father exclaimed that he had inadvertently missed one of the three names that he intended to give to his new son. He wanted to give his son the names *Yisrael* (in memory of *R' Yisrael Baal Shem Tov*), *Eliyahu* (in memory of *Hagaon R' Eliyahu miVilna*), and *Yehoshua* (in memory of the author of the *Pnei Yehoshua*). He was perturbed that he had missed the name *Eliyahu*. One of the *Rabbanim* attending the *brit* told the father that he had in fact given all three names to his son. Explain.

23. In Jewish life, the religion of the child always follows the religion of the mother. If the mother is Jewish, then automatically the child is Jewish. How do we see from the Hebrew words of mother and child, that the child's religious affiliation follows the mother?

24. Complete the following Jewish mathematical progression: 3, 6, 8, 11,…?
25. Your father is my father; your grandfather is my husband; I am your sister; and you are my son. I am mentioned in the *Torah*. Who am I?
26. Beginning with number one, find an actual reference to numbers one to forty two mentioned specifically in the *Torah* or in *Tanach*? Obviously, numbers one to seven are found during the days of creation. But how far beyond seven can you go (for some of the numerals, there are many answers; I have provided only one for each numeral)?
27. Where in *Parshat Bereishit* do we derive the principle of *"shlucho shel adam k'moto"*?
28. A *"midrash pli'ah"* – "wondrous midrash": *"Af al pi ra'iti, af al gav lo ra'iti, v'im ra'iti, tzarich lomar baruch meshaneh habriyot."* Explain?

BRAINTEASERS ANSWERS

1. "Whistle" in Hebrew is "*tishrok.*" It is spelled "*tav shin reish kuf.*" These are the last letters of the Hebrew alphabet, backwards. "The fish comes" in Hebrew is "*hadag ba,*" spelled "*heh daled gimmel bet alef.*" These are the first letters of the Hebrew alphabet, in reverse order from fifth to first. Hence, "Whistle" until "the fish comes," backwards, refers to the entire Hebrew alphabet, which is the foundation of the entire *Torah.*

2. *Emet* is made up of *alef, mem* and *tav.* The *Kotzker Rebbe* notes that if you look at how these letters are constructed, each letter has a firm base and the letters are positioned at the beginning, middle and end of the alphabet. Truth stands alone and is solid! *Sheker* is made up of *shin, kuf* and *reish,* each letter being very unstable in its construction. The three letters are grouped together at the end of the alphabet. Lies require other lies to cover them up. Falsehood cannot stand alone.

3. In Hebrew, these are all homographs – that is, they are pairs of words that are spelled the same but pronounced differently.
   1. Water/from the sea = *mayim/miyam*
   2. Atonement/like a cow = *kapara/k'para*
   3. An onion/in the shade = *batzal/b'tzeil*
   4. Three/that he kneaded = *shalosh/shelash*

   In Hebrew, these pairs of words are all spelled exactly the same!

4. The last verse in *Parshat Shlach* begins and ends with the same three words: "*Ani Hashem Elokaychem*" – "I am *Hashem* your G-d who took you out of the land of *Mitzrayim* to be your G-d, I am *Hashem* your G-d." When we recite this verse in our *tefillot* as part of the *Shema,* we add the word "*emet*" – "truth" – at the end of *pasuk,* as though this word belongs as part of the verse. This, however, is not the way the verse appears in the *Torah.* Therefore, this is the verse, where the first three words are the same as the last three words, and where *Moshe* did not say the word "*emet*" although when we read the verse, we do say "*emet.*"

5. The word "*margaliyot*" (pearls) is made up of the word "*raglov*" surrounded by a "*mem*" and a "*tav*" or the word "*met.*"

6. The *Vilna Gaon* says that *Sefer Devarim* hints to everything that will occur during the sixth millennium of creation and each *parshah* hints to one of the ten centuries (*Nitzavim-Vayeilech* are considered one *parshah*). Therefore, *Parshat Ki Teitzei,* which is the sixth *parshah,* corresponds to the century in which the *Vilna Gaon* lived. He answered, "in this *parshah,* we read '*even shleima*'" (*Devarim* 25:15). *Even* can be divided into "*alef ben*" which stands for "*Eliyohu ben*" and "*Shleima*" has the same letters as *Shlomo* (the *Vilna Gaon*'s father). The *Sefer Daat Yoel* continues that everyone knows

what happened at the end of the seventh century, the *Shoah*, and the seventh *parshah* discusses the curses. The eighth *parshah*, *Nitzavim-Vayeilech*, discusses *Teshuva*, which is why today we see so many *Baalei Teshuva*. (*Peninim Mishulchan HaGra*).

7. Three answers:
    1. *Achav*, can be divided into the words *ach* (brother) *av* (father); i.e., uncle.
    2. *David* (*daled, vov, daled*) can be read as "*dod*" or uncle.
    3. *Dishon* (*Bereishit* 36:21) who was, in fact, the uncle of *Dishon* (*Bereishit* 36:25).
8. There is an individual called "*savta*" or grandmother (*Bereishit* 10:7).
9. *Nachor*'s grandfather was also called *Nachor* (*Bereishit* 11:24–26).
10. It is a small *alef*. It appears as the fifth letter of the first word of the first sentence in the first *perek* of the third book (the *alef* of *Vayikra*).
11. The *gemara* in *Shabbat* (88a) speaks of the giving of the *Torah* as a three part *Torah* (*Torah, Neviim, Ketuvim*) given to a three part people (*kohen, levi, yisrael*) through a third born (*Moshe*, after *Aharon* and *Miriam*), on the third day of abstinence in the third Month (*Sivan*).
12. It is a grain of salt. If you take something with "a grain of salt," it means that it is not important. But when you bring a *korban* (sacrifice), you must always bring it with salt. (*Vayikra* 2:13).
13. He was reading *Shemot* 13:10, specifically the words "*miyamim yamima.*"
14. A little background. This popular legend has *Rashi* travelling somewhere in Europe, wanting to meet other *Torah* scholars. One has *Rashi* travelling to Toledo to visit *Rav Yehuda Halevi*; this could be plausible as they lived in the same time period. Another version has him travelling to meet the *Rambam* which would be impossible as their lives did not overlap; alternately, he was meeting the *Ibn Ezra*, whose life did overlap with *Rashi* but their meeting would have taken place when the *Ibn Ezra* was a very young man, as at best, *Ibn Ezra* would have been in his teens when *Rashi* died. Yet another says the story did not involve *Rashi* at all but rather *Rav Shlomo Kluger*. In any case, the common thread has someone called *Shlomo* showing up at the home of another *Torah* scholar, who is not home. The servants, thinking that the visitor is a pauper seeking a donation, dismiss him and then discover that a valuable coat or robe is missing from the vestibule where the visitor had been waiting. They chase him and force him to pay for the missing garment. The visitor protests but eventually, realizing he has no choice, pays for the garment and then leaves the cryptic message on the door. When the homeowner/*Torah* scholar returns home and sees the cryptic message, he asks his servants to find the man who had written the message. When *Rashi*, or whoever it really was, returns to the house, he takes his quill and scribes the vowels under each of the five words and

only then, they are able to read the message *"shelama shilma Shlomo salma shleima"* – "why had *Shlomo* (*Rashi's* given name) been required to pay for a complete article of clothing?" Each of the five words in the sentence are spelled with the identical four letters, *shin, lamed, mem* and *heh*. Realizing that this was no ordinary visitor but rather a man of great wisdom, he is invited into the home and the homeowner and visitor share words of *Torah*.

15. Two answers:
     1. The Hebrew word for thirty is *"shloshim."* The Hebrew letter which has the value of thirty is *"lamed."* If you take the *"lamed"* away from the word *"shloshim,"* you are left with the letters that spell *"shishim"* which is the Hebrew word for sixty.
     2. Thirty minus thirty equals 0, which is the letter *"samech"* as we write it in script. *"Samech"* has the numerical value of 60.

16. They are all connected to the number 248. *Avraham* is 248 in *gematriya*; there are 248 organs in the human body; there are 248 words in *Krias Shema* (if one includes either *"kayl melech ne'eman"* when *davening* alone or *"Hashem elokaychem emet"* when *davening* with a *minyan*); and it takes approximately 248 years for Pluto to revolve around the sun (actually, it takes 247.9 Earth years for Pluto to make one orbit around the Sun).

17. In *Parshat Beshalach, Hashem* promises *Bnai Yisrael* that they would no longer have to see the Egyptians… *"ad olom"* – "forever" (*Shemot* 14:13). And yet a number of *pesukim* later (*Shemot* 14:30) we find that *Bnai Yisrael* saw the Egyptians *"met al sfat hayam"* – "dead on the side of the sea." The *Torah Temimah* cites these seemingly contradictory statements as proof that *Reuven* was permitted to do the *Tahara*, now that *Shimon* was no longer alive.

18. The chapter is *"L'David Mizmor"* (*Tehillim* 24). This chapter is said as the *"Shir Shel Yom Rishon"* – "Song of Sunday" and is also said at the end of the *Torah* reading when the *Torah* is returned to the *Aron Hakodesh* (except on *Shabbat* Morning). It is therefore said every week at *Shabbos minchah* at the end of the *Torah* reading, Sunday as the *Shir Shel Yom*, Monday and Thursday at the end of the *Torah* reading, *Rosh Chodesh* at the end of the *Torah* reading, *Yamim Tovim, Chanukah* and *Purim* at the end of the *Torah* reading and on fast days at the end of the *Torah* reading. The solution to the riddle is as follows:
     1. One day alone would be a Thursday.
     2. Two days in a row would be when *Rosh Chodesh* falls on a Wednesday (Wednesday and Thursday).
     3. Three days would be every week (*Shabbat*, Sunday and Monday)
     4. Four days would be when *Rosh Chodesh* falls on a Tuesday (*Shabbat*, Sunday, Monday and Tuesday).

5. Five days in a row is when *Rosh Chodesh* falls on a Friday (Thursday, Friday, *Shabbat*, Sunday and Monday).

6. Six days in a row is when *Rosh Chodesh* falls on a Tuesday and Wednesday (*Shabbat* until Thursday).

7. Eight days would be when the first day of *Chanukah* falls on a Thursday (Thursday to Thursday).

8. Nine days would be when the first day of *Chanukah* falls on a Wednesday (Wednesday until the following Thursday).

9. Ten days is when the first day of *Chanukah* falls on a *Shabbat* (*Shabbat* until the following Monday).

10. Eleven days is when the first day of *Pesach* falls on a Tuesday (*Shabbat* until the following Tuesday).

11. Twelve days is when the first day of *Chanukah* falls on a Friday (Thursday until the following Monday).

12. Thirteen days is when the first day of *Sukkot* falls on a Tuesday (*Shabbat* until the following Thursday).

The attempt to include seven days as seven days of a *Pesach* that begins on a Wednesday in Israel fails as the first day of *Pesach* can not be a Wednesday. The first day of *Pesach* can only fall on a Sunday, Tuesday, Thursday or *Shabbat* and if you try any of these four possibilities, you will always end up with more than seven consecutive days.

19. The words are "*haya*" – "it was" and "*yehi*" – "let it be." When a *vav* is added to "*haya*" which is in past tense, the word becomes "*vehaya*" – "and it will be" which is in the future tense; and when a *vav* is added to "*yehi*" which is in the future tense, it becomes "*vayehi*" – "and it was" which is in the past tense. (*Peninim Mishulchan Hagra, Bereishit* 14:1).

20. *Eisav's* son *Reu'el* had a son called *Nachat* (*Bereishit* 36:13) and we can therefore say that *Eisav* had "*nachat*" from his *mishpacha*. So when we wish our friends the blessing of "*nachat*," we must have in mind that we are not looking for *Eisav's* type of *nachat*, but rather true *yiddishe nachat*!

21. The *gemara* (*Gittin* 70a) states "Eat to fill a third of your stomach, and drink to fill another third, and leave a third empty, so that when you become angry you will become full." There is another *gemara* (*Nedarim* 22a) that deduces from a *pasuk* (*Devarim* 28:65) that anger only occurs in *Bavel* or in the *Diaspora* exile, but does not occur in Israel. Therefore if one resides in Israel, he has one third of his stomach empty and available for additional food and drink!

22. The *Rabbi* correctly noted that by combining the last two letters of *Yisrael* with the first three letters of *Yehoshua*, you have the name *Eliyahu*.

23. The Hebrew word for mother is "*eim*," spelled "*alef, mem*." The Hebrew word for child is "*ben*," spelled "*bet, nun*." The letters of "*ben*" directly follow the

letters of *"eim"*; *"bet"* following *"alef"* and *"nun"* following *"mem."* Hence, here is a hint that the religion of the child directly follows the religion of the mother.

24. The next three numbers are 14, 17, 19. These seven numbers represent the seven leap years in every 19 year cycle in the Jewish calendar.

25. I am either one of the daughters of *Lot* speaking to *Amon* or *Moav.* Your father *Lot* is my father; your grandfather *Lot* is my husband; I am your sister, because we have a common father, *Lot*; and you are my son.

26. Answer:

    1. *yom echad* (*Bereishit* 1:5)

    2. *yom sheni* (*Bereishit* 1:8)

    3. *yom shlishi* (*Bereishit* 1:13)

    4. *yom revi'i* (*Bereishit* 1:19)

    5. *yom chamishi* (*Bereishit* 1:23)

    6. *yom hashishi* (*Bereishit* 1:31)

    7. *sheva shabatot temimot* (*Vayikra* 23:15)

    8. *shemoneh* (*Bereishit* 22:23)

    9. *b'tisha lachodesh* (*Vayikra* 23:32)

    10. *b'asor lachodesh* (*Vayikra* 16:29)

    11. *achad asor kochavim* (*Bereishit* 37:9)

    12. *bnei yaakov shneim asar* (*Bereishit* 35:22)

    13. *parim bnei bakar shlosha asar* (*Bamidbar* 29:13)

    14. *avadticha arba esrei shanah* (*Bereishit* 31:41)

    15. *bachamisha asar yom* (*Vayikra* 23:39)

    16. *sheish esrei nafesh* (*Bereishit* 46:18)

    17. *Yosef ben shva esrei* (*Bereishit* 37:2)

    18. None in the *Torah* (we cannot accept the 318 person army of *Avraham* – *shmoneh asar u'shlosh meiot*) but numerous in *Tanach* – *shemoneh esrei shana l'Nevuchadnetzar* (*Yirmiyahu* 32:1)

    19. None in the *Torah* (we cannot accept *Nachor*'s age of 119 years – *tsha esrei shana u'me'at shana*) but numerous in *Tanach* – *shnat tsha esrei shana l'Nevuchadnetzar* (*Yirmiyahu* 52:12)

    20. *esrim kesef* (*Bereishit* 37:28)

    21. *haechad v'esrim lachodesh* (*Shemot* 12:18)

    22. Closest in the *Torah* is *shnayim v'esrim elef* but that really means 22000; in *Tanach* – *l'gamul shnayim v'esrim* (*Divrei Hayamim* 1:24:17)

    23. Closest in the *Torah* is *shlosha v'esrim elef* but that really means 23000; in *Tanach* – *b'shlosha v'esrim bo* (*Megillat Esther* 8:9)

    24. *esrim v'arbaah parim* (*Bamidbar* 7:88)

    25. None in the *Torah* but many in *Tanach* – *b'esrim v'chameish shanah* (*Yechezkel* 40:1)

26. None in the *Torah* but many in *Tanach* – *bishnat esrim v'sheish shanah* (*Melachim* 1:16:8)

27. None in the *Torah* but many in *Tanach* – *bishnat esrim v'shiva* (*Melachim* 1:16:15)

28. *Orach hayeriah ha'achat shemona v'esrim* (*Shemot* 26:2)

29. None in the *Torah* and few in *Tanach* – *machalafim tisha v'esrim* (*Ezra* 1:9)

30. *shloshim yom* (*Devarim* 34:8)

31. None in the *Torah* and few in *Tanach* – *shloshim v'echad* (*Yehoshua* 12:24)

32. *shtayim u'shloshim* (*Bereishit* 11:20)

33. *u'shloshim yom u'shloshet yamim* (*Vayikra* 12:4)

34. *arba u'shloshim* (*Bereishit* 11:16)

35. *chameish u'shloshim* (*Bereishit* 11:12)

36. None in the *Torah* and few in *Tanach* – *shloshim v'sheish* (*Divrei Hayamim* 2:16:1)

37. None in the *Torah* and few in *Tanach* – *shloshim v'sheva* (*Melachim* 2:25:27)

38. *shloshim ushemonah* (*Devarim* 2:14)

39. None in the *Torah* and few in *Tanach* – *b'shnat shloshim v'teisha* (*Divrei Hayamim* 2:16:12)

40. *ben arba'im shanah* (*Bereishit* 25:20)

41. None in the *Torah* and few in *Tanach* – *arba'im v'achat shanah* (*Melachim* 2:14:23)

42. *arba'im u'shtayim ir* (*Bamidbar* 35:6)

43. We could not find a 43, so that is where we stop this question!

27. In *Bereishit* 2:17, *Adam* is told by *Hashem* that if he eats from the "*eitz hadaat*" – "the tree of knowledge," he will surely die. But we know that ultimately *Adam's* punishment was not death, but rather expulsion from the *Garden of Eden*. Therefore we see that "*shlucho shel adam*" – "the sending out of *Adam*" from the *Garden of Eden* was "*k'moto*" – as though he had died.

28. The wondrous midrash reads, "*af al pi ra'iti*" – "I have seen a nose above a mouth"; "*af al gav lo ra'iti*" – "I have not seen a nose on a back"; "*v'im ra'iti*" – "and if I actually see a nose on a back," "*tzarich lomar baruch meshaneh habriyot*" – I will have to recite the special blessing that one is supposed to say upon seeing an exceptionally strange-looking person.

Sources Cited

The following is an alphabetical listing of sources quoted in the book, either by name of the *sefer* or its author. In the cases where specific *sefarim* are quoted, I have provided the name of the author, dates of birth and passing, if known, and the countries where the author lived. In cases where I have quoted a *Rav* without a reference to a specific text, I have simply listed the name of the *Rav* with his information.

Aderet Eliyahu, Rav Eliyahu Kramer, Vilna Gaon (1740–1800) Lithuania

Arizal, Rav Yitzchak Luria, (1534–1572) Israel

Artscroll Stone Chumash, USA

Asara Ma'amarot, Ramah miFano, Rav Menahem Azariah da Fano (1548–1620) Italy

Aderet Zekeinim, Rav Menachem Mendel Auerbach (1620–1680) Vienna

Avudraham, Rav David Avudraham, (14th century) Spain

Ba'er Heitev, Rav Yehudah ben Shimon Ashkenazi (1730–1770) Germany

Baal Haturim, Rav Yaakov Ben Asher aka Rabbeinu Asher, (1269–1343) Germany; Spain

Bartenura Al HaTorah, Rav Ovadiah ben Abraham, (1445 n-1515) Italy and Israel

Bayit Chadash, Rav Yoel Sirkis, aka (also known as) the Bach, (1561–1640) Krakow, Poland

Be'er Mayim Chaim, Rav Chaim of Chernovitz, (1760–1816) Ukraine

Ben Ish Chai, Chacham Yosef Chaim, (1832–1909) Iraq

Ben Yehoyada, Chacham Yosef Chaim, (1832–1909) Iraq

Binat Nevonim, Rav Nisan Markel, (1877–1947) Poland; Buffalo, NY

Biur Halacha, Rav Yisrael Meir (HaKohen) Kagan, aka Chafetz Chaim, (1838–1933) Radin, Belarus

Bnei Yissaschar, Rav Zvi Elimelech Shapiro of Dinov (1783–1841) Hungary

Chafetz Chaim, Rav Yisrael Meir Kagan (1838–1933) Poland

Chatam Sofer, Rav Moshe Sofer Schreiber, (1762–1839) Pressburg, Austrian Empire

Chayei Adam, Rav Avraham Danzig, (1748–1820) Poland

Chazal Tzion, Rav Raphael Immanuel Ricchi, (1688–1743) Italy

Chiddushei HaRim, Rav Yitzchak Meir Rotenberg-Alter known as Gerrer Rebbe, (1799–1866) Poland

Chizkuni, Chizkiyah bar Manoach, (13th century) France

Chochmat Adam, Rav Avraham Danzig, (1748–1820) Poland

Chomat Anach al HaTorah, Rav Chayim Yosef David Azulai Chida (1724–1806) Israel; Italy

Daat Zekeinim, Torah Commentary compiled by Baalei Tosafot (1100–1300) France; Germany; Italy; England

Derech Eretz Zuta, one of the minor tractates of the Talmud

Eretz Hachayim, Rav Klonimus Kalman Shapira aka the Piasechner Rebbe (1889–1943) Poland

Haflaah, Rav Pinchas HaLevi Horowitz (1731–1805) Ukraine; Germany

Hagada Ki Yishalcha Bincha, Rav Moshe Bogomilsky, Contemporary Rabbi, USA

Haktav V'Hakabbalah, Rav Yaakov Tzvi Mecklenburg, (1785–1865 CE) Germany

Hon Ashir, Rav Immanuel Ricci, (1688–1743) Italy

Ibn Ezra, Rav Abraham ben Meir Ibn Ezra (1089–1167) Spain

Iggrot Moshe, Rav Moshe Feinstein, (1895–1986) Russia; USA

Ish Uveito, Rav Eliyahu Kitov (1912–1976) Poland; Israel

Kaf Hachaim, Rav Yaakov Chaim Sofer (1870–1939) Iraq; Israel

Keset Hasofer, Rav Shlomo Ganzfried (1804–1886) Ukraine; Slovenia

Kitzur Shulchan Aruch, Rav Shlomo Ganzfried (1804–1886) Ukraine; Slovenia

Kli Yakar, Rav Shlomo Ephraim Luntchitz (1550–1619) Poland; Czech

Kotzker Rebbe, Rav Menachem Mendel Morgensztern of Kotzk (1787–1859) Poland

L'orah Shel Torah, Rav Yaakov Auerbach, (1940–2015) Israel

Levush, Rav Mordechai Yaffe, (1530–1612) Prague; Poland

Maaseh Rokeach, Rav Eliezer Rokeach (1665–1742) Amsterdam

Magen Avraham, Rav Abraham Abele Gombiner (1635–1682) Poland

Maharal of Prague, Rav Yehuda Loew (1512–1609) Prague

Maharil, Rav Yaakov Moelin (1325–1427) Germany

Maharsha, Rav Shmuel Eliezer Halevi Eidels (1555–1631) Poland; Ukraine

Maharshal, Rav Shlomo Luria (1510–1573) Poland; Lithuania

Maharsham, Rav Meir MiRotenberg (1215–1293) Germany

Maor V'Shemesh, Rav Klonimus Kalman Halevi Epstein (1753–1825) Krakow, Poland

Matteh Moshe, Rav Moshe ben Avraham of Przemusl (1550–1606) Poland

Meam Loez, Rav Yaakov Culi (1689–1732) Jerusalem; Turkey

Medrash Abba Gorion, Rav Abba Gurion of Sidon (2nd century) Israel; Babylon

Mekhilta d'Rabbi Yishmael (135 CE) Israel; Babylon

Meorei Ha'Aish, Rav Ari Kahn, USA; Israel

Meshech Chochma, Rav Meir Simcha of Dvinsk, (1843–1926) Lithuania; Latvia

Metzudat David, Rav David Altschuler (1740–1780) Prague

Minchat Elazar of Munkatch, Rav Chaim Elazar Spira (1868–1937) Hungary

Minchat Shai, Rav Yedidyah Solomon Norzi (1560–1626) Italy

Mishnah Berurah, Rav Yisrael Meir Kagan aka Chafetz Chaim (1838–1933) Poland

Mizrachi Al HaTorah, Rav Eliyahu Mizrachi (1455–1525) Turkey

Moshav Z'keinim al HaTorah, Rav Solomon David Sassoon (1915–1985) England; Israel

Nachal Kedumim, Rav Ary Nahum Lubetski (Printed 1931) Poland

Nachalat Yaakov, Rav Yaakov Naumberg (c. 1560) Germany

Nachalei Binah, Rav Chaim Yehuda Katz (Contemporary Rabbi) Brooklyn, NY

Nefesh Chaim, Rav Chaim Pelagi (1788–1868) Turkey

Niflaot Mitoratecha, Rav Mordechai Nachman Aronovsky (Printed 2004) Jerusalem

Nishmat Adam, Rav Avraham Danzig (1748–1820) Vilna

Noda B'Yehuda, Rav Yechezkel ben Yehuda HaLevi Landau (1713–1793) Prague

Ohaiv Yisrael, Rav Avraham Yehoshua Heschel, the Apter Rav (1755–1825) Poland

Ohel Rachel, Rav Chaim Lieberman, NY

Ohr HaChaim, Rav Chaim Ibn Attar (1696–1743) Morocco

Or Zarua, Rav Yitzchak ben Moshe of Vienna (1200–1270) Bohemia Vienna

Otzar Chaim Al HaTorah, Rav Chaim Yaakov Zuckerman (1895–1971) Jerusalem

Otzar Taamei Haminhogim, Rav Avraham Sperling (1851–1921) Lemberg

Pardes Yosef, Rav Yosef Patzanovski (d.Lodz Ghetto 1942) Poland

Parpera'ot la-Chokhmah, Rav Noach Mindes Lipshutz (1775–1797) Vilna

Parshat Hashavua on the Internet by Rav Kalman Kaminer/Dr. Avraham M. Speiser

Peninim Mishulchan Hagra, Rav Eliyahu Kramer, aka Vilna Gaon, (17201797) Lithuania

Pirkei D'Rabbi Eliezer, Eliezer ben Hyrcanus (1st or 2nd century) Israel

Rabbeinu Bachya ben Asher ibn Halawa (1255–1340) Spain

Rabbenu Yona, Rav Jonah ben Abraham Gerondi (d. 1264) Girona, Catalonia

Radak, Rav David Kimchi (1160–1235) France

Radziner Rebbe, Rav Mordechai Yosef Leiner (1801–1854) Poland

Ralbag, Rav Levi ben Gershon (1288–1344) France

Ramah MiFano, Rav Menachem Azaria (1548–1620) Italy

Ramah, Rav Moshe Isserles (1530–1572) Krakow

Rambam, Rav Moshe ben Maimon, (1138–1204) Spain; Egypt

Ramban, Rav Moshe Ben Nachman, (1194–1270) Spain; Israel

Rashbam, Rav Shmuel Ben Meir (1083–1174) France

Rashi, Rav Shlomo Yitzchaki, (1040–1105) Troyes, France

Rav Adin Even Yisrael Steinsaltz (1937–20230) Jerusalem

Rav Aharon Adler, Contemporary Author, Israel

Rav Aharon Lichtenstein (1933–2015) Paris; USA; Israel

Rav Akiva Eiger (1761–1837) Austria-Hungary

Rav Ari Kahn, Meorei Ha'Aish (Contemporary Rabbi) USA; Israel

Rav Aryeh Kaplan, Jewish Meditation (1934–1983) New York

Rav Chaim Halberstam of Sanz, Divrei Chaim (1793–1876) Poland

Rav Eliezer Deutsch (1850–1916) Hungary

Rav Isaac Halevi Herzog (1888–1959) Poland; Ireland; Israel

Rav Isaac Turnau (14th Century) Austria

Rav Levi Yitzchak of Berditchev (1740–1809) Ukraine

Rav Matityahu Glazerson, Music and Kabbalah, Contemporary Rabbi, Israel

Rav Menachem Ziemba, (1883–1943) Poland
"Hashem Yinakem Damo" – (Rav Ziemba was murdered by the Nazis in the Warsaw Ghetto)

Rav Mendel MiRiminov (1745–1815) Poland

Rav Mordechai Gifter (1915–2001) Cleveland

Rav Naftali MiRopshitz (1760–1827) Galicia

Rav Saadia Gaon (882–942) Babylon

Rav Shimshon of Ostropoli (1599–1648) Poland

Rav Shmuel Shmelke Halevi of Nikolsburg, (1726–1778) Moravia

Rav Tzvi Hirsch MiZidikov (1763–1831) Poland

Rav Yaakov Yisrael Kanievsky, Steipler Rav (1899–1985) Israel

Rav Yaakov Emden, Yaavetz (1697–1776) Germany

Rav Yehoshua Leib Diskin, Maharil Diskin (1818–1898) Belarus; Jerusalem

Rav Yitzchak Ginsburg, USA; Israel

Rav Tzidkiyahu Ben Avraham Anav Harofeh (1210–1280) Italy

Rokeach, Rav Eliezer Rokeach of Worms, (1176–1238) Germany

Saadiah Gaon (882–942) Egypt; Iraq

Sefer Chassidim, Rav Judah ben Samuel of Regensburg (1150–1217) Germany

Sefer Hachinuch, Anonymous (13th Century) Spain

Sefer Haminhag, Rav Isaac Tyrnau (14th century) Austria

Sefer Hatodaah, Rav Eliyahu Kitov (1912–1976) Poland; Israel

She'elot U'Teshuvot Trumat Hadeshen, Rav Israel Isserlin (1390–1460) Germany

Shemen Hatov, Rav Shmuel Shmelka ben Tzvi Hirsch Horowitz (1726–1778) Poland; Moravia

Shnay Luchot Habrit, Rav Yeshaya Halevi Horowitz aka Shelah Hakadosh (1558–1628) Prague

Shulchan Aruch, Rav Yosef Caro (1488–1575) Tzfat, Israel

Siftei Chachamim, Rav Shabetai Bass (1641–1718) Prague

Smichat Chachamim, Rav Naftali Katz (1649–1718) Frankfurt, Germany

Taamei Haminhagim, Rav Avraham Yitzchak Sperling (1851–1921) Lvov, Poland

Talelei Orot, Rav Yissachar Dov Rubin (1962–2008) Bnei Braq

Targum Onkelos, Onkelos (35–120) Israel

Targum Yonatan, Rav Yonatan ben Uziel (1st Century) Israel

Terumat HaDeshen, Rav Israel Isserlin ben Petachia, (1390–1460) Austria

Tiferet Yonatan, Rav Yonatan Eybeschitz (1690–1764) Germany

Toldot Aharon, Rav Aharon of Pizaro. (16th Century) Nikalaro, Italy

Torah Ladaas, Rav Matis Blum, Contemporary Author (d. 2020), New York, USA

Torah Temimah, Rav Baruch Ha-Levi Epstein (1860–1941) Lithuania

Torah Tidbits, Weekly Publication of OU Israel, Phil Chernovsky

Torat Kohanim, aka Sifra – Halachik midrash to Vayikra

Tosafot, Medieval Commentary of the Talmud

Turei Zahav, Ta"z, Rav David Ha-Levi Segal (1586–1667) Poland

Tzror Hamor, Rav Avraham Saba (1440–1508) Spain; Portugal; Morocco

V'Dibarta Bam, Rav Moshe Bogomilsky, Contemporary Commentary, USA

Vilna Gaon, Rav Eliyahu Kramer (1720–1797) Lithuania

Wellsprings of Torah, Maayan Shel Torah, Rav Alexander Zusia Friedman (1897–1943) Poland

Yabia Omer, Rav Ovadia Yosef (1920–2013) Iraq; Egypt; Israel

Yalkut Shimoni, Rav Shimon of Frankfurt (13th Century) Germany

Yesodai Yeshurun, Rav Gedaliah Felder (1921–1999) Galicia; Toronto

Zohar, Rav Shimon Bar Yochai, Israel

Notes

Notes

About the Author

David Woolf was born in England and grew up in Toronto. His professional activity was in the plastics industry. His communal activity included more than three decades running the youth minyan at Congregation B'nai Torah in Toronto, forty years as the lay head of NCSY Canada, and involvement on the lay boards of JFCS, COR Kashruth Council and Jews for Judaism. He and his wife Fran, make their home in Toronto, Canada and Hashmonaim, Israel. They love travelling and meeting with Jewish communities in the countries they visit, and he hopes one day to be recognized by Guiness World Records as having served as *"baal kriah"* – "Torah reader" in the most countries in the world (over 30 thus far and still counting). They have been blessed (*bli ayin hara*) with 5 children and 16 grandchildren (*kain yirbu*).

Printed in Great Britain
by Amazon